Schriftenreihe „Moderne Südasienstudien – Gesellschaft, Politik, Wirtschaft“

The series „Modern South Asian Studies – Society, Politics, Economy“

herausgegeben von
is edited by

Prof. Subrata K. Mitra, Ph.D,
Ruprecht-Karls-Universität Heidelberg
Prof. Dr. Dietmar Rothermund,
Ruprecht-Karls-Universität Heidelberg

Band 4

Silvan Siefert

Social Security in India and China

Reforms, Development and Determinants of Social Security Provision in India and China (2004–2009)

Nomos

Die Deutsche Nationalbibliothek verzeichnet diese Publikation in der Deutschen Nationalbibliografie; detaillierte bibliografische Daten sind im Internet über http://dnb.d-nb.de abrufbar.

Zugl.: Heidelberg, Univ., Diss., 2015

ISBN 978-3-8487-2682-0 (Print)
ISBN 978-3-8452-7019-7 (ePDF)

1. Auflage 2015

Table of Contents

List of Diagrams and Figures 13

List of Tables 15

List of Abbreviations 19

I. Introduction – Social Security Provision in India and China 21

1.1 The Puzzle 23

1.2 Research Questions and general Assumption of the Study 25

1.3 Methodolgical Approach 27

1.4 Aim of the Study 29

1.5 Academic Relevance 29

1.6 Review on the Public Policy Literature 36

1.7 Design of the Study 42

II. Method 44

2.1 A Most Different Case Design 44

2.1.1 Oranges and Apples: Can Democracies be compared to non-Democracies? 45

2.1.2 Exploring the Puzzle: Social Security Provisions and Regime Type 48

2.1.3 Social Security and 'Good' Governance 50

2.1.4 Can Asia be compared to Europe? 52

2.1.5 China and India: Same Path, different Goals? 54

2.2 Towards a comparable Definition of Social Security 56

2.2.1 In Pursuit of a Working Definition 59

2.2.2 India and Chinese Concept of Social Security: Same Word, different Meaning 61

2.2.3 Working Definition for Social Security 62

2.3 Welfare Literature and the two Cases 63
2.3.1 Three classical approaches in theoretical reasoning and their implications 64
2.3.2 Towards an actor-orientated approach 67
2.3.3 Path-dependency and Social Security Provision 69
2.3.4 Critical Evalution on the existing Typologies 70
2.3.5 Expanding the View – Welfare Regimes Types in autocratic Systems 72
Typology of Social Political Regimes in non-Democracies 73

2.4 Method of Process Tracing and the Analytic Narrative 76
2.4.1 Narrative, Path-Dependency and Critical Junctures 79
2.4.2 Narratives of Social Security Policy Development 81

2.5 The theoretical Framework and the Working Model 82
2.5.1 New Institutionalism in Comparative Political Literature 83
2.5.2 Relevane of Culture and Social Preferences in Literature 84
2.5.2.1 New Institutional Logic of Inquiry 87
2.5.2.2 A Sequence Model of Social Security Provision 92
2.5.2.3 Definition of Institutions: Why they matter? 93
2.5.3 A New Institutional Model: Politics, Policy and Polity 96
2.5.4 Comments on the applied theoretical Model 100

III. Descriptive View on India and China 101

3.1 Descriptive Inquiry and the analytic Narrative 101
3.1.1 Regional Differences 103
3.1.2 Social Security Provision: The Gap between Objectives and Outcomes 105
3.1.3 Female Participation in the Work-force 112
3.1.4 Vulnerability 114
3.1.5 Comments on Social Security Provision in China and India 116

3.2 Historical Development of Social Security Politics 117
3.2.1 General reflection on the Path-Dependency of Social Security Provision 117
3.2.2 Social Security Policy Trajectories 118
3.3 Same Goal, different Paths: Evolution of the Chinese case 120
3.3.1 Following Socialistic Vision, 1949 to 1977 121
3.3.1.1 The Iron Rice Bowl: Left-totalitarian Welfare Regime and its Features 122
3.3.2 The First Period: Coming crises, hard figures vs. Socialistic Vision, 1978 to 1992 125
3.3.3 The Second Period: A Conflict of Visions, 1993-2004 129
3.3.3.1 Reform Period and Blueprint for today 130
3.3.3.2 Evolution of a pluralistic System in China 133
3.3.3.3 Introducing market-orientated Social Security Schemes in a pluralistic Setting 134
3.3.4 The Second Period: Social Security Politics, 1993-2004 140
3.3.5 The Third Period: Balanced economic and social Development, 2004 to 2009 160
3.3.6 Welfare Regime with Chinese Characteristics 162
3.3.7 Comments on Social Security Provision in China 166
3.4 Same Goal, different Paths: Evolution of the Indian case 167
3.4.1 Following a socialist Vision, 1949-1977 169
3.4.1.1 Continuity and Departure of Social Security Provision in the 1960s 171
3.4.2 The First Period: Blueprint for the modern Welfare Regime, 1978 to 1992 180
3.4.3 The Second Period: Performance has Priority, 1993 to 2004 185
3.4.3.1 Social Security Provision in the late 1990s and early 2000s 191
3.4.3.2 India's Social Security and typical Deficits, 1991-2004 192
3.4.3.3 Expanding the Safety Net for elderly people 193
3.4.3.4 Three Categories: the Range, Ccope and Deficits of typical pension schemes 194

3.4.3.5 Social Security and Health insurance in the unorganised sector 200
3.4.3.6 Social Security Schemes for the unorganised Sector 205
3.4.4 The Third Period: Balanced economic and social Development, 2004 to 2009 207
3.4.4.1 The NREGA and Social Assistance in India 208
3.4.4.2 Initiatives to improve the Social Security of unorganised Workers 211
3.4.5 Welfare Regime with Indian Characteristics 214
3.5 Comments on the historical descriptive Perspective 218

IV. Economical-descriptive Approach 220

4.1 Elaboration of Wagner's Law in times of austerity 222
4.2 Economic Growth and institutional Causality 223
4.3 Explanatory Power of the demographic Growth 225
4.3.1 Economic Constraints on Social Security Policy Performance 226
4.3.2 Budget Restrictions: Debts and Revenues 228
4.3.3 Budget Restrictions: Programm Concurrency 229
4.4 Social Security Provision in Times of Global Economies 230
4.4.1 Changing Employment Situation, Trade Openness and Social Security 234
4.5 Economical, Social and Demographic Factors 235
4.5.1 Demographic Change and Public Policy 237
4.6 Comments on socio-economical Determinants 241

V. Social Security Provision, State Capacity and Regime Type 242

5.1 In Pursuit of Regime Type: General reflection 242
5.1.1 Defining Regime Types 243
5.2 Assumed institutional Causalities and Social Security 246
5.3 Social Expenditure: Assumed Effects and the Reality 250
5.4 Remark on the Regime Type and Social Security 252

VI. State format and Social Security Provision 254

6.1 Institutional Constrains on Policy Making 254

6.1.2 Autocracies, Democracies in Developing Countries, and institutional Veto Points 256

6.1.3 MDCD and the Issue of Comparison 257

6.2 Descriptive Perspective: Constitutional and institutional Constrains 261

6.2.1 Institutional veto points in China and India 262

6.3 State Format: National Level and Decision Making 264

6.3.1 India's resilient Democracy 264

6.3.1.1 Constitutional and institutional Features of India's Political Regime 266

6.3.1.2 Lok Sabha and Raj Sabha: Social Policy Making 267

6.3.1.3 Social Policy Making: Involvement of Legislative and Executive 271

6.3.1.4 The Indian Social Security Administration 272

6.3.2 Political Chain of Command and Control in China 277

6.3.2.1 CCP the Locus of Political Life 277

6.3.2.2 The Politburo: A key actor 282

6.3.2.3 The Chinese State, Social Security and Administration 283

6.4 The State Format: Federalism and Decentralisation 289

6.4.1 State Format and Social Security in India and China 290

6.4.1.1 Chinese-Style Federalism 291

6.4.1.2 India's unusual Federalism: a Balance of self and shared Rule 294

6.4.1.3 Pluralism: Performance differences on Local Levels 298

6.4.2 Comments on the State Format 303

6.5 Bureaucracy and Longitude of Policy Making 305
6.5.1 Chinese Bureaucracy and Long-term Planning 306
6.5.1.1 Qualitative Constraints on Chinese Bureaucracy 306
6.5.2 India's Bureaucracy and Long-term Planning 308
6.5.2.1 Qualitative Constraints on India's Bureaucracy 309
6.5.3 Comments on bureaucratic Efficiency 310

VII. Political Parties and Social Seucirty Provison 312

7.1 Political Parties, Party Effect and Policy Outcomes 313

7.2 Political Entrepreneurs in India and China 316
7.2.1 Relevance of Party Politics and Ideology 318
7.2.2 Leading Political Parties in India and China 319
7.2.2.1 The Asian Case and why parties matter 319
7.2.2.2 The INC in the Indian political system 320
7.2.2.3 The 1990s: The End of Personal Rule and Ideology? 332

7.3 Expanding the Veto Player Theorem 335
7.3.1 Beyond the Veto Player Theorem – The Asian cases 336
7.3.2 Political Parties as Engines for Clientelism 337
7.3.3 The Case of Patronage-client Networks 338
7.3.3.1 Indian Democracy, Vote Banks and Patronage 339
7.3.3.2 Veto Players and Co-regents in China 340

7.4 Comments on Party Politics, Ideology and Social Security 343

VIII. The Constitution, Rule of Law and State Capacity 345

8.1 Rule of Law, Constitution and Social Security 345
8.1.1 Democracies and Rule of Law 346
8.1.2 The Rule of Law and Constitutions in Autocracies 347
8.1.3 Law, the Constitution and Social Security Provision 347
8.1.4 Comparing China and India 348

8.2 The Chinese Case: From '人治' to '法治' 349
8.2.1 The Constitution and Social Security in China 351

8.2.2 The Constitution of 1982 and Social Security 352
8.2.3 The Constitution: Constraints on Civil Rights 354
8.2.4 Laws and Constraints on Social Security in China 356

8.3 The Constitution and Social Security Politics in India 357
8.3.1 The Supreme Court and Social Security 358
8.3.2 Social Security Laws in India 361

8.4 Comments on the Constitutions and Social Security Laws 364

IX. Cooptation, Labour Organisations and Social Security 365

9.1 Critical Elaboration of the typical Logic of Inquiry 366

9.2 General Reflections on Unionism and Social Security 373

9.3 Production Regimes and organisational Power 375
9.3.1 Measuring the Level of Organised Interest 375
9.3.2 China's autocratic Cooperatism 378
9.3.3 India's State Capitalsim and Organised Labour 379
9.3.4 Remarks on Typology and the Hybrid Types 380

9.4 The party-centred Approach for India and China 381
9.4.1 The Trinity of Party-State-Union 381
9.4.2 Social Policy Making and the Party-State-Union Relationship 383
9.4.3 Patronage in the Political Decision Making Process 384
9.4.4 Constraints on the internal Decision Making Process 386
9.4.5 Organised Labour and the Logic of Influence 388

9.5 Political Patronage and the Party-Union Relationship 389

9.6 Comments on Organised Labour and its Political Power 396

X. Conclusion 398

Bibliography 407

List of Diagrams and Figures

Figure 1:	Huntington-Gurr 'polarisation' model	89
Figure 2:	Extended model on structural change	91
Figure 3:	Three Sequence Model	93
Figure 4:	Three Political Simensions of Social Security Provision	97
Figure 5:	Sequence of regime-related and institutional Effects on the Welfare Regime	98
Figure 6:	Assumed Variables determining Social Security in India and China	99
Diagram 1:	Comparison of the proportion of older persons receiving a pension 2000 and 2010–12	110
Diagram 2:	Replacement rate in cases of disability	111
Diagram 3:	Public Social Protection Expenditure (percentage of GDP) and Income Equality (Gini coefficient), latest available year	115
Diagram 4:	Gross Domestic Product per Capita	227
Diagram 5:	Degree of Trade Openness	232
Diagram 6:	Fertility Rate	240
Diagram 7:	Public Social Expenditures since 2000	250
Diagram 8A/B:	Trends in Social Expenditures	252
Figure 7:	Paths to Public Policy Formation	267

Figure 8:	Check and Balances in India	268
Figure 9:	India's central Social Security Administrational Bodies	273
Figure 10:	CCP's Central Organisation and Institutions	278
Figure 11:	Structure of the Chinese State - 中国的民主政治建设白皮书	279
Figure 12:	Governmental Administrative Structure in the CPR	292

List of Tables

Table 1:	Social Security related Determinants	101
Table 2:	Regional differences in the HDI	103
Table 3:	Existence of Statutory Programmes	105
Table 4:	Data related to the socio-economical Vulnerability: Income	107
Table 5:	Legal Coverage of various Schemes (for 2007)	108
Table 6:	Unemployment: Indicators of Effective Coverage	109
Table 7:	Female Participation Rate	112
Table 8:	Data related to the socio-economical Vulnerability (life expectancy)	116
Table 9:	Comparative View on Social Security in India and China	119
Table 10:	Legislation and area of law making (1993-1997)	131
Table 11:	Rural Pension Scheme (1992-1994)	144
Table 12:	Types and coverage of Health Insurance in 2003	148
Table 13:	MSLS - Scheme, Coverage and Benefits	154
Table 14:	Development of Social Security Politics in China (1949-2009)	164
Table 15:	State and Welfare in India (1949-2009)	168
Table 16:	Early Social Security Legislation in India	171

Table 17:	Major social Security Legislation in India	191
Table 18:	India's welfare categorisation	214
Table 19:	Economical Data	227
Table 20:	KOF (1980-2009)	233
Table 21A:	Sectoral composition of GDP (1980-2006)	234
Table 21B:	Employment structure and sectors	234
Table 22:	Population Aging	238
Table 23:	Regime Types in India and China over time	245
Table 24:	Social Expenditures in percentage of the GDP	251
Table 25:	Constitutional Structure and Veto Players, 2000-2009	262
Table 26:	World Governance Indicators (2000-2009)	263
Table 27:	Law Initiatives	280
Table 28:	State Format and Policy Performance	290
Table 29:	Revenue ration of the Central Government (1980-2004)	293
Table 30:	Regional differences in the monthly benefits of the MSLS	301
Table 31:	Constitutional and institutional Features of India and China	319
Table 32:	Elections and the INC (1971-2004)	322
Table 33:	Electoral Success of the INC and the Nehru-Gandhi Dynasty	325

Table 34: UPA, multi-party Coalition and Constrains on Policy Making 329

Table 35: Political Issues of the UPA Coalition 330

Table 36: Constitution and Social Security in China 351

Table 37: Social Security Legislation in India (1950-2007) 362

Table 38: Revenue of the ACFTU 395

Table 39: Dependence of Labour Confederations 397

Table 40: General assumed institutional Effects 399

Table 41: Implications of the institutional and non-institutional Factors 400

List of Abbreviations

ACFTU	All Chinese Federation of Trade Union
BJP	Bharatiya Jamata Party
BPL	Below the Poverty Line
CBI	Central Bureau of Investigation
CCP	Chinese Communistic Party
CPR	Chinese People Republic
GoI	Government of India
GNP	Gross National Product
GDP	Gross Domestic Product
GDR	German Democratic Republic
IAS	Indian Administrative Service
ICS	Indian Civil Service – former 'term' for the IAS in colonial times
INC	Indian National Congress
INTUC	Indian National Trade Union Congress
ILO	International Labour Organization
IMF	International Monetary Fund
LF	Left Front
MOCA	Chinese Ministry of Civil Affairs
MOF	Ministry of Finances
MOJ	Ministry of Justice
MOLE	Indian Ministry of Labour an Employment
MOLSS	Chinese Ministry of Labour and Social Security
NGO	Non-Governmental Organisation
NPC	Chinese National People Congress
PRC	Chinese People Republic
PRIs	Panchayat Raj Institutions
SC	Chinese State Council
SC	Scheduled Castes
UDSSR	Union of Soviet Socialist Republics
UPA	United Progressive Alliance
WHO	World Health Organization
WTO	World Trade Organization

I. Introduction – Social Security Provision in India and China

'Social Security is one of the important dimensions of the development process. It assumes a place of special significance in the developing countries, where poverty, destitution and income inequalities abound in large measure. While growth is an important precondition for expanding the scope of social security, no less important is the need for adopting special social security policies.'[1]

The contemporary public policy of the Republic of India and the People's Republic of China is rife with contradiction. It is also characterized by a significant gap between policy objectives and policy goals. The latest Social Security Report (2015) by the International Labour Organisation, 'World Social Protection Report 2014/15: Building economic recovery, inclusive development and social justice,' states that more than 70 per cent of the world population in general and a substantial portion in China and India lack proper social protection. The report states that the two middle-income countries, China and India, 'have significantly extended various elements of their social protection systems, particularly since the early 2000s, with remarkable outcomes' (2015:141) but still have a long way to go. The financial crisis of 2007/2008 has painfully illustrated the lack of proper social security in both developing countries.

In the twenty-first century both modern states have issued various bold reform plans to strengthen their commitments to expanding existing social security. In India the United Progressive Alliance (UPA) coalition government announced its plans to tackle socio-economic deprivation and released two major legislatures as well as a series of new social security programmes, which primarily opted to provide coverage for the 'poorer' segments of society in rural as well as urban areas. Similar to India, the Chinese Communist Party (CCP), under the newly nominated party leader Hu Jintao (2005:11), proclaimed the concept of the '和谐社会' ('*harmonious*

1 Derived from the address of Professor Shri K.C. Pant, acting former Deputy Chairman of the Planning Commission, to the International Conference 'Social Security Policy: Challenges before India and South Asia' held on 1st November 1999 (quoted in Rao's paper 2005:38-39).

society') and attempted to issues various social policy reforms to achieve the aspired universal social security coverage.

From a historical perspective, despite divergent political systems both states have witnessed, during almost precisely the same time periods, deep policy changes and transformative socio-economic processes that challenge existing, inadequate social security provisions.

In their political ambitions to transform from agrarian *third world* countries into modern advanced industrialized countries, India and China adapted foreign development strategies, and political, institutional, as well as constitutional context-specific features. Beginning in the post-World War II period and even without the dreadful experience of the 'sheep ate man' capitalism of the classical industrial revolutions in Europe, to quote Barrington Moore (1966)[2], both newly founded states attempted to combine the process of industrialisation with generous welfare systems. Unrealistic policy objectives, poor economic conditions, as well as overburdened state administrations led to economic and human disaster. Mao Zedong's 'Great Leap Forward' ended in the 'Great Famine' with the death of 36,000 million. Deng Xiaoping's 'Four Modernizations' broke with the old Soviet development model by starting the partial liberalization and market reform of the social security system. In India the monsoon failure of 1965/66 and near famine underlined the failure of Jawaharlal Nehru's 'mixed economy' and led to policy change. Nehru's daughter Indira Gandhi attempted to solve the problem of low human development by strengthening the central state and deeply subsidising poverty reduction measures without tackling the economic model. In the 1980s India's eroded economy and financially overburdened state teetered on state bankruptcy.

In the 1980s both governments gradually converted to neo-liberal policy making. The prevalent belief in the 'trickle-down effect' gave rise to bold structural reforms, which were not accompanied by adequate social security provisions. The rapid economic and social transformation that ensued in India as well as China illustrated the shortcomings of a broken social security system. The countries' comparable historical development and similar policy strategies—resulting from the earlier adoption of the Soviet development model—are interesting to analyze. Drawing on a lib-

2 Barrington Moore refers to the law of enclosure or 'enclosure of the common' which resulted in agrarian revolution in sixteenth-century England. See Barrington Moore. 1966. *Social Origins of Dictatorship and Democracy, Lord and Peasant in the Making of the Modern World.* Boston: Beacon Press.

eral theoretical perspective, we will see that the higher performance level of the social policy of the People's Republic of China, as compared to the Republic of India, provides a substantial piece of the puzzle regarding the interaction of regime types, policy performance and state capacity in modern times.

1.1 The Puzzle

If one were to ask what social security policy is and means in relation to assumed institutional causalities in these two countries and their historical experiences, then one would be puzzled in the search for answers. 'Public policy' is a self-evident concept for any modern state and as such it appears to have been a phenomenon of governance for political regimes all over the world since the mid-twentieth century. In contrast to the vast amount of literature on the subject, this study does not question the ability of both governments[3] to produce stable and resilient political systems[4] without falling prey to political instability[5] from their transformation from

3 Government is considered as 'those 'mechanisms' through which ordered rule is maintained' (Lane and Errson 2002:271). It is worth noting that rules as general guiding norms for conduct or actions are seen as the 'main building block of governance' (Mitra 2008:17) and the related governmental institutions are considered as 'interacting sets of humanly devised constraints that shape human interaction' and political processes (North 1990:5) Furthermore, the related term 'governance' (used throughout this study) describes 'all processes of governing, whether undertaken by a government, market or network, whether over a family, tribe, formal or informal organization or territory and whether through laws, norms, power or language' (Besvir, Mark. 2013. *Governance: A very short introduction*. Oxford: Oxford University Press). Governance is used without normative considerations. It is not measured in terms of 'good' or 'bad' governance (see 2.3.1). To measure the performance of institutions this study uses qualitative data as well as the World Governance Indicators (WGI) (Kaufmann et al. 2006, 2008). The methodology as well as the WGI will be discussed at length in Chapter 2 (see also Appendix for technical notes in the index).

4 Assessment of the resilience of the regime type is discussed later (see table 22, Hadenius & Teorell 2007).

5 Following the liberal argument of Huntington (1968, 1991) and others (Gurr 1990), young modern states tend to be 'overcharged' by the rapid economic and social changes which produce an overwhelming public demand for public goods, services and social rights. Accordingly, young modern states are not well equipped to handle the issues. As a consequence, socio-economic deprivation, protests and violence

agrarian developing[6] countries into so-called emerging markets.[7] Most interesting in light of the study's objectives is the development of social security provisions and the question of the institutional causalities of regime type, state capacity, and institutional performance in the field of social security policy.

Of course, the question of social security provisions is a smaller part of the highly complex development of these two modern states. Contemporary Sino and Indian social security politics is a policy field of contradiction between assumed institutional causalities and institutional output performance. The complexity of social security provisions in India and China is embodied in the conflict between the deep decentralisation of provisions and the issuing of centralised policy goals mainly focused on the formal industrial and administrative sectors covered in the five-year plans. Even more interesting is the critical evaluation of the classical liberal reasoning in Tocqueville's (1990) *Democracy in America* and recent accounts in po-

---

tend to break out and threaten the legitimacy of the state itself. Legitimacy can be measured in both cases by the World Governance Indicators (table 26) for 'political stability,' qualitative data, as well as the 'continuity' of the political regime itself (Hadenius and Jan Teorell 2007, and see Chapter III).

6 There exist various definitions that attempt to adequately conceptualize 'developed' and 'developing' countries in literature as well as in the public debates. The literature based on the categorisation of international associations, such as the United Nations, the IMF and Morgan Stanley Capital International shows inconsistent results with regard to the clear categorisation of countries, with the most prominent example being Singapore's changing categories (The Economist 2006b). Accordingly, the study defines 'developed' countries – often collectively referred to as the '*rich-man's club*' – as all pre-1994 OECD membership countries, and thus an '*ex negativio*' definition is used to categorize the rest (and the majority) as 'developing' countries, which were not members of the OECD in 1994, such as India, China, South Africa, Brazil, as well as Poland, Mexico and so on (OECD 1999, The Economist 2006b). Another note has to be added in this context: the term 'emerging markets' or 'emerging economies', which has lately been used to describe the more economically successful developing countries, is used in the research without notation and only to underline the rapid economic development and increasing role in the international market of the two 'developing' Asian countries, China and India, since the late 1980s. Another side note is maybe useful in the current debate to remind the reader that 'China and India were the world's biggest economies until the mid-19th century, when technology and a spirit of freedom enabled the West to leap ahead' (The Economist 2006a).

7 See chapter 7 in which a close investigation of the economic performance of both countries is conducted. See also the World Bank reports (1995, 2000b, 2005, 2008, 2014), Swamy (2011), and OECD (2010c).

litical science and economics on the causal relationship between democracy and the quality of social and individual life (Lipset 1961, Potter et al 1977, Huntington 1999, Halperin et al. 2010). Following the general assumption of these accounts regarding the 'comparative advantage' of democracies in providing public goods, the higher performance of China compared to India in the provision of social security is puzzling. Take a closer look at the contemporary figures related to social security (see Chapter II): China is performing better than India not only in the economic sphere but also in the realm of social security provisions and human development.

The study claims that social security policy in both countries has to been understood as part of a larger puzzle. To successfully investigate the nature of the puzzle, the bundle of institutions involved in the process of providing social security have to be understood as determining state capacity.

1.2 Research Questions and general Assumption of the Study

Contrary to the classical assumption of western liberal theoretical reasoning (Dahl 1970, 1999, Kohli 1987, 1989, Lipset 1999, and/or Halperin et al. 2010) and empirical inquiries (Potter et al. 1997, Acemoglu & Robinson 2012, Acemoglu 2014), China seems to be doing much better than India in terms of social security provisions. Thus, the study attempts to answer the following core research question:

Why is the People's Republic of China outperforming the Indian Democratic Republic in providing social security?

In pursuing the leading core question the study aims at an empirical and theoretical investigation of political institutions and their relevance for the development of social security in both countries. The following catalogue of sub-questions will help to elaborate the main research question:

To what extent can two differently designed and functioning political systems be compared to each other in their institutional performance?

To what extent does institutional causality[8] *determine the development, features and characteristics of contemporary social security provision (2004-2009) in India and China?*

In response to the above stated questions, the following inquiry takes up the relevance of regime type. Is state capacity more relevant than the assumed institutional causalities for institutional performance in providing social security? Social security is seen as a complex policy field affected by other policy fields, as well as institutional and non-institutional factors. Accordingly, it is argued that social security provisions are shaped primarily by a bundle of state instruments, such as the state format (Lijphardt 2000), bureaucracy (March and Olsen 1989, Potter 1996, Rao 2011), planning and financial competency (Wagschal 1996), political party, and collective actors (Hibbs 1977, 1994, Schmidt 1983, 2002, Mitra 1994b). Non-institutional factors, such as socio-economic conditions, so-called problem pressure by other policy fields, socio-economical changes, tradeopeness and corruption, will be treated as ***control variables*** (Wagner 1911, Wilensky 1975, World Bank 1997, 2010, 2011, Wagschal 1996).[9] The study focuses on providing a theoretical as well as empirical analysis of the key controversial political and non-political factors influencing social security provisions and related policy performance in non-western contexts under atypical conditions. Moreover, the study aims to provide insight into the similar political logics, institutional and constitutional constraints, as well as problem pressures on social security provisions in India and China.

8 There is much empirical evidence of the comparative advantage of democracies and the positive effects of institutional features, such as recurrent electoral cycles of free and fair elections, and political competition and participation, on the extension of social policy expenditures and social security (Almond and Verba 1963, Huntington 1991, Linz and Stephan 1996, Lipset 1981, Przeworski 1991, Brooker 2009, and Halperin et al. 2010, Acemoglu, 2014, Acemoglu & Robinson, 2012). As Manfred G. Schmidt (2012) notes of the relationship between the comparative advantage of democracies – especially young democracies – and cross-national variations in policy performance the postulated causal link between democracy and high levels of policy performance, as well as the explanatory potential of comparative studies, has to be critically analysed for each case.

9 A detailed investigation of the determinants as well as a working model will be presented in chapter 2.

1.3 Methodolgical Approach

The main objective of the comparative political perspective is to analyse the role, function and behaviour of the principle actors across countries[10] (Kalleberg 1966, Wallerstein 1974) through a descriptive analysis of the political processes and cross-national phenomena per se (Apter 1965, Lane and Errson 1994, 2002).[11] In effect, comparative approaches cultivate a sophisticated logic of inquiry in including various schools of reasoning to provide an adequate theoretical and methodological frame for explaining cross-national variations in policy performance, outputs and outcomes[12].

Many scholars in comparative political science argue that a *most different case design*[13] is in demand as a competitive theoretical approach (Ward and Rustow 1964, Dahl 1966, Budge et al 1976)[14]. Derived from comparative political science, welfare state as well as autocratic literature, a set of *working hypothesis* will be formulated and tested. Yet, it is worth mentioning that democratic and non-democratic institutions can only be

10 Traditional fields of interest in comparative politics are variations in democracy (Dahl 1971), electoral or party behaviour and the political system (Sartori 1976, Beyme 1985), and political stability (Bartolini and Mair 1990:35sp) across countries.

11 In their book *Comparative Politics: An Introduction and New Approach* Lane and Errson (1994) provide an impetus for a critical discussion of new theoretical reasoning in comparative political science.

12 For a detailed discussion of the usefulness of a comparative approach, see Durkheim (1965:216).

13 The conducted comparative analysis of a democratic and an autocratic regime and their divergent institutional, historical as well as economic conditions presents a typical MDCD (Schmidt 2000b:521).

14 In joint studies, for example by Ward and Rustow who compared Japan and Turkey in 1964, the choices of elected cases is often directly related to the involved authors. Including more countries in a cross-national study could easily lead to a quality problem, lack of specific information and ad-hoc generalized conclusions. Famous comparative studies highlight the need for a narrowed research focus on particular institutions such as the monarchy (Fusilier 1960), parliaments (Beyme 1970), electoral systems (Lijphart 1993), and political parties (Sartori 1976, Beyme 1985) than on country as a whole. These studies in the field of comparative studies strengthen the case for an individual synthesis of at least two cases. Comparing India and China will assure in-depth theoretical and empirical research findings, allowing explanation and generalization of the national variations (Verba 1986:28).

compared to each on a macro-level (Wintrobe 1998, Gandhi and Przeworski 2006/2007, Stykow 2013). The study does not aim to compare the Indian and Chinese cases in detail but with respect to the impact of specific institutional causality on social security outputs and outcomes. The theoretical analysis explores the extent to which institutional determinants are comparable and relevant for social security outputs and outcomes.

The study approaches these two problems from the perspective of macro-analysis, meaning it examines data about macro-political institutions as well as social security related policy performance. Such a macro-analysis is based upon two requirements: First, institutions can be clearly identified at the macro-level as well as separated from other types of entities in social reality, such as social and economic conditions, the interests of actors, and culture. Second, there is a set of policy outputs and outcomes which vary and warrant a search for institutional effects. Outcomes are not to be analysed merely by means of preferences or culture, but it is believed that institutions play a role in determining political performance. This is basically a causal notion, meaning that we must be able to observe some form of constant conjunction between an institution and its effects (Weaver and Rockman 1993; Colomer 1996; Keman 2002, Schmidt 2007).

Accordingly, by default the ***independent variable***, the ***regime type***, and its implications for social security and the welfare regime, are elaborated. Following the pioneering work of Franzis Castles the ***social security expenditures***[15] are ***the dependent variable***, leaving out social preferences which will be analysed using the institutional 'chain of command' by an *actor-oriented institutional approach* (Scharpf 1990, Thelen and Steinmo 1992, Czada et al. 1998, Keman 1998, 2002:10). As a consequence ***institutions*** are treated as ***intervening variables***. First, institutions have to be defined and separated from other entities. Second, the conjunction between institutions and its effects on outputs and outcomes has to be observed. For the macro analysis, it is imperative to define the terminology. In addition, to investigate and explain cross-national and country variations across time and various polities, the regime type is not the only ex-

15 Measured in percentage of the GDP.

planatory variable, as the country-specific institutional design has to be taken into account (Schmidt 1980, 1998, 2000a).[16]

1.4 Aim of the Study

This dissertation aims to provide an empirical and theoretical analysis of the interaction of state capacity and social security policy performance. Such an analysis not only offers an important contribution to the field of political science but also provides a wider understanding of social security provisions in developing countries under different political, social and economic conditions. In particular, the empirical inquiry aims to carefully elucidate, categorise and document contemporary social security provisions in India and China as well as its strengths, deficits and development. Moreover, the account pulls together historical as well as contemporary data, granting the reader a wider view of various macro-level and single-case studies.

The theoretical aim is to identify the shared defining processes of social security provisions across different political systems. Moreover, the study generates a general working model under the umbrella of an institutional research design. The working model is based on various working hypotheses derived from the most relevant schools in comparative political science, with a view toward offering a holistic approach to the puzzle of social security provision in developing countries.

1.5 Academic Relevance

The academic relevance is twofold: theoretical and empirical. The theoretical relevance is closely linked to the comparative enterprise stated above; a short thematic approach to the subject and related discourse in comparative political science is in demand for defining the field of social security

16 The institutional approach and its implications will be discussed and presented in the remainder of the introduction. See, for instance, North (1990), Thelen and Steinmo (1992), and Mitra (1994b, 1999a/b, 2013).

politics within the broad literature on public policy.[17] The general understanding of social security in comparative political science is characterised by theoretical and empirical insights based on the development of the United States and European countries (Castles 1998, Daalder 2002: 19-21, Kersbergen and Becker 2002:185-87). A consequence has been a normative overtone in political science, which emphasizes the merits of democracy and its comparative advantage compared to all other forms of governments (Dahl 1971, 1998, Haperlin et al. 2010). Another aspect is closely related to the historical experience of modern advanced democracy and the resulting theoretical argument that a high level of economic growth is either a pre-condition or consequence of democracy.[18]

Accordingly, two challenges, a normative and an empirical one, have to be considered in analysing non-western cases. When examining the philosophical grounding of the contemporary academic debate on the welfare state, it is distinctly visible that the liberal bias and western state philosophers, such as John Locke or Alexis de Tocqueville (1990), constitute the philosophical grounding of comparative theories (Schmidt 2000b:466-67). It is worth mentioning that state philosophy is not restricted to the modern western context; in its roots it can be traced back to ancient traditions of reasoning all over the world. However, the hegemony of the West is not merely restricted to academic discourse (including that of comparative political science) but can be traced back to the successful implementation of Western concepts of the state in the postcolonial and developing countries which ironically referred to these concepts to emancipate themselves from foreign western influences (Yang and Li 2013:61-65). As a consequence, western concepts and institutions have taken over; however, cultural contextual and informal patterns have heavily shaped the functioning of these institutions and produced country-specific versions (Mitra 1994a, 2008). This merging process challenges the theoretical arguments of Max Weber (1976) and Samuel Huntington (1996)[19] that culture and civilisation ex-

---

17 It is worth mentioning that the following section aims to provide only a thematic approach and is not designed to provide an intellectual history of comparative politics as a sub-field of political science.

18 See, for instance, Seymour M. Lipset (1959) or Robert Dahl (1971, 1989) on the assumed causality of high levels of economic growth either as a pre-condition or a consequence of democracy.

19 See Huntington's (1996) introduction in his widely cited work '*Clash of Civilizations'*.

clude each other. For instance, India represents a perfect example of combining modernization and cultural habits in the successful adaptation of the social caste system in the modern labour market, in which various employment[20] is directly associated with a distinctive caste even in modern times. Another aspect is the mutual respect and trust in the competency of bureaucrats to decide on the behalf of Chinese citizens, which can be traced back to the ancient times of the Chinese dynasties (Li 2010:18-19, NZZ 2004). These culturally rooted concepts and interaction patterns, such as client-patronage networks and/or gift exchanging as a form of respect, have been adapted to the new political and institutional realities as informal institutional patterns which accelerated merge, resulting in social acceptance of the modernization process (Li 2010).[21]

A distinctive indicator of this emerging process as well as of the search for independence is the re-'invention' of indigenous cultural concepts to legitimate the modern state (Anderson 1996, Hobsbawm 1982). In India's and China's search, the rise and fall of former empires have impelled various outstanding state-philosophers, including Kautilya and Confucius.[22] Undeniably, different traditions of logic, ideology and political theory have had their influence on the perceptions of decision-makers (Hibbs 1977, 1992, Kerbergen 1995, 1999, Pennings 2002:99).[23] Since their experiences with colonial rule both states have been wary of referring to foreign influences and have tended to refer to their own experiences with state-craft, philosophy and civil rights. In China the 'mandate of heaven' and Confucian theoretical reasoning of the state have survived the rise and fall of ancient dynasties to be relocated and reinterpreted for the increasingly inventive character of the state in improving social security and tackling socio-economic realities in the twenty-first century (Li 2010, Guo

---

20 See the appendix I for a detailed discussion on employment, formal and informal sector or so-called organised and unorganised employment.

21 For a resourceful contribution to the issue of informal clientelism in both countries, see the accounts of Wedeman (2004, 2012), Bardhan et al. (2008) and Hicken (2011).

22 For a discussion of the topic see Sujian Guo (2013a) '*Political Science and Chinese Political Studies*' or Cheung, T. 1989. *Confucian Ethics and the Order Complex*. Taipei: Juliu. And for the Indian case see the contribution made by Michael Liebig. 2014. *Endogene Politische-Kulturelle Ressourcen*. Baden-Baden: Nomos.

23 For Pennings (2002:99) the 'two central concepts which structure the behaviour of parties and voters are ideology and institutions' and their implications for party politics as well as electoral behaviour.

2013b, Bo 2013). Similar to China, in India the political as well as academic discourse has been strongly focused on the historical traditions and cultural merits of philosophy and state-craft in ancient times (Liebig 2014). In addition, the question arises: in how far do differences in the historical experience affect the calculus of the modern state?

Another, closely related, issue is the empirical challenge of two cases, which do not converge with the classical historical experiences of modern western countries (Adas 1989:69-71).[24] Several characteristics reveal the differences in the development of the two developing countries compared to advanced industrial ones. One of relevance is colonialism and the resulting 'drain of wealth' and resources, which has hindered the ability of the developing countries to witness their own industrial revolutions under colonial rule.[25] In particular, the industrial revolution and experiences with the consequences of 'capitalism' have incited the rise of organised labour and the modern welfare state (Korpi 1989, Esping-Andersen 1985). The central role of regime type in most comparative political studies does not imply that it is the only explanatory variable. How and to what extent does the regime type matter for social security policy making and what are the explanatory determinants to explain cross-national variations?

In academic discourse the issue of social security and the interventionist character of states has been tackled by classical writers, such as Aristotle, Dante, Machiavelli, Locke, Montesquieu and Tocqueville and the authors of the Federal Papers.[26] Moreover, given fierce present-day debates on the issue of intervention, as well as the increasing fiscal appetite of social security systems, it seems that the relevance of the character and efficiency of social security is more an issue than actual policy outcomes (Pierson 1994, Kitschelt and Obinger 2003). Although social security provisions are generally present in all modern states, the level of state-provided social security, services and benefits, as well as the character of these policies, varies across countries even under similar or at least comparable political,

---

24 In his book 'Machine as the Measure of Men' Michael Adas coins the term 'asian mode' to describe the atypical development of the Asian cases (Adas, Michael. 1989. *Machine as the measure of men. Science, Technology, and Ideologies of Western Dominance*. Ithaca, NY: Cornell University Press.

25 See Bose, S. and A. Jalal. 2011. *Modern South Asia. History, culture, political economy*. London: Sage.

26 For a sophisticated overview of the classical authors and their theoretical reasoning see Manfred G. Schmidt's (2000b: 466sp) and/or Hans Daalder's article (2002:16) 'Development of the study of comparative politics'.

historical and social conditions (Castles 1998:312-336). The paradox has challenged comparative scholars to explain these cross-national variations and the driving forces behind the differences in social security provisions, in particular between the modern industrial countries (Daalder 2002:17-21). In the last decade comparative political science has witnessed an outpouring of conducted studies which deal consciously with modern welfare regimes in times of globalisation, demographic growth and capitalism.[27] The main body of literature, however, has been limited to an analysis of welfare politics in rich countries, the related historical development of the modern welfare state, and studies comparing 'rich' and 'poor' countries.[28] Conducted case studies focusing on developing countries tend to remain limited in their range and scope. Furthermore, many of the conducted cross-national studies on these countries are not really comparative.[29] Although these studies tend to draw on country-specific data, the research questions commonly focus on generalized political, sociological, or even psychological issues instead of comparable policy analysis of the determinants of policymaking. Another issue is of a methodological nature and concerns the comparability of cross-national variables. Compared to the western European cases and the groundbreaking Luxemburg study in the late 1980s (Luxembourg Income Data Study 2014), the empirical data on social security schemes and programmes in developing countries, such as the size of the public sector, is limited.[30] The issue of missing empirical accounts is also directly related to the fact that most of the conducted case studies on the development and actual social security provision in these countries, such as India and China, are written in the format of commentary, policy recommendations and local single case studies lacking any indepth comparative analyses to explain the cross-national

27 See, for instance, such widely cited works as those of Wilensky (1975), Esping-Andersen (1990), Pierson (1994, 2002).

28 For instance, comparing 'rich' or advanced modern industrial countries to each other (Kersbergen 1995, 2002, Schmidt 1998), 'rich' and 'poor' countries (Zöllner 1963, Mesa-Lago 1985), or historical analysis of the development of advanced industrial countries (Abelshauser 1987, Schmidt 2012a).

29 Although these one-case studies of specific social security schemes and programmes provide indepth data, they allow only limited generalization, (e.g. Wadhawan 1987, Gupta 2003, Zheng 2004, White 2006, Rao 2007, 2011, Ambasta, Shankar and Shah 2008, Sülzer 2008, Shah 20009, Shankar and Asher 2011).

30 The issue of empirical data and its reliability will be discussed in the following chapter.

variations and similarities in social politics.[31] Interestingly, in both countries social security provision has been a political as well as ideological issue and therefore retained a prominent place in policymaking. To sum up, the analysis of social security provisions is compared to other fields of research that are relatively underdeveloped (Sankara, Subrahmanya and Wadhawan. 1994, ILO 2010a, 2015). [32]

Through there is consensus that regime type plays a significant role in the political development of the modern state, scholars disagree on its relevance as a sole explanatory variable, especially for developing countries.[33] Compared to non-democracies, most 'established' democracies in the OECD have comparative advantages compared to their non-democratic counterparts, such as political equality, higher levels of economic and human development, as well as social security coverage (Schmidt 1999a, 2005, Kaufman et al. 2008, Halperin et al. 2010, Acemoglu & Robinson 2012, Acemoglu 2014). It would be too simplistic to argue that democracy per se provides comparative advantages in the provision of social security, as well as human and economic development (Dahl 1971, 1998, Lijphart 1996, 1999). The cross-national differences between democracies in Europe, such as the gap between Spain and Scandinavian countries in terms of welfare, economic and social development, call for a more critical evalua-

---

31 See, for instance, the single case studies provided by various scholars (Rao 2011, Suryanarayana, M. H. 1983, Som, B.N. 1994, Sülzer, Rolf. 2008, Tang, J. 2005, Wang 2005, World Bank 2009b/c, MoF 2013)

32 Various sources validate the political relevance of social security politics for political parties in general (Hibbs 1994, Pennings 2002) and for India (Hindu 2004, Nagaraj 2012:36, Kohli 2012, The Economist 2014f) as well as China (Lieberthal 1992, ibid and Lampton.1992, Xinhuanet 2005, Xinhua News Agency 2007).

33 The last decade has witnessed an outpouring of comparative political science literature offering a closer focus on autocracies, hybrid systems, or so-called 'anocracies,' as well as a critical look on the postulated 'comparative advantage of democracies'. A broad range of innovative studies on non-democracies has cultivated a sophisticated understanding of the functioning of non-democracies (Gandhi and Prezworski 2006, 2007a/b, Kailitz 2009), their survival (Gerschewski 2010, Gerschewski, Merkel, Schmotz, Stefes 2013) as well as their policy performance in comparative perspective (Wurster 2011). The studies have accumulated evidence of the resilience of autocratic states as well as their relatively better policy performance in some policy fields (e.g. economic policymaking) compared to their democratic counterparts.

tion of the assumed comparative advantage that has dominated comparative political discourse analysis for several decades.[34]

In particular, the cases of India and China invite us to challenge the hypothesis and question the classical accounts of the explanatory potential of regime type, such as Atul Kohli's (1987, 1989, 2004), to explain the maturity of the welfare regimes in both countries. As accurately summarized by various case studies[35], India's democracy is still, after half a century of political stability, challenged by mass poverty, unemployment and low living conditions. Contrary to the assumed regime-related effect, the Chinese autocratic system seems to be better off than India's democracy.

Another classical explanation has been provided by economic approaches (Wagner 1911, Wilensky 1975, 1981). Such approaches have focused their attention on the connections between economic conditions, the level of welfare provided by the state, and the consequences for the macro- and micro-level (Barr 1993). The paradox in India and China has been that both governments have not followed the common trajectory of modern Western welfare regimes. Contrary to their western counterparts, India and China implemented generous social security systems for the urban population before having the economic prosperity to back it up (Teiwes 1995, Nagaraj 2000, 2012a). The development strategies have relied on the trust of both governments in the merits of the Soviet planning model and assumed economic take-off. How could both states, despite socio-economic hardships, successfully achieve development and modernization? In the tradition of a critical logic of inquiry into assumed regime effects, the accumulated descriptive data for India and China suggest strong validation of such an argument. Taking a closer look at the descriptive outcomes—that is, the number of 'absolute' poor people[36]—related to social security provisions, the core question seems to be valid: *Why is the People's Republic of China performing better in providing social security compared to the Indian Democratic Republic?*

---

34 See the OECD statistical reports (1999, 2010a) for a detailed investigation of the cross-national differences between European countries in terms of variations in economic and social policy performance.

35 Principal investigations have been conducted by Guhan (1993, 1994), Drez and Sen (1995), Nagaraj (2012a), Sen and Rajasekhar (2012), and Chibber (2012).

36 See Chapter 3.2 for a descriptive investigation of determinants related to social security as well as the World Bank reports (2007, 2008) and database (2014).

Answering the question of the driving factors behind the simultaneous periods of social policy changes is not only interesting in light of the fierce debate on the interventionist character of the state in science, politics and public discourse. This issue and its theoretical implications affect not only the advanced industrial countries but also developing countries such as India and China.[37] More specifically, with respect to what Karl Marx has called the '*Asian mode*' of (quoted by Adas 1989:236-41) development of both non-western countries, the general theories have to be elaborated in their range and scope to explain and investigate the country-specific evolution of social security as well as the underlying assumption regarding political processes, structure and agency.[38]

1.6 Review on the Public Policy Literature

Studies on public policy and its sub-field of social security provisions have mainly concentrated on advanced industrial countries (Kersbergen 1995, Pierson 2001, Schmidt 1998, 2012), the historical development of social protection in these countries (Abelhauser 1987, Hockerts 1986), comparisons of advanced industrial and developing countries (Zöllner 1963, Mesa-Lago 1997, Schmidt 1998), and also case studies of eastern European countries under autocratic rule and in the transition that followed (Flora 1986, Beyme 1994, Schmidt 2000a, Zacher 2001, Shevtsova 2007).[39] Studies comparing the rich industrial democracies to either poorer non-Western democracies, such as India or young democracies, or to non-democratic regimes, such as China and Cuba, have gained less academic attention (Zöllner 1963, Mesa-Lago 1997, Schmidt 1998:229-31). In comparative political science the amount of studies conducted on the variations of public policy in autocracies and democracies are relatively

37 Various cross-national as well as country-specific studies have repeatedly argued for the general relevance of the issue (World Bank 1986, 200b, 2001, Pierson 1994, WHO 2000, Keman 2002, Kersbergen and Becker 2002, Chan et al. 2008, Mishra and Raveendran 2011).

38 Chapter 2 provides a theoretical and methodological elaboration.

39 Shevtsova (2007) points out that the transforming post-communistic regimes tend to take over Western democratic structures but not their functioning. Thus, he (2007:63) refers to the process in Russia as an 'imitation of democracies' or a 'lost' transformation.

low and the topic has gained less attention compared to other fields of interest.[40]

The lack of comprehensive studies comparing non-democratic and democratic developing countries necessitates the following study. While most of the existing country-specific and comparative studies are engaged in determining the degree of democratic rule and political participation, the studies on elections and electoral participation have created a sense of the importance of collective social demands and organised interests. The so-called bottom up or survey studies on political participation are traditionally strong in the fields of politics, anthropology and sociology in the studied countries (Mitra and Singh 1999, Mitra 2002, 2013).

The electoral success of national and regional parties and the resulting variations in the policy choices and performance of the individual state has always been a prominent topic. The ambitious pioneering work of Mitra and Singh (1999) has produced a landmark study linking survey data on electoral behaviour, individual perceptions, and the strategies of political parties to gain electoral victories on national and local levels relying on different kinds of social minority or majority groups. Various conducted political studies on the electoral behaviour of individuals and social groups (Bardhan 1987, 2007, Mitra 1991, 2002) have documented and evaluated the role of societal groups and organised interests in India.[41] The historical descriptive accounts of the political ties of labour organisations and political parties have produced a sophisticated literature. Prominent authors, such as Dietmar Rothermund (1995c) and others (Kennedy 1968, Harris 1984, Sharma 2006, Das 2011), have systematically described the development and interaction of labour organisations and political actors in India from colonial times until today. All these authors and their accounts point out that the informal dimension (Merkel and Croissant 20000:3-6, Scott 2011) heavily affects decision making, bureaucratic ef-

40 Comparative research in the sub-field has gained more attention in the last three decades and produced a number of sophisticated studies (Zeifel and Navia 2000, Schmidt 2005, Gandhi 2007b, Wurster 2011, Kailitz and Köllner 2013a).

41 Bradhan (2004, 2007) has repeatedly argued for the measurable political impact of organised interests, such as business and farmers, on political decision-making. Undoubtedly, the political impact of rich farmers and business steadily increased in the 1980s. In the late 1980s the government took the advice of business organisations in its 'liberalization' of policies without including organised labour associations in the process (Sharma 2006).

fectiveness, *rule of law*[42], and policy performance on all levels. Furthermore, Bardhan's (1984, 2007, and 2008) account of social security provisions portrays the demand for better representation of organised interests in national policymaking, particularly in the context of the shifting power balance in favour of business in the late 1980s and early 1990s (Kohli 2012).[43]

In academic research on China the attention of various scholars, especially American political scientists, has concentrated on Chinese politics at the street level. Dorothy J. Solinger's book *Contesting Citizenship in Urban China: Peasant Migrants, the State and the Logic of the Market* (1999) has encouraged further survey studies of the topic (Zhang 2001, Wang 2005). In research on the degree of democracy in China the conducted studies on proletarian politics have highlighted the available participation opportunities of workers for political decision-making (Gallagher 2002, 2005).[44] For all the differences, these studies (Chan 2001, 2005, Lee 2007, Pun 2005) document similar processes across both countries, and draw a distinct picture of the importance of intra-institutional arrangements and the related impact of organised interests (Rothermund 1995c, Metcalf and Li 2005, M. Liu 2011, Qi 2013), formal and informal institutional patterns (Bardhan 1984, 1997, 2008, Azari and Smith 2012), and party and elite perceptions (Nathan 1973, Mitra 1994b, Ngok and Zhu 2003, Wagner 2006).[45] A quick glance at recent publications, particularly on intra-country variations of social protection, the institutional competency of local administration, and the path-dependency of social security provision, reveals a consistent emphasis on contemporary perspectives of so-

42 See appendix I for a detailed definition of rule of law.

43 In the mid-1980s the INC government under Rajiv Gandhi, a former business man himself, attempted to strengthen the business community and its political impact in order to gain additional input on economic policies as well as the needed structural reforms (Rothermund 1993, 1995).

44 The studies conducted by Elizabeth Perry (2001, 2002), Li Xun (Perry and Xun 1996), and others analysed the political role and participation opportunities for workers on various political levels. Recently feminist Hong Kong authors have concentrated on the situation of female workers in the export sector and the effects of economic and social politics on their socio-economic situation (Chan 2001, 2005, Lee 2007, Pun 2005).

45 For insight into the rational calculus of local elites in India's political arena, see Subrata K. Mitra (1991) '*Room to Manoeuvre in the Middle: Local Elites, Political Action and the State in India*'.

cial security politics in developing countries (Ahman et al. 1991, Sen and Dreze 1990, Sen 1997, World Bank 1997, Sankaran, Subrahmanya and Wadhawan 1994, ILO 2010a).[46]

Limitations of the existing public policy literature for India and China

Most of the research thus far conducted on India and China lacks clarity on the determinants, policy processes and involved actors in social policy behaviour and implementation. In particular, the implementation process, and the gap between policy objectives and outcomes, has been a rather theoretical topic (Chan et. al. 2008:128, Rao 2011:252). In fact, public policy in India and China has not been a prominent academic topic either in the social sciences generally or in political science in particular. Country-specific studies on public policy and related social security, social assistance, and labour market programmes, schemes and services, as well as their implication for societies in India and China, emerged in the 1970s but witnessed a steady increase in the 1990s; yet the conducted studies remain very limited in number and theoretical scope.

Much of the research has been in the form of commentaries, policy advice, or case studies restricted to the micro level—i.e. the village level and the situation of local minorities—which is distinctly visible in the current wealth of studies on the millennium goals[47]. Briefly put, political scientists have paid less attention to social security provisions than to political parties, elections, and country-specific institutional arrangements (see Schmidt (1999b:44) for a critical elaboration on the shortcoming of academic inquiry). The reason may be that the data on social security policy outcomes in both developing countries is only partly tracable to statistical accounts and existing pluralism also enhances the complexity (World Bank 2010, 2011).[48] The relevance of social security for human develop-

46 See the introductory chapter to the edited volume '*Social Security in Developing Countries'* by Ahman et al. (1991) as well as Sen and Dreze (1990) on the importance of social security in their article 'Social Security in Developing Countries' in the same volume.

47 For a comprehensive selection of various authors on the topic and the challenges that the Millennium Goals raise for, India see R. K. Mishra and Jayasree Raveendrans' (2012) (eds.) '*Millennium Development Goals: The Indian Journey*'. A general survey of the millennium goals is provided by the ILO (2006:2-4).

48 The issue of data accountability will be discussed later in chapter 2.

ment is undeniable and has been documented by various studies (ILO 1984, 2001, World Bank 1986, 1990b, 1997, 2005, 2011 WHO 2000). But by no means does the existing literature address the whole complexity of social protection; most of the existing studies are only concerned with the outcomes and level of economic and human development,[49] or with a specific social security scheme—i.e. pension schemes (Hurst and O'Brian 2002, Shah 2003, Rao 2007, 2011), nutrition (Suryanarayana 2001), and food security (Radhakrishna and Subbarao 1997).[50] Comparative analyses of social security provisions between developing countries are rare in the literature.

In the country-specific literature on social security in India, Atul Kohli (1987, 2012), Amartya Sen and Jean Dreze (1991), among others (Ahmad 1991, Burgess and Stern 1991, Guhan 1993, 1994), are all engaged in the documentation and evaluation of national and local social security provisions. In the Indian case, however, the number of sophisticated studies on social security administration, social security policies and its features is limited. In the 1990s some scholars (Chattterjee et al. 1994, Lynn 1994, Rastogi 1994, Som 1994), in close cooperation with Indian institutions and under the umbrella of the Friedrich Ebert Stiftung, tried to tackle the topic of social security politics and social security administration and produced case studies on various social security schemes and the evolution of their range, scope and administration over time. A landmark study has been Kohli's (1999, 2012) historical and political account[51] of the changing logic of national politics and its direct effects on the attempt to expand social security strategies under the doctrine of the Five Year Plan for rural areas. It is worth noting that the issue of social security provisions has gained more attention and that non-Indian authors have taken a closer look

49 See various articles, reports and studies conducted by the World Bank (2010, 2011), ILO (2010) and the Asian Development Bank (2008, 2012). See, in particular, the conducted project on social security and the estimated *Social Security Index (SPI)* provided by the Asian Development Bank (2008, 2012).

50 See, for instance, Rao's (2005) or Shah's (2003) studies for detailed and indepth analyses of the national pension scheme and its implication for Indian households.

51 Kohli (1999, 2012) stresses the relevance of the democratic regime effect and comparative advantage, which is not taken for granted in the conducted study. Hence, following the general argument in the proceeding comparative part of the study, the assumed regime effects are analysed, compared and discussed at length to provide insight into the relevance of regime effects for modern states' policy-making in the sub-field of social security.

at the development of such provisions.[52] As mentioned before, however, the theoretical and comparative scope of the studies to date has been limited (Shah 2003, Shankarand Asher 2011).

Compared to the literature on studies of India, studies on China have steadily increased in number since the 1990s; however, the bulk are restricted to purely historical accounts, commentaries, and/or case studies of existing programmes (World Bank 1990a/b, 1996, 2002, 2003, Mu and Liu 2006). An investigation of the development and political logic of social security provisions in China reveals the close linkage between the commitment of the central government to an urban-focused security net and the limited coverage for rural or informal employed citizens. Joseph Fewsmith (2001), Chen Weixing and Yang Zhong (2005), among others (Gang and Xiaobo 2005), have evaluated the Chinese experiences in social security provisions, and their institutional, constitutional, financial and programmatic limitations (Swank and Hicks 1985, Tsebelis 1990, Wagschal 1996, Kersbergen 1999, ibid and Becker 2002, Rao 2011), to establish a 'safety net' with only minimum benefits in urban and rural areas (Asian Development Bank 2013).[53]

What all these authors share in common in the two contexts is summarized by Susanne Shrik (2007), who emphasizes the increasing role of domestic social politics in overcoming the limited range, scope and bias of social security policies to raise adequate social protection for all segments of society. Under such circumstances a question arises: What are the determining institutional variables for social security provisions and their relevance for the development of both countries? Both the general as well as country-specific academic discussions on social security provisions point to more or less the same conclusion: that adequate social security must be an essential feature of our social and economic future (World Bank 1996, 1997, 2010, 2011, Rao 2007, Chan et al. 2008, Sülzer 2008, Hurst 2009, D. Liu 2011, Nagraj 2012a).

52 Insight into the planning process in the 1980s is provided by the official document 'A Technical Note on the Sixth Plan of India (1980-1985)' issued by the Planning Commission (GoI 1981).

53 The Asian Development Bank (2013) has conducted an evaluation of social security in Asia; however, the measurement is 'problematic' in that one of the main categories is chiefly concerned with the effect of social security in lifting the absolute poor out of their socio-economic situation. Accordingly, employment-related social security is less relevant than social assistance programs in the construction of the index.

1.7 Design of the Study

The study and its division into nine parts provide insight into the issue of social security provisions in India and China. Each part deals with an issue related to the core question and the determinants of social security provisions under different political, social, and economic conditions.

The three chapters of the thesis are meant as a general survey. The introduction evaluates the topic, its academic relevance as well as the research puzzle. The second chapter aims to provide a short discourse on the comparative approach in political science. Amongst other things, the comparative literature, commonly assumed 'comparative advantage' of democracies, welfare typologies and research method will be discussed. Following the theoretical investigation, the working model for evaluating state capacity is presented. The proceeding chapter attempts to illustrate the merits of a historical-descriptive approach. Accordingly, the contemporary social security related data for each case is presented and compared. In the second part, the 'structured' and 'focused' investigation categorises, documents and analyses social security development in India and China since the 1950s.

The theoretically-driven inquiry starts in the fourth chapter. This chapter tests the common working hypothesis of socio-economic schools. In pursuit of the causal relation between social security performance and socio-economical determinants, the study investigates economic growth, demographic tendencies, budget restrictions and trade openness. Chapter five engages in a theoretical and empirical inquiry of the dependent and independent variables, testing the relationship between regime type and social security expenditures. The following five chapters aim at a theoretical and empirical analysis of social security policy performance with respect to the earlier new-institutional working model. In fact, chapter six shows in what way institutional constraints determine the 'room to manoeuvre' in China and India. As mentioned before, each case will be reviewed in itself due to the complexity of the autocracy-democracy differences. Much attention is paid to the 'chain of command' of decision-making, veto players and co-regents as well as the state format and related bureaucratic efficiency. Chapter seven inquires into the relevance of the two dominant political parties, namely the INC and CCP, and their programmatic changes in time. Chapter eight attempts to demonstrate how far constitutionally granted social rights and the degree of 'rule of law' matter for social security provisions. The last chapter introduces the power resource theorem and investigates the relationship between unions, production regimes as well as political systems.

The conclusion reconsiders the accumulated theoretical working hypotheses to date and the empirical evidence. Based upon the earlier finding it attempts to solve the puzzle at hand by answering the core question. In pursuit of the research goal the relevant findings will be formulated in the presented thesis.

II. Method

The chapter is designed to provide a basic understanding of the theory and methodology underpinning the working model and assumptions used throughout the study. Accordingly, it will begin with a short introduction to the merits of the current intellectual and critical discourse on the postulated comparative advantages of democracy for contemporary political science (Dahl 1971, 1994, Lane and Errson 2002). It should be mentioned that the following chapter does not provide a full intellectual history of comparative political science as a sub-discipline.[54] Rather it concentrates on the applicable selection of the relevant theoretical and methodological approaches for the purpose of creating a theoretical tool-box for comparing India and China in the policy sub-field of social security. Consequently, in the following sections, the most prominent schools of reasoning in comparative political science are critically discussed to elaborate their key assumptions and the resulting relevance of their insights for the research design by answering the following general questions: What are the implications of regime types for social policy making? What are the relevant political factors shaping the policymaking process, structure and agency? How and what political and non-political factors affect the process of social policymaking? And what are the political implications of divergent historical, economic and social conditions?

2.1 A Most Different Case Design

The main objective of comparative political approaches is to account for the relationship between institutional structures determining the '*room to manoeuvre*' (Apter 1965, Lane and Errson 1994, 2002) and the role, func-

54 See other accounts, such as Prezworski and Teuner (1971), Penning (1999, 2002), Daalder (2002:17-19) for an intellectual history as well as methodological overview of comparative politics.

tion and interests[55] of the involved actors across countries (Kalleberg 1966, Wallerstein 1974).[56] In contrast to the comparative approach, conducted case studies and monographs for a single country are limited in scope. Although they offer qualitative indepth data, their explanatory potential is limited (Eckstein 1966, Lijphart 1968); for generalizable theoretical predictions two or more cases have to be compared (Ward and Rustow 1964, Dahl 1966, Budge et al 1976)[57]. Hence, for the theoretical and empirical analyses of the determining variables for social protection in the two different political systems of India and China the study will rely mainly on the *new institutional* approach. Comparative politics offers various theoretical schools which allow such an undertaking due their 'use of attributes of macro-social units in explanatory statements' (Ragin 1987:5). The theoretical advantage of the comparative approach is its ability to explain the potential political power of trade unions by analysing their influence on political processes, policy outputs and outcomes.

2.1.1 Oranges and Apples: Can Democracies be compared to non-Democracies?

As Geddes points out 'different kinds of authoritarianism differ from each other as much as they differ from democracy. They draw on different groups to staff government offices and different segments of society for

55 Traditional fields of interest in comparative politics are variations in democracy (Dahl 1971), electoral or party behaviour and the political system (Sartori 1976, Beyme 1985), and political stability (Bartolini and Mair 1990).

56 In their book '*Comparative Politics: An Introduction and New Approach*' Lane and Errson (1994) provided an impetus for a critical discussion of new theoretical reasoning in comparative political science.

57 In joint studies such as Ward and Rustow's (1964) comparison of Japan and Turkey, the choice of the elected cases is often directly related to the involved authors. Including more countries in a cross-national study could easily lead to a quality problem, lack of specific information and ad-hoc generalized conclusions. Famous comparative studies highlight the need for a narrow research focus on particular institutions such as monarchies (Fusilier 1960), parliaments (Beyme 1970), electoral systems (Lijphart 1993), and political parties (Sartori 1976, Beyme 1985) rather than the country as a whole. These studies in the field of comparative studies strengthen the case for an individual synthesis of at least two cases. Comparing India and China will assure indepth theoretical and empirical research findings, explaining and generalizing the national variations (Verba 1986:28).

support. They have different procedures for making decisions, different ways of handling the choice of leaders and succession, and different ways of responding to society and opponents (1999:121)'.

In the last two decades an interdisciplinary consensus has evolved that not only political parties[58] but also institutions, formal as well as informal, play a crucial role in determining policy processes, structures, and interaction patterns (Köllner 2013:272-6). A landmark study of the institutional and actor-orientated turn in comparative political science has been the widely cited historical work of Douglas North (1990, 2008) on the rise and fall of nations.[59] In the 1950s and 1960s an increasing number of newly independent developing countries emerged from the old declining imperial order (Huntington 1991, Beyme 1994).[60] The 'wind of change' of the second wave of decolonisation produced significant pressure for comparative political science in studying these non-Western political systems and comparing them to Western countries (Huntington 1991, Daalder 2002:17-18). In general, the core question of the study concerning democracies and autocracies is this: Do democracies have a comparative advantage compared to non-democracies in providing social security? Or can '*apples be compared to oranges*'?[61]

To the above stated problem, Adam Przeworski and Henry Teune (1970:25) remind their readers that both are fruits at a higher level of analysis. In this regard, historical studies echo a point made by Aristotle, Plato, Cicero, as well as the authors of the *American Federal Papers*, and even egalitarian democrats, such as Montesquieu (Merkel 1999:12, Schmidt 2000b: 467, Daalder 2002:16). All of them agree that democracy

58 From the beginning a rational definition by Anthony Down has been applied. For Down (1957:24-25) '*a political party is a coalition of men seeking to control the governing apparatus by legal means. By* ***coalition****, we mean a group of individuals who have certain ends in common and cooperate with each other. By* ***governing apparatus****, we mean the physical, legal and institutional equipment which the government uses to carry out its specialized role in the division of labour. By* ***legal means****, we mean either duly constituted or legitimate influence* [emphasis made by authors].'

59 See Kathleen Thelen's (1999) article 'Historical Institutionalism in Comparative Politics' on the issue.

60 See 'waves of democratization' (Schmidt 2000a:463 sp).

61 A common illustration used in comparative political science textbooks to emphasise the various differences of political regimes (Przeworski and Teune 1970, Schmidt 2000a).

is a powerful but at the same time an imperfect system and therefore they tend to question the comparative advantage of democracy and its pluralistic interest mediation or so-called '*tyranny of the minority*' (Merkel 1999:12-13, Schmidt 1999a).

While some decades ago the socialist/communist regimes slowly collapsed in Europe due to their ambitious extension of the welfare state and lack of economic support for social security provisions, their democratic counterparts succeeded in combining welfare, political stability and economic growth (Fukuyama 1992)—resulting in the postulated assumption by various scholars that established democratic systems are superior to other regime types in various policy fields, such as the provision of welfare (Lipset 1999, Halperin et al. 2010, Acemoglu & Robinson 2012, Acemoglu 2014). Not surprisingly democracies in advanced industrial countries tend to have higher levels of policy performance in most sub-fields compared 'poorer' non-democratic countries; however, from a cross-national perspective the OECD countries vary in their level of welfare and economic growth (Schmidt 1983, Cusack 1995, OECD 1999, Garrett and Mitchell 2001).

In fact, democracy and the welfare state seem to have similar goals and an inherently egalitarian character. Yet as Dieter Nohlen (1999) points out, the Hungarian monarchy and German Reich, which introduced the first social security, health care and pensions schemes in the late nineteenth and early twentieth centuries, had neither a democratic nature nor democratic ambition in mind.[62] Therefore it is not surprising that comparative studies have accumulated evidence that democracy per se does not automatically generate a higher level of human or economic development (Helliwell 1994, Doucouliagos u. Ulubaşoğlu 2008:61).[63] As pointed out by comparative political scientists, for instance Manfred G. Schmidt (1999b, 2000a, 2013) or Stephan Wurster (2011), autocratic regime types

---

62 It should be noted that the historical roots of social policies can be traced back to the conservative Danube Monarchy which implemented social services, such as pensions, for bureaucrats and military servants to ensure and honour their loyalty. The German Reich under the chancellor Bismarck pioneered an authoritarian welfare state in 1871 to counter the negative effects of ongoing urbanisation and industrialisation which denounced the traditional social security nets and promoted socio-economic insecurity and inequality (Austin 1966, Dahrendorf 1971:68).

63 In their study Doucouliagos u. Ulubaşoğlu (2008:61) point to the fact that comparative political scholars still struggle to explain the relationship between regime type and economic growth of a country.

can also provide high levels of welfare—equal to those of their democratic counterparts—for their citizens.[64] High levels of social policy outcomes, such as welfare expenditures and public goods, are phenomena neither restricted to democracies in general[65] nor to advanced industrial OECD democracies specifically. In response to the findings, high(er) levels of policy performance cannot be associated to democracy per se (Schmidt 1983, 1999a/b).

2.1.2 Exploring the Puzzle: Social Security Provisions and Regime Type

In his hallmark study on the relationship of democracy and public policy, Alexis de Tocqueville (1990) critically evaluated the tendency of democracy to continually expand public policy expenditure for various regime-related institutional reasons.[66] In the tradition of Tocqueville and students of liberal theory, the outcomes of comparative political studies on social security provisions between 'richer' and 'poorer' countries (Zöllner 1963, Mesa-Lago 1985, 1997 and Schmidt 1998) validated the comparative advantage of democracies in having a positive effect on increasing public policy expenditures (Halperin et al. 2010, Acemoglu & Robinson 2012, Acemoglu 2014). Although reviewing the development of increasing public policy expenditure in the industrial advanced democracies—the assumed causal regime effect by Tocqueville (1990) and Wagner (1911)—seems to be right in most cases, it cannot be universally adopted. Contemporary comparative political science and recent studies on social security provisions in the OECD countries (Schmidt 1983, Western 1989, Cusack 1995, Kersbergen 1999, Garret and Deborah 2001) as well as worldwide (World Bank 2007, 2008) have refuted the simplistic universal assumption. More recently, in a comparative analysis of public expenditures for the year of 2009, conducted on 112 democracies and autocracies world-

64 It should be taken into consideration that even in a cross-national comparison the budget deficit is not restricted to the regime type (Wurster 2011).

65 The former left-totalitarian Soviet countries achieved high levels of social welfare equal to their democratic counterparts (Schmidt 2012a).

66 Tocqueville does not only praise democracy. He (1990:130) also offers some critical notes concerning short-term policy behaviour, arguing that promoting expanding public welfare can also endanger the long-term decision-making and 'learning capacity' of democracies if politicians are more interested in the present than in the future of the country.

wide, Stephan Wurster (2011) concluded that the public policy deficit is not linked to the degree of democratization.[67] Meanwhile the growing number of recent studies in comparative political science on autocracies and democracies points to the relevance of institutional features for the policy performance of all types of political systems (Brownlee 2007, Gandhi and Przeworski 2006, 2007a/b, Gandhi 2008, Hadenius and Teorell 2007). Comparing China and India in terms of their national security systems illustrates the need for a more adequate 'inquiry' of the relevant variables of social security provisions that does not rely only on the assumed comparative advantage of democracies in producing higher levels of public policies.

It would be simplistic to argue that regime type can fully explain the characteristics and development of social security provisions in both countries (Castles 1998:312-15). What emerges from the recent institutional turn in comparative political science and the wealth of literature on the institutional rational choice approach is the prospect of the relevance of country-specific formal and informal institutional determinants for overall policy performance (Mitra 1991, 2002, 2013: 228, Richter 2007, Gandhi and Przeworski 2006, Gandhi and Prezworski 2008). In response, the formal and informal elements of the party-state-society dimension shape the policy processes, structures and abilities of actors to modify them in their favour and consequently determine the policy choices of third world autocracies (Merkel and Croissant 2000:3-5) as well as democracies (Helmke and Levistski 2006). In this regard, following David Easton (1965), democracies have an advantage due to their input dimension and resulting citizenry feedback or '*government by the people*'. Similar to any other determinant, the openness of the opportunity structure varies depending on cross-national perspective, determining the available impact of organised interests, such as labour organisations, as well as other pressure groups (Pizorno 1978, Lehmbruch 1991, Pierson 1994).[68] Nowadays there

67 In his conclusive remarks Stephan Wurster argues for the relevance of GDP per capita as an explanatory variable for cross-national variations in human development (2011). Although China and India can be taken as examples of the causal link of human development and GDP per capita, the causality cannot be expanded to social expenditures and the efficiency of social security politics.

68 The widely cited and also criticized 'new politics of the welfare state' argument made by Paul Pierson (1994, 1996, and 2001) is critically evaluated on empirical and theoretical grounds later in this thesis.

is little dispute that state authorities are in need of aggregated information and expert knowledge on the scope and range of relationships between social security provisions and socio-economic realities.[69] Interestingly, non-democracies tend to have limited or even missing input functions, such as elections and/or participation opportunities; however, these systems tend to establish strong 'cooptation' ties to socio-economic elites, such as organised labour or ethnic groups, to compensate for their input deficit and gain additional feedback on policy choices (Gandhi and Prezworski 2006:4-6, Gerschweski et al. 2013).[70]

2.1.3 Social Security and 'Good' Governance

All this, in turn, raises the issue of the comparability of political processes, structures, and agencies in both contexts: *Can apples be compared to oranges or what are the institutional variables for the development of national security politics in both political regimes?*

In addition to the above stated question, another question arises: *What are the determinants for determining state capacity in India and China*? Under the commonly accepted premise that political stability, legitimacy, orderly rule and public support[71] of the state directly correspond to a significant degree to its social security provisions and performance, state governments need to exercise '*good*' governance (Norris 2000).

But what is *good* governance in the context of developing countries? *Good* governance has been long considered a model of success for advanced industrial countries. A good deal of the literature on good governance was inspired by this narrow view (Norris 2000, 2005). Correspondingly, governance has been evaluated on the basis of financial outputs and other measurable effects of policy outcomes. This underlying dynamic is

69 Even in a scenario with perfect information the state needs an administration to plan, modify and administer social security schemes and programmes as well as state revenue to fund its programmes (Wildavsky 1980, March and Olsen 1989, Potter 1996, Busemeyer 2006).

70 See also Kailitz and Köllner (2013:17-18) for a sophisticated discussion of the relevance of cooptation and cooperation in autocratic systems as an instrument for legitimacy and political stability.

71 See also Samuel Huntington's (1968, 1991) liberal and Douglas North's (1990) historical institutional works on the 'rise and fall of nations' in times of rapid economic and social change.

the rationale for the evaluation of social policy performance in developing countries compared to advanced industrial countries (Zöllner 1963, Mesa-Lago 1997). This narrow output-oriented perspective on the political performance of developing countries has been worrisome to scholars and students of institutionalism engaged in country-specific studies (Mitra and Singh 1999, Mitra 2000, 2002, 2013, Yang 2006a, 2006b, Guo 2013a/b).

Given this serious problem, since the 1990s various institutional-oriented studies have offered evidence of the duality of governance and the relevance of formal and informal institutional conditions, including institutional, economic, as well as human development. As Subrata Mitra (2005:4) points out, governance has a dual character because two sets of considerations have to be balanced: on the one hand, the existing institutions, related formal and informal rules, policies and law, which place significant constraints on the policy maker; on the other hand, the personal perceptions of elites, factionism[72], ideology[73], organised interests[74] and

---

72 For a detailed discussion of the increasing relevance of factionalism for politics, see Dittmer and Wu (1995), Dittmer (1995), and Hung (2001) for China and Kothari (1970) as well as Dyke (2007) for India. It should be mentioned that contemporary scholars on the CCP have problems in using the concept of factions for internal party dynamics in the CCP (Dittmer and Wu 1995). Although the CCP has always witnessed internal party struggle and changing groups seeking political power (i.e. Shanghai faction), the dynamic, collective behaviour and characteristics of these coalitions cannot be easily determined or compared to typical factions in other political parties (Köllner and Basedau 2006:14, Lam 2011). Since the 1980s and the fierce internal party power struggle between liberals and left-winged groups, a common consensus has evolved to refer to these groups as 'clusters' (Fewsmith 2001).

73 According to Budge (1994) and Paul Pennings, ideology is defined as 'a set of ideas which provides a guideline for political actions' and, as Keman (1997b) correctly adds, similar to institutions ideology also determines and at the same time restricts to a decent degree the available public policy choices and public actions.

74 For a comparative and systematic approach the unlimited numbers of country-specific interest and/or demand groups have to be specified and simplified to be comparable. Thus, in a generalizing and simplifying habit of thinking three main competing kinds of societal organised interests are distinguished which matter for the distinct development of the welfare state in both countries: businesses, rich farmers, and labour. Note the importance of rich farmer associations for political alliances,as in Sweden or the USA (Esping-Andersen 1990, 1999). Generally speaking, it is assumed that strongly coordinated business and farmer associations are opposed to the maturity of the welfare state and that organised labour is in favour of the expansion of social security and services. As pointed out by Korpi (2010:80), the ability of specific organised interests to modify policy processes,

socio-economic reality shape the '*room to manoeuvre*' (Mitra 1991) for the decision-maker in the party government.

In pursuit of '*government for the people*' policymakers in democracies and autocracies as well as political scholars have to take these two sets and their restrictions into consideration in formulating or explaining policy choices in developing countries.

2.1.4 Can Asia be compared to Europe?

In their prominent and widely cited work '*The Politics of the Developing Areas*' Gabriel Almond and Coleman (1960) stress the fact that countries around the world differ not only in their cultures but also in their overlapping interactions, perceptions, and results of modern and traditional influences on politics, economy and society. It seems that the commonly used definition of the modern welfare state, as well as the literature on the modern welfare state, reveals Almond and Coleman's theoretical and analytic limitations in investigating Western advanced industrial capitalistic democracies[75]. The debate on the applicability of Western theories and concepts in non-Western cases has been an issue even for prominent poltical scholars such as Giovanni Satori (1970).[76]

---

structures, and agencies determines to a decent degree the 'distribution process in society; the social consciousness of the citizens; the level and patterns of conflict in society; *the shaping and functioning of social institutions* [emphasised by author]'. Although Korpi (2010:80) focuses on advanced Western countries, the universal implications for the political relevance of organised labour can be used as an introduction to the nature of the political relevance of organised interests.

75 As mentioned before, since the corporate debate, research has overwhelmingly focused on the relation between regime type, governmental institutions, organized labour and markets in different political, social and cultural settings (Lehmbruch1984, 1993). Various studies have explored the variations in interest mediation and the resulting effects on policy outcomes, economic performance, as well as the resolution of societal conflict. The corporate debate has added a new perspective on institutionalized interaction patterns, expanding the pluralistic approach to, and the indepth knowledge of, the distinct contexts in various countries through cross-national studies of the topic.

76 See Sartori's (1970:1033-1053) widely cited article 'Concept Misformation in Comparative Politics' on the issue of comparability and theoretical modification.

Persuasive evidence is given in the pathbreaking indepth research of Esping-Andersen (1990),[77] which offers a critical evaluation of the concept but is arguably not able to overcome contextual limitations.[78] Although the welfare state literature and most of the conducted studies on modern welfare regimes have revealed a considerable understanding of the processes, determinants and development of the modern state, the typologies and analytic frameworks are mostly restricted to western European cases and even in the more 'homogeneous' cases the country-specific welfare systems cannot be easily attributed to typologies (Castles 1998:312-14, Schmidt 2003, 2012a). Common assumptions of party politics and social expenditures are inadequately equipped to explain governance in both the Mediterranean welfare regimes and the Asian or South-American cases (Lessenich 1994, Nohlen 1999, Keman 1997c, 2002).[79]

Moreover, the development of welfare regimes in Asian countries in particular, under different political, social and economic conditions, produces methodological problems and underlines the need for reflection on the general categories, definitions, analytic framework and assumptions. In general Indian and Chinese scholars have no problem with Western theories, and agree that they can be applied to both countries in a limited way; yet disputes remain regarding the general application. Obviously, it is difficult to explain country-specific development using theory and methodology based on another cultural, historical and geographical context (Croissant et al. 2000). The resulting dilemma that political scientists face in conducting country-specific studies can be phrased as a question: Can general theories based on Western experiences be applied unproblematically to a different context? Sanfor Schram (2005) questions the goal of political science and the potential of various approaches to explain or understand political phenomena.

---

77 Esping-Andersen's (1990, 1994) works are reflective of the gradual shift in the sub-discipline away from the traditional economic approach (Barr 1993) towards a combined economic and sociological perspective under the sub-discipline of 'economic sociology'.

78 Esping-Andersen's (1990) pathbreaking work *Three Worlds of Welfare Capitalism* pioneered the dominant typology for welfare regimes in Western advanced capitalistic systems. His typology of welfare states offered a standard means to categories the typical welfare regime in the advanced industrial nation.

79 See Lessenich's article (1994) for a critical evaluation of the shortcomings of Esping-Andersen's typology (1990) for analysing the development and features of Mediterranean welfare systems.

To the above stated problem, another challenge, Almond and Coleman (1960) note, is grounded in the theoretical dimension and required modification of Western concepts, theories and causal implications, based on historical, political and social experiences and developments, for the Asian context.[80] Although David Easton (1965) and his pioneering work supplied an adequate system theory of different kinds of political systems, a major challenge for comparative political science has been the issue of how to treat and study the country-specific development of non-Western countries which test Western liberal theoretical assumptions regarding the typical development and functioning of modern states.

A so-called 'one-dimensional' approach cannot provide adequate explanation for variations. Douglas North's (2008) theoretical interpretation cultivated a theoretical and logical approach to explain the contemporary development on an abstract level as well as take into account the country-specific implications for contemporary politics. New institutionalism emerged as a new and powerful research approach for explaining, exploring and understanding country-specific institutional development, design and interaction patterns (Thelen and Steinmo 1992, Mitra 1994, 2005, 2013:229-33). Since 1990s, students of new institutionalism have modified and expanded research approaches and methods, producing sophisticated comparative studies on the country-specific political systems, related processes, structures and agencies of non-Western countries such as India (Mitra 2000, 2005, 2013:228) and China (Lieberthal and Oksenberg 1988, Lieberthal 1995, White L. 1998, 1999, 2009).

2.1.5 China and India: Same Path, different Goals?

Contrary to their Western counterparts, modern institutions in both countries have not evolved over time from the bottom to the top and could successfully establish themselves in their current form in the political, cultural and economic arenas (Mitra 1994a, 2002, 2013, Guo 2000, 2013b). Consequently, a common theme in the sophisticated political science literature on the Asian context (Croissant et al. 2000, Mitra 1994a, 2013, Guo 2013a, Ming and Li 2013) is the need to modify theoretical assumptions

80 Subrata Mitra (1999b, 2005, 2011) has repeatedly stressed the need to adapt Western theories to the Asian context and the specific conditions and development of Asian institutions and society.

for the Asian case. In the domestic political science discourse, scholars have pronounced the 'uniqueness' of both countries' development with regard to their cultural contexts and historical experiences (Tsou 1969, Jones 1981, Mitra 2005, 2013:227). Colonialism, Western dominance and globalization have brought capitalist market systems, modernization processes and political institutions (Bose and Jalal 2011).[81] On a macro level the processes and structures are the same but the country-specific characteristics of the formal and informal mechanisms for solving societal conflict have followed their own evolution (Mitra 1994a/b, Teiwes 1995). In time and space these mechanisms have adapted to country-specific historical, economic and political experiences and moments since the 1950s.[82]

The Chinese case: illustrating the requirement of adaptation

In China the notion of the '*welfare state*' or '*social state*' '社会福利国家' ('*shèhuì fúlì guójiā*') is only used for describing the welfare state in the Western industrial nation, which is seen as an advocate of private capitalism (Kaufmann 2009:190).

Relevant here are the differences in the definition of 'welfare'. The commonly used broad concept of 'public welfare' in literature refers to a range of schemes, programmes and services to increase the socio-economic security of citizens in the areas of education, health care as well as social security (McLean and McMillan 2013:570). In contrast to the broad Western definition of *social welfare* the Chinese term for welfare '社会福利' ('*shèhuìfúlì*') is restricted to a component of the broader category of '社会保障' ('*shèhuì bǎozhàng*'). The Chinese welfare system does not opt to guarantee minimum living standards for the citizen.[83] It is worth noting, as Dongmei Liu (2011:55-6) emphasises in her law study, that welfare does not aim to provide a security net for the individual but to improve the overall living conditions of the society, which again highlights the consti-

81 Cit op.
82 Chapter 3 provides an inquiry into the historical development of social security in India and China.
83 See Zheng, Hangsheng's (2004) report '郑杭生, 中国社会发展研究报告 ('*Research Reports on China Social Development 2004*')' for an investigation of the subject.

tutional preamble that the state provision of social security has to be 'compatible with the level of economic development'.[84]

In response to the problem stated above, the notion of the welfare state is replaced by the broader and value-neutral concept of the welfare regime, which grants a comparable category to explore social security provisions in cross-national perspective.

2.2 Towards a comparable Definition of Social Security

To address the above stated problem, a theoretical inquiry into the general definition of social security and its usefulness for the task ahead is in demand. Following Karl Marx's earlier argument on the '*Asian Mode*', it is interesting to note that most analyses based on country-based analytical descriptions of social security tend to offer little comparative information. What is lacking in most case studies of Asia seems to be a truly comparative set of theoretical definitions of social security. The issue is closely related to the complexity of the topic itself as well as the available range and scope of definitions.

What is social security? One could claim that, from the vantage point of most critics, social security provision is all about policy output legitimacy: first, there are those who argue that social security enables the state to react to socio-economic realities without intervening in free market forces; second, those who emphasise the very different capacity of social security to give the state an instrument to alter the outcomes of free market forces; third those who combine both previous statements and emphasise the relevance of social security provision as an instrument of the state to ensure the loyalty or public support of the majority of society. What these accounts miss, without denying the relevance of output legitimacy, is the complexity of social security provisions and the gap between policy objectives and policy outcomes due to mismanagement and misconceptions related to the missing administrative as well as financial resources and/or missing participation (Wagschal 1996, Castles 1998, 1999, Chan et al

84 See article 14 of the Chinese Constitution. A detailed investigation of social security as well as the related social rights of citizens in law and the constitution is conducted in Chapter 8.

2008, Rao 2011).[85] Undeniably, the policymaking process is determined to a decent degree by the assumed requirement of balancing pragmatic needs and ideological party guidelines[86]; however, the resulting social security provisions and the provision of welfare is much more complex and restricted by different kinds of constraints (Mitra 1991, 1999a, March and Olsen 1989). Even in the first step of political decision-making, constitutional and institutional constraints (Colomer et al. 1996, Shepsle 1997, Scharpf 1998, Schmidt 2000a), restrictions by the state budget (Tarschys 1985, Wagschal 1996, MacKinlay 1997), policy trajectories (Rose and Davis 1984) as well as the pressure of other policy fields (Schmidt 2003, 2005, Zohlnhöfer 2009)[87] and pressure groups (Immergut 1992, Pierson 1997) shape the '*room to manoeuvre*' (Mitra 1991, 2013). Following policy objectives, the provision of social security is jeopardized by the competence of the social security administration (Olsen 1998, Lehmbruch 1999), the state format, the funding and administration of schemes and programs, as well as changing socio-economic realities (Wilensky 1975, 1984, Wagschal 1996).[88]

In general, social security has not been effective and has even resulted in the direct opposite of its intended goal. In addition to the classic example of the downfall of the USSR in the late 1980s, the early experience of the Soviet development strategy in India and China has provided evidence of the negative side effects of overambitious social security politics, which have taken a heavy toll on economic resources and in the end not legitimated the system but accelerated the pressure for systematic reforms (Fukuyama 1992, Beyme 1994). Contrary to the USSR, India and China were able to cope with the negative consequences of their generous social security systems and policy objectives, providing full employment, gener-

---

85 See, for instance, the studies conducted by the World Bank (Kaufman et al. 2009, 2010) and/or case studies on the relevance of the social security administration for policy outcomes in India and China (Rao 2011, Rastogi 1994, Rohenstein, and Teorell. 2008, Shi 2006).

86 In his study on the USA and its public expenditures McDonald et al. (1999) found a strong measurable effect of Left-Right party priorities on public expenditure.

87 In particular, the pressure of actual challenges, such as needed state intervention in environmental, national security or economic issues, has a significant impact on the 'room to manoeuvre' for policymakers and results in available resources for social security provisions (Schmidt 2000a, 2012).

88 See also the Public Administration literature (Wildavsky 1980, March & Olsen 1989).

ous welfare and health care benefits in times of financial trouble and failing to fall prey to social unrest and political instability (Teiwes 1984, Schmidt 1999b).[89] Through the introduction of the capitalist market economy in the 1980s in China and in the 1990s in India, the limited social security coverage for rural and poorer segments of society became distinctly visible. The changing realities accelerated the demand for structural reforms in various policy fields, including social security provision. Both governments initiated a process of continual reform, became more and more pluralised, and modernized their social security administration in the 1990s to unburden the national bureaucracy as well as improve social security coverage for the rural and urban population until 2009.[90]

Contrary to the argument that social security provision has been a mere by-product of the economic transformation process, the welfare regimes in India and China have not transformed into classical 'liberal' welfare systems in times of accelerated liberalization and increasing trade openness[91] but instead proceeded in the twenty-first century to expand their *social-democratic/socialistic* character in opting for 'universal' social security coverage for all parts of society.[92] Accordingly, social security provision has to be elaborate and not reduced to a pragmatic tool to support economic growth; it needs to function as an instrument in the state arsenal to

---

89 For empirical evidence of the resilience of Indian democracy, as well as an analysis of the reasons, see Subrata K. Mitra (2005) '*The Puzzle of India's Government: Culture, Context, Comparative Theory*' or Rudolph and Rudolph (1968) '*In Pursuit of Lakshmi: The Political Economy of India*'.

90 In 2005 the president and leader of the CCP, Hu Jintao, announced the goal of improving coverage for urban and rural populations (Hu 2005). In 2004 India's newly elected UPA government said that a crucial point of its agenda is to 'enhance the welfare and well-being of farmers, farm labour and workers, particularly those in the unorganised sector, and assure a secure future for their families in every respect' (Hindu, 2004-04-28). What both share in common, at least rhetorically speaking, is the political ambition of setting up universal social security for the total population. The performance of both governments in the provision of social security will be elaborated throughout the study.

91 See the subsection on 'trade openness' (table 20).

92 The definition of 'liberal' welfare regime is used in reference to Esping-Andersen (1990). As argued in Chapter 3, his typology is not equipped to provide a clear categorisation of Asian welfare regimes. Accordingly a theoretical discussion of the limits of the typology is conducted in Chapter 3 as well as an indepth elaboration of the welfare regimes in China and India.

modify the outcomes of the ongoing modernization process in the nation's favour (Chan et al. 2008:186, Nagaraj 2012a, Kohli 2012:201, 215-17).

2.2.1 In Pursuit of a Working Definition

As emphasised in 1995 by the acting General Director of the ILO: 'Social Security Schemes in developing countries generally apply to wage earners in stable jobs in an Industrial Urban setting. Other categories of workers and especially the overwhelming majority of the working population who live in rural areas remain uncovered. Thus the gap between the relatively well off and poor may well be increased rather than diminished by such schemes. Many schemes inherited from colonial regimes benefit those who occupy a commanding position in the power structure including the military and civil service, the prosperous and better educated in other occupations. Some assistance schemes such as family benefits are patterned on schemes in the developing countries devised for very different demographic situations. Moreover, when social protection schemes are financed by state revenue derived from indirect taxes, which is sometimes the case, part of the cost of the benefits paid to the already better off bears more heavily on the poorest'. (ILO 1995:57)

Before proceeding to the problem and theory-driven analysis, we need to ask: what is social protection or security about? As mentioned before, the definition of social security or protection—terms that are often used as synonyms—has to be critically evaluated for the purpose of the study. While a coherent definition of social security is missing, the crux of most existing approaches is that such a definition either has a normative character or has been devised with regard to social protection and the socio-economic situation of advanced industrial countries. Leaving out the normative definitions, which lack a flexible and comparison-friendly framework, it is useful to summarize briefly the common definition of social security in the Western context before proceeding to provide a more adequate definition with regard to the subject of the study.

In 1958 the ILO counted social security as the 'the result achieved by a comprehensive and successful series of measures for protecting the public (or a large sector of it) from the economic distress that, in the absence of such measures, would be caused by the stoppage of earnings in sickness, unemployment or old age and after death; for making available to that same public, medical care as needed; and for subsidising families bringing up young children' (ILO 1958). Nearly twenty years later the ILO's characterization of social security has been significantly reformulated in the sense that social security is defined as the 'protection given by society to its members through a series of public measures from economic and social distress that otherwise would be caused by stoppage of or substantial reduction of earnings resulting from sickness, maternity, employment, injury, unemployment, invalidity, old age and death; the provision of medical care and the provision of subsidies for families with children' (ILO 1984:3), with the ILO highlighting later in the same report that 'the security [is] furnished through appropriate organisation against certain risks to which its members are exposed. These risks are essentially contingencies against which the individual of small means cannot effectively provide for by his own ability or foresight alone or even in private combination with fellows' (ILO 1984:83).

What these stated characterizations of the ILO share in common is the typically restricted view of social protection in modern developed countries as an integrated strategy to cushion sharp decline in individual income. Such a restricted view has been criticised as failing to grasp the function of social protection in developing countries.

Amartya Sen and Jean Dreze (1989) characterize the ideal-typical function of social protection in a broader perspective as 'an objective to be pursued through public means rather than … a narrowly defined set of particular strategies.' Their point of view emphasizes that the tight coupling of socio-economic deprivation and the vulnerable socio-economic status of groups has to be addressed through social security politics in developing countries or that 'the basic idea of Social Security is to use social means to prevent deprivation and vulnerability to deprivation' (Dreze and Sen 1991). In tandem with Amartya Sen and Jean Dreze (1991), a good deal of authors[93] question the restricted view of social security as merely an instrument to reduce decline in income. What all these works have in common is a broad perspective on social security provision as an instrument to shape socio-economic realities. These authors all point to more or less the same argument: that social security provision in developing countries has to address vulnerable and low income groups to tackle socio-economic deprivation.

93 Particular contributions have been published by Ahmad (1991), Burgess and Stern (1991) and Guhan (1992).

Robin Burgers and Nicholas Stern (1991:43) note that 'Deprivation and vulnerability are integral to the lives of many in poor countries. In developed countries unfavorable outcome in economic activity frequently means real hardship but in poor countries they often lead to death or destitution. (…) Accordingly, we define the objective of Social Security as being the prevention by social means of very low standards of living irrespective of whether there are the results of chronic deprivation or temporary diversity. The term Social Security may then be viewed as a means of success in meeting this objective'. [94]

For all the existing differences, these authors' accounts make very similar and consistent comments on the necessity of broadening the perspective on social security to facilitate economic security for all segments of society so that it not only aims to rectify employment situations but also to introduce programmes and schemes aimed at improving vulnerable groups and their endowments, exchange entitlements, real incomes and social consumption (Guhan 1994). For Rao (2007:4-5) providing economic security includes creating 'opportunities and building capacities, institutional as well as individual, for utilization of such opportunities for economic security provided by the society as a whole or by the institutions in it like families, communities, social groups, markets, individually or collectively for the 'social well being' of an individual for his journey from the date of birth to the date of death.'

2.2.2 India and Chinese Concept of Social Security: Same Word, different Meaning

Unlike India, where the British Raj established Western concepts and terminology, in China the term 'social security' '社会保障' ('shèhuì bǎozhàng') refers to the ILO definition of social security (1984) and has been officially adapted by the CCP's Central Committee in the 'Sugges-

94 Similarly, the Indian National Academy for Training & Research in Social Security (NATRSS) (1998:3) defines social security as 'the security that society furnishes through appropriate organisation against certain risks to which its members are perennially exposed. These risks are essential contingencies against which the individual of small means cannot effectively provide by his own ability or foresight alone or even in private combination with his fellows. The mechanics of social security therefore consists in counteracting the blind injustice of nature and economic activities by rational planned justice with a touch of benevolence to temper it'.

tions of the CCP for the 7th Five Year Plan'.[95] Upon its suggestion the term was instantiated in the 7th Five Year Plan for 'economical and social development (1986-1990)' published in 1985 (Shi 1990). Interestingly, despite the reference to the ILO definition Chinese scholars have so far failed to devise a common definition of social security. It is used in an ad-hoc manner and associated by scholars and government officials with the granted 'right to material assistance from the state and society when they [citizens] are old, ill, employment-related accidents, disabled or in cases of natural catastrophes'.[96] In a broader understanding, social security is used in official documents for social security, social assistance, social welfare, medical health care, and state- and employer-provided services. It is worth noting that social security is not only seen as an instrument to guarantee minimum living standards but also as a means to improve overall socio-economic living conditions of society (D. Liu 2011:96-97).[97]

2.2.3 Working Definition for Social Security

The revision of the definition by the ILO (1984:3) captures the point and will be used as a working definition throughout the study: 'The protection which society provides for its members, through a series of public measures, against economic and social distress that otherwise would be caused by the stoppage or substantial reduction of earnings resulting from sickness, maternity, employment injury, unemployment, invalidity, old age, death, the provision of medial care, and the provision of subsidies for families with children.' In general social security programmes around the

95 The term 'social security' is relatively young and was introduced by the former non-communist Chinese government in the late 1930s. It is an adaptation from the American '*Social Security Act, 1935*' (D. Liu 2011:96).

96 Zheng, Gongcheng (2004:29-31) emphasises this point in his article '郑功成，自然灾害与社会安全 ('natural catastrophes and social security')' and provides insight into existing state social security schemes to cover natural catastrophes and economic uncertainties of citizens.

97 In his article Jun Tang (2002:204-6) 唐钧，中国社会救助制度的变迁与评估 ('*Commentaries on the Chinese social assistance system*')' gives a short overview of the concept of social assistance in China.

world and across countries can be distinguished by their range, scope and contribution modalities.[98]

In the OECD Report (2007) 'Statistics and Indicators for 30 Countries' [99] a useful working definition is provided: 'social security schemes are schemes imposed and controlled by government units for the purpose of providing social benefits to members of the community as a whole, or of particular sections of the community' and 'they generally involve compulsory contributions by employees or employers or both, and the terms on which benefits are paid to recipients are determined by a government unit. Social security funds have to be distinguished from other social insurance programmes which are determined by mutual agreement between individual employers and their employees.'

2.3 Welfare Literature and the two Cases

An investigation of academic discussions of the nature of the welfare state is useful in evaluating the variables for state capacity. Comparing India and China on an empirical and theoretical level with the typical modern welfare state in the OECD, such as one of the Scandinavian countries, is not of concern here. Both Asian governments have limited their social policy outputs, in terms of the proportional amount of social expenditure for social security, due to the pressure of other policy fields, such as defence, security and economy.

Another issue or problem for the provision of social security is the amount of people under the poverty line (see the next chapter's descriptive section, table 4). Although in the last couple decades new institutionalism has given way to sophisticated comparative research on democracies, autocracies and hybrid regimes, the impetus for the study of welfare regimes has been positively affected by welfare discourse.[100] It should be noted at

98 In its descriptive reports on social security around the world the United States Social Security Administration (SSA 2002, 2005, 2006, 2008, and 2012) includes statistical data on social security and a general and comparable definition of the existing types of social security schemes.

99 See http://stats.oecd.org/glossary/detail.asp?ID=2496 (2015-01-01)

100 In particular, rational choice institutionalism has proven extremely useful for the investigation of the nature of policymaking in autocratic regimes such as China. Recent studies conducted by Chinese scholars rely on the theoretical assumption of rational choice (Guo 2013a).

the outset that welfare discourse includes not merely an intellectual history but also the relevant theoretical approaches of the current discourse.

2.3.1 Three classical approaches in theoretical reasoning and their implications

The recent debate on the welfare state and the impetus of the new institutionalism has produced a common consensus on two central concepts of institutional variables which structure welfare regimes and social security provision to a decent degree (Hewitt 1977, Esping-Andersen 1990, Ostrom 1990, Shepsle 1997, North 2008). In the academic discourse on the welfare state, three major approaches can be separated which shape the current understanding of the welfare state in literature.

For an investigation into the current academic discourse[101] on the topic the three major schools of theoretical reasoning, which have significantly shaped the current debate, will be briefly introduced. The first two, traditional institutionalism and functionalism, are relevant, however, whereas the third source, the group theories, are not a unified school per se. Yet the latter will be discussed in detail because they have significantly shaped the theoretical and methodological logic of inquiry in the welfare literature.

Let us begin with **classical institutionalism,** which has cultivated the long-standing and generally agreed-upon fact that institutions matter. Students of classical institutionalism have argued that institutions are the major determinants which structure the available behaviour patterns and potential outcomes, as well as limit the access of involved actors and their chances to enforce their perceptions (Shepsle 1997). According to this line of argument, a distinct set of institutions structure the welfare regime, policymaking and outcomes, separate from political and social pressure—which strongly suggests that 'in contrast to approaches that seek the root of political activity in social forces, the cases discussed here show that politics can be independent of social power' (Immergut 1992:243). In the second part of the twentieth century, the rise of young democratic states from colonial dependency and in most cases the authoritarian power of po-

101 The development of modern comparative politics is largely a consequence of increasingly indepth knowledge of individual countries and political contexts based on modern data collection methods and the critical evaluation and evolution of classical theories (Blondel 1969, 1973, Keman 1997b).

litical elites, bureaucratic governors, or the military could not be explained by the limited theoretical and methodological perspective of classical institutionalism (Immergut 1992, Daalder 2002). The resulting critical debate cultivated a positive climate for more sophisticated approaches in political science. A watershed event was the emergence of New Institutionalism in the 1990s, which expanded the classical institutional approach with a more actor-oriented perspective and a sophisticated theoretical and problem-driven research design. Contrary to classical institutionalism the role and function of the involved actors and their rational behaviour gained attention. The impact of *New Institutionalism* on the discipline of comparative politics cultivated an understanding of the relevance and nature of institutions for policy processes, structure, agency and related outcomes (Shepsle 1997)[102].

Functionalism (similar to early Marxism) explained the evolution of the welfare state as a reaction to modernization and the industrialization process. However, functional accounts criticised the contemporary Marxist theory of modern capitalism as conceptually and empirically limited (Goldthrope 1984:315). Liberal reasoning produced a long-term concept to grasp the multidimensional impacts of the industrialisation process (Kerr 1960, 1973), which on the one hand applied similar deductive methods to explore socio-economic processes such as Marxism but on the other hand directly criticised Marxist interpretation (Kerr 1983, Goldthrope 1984:315-16). Hence, it is argued that the driving force of historical development is not class and societal conflict but instead the political elites' perception of and response to mass public pressure. In addition, the basic assumption underlying the functionalist approach[103] is that the welfare state is heavily affected by country-specific variations in the development, labour market structures and performance of domestic economies and shifts in the societal demands of citizens. It has therefore been repeatedly argued that industrialization or modernisation processes weaken the efficiency of the existing traditional security net in society, which has been provided by the family, church and kinship. It is assumed that the state reacts to citizens' demands for social protection, services and new collective

---

102 Students of traditional institutionalism emphasised the independence of institutional processes. In their perspective societal or political interests did not affect institutional choices and outcomes.

103 For functionalistic accounts of the nature of the welfare state see Lebeaux (1958), Pryor (1968) and/or Wilensky (1975).

goods. Thus, it has been argued that the central role of welfare states in modern advanced industrial countries is to satisfy these new societal demands that in turn determine the shaping of the welfare state (Wilensky 1975, Kerr 1983, Flora 1986).

Another point of departure in exploring the welfare state are *group theoretical approaches* derived from the recent debate on the welfare state and the role of societal and political actors. Following the 'logic of industrialization' and the development of welfare regimes under Social Democratic governments in advanced industrial countries the process of welfare expansion is directly linked to the 'Social Democratization of Capitalism'. Similar to functionalism the approach emphasises the importance of societal demands for the welfare state; but contrary to functionalism it stresses that class coalitions between political parties and interest groups, namely social democratic parties and labour organisations, are crucial for the welfare state. In addition, group theory-related studies emphasise that 'the history of political class coalitions is the most decisive cause of welfare-state variations' (Esping-Andersen 1990:1). Various case studies on welfare states and the social democratic party model argue for the relevance of the partisan effect on social spending.[104]

From the results of the vast numbers of cross-national and country-specific studies on modern welfare regimes in the OECD nations, students of comparative politics, such as Hewitt (1977), strongly suggest that political parties and the composition of government matters. Evidence in support of the hypothesis can be derived from the development of welfare regimes in Western Europe in the 1960s and 1970s, which exemplify broad patterns that suggest the composition of the party government matters (Goldthrope 1984, Cameron 1984, Lehmbruch 1984). In settings with strong Social Democrats, which in most cases relied for their electoral support on associated labour organisations, the resulting Social Democratic party government nurtured the expansion of the modern welfare state and '*égalité des conditions*'[105] (Schmidt 1983, Cameron 1984). A common consensus in the literature has linked the political power of pro-welfare parties, such as

104 For a detailed discussion of the partisan effect see various authors, such as Hewitt (1977) and Manfred G. Schmidt, for a detailed discussion on the topic (2002).

105 '*égalité des conditions*' in the notion of Tocqueville (1990), cit op.

Social Democrats and/or Christian Democrats[106], to their available support by trade union organisations (Korpi 1978, Esping-Andersen 1990). Various cross-national quantitative approaches explore the link between the social democratic party, labour organisations and the welfare state (Hewit 1977, Korpi 1983, Swank and Hicks 1985). A common consensus in literature on the welfare state is that the extension of the welfare state is directly linked to the political weakness of conservative parties (Castles 1978) and the ability of social democrats to build political and class coalitions (Esping-Andersen 1985)[107]. In addition, the students of the power resource theorem argued that the political power of social democrats is determined by the relative power of associated labour organisations (Stephens 1979, Esping-Andersen 1990). Since the late 1980s most cross-sectional and pooled time studies on the welfare state and the social democratic thesis have identified the political power of social democrats as the main variable for the extension of social policymaking and therefore the focus has shifted to the elaboration of social democratic political power as an explanatory variable for variations in country-specific outcomes of social policymaking (Griffin et al. 1989, Korpi 1989, Alvarez et al. 1996).

2.3.2 Towards an actor-orientated approach

In the course of theoretical reasoning and the context of the *structure-agent debate*, Korpi (1983) expanded the limited terms of much of the academic debate. He strongly argued, on the basis of empirical observations, for the relevance of trade unions as collective actors and supporters of the expansion of the welfare state. His postulated link between strong

106 Expanding the causality of the '*Social Democratic*' model, Manfred G. Schmidt (1983) and others evaluated the same partisan effect of Christian Democrats on the expansion of the welfare state in the 1980s.

107 A prominent research topic in the bulk of cross-national studies has been the Scandinavian countries and their traditionally strong social-democratic parties and high levels of welfare expenditure, such as the Swedish case, which has commonly been used as an example of the postulated causal link between a social-democratic majority and expansion of the welfare state (Esping-Andersen 1985a, Esping-Andersen and Kropi 1986). It is worth noting that Therborn (1989) has argued that the high solidarity and resulting welfare in Sweden has to be understood not as a consequence of democracy but in terms of the historical experiences of the country.

union organisations in terms of union coverage and the success of social democrats in election processes could be easily validated for most of the OECD countries (Schmidt 1983, OECD 1999). In addition Korpi (1983, 1989) formulated his power-resource argument that the higher the organizational coverage of wage earners the higher the extension of the welfare state and related '*de-commodification*'. Following the power-resource argument strong welfare is evidence of the relative power of working-class organisations and social democrats. In effect, the underlying pre-condition of social democratic power are strong labour organisations (Stephens 1979).[108] The resulting debate on the 'social democratization of capitalism' has either focused on the distributive performance of the welfare state to produce equality or the specific institutional outcomes of the welfare state (Western 1989, Esping-Andersen 1985a, 1990, Kersbergen and Becker 2002).

The welfare state is not restricted to Social Democracy. The postulated link between the relative power of the labour movement and the extension of the welfare state is not unchallenged. Cameron (1978, 1984) and other scholars critically evaluated the Social-Democratic model, with Cameron arguing that the extension of the welfare state is directly related to the economic performance and size of a country's economy.[109]

Students of the welfare state have provided evidence that there is considerable variation in the variables as well as the postulated causality. Another objection is that Social Democratic majority governments tend to promote the expansion of the welfare state; however, other parties, such as Christian Democratic or Left-totalitarian parties, are in favour of social policies. Also in recent times of austerity and budget restrictions even Social Democratic majorities are no guarantor of an increase in social expenditures. Neither do social democratic governments produce better social

108 Various corporate studies have produced theoretical and methodological measurements; see, for instance, Cameron (1978, 1984), Schmidt (1983), and Scharpf (1984, 1998). In addition, the methodological framework developed in the corporate debate and related studies on the industrial relation system are central points of reference for most of the conducted studies on the relevance of labour unions for public policy.

109 In the same vein Katzenstein (1985) further developed the argument that small open economies tend to promote democratic corporatist arrangements to guarantee socio-economic equality in exchange for international competitiveness.

policy outcomes or higher socio-economic equality than their counterparts (Titmus 1974, Keman 1990, OECD 1999).[110]

2.3.3 Path-dependency and Social Security Provision

The critical reflection on the '*Social Democratic bias*' has revealed the requirement for sophisticated research on the link and given way to various studies on social policies—such as pension systems (Myles 1989), sickness insurance (Korpi 1983, 1989), pension rights (Palme 1990) and labour market policies (Esping-Andersen 1990, 1998)—stressing the need to explore the institutional design of the specific welfare state and related effects on policy choices and outcomes. In his popular research Paul Pierson (1994, 1996, 2000) reflects at length on the welfare state. Pierson argues in his (1994) study '*Dismantling the Welfare State?*' that despite political and financial pressure on the welfare state, 'the welfare state stands out as an island of relative stability' (1994:5). His argument in '*New Politics of the Welfare State'* (1994, 1996, 2001 and 2003) is for strong path-dependency of social policies.[111] Following the line of new institutional reasoning, the weakening of traditional support for the welfare state, such as that provided by Social or Christian Democrats and related labour organisations, does not automatically result in weakening support for the welfare state or the elected political parties. It is worth noting that social policies produce their own supporters, such as interest groups (Pierson 1996, 2001). Hence, the 'frontal assaults on the welfare state carry tremendous electoral risks' (Pierson 1996:178) as well as institutional opposition by majority as well as minority institutions empowered by formal and/or informal institutional features with a veto ability (Schmidt 1998, 2002, Przeworski and Gandhi 2007 a/b).

Meanwhile, the controversy has resulted in critical evaluation of '*welfare statism*' in general, and of the determinants and resulting theoretical

110 The cases of several countries, such as the Netherlands, disproved the argument that Social Democratic majorities are a necessary pre-condition for '*welfare statism'* and high levels of socio-economic equality (Castles 1978, 1985, Stephens 1979, Wilensky 1981).

111 Moreover, changes in the composition of governments, such as the takeover by liberals, will not produce proclaimed cutbacks to the welfare state. As argued by Paul Pierson (1994, 1996) the reason is that the beneficiaries of social services (i.e. pensioners) act as a powerful pressure group.

assumptions specifically (Kersbergen and Becker 2002:193). Three main shortcomings of the early studies questioned the theoretical argument on the variables explaining the development and cross-national variations in the social policy performance, choices and character of welfare regimes.[112]

The comparative measurement mainly focused on the aggregated data on income distribution, which was problematic on technical grounds. Before the 1990s comparative empirical data was missing in this field of research on social policy outcomes in the conducted comparative studies. In the 1990s the *Luxembourg Income Study* produced a landmark study and for the first time offered a cross-national database for comparable empirical data (Mitchell 1990)[113]. Another problem in determining the effects of welfare programs is the time variable. On the one hand, the effects of social policies tend to reduce their significant outcomes over time (LeGrand 1982, Esping-Andersen 1990). On the other hand, the impact of path-dependency and the policy trajectories of social policy make it hard to attribute social outcomes to a distinguished set of government characteristics (Pierson 1994, 1996).[114]

2.3.4 Critical Evalution on the existing Typologies

In effect, in the 1990s witnessed an outpouring of sophisticated studies on the modern welfare regimes and cluster studies. These inquiries (Esping-Andersen 1990, Kersberger 1999, 2000, Casltes 1999) not only offered empirical data but also initiated a critical debate related to empirical

112 Mostly all of these studies used the amount of public expenditures as a core variable. Although the public expenditures offered reliable and comparable data, the outcomes could not clearly distinguish the assumed effects of Social Democrats on social expenditures (Esping-Andersen 1990, ibid and Korpi 1986).

113 Before the publication of the *Luxembourg Income Study* and its comparative data catalogue, for nearly all Western European countries the comparative measurement of income distribution could only account for transfer payments which excluded non-cash services (Ringen 1987). For a detailed discussion of the issue see D. Mitchell's Ph.D. thesis (1990).

114 Policy trajectories (Steinmo and Thelen 1992, Schmidt 1999a, 2012a), constitutional and institutional veto players (Tsebelis 1990), electoral promises (Lane and Errson 2002) as well as financial budget restrictions (Swank and Hicks 1985) produce constraints on the '*room to manoeuvre*'.

deficits and assumed theoretical implications, such as the *Social Democrats Theorem*, of former comparative conducted researches. The controversial and critical reflection on the shortcomings of decent typologies in the welfare state literature cultivated a vivid debate on theoretical and methodological issues. The recent empirical-analytical findings on the development of the current welfare regimes in the OECD countries questioned the limitation of the old assumption and typologies (OECD 1999). Titmus (1977) gave impulse to rework the existing theoretical categories of welfare regimes and stresses the need to distinguish between '*social security state*' and '*social welfare state*'. Similar to Titmus (1977), Therborn (1986, 1987a)[115] repeatedly emphasised the need for improvement and argued to include not only policy outcomes but also policy choices in any model on the welfare state to explain cross-national variations effectively. In his perspective the *Social Democratic welfare state* could only be considered in relation to the political commitment of full employment (Therborn 1987a). Taking up various points of critique Esping-Andersen (1990) established in his path-breaking work a categorisation for the common welfare regimes in the OECD nations. He avoided the old class reductionism because one '*cannot assume that socialism is the natural basis for age-earner mobilization*' (1990:17). Esping-Andersen distinguishes three types of welfare regimes, related social policy styles of Liberal, Social Democrats and Conservative regimes. He further argues that the success of political parties is also influenced by its ability to *re-interpreted* workers' demands gain support of the mass labour organisations (Esping-Andersen 1990).[116] While his typology is offers three broad categories for the development of typical welfare regimes it is limited to the Western European context and can not account for the specific development of welfare regimes in other parts of the world. The suggested theoretical expansions,

115 Another account is provided by T. Therborn's In his article '*Capital and suffrage*' Therborn (1977) argues that universal suffrage is a result of the growing importance of the working class in the process of industrialization which suffered under the industrialization process as well as in the Great War.

116 Goldthrope (1984) work and the included article by various students of corporatism contribute to the academic understanding for the relevance and determinants of organised labour. The volume also contributes to foster a common understanding for the political impact of unions on the decision making as well as implementation process (Lehmbruch 1984) as well as provide a sophisticated elaboration of the determinants for the political and economical power of organised labour in democracies (Cameron 1984).

for example an Asian welfare regime[117] (Goodman and Peng 1996), Mediterranean type[118] (Lessenich 1994) as well as a special category for Australia and New Zealand (Castles and Mitchel 1993), had their own deficits and could not establish themselves due to the broad variations of welfare regimes in the conducted countries.

2.3.5 Expanding the View – Welfare Regimes Types in autocratic Systems

In effect, the 1990s witnessed an outpouring of sophisticated studies, including cluster studies, on modern welfare regimes. These inquiries (Esping-Andersen 1990, Kersberger 1999, 2000, Casltes 1999) not only offered empirical data but also initiated a critical debate related to empirical deficits and assumed theoretical implications, such as the *Social Democrats Theorem*, of comparative research. The controversial and critical reflection on the shortcomings of decent typologies in the welfare state literature cultivated a vivid debate on theoretical and methodological issues. The recent empirical-analytical findings on the development of current welfare regimes in the OECD countries question the limitations of the old assumptions and typologies (OECD 1999). Titmus (1977) provided the impetus to rework existing theoretical categories of welfare regimes and distinguish between the '*social security state*' and the '*social welfare state*'. Similar to Titmus (1977), Therborn (1986, 1987a)[119] repeatedly argued for the requirement to take policy choices into account. In his perspective the *social democratic welfare state* could only be considered in relation to the political commitment of full employment (Therborn 1987a). Taking up various points of critique in his pathbreaking work, Esping-An-

117 Goodman and Pengs' (1996) article '*The East Asian welfare states: peripatetic learning, adaptive strategy, and nation-building*' in which both authors have developed a category for Asian context based on the Japanese development.

118 The Mediterranean state, such as Italy, can not be easily included in Esping-Andersen's typology (1990) due to the variations in the historical and political conditions. Lessenich (1994) illustrates the unique features of contemporary Mediterranean welfare regimes as well as a critical elaboration of Esping-Andersen's typology.

119 Another account is provided by T. Therborn's article '*Capital and suffrage.*' Therborn (1977) argues that universal suffrage is a result of the growing importance of the working class in the process of industrialization.

dersen (1990) established a categorisation method for the common welfare regimes in the OECD nations. He avoided the old class reductionism because one 'cannot assume that socialism is the natural basis for age-earner mobilization' (1990:17). Esping-Andersen discerns three types of welfare regimes related to the social policy styles of Liberal, Social Democrat and Conservative regimes. He argues that the success of political parties is also influenced by their ability to *re-interpret* workers' demands to gain the support of mass labour organisations (Esping-Andersen 1990).[120] While his typology offers three broad categories for the development of typical welfare regimes it is limited to the Western European context and cannot account for the specific development of welfare regimes in other parts of the world. The suggested theoretical expansions of, for example, an Asian welfare regime[121] (Goodman and Peng 1996), the Mediterranean type[122] (Lessenich 1994) or the special category of Australia and New Zealand (Castles and Mitchel 1993), have their own deficits and cannot establish themselves due to the broad variations of welfare regimes in the conducted countries.

Typology of Social Political Regimes in non-Democracies

Comparative political literature has been nurtured by a sophisticated autocratic literature (Linz 1975, Kailitz and Köllner 2013), which has developed multiple variables to distinguish autocracy. The generalisation of the social policy choices and outcomes of autocratic regimes allows for simple categories of autocratic regime types. Three main types can be distinguished: *fascist* welfare regimes, *socialist* welfare regimes, as well as the so-called *Newly Industrializing Countries*.

---

120 Goldthrope's (1984) work and an article by various students of corporatism contribute to the academic understanding of the relevance and determinants of organised labour. The volume also contributes to fostering a common understanding of the political impact of unions on the decision-making and implementation processes (Lehmbruch 1984), as well as provides a sophisticated elaboration of the determinants of the political and economic power of organised labour in democracies (Cameron 1984).

121 See Goodman and Pengs' (1996) article 'The East Asian welfare states: peripatetic learning, adaptive strategy, and nation-building' in which both authors develop a category for the Asian context based on the development of the Japanese case.

122 see footnote 118.

First, typical *fascist* autocracies have the aim of implementing high levels of discriminating welfare schemes. The programs are often direct and exclusive in their arrangements. The typical example is the Third Reich. The social policy included a vast range of various social programs and security systems to support families, workers and soldiers. The fascist government continued and extended the policies of the German Reich of 1871 and the Weimar Republic. The direct and exclusive character of the programs and schemes included only members of the *Volksgemeinschaft*. The membership was based on the racial ideology of the Third Reich and excluded all others who did not fulfil the racial categories of the *Volksgemeinschaft* (Schmidt 1999, 2012).[123]

Second, in *socialist or left-totalitarian* states, the overall objective of social security politics is similar to fascist regimes: to produce output legitimacy. Similar to the fascist welfare regime the left-totalitarian one opts for high levels of welfare and social security but (in contrast to the limited scope of the fascist regimes) universal access for all citizens (Schmidt 1999b). The post-war *left-totalitarian* regimes tend to have the highest levels of social welfare spending compared to other autocratic regimes. In this regard the German Democratic Republic, and the Hungarian and Czech Republics can be characterized, as mentioned before, by high levels of social expenditure due their historical and ideological roots (Schmidt 2013). The discrepancy between high social expenditures and low levels of economic growth increases the pressure on the welfare regime in the long run. The same can be observed of the *left-totalitarian* regimes in Latin America, which tended to overburden the state's capacity due to high levels of social expenditure (Nohlen 1998, Schmidt 1999, Wagschal 1996, The Economist 2014h). In Argentina Juan Peron imposed a kind of protectionism with socialist features and high levels of public expenditure from 1946 until 1955. Similar to the middle-European *left-totalitarian* regimes, his regime's overstretched social policy choices had negative long-term implications for economic development and the state budget of his government and succeeding ones (Hirschmann 1979).[124]

---

123 For a detailed analysis of the Third Reich's social security system, see Manfred G. Schmidt (1999:582-84).

124 In his work, Hirschmann (1979) grants the reader an indepth analysis of social security provision and related human as well as economic development in Argentina under the presidency of Juan Peron.

Third, the development of many of the South-East Asian autocratic countries emphasised the demand for a theoretical stretching or expansion of Western-oriented typologies. In the literature on the economies of the South-East Asian countries scholars generally agree (Goodman 1996) on the category of the so-called *Newly Industrializing Countries* (NIC). Based on the experiences of the authoritarian regimes in South-East Asia in the post-war period, Asian scholars constructed their own typology. It is argued that the governments in the NICs pay close attention to economic growth and social security politics is only an instrument in the arsenal of the state to guarantee economic performance and a healthy and cheap labour force. The welfare regimes in NICs set up discriminating social security with minimal benefits for the urban working-aged population (Swamy, 2010). The range and scope of welfare policies are mainly restricted to urban areas and coastal provinces and aim to improve urbanization.

The typology seems close to Karl Marx's categorization of the Asian case as the '*Asian Mode*'[125] because of its different development.[126] In comparative studies the European cases have been under the scrutiny of intensive theoretical and empirical studies. The typologies that have been developed on the basis of the experiences of Western cases did not fit the Asian context. In effect, as mentioned before, the theoretical discourse has been limited, which is reflected in the NIC category. The relatively broad typology is more or less a catch-all category which fits for nearly all developing countries.

A critical review of the concept illustrates that the NIC typology greatly overlaps with the fascist or liberal welfare regime. The only difference in the fascist one is in the range and scope of social policies from the ethnic category with a high level of benefits to an economic one with only minimal benefits for the target group. But the category also overlaps with the liberal welfare regime category of Esping-Andersen (1990) and therefore offers only marginal benefits for close investigation and categorization.

Why is the Chinese autocratic system not following the classical policy choices and development of other left-totalitarian regimes in Europe? A point of departure is given by recent studies and the empirically validated

125 Quoted by Michael Adas (1989:236-38), cit op.

126 The development of the Asian states can not be explained by traditional Marxism because of the missing industrialization and class structure (Adas 1989).

argument that economic and political *transformation processes*[127] can have significant effects on social security politics.

It goes without saying that these categories describe ideal types on a higher level of abstraction. Cross-national comparisons of autocratic regimes as well as democracies have provided empirical evidence that even states operating under the same political system vary in their institutional design, resulting social output, and policy performance. Despite the fact that in most cases the country-specific regimes cannot easily be attributed to one category, these models with high levels of abstraction are indeed important methods for comparative political inquiry. Although both cases are not easily associated with one type of welfare regime, the issue at hand is the extent to which these categories account for cross-national variations and help to explain the development of contemporary welfare regimes.

2.4 Method of Process Tracing and the Analytic Narrative

Why do nations respond in such different ways to endemic crisis? For Charles Tilly (2005:10) anyone 'who wants to explain political structures and processes in the present state of knowledge does much better sorting out the more limited causal mechanisms that produce change, variation, and salient features of those structures and processes' (Tilly 2005:10). Accordingly to Tilly's (1970, 2005) analysis of actual political processes, the narrative approach not only offers indepth understanding of the country-specific context, but also provides distinct data on the reasons why, under the guidance of rationalism, countries or politicians follow or depart from policy trajectories during critical junctures.[128] Critical junctures are events in which external or domestic processes result in changing trends for the

---

127 See Wolfgang Merkel (1999, 2004).

128 Paul Pierson (2004) notes of critical junctures that they 'are 'critical' because they place institutional arrangements on paths or trajectories, which are then very difficult to alter.' Also Capoccia and Keleman (2007:343) characterize critical junctures as 'a situation in which the structural (that is, economic, cultural, ideological, organizational) influences on political action are significantly relaxed for a relatively short period, with two main consequences: the range of plausible choices open to powerful political actors expands substantially and the consequences of their decisions for the outcome of interest are potentially much more momentous'. As Thelen and Steinmo (1992:16-18) further remark, these critical

economic, social or political processes realities threatening the status quo and the legitimacy of the state (Gerschewski et al. 2013:106-8). These events and the ability of the state to react to the new circumstances determine the development and policy output of the modern states in times of crisis.

Comparative politics and political science in general have been called upon to adequately explain why nations often stick to policy trajectories even challenging times which produce significant pressure to adjust or even reject former policy trajectories (North 1990, Hall 1986 Mahoney and Thelen 2010). A strong controversy on the topic and reasons for radical policy changes has erupted on different occasions involving various explanatory approaches.[129]

One point of departure has been formulated by the '*incrementalism*' argument (Davis et al. 1966) for the veto capacity of bureaucratic inertia and stand-offs against the attempts by the party government to initiate structural changes. Although the cooperation of bureaucracy has had a direct influence on policy planning and implementation, the degree of bureaucratic opposition is limited mostly to the quality of policy implementation. A coherent body of studies has accumulated evidence of the minor relevance of so-called '*incrementalism*' for policy processes, planning and implementation (Castles 1982, Schmidt 1980, 1996a/b, 2002, Keman 1984, 2002b).

A more fruitful approach for the investigation of policy trajectories is provided by historical institutionalism and Douglas North's prominent work (1990) on the methodological and theoretical challenge to explain the rise and fall of nations—by referring to their institutional trajectories or '*institutional change*' and the concept of critical junctures, which is essential to the logic of inquiry adapted by historical institutionalism.[130] In the wake of historical institutionalism Paul Pierson (1994, 1996)[131] has examined the relevance of path dependency for explaining current welfare

---

junctures are exogenous factors and cannot be explained by the country-specific institutional setting or development alone.

129 In this context only the main relevant approaches for the research are discussed.

130 While such structural reasoning has been criticised for its 'structural bias' (Joppke 1993, Goodwin and Jasper 1999), the contextual principles in decision-making can account for cross-national variations.

131 Furthermore Pierson constructed a general typology for categorizing welfare regimes (Pierson 1996).

regimes, policy choices and outcomes. His article (1996) on the categorization of welfare regimes emphasizes the importance of path-dependent policy trajectories for today's decision making.

(i) First, one main reason why governments follow policy trajectories is the fact that 'each step along a particular path produces consequences which make that path more attractive for the next round (Pierson 2000:253).'

(ii) And second, the country-specific policy choices in the past and present depend on the institutional context and involved actors, which produce either pressure for or opposition against policy choices. As he highlights, besides the institutional veto players, welfare policies tend to build their own collective actors and pressure groups.[132] These groups can have significant relevance as veto players.

The causal logic behind the path-dependency argument is that policy choices made as a reaction to critical junctures in history have lasting impacts (Thelen and Steinmo 1992, Streeck and Thelen 2005:8-9). There is little dispute nowadays on the theoretical and practical relevance of 'crises' or 'unsettled times' in which the status quo is breached (Swidler 1986, Capoccia and Kelemen 2007:341). These events or junctures, as Pierson emphasises, 'are 'critical' because they place institutional arrangements on paths or trajectories, which are then very difficult to alter.' These junctures are 'relatively short' in time and have a 'substantial' chance of affecting policymaking (Pierson 1994, 1996, Capoccia and Kelemen 2007:348), or in other words they are 'structural (that is, economic, cultural, ideological, organizational) influences on political action [that] are significantly relaxed for a relatively short period, with two main consequences: the range of plausible choices open to powerful political actors expands substantially and the consequences of their decisions for the outcome of interest are potentially much more momentous' (Capoccia and Kelemen 2007:343).[133]

---

132 The supportive pressure groups for welfare programs typically consist of their beneficiaries, such as retirees who are interested in ensuring the program to secure their material benefits (1996, 2001).

133 In their work '*Designing Social Inquiry*' (1994:77-80) Gary King, Robert O. Keohane, and Sidney Verba highlight the merits of counter factual analysis for historical studies, which, however, demands theoretical consistency and follows logical and methodological rules for assessing plausibility. For a discussion of the elaboration on the counter factual approach see also Fearon's (1994) article

2.4.1 Narrative, Path-Dependency and Critical Junctures

The rise of historical institutionalism since the early 1990s has been explained by the lack of coherent and analytic methodology from the narrative perspective (North 1990, Greif 1995, 2004, Hall and Taylor 1996, Capoccia and Kelemen 2007, Mitra 2013:228-29).[134] Interestingly, the sub-field of comparative study has always been interdisciplinary and the accounts of historical scholars have significantly aided in the exploration and understanding of country-specific developments (Black 1966, Tilly 1975, 1990). With a wealth of country-specific and comparative literature engaged in a wide application of historical descriptive approaches under the guidance of new institutionalism, comparative politics and its subfields witnessed the revival of narrative perspectives, which, however, are in need of a structured and focused approach. It is worth noting Castles' (1985) remark: history not for its own sake, but history as a means to theoretical understanding.'

As Castles (2000, 2002) reminds the reader, indepth historical accounts reflect empirical strengths and theoretical weaknesses at the same time. Notwithstanding plausible arguments that history matters, a structured and focused methodology is in demand in such a narrative approach. Obviously there are different ways of integrating historical data.[135]

In the 1950s comparative discourse was challenged to provide an adequate understanding of the rise, development and fall of the newly independent postcolonial states in Africa and Asia. The explanatory limitation motivated not only political scientists, such as Easton (1965, 1975)[136], but also academics from other disciplines to generate a general research methodology for comparative case studies. In their joint article published in 1955 Roy Macridis and Bernard Brown criticised existing comparative political discourse for its limitations. Most of the comparative historical studies consisted of single case studies, which tend to be less theory-ori-

---

'*Counterfactuals and Hypothesis Testing in Political Science*'. The counter-factual method will not be used in the study.

134 For a detailed account of historical institutionalism and its relevance for providing an essential methodological contribution to comparative political theory, see Kathleen Thelen's (1999) article on Historical Institutionalism.

135 In their prominent work Przeworski and Teune (1970) discuss the usefulness of statistical indicators for testing assumed development models.

136 David Eaton's system theory (1953, 1965, 1975) and its implications for comparative political science and theories are discussed later in the study.

ented and rather '*atheoretical*', monographic and descriptive (Macridis and Brown 1955).[137] Interestingly, the same holds true for comparative political case studies.[138] These conducted case studies lacked a coherent focus and comparable variables. Accordingly historical scholars engaged in comparative studies agreed on the requirement of a general and standardized methodology. This initiated a debate by various scholars on a general analytic method of historical narration, which was fuelled by the attempt to not only generate a general method but also discourage decision-makers from relying on a single historical approach to one particular event (George 1979).[139] In his widely cited article on American politics, Theodore Lowi (1964) formulated the major points which have to be taken into account in a sophisticated, focused, and structured narrative analysis. George and Bennett (2005) summarised the methodological insights of over nearly half a century of critical debate on general methodology and published a chapter 'The Method of Structured, Focused Comparison' on the 'structured and focused' methodology of narrative case studies.[140]

'Structured' means that the conducted narrative analysis attempts to answer general questions that 'reflect the research objectives and that these questions are asked for each case under study to guide and standardize data' (Haney 1997, George and Bennett 2005:67). General questions are as follows:

(i) How and why did social security provision evolve in both countries?
(ii) What are the implications of late twentieth-century economic transformation processes for social security provision?

---

137 R. Macridis and B.E. Brown (eds.). 1955. *Comparative Politics*. Homewood, Ill.: Dorsey Press.

138 Sidney Verba (1967: 116-118) remarks of Robert A. Dahl's (1966) prominent book '*Political Oppositions in Western Democracies*' that it 'highlights a problem that arises in the multiauthored book. There are great advantages in having a large number of country specialists, but specialists are hard to discipline. In *Political Oppositions*, the major theoretical chapters that attempt to tie together the individual country chapters are found at the end of the book. ... If we want to have as collaborators men of the stature of the authors of this book, we must let them go their own way [emphasised by author].'

139 See Robert Yin and Karen A. Heald (1975) and Patrick J. Haney (1997). All three authors have been engaged in survey case studies which combine structured and focused methodology.

140 See also Bates and colleagues' (1990) theoretical chapter on the compatibility of the narrative approach.

(iii) What is the role of regime type and ideology in shaping the character of the welfare regime as well as the range and scope of social security?
(iv) In what way do constitutional and institutional actors determine the development of social security provision and produce constraints for decision makers in carrying out policy guidelines?

'Focused' means that the narrative perspective is limited in scope and 'deals only with certain aspects of the historical cases' (George and Bennett 2005:67).[141]

(i) In addition to this functional argument the time frame under investigation is limited to the period between 1949 and 2009.
(ii) Furthermore the historical descriptive perspective on cases is limited in its range and scope to relevant processes, events or so-called *critical junctures* and structural changes which are related to the evolution of social security provision.

Of course some of the findings are contested. For example, although some events produce significant pressure for policy changes – as expected – former policy trajectories persist (Greif 1995, 2004). Notwithstanding the plausible arguments for the relevance of critical junctures (Capoccia and Kelemen 2007), policy trajectories continue even against the backdrop of socio-economic realities. This might be due to institutional and constitutional determinants, including the underlying logic of the policymaking of the ruling elites, which shapes the '*room to manoeuvre*' and the ability of party governments to engage in decision-making.

2.4.2 Narratives of Social Security Policy Development

> '*The method also requires that the study of cases be 'focused': that is, they should be undertaken with a specific research objective in mind and a theoretical focus appropriate for that objective*' (ibid 2005:72).

(i) Basically the research question is to estimate the major driving force for the evolution of social security provision in both cases.

So, the question arises of how to explain, based on a causal theoretical research design, social policy choices and welfare regimes under changing

---

141 Dwaine Mefford (1987) discusses the merits and methodology of a general '*focused*' comparison as well as the relevance of the involved actor's cognitive processes.

political, economic and social conditions. The question has been the concern of recent academic discourse on the welfare state (O'Connor 1990, Pampel, Williamson and Stryker 1990).

(ii) With respect to the demand for a sophisticated theoretical research design to provide a causal explanation of the development of social security politics, the study relies on a combination of various theoretical and methodological approaches under the umbrella of new institutionalism to verify and prove the assumed causal explanation given by the historical descriptive approach.

The vast amount of cross-national quantitative findings and different measurements of the welfare level have produced *empirical confusion* (Huber and Stephens 1993). The empirical confusion is related to the fragmentation of theoretical approaches in welfare studies (Hicks and Misra 1993). In addition, Hicks and Misra (1993) stress the necessity of a coherent *meta* theory to solve the empirical problems at hand: The '*political resource approach*'[142]. It should solve the theoretical fragmentation and also reduce related empirical problems. The political resource theory is more a combination of different theoretical approaches, which offers a broad flexibility to analyse the welfare regime compared to the narrow perspective of only one theory. As discussed in earlier sections of the chapter, it should be noted that the combination of hypotheses of different schools of reasoning has to be handled with care; however, 'their separation in this work, as in the literature, is artificial' (Wilensky and Turner 1987: 383).

2.5 The theoretical Framework and the Working Model

In the remainder of the following section of the introduction, the study presents the general framework of the analysis, the theoretical argument, assumed sequences and variables, as well as a working model.[143] As men-

142 For a principal investigation, see Hicks and Misra (1993) who identified '*theoretical fragmentation*' as a main reason for the inconsistent and contradictory findings in comparative studies of similar cases. In their work they attempted not only to solve theoretical issues but also to formulate the '*political resource*' approach, which combines various theoretical and methodological approaches to gain insight into the complexity and causalities of the cases.

143 It goes without saying that the general theoretical grounding of the working model and the academic discourse in comparative political science will be presented, elaborated and critically discussed at length in the second chapter.

tioned before, the aim of the conducted study is to prove the relevance of the intra-institutional features of modern states for the related social security provision and its performance over time. Accordingly, the leading hypothesis is that the 'state capacity and not the regime type determines social security performance.' In addition, the study holds the view that regime type has an impact on institutional performance in general but that the country-specific variations in the state capacity to deliver policy choices are the product of the dynamic evolution process of the institutional arrangement. Hence, the country-specific social security system and policy outcomes have to be understood in regard not only to the regime type but also the country-specific evolution of the institutional setting and its resulting ability to deliver policy choices.

2.5.1 New Institutionalism in Comparative Political Literature

For a good reason the institutional orientated approaches are traditionally strong in the existing literature in comparative political studies on the development of the democracies in developing countries (Lijphart 1996, Merkel and Croissant 2000, North 2008, Scott 2011).

A sophisticated institutional orientated literature has evolved on the Indian case and its country-specific development of the state institutions, political economy and democratic institutional patterns (Morris-Jones 1968, Manor 1988, Jenkins 1999, Rösel 1994, and Mitra 2011, 2013) . In particular, a field of interest has been the expansion of the federal structure in 1992 in which a third tier of electoral community administration on the village level or so-called 'PRIs' (Panchayat Raj Institutions), has been introduced (Mitra 2002, Besley, Pande and Rao 2005).

New institutionalism has also been prominent for comparative studies on non-democratic system in general and for the Chinese case in specific (Guo 2013a/b). Recent literature on the political economy (White 1998, 1999, 2009, Law 2002) has critical evaluated the decentralisation process since 1989 (Li and Rozelle 2003, Cai and Treisman 2006, Pearson 2005). Particularly the policy performance of local authorities has become a prominent topic: impact of decentralisation (Zheng 2007), local economical policies (Steinfeld 2002), taxation reform (Bernstein and Lü 2008) and variation in local management (Segal 2003, Thun 2006) have been evaluated to investigate intra-country variation of policy outcomes.

2.5.2 Relevane of Culture and Social Preferences in Literature

As will be argued throughout the study, India and China have witnessed comparable historical experiences and socio-economic challenges as well as atypical transformation processes from impoverished colonial countries to modern states.[144] Comparing the CRP and the Indian Republic represents a most different case design (MDCD) with respect to the divergent political regime types in both cases (Przeworski and Teune 1970, Pennings et al. 1999, Schmidt 2000).[145]

As Rudolph and Rudolph (1968) argue, both modern nation states have evolved from ancient empires. Even today decision-makers are expected to convey legitimacy and accordingly often proclaim the overlap of ideological and historical roots (Andersen 1990).[146] This complex outcome or so-called 'invented tradition'[147] has merged together with new modern Western influences in the construction of a modern society and nation state (Andersen 1990, Rothermund 1993, Saich 2001).

Both nation states have set up modern Western state institutions in non-Western contexts and under different political, social and historical experiences. Despite the challenges of the adaptation processes, whether the peaceful democratic freedom struggle or the violent communistic revolution, both modern states have successfully constructed a resilient institutional framework to hold together the modern nation state even in times of despair. It has been argued that the key to their success is rooted in the attitude of political elites insistent on rooting the modern functioning of the political and administrative system in traditional society. In effect, in the land of the '*Tiger*' and '*Dragon,*' time is not always linear and national history is constructed and reinterpreted. It seems to be true that the old myths and gods are not dead and the traditional concepts of old philoso-

144 In the introductory part of chapter 3, a descriptive perspective of social security-related determinants as well as similar challenges of social security policymaking and delivery is provided.

145 For a detailed discussion of the issue see the textbook '*The Logic of Comparative Social Enquiry*' published by Prezworski and Teune (1970).

146 In the tradition of reinterpreting history, Mao Zedong is depicted as the father of the nation as well as the Communist Party who continued the tradition of Chinese state philosophy (Bouye et al. 2002, NZZ 2014a).

147 For a brief discussion of nationalism and invented tradition, see Anderson (1982). As Eric Hobsbawm (1982) stresses, reinterpretation or invented tradition is in demand in the search for historical roots.

phers, such as Kautilya and Confucius, are present in public and political life.

Until today the traditional trust in bureaucracy and its postulated '*mandate from heaven*' dating back to ancient times and prominent state philosophers, such as Confucius, is still present in China and used to legitimate the modern state (NZZ 2004, Li 2010:30-33). In the tradition of Confucius' state philosophy the rulers and his advisers had a high rank in society, and even today Chinese officials and administrative employees are ranked highly among citizens (NZZ 2004). A mutual respect exists between officials and citizens even against the background of corruption, inefficiency and mismanagement.[148] Bouye, Denton, and Dickson have noted that corruption has 'always been a way of life in China' (2002:301).

India's deeply fragmented society and nation state is founded on a constructed past and strong patriotism. The process of nation-state building has been accelerated and even enforced by the dreadful experience of the constant military clash with Pakistan.[149] Thus, cultural values, concepts and historical experience matter for the modern state. India's democratic state has established a policy of secularism but cannot overcome the underlying potential of religious violence dredged up by historical experiences (Rothermund 1993, Mitra 1994b, 2009). A horrific consequence has been the repeated religious riots of the Hindu majority against Muslim minorities, to mention only Ayodhya[150] in 1992 or the violent outbreaks against the Muslim community in Gujarat 2002 which were supported by the local law enforcement and the local BJP government under the leadership of Narendra Modi, former Chief Minister of Gujarat and recently elected Prime Minister of India (Jürgenmeyer 1995:83-86, Venkatesh 2005, Wagner 2006:131).

As accurately illustrated by the Chinese case and the recent open outbreaks of ethnic and religious violence toward minorities, such as the Uighur in Xinjiang, or by the public uprisings for more autonomy and po-

---

148 As a sign of public respect, gifts (which would be seen as bribes in the Western context) are traditionally given to authorities and officials (NZZ 2014a).

149 Mitra (2014) and Rothermund, Dietmar. 2002. *Krisenherd Kashmir. Der Konflikt der Atommächte Indien und Pakistan*. München: Beck.

150 For historical perspectives of the Ayodhya incident and the historical roots of the potential for religious conflict in India, see C. Jürgenmeyer (1995:83) '*Koexistenz und Konflikt zwischen indischen Relgionsgemeinschaften. Das Beispiel Ayodhya.*' The author addresses historical and contemporary religious cleavages.

litical participation of the kind recently seen in Hong Kong[151], the iron grip of oppression cannot suppress such demands (The Economist, 2014g, 2014e). Of the various types of political regimes, democracy, however, seems to be the one best equipped to deal with such problems. It seems plausible, taking the Indian case into account, that self-rule and a decent degree of ethnic autonomy and secularism give way to the transformation of rebels into citizens (Mitra 2002, 2009, 2013). Transforming the potential for societal conflict into political capital within the boundaries of democratic institutions, the violent riots are exceptions to day-to-day business.

Put briefly, culture, or to be more specific, social preference, matters. There is little dispute nowadays that India and China are, to a decent degree, 'unique' in their development and that country-specific cultural concepts shape the perceptions of actors and patterns of interaction in politics and public sphere; however, these determinants are measurable or comparable not only from country to country but also from individual to individual. Every person has his or her own experiences, cultural understanding and resulting behaviour, which is arguably a combination of 'zwecks' and 'value' rationality (Böcher and Töller 2012). An empirical validation of culture and its impact on policymaking is not the purpose of this study.[152] Hence the premise is that culture matters; however, it is not used as a variable for the comparative approach, which attempts to provide insight into the comparable determinants of social security provision in China and India.

It goes without saying that the notion of India's and China's '*uniqueness*' gains relevance only in so far as universalism and abstract reasoning tend to ignore the influence of cultural uniqueness. The intellectual merits of the uniqueness thesis cannot help to overcome the missing empirical validation as well as the fact that every individual develops his or her own dynamic perceptions and values despite cultural bias (Jones 1981, Li

151 It is worth noting that in the long run the CCP's refusal to negotiate and its willingness to use its monopoly of legitimate power against any public uprising have achieved, at least temporarily and superficially, what could be called 'social harmony'.

152 For a principal investigation of culture and freedom, see the recent work of Welzel, Christian. 2013. *Freedom Rising. Human empowerment and the quest for emancipation*. New York: Oxford University Press.

2010, Böcher and Töller 2012).[153] How to solve this problem? Departing from Max Weber's (1976)[154] prominent concept of '*Zwecksrationalität*,' the rational choice approach, coined by William Riker (1975), generated a theoretical approach that extends beyond the 'uniqueness' of one culture to grasp the patterns of policymaking under different political, economic, and social conditions. A point of departure for this study is the logic of rational choice[155], whereby actors are seen as rational individuals determined by a combination of 'zwecks as well as value rationality' (Böder and Töller 2012:190). Furthermore, it is assumed that actors possess a 'learning-ability' (ibid). At the end of the day, from a new institutional point of view, the modern state is a set of modern institutions that have been implemented and adapted to the country-specific context over time. Accordingly, institutional arrangement—its design and performance—varies from country to country even under similar regime types, thus setting the 'rules of the game' for the involved actors (Keman 1998, 1999, 2002a:6-8).

2.5.2.1 New Institutional Logic of Inquiry

In addition to the challenges stated above, it is crucial to evaluate the involvement of political parties (Hibbs 1977, 1994, Schmidt 1983, 2000, 2004), organised labour (Korbi 1989), institutions (North 1990, 2008, Steinmo and Thelen 1992), and constitutions (Austin 1966, Dahrendorf 1977) in social policy delivery in order to investigate the nature of social security provisions, including the range and scope of security policies and its determinants, from a theoretical point of view. Consequently, the main objective of the application of the new institutional-oriented approach is to locate the relevant determinants of the party-state-society relationship in shaping policy formation and outcomes. According to the approach, political institutions, as Mancur Olsen (1998:95) notes, 'are the building blocks

---

153 As Jones (1981:160) and Li (2010) remark, history in Asia and Europe has to be analysed from a neutral and comparative perspective.

154 The rational choice approach in the tradition of rational choice scholars such as Riker (1975), and its implications for the logic of inquiry, will be discussed at length in the theoretical section of the study.

155 The rational choice approach allows us to test and verify general assumptions about the behaviour of political decisionmakers and other involved actors under the premise that their rational behaviour maximizes their interests.

of political life. They influence available options for policy-making and for institutional change. They also influence the choices made among available options.' Hence, institutions are seen as crucial pillars in cultivating the existing formal and informal rules, elements, and patterns of exchange in a system and are treated as intervening variables shaping the policy process, structure and agency.[156]

A point of departure in investigating the policy process is provided by Douglas North's (1990) widely cited contribution to the rise and fall of nations, in which he points to the fact that institutions shape the arena where actors interact with each in a political system. In his analysis, North (2008) strongly suggests that, in addition to actors, social-economic realities and institutions shape the policy process. Accordingly, the survival of the state in times of socio-economic or political challenges, or so-called structural change, depends on the ability of political actors and institutions to successfully adapt their policy instruments to the new realities.[157] Structural change, as noted by Atul Kohli (1991), produces social inequality, relative deprivation, and a collective identity, which in most cases lead to political mobilisation, social unrest and collective violence threatening the legitimacy of the state. In effect, states can successfully overcome and confront structural changes with a combination of structural reforms involving institutions and state instruments—what North (1990, 1995, 2008:92-93) or recently Mahoney and Thelen (2010) have coined gradual 'institutional change' that avoids falling prey to an overburdening of the system.[158]

Similar to North's (2008) historical institutional argument, other prominent studies of liberal theory, such as those by Samuel Huntington (1968:55, 1984, 1991), Robert Gurr (1970), O'Donnell (1994) and Gabriel Almond (2000), have, in their political analysis of the disjuncture between stable and fragile political regimes, repeatedly argued for the relevance of

156 It is worth noting that the impact of informal institutional patterns can only be assumed and not measured well. Therefore the major focus is given to formal institutional constraints. The informal dimension of policymaking is taken into account to explain atypical sequences, policy choices and/or variations. The issue will be discussed in detail in the theoretical and methodological section.

157 As previously discussed, critical junctures refer to economic, social or political processes that challenge the state in its ability to ensure orderly rule and legitimacy (Gerschewski et al. 2013).

158 See Douglas North's article (1995:16-20) 'Five Propositions about Institutional Change' in which he discusses the proposition of institutional change.

political parties and institutions as major determinants of policy choices and policy outcomes.[159] These accounts provide an adequate understanding of the relevance of social security policies as an instrument of policy output performance. The sequence of loss of legitimacy described by these authors can be best categorised as the '*Huntington-Gurr 'polarisation'* model' (Mitra 2012:14):

Figure 1: Huntington-Gurr 'polarisation' model

Structural Change	⇨	Social inequality, relative deprivation, Ethnic identity	⇨	Political mobilisation, collective violence, de-institutionalisation	⇨	Political disorder	⇨	Loss of legitimacy

Source: Mitra (2012:14)

These authors point to more or less the same conclusion: that in young democracies in which the liberal and constitutional character is declining and the power of the executive is increasing in the attempt to overcome structural change—i.e. rapid social or economic transformation processes (Huntington 1991, O'Donnel 1994, Merkel 1999:35)[160]—the shift in the balance of power affects the institutional capacity to cultivate and enforce the '*rules of the game*' in any political regime (see figure 1 above).[161]

In effect, it is argued that the country-specific institutional design, features and characteristics are essential variables in determining the ability for 'institutional change' (North 1990:3-6, 1995, 2008, Mahoney and Thelen 2010) and the resulting adaptation capacity of political systems in times of rapid social and economical transformation (Pierson 1994, 1996, Mitra 1994b, 1999a, Kersbergen and Becker 2002). Consequently the

---

159 What these authors share is the view of the 'worst case scenario' summarized by Samuel Huntington (1968:55) in his abstract model, which describes the overcharging of young democratic states to satisfy public demands, resulting in socio-economic deprivation and violent protests (see figure 1.3).

160 In literature it is described as the 'cycle of crisis' (O'Donnel 1994, Merkel 199:35).

161 It is assumed that the same process can be associated with non-democracies. Of course, the concentration of power in the executive already exists in non-democratic regimes (Kailitz 2009a, Gerschewski et al. 2013:106-8). Yet, even against the backdrop of features such as oppression, autocracies and other non-democratic systems have to maintain at least some kind of legitimacy to establish orderly rule. If not, these systems can also easily fall prey to the 'cycle of crisis' (O'Donnel 1994) or the 'Huntington-Gurr 'polarisation' model (figure 1.3).

question arises: which variables affect the policy process, choices, and resulting social security politics, as well as the range and scope of policies?

From a neo- or new institutional perspective, the possibility that the political process can provide an effective resolution in producing coherent, effective and legitimate policy outcomes is directly linked to *institutional change* which in a second step can create resilience (Remmer 1997:36, March and Olsen 1984, North 2008, Mahoney and Thelen 2010).

Following this logic, there is a way in which *institutional change* can not only transform societal interest in political outcomes (Remmer 1997:50) but also create what Mitra (1991, 2013) calls the '*room to manoeuvre'* by offering decisionmakers flexibility in their political reactions to structural changes. In general, *institutional change* describes a positive process initiated by political actors to adapt institutions, policy choices and outcomes to current demands (Mitra 1991, 1994a, 1999b, 2005:16).

What is essential is not the political stability of the nation-building process but the process of institutional change or the ability of the state government to adapt policy formation and outcomes to current socio-economic challenges (North 2008: 92, 118-21). Previous analysis has concluded that social security politics are more than the balancing of competing paradigms between ideologies and pragmatics in the political arena, but the sum of institutional and agitational politics. In addition to the party (Schmidt 1996a, 2002), the policy formation of the party government can be affected by organized interests (Korpi 1989), socio-economic conditions (Wagner 1911, Wilensky 1975) and institutional as well as constitutional constraints (Tsebelis 1990, 1995, 1999, Immergut 1992, Schmidt 2000a).

Figure 2: Extended model on structural change

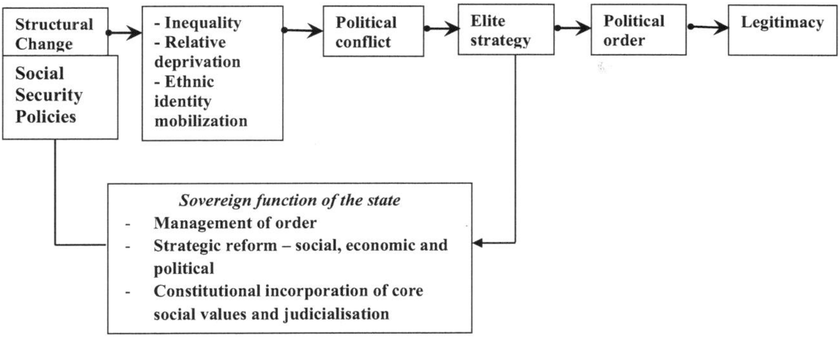

Source: Adapted by Subrata Mitra (2013:232)[162]

Accordingly, the party government's ability to execute coherent policy is directly related to the number of existing majority and minority veto points (Tsebelis 1990, Schmidt 2000a, 2004) and the overall ability of the party government to overrule such oppositions. Another assumption of system theories (Easton 1953, 1965) and the democratic liberal school (Dahl 1971, Lipset 1999, Lane and Ersson 2002) is that democracies tend to be more effective in adapting their policy choices to contemporary challenges due to the openness of the political system for 'inputs'. Decision-makers are in search of positive feedback (Easton 1975, Pierson 1994, 1996).[163]The challenge of 'structural change' in its various dimensions can be met by responsible policymaking which relies on positive feedback; however, recent studies on autocracies demonstrate that such regimes rely on 'cooptation' with socio-economic elites or organised interests to compensate for their limited input dimension (Köllner 2008: 362, 2013, Gerschweski 2010:46, Wischermann 2013:324-27).

---

162 The model is based on the common agreement among comparative politicians on the causality of structural change and the need for effective and coherent policy making to counter the negative effects, such as socio-economical inequality, decline of trust in the political system, political and social conflict (Huntington 1968, Kohli 1991, Mitra 2005, 2014).

163 David The theoretical approach of Easton's (1953, 1965, 1975) classical system argues for the relevance of 'positive feedback for any regime in increasing its responsibility to meet current socio-economic demands, problems as well as short comings of either policy making or provision.

As outlined above, political elites tend to reach general conclusions by dealing with structural change through reliance on two instruments. First, party governments tend to rely on state institutions, as well as law and order to (re-)establish orderly rule.[164] Second, they actively initiate policies and policy reforms, such as social security, to tackle the consequences of structural change and reduce the possibility of 'public unrest' based on socio-economic deprivation in the long run.[165]

2.5.2.2 A Sequence Model of Social Security Provision

In his widely known and cited question '*Who gets what, when and how?*' Harold Lasswell illustrates the usefulness of a generalized and simplified model of the interaction patterns of institutions and institutional actors, which carries the advantage of a higher level of abstraction.

A decent degree of quantification is needed to pass from a theoretical to a working model of social policymaking in which predictions of the determinants of policy choices, outputs and outcomes can be generated. Accordingly five intervening variables are identified via the insights of various comparative schools of reasoning.[166] This study attempts to provide theoretical and empirical evidence of the relevance of intra-institutional determinants of social security politics, policy behaviour, policy trajectories, and the resulting range and scope of policies (Scharpf 1990, 1999, Pierson 1996, Mitra 2013).

The abstract model offers a heuristic device for understanding the determinants of social security politics, polity and policy provision. It is worth noting that the theoretical model, which is based on commonly identified

164 In particular, non-democracies tend to use oppression as an instrument against public protests, freedom of speech, and opposition (Köllner 2008:362-8). The case of China illustrates various historical examples of the effectiveness of oppression, i.e. the violent breakdown of the Tiananmen Square protests in 1989 (Kailitz 2009).

165 It is worth noting that social politics is a state instrument that provides effective resolution to socio-economic challenges but varies widely in its agenda setting and policy character depending on the composition of the party government, the involved societal actors, and the formal and informal framework which structures the policy formation process and its outcomes (Keman 2002, Schmidt 1994a).

166 See Chapter 2 for a discussion of different schools of reasoning and their theoretical and methodological consequences for the research design.

variables of the policymaking process, is therefore not irrelevant for the task ahead.[167]

Figure 3: Three Sequence Model

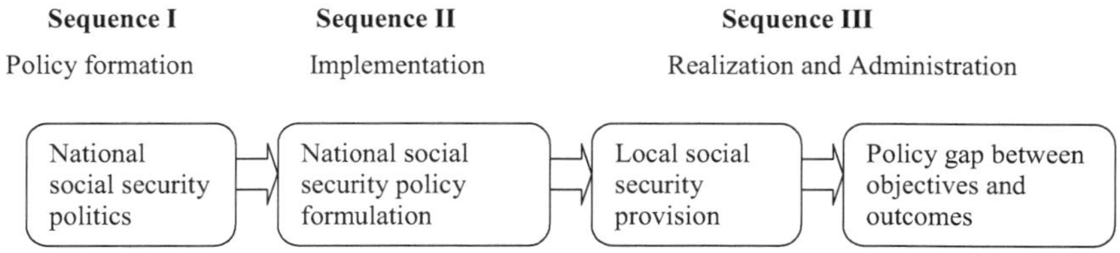

Source: author's own figure

As indicated in figure 3, social security provision is an ongoing process, starting at the 'high' level of politics and interest aggregation, then moving to policy formation, followed by the implementation and realization sequence. In all these sequences, formal and informal institutions (*polity dimension*) determine the '*room to manoeuvre*' or '*rules of the game*' for the formulation and provision of social security schemes and programmes. Furthermore, the gap between national policy objectives and local outcomes is directly related to the *intervening variables* and their effect on the ability of local authorities to realize the policy goals.

2.5.2.3 Definition of Institutions: Why they matter?

The first task for an institutional approach is to define, explain, and understand institutional effects on political processes, structures and behaviours (Mitra 2005:1-4). What are institutions? How does one distinguish between formal and informal institutions? And are there institutional effects on the efficiency, legitimacy and decision-making of political systems? These questions bring relevance to comparative politics and have been taken into account by sociologists and political scientists in their hope of providing satisfactory answers. In both the disciplines of sociology and

167 Even if the data analysis departs from some of the conceivable and assumed linkages, as Hans Keman (2002:13) reminds the reader, such a model is not 'irrelevant' for the scientific purpose of offering insight into the complexity of the policymaking process.

political science, scholars have been engaged in the definition of institutions and have developed various concepts in a broader and narrower sense (Köllner 2012:11-12). Richard Scott (2008:48)[168], who published a working definition of institutions, combines both the broader and narrower perspective: 'Institutions are comprised of regulative, normative and cultural-cognitive elements, that, together with associated activities and resources, provide stability and meaning to social life.' A point of departure has been actor-oriented institutionalism. Institutions are conceived as an 'irretrievable source of political action' (Héritier 1998:33), which accordingly to March and Olson (1989) can be seen as a number of interconnected rules and/or routines shaping policy processes, structures, agencies, and consequently policy outcomes. The main objective of the analytic concept is to sketch out the various stages, processes and actors involved in the policy process based on shared elements that present the process of policy formation in each case. It is argued that formal institutions grant 'corridors of action' (Scharpf 1987) but policy outputs and outcomes can only be understood in reference to the involved actors, and their perceptions as well as influence. In democracies formal institutions are crucial to providing traceable legal regulations pertaining to the division of power, responsibilities and processes through which politics is discussed and conducted. Formal institutions in a broader sense provide the '*metarules*' for involved individual and collective actors, such as constitutional regulations on the power of the executive and legislature as well as norms and rules for the political arena (Beyme 1994b:233). American scholars writing on the US Senate agree that institutions and formal rules determine the efficiency of institutional interaction and limit '*cycling*' effects in the policymaking process (Shepsle and Weingast 1981).[169]

---

168 In his work '*Institutions and Organisations: Ideas and Interests*' Scott draws on the work of psychologists, political scientists, and other theorists to illustrate the existing 'richness' and 'diversity' of the academic tradition as well as present his own theoretical framework for defining, exploring and understanding modern 'institutions'.

169 The 'cycling effect' is a common term used to refer to the inability of the legislature to quickly produce consensual outcomes in majority systems. In the context of the USA Tullock raises the question: 'Why so much stability?' Shepsle and Weingast (1981) provide an answer with their 'structured-induced equilibria'—legislature devices, committees, and floor amendment rules restrict the available outcomes and therefore reduce the time and cost of policymaking as well as pro-

Contrary to their formal counterparts, informal institutions set up '*filters*' or '*frameworks*' for political actions by either reducing or increasing the probability of decent behaviour and interaction patterns that political actors use to affect policy processes and structures (MacIntyre 2003:102-103). A good deal of the literature on institutionalism argues for the negative effect of informal institutions on political stability, legitimacy and efficiency. At the same time, a substantial body of literature offers evidence of the positive effects of informal institutions, such as political legitimacy and 'social efficiency,' which fill the gap between the formal institutions and complement their functioning (Köllner 2006:39-42, Radnitz 2011:361-365).

A second task and a suitable field to explore is related to the understanding of formal and informal institutions and their ability to structure the interaction patterns, behaviour and access to power for actors: that is, the responding behaviour of political actors. For this purpose, new institutionalism[170] is treated as an actor-oriented approach in the manner of rational-choice theory (Riker 1975).[171] Contrary to the much-maligned behaviouralism,[172] which lacks an abstract level of analysis and produces mixed findings, rational-choice theory offers a simplified theoretical and logical design based on the rationality of political actors to explain and predict patterns of behaviour. Methodologically, rational choice depends on the '*economic-man model*' and emphasises the crucial role and function of individuals in political processes and outcomes. The actor-oriented component of institutionalism adapts the rational-choice theory and underlying game theory for the collective purpose of explaining the role of actors inside the given *room to manoeuvre* structured by institutions (Mitra

---

duce more stability. Accordingly, the argument supports the institutional view that institutions limit the 'room to manoeuvre' for decision makers.

170 New, Historical and Rational Choice Institutionalism have become prominent theoretical approaches to the role and function of political processes and policy performance in providing public goods in democracies and autocracies (North 1990, Keman 1998, 1999, 2002, Gandhi and Prezworski 2007a/b).

171 Rational-choice and institutionalism have been treated for a long time as different theories in terms of their different methodological foundations—rational-choice approaches rely mainly on an individual-oriented economic-man model and institutional approaches rely mainly on a collective model (Jing and Wang 2013:96)

172 See Robert Dahl's (1961) prominent article 'The Behavioural Approach in Political Science: Epitaph for a Movement to a Successful Protest' in the American Political Science Review.

1991, 2005, 2013, Jing and Wang 2013:95-96). The sub-field of country-specific institutional design raises the perennial debate among comparative political scientists on how to conduct comparative studies (Prezworski and Teune 1970, Penning 1999).[173]

2.5.3 A New Institutional Model: Politics, Policy and Polity

It is argued that the process of social security provision involves the three dimensions of *politics, policy* and *polity* and varies from country to country—even under similar political, social and economic conditions.

Polity: polity are the formal and informal '*rules of the game*' or humanly constructed constraints derived from formal and informal institutions. These *rules* shape and determine the access and characteristics of the political interaction process, the resulting '*room to manoeuvre*,' as well as the provision of social security (North 2008, Mitra 2013, 2014[174]). As Olsen (1998: 95) notes, political 'institutions are the building blocks of political life. They influence available options for policy-making and for institutional change. They also influence the choices made among available options.' Institutions are furthermore crucial not merely for the political process of decision-making but also for the provision, including the implementation, administration and monitoring, of policies (Wildavsky, 1980, March and Olsen, 1989, Kaufman et al., 2013).

Policies: social security policies or social policy formation aim to produce public welfare (i.e. social security) for citizens to regulate and resolve the potential for societal conflict. The process of policy formation is a state instrument for intervening in economic or social processes. Social security policies are therefore a means to an end—the end being to solve socio-economic conflicts by granting public welfare and a social security net to citizens in times of socio-economic uncertainty (Olsen, 1989, Keman, 1999, Schmidt, 1999) and at the same time to produce measurable

---

173 See also Hans Daadler's article (2002) 'The Development of the Study of Comparative Politics' for a sophisticated approach to, and intellectual history on, the origins and development of modern comparative politics.

174 Permission has been granted to cite Subrata K. Mitra's unpublished paper 'Public service delivery and multi-level governance in India: Politics and the room for innovation,' which was presented at the international conference on public service delivery in Bangladesh (November 2014).

policy output performance (Easton, 1965, Castles, 1998, Schmidt, 2000, 2005, 2013).

Figure 4: Three Political Simensions of Social Security Provision

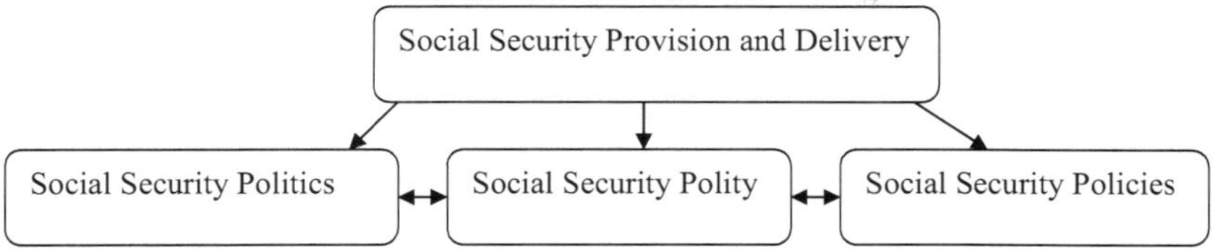

Source: author's own figure

As indicated in the figure 3 as well as 4, social security provision combines the three main dimensions of politics, policy and polity, which interact with each other:

Politics: social security politics is the political process or 'black box' (Easton 1965) determined by the 'paradox between societal conflict and political consensus' (Thelen and Steinmo, 1992, Schmidt, 1999, Keman, 2002a:9). In the social security political process the involved actors, such as political parties, organised interests and pressure groups, interact with each other to achieve political consensus on the issue of social policy formation (Czada et al., 1998, Mitra, 1991, 2002, 2013).

To sum up, it is assumed that polity determines the *'room to manoeuvre'* for politics as well as the provision of policies. Politics shape the range and scope of policies as well as to some degree the institutions involved in the process and policies that provide the state with the ability to regulate socio-economic conflicts and allocation processes. Accordingly, as argued throughout the study, social security provision is a complex product of country-specific institutions, involved actors as well as policy trajectories harnessed by the state to react to, intervene in, and control changing socio-economic realities, as well as to legitimate the political status quo by ensuring a *structure-induced equilibrium* (Colomer, 1996, Shepsle, 1997). Before moving into the study of social security provision in the field of high politics, it is essential to answer the following question: What is the impact of regime type on institutional design and social security provision?

From a theoretical point of view the research gathers evidence on the question of to what extent political regime type matters for the character of the welfare regime as well as the range and scope of social security politics. In contrast to accounts such as that provided by Kohli (1987, 1989), regime type is considered as a relevant but not explanatory variable in explaining cross-regime differences in the format, functioning and effectiveness of the state apparatus and the character of social security provision (Castles, 1998, Keman, 2002).[175] Accordingly, the merits of democratic rule in terms of public participation, protection of civil rights and higher responsiveness (Dahl, 1998, Lane and Errson, 2002) are not discussed here; however, the assumed comparative advantage of democracy per se in providing higher levels of welfare, social security and policy performance is critically evaluated by comparing social security provision in the democratic Republic of India to the left-totalitarian CPR. In fact, the study claims that the development of country-specific social security provision in both cases follows a similar logic which has been steered by the leading political parties, socio-economic realities and pressure groups.

Figure 5: Sequence of regime-related and institutional Effects on the Welfare Regime

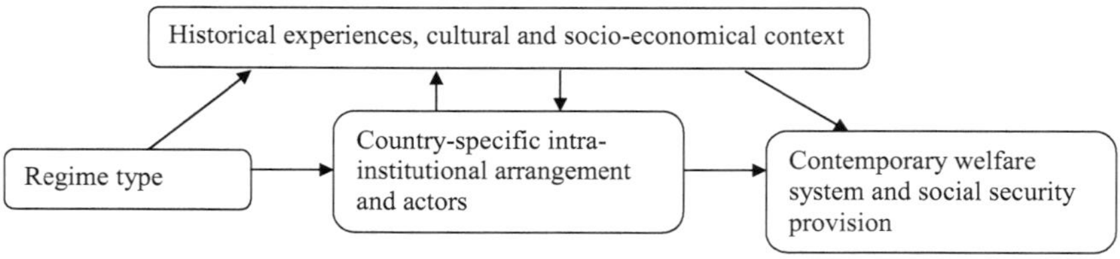

Source: authors' own assumptions

As indicated in figure 5, the point of departure is the institutional arrangement, which has to be considered as an *intervening variable* that varies in design and across various polities from country to country and over time (Keman 2002:7, 21). In addition, regime type is relevant in shaping the formal institutional arrangement but the study argues for the actor-oriented institutional view (Steinmo and Thelen 1992, Czades et al 1998, Keman 1998, Scharpf 1999); in other words, the resulting formal and informal institutions and exchange patterns, such as the state format (Tilly 1975), the division of power (Tsebelis 1995), the efficiency of the bureaucracy

175 In his cross-national study Castles (1998:312-336) reminds the reader that public policy varies from country to country as well as in time despite the backdrop of similar political regime types.

(March and Olsen 1989, Hicken 2011), constitutional and institutional constraints (Schmidt 1999a[176]), the political power of organised labour (Korpi 1978, Bardhan 1984, 2008) as well as socio-economic realities (Wilensky 1975, 1981) determine the *'room to manoeuvre'* for political parties[177] (Hibbs 1994, Wagschal 1996, Wagschal and Obinger 2002) and the resulting characteristics, features, and outcomes of the social security provision process. As indicated before, the model follows a liberal reasoning[178] and offers a dynamic interpretation of the gap between regime type and assumed characteristics and outcomes of social security provision.

Figure 6: Assumed Variables determining Social Security in India and China

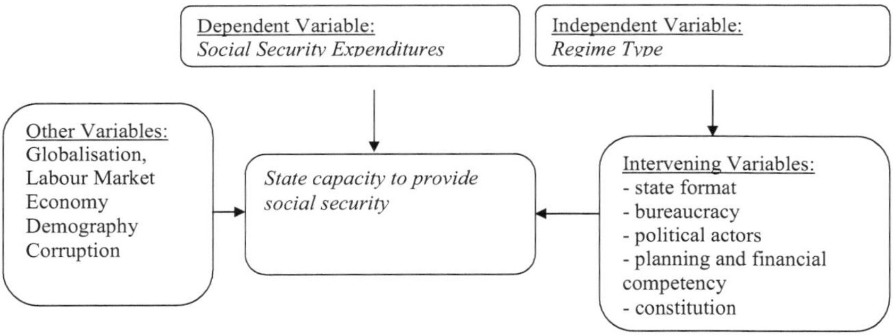

Source: authors' own model

There is little dispute nowadays that the postulated five institutional actors or dimensions—the state format (Tilly 1975, Lijphart 1999, Schmidt 2000, Braun 2000, Dyke 2007), bureaucracy (Wildavsky 1980, March and Olsen, 1989, Potter 1996, Rao 2011), constitutional and institutional fea-

176 In the tradition of the veto player theorem (Tsebelis 1990, 1995), institutional constraints are provided by majority and minority veto points (Schmidt 2000). Constitutional constraints include the rule of law as well as social rights embedded in the constitution that produce pressure for the provision of social security (Rawls 1972, Kaufman et al. 2008, Rao 2011).

177 It is argued that the party composition and assumed typical party effects determine, in addition to the previously mentioned constraints, the social policy choices of the party government (Schmidt 1983, 1999a, 2000a, 2012), as well as affect the development, outputs and outcomes of social security provision.

178 See North (1990), Huntington (1984) and/or March and Olsen (1990).

tures (Tsebelis 1995, Barros 2002, Mitra 2013) as well as the impact of political and collective actors (Hewitt 1977, Korpi 1989, Schmidt 2000a) —are crucial variables of social policy formation and provision in democracies as well as autocracies.[179] Contextual pressure, party priorities, government policies and other determinants vary according to cross-national perspective.[180]

2.5.4 Comments on the applied theoretical Model

To quote Esping-Andersen (1990:32) 'a theory that seeks to explain welfare state growth should also be able to understand its retrenchment and decline,' as it is neither theoretically nor empirically sound without simplifying the theoretical assumption and thereby sacrificing explanatory power (King, Koehane and Verba 1994:103). It should be mentioned that the presented hypotheses might have time-related limitations on their explanatory power in times of welfare expansion or retrenchment. Hence, as part of the empirical evaluation of the hypothesis, consideration will be given to ways to guarantee explanatory power. According to Peter Hall (2003:293), the presented hypotheses have been selected to explore the causality of social security political outcomes and the related impact of involved variables. All variables are stated in a fashion that allows their falsification or verification based on the empirical findings. The former is best addressed by King, Koehane and Verba (1994:101), who argue that theoretical assumptions do not have to be correct to produce useful research outcomes, as the presented tool-box, according to the tradition of the 'political resource' approach (Hicks and Misra 1993), grants a theoretical guideline based on the assumptions underlying the proposed comparison of social security provision in India and China between 2004 and 2009.

---

179 See for example Gandhi and Prezworski (2006, 2007 a/b).
180 See Zohlnhöfer's article (2009), cit op.

III. Descriptive View on India and China

The previous chapter addressed the theoretical and methodological issues of comparative politics as applied to the challenge of comparing the development and characteristics of two non-Western and politically divergent cases. This chapter provides a descriptive and historical inquiry into data related to contemporary social security, and its historical development, before concluding with an attempt to categorise the welfare regimes under scrutiny.

3.1 Descriptive Inquiry and the analytic Narrative

In order to arrive at a thorough understanding of country-specific social security provision, a descriptive perspective on social security-related data is necessary. Such a perspective will illustrate the intrinsic theoretical assumptions and assumed political impacts of various exogenous and indigenous variables used in the working model. Interestingly, India and China are currently facing comparable socio-economic and demographic challenges in their ongoing transitions from impoverished developing countries to successful international emerging markets—testing the actual accountability of and support for the government in power.

Table 1: Social Security related Determinants

country	**population (million)**	**population aged 65+ (%)**	**Dependency ratio**	**Life expectancy at birth (years)**		**Statutory pensionable age**		**GDP per capita (US$)**
				men	**women**	**men**	**women**	
China 2002	1,275	6.9	46.4	69.1	73.5	60	60	3,976
China 2004	1,275	6.9	46.4	69.1	73.5	60	60	4,020
China 2006	1,303	7.6	40.8	70.8	74.6	60	60	5,896
China 2008	1,351	8.4	38.9	73.3	74.9	60	60	6,757

country	population (million)	population aged 65+ (%)	Dependency ratio	Life expectancy at birth (years)		Statutory pensionable age		GDP per capita (US$)
				men	women	men	women	
India 2002	1,008	5	62.5	63.6	64.9	55	55	2,358
India 2004	1,008	5	62.5	63.6	64.9	55	55	2,840
India 2006	1,103	5.3	59.7	63.2	66.7	58	58	3,139
India 2008	1,220	5.3	56.3	63.2	66.4	58	58	3,452

Source: SSA reports on Asia and Pacific (2004, 2005, 2006, 2008)

From a comparative perspective, the argument does not hold. In terms of economic data, it is distinctly visible that China outperforms India in terms of growth. Compared to India, China could realize much higher economic growth in the next decade and is ranked as an *upper-middle income country*[181]. In effect, China has a relatively higher GDP per capita compared to India (table 1), which is only ranked as a *lower-middle income* country based on GDP per capita[182] (Pallares-Miralles et al.2012, World Bank 2014).

Whatever the disagreement on the role of political and institutional determinants most approaches identify economic and social realities as highly relevant determinants for social security provision (Wilensky 1975, Wagschal 1996). Both countries, India and China, represent the largest countries in the world in terms of territory, with a population surpassing one million people. Although the Chinese demographic growth ratio is lower (0.6 exponential growth rate per year) due to the one-child policy, it still outmatches the Indian population which is constantly growing by an

181 According to the official measurement of the World Bank (2014), economies are generally categorized by GNI per capita, which is calculated using the World Bank Atlas method (2014). The groups are categorized as low income (1,035 or less US $), lower middle income (1,036 to 4,085 US $), upper middle income (4,086 to 12,615 US $) and high income (more than 12,616 US $).

182 From 2000 to 2010 the ranking for both countries did not significantly change (World Bank 2014).

average 1.4 exponential growth rate per year (2006 to 2009). In both cases the dependency ratio[183] dropped over time.

3.1.1 Regional Differences

Regional variations are commonly phenomena._It is not surprising considering the vast territories and populations that the overall HDI[184] value varies dramatically from locality to locality in both countries:It is not surprisingly in regard to the huge territory and amount of population the overall HDI[185] value varies dramatically from locality to locality in both countries. What is surprisingly, are the huge regional differences can be observed regarding the human development.

Table 2: Regional differences in the HDI

China	HDI 2008	India	HDI 2007/08
Shanghai	0.908	Kerala	0.79
Beijing	0.891	Delhi	0.75
Tianjin	0.875	Himachal Pradesh	0.652
Guangdong	0.844	Goa	0.617
Zhejiang	0.841	Punjab	0.605
Jiangsu	0.837	NE (excluding Assam)	0.573
Liaoning	0.835	Maharashtra	0.572
Shandong	0.828	Tamil Nadu	0.57
Jilin	0.815	Haryana	0.552
Hebei	0.81	Jammu and Kashmir	0.529
Heilongjiang	0.808	Gujarat	0.527
Fujian	0.807	Karnataka	0.519

183 The dependency ratio is constructed from the sum of the population aged 14 or younger plus the population aged 65 older, which is then divided by the population aged 15 to 64 (SSA 2012).

184 The Human Development Index (HDI) is used here as an indicator to illustrate the intra-national differences in overall human development because it allows us to rank both countries and their sub-regions. For a discussion of the methodological issues, strengths and limits of the HDI see the Appendix II.

185 The Human Development Index (HDI) is used here as an indicator to illustrate the intra-national differences in the overall human development because it allows to rank both countries and their sub-regions to each other. For a discussion on the methodological issues, strengths and limits of the HDI see the Appendix II.

China	HDI 2008	India	HDI 2007/08
Inner Mongolia	0.803	West Bengal	0.492
Shanxi	0.8	Uttaranchal	0.49
Henan	0.787	Andhra Pradesh	0.473
Hubei	0.784	Assam	0.444
Hainan	0.784	Rajasthan	0.434
Hunan	0.781	Uttar Pradesh	0.38
Guangxi	0.776	Jharkhand	0.376
Xinjiang	0.774	Madhya Pradesh	0.375
Shaanxi	0.773	Bihar	0.367
Ningxia	0.766		
Sichuan	0.763		
Jiangxi	0.76		
Anhui	0.75		
Qinghai	0.72		
Yunnan	0.71		
Gansu	0.705		
Guizhou	0.69		
Tibet	0.63		

Source: various scources[186]

As indicated in the previous table, there is an extremely wide divergence within both countries, which is illustrated by the HDI and its regional measurement. Interestingly, there is a distinctly visible causal relationship between the economic performance and resulting human development of a region, such as a province and/or union state (Hurst and O'Brian 2002, Rao 2007:141, Hurst 2009:17-25, Mishra and Raveendran 2011, Kohli 2012:208, Mitra 2014).[187] In particular, the poorer regions and their local governments are obstructed in their ability to facilitate social security for citizens in cases of financial hardship, disability and sickness (Guhan 1994, Wong 1998, Prabhu 2001, Sen and Rajasekhar 2012, Mitra 2014).

186 UNDP. 2013. *China National Human Development Report 2013*. Beijing: China Translation & Publishing Corporation and Ministry of Women and Child Development. 2009. *Gendering Human Development Indices*. New Dehli: GoI.

187 See Mishra and Raveendran (2013) for an elaboration of the 'Millennium Development Goals' in India and the gap between 'rich' and 'poor' union states. Also in China geographical situation seems to be the main determinant; the coastal and south regions score much higher values than the northern inland provinces.

For a closer inquiry a general perspective on the existing social security provision is necessary.

3.1.2 Social Security Provision: The Gap between Objectives and Outcomes

Lately several middle-income countries, including China and India, have significantly extended their social protection systems by adding new components. In China for instance, a remarkable policy development has been the 'household minimum income support', 'child and family benefits' as well as improvement of 'health care' coverage. In India the government strengthen the social security system. The new 'public unemployment program' and extension of the social pensions and maternity benefits provide now to a decent degree social security for the majority of poor people (ILO 2015:141).

Table 3: Existence of Statutory Programmes

Coun-try	Number of policy areas covered by at least one programme		Existence of a statutory programme							
	Number of policy areas covered by at least one programme	Number of social security policy areas covered by a statutory programme | Strict definition	Sickness (cash)	Maternity (cash)[1]	Old age[2]	Employment injury [3]	Invalidity	Survivors	Family allowances	Unemployment[4]
China	8	Comprehensive scope of legal coverage | 8	x	x	x	x	x	x	x[188]	x
India	7	Semi-comprehensive scope | 7	x	x	x	x	x	x	[189]none	x

Source: SSA reports on Asia and Pacific (2004, 2005, 2006, 2008)

188 The strict '*one child policy*' had its exceptions for rural families and minorities. Also in the past decade the Chinese government paid attention to the decline in the birth rates and revisited the policy.

189 India has left behind the attempt of forceful family allowance in the 1970s, with instruments such as mass sterilization, and follows another strategy since the 1990s. The new policy guideline has a passive character and is limited in its benefits to for only one up to two children. http://www.archive.india.gov.in/sectors/commerce/insurance.php (2014-01-05).

As indicated in table 3, both countries have set up a robust legal framework for cases of sickness, maternity, old age, invalidity, injury as well as unemployment. Interesstingly, India compared to China has still not legally covered the family allowance which requiring employers to pay family benefits to their workers. While remarkable progress has been achieved in both countries, China compared to India has significantly extended various elements of their social protection systems, particularly since the early 2000s, with remarkable outcomes.The challenge, however, is to provide adequate social security for the total population and in particular the segments outside formal employment structures, such as informal workers, the long-term unemployed, and old people (ILO 2005, 2006, 2010a).

Economic deprivation is multidimensional in the sense that the economically deprived 'tend to cluster along with caste and gender as characteristics that define who is poor and deprived in terms of social protection' (Sen and Rajasekhar 2012:95).[190] As noted before, social security aims to tackle the multiple dimensional reasons for the economic uncertainties of citizens. Accordingly a relevant non-institutional determinant of public policy in developing countries is '*socio-economic vulnerability*' or the pressure of changing socio-economic realities. Most interesting is the large variation in the level of *socio-economic vulnerability*[191] between India and China. As indicated in table 4, China managed to reduce absolute poor and informal non-waged workers in the last decade, resulting in a '*low vulnerability*' rating compared to India's '*very high vulnerability*' rating (ILO 2010:191-94). [192]

---

190 As Gita Sen (1997) notes, poverty and economic deprivation are 'group phenomena' and therefore any approaches have to tackle both of them to achieve any long-term success.

191 In the World Social Security Report 2010/11 the ILO defines vulnerability in terms of the proportion of the population living below 2 US $ a day and the amount of non-waged workers. In most cases the two categories overlap to a decent degree (ILO 2010a:191-193).

192 The categorization is based on the amount of population living below 2 US $ per day, including the percentage of non-waged workers assumed to have neither legal nor voluntary social insurance coverage (World Bank, 2011, ILO 2010a: 186-88). The data has been retrieved from the online data bank of the ILO (2009h) '*Key Indicators of the Labour Market*' (see table 2+A7D).

Table 4: Data related to the socio-economical Vulnerability: Income

country	People living on less than		Gini index	Non-wage workers as a percentage of total employment
	1.25 US$ PPP a day	2 US$ PPP a day		
China	15.9	36.3	35.4	20-40
India	41.6	75.6	34.5	75+

Source: World Bank (2009a), ILO (2009b)

As indicated in the data sample (Table 2 and 4), India's significant deprivation problem is clearly linked to missing social security for the large numbers of non-waged workers (estimated at above 75 percent of the total work-aged population) (ILO 2010a). China has only 15.9 percent of its population living in absolute poverty or below the poverty line—defined as 1.25 US $ (PPP a day) and 36.3 percent below 2 US $ (PPP a day). Additionally, China is ranked in the category of medium-level of poverty (25.1 to 50 per cent) in terms of the proportion of the population living on less than 2 US $ (PPP per day) (WHO 2000, World Bank 2009a, ILO 2010a).[193] Contrary to China, India is ranked as highly vulnerable. In India 41.6 percent of the population are living in absolute poverty or below 1.25 US $ (PPP a day), and 75.6 percent below 2 US $ (PPP a day). As indicated before, the number of people living on less than 2 US $ (PPP day) and non-waged workers are correlated, which is demonstrated in the fact that the number of non-waged employees in an unorganised employment situation are up to 91 percent; for China it is estimated that roughly 20 to 40 percent of the workforce are non-waged workers (Planning Commission 2008, World Bank 2009a, ILO 2009a, ILO 2010a:189).

Limited social security provision for the old-aged population is another typical feature of third world countries. In particular non-waged workers and rural citizens suffer as a result of the missing coverage or provision of social security schemes, services and benefits (Sen and Dreze 1990, ADB 2008, 2013, Sen and Rajasekhar 2012:95). For 2000 the Indian Government estimated that roughly 5 to 6 percent of the estimated 362 million informal workers are covered by a social insurance scheme (GoIc 2007c: 152). In the following years the Central Government paid more attention

193 Other countries are South Africa, Botswana, the Republic of Moldova and Turkmenistan (World Bank 2009a).

to expanding coverage and implemented national pension schemes (Sülzer 2008). As a result, in 2007 an estimated 24 percent of the population older than 65 years was effectively covered and received benefits from a pension scheme. China has achieved roughly ten percent more and can cover 33.4 percent of its pensioners.

Table 5: Legal Coverage of various Schemes (for 2007)

country	**Legal employment injury coverage as a percent of the working-aged population**		**Share of population aged 65+ in receipt of pension in percent**	**Legal coverage for old age as a percent of the working-aged population**	
	Mandatory	Voluntary	All programmes	All programmes	Contributory only
China	13.5	0	33.4	25-50	27
India	7.5	0	24	25-50	29

Source: (Pallares-Miralles et al. 2012: 183-87, 251)

As illustrated in both tables (5 and 6), the real time coverage is relative low. As indicated by the legal coverage numbers presented in the table above (table 5), there seems to be a structural deficit of coverage. Similar to pension, the legal employment related injury coverage covers only 13.5 percent (121,733,000 subjects) of the working-aged population in China and merely 7.5 percent in India (Pallares-Miralles et al. 2012: 253).

Table 6: Unemployment: Indicators of Effective Coverage

Percentage of unemployed receiving unemployment benefits [b]																			
2000		**2005**		**2007**		**2008**		**2009**		**2010**		**2011**		**Latest available year**					
Contributory and non-contributory schemes	Real year	Contributory and non-contributory schemes	Real year	Contributory and non-contributory schemes	Real year	Contributory and non-contributory schemes	Real year	Contributory and non-contributory schemes	Real year	Contributory and non-contributory schemes	Real year	Contributory and non-contributory schemes	Real year	Contributory schemes	Non-contributory schemes	Contributory and non-contributory schemes	Male	Female	**Latest Year**
9.9	2000	20.0	2005	17.1	2007	14.8	2008	14.0	2009	9.2	2010	9.1	2011	9.1	0.0	9.1	…	…	2011
n.a.	…	n.a.	…	n.a.	…	3.0	2008	n.a.	…	n.a.	…	n.a.	…	3.0	0.0	3.0	…	…	2008

Source: ILO[194]

Another typical feature for *third world* countries, such as India and China, is the low coverage of the so-called 'right to income security in old age', as articulated in the international labour standards.

Diagram 1: Comparison of the proportion of older persons receiving a pension 2000 and 2010–12

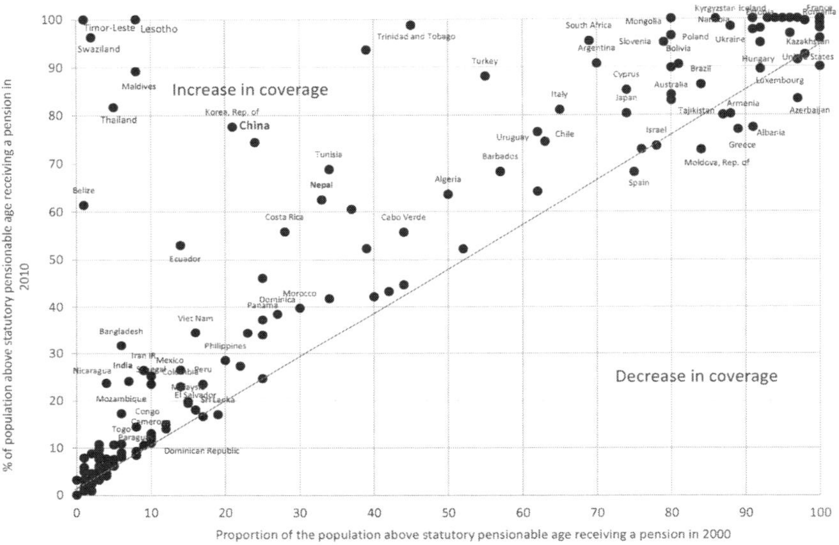

Source: http://www.social-protection.org/gimi/gess/RessourceDownload.action?ressource.ressourceId=42999.

As illustrated in the diagram, in China a total of 74 percent of the eldery receive pension compared to only 24 percent in India in 2010 to 2012.[195] Both countries have extended their pension provision since the 2000 remarkable. India's social pension at least began to tackle the missing coverage and Chinese pension reforms significantly boosted the coverage.

In particular non-wage workers and rural citizens are suffering by the missing coverage or provision of social security schemes, services and

194 http://www.social-protection.org/gimi/gess/RessourceDownload.action?ressource.ressourceId=37697 (2015-06-01).

195 http://www.social-protection.org/gimi/gess/RessourceDownload.action?ressource.ressourceId=44420 (2015-05-05).

benefits (Sen and Dreze 1990, ADB 2008, 2013, Sen and Rajasekhar 2012:95). For 2000 the Indian Government estimated that roughly 5 to 6 percent of the estimated 362 million informal workers are covered by any social insurance scheme (GoIc 2007c:152). In the following years the Central Government paid more attention to expand the coverage and implemented national pension schemes (Sülzer 2008). As a result, in 2007 estimated 24 percent of the population above 65 years are effectively covered and actually receive benefits from a pension scheme. China has at least achieved roughly ten percent more and can cover 33.4 percent of its pensioners:

Social protection programs play a key role for financial support of persons with disabilities. Since the mid of the twentieth century, India and China have made progress in extending social security coverage and building comprehensive social security systems for the working-aged population with variations in their outcomes.

Diagram 2: Replacement rate in cases of disability

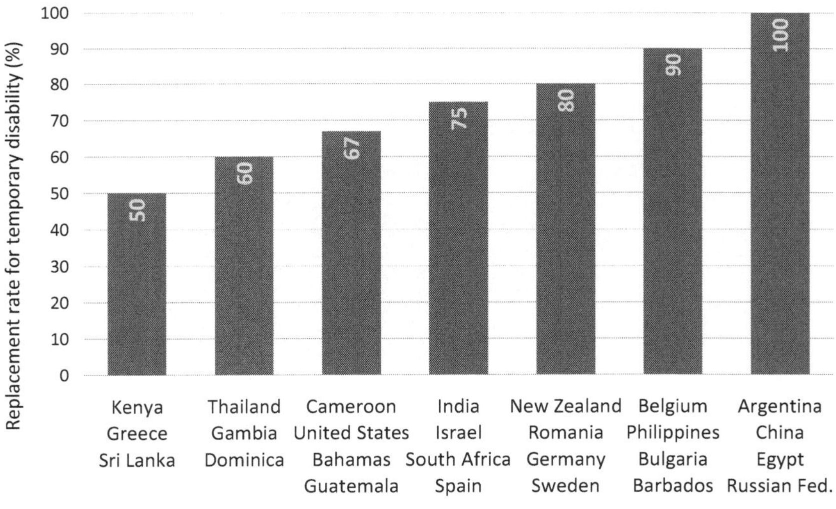

Source: ILO (2015)[196]

196 http://www.social-protection.org/gimi/gess/RessourceDownload.action?ressource.ressourceId=37030.(2015-05-01).

China has achieved a 100 percentage replacement rate in cases of employment-related disability. India could only muster 75 percent coverage, but still relative good compared to other countries, i.e. Sri Lanka or Thailand.

3.1.3 Female Participation in the Work-force

As indicated by the legal coverage numbers presented in the table above (diagram 1 and 2), there seems to be a structural deficit of coverage. As with pensions, the legal employment-related injury coverage covers only 13.5 percent (121,733,000 subjects) of the working-aged population in China and merely 7.5 percent in India (Pallares-Miralles et al. 2012: 253).

Female participation is another issue closely related to socio-economic deprivation and the limited scope of existing schemes for these target groups (Bussemaker and Kersbergen 1999).[197] In particular India's highly fragmented society cultivates the most unequal gender relations in terms of wage and income level, employment opportunities, and access to social security, health care, education, and sanitation (WHO 2000, NCEUS 2006, 2007, Rao 2011). A clear indicator is the traditional role of women and the related low labour participation rate compared to China:

Table 7: Female Participation Rate

	Female labour force participation rates at					
	aged 16-64 (in percent)			aged 65+ (in percent)		
Year	2000	2005	2010	2000	2005	2010
China	74.8	73.2	72.5	8.1	8.9	9.4
India	35.2	34.7	35.3	3.8	2.7	2.1
Asia	55.8	54.8	54.4	11.2	11.2	11.4

Source: ILO (2009a, 2009e)

197 In their comparative study Bussemaker and Kersbergen (1999) inquire into the relevance of female participation for the socio-economic situation as well as the causal effect of fair arrangements for day care and maternal and paternal leave, which promote female participation in the workforce. Bussemaker, J. and Kersbergen, K. van. 1999. 'Contemporary social-capitalist welfare states and gender inequality', in D. Sainsbury (ed.), *Gender and Welfare State Regimes*. Oxford: Oxford University Press.

The resulting low participation of female workers (table 7) in the urban workforce and the limited access to social security benefits is taking its toll on the well-being and financial situation of households (table 1). India's commitment to producing appropriate social security for the formal workforce has resulted in the implementation of a well-funded and well-designed bundle of employment-related social insurance (Rao 2007:85, 2011:72, ILO 2010a, Nagaraj 2012a:52-53). Although India's social insurance system for formal employment provides an adequate security net to cover the socio-economic uncertainties of the workforce, the overall performance of the state in providing improved social security coverage is relatively low. Briefly put, formal social security coverage is limited. An estimated mere 2 percent of the working-age population is covered by social security schemes (Pallares-Miralles et al 2012:143). Consequently, a shocking majority of roughly 98 percent of the workforce in India are operating outside the coverage of the employment-related social insurance system for formal employment. Informal employment and substantial urban poverty are affected by a lack of social insurance coverage, low wages, bad working conditions and deprivation (Pallares-Miralles et al 2012).[198]

China has a much higher participation ratio for males to females than India (table 7). Regarding access to social security, health and job opportunities China's active labour policy has sought to address the gender dimension of economic deprivation and could provide much higher female participation in the urban working force—in addition to cash transfers for unpaid women and access to social security—than the Indian case.[199] Since the radical policy changes under Deng Xiaoping in 1978, the CCP has been eagerly engaged in providing economic and social development. Interestingly, Deng Xiaoping seems to realize Mao's '*getting rich is glorious*' philosophy; however, his course of radical policy changes involves modifying the communist agenda and incorporating a capitalist market system under the 'social market economy' (SC 2006).[200]A third observa-

198 See the official report of the Indian NCEUS (2006) 'Report on the Unorganised Sector' as well as the follow-up report (2007) for a detailed inquiry. Both reports highlight the need for structural reforms in the social security system to grant minimum coverage for the millions of unorganised workers.

199 Details on social security schemes and programmes will be discussed later.

200 Although the target correlation for more economic growth and decent universal social security has not changed, the radical structural reforms of the 'Four Mod-

tion is the increasing pressure of demographic growth for both welfare regimes. The life expectancy in both countries has improved over the last decades (Table 1, 22) and meanwhile the percentage of older people is increasing steadily which is challenging in various ways for the future development.

A third observation is the increasing pressures of demographic growth for both welfare regimes. The life expectancy in both countries has improved during the last decade (Table 1 and 8) and meanwhile the percentage of older people is increasing steadily which is challenging in various ways for future development.

3.1.4 Vulnerability

Social security policies attempt to break the 'vicious cycle of poverty and vulnerability' (ILO 2015:9). The ILO Recommendation No. 202 and its realization aims to prevent or alleviat poverty, vulnerability and social exclusion through income security guarantees.

ernizations' and the resulting abandonment of the 'closed-door' policy in favour of capitalism represent policy changes that radically depart from those of Mao (Guo 2000, 2013b).

Diagram 3: Public Social Protection Expenditure (percentage of GDP) and Income Equality (Gini coefficient), latest available year

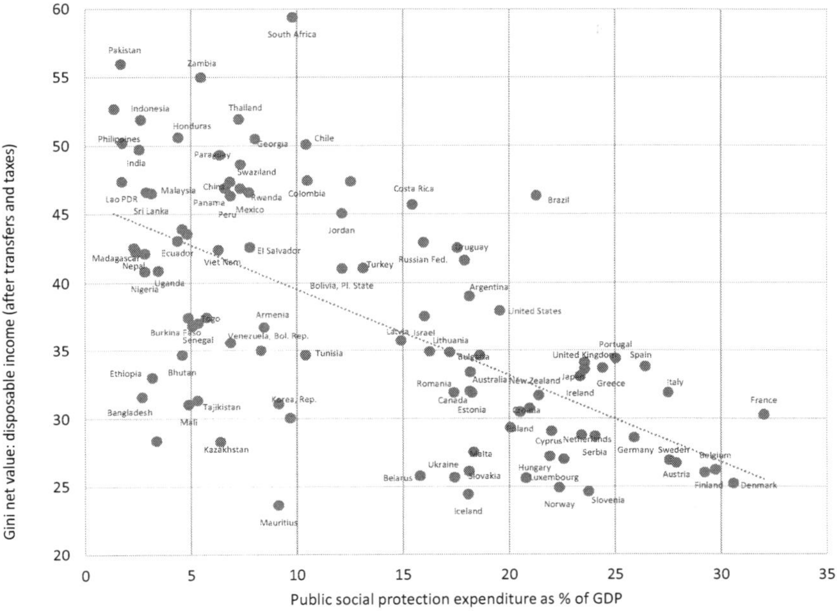

Source: ILO[201]

The present correlation in the diagram 3 provides an interesting fact. The causality between public social protection expenditure and inequality is less causal than for poverty and inqeualiry. Nevertehless, the outcomes for India and China seem to validate the suggestatin by the ILO (2015:155) that '*higher levels of social protection expenditure are associated with lower levels of inequality*'.

In regards to life expectancy, India has also made clear gains, though it scores below the Asian average, with Chinese life expectancy in 2009 having been roughly ten years above the Indian one.[202]

---

201 http://www.social-protection.org/gimi/gess/RessourceDownload.action?ressource.ressourceId=42217 (2015-01-01).

202 For a detailed analysis see the '*World Social Security Report 2010/2011*' (2010) and online statistics published by the ILO (2009b) on the issue of demographic growth in a comparative perspective.

Table 8: Data related to the socio-economical Vulnerability (life expectancy)

	Life expectancy at							
	Male (all ages)		Female (all ages)		20 years (both sexes)		60 years (both sexes)	
Year	2000	20009	2000	2009	1995-2000	2005-2010	1995-2000	2005-2010
China	69.8	71.6	72.9	75.1	53.7	55.7	18.9	20.4
India	60.3	62.6	62.3	65.6	48.8	50.4	15.8	16.9
Asia	65.1	67.5	68.5	71.2	52.2	54	17.7	19

Source: World Bank (2009a)

Meanwhile, urban poverty is sharply increasing. Socio-economic deprivation affects both the urban working-age population as well as retirees who find themselves facing financial difficulties.[203] In particular, those aged 65 years or older are suffering increasing living costs because a large part of the target group is not entitled to pension benefits (table 5) or the schemes provide only minimum yearly benefits. In India 24 and in China 33.4 percent of the population aged 65 or older is not entitled to any kind of pension benefit.

3.1.5 Comments on Social Security Provision in China and India

At comparable outset, India and China were starting to build a coherent social security system; today, both have made remarkable development. What is more, the so-far conducted inquiry of social protection coverage and benefits as well as the related social security data on human development indicate that China is doing better than India.

203 For further studies on the issue of old age poverty see the World Development Indicators (World Bank 2002, 2007, 2008, 2009a) and various case studies (Zhiyuan et al. 2000, Rao 2007, 2011 ILO 2010).

3.2 Historical Development of Social Security Politics

In the following historical-descriptive part of the study, the social security development of India and China is presented. The historical-descriptive observations are limited in two ways: first, in their time frame of 1949 through to 2009, and second, in the historical account on social security politics, which is 'structured' and 'focused' to transform 'descriptive historical' accounts into 'analytic ones' which are 'theoretically relevant' (George and Bennett 1998:14).[204] Accordingly, an investigation of social security development and reforms was conducted by carefully elucidating, categorising and documenting the kinds of changes that have been taking place.

3.2.1 General reflection on the Path-Dependency of Social Security Provision

It is an accepted point of view in comparative political literature that 'time' has an effect on policy choices and outcomes (Thelen and Steinmo 1992, Esping-Andersen 1996:24, Mitra 2013:228-29).[205] A narrative perspective 'pays close attention to stories, accounts and context' (Bates et al. 1999) and gives, according to the historical account of Thucydides (1951) on the Peloponnesian War, explanation for human behaviour. It should be noted that the narrative approach also has its methodological limitations, and that historical sources and documents have to be handled and analysed with care (Goldthorpe 1991, Rothermund 1995, George and Bennet 2005). The sheer amount of qualitative information alone makes case selection necessary in order to clarify, explore and analyse the relevance of events, processes and agency by 'explicit and formal lines of reasoning, which facilitate both exposition and explanation' (Bates et al. 1999, Fogel and Elton 1983).[206] In the ideographic tradition (Geertz 1973, Stone 1979 and Tilly 2005) the narrative perspective allows the inclusion of the 'historical turn in the social sciences' (McDonald 1996a:10) to 'produce understand-

204 See chapter two for a discussion of the narrative approach.

205 See also Putnam (1994) or Pierson (1997, 2002) and Norht (2009).

206 Fogel and Elton (1983) stress the fact that historical events can be theoretically explained by referring to statistical reasoning, including market transactions, and birth and/or death rates.

ing via richness, texture and detail' (Ortner 1996:281). The path-dependent approach can help to explain certain policy outcomes as the result of historical experience (Rose and Davies 1984, Bates et al. 1999).

Hypothesis 1: *Decisions and policy choices in former periods narrow the available options for current decision makers.*

Put briefly, path dependency matters for policymaking (Tilly 1970, Armingeon 1994, Capoccia and Kelemen 2007). For a narrative analysis a long time frame has to be included to grasp the path-dependent processes of social welfare policies (Pierson 1996, 2001) and the resulting implications for the contextual relationship between involved actors, institutions and social security politics in China and India. In the same fashion of the single case studies conducted by Lipset, Trow and Coleman the ambition is not to produce 'particularizing' but instead comparative and to some degree 'generalizing' analysis.

3.2.2 Social Security Policy Trajectories

In the burgeoning literature on the rise and fall of modern states in developing countries in the last several decades, scholars commonly agree that policy choices, including the sub-field of social security politics, in developing countries cannot be compared to the trajectories in European countries due to variations in socio-economic and political conditions and historical experiences (Bonoli et al 2000, Castles 2002:215-17, Kersbergen and Becker 2002:185-89).

Contrary to their European counterparts, India and China have experienced similar critical junctures and experiences in the attempt to construct their own unique modern states, economies and welfare regimes. The development of social security provision in both countries has had to face simultaneous 'challenging' starting conditions, such as large territories and populations, and resulting socio-economic diversity, which in turn have produced significant challenges in matters related to governance, bureaucracy and/or centralism (Rothermund 1995a, Swamy 2010). What both countries share in common is the linearity of significant critical junctures and resulting socio-economic challenges for the domestic party governments in which the limitations of former social security policies have become distinctly visible. Interestingly, *four periods*[207] clearly stand out in the evolution of social security politics in both countries, in which the vision and logic of the leading political party has steered policymaking:

- ***Post-WWII period**: 'Following the socialist vision'*, 1949 to 1977[208]
- ***1st period**: 'Blueprints of the modern welfare regime', 1978 to 1992*[209]
- ***2nd period**: 'Performance has priority', 1993 to 2004*
- ***3rd period**: 'Balanced economic and social development'*, 2004 to 2009

As summarized in the following table 9, both governments have reacted in similar ways by adapting the state's role in providing social security to changing realites. The pace and nature of the country-specific development processes is closely linked to the constant adaptation and reconfiguration of social security politics to the issues at hand.

Table 9: Comparative View on Social Security in India and China

Year	Era	State's role in development	State's role in social development	State's guiding principle
1949-1960s	Nehru	High	Low	Socialistic welfare regime, 'mixed economy'
	Mao	High	High	Socialistic welfare regime; 'iron rice bowl'

207 A note of clarification is needed to underline the fact that the historical-descriptive analysis is limited in its scope to providing a 'structured' and 'focused' perspective on social security and related events; however, it does not give an entirely historical recap of the historical and political development in both countries since the early 1950s. These time periods reflect the moments in time in which public policy and its sub-field of social security politics have been reconfigured and adapted to new socio-economic realities and/or elites' perceptions.

208 For a comprehensive understanding of the significant changes in social policymaking since 1978, the post-World War II period will be briefly described. For both countries the period is directly associated with the leading roles of Mao and Nehru as well as the impact of their policy choices on the future of the countries (White 1993, Dua 1994).

209 In the pre-1978 period both states set out to modify their welfare regimes and significantly reconstructed the range and scope of the former social policies. The older social policy strategies were unable to produce adequate policy performance to address socio-economic realities and in the long run burdened the financial capacity of the developing countries. Therefore from 1978 onwards both governments broke with the former policy choices. The approved policy outputs and outcomes still affect current policy decisions and the overall development of the welfare regime in both cases (Rothermund 1995, Mitra 1994b, Guo 2000).

	Indira Gandhi	High	Medium	Social democratic orientated welfare regime
1960s-1990s	Deng	High	Low	Cutback of welfare regime
	Liberalisation (1993-2004)	Low	Low	Market-orientated policy making
1990s-2000s	Liberalisation (1993-2002)	High	Low	Market-orientated and liberal social policy reforms
	UPA (2004-2009)	Low	Increasing	Combination of liberal and socialistic policy making; universal social security coverage with low benefits
2000s-2009	Hu Jintao (2002-2009)	Medium	Increasing	Combination of liberal and socialistic policy making; universal social security coverage with low benefits

Source: author's own table

3.3 Same Goal, different Paths: Evolution of the Chinese case

The unique development of China's social security provisions and policy trajectories depended largely on the strategy of constant 'step by step' reformation or, to quote Chinese officials, 'crossing the river by groping for stones' (quoted in Qian and Wu 2001:1).[210] Similar to the health[211] and labour market[212], social security should not be reduced to by-products of economic development or fiscal constraints (Ma and Hou 2005). Over the last few decades the CCP leadership has followed the guidelines developed by Deng Xiaoping to build a national security system with universal coverage and minimum benefits for the total population. In the twenty-

210 Qian, Y. and J. Wus' paper (2001) 'China's transition to a market economy: how far across the river?' presented at the Conference on Policy Reform in China at the Centre for Research on Economic Development and Policy Reform, 16-18 November, Stanford University, California [quoted by Chan et al. 2008:43].

211 On the constant cutbacks in health care and the privatization of hospitals and clinics, see the official statistics and reports (MoH 2004, 2009).

212 The path dependency of labour market reforms and reduction of employment in the SOEs has been discussed in Solinger's article (2001), which offers a historical descriptive perspective of the development.

first century Jintao Hu, Deng's favourite official, announced a shift from Deng's 'performance has priority' to the 'society with modest welfare level' in 2002, ending in the 'harmonious society' (Information Centre of the SC 2004b).

3.3.1 Following Socialistic Vision, 1949 to 1977

The first critical juncture in the Chinese case was the foundation of the CPR in 1949. After the violent revolutionary struggle the communist government officially took political control of the country and set out to establish a '*classless*' communist nation, or in Mao's words, '*the People's Democratic Dictatorship*'.[213] The narrative of the creation of the Chinese Communist Republic, together with its first decade of rule, is interwoven with the story of Mao's personal leadership and his ambitious vision to transform China into a typical left-totalitarian welfare regime (Guo 2000:69 sp).[214] The years of civil war left the country impoverished, with a state overburdened by social security politics and the modernization attempts crippling fiscal, human and economic development. In effect, these developments left the succeeding government no other choice than to start deeply structural reforms of the economic and welfare regime (Wong 1998:63).[215]

213 In his essay '毛泽东, 论人民民主专政 ('On the People's Democratic Dictatorship')' Mao Zedong (1991:273) pffers insight into his political philosophy: 'Who are the people? At the present stage in China, they are the working class, the peasantry, the urban petty bourgeoisie and the national bourgeoisie. These classes, led by the working class and the Communist Party, unite to form their own state and elect their own government; they enforce their dictatorship over the running dogs of imperialism – the landlord class and bureaucrat bourgeoisie, as well as the representatives of those classes, the Kuomintang reactionaries and their accomplices – suppress them, allow them only to behave themselves and not to be unruly in word or deed. ... Democracy is practiced within the ranks of the people, who enjoy the rights of freedom of speech, assembly, association and so on. The right to vote belongs only to the people, not to the reactionaries. The combination of these two aspects, democracy for the people and dictatorship over the reactionaries, is the people's democratic dictatorship.' For a detailed discussion of Mao's state philosophy, see for instance Sujian Guo's book (2000).

214 The left-totalitarian welfare regime, its characteristics and features, will be discussed in the following chapter.

215 For a comprehensive overview of Mao's welfare system, see Dixon (1981).

3.3.1.1 The Iron Rice Bowl: Left-totalitarian Welfare Regime and its Features

In the early years the communist government adapted the Soviet central planning model and instantiated a generous left-totalitarian social security system. The first official act was to abolish all laws of the former government and reformulate policies and laws concerning all areas of political, social and economic life (Teiwes 1995). In 1951 the first legislation was drafted concerning social security and was the target of *socialist/communist* ideology aimed at empowering workers in the production process, improving their social security, and providing life-long full employment (Zedong 1991).

In the spirit of socialism, the social security schemes were entirely funded through the contributions of employers, with the state as the major employer. The generous social security system, in combination with the guarantee of lifetime employment for the urban workforce, has often been described as the '*iron rice bowl*' (Drouin and Thompson 2006:17).

To accomplish the goal the CCP issued the 'Regulations Concerning Labour Insurance' in 1951. The draft put into practice a social insurance system for workers covering all relevant areas, including retirement, disability, death, sickness, maternity, work-related injuries, and medical care (Zhang 2004). While in the beginning the system was designed only for government employees and urban economic entities with at least 100 employees, the social security system was expanded to include all urban enterprises in 1955[216]. In addition, the government built a universal guaranteed employment policy as well as comprehensive welfare services for the urban working force. In 1954 the central government designed and relied on a Soviet-oriented social security system which was administrated by the local trade union branches under the authority of ACFTU[217]. Undeniably, the generously designed welfare regime and full-employment policy

216 Rural farmers, agricultural workers and workers in economic entities in rural areas were excluded.

217 The ACFTU was under the direct control of the Ministry of Labour in Beijing. The national fund consisted of 30 percent and was administrated by the ACFTU. In addition, the major part of the contribution was under the control of the local union committee, which regulated, monitored and administered pension payments. The collected money was split between local and national pension funds, both managed by the ACFTU and its local branches (Metcalf and Li 2005).

overburdened the administrative and financial capacity of the state (Teiwes 1995, Zhang 2004). The 'extravagant' qualities of the left-totalitarian welfare regime is reflected in the inefficiency of the pension system, which lacked both the postulated universal coverage and financial funding. Pensions were funded by 3 percent of the beneficiary's wage (Zhang 2004).

In the early stage the pension scheme covered roughly 8 million employees but due to the requirement of 25 years of service[218] only a minimal number of roughly 20,000 pensioners were entitled to pension payments in the 1950s. However, the low contribution rate of 3 percent could only cover the related administrative costs of setting up the pension system and the system struggled to provide payment to the minimum number of recipients (Drouin and Thompson 2006:17).

Under the umbrella of the centrally planned economy, labour bureaucratic institutions were set up all over the country to regulate and control employment. As a consequence of centralisation the state authorities took over economic planning, the creation of employment, and the assignment of workers to job opportunities (White 1989, Chan et al 2008:28-29). In 1958 the central government introduced the *danwei* system for urban workers and the commune system for the rural population as controlling mechanisms (Gang et al 1998). In the urban enterprises workers were grouped together in the *danwei units*. These small work units became the second smallest social unit for the workers after the family and provided welfare, salaries, housing, food and pensions for the workforce (Leung and Nann 1995:57)[219].

---

218 At the age of 60 retirees with at least 25 years of service, or at the age of 50 or 55 with 20 years of service, are entitled to pension benefits between 50 to 70 per cent of their former salary.

219 In his famous study '*Communist Neo-Traditionalism: Work and Authority in Chinese Industry*' Andrew Walder (1986) describes the relationship of workers and work units as an '*organised dependency*'. Workers and management depended on each other in the Chinese planned economy. While the SOEs determined the workers' social, political and economic life, they had to depend on the cooperation of the workers to fulfil their quotas and state-assigned duties (Walder 1986). According to the Soviet-proclaimed development model jobs were created and assigned by the danwei system. Until the reforms in the 1980s, the danwei system promoted lifelong employment as well as the opportunity to pass one's job to one's child (Korzec 1992).

For rural areas Mao Zedong enacted the *Resolution on the Establishment of the People's Communes in Rural Areas* in 1958, which marked the beginning of the commune system. More than 26,000 communes were founded all over China to regulate and control all aspects of life and safeguard equality. 'The people's communes are to be established … in which the workers, peasants, soldiers, students, and businessmen will help each other and work together.'[220] A commune was 'a highly centralised unified management and egalitarian distribution system, which distributed daily necessities to its members' (Qi 2000:15) and took over the social welfare function as well as employment (Gang et al 1998). China's closed economy could not generate the economic growth or job opportunities to provide additional employment; typical for state capitalism with full employment the existing employment was oversaturated which in a short time resulted in a dramatic drop in productivity (Teiwes 1995, Chan et al. 2008).

As Richard Lowenthal (1970) puts it in '*Development vs. Utopia in Communistic Policy*' the success of Mao Zedong's centrally planned economy also failed to appear and the generous social security system and closed door policy could provide neither economic nor social development in the long run (Zhiyuan et al 2000:20-21).[221] The overall low productivity reduced Chinese economic development and the financial revenue of the state. Furthermore, the collective social security system, especially the pension scheme, could not provide the postulated coverage and constantly overstretched the state budget and administrative capacity (Lieberthal and Lampton 1992).[222]

In 1966 the failed hopes of the left-totalitarian planned economy regarding full employment and social security could no longer be denied, and even before Mao's death in 1976 the pension system had to be dismantled (Tsou 1983, Lieberthal and Lampton 1992:1-30). Most of the less productive enterprises could often not provide adequate social security or pension payments (Guo 2000, 2013b).

---

220 '*Resolution on the Establishment of the People's Communes in Rural Areas*' quoted by Qi (2000:15).

221 For a general and early discussion of the limits of communist policymaking, see Chalmers Johnson's (1970) work '*Change in Communistic Systems.*'

222 Kenneth G. Lieberthal and David M. Lampton (1992) provide a range of essays on the post-Mao period in their work '*Bureaucracy, Politics, and Decision Making in Post-Mao China.*'

3.3.2 The First Period: Coming crises, hard figures vs. Socialistic Vision, 1978 to 1992

In 1976 the consequences of the 'Great Leap forward', the 'Great Famine' and the 'Great Proletarian Revolution' marked another critical juncture for the CPR. Mao's reign had totally eroded Chinese economic performance and social well-being as well as left the country impoverished (Wong 1998:63, Xia 2013:43). In the 1970s the half-hearted reform ambitions of Mao's successor Hua Guofeng could no longer handle the high level of unemployment or *'people waiting for jobs,'* among other grievances concerning the Chinese economy (Wong and Ngok 1997). In the following years the internal power struggle consumed all the attention of the government in its search for structural change and resulted in the continuation of the totalitarian agenda under Mao's successor Hua Guofeng. Based as it was on outdated and inadequate policy strategies, the government's attempts accelerated increasing economic and social problems.[223]The resulting socio-economic grievances of the Chinese population produced significant pressure for structural reform and coincided with the increasing burden of running a left-totalitarian welfare system which could neither improve living standards nor provide universal coverage for a hungry population. Frederick Teiwes' (1995) analysis in '*The Paradoxical Post-Mao Transition. Form Obeying the Leader to 'Normal Politics'* notes the tension between continuing Mao's communistic politics and the demand for structural reformation that prevailed during the post-Mao period.

Consequently, in 1978 political and policy change was inescapable. The new and pragmatic leader Deng Xiaoping announced the enactment of ambitious structural reforms[224] of agriculture, industry, national defence and science as well as social security. The first major reformation was the Household Responsibility System in 1978, which marked the beginning of a new era of development in the economy as well as in social security po-

223 The government heavily focused on the creation of job opportunities at all cost, investing more money to build factories and create job opportunities. Another desperate measure was forcing the SOEs to recruit the masses of unemployed, which resulted in a dramatic reduction of productivity per worker because 'five people were doing the job of three' (Feng 1982:16-17).

224 The blueprints for the reforms were drafted by the former premier Zhao Enlai. Enlai's structural reforms did not gain the approval of Mao Tse Dong and were dismissed until 1978 (Chan et al. 2008:28 sp).

litics[225]. In the same year, the Central Government issued Document 104 of 1978 on the Third Plenary Session of the 11th Party Central Committee to reform and regulate the ad hoc social security system of former periods. Central government regulation officially included not only the SOEs and government institutions but also other collective entities on the behalf of the government in its takeover of regulations; the provision of social security, including pension, maternity, illness and employment related accidents, was transferred to the employers' responsibility (Drouin and Thompson 2006:17). In particular, the benefits were generously adjusted to current price levels, which included reform of the pension requirements[226] for urban employees to provide employment for the growing number of younger job-seekers joining the labour market (Drouin and Thompson 2006).

Furthermore, Deng introduced various other market-oriented social security pilot projects[227] and set the stage for developments in social security politics to address the new socio-economic changes (Tsou 1983, Lieberthal and Lampton 1992). In the mid-1980s the pace of economic reform produced three major challenges and accelerated the requirement for structural changes in the labour market, employment policy, and social security:

First, the capacity of the state to provide full employment and control the labour market effectively vanished in regard to ongoing demographic growth of the workforce in the early 1980s and private employment op-

225 The rural reform allocated property to the responsibility of individual farmers. The result of the new reform for wheat production in the Anhui Province tripled (Liu 1992). The local success promoted the reform that was adopted by the central government and set up nation-wide. The annual growth rate in agrarian production increased to 7.9 percent until 1984 (Wang 1994).

226 The pension requirement was lowered from 25 years to only 10 years of service for male employees and the benefit rate of pension payment was standardized based on years of service. Retirees with ten to fourteen years gained 60 per cent of their age, 15 to 19 years gained 70 per cent and beneficiaries above 20 years a payment rate of 75 per cent. As a consequence of the reform, in the first 12 months the number of pensioners nearly doubled and increased from 3.14 million to 5.96 million (Drouin and Thompson 2006:17-18).

227 In the report of the World Bank, Liu and Yang (2004:73) conclude that the 'overall process is throughout experiments and then the central government develops models later to be adopted (and adapted) on national scale.''

portunities in the mid-1980s. Both the increased unemployment[228] and economic privatization in the 1980s accelerated the pressure for structural changes in the labour market (Wong 1998).

The central government recognised the problem and passed the 'three-in-one' labour policy which relaxed the iron grip of the state on the labour market. The 'government would no longer take full responsibility for providing a job for everyone and the job market was to developed' but employment in the SOEs was still in the hand of the state (Gang et al 1998:31). In giving up the ambition of full employment the state slowly remodelled the old egalitarian wage system into a performance-based labour contract system. At first the contract system was tested in pilot projects in a few cities, which persisted until 1980 and was slowly expanded in 1983. In the following years the state introduced more policies to ensure the functioning of the labour market. Unemployment was tackled through the introduction of public employment agencies and retraining centres to guarantee re-employment and offer information about self-employment (Lee 2001).

The creation of a free labour market depending on the supply and demand mechanism also produced negative side effects. Employment patterns in the SOEs changed from full to contract employment for new recruits but the lifelong employment contracts created before the reforms prevailed until 1993. In the same period the level of unemployment further increased[229]. As a reaction, the SC passed an unemployment insurance scheme in 1986 to react to the growing numbers of unemployment due to the government's labour market reforms.[230] Yet, in 1988 the SC officially legalized the existence of private enterprises as well as defined their rights and duties in the *Temporary ordinance on China's private enterprises* (SC 1988b).[231] Since the mid-1980s the dwelling private entities have taken

228 In 1979 the urban unemployment increased to 5.4 percent including 5.7 million people (China Labour Statistical Yearbook 1997:8).

229 While the private enterprises' gross output value gained an increase of only 7 to 33 percent until 1997, their state-owned counterparts suffered a loss in gross output value from 57 to 27 percent in the same period (Liu 2000).

230 See also the '*Regulations on unemployment insurance*' (SC 1993).

231 Short-term employment in SOEs increased from 7 to 51.6 percent in 1986 to 1997 (Bloom et al 2002).

the lead in terms of economic performance and after 1988 the number of private enterprises and their employees sharply increased.[232]

Second, structural reforms to the labour market, demographic growth, and employment patterns tested the capacity of the existing social security system. The social security system's administrative and financial resources could neither handle the increasing number of beneficiaries nor cope with the growing private sector. In the attempt to reduce the costs of the social security system the NPC published the *Law of the People's Republic of China on Enterprise Bankruptcy* in 1986. The law dismantled the bankrupt SOEs and divested the communes of their function to provide jobs and welfare to older workers.

The downstream implication of the law was an obvious break with the former universal social security system mainly based upon the SOEs as a contributor for welfare. In addition, the SOEs had no longer any need to fulfil their traditional function of providing financial, medical and education support and protection of housing for disadvantaged groups in rural and urban areas (Chan et al 2008:169-71). As a direct reaction to the *Law of the People's Republic of China on Enterprise Bankruptcy* the SC put into pratice the pension system scheme or so-called *Decision on old age pension insurance scheme for enterprise workers* to assure the welfare of the pensioned SOEs workers who lost their entitlements due the reforms (SC 1991). Finally, the law marked the beginning of the reconstruction of the social security system. The new, more market-oriented character of social security is distinctly visible in the pension scheme available only to retired employees in the urban SOEs (Dong 2001, Chan et al. 2008:30-32).

Third, in dismantling most of the SOEs and communes of their role as contributors of welfare the local governments had to take over their functions. Thus, slowly but steadily the increasing responsibilities overburdened local administrative and financial capacity beginning in the mid-1980s.[233] Education was seen as the key to solving poverty in the long run. In 1986, the NPC imposed the *Compulsory Education Law of the*

232 Private enterprises growth rate jumped from 90,581 to 1,508,857 in 1989 to 1999 (Kanamori and Zhao 2004).

233 Furthermore, the central government expanded education and health programmes to tackle the increasing income inequality which was resulting in an increasing number of poor people without access to education or health care (Zhang 2005, Chan et al. 2008:30ff, 148 sp).

People's Republic of China which represented an education scheme to ensure nine-year compulsory education for children. Also the central government expanded the local authorities' competence in education to safeguard successful implementation. Another main field of interest concerned health care.[234]

3.3.3 The Second Period: A Conflict of Visions, 1993-2004

In 1986 the central government reacted to the three major challenges and accelerated the liberalization of the labour market as well as dismantled the former *iron rice bowl* in a more market-oriented approach. Beginning with the transformation of the old permanent employment guarantee, the government deregulated the labour market and set up a new contract-based employment system. It is worth noting that in the course of deregulation and the resulting vagaries of employment the government introduced additional unemployment insurance, especially designed to cover the unemployment of former SOEs' employees (Josephs 1990, SC 1986). The shift towards market-oriented structures resulted not only in the reform of the labour market but also in adjustments to the social security system. In an ambition to create the conditions for the economic prosperity of the SOEs and attract foreign enterprises the central government shifted the responsibility for the administration of social security funds towards local administration. In 1986 the *State Council Document 77* was issued to address the reconstruction of the social insurance administration.[235] The central government instructed the local authorities to build social insurance agencies and social security funds to administer, monitor and provide social benefits. The newly created insurance agencies have to administer and collect contribution fees from employees. For the first time, employees have to pay into their unemployment insurance and pen-

234 Rural areas notoriously suffered under limited access to health care schemes due to the privatization of most clinics and the reform of the SOEs (PTDRC 2006, Dong 2001). As a result, the local authorities were pressured to fund and administer the new programs and provide coverage to all recipients, especially in the rural underdeveloped provinces (Chan et al 1999, 2008:195).

235 The SC published the '*Provisional regulations on the implementation of the labour contract system in state-owned enterprises*' in 1986.

sion scheme, as contributions are no longer entirely paid by employers (Drouin and Thompson 2006:18).

3.3.3.1 Reform Period and Blueprint for today

In 1991 the introduction of the *Code of Civil Procedure* marked the beginning of a 'new chapter for market-oriented labour relations' (Chan et al. 2008:32), which 'promoted the market competition mechanism of survival of the fittest' (Li 2001). In the Third Plenary Session of the 11th Central Committee of the CCP, it was announced that the new policy guidelines would 'pay attention to the Chinese national character while incorporating foreign experience in order to safeguard the predominant position of the state economy and distribution according to work, and embody the essence of our socialistic system while following the common law of a market economy' (quoted by Guo 2000:105).

In 1993 during the 14th session of the Central Committee of the CPP, the Committee officially published the 'Decision on Issues of Building a Socialist Market Economy'.[236] Accordingly, in the early 1990s the central government's overall objective was the improvement of economic performance and it therefore accelerated the process of transforming the SOEs into profit-generating economic entities.

In 1993 the *Company Law* proceeded with the task and dissociated the SOEs from their traditional function of providing welfare schemes to the workforce. In effect, the SOEs would no longer provide pensions, housing, health, education, and insurance schemes to workers and could concentrate on being modern economic entities (Qin 1999). In addition, the CCP was under pressure to close the gap. In 1993, in the aftermath of the National Party Congress in 1992, the elected Central Committee[237] published guidelines in pursuit of (1) improved coverage of pension and unemployment insurance as well as insurance for employment-related acci-

236 The 14th November 1993 meeting of the Central Committee of the CCP saw the publication of the '中共中央关于建立社会主义市场经济体制若干问题的决定' ('Decision on Issues of Building a Socialist Market Economy'). The official report was published 17. 11. 1993 in the 人民日报 (RMRB).

237 The Central Committee is elected by the National Party Congress and represents the highest executive organ to announce the policy guidelines for subsequent years. It decisions are binding.

dents;[238] (2) the design of a rural pension system and medical system;[239] and (3) the implementation of a coherent social security administration.[240]

The main focus of the legislature and policymaking was to support the economic productivity of the SOEs, as was distinctly evident in the outcomes of law-making:

Table 10: Legislation and area of law making (1993-1997)

Economic laws/ regulations	Administrative and institutional system	Criminal and civil lawsuits	Social security, Health, Science, Culture, and Environmental Protection
54	25	28	18

Source: Hina Renmin University's (1998) Research Report on Chinese Social Development 1996-1997 (1998:65).

As indicated in table 10, social security, health, science, education and environmental protection have gained less attention in law-making.

The various attempts by the legislature to promote the productivity of the SOEs and reduce their fiscal burden for the state gained only limited success which resulted in the dissatisfaction of the CCP with the pace and success of the privatization process. As a consequence, the Central Committee under Deng Xiaoping launched the deep reconstruction of the current economic system and its conversion to a 'socialistic market economy' (Dodds 1996), followed by the official announcement of the *Decision on issues concerning the establishment of a socialistic market economic structure* by the People's Party in 1993 (CCPCC 1993). The document marked the beginning of the partial liberalization of the SOEs. While the first attempts to reform the SOEs in 1984 could not overcome the old patterns of central and local state dependency, the new reform managed to do so.[241] Central government and state authorities agreed to no longer inter-

238 See decision No.27 published by the Central Committee in 1993.

239 See decision No.27 published by the Central Committee in 1993.

240 See decision No.28 published by the Central Committee in 1993.

241 In 1984 the Chinese Communist Party Central Committee (CCPCC) under Deng Xiaoping initiated the new economic reformation of the economy. In the *Decisions on the reform of the economic system* the government recognised the role of private entrepreneurs beside the SOEs. The main ambition of the reforms was to promote productivity, as 'the policy of encouraging some sections of people to get rich is compatible with the logic of the development of a socialistic society' (CCPCC 1984). In addition, the SOEs would become more efficient. To increase

vene in the SOEs management and productivity decisions. In addition, to ensure the market-oriented success of the SOEs, the government reorganised the existing enterprises into shareholding or contracted enterprises or even sold or shut smaller SOEs down if necessary.

The reorganisation was officially approved and issued in company law, published in 1994, 'in which the state has sought to transform SOEs from administrative agencies into business enterprises' (Wedeman 2004:79). The success of the '100-Firm Corporation Experiment' pioneer project in which the government transformed former SOEs into limited shareholding corporations (Zhiyuan et al. 2000) created a new consensus in the central government that 'the state should be a passive shareholder, ... without the power to control the corporation's day to day operations' (Zhiyuan et al 2000:6). The government made the commitment to accept the autonomy of the new SOEs and focus its attention on macro economic guidance: 'The main duties of the government are to formulate and implement macro economic policies, establish basic facilities and create a favourable economical environment' (CCPCC 1993). In addition the 'government will use economic, legal and administrative measure to manage the economy, it will not directly intervene in the production and management activities of enterprises' (CCPCC 1993). Two main objectives were accomplished:

First, the SOEs' ownership as well as property rights were clearly defined. In the course of action, the SOEs gained autonomy in the day-to-day operations and the involvement of state authorities was heavily reduced to support the economic effectiveness of the entities (Gang et al 1998:18). *Second*, the state was able to get rid off the large proportion of non-profit-making SOEs and their burden on the state budget, as well as to improve the overall economic output of the economy to legitimize the political power of the CCP (Chan et al 2008:34-35).

As a reaction, in 1994 the SC announced the new labour law in which the main concern was to regulate unemployment for reason of maternity, accident, or illness, as well as the pension insurance system for employees

productivity the government decided to grant independent management to the SOEs. Central and local governments were no longer in charge of management and business. However, the ownership of the SOEs remained in the hands of the state as did the control of major economic sectors. Central and local government could still give advice to the SOEs. Also macro-economic development was state business, which determined economic strategies, technical and skill development as well as social welfare schemes (Chan et al 2008:30).

in the new environment.[242] The focus of the legislature was placed on the pension system.[243]

3.3.3.2 Evolution of a pluralistic System in China

In the early 1990s the increasing complexity and costs of maintaining the social security schemes, programmes and services accelerated the pace of decentralization for social security and the pension scheme (Yu 2010, D. Liu 2011:112 sp). The Central Committee paid close attention to the financial dimension and increased the contribution of employees.[244] In another attempt to further decentralize, the central government shifted responsibility from local governments to the newly introduced social insurance agencies in 1991. The ongoing decentralisation promoted pluralism and harsh variations in the social security and pension system (see diagram 1, Chan et al 2008:45, 56). In 1991 the local governments set up insurance agencies at the provincial, municipal and federal levels to administer the various social funds for the different types of enterprises (D. Liu 2011:133-137) and the responsibility for social security was deeply decentralised (Lieberthal 1995, Yang and Li 2013:61, Wang and Gong 2007). The central government encouraged local authorities to introduce their own pilot projects in social security, especially in rural areas to expand the urban-focused coverage of the social security system (Hong and Wang 2002:108-9). In a relatively short time the central government could access various local approaches and select the best functioning pilot project to introduce in other parts of China in need of improvement (Horsley 2004, D. Liu 2013:120).[245]

The first task of the central government was the standardization of the pension reform. In the same year (1991), the *State Council Document No. 33* was published to address the complexity of the pension system, and proposed a national three-tier pension system for all employees.[246] In 1993

---

242 For details see the labour law of the CPR, 1994, and in particular § 73.

243 See decision No. 27 published by the Central Committee in 1993 and its strong case for the regulation of pension insurance.

244 See again decision No.27 published by the Central Committee of the CCP.

245 The strategy was used before in the context of the special economy zones (Hurst 2009).

246 First tier included a basic pension for all employees financed by the contributions of the employer and the employee. Second tier consisted of a supplemental pen-

the Central Committee suggested setting up public funds and individual funds for the pension system. In 1995 the SC approved and published regulations.[247] Local authorities had to set up a pension pool for the different types of enterprises and had to administer the different pension contributions, schemes and claims (China Daily Online 2007). From 1995 to 1997 the pension system was tested in various locations and the SC opted for a nation-wide standardization of the pension system.[248] The formulation attempt and resulting debate on the reconstruction of a national pension system could not produce a coherent strategy. Therefore the central government fell back on the traditional 'trial and error' method and initiated various pilot projects aimed at providing a solution for rural areas.[249] In the meantime, the old pension scheme of 1986 persisted due to the missing consensus on range, scope and modalities (Darimont 2004, D. Liu 2011:113).

3.3.3.3 Introducing market-orientated Social Security Schemes in a pluralistic Setting

In the early 1990s the puzzle of achieving economic performance for the SOEs convinced the CCP of the urgent need for structural reforms to solve

---

sion funded by enterprises and third tier a voluntary pension paid by the individual worker.

247 '国务院关于深化企业职工养老保险制度改革的通知' (*Circular of the State Council on Deepening the Reform of the Pension System for Staff and Workers of Enterprises'*) published 1st March 1995. The 'aim of the reform of the pension system for staff and workers of enterprises is to basically establish by the end of the century a pension system which will meet the requirements of the socialist market economic system, and apply to the staff and workers of enterprises of all kinds and individual laborers in cities and towns, have multiple financial resources and multiple categories of insurance, combine a collection of insurance funds from society with individual accounts, balance rights with obligations and adopt socialized management and service,' available at http://www.lawinfochina.com/display.aspx?lib=law&id=12196&CGid= (2014-12-12).

248 SC published the '*Circular of the State Council on Establishing the Standardized Basic Pension'* for urban workers, the scope of which will be expanded to the rural population in 2007 (Darimont 2004:208 sp).

249 The majority of social security schemes, programmes and services have been designed for the urban workforce. Accordingly, the rural areas and their citizens have been excluded from most of the social security system's benefits and/or gained only marginal support compared to urban dwellers (Chan et al. 2008:81).

two major problems. *First*, keeping the relatively high number of smaller and profit-losing SOEs going cost the government additional resources and burdened the state budget. Further, the existing welfare administration and provision was mainly in the hands of the SOEs, which reduced their economic capacity (Chan et al. 2008:98-99, D. Liu 2011:109).

Second, and more importantly, the flagships of the SOEs constantly criticised the negative effect of strong political influence on management and day-to-day work which reduced their international competitiveness. In pursuit of economic growth the CCP willingly granted the SOEs more managerial independence and heavily reduced the state's supervisory role (Lee 2001, Dodds 1996:695, Wong 1998).

In recognition of the problem, the CCP's policies set out to reduce the state's involvement in the SOEs and the burden of non-wage costs for the SOEs in order to guarantee their economic performance (Feinermann 1991:65-66). In 1993 the SC issued the *Company Law* to transform the SOEs in modern market-oriented entities. The *Company Law* did not only grant the SOEs more managerial independence in decision-making but also dismantled them from providing social welfare, including pension to former employees. Furthermore, life-long employment was replaced with contract employment. In particular, the reform had a significant effect on employment and recruitment patterns by giving SOEs the leeway to get rid of working-aged employees above 40 years and retirement obligations to former employees (Chan et al. 2008:33-36). Politically speaking, the central government encouraged the SOEs to transform into internationally competitive enterprises even in exchange for massive job losses. In the following years, the SOEs dismissed large numbers of their employees, with the vast majority comprising older workers above the age of 40. The continuing job losses, or so-called '*lay-offs*,'[250] in the SOEs enormously increased the unemployment rate and put substantial pressure on the central government to provide employment opportunities for the working-aged population (Chan 2001, Lee 2001, Gallagher 2002:340-341).

250 The UNDP Report (1999) estimated that the number of laid-off workers increased from three million in 1993 to approximately 18 million in 1998.

RSCs: illustrating the deficits in policymaking and provision

A clear indicator of the limited capacity for input and the missing available democratic mechanisms for participation, as well as their potential to damage the government's credibility, is shown in the relatively slow reaction of the state party to the immediate problem. Following its typical pattern of behaviour, the central government initiated a pilot project in 1996 by opening the *Reemployment Service Centres* (RSCs) in several cities which had suffered disproportionate job losses (Hurst 2009:68-69).[251]

The RSC policy is best described as an active labour market scheme. The RSCs were designed as community facilities to provide a range of services and retraining opportunities to *laid-off workers*.[252] They provided more than re-employment and training opportunities for workers and were designed not only for the purpose of managing the job losses in the SOEs[253]. In particular, the RSC combines a variation of social security packages, including services granting their beneficiaries re-employment opportunities, monthly unemployment benefits as well as social insurance coverage for a limited time (Hurst 2009:66, 135). The central government attempted to realize its commitment, initiated by Deng Xiaoping and his concept of the 'socialistic market economy', to set up a functioning but market-oriented social security system to tackle the realities of economic transformation (Chan et al. 2008:32-34). The new dynamics of the labour market and the large amount of pensioners with financial difficulties due to the dismantling of the SOEs, as well as the act of divesting the SOEs of their responsibility to provide pensions, increased the pressure to reform the poorly designed pension system. In 1995 the SC issued the standardization of the pension system and published the '*Circular on Deepening the Reform of the Old Age Pension System for Enterprise Employees*'.[254]

251 Two year later, in 1998, the setting up of local RSCs was made mandatory for all urban SOEs.

252 For a discussion on the term of laid-off workers see the appendix.

253 The SC stopped the project in 2000 due to only modest success (Hurst 2009).

254 The national scheme and its three divergent components have to be understood as part of the 'trial and error' tradition. The SC announced the introduction of one national pension system for all employees in 2000. But the SC outlined three different approaches to the contribution rates for employers and employees to achieve the goal of a unitary pension system on the national level. Local governments were free to choose any of the approaches. The resulting vagueness enforced the SC in 1997 to define one approach for all provinces. However, the ap-

Similar to the pension system initiatives, the SC and the Ministry of Labour and Social Security (the MoLSS, today the Ministry of Human Resources and Social Security) began to tackle the outdated social security system in 1996. MoLSS published regulations for the Occupational Injury and Disease Insurance and its financial pooling to strengthen the social security of urban workers in cases of employment-related accidents, disability or illness (D. Liu 2011:114-16). In addition to the problem of laid-off workers the government had to issue the collapse of the health care system in the early 1990s.[255] In effect, the structural reforms dismantled the traditional contribution function and gave rise to new employment trends in which a large proportion of the working-aged population were employed by private enterprises which would not have been included in the old coverage and contribution patterns of the health care system (Chan et al. 2008:141). It took until 1998 for the SC to announce the problem and produce a coherent reform attempt for the inadequate health insurance system. In 1998 the SC announced a Basic Health Insurance System which was planned to replace the Labour Health Insurance System and the Government Health Insurance System in 2000 to 2001.[256] Over the years the CCP ambitiously concentrated on the provision of output performance in terms of economic growth (Kailitz 2009a). In 1999 the CCP leadership under chair of Chinese President Zemin Jiang accelerated the pace of liberalisation and officially quit the socialist market economy with the official document on *Decisions on the reform and development of SOEs*.[257]

---

proach determined the base pension rate to be 20 per cent of the average local wage in the province but did not produce a coherent framework concerning administration and funding of the scheme (Drouin and Thompson 2006:18, ILO 2010b).

255 It should be stressed that the SOEs' reforms and the dismantling of welfare provision had a strong impact on the need for structural reform of the welfare system on all levels, such as administration, funding, as well as provision. Before the reforms the SOEs were a major pillar of the provision of welfare schemes, services and benefits for the workforce as well as provided life-long employment and pension schemes for their employees (Yiyong 2001, Hurst 2009:66).

256 The Basic Health Insurance System was designed in response to the employment situation and is based, in constrast to the old insurance system, on a combination of individual contribution and social pooling (Hurst 2004, 2009:74-76).

257 The document is based on the earlier enterprise reform system of 1997 aimed at accelerating the pace of economic transformation and achieving higher economic performance (Ma and Hou 2005). In order to pursue the ambitious goal, the document introduced a huge range of different types of companies ranging in their

The central government expanded the coverage of employment-related social security beyond the state sectors, increasing its discriminating character (Drouin and Thompson 2006:18-19).[258] President Jiang defended the structural strategy because 'a socialistic state does not need to have the state sector as the predominant actor in the economy to maintain its socialistic nature' (quoted in Gang et al 1998:18).

Shequ system – an example for urban focused focus of policy making

An important and typical example of Chinese policymaking, missing coherent strategy and sub-optimal outcomes is the '*shequ system*'. Its development emphasises the seemingly—in all social security schemes—present logic of '*crossing the river by groping for stones*' as well as strong path dependency (quoted in Qian and Wu 2000:1).[259]

During the reform era of the late 1980s and early 1990s, the key issue of the legislature was two-fold. On the one hand, it was concerned to accelerate the privatization and decentralisation of economic entities to jointly shoulder economic growth. On the other hand, it aimed to tackle structural reforms and the eroded employment-related social insurance system (i.e. the *danwei system*)[260] (Hurst 2009:65).

In the issued legislation the state officially permitted SOEs to rely on the so-called 'lay-off strategy' to enhance competitiveness by reducing the labour costs[261]. The sanctioning of the employment policy resulted in a peak unemployment rate. In 1997 the rate jumped rapidly to 11,510,000

---

ownership from traditional state-controlled to fully privatized enterprises; it stressed the need to adopt the welfare system (Green 2004:19).

258 In urban areas the firms provide higher salaries and a wider range of compulsory social security, pension and health schemes and programs than in the rural, less economically developed provinces (Wong 1998). The same holds true for the Indian context (Nagaraj 2000, 2012a:54-58).

259 Quoted in Qian Y. and J. Wu . 2001. 'Chinese transition to market economy: how far across the river?' presented at the Conference on Policy Reforms in China at the Centre for Research on Economic Development and Policy Reform, 2000-11-18/20. Stanford: Stanford University Press.

260 In the late 1980s reforms to the SOEs and labour market resulted in the erosion of the *danwei* or work units including its welfare schemes and services.

261 For the norm shift in politics and the acceptance of employment reduction measures to enhance the competitiveness of the SOEs, see Steinfeld (2004), Chai (2005) and Pierson (2005).

unemployed workers (Jiang et al 1998). Various studies sponsored by the state government announced that the unemployment would affect up to 2 million people by the end of 1998 (Wong and Ngok 1997:335, Yiyong 1998, Cook and Jolly 2002). Taking the problem seriously, the government decided on the Fifteenth Party Congress to take measures to prevent the wildfire of job loss. The CCP leadership set up a '*Work Conference on Basic Livelihood Protection and Re-employment of Laid-off Worker in SOEs*' under the supervision of the SC. The consensus of the conference in 1998 resulted in the introduction of the *shequ system*, a modified version of the former *danwei system* (Zemin 1997).[262]

Accordingly, in 1998 the *shequ system* was instantiated in various cities to expand the existing RSC program and tackle the issue of increasing numbers of laid-off workers. As a result, the legislature expanded the local governance structure to cushion the growing socio-economic problems on local level (Chan et al. 2008:98). The new '*shequ* or *community'* unit was imposed on a local urban level to fill the gap for the long-term unemployed after the expiration of the RSC[263] (Hurst 2009:66, 135-36). The role of the program is to provide various services, such as information, education and training for re-employment. As a main service provider on the local level for the unemployed the *shequ* provides facilities for external[264] and internal services and a community for the unemployed. Indeed, the *shequ* system has to be understood foremost as a reform of the *danwei* system meant to cope with socio-economic realities and cushion the hardships of unemployment related to the economic transformation process. In this context Yiping and Qi (2005) emphasise that the main ambition of the project was to transform the '*danwei man*' into the '*society man*,' or the laid-off worker into a 'useful' member of society. Again Ma and Hou's (2005) assumed separation of policymaking and budget demands seems valid. The costs of the *shequ* could be heavily reduced due to the fact that the old *danwei* facilities were taken over; still the *shequ* system is first and

262 See Jiang Zemin's report '在中国共产党第十五次全国代表大会上的报告 ('*Report of the 15th Party Congress of the CCP*')', in: 人民日报 (RMRB), published 1997-09-22.

263 Officials anticipate a growing internal competition for the SOEs and expect that the laid-off workers will permanently lack job opportunities (Hurst 2009:66).

264 The All China Women's Federation has utilized the *shequ* facilities for their own unofficial re-employment, education schemes, programs and community meetings (Yiyong 2001: 16 sp). These informal programs, such as '*Hope Schools*' for female drop-outs, are not state financed (Chan et al. 2008:54).

foremost a government solution intended to expand the welfare of the long-term unemployed and not to reduce social welfare costs. While the RSC for laid-off workers was restricted in its time frame[265], the *shequ* was conceived as a permanent local institution to cope with short- and long-term unemployment[266] (Hurst 2009:135).

The pluralistic structure of the Chinese social security system has a clear effect on the *shequ* system, resulting in three different types which can be distinguished mainly in terms of the independence of the *shequ* (Yipeng and Qi 2005:147). The first type is a weak '*Shenyang model*' or joint operation in which the authority of the local authorities, state organisation and *shequ* is balanced. In the second type or the so-called '*Shanghai model*' the *shequ* is 'coopted by the increasingly powerful local street committee' (Hurst 2009:135). Third, an autonomous *shequ model*, often referred to as the '*Jianghan model*', supports and expands the range and scope of the existing local social services (Yipeng and Qi 2005).

3.3.4 The Second Period: Social Security Politics, 1993-2004

From 1993 to 2003 various kinds of social insurances for the urban working-aged population were designed and implemented. The Chinese government slowly but steadily expanded the coverage of social security for the target group. Despite the officially announcement by the SC in 2002 that 'with the progress of history, the old labour and social security system had become inadaptable to the requirements of economic and social development' (Information Office of the SC 2002), the authorities ensured the continuation of various older social security schemes, dating back to the 1950s and 1970s, to fill the gap. Policy trajectories, experiences and old programmes were constantly revamped or even continued. In 2000 the SC announced the '*Notification on the Pilot Project for improvement of the*

265 The program was terminated in 2003, and access only available for laid-off workers until 2000; since then no more recipients have been accepted into the program (Hurst 2009:66)

266 In 2008 the *shequ* system was still in the early stages of development in terms of coverage and was restricted to the urban metropolis that represents the traditional focus of Chinese welfare (Yipeng and Qi 2005:147, Hurst 2009:83, 134).

social security in cities,'[267] reflecting the slow but steady policy change in social security provision from Deng Xiaoping's '*socialistic market economy*' to Jintao Hu's (2005) '和谐社会' (*'harmonious society*').[268]

The urban Pension Scheme: Strengths and Deficits

The urban pension scheme is the flagship of employment-related social security in China, with 223 million beneficiaries in 2009. The pension system reflects the focus of social security politics for older generations as well as two systemic problems of social security provision (Hurst and O'Brian 2002:370-74, Chan et al. 2008:73-74): inadequate funds and narrow coverage[269] (Liu and Yang 2004).[270]

The events following the implementation of the *Bankruptcy Law 1986* and the divestment of the SOEs from their welfare function, including the provision of pensions, resulted in the reduction or even cessation of pension payments for 1,510,000 pensioners (Wong 1998, Hurst 2004:99-101). Accordingly, the old pension funds were inadequately equipped to face the increasing number of 'early' pensioners.[271] A persistent problem of the pension scheme is its low benefits rates. An indicator is the drastic increase of old-age poverty even for beneficiaries of the program.[272]

---

267 See the official announcement published by the SC (2000) '国务院关于完善城镇社会保障体系的试点方案, 国发 (Notification on the Pilot Project for improvement of social security in cities)', 42 号, released 2000-25-12.

268 See article 1 of the official notification from 2000.

269 Disability is also covered if the beneficiary is totally disabled, fulfils the requirement of having at least 10 years of service, and is 50 years old if male, or 45 years if female. Younger and fully disabled people can apply for a pension of 40 per cent of their previous salary (Chow 2000).

270 As previously indicated, local authorities had to cover the welfare and pension of SOEs' employees.

271 Normally pension schemes can be accessed by workers who have at least 15 years of employment experience. In China the retirement age for the employed is 60 years of age for male salaried workers, 55 years of age for female salaried workers, and only 50 years of age for women with flexible contracts. In this context pension schemes have been used by the government to realize a rapid reduction in the large amount of older laid-off workers. Similar to workers with hazardous work environments, employees of bankrupt SOEs with 15 years of service gained a 5-year reduction on their retirement age (Hurst 2009:37sp).

272 Since June 1998 the retirement payment consists of a two-part transition benefit —a basic and an individual account benefit. The basic benefit is equal to 20 per-

In the late 1990s the CCP set out to tackle the structural problems of the urban pension system without much success. Challenged by increasing complexity and administrative burdens, the SC began to address financing basic pensions in 1995.[273] In the second step, in 1997 the SC *Decision on establishing a uniform basic old age insurance system for enterprise employees* (SC 1997a) set a standard level of contribution for employees and employers, addressing issues concerning the regulation of the social pooling of the basic old age pension insurance at the provincial level as well as transferring *occupational* pooling to local level (Sc 1998).[274] Although the reforms were sound on paper, neither the financial deficit nor the newly emerging issues could be solved. The SC followed the 'Chinese way' and started a trial pilot project for a newly designed pension scheme in Liaoning Province. In 2001 the scheme was expanded nation-wide. The reforms in 2001 as well as 2005[275] aimed to standardize the payment modalities[276] as well as access for pension schemes for the increasing numbers of urban workers with flexible contracts.[277]

Taking a look at the demographic tendencies, sharpened by the one-child policy as well as enduring low financial benefits and old-aged poverty, one realizes that the reforms have been short-sighted (World Bank 1997, WHO 2000, NZZ 2014c). In particular, in the last years the nominal

cent of the average wage in the year prior to the individual's retirement. The monthly benefit based on the individual account is the balance in the worker's account at the time of retirement divided by 120. Initial retirement benefits are to be adjusted each year by an amount established by each provincial government. The adjustment is intended to take into account changes in wage and price levels and the financial conditions of the programmes in the respective provinces (Mu and Liu 2005).

273 In the published Document No.6 1995 the SC addressed the problem of financing and proposed two available options for local governments.

274 See Huaizhon Mu and Qingrui Liu's (2005) article '穆怀中/柳清瑞, 中国养老保险制度改革关键问题研究' ('*The Research on the Key Issues about China's Pension System Reforms*') for an elaboration of the pension reforms and their implications for social security provision, funding and benefits.

275 SC's (2005) *Decision on improving enterprise workers' basic old age insurance.*

276 Pension schemes are financed by the employer and employee. The contributions of the employers vary from locality to locality but are normally around 20 per cent of earnings. From 2001 to 2005 the individual contribution of the employee was gradually increased up to 8 per cent of his earnings (Drouin and Thompson 2006:40, Mu and Liu 2005, ILO 2010b).

277 Workers with flexible contracts have to pay an insurance premium of 18 per cent of the average regional salary (Chan et al. 2008:64).

wages and therefore the entitled retirement benefits grew faster than the pension reserves.[278] In 2003 the local governments together contributed 54.4 billion, roughly 20 percent of their budgets. In addition the central government had to contribute an additional 47.4 billion to ensure the funding of the pension system (Ministry of Finance 1999-2007). Official statistics show that by 2006 a total number of the 141.31 million urban employees had participated in the old-age insurance programs; however, the program only covers 50 percent of urban employees. Furthermore, the number of pensioners gaining benefits from the pension scheme is also a modest 46 million, due to the fact that the pension scheme only covers government employees (MoLSS 2007).[279]

Voluntary rural Pensions: Planning Challenges and Program Concurrency

The lack of rural pensions has been a long-standing issue. The situation considerably worsened after the decline of the rural 'cooperative medical system' in the early 1980s. Following the common strategy of social security provision, the CCP initiated a series of pilot projects in rural counties. These pilot projects were characterized by a high degree of self-administration on the part of local governments to allow on-the-go adaptation and modification. One of these programmes was the voluntary rural pension scheme in 1992 under the authority of the MOCA.[280]

As indicated in next table 11, in a short time the well-designed and well-funded scheme gained popularity and was even introduced in more than six rural provinces. The contributions have been higher than the expenditures; however, the ratio of recipients has been relatively low (see

---

278 Between 1990 and 2000 government bonds for the pension system could only achieve an average of 10.2 percent. In contrast, nominal wages grew at an average annual rate of 15.9 percent.

279 See the '2007 Statistical bulletin for Labour and Social Security' (MoLSS 2007).

280 The pension scheme was a group-based target for workers of town and village enterprises. The contributions are voluntary. Starting at age 60 the recipient is paid an annuity-based monthly paid pension equal to the balance in the account divided by 180 at the moment of retirement. A guarantee was granted for at least 120 monthly payments for the beneficiary's survivor in case of early death before the age of 70. The average pensioner received just over ¥ 80 per month in 2002. In 2002 there were 54.6 million accounts in total and 1.2 million retirees received ¥ 1.2 billion (Shi 2006, Herd 2010).

also table 11 and diagram 1).[281] Furthermore, the number of participants steadily increased until 1998 but then completely stagnated. Against the background of success, the CCP decided—in an act of supreme coordination—to reassign the responsibility for the program to the Ministry of Labour and Social Security in 1999. The joint venture could not arrive at a coherent strategy for the future of the program.

Table 11: Rural Pension Scheme (1992-1994)

Year	1992	1995	1996	1997	1998	2000	2001	2002	2003	2004
Numbers of insuranced (million)	26	51.4	65.9	82.8	80.3	61.7	60	54.6	54.3	53.8
Numbers of pensioners (million)		0.3	0.3	0.6		1	1.1	1.2	2	2.1
Contribution collection (billion Yuan)		3.7	4.4	4.2	3.1	1.4	1.7	2.5	3.6	x
Pension expenditure (billion Yuan)		0.1	0.2	0.3	0.5	0.4	0.5	0.5	1.5	x
Accumulated funds (billion Yuan)	0.8	6	10	14	16.6	19.6	21.6	23.3	25.9	28.5

Source: Shi (2006:801), Chinese Statistical Yearbook various issues

Moreover, mismanagement and insecurity resulted in a sharp drop in coverage from 82.8 million to only 53.8 million from 1997 to 2004.[282] Hence,

281 Of the contribution 85 percent of individual funds are managed by the local county administration and the rest are taken by the provincial government to provide reinsurance claims. In 2002 only 45 per cent of the contributions came from 4.1 million individual participations. The rest have been funded by the local government and roughly 0.67 million by the TVEs due to the central government encouraging the TVEs to charge for social security costs. A fee of three per cent of the individual contributions is taken by the local government to finance the administrative costs of the scheme. At the end of 2002 there were 54.6 million accounts in total, credited with a total sum of ¥ 23.3 billion, suggesting an average balance across all accounts of only about ¥ 433 (Statistical Yearbook 2007).

282 See Wang, Y. 2005. 'Reform of China's Pension System', *China & World Economy, vol.* 13, no. 3:44–55.

the schemes ran into serious problems. Several important issues stand out when it comes to the efficiency of the voluntary rural pension scheme. Beneficiaries will likely gain a benefit of around 40 percent of their local average earnings in exchange for lifetime payments of roughly 8 percent of average local income. The major problem is the modest coverage. One reason for the low frequency is that the programme is based upon individual voluntary contributions.[283] Furthermore, the program concurrency to the MSLS has not been taken into account. Most rural participants can only afford one pension scheme at a time (Herd 2010, D. Liu 2011:148, 150). To sum up, the report of the World Bank concludes that the voluntary pension 'scheme was unsuccessful and the coverage was small' (White 2006). In retrospect, the voluntary pension scheme ran into the same problem as the current urban pension scheme concerning its long-term funding and was jeopardized by ineffective central planning.

Health Insurance: The Issue of a missing coherent National Strategy

Another example of the lack of a coherent national social security system is provided by the Chinese health care system. Before the reforms in 2009 it was characterised by the central government's struggle to improve universal health care and by the low budget of local authorities to deliver and maintain the needed facilities as well as the inability of the central government to formulate a coherent national policy until 2007 (Liu an Yi 2004).[284]

A missing coherent health policy on the national level, various different pilot projects, and variations in local health care schemes all over the CPR produced pressure on the central government to pursue a series of reforms. In their report for the World Bank, Liu and Yang (2004:73) conclude that the 'overall process is thorough experiments and then the central govern-

283 Another problem that could explain the central government's attitude is related to the program itself. The low rates of return, the administrative and financial costs, and the competition of private insurance companies are obstacles to be taken seriously (Leisering et al 2002:19). In rural areas the responsibility to contribute to social protection for old age shifted from communities to families (Chan et al. 2008:67).

284 In 2007 the CCP started the pilot project for 'unitary' social security in urban and rural areas, which resulted in the reform of the rural health insurance system in 2009.

ment develops models later to be adopted (and adapted) on the national scale. The health reforms have been passive, partial, and uncoordinated. As a result, it is often the case that one problem has not been solved by a reform, new problems have been brought out'. Since the end of the commune system the CRP has struggled to provide rural social security coverage and adequate funding for urban health care facilities (NFSH 2000).[285]

The attempt to set up a nation-wide health insurance program for urban workers is what drove the central government, namely the SC, to introduce the pilot project[286] of the *Basic Health Insurance System for Urban Employees* (BHIS) in 1998.[287] The BHIS could not stand up to the task. Against the background of constant adjustment the BHIS was unfit to accomplish the task of unifying the various existing local schemes under the umbrella of one nation-wide health system for urban citizens. As a consequence, most of the local schemes co-exist beside the BHIS, increasing the complexity of administration and funding. A traditional issue of social security is low coverage and narrow scope of specific schemes.[288] The SC had to expand the access modalities twice: in 2003 access was made available to the increasing numbers of the self-employed and in 2004 to employees in non-public enterprises. Against the background of the constant expansion of access modalities the participation rate was modest.[289] At the end of 2006, the BHIS covered 41 percent of the urban workforce and 42 million retirees (Ministry of Labor and Social Security 2007).

285 Missing health insurance for rural residents is a perfect example of the gap between policy objectives and implementation. It was assumed that the scheme would sharply increase coverage without much success, due to missing public information, cooperation and an overcharged bureaucracy (Rao and Mander 1996).

286 The newly designed insurance scheme was tested in different cities in the 1990s. After the intensive testing phases, the central government evaluated its efficiency and began to implement the program on a national scale in 1999 (Xu 2007).

287 Before the BHIS China's health care system in cities could be divided into two separate schemes dating back to the early 1950s. The first scheme covered employees and retirees from government institutions and civil services. The second scheme covered employees and retirees from urban enterprises (Xu 2007, D. Liu 2011:135f, 138sp). Therefore, BHIS attempted to incorporate the existing health insurance for civil servants, urban and public workers.

288 The same holds true for the BHIS, which in the beginning only covered the public sector, such as employees and retirees of government agencies, public institutions, party organizations and non-enterprise institutions.

289 In 2003 only 80 million people participated in the BHIS, which covers only a marginal portion of the urban workforce and government employees.

Another issue has been the organized strategy to privatize the health care sector, which did not improve the health care system and/or coverage. In the 1990s the CCP trusted in the market to solve the problem and privatized the cost of health care facilities and services (Sun 2002).[290] In addition the BHIS attempted to reform the access to hospitals and shift the responsibility for dispensing pharmaceuticals from hospitals to independent pharmacies (Chow and Xu, 2002, Drouin and Thompson 2006:43).[291]Another constraint on the BHIS is the missing coherent regulations for contributions, benefits and funding.[292] The demographic 'aging' of the population, low rent potential of pension investment funds and increasing medical costs are even today challenging the financial capacity of the BHIS.

As indicated (see next table 12) the CCP has traditionally been challenged by the overall missing or 'non-existing' state-provided health insurance for rural areas. Moreover, similar to the pension scheme (see the previous section), the benefits are relatively low, not to mention the discriminating access modalities for additional services. [293]

---

290 Sun, S. H. 2002. 'The transition and evaluation of China's medical protection for enterprise workers', in G.C: Zheng (eds.), *The transition and evaluation of Chinese social security system*, pp. 119-159. Beijing: People University of China Press.

291 Before the reform of the BHIS hospitals received government subsidies, which made up roughly 25 per cent of their revenue. In the new context, these costs will be taken over by insurance and no longer subsidized by the government. For a detailed discussion of the privatization of the Chinese health care system see the Ministry of Labor and Social Security, 2007.

292 Health insurance is financed entirely from worker and employer contributions. The average employer contribution rate in 2007 was 6 percent. However, the contribution rate varies form county to county and is not standardized. Approximately 30 percent of the payment is transferred to the employee's account and the rest of the employer's contribution is used for funding the BHIS. On the contrary, the employee's contribution of 2 per cent of his salary is directly transferred to his individual account. Employees have to pay two percent of their salary payment as premium. Administrative costs for collecting, controlling and maintaining the scheme and funds are separately paid by the local government (Drouin and Thompson 2006:44). Retirees do not pay any contributions, but are enrolled for coverage financed from the employer contributions. Their coverage comes through the pool, which covers the locality of their permanent legal residence (Dong 2001).

293 The scheme is discriminating in the sense that the entitlement to the previous public sector schemes is a requirement to access certain additional services.

Table 12: Types and coverage of Health Insurance in 2003

Medical scheme	Urban	Rural
Cooperative insurance	6.6	9.6
Compulsory insurance for urban workers	30.4	1.5
Catastrophic disease insurance	1.8	0.1
Government scheme	4	0.2
Labour insurance	4.6	0.1
Other types	2.2	1.2
Commercial insurance	5.6	8.3
Sub-total	55.2	21
Self-payment	44.8	79

Source: MH (2007); Chan et al. (2008:133)

A representative of the Pingan Insurance Company remarked that it is '*just like having no medical benefit at all. They are not covered much by the public fund and mostly have to rely on their own ability to pay*' (cited by Dong 2001:19). The statement summarizes the evidence presented in table 12 that reveals that only 55.2 percent of the urban and 21 percent of the rural population are covered.[294]

The issue of missing rural health care is directly linked to the economic transformation and collapse of the former 'cooperative medical system' in the late 1980s. In 2002 the central government under Hu Jintao set out to solve the issue of missing social security and health care coverage in rural areas (Hu 2005). The Chinese government followed its typical strategy of initiating different types of pilot projects in various counties to optimize the administration, funding, as well as coverage of health care schemes under the umbrella of the policy agenda to set up a 'unitary' urban and rural social security system (Sen et al. 2002). A consequence of the missing health care programs has been a sharp increase in out-of-pocket health care costs for the individual, which has produced a barrier for poorer people who are unable to access the benefits of modern health care.[295]

294 Another problem of the compulsory health insurance is the very limited financial coverage in cases of hospitalization (Dong 2001). In his case study, Dong (2001:19) demonstrated that a middle-aged worker in Shanghai could save a maximum of 300 Yuan in his health insurance account to cover his medical costs.

295 See the special report by Wagstaff et al. (2009:19 sp) for the World Bank on the issue of increasing out-of-the-pocket costs.

Unemployment Insurance: Modest Coverage and low Benefits

Contrary to other social security schemes unemployment insurance is directly linked to employment policy and its responsiveness to economic realities. In the post-Mao period the CCP faced a jump in the urban unemployment ratio; from 1978 to 1979 alone, the number of registered unemployed reached 5.3 and accelerated to 5.7 million (Chinese Labour Statistical Yearbook 1997:8).[296] In the post-Mao period officials had to accept the fact that unemployment is and will be an issue for the CPR. Still it took the central government until 1986 to formulate unemployment insurance exclusively for SOEs employees (SC 1986). In 1993 the new labour law also addressed the issue of reforming the unemployment insurance contribution. Similar to any other policy reforms in the era of economic transformation, the focus of the central government was on unburdening economic entities. Accordingly, the contribution rate of 1 percent of the payroll was lowered to only 0.6 percent (SC 1996).[297] It has been a hallmark of the introduction of '*general*' unemployment insurance and the extension of the coverage of the existing unemployment payment scheme because the older scheme did only cover unemployment in the state or collective-owned sector (Chow and Xu 2002; Leung 2006).[298]

From 1980 to 2002 the rapid economic transformation, relaxation and liberalization of the labour market as well as the SOEs' reform resulted in increasing 'problem pressure,' with rapidly expanding numbers of 'laid-off workers' and unemployed (Chan et al. 2008:33-35). In particular, the earlier unemployment insurance program was unfit to deal with the issue of 'laid-off' workers, which was an artificial category created by the government to decrease the official unemployment numbers.[299]

296 In rural areas the number is estimated to be above 15 million (Chinese Labour Statistical Yearbook 1997)

297 See § 73Chinese labour law (1994). Before the 1980s the prohibition of the private sector in the Chinese economy and state-controlled labour-market unemployment was not a major issue for the party government despite the increasing numbers of people without a job (Leung 2003, 2006).

298 In 1979 at least 15 million people in rural areas were 'waiting' for job opportunities (D. Liu 2011:205). The '失业保险条例' ('*Regulation on Unemployment Insurance*') was published 22. 01. 1999.

299 Until 1994 12 percent or 12 million former SOEs' employees were '*reemployed*' and became '*laid-off*' workers (Hurst and O'Brian 2002: 350f, D. Liu 2011:206).

The CCP had to take the issue of employment seriously due to its ideological ambition of being a proletarian party and its requirement for output legitimacy, which was jeopardized by high levels of unemployment. In effect, in 1998 the '*Two Guarantees*' and '*Three Security Lines*' for laid-off workers[300] were introduced. In combination with the RSCs the schemes guaranteed cash benefits for the provision of a minimum living standard, the payment of pension benefits, and support in finding new employment opportunities.[301]

Against the background of ideological as well as pragmatic pressure the unemployment insurance offered only little comfort to the unemployed and coverage has traditionally been low.[302] Three years later, the official urban unemployment rate was 4.1 percent and an estimated 8.5 million people. The gap between beneficiaries and the officially registered unemployed further widened (Ministry of Labor and Social Security 2007).[303] Various reasons can account for the traditionally low participation ratio.[304] One problem is that according to the modalities of the program, workers are only entitled to benefit payments if they have been employed and paid insurance contributions for one year.[305] Another is the administrative hur-

300 All laid-off workers still without employment in 2005 were entitled to the general unemployment scheme. See the '国务院关于进一步加强就业再就业工作的通知 ('*Regulation of the SC promoting employment and re-employment*')', 2005-11-08.

301 In 2005 the SC imposed the closure of all re-employment centres of the *Reemployment Service Centres* until 2006, which were replaced in function by public reemployment institutions. The Central Committee issued the document titled '中共中央国务院关于切实做好国有企业下岗职工基本生活保障和再就业工作的通知' concerning the new guidelines for the guaranteed minimum living standards, reemployment schemes and unemployment insurance for laid-off workers, published in 09. 06. 1998.

302 In 2003 at least 8 million urban workers were reportedly unemployed but only 4.5 million received unemployment insurance payments (Chinese Statistical Yearbook 2004).

303 In 2006 the participation rate declined to 40 per cent, representing 3.3 million beneficiaries (Ministry of Labor and Social Security 2007).

304 It should be noted that the program was introduced in 1999.

305 The cash benefits are only given to workers whose unemployment is involuntary and the workers have to be registered and ready to take up any job opportunity or re-employment program offered by the employment office. Also the entitlement to payment requires monthly reports at the employment office. The unemployment insurance mainly pays cash benefits for a limited period of time depending on the recipient's participation. One and less than five years entitle the recipient

dles and regulations that consume the time and efforts of any recipient seeking to gain access and steady benefits. In 2009, the same problem persisted: 120 million participants were registered of the roughly 8.86 million people unemployed (China Daily 2009). Last but not least, the temporary benefits are relatively low.[306]

Maternity Insurance: Longitude and Commitment of Policy Making

Maternity protection[307] has always been an essential part of employment-related social security for any modern democratic or non-democratic social security regime (SSA 2010, 2012). In 1951 under Mao Zedong maternity protection was issued alongside other employment-related social security schemes to ensure the well-being and steady increase of the labour force. Even in times of structural reform, maternity benefits have not been touched; however, the funding was redesigned in 1988 under Deng Xiaoping's motto of economic 'performance has priority' (D. Liu 2011:189).[308]

---

to benefits for up to one year; for above five years but less than ten years the time is expanded to 18 months, and contributors to social insurance for more than ten years gain 24 months of unemployment insurance payments. In cases of death of the recipient, the entitled benefits of unemployment insurance can be used by the survivor to cover funeral costs.

306 The amount of received cash benefits is adjusted by the county and normally is between 60 and 80 per cent of the local minimum wage. However, it also covers a broad range of other expenditures, such as medical care, funeral costs, subsidies for costs related to labour exchange, and re-employment centre services, such as vocational training. In 2002 the main expenditures with 60 per cent of the unemployment insurance were cash benefits; only 18 per cent were subsidies for reemployment measures and 10 per cent were payment for training and labour exchange services (Zhang 2005: 174, D. Liu 2011:143)

307 The maternity insurance covers all pregnant women in urban and public workplaces which contribute to the scheme. Either the enterprises have to participate or they (particularly government institutions) have their own maternity schemes and pay the cost directly to the individual. See also the official '*Regulation no. 504*' published 14.12.1994 by the Ministry of Labour.

308 Before 1988 the maternity costs had to be self-financed by the employers and in the aftermath of the ongoing attempt of the CCP to improve the economic performance of the SOEs, economic entities were unburdened of the obligation to pay the whole cost. Accordingly, the CCP deemed that local governments had to contribute to the maternity protection costs (Zhang 2004).

Similar to any other social security a national policy was missing for regulating the public funding of the contributions paid by the employees and local governments (Zhang 2004). In 1994 the central government reacted and the Ministry of Labour issued the '*The Temporary Administrative Regulation on the Maternity Insurance Scheme for Enterprise Workers*,' which standardized maternity protection contributions, funding, as well as benefits.[309]

Another important change (and an atypical feature for a left-totalitarian welfare regime) to maternity protection concerns state-issued family planning, marriage laws, as well as the one-child policy.[310] The costs of giving birth and any surgery costs related to family planning are paid out of the social fund; also, for the time of maternity protection women receive at least 90 days of their normal salary to tend to the well-being of their families.[311] In 2009, 80 million recipients were registered, which is relatively low considering the high female participation rate in the workforce (table 7).

Employment Injury Insurance: Addressing Unemployment

A cornerstone of any employment-related social security system is the provision of benefits in cases of employment-related injury. Similar to maternity insurance, the scheme can be traced back to the early labour law regulations in 1951 in which employers were made responsible for the provision of medical costs and the lost wages of injured employees. Both schemes have been under the authority of the Ministry of Labour (since

309 Employers of urban enterprises and the state in its function as employer of public administration have to contribute to the social funds. National regulations suggest a contribution rate of less than 1.0 percent of the wages, but the actual rate is normally only around 0.6 to 0.8 percent of the payroll. The related costs for maternity can be refunded by employers out of existing social funds (Regulation no. 504, cit op.).

310 Any pregnant women covered by employment-related maternity protection gains maternity payment only if the pregnancy is in compliance with the *Marriage Law* and needs official documentation.

311 In 2002, maternity social pooling covered up to 34.8 million women in urban enterprises. For details see *Regulation no. 504* cit. op.

2008 for Personal and Social Security).[312] The employment injury scheme reflects the ongoing adaptation process of any social security scheme to optimize funding and administration. After the dismantling of the SOEs' welfare function, social funds were introduced between 1996 and 2003 in addition to other needed adjustments.[313]

In its range, scope and coverage the scheme is comparable to maternity insurance.[314] In particular, the coverage has been modest. Only 44.1 million urban workers were covered in 2002 and large numbers of employees outside the public sector have to rely on the liability of the individual employer (Drouin and Thompson 2006:47). Accordingly, employment-related insurance is suffering of low participation due to the exclusive coverage of public and state-owned economic entities as well as public servants.

MSLS: A pioneering Project and its programmatic and ideological Constraints

Social assistance in China is provided mainly by the *Minimum Standard of Living* (MSLS) for the urban and rural 'poor' population. The MSLS is divided in the urban version, referred to as 'urban' MSLS, and the rural

312 Currently, the schemes are still under the authority of the Ministry for Personal and Social Security; however, the responsibility for the management of social funds lies with the social security administrative body. Social security administration is under the authority of the Ministry but has been granted legal authority in issuing administrative laws concerning administration, monitoring and funding.

313 See for instance § 6, 16, 24 and 29 of the 社会保险基金财务制度 ('*Financial Regulation for Social Security Funds*'), 财社字(1999) 60 号,15. 06. 1999.

314 All urban enterprises and civil institutions have to contribute to the social funds or the employers have to pay the costs for lost wages and medical care directly. Furthermore, the social pool also contributes cash benefits for workers with long-term disabilities. The worker can receive either a lump sum or monthly payment for his work-related disability. Benefits are conducted by the local Labour Assessment Commissions on the county level, including members of the insurance company, the civil service, and the labour union (Zhang 2004). The social pooling is administrated by the social insurance companies on the county level. On the jurisdictional level the government has introduced employment injury pools to cover the medical care and lost wages of recipients. The pool is financed only by employers' contribution of approximately 1.0 per cent of the payroll, and the contribution rates vary across counties and according to the working conditions of the enterprise (Herd 2010).

counterpart as the 'rural' MSLS or the *Five Guarantees* (Herd 2009, 2010). Characteristic of Chinese social security the separation of the MSLS has produced a discriminating character in favouring urban recipients (Xinhua News Agency 2006b). The central government's motto that 'performance has priority' has translated into it following a rational calculus in designing the MSLS, which grants only minimal benefits to meet the costs for essential items for living (see table 13).

Table 13: MSLS - Scheme, Coverage and Benefits

Year	2005	2006	2007	2008
	Amount as percent of area disposable income			
Income threshold for benefit				
Urban	17.8	17.7	15.9	15.5
Rural	28	23.7	20.3	20.7
Average benefit				
Urban	8.3	8.5	8.9	10.4
Rural	14	11.5	10.7	12.4
Average income of beneficiaries (before benefit)				
Urban	9.6	9.2	7	5.2
Rural	14	12.2	9.6	8.4
	Beneficaries as % population per area			
Coverage ratio				
Urban	4	3.9	3.8	3.9
Rural	0.8	3.1	3.8	6.7
	% total household income per area			
Beneficaries household				
Urban	0.33	0.33	0.34	0.4
Rural	0.19	0.21	0.53	0.99
Public expenditure on MSLS				
Urban	0.11	0.11	0.1	0.13
Rural	0.02	0.03	0.03	0.11
Total	0.13	0.14	0.13	0.24

Source: MoCA (2009), Herd (2010:11)

The 'income threshold for beneficiaries' has only marginally increased without taking into consideration the increasing living costs of roughly two percent for rural as well as urban households (table 13, World Bank 2010, 2014). Furthermore, similar to most of the other social security schemes, the MSLS has only marginal coverage despite the much higher number of total poor. The jump in the rural coverage from only 3.8 in 2006 to 6.7 in 2008 as well as the improvement in 'total household income' (0.53 to 0.99 percent) is directly linked to the additional funding of social security issued in 2007 by the SC (from 0.03 in 2006 up to 0.11 in 2008). The urban coverage as well as public expenditure remained constantly low and does not match the higher urban unemployment rate. What these numbers indicate coincides with the findings of several studies (Cook and Jolly 2001, Mei and Lu 2005, Zhang and Tang 2005) which provide evidence of the limited financial ability of social assistance to meet the demands of its recipients.

In effect, 50.6 percent of the urban beneficiaries of MSLS are in need of supplementary support because the average monthly benefits of the MSLS are only 22.2 to 9.2 percent of the standard income of a citizen (Zhang and Tang 2005).[316] Consequently, as Cook and Jolly (2001:18-19) remark, MSLS beneficiaries struggle in their daily life due to "no good clothes to wear, family has poor equipment, difficulty getting food and clothes, no money to pay heating or rent, no ability to pay back loans, do not dare to borrow money and cramped living space." The gap between the offered local benefits of the MSLS and the national minimum wages is an essential part of the underlying logic of social assistance to provide only minimal benefits and encourage people to take a job instead of relying on social assistance by the state (Zhang and Tang 2005, Xinhua News Agency 2006b, D. Liu 2011:148 sp). Another structural limitation of social assistance in China concerns the health coverage for recipients of the MSLS. As mentioned before, health care in China is dominated by out-of-pocket costs for individuals due to the low benefits of the existing schemes and the privatization of health care facilities.[317]

The Urban MSLS: In pursuit of Universal Coverage

The Commitment of the Central Government set up adequate social security measures to address the increasing problem of urban poverty in the 1990s, leading to the creation of the Minimum Standard of Living (MSLS) (Appleton and Song 2004). The social assistance program transformed

316 The national study included 1,257 responders in 36 cities (Zhang & Tang 2005).

317 Sun (2005) reported that only 7.3 percent of 686 MSLS families would go immediately to a hospital and 20 percent would delay the treatment if possible. The reason is that the majority of MSLS recipients, 89.3 percent, have to pay all their medical costs out of their own pocket (MoCA 2009).

from ad hoc local schemes[318] introduced in 1993 to the national flagship in urban poverty reduction and social security in 1997. In 1999 at least 581 cities and 1121 counties are covered by the MLSS. The social assistance program is under the control of the Ministry of Civil Affairs (MOCA) and was designed to provide 'provide a basic living for individuals or families to overcome their difficulties, maintaining social stability and promoting social development' (Shanghai MCA 1996). In particular, the MLSS represents a social assistance program responsible for ensuring the social security net and minimum living standards for poor and vulnerable households in urban areas (Xinhua News Agency 2006b).

In 1999 the MOCA laid down a broad regulatory framework but did not standardize the requirement to access the program, the financing, or the level of benefits paid to recipients of the scheme. In 2000 the MOCA encouraged local government units to implement their own MSLS. Due to the broad framework of the MSLS the local administration imposed its own supplementary regulation. In addition, the financing and operation of the scheme varies from city to city (Asian Development Bank, 2004).

The cost of the programme is split 60 to 40 between the central and local provincial government. Before 1999 the schemes were financed solely by local governments. Between 2000 and 2003 alone, the demand for the MSLS exploded from only 4 million to 22 million recipients. The total cost of the program in 2003 increased to ¥ 15.1 billion. Therefore, the contributions of the central government sharply increased from ¥ 0.8 billion to ¥ 9.2 billion in the same period (Hong & Wang 2002, Chen & Barrientos 2006: 10-11).

The MSLS is designed as a group-based target program for 'city dwellers with non-agricultural households and where the average income of family members is below the level of the minimum living standard of a region' (Sc 1997b). The definition included de facto unemployed workers, low-income households and households without dependants or any income and working ability. Only three years after its introduction the number of beneficiaries jumped from 0.5 to 21 million. In 2006 roughly 74 percent of the urban poor or 22.64 million people were covered by the

318 The MSLS was introduced at the city level in Shanghai in 1993; due to its success it was extended to other large cities. In May 1995 the MLSS covered six large cities: Shanghai, Xiamen, Qingdao, Dalian, Fuzhou and Guangzhou (Hussain 2003).

MLSS (Chen and Barrientos 2006:9).[319] The access for potential beneficiaries is mainly based on the existing *hu kou* system or people registration system. The registration system divides the population into non-agricultural and agricultural residents as well as captures their per capita income (Herd 2010).

Consequently, the MSLS provides no coverage for rural migrants living under the local poverty line in cities. Benefits of the MSLS vary from city to city due to the local poverty line (Xinhua News Agency 2006b). The cash benefits of the program are supposed to cover the gap between per capita household income and the local poverty line. As a consequence, the benefit payment is directly associated with the local minimum poverty line set by the city administration. In most cases the local poverty line is based on fiscal capacity and generally arbitrary without a research base.[320] The adjustment rate for the poverty line (to increasing costs of living) is not standardized.[321] Hence, the minimum living standards ranged in the year 2005 alone from ¥ 161 per month to ¥ 330 per month in different parts of China (Chen and Barrientos 2006).

The MSLS has been criticised for its limited coverage of '*absolutely poor*' urban households, as it excludes the large number of marginally poor households and also rural migrants living in poverty in the cities (Xu 2007:11). Furthermore, the lack of a national coherent poverty line has resulted in the fact that the regulation of the local poverty line is often misused by authorities to reduce the number of potential beneficiaries for the MLSS. Economically disadvantaged cities lack both the financial funds and the administrative capacity to provide the needed coverage (Wang

---

319 In 2006 the number of beneficiaries varied from city to city; in Hubei there were 1.67 million registered beneficiaries, in Heilongjiang 1.59 million, Jilin 1.46 million, Sichuan 1.46 million, Hunan 1.43 million, and in Beijing only 160,000 due to the local poverty line (Xu 2007:4).

320 Actual poverty lines vary markedly across provinces, cities, districts and counties, ranging from less than ¥ 150 (US$ 20) in six provinces to ¥ 330 in Beijing in 2007. However, many city administrations have set the minimum living standard based on the cost of 20 essential items of goods and services (Hong & Wang 2002).

321 The local poverty line is set and adjusted by the local city government in consideration of the local minimum wage rate. In Beijing the poverty line was announced to be ¥ 273 in 1999, ¥ 280 in 2000, ¥ 285 in 2001, ¥ 290 in 2002 and 2004, ¥ 300 in 2005, ¥ 310 Yuan in 2006 and ¥ 330 in 2007 (Xu 2007).

2002, Hussain, 2003)[322]. Another problem is related to the local government's ability to determine the income of households.

The used method of a means-test followed by community screening has been subjected to heavy critique due to its unreliable data (Xu et. al. 2007). Above all, the benefits are often calculated 'too low' and do not meet the beneficaries' basic costs of living for medical care, education and housing (Chen and Barrientos 2006).

Five Guarantees: Providing minimal Social Assistance

Similarly the rural version of the MLSS' minimum social assistance program, or so-called *Five Guarantees*, has to be financed by the local governments. In 1993 the pilot project was introduced but it took 13 years for the central government to put the Five Guarantees for rural citizens into practice on a nation-wide level (Zhang 2004, Wang 2004). In 2007, on the recommendation of the Central Committee for improving rural social security coverage, the SC announced the nation-wide introduction of the scheme.[323]

Despite the slow but controlled reduction of economic growth the party government engaged in fulfilling its commitment and expanded the financial funds, coverage and range of the *Five Guarantees*, the flagship for rural social security. It was designed as a rural counterpart of the MLSS, using the (above described) mechanisms to identify potential beneficiaries and provide benefits based on the estimated minimum cost of living for poor households.[324] It is worth noting that the *Five Guarantees* scheme had significant problems in its pilot-project period in the early 2000s. Whereas the MLSS represented a sophisticated approach for the central government and local authorities to tackle urban economic deprivation, in the rural areas the MLSS grew less accommodating than in the urban ar-

322 Since the Central Government Tax Reform in 1994 the local governments have lost their additional income source and their budgets are heavily overburdened. Therefore local authorities tend to reduce their local social expenditures by tightening the requirements for social assistance programmes (Chan et al. 2008:81).

323 See '国务院 关于 在 全国 建立 农村 最低 生活保障制度 的 通知 ('The Notice of the State Council on Establishing the Rural Minimum Living Standard Security System across the Country')' announced on the 11. 07. 2007.

324 The benefits payments vary from locality to locality because the local authorities estimate the local costs for the '*products for a person to survive*' (Herd 2010:10).

eas. Therefore, in early 2000 the MLSS failed to achieve significant coverage for rural recipients. While in 2003 around 2,037 counties of 15 provinces had introduced the MSLS, the programmes covered only 4 million recipients or 0.4 percent of the rural population. Local authorities where free to provide the MLSS and the central government tended to encourage only local authorities that could finance the MSLS to effectively to introduce it (Information Office of the SC 2004a). In the mid 2000s the local authorities responded differently in providing social security for the poor rural population.

Not surprising considering the pluralistic setting, local authorities have designed their own social assistance programmes. Futher, target group social assistance programmes for '*households with special difficulties*' have been installed by the government (Tang 2005).[325] In the case of the *Five Guarantees*, villages, communities and/or township governments had to absorb the financial burdens of the social assistance scheme and consequently assume responsibility for the registration, administration and payment of the scheme (Wong 1998). Furthermore, in the attempt to reduce financial pressure the central government took the collective *village enterprises* (TVEs) under its umbrella to contribute additional funds for the local provision of the *Five Guarantees* (SC 2006).

The *Five Guarantees* scheme has two strains of social assistance for rural poor household. The first strain is the focus care, which provides collective care to mainly older people. Similar to other social assistance programmes, the *Five Guarantees* started as a pioneer project in two provinces, Guangxi and Shanxi. In 1999 the programme was expanded to 11 provinces across China. Without a doubt, the scheme has been in demand. In 2003 the communities or township governments set up 24,000 old age homes to provide care to 503,000 elderly residents (Hong et al 2004).[326] The second strain of dispersed care offers elderly people regular and individual care. These services are conducted by residents who agree to take over the regular care under the '*Five Guarantees Caring Agree-*

325 In the period between 2003 and 2007 the special programme for absolutely poor households was realized separately, which reduced the overall number of beneficiaries for the main scheme. In 2006 the issued directive published by the SC resulted in the inclusion of the scheme and the target group in the *Five Guarantees* scheme (Herd 2010).

326 See also the '*Ordinance on the management of rural old aged homes (tentative)*' issued by the Ministry of Civil Affairs (MCA 1997).

ment' for additional benefits for their services. Another relevant dimension is the amount of benefits. The MSLS is designed to provide only minimal benefits for its beneficiaries and is adjusted to the local MCL line. Therefore the granted benefits are not higher than the minimum wage to motivate employment. In fact, there is only an 11 percent reduction in the poverty rate after the payment of benefits (Wang 2007)[327].

The increasing demand for social assistance and the variations of provided benefits across provinces have produced disharmony. In 2006 the central government published an *Ordinance on the implementation of Five Guarantees in rural areas* (SC 2006) to regulate and standardize the social assistance as well as the financial base of the scheme. In 2005 the MSLS covered 4.4 million[328] and an additional 8 million beneficiaries were covered by other local schemes. In early 2007, with the enactment of the SC, the coverage of the MSLS sharply increased to 15 million rural residents and a total expenditure of ¥ 4.16 billion (China Daily Online. 2007, Chan et al 2008:70).

3.3.5 The Third Period: Balanced economic and social Development, 2004 to 2009

Since the 16th Party Congress in 2002 and Hu Jintao's official pledge for a '建设小康社会' (society with modest welfare), social security provision in China has moved toward improving urban and rural social security coverage. In 2004 the Information Centre of the SC (2004:20) published 'China's social security white paper' which underlines the policy guidelines as follows: 'In light of China's actual situation and adhering to the principle of "putting people first," the Chinese Government attaches great importance and devotes every effort to establishing and improving its social security system. The Constitution of the People's Republic of China stipulates that the state shall establish and improve a social security system cor-

327 Furthermore, the 2004 Urban Employment and Social Protection Survey show that there are substantial errors in MLA allocation: 40% of the recipients are not entitled to it, and 61% of those who are entitled to it fail to receive it (Wang 2007). Intrusive methods have been used to administer the system to identify beneficiaries.

328 In 2006 the *Five Guarantees* scheme covered 3.2 million rural residents (China Daily Online 2006)

responding to the level of economic development. The Chinese Government regards economic development as the basic prerequisite for improving people's livelihood and effecting social security.'

In the 16th plenary session the Central Committee published the 'Decision of the CCP Central Committee on Several Issues in Perfecting the Socialist Market Economy' following the experience gained by the pilot project in Liaoning. In the following year (2004) a constitutional preamble was passed which determined the creation of 'a sound social security system compatible with the level of economic development.'[329]

A major reason was the new phenomena of '*poverty risk*' in cases of illness or old age (Darimont 2004:67-8). Health insurance for members of the urban population who were not employees in urban enterprises or administration was still missing in 2005, and the low benefits and coverage of only 64 percent of the employment-related pension for employees in urban enterprises was a source of concern.

In 2007 a critical juncture occurred in form of the 17th National Congress and the opportunity for a change in CCP leadership to set the policy guidelines for the next five years and to nominate the candidates for the Politburo. Although the National Congress is relevant for policy choices, the personal change in the Politburo, which represents the key institution and highest policy-making body[330], is more significant. In 2007 a good proportion of the Politburo had reached official retirement age and consequently Jintao Hu[331] had the opportunity for the first time since 1978 to nominate his favourite members to seize control of the Politburo.

Under the new political realities of 2007, the CCP leadership at the 17th National Congress announced its policy objective of improving the national social security system by increasing available funding for the nationwide implementation of the '*Five Guarantees*' (China Daily Online 2007).[332]

---

329 See the contemporary constitutional amendment, article 14.

330 The Politburo is the 'CCP's central locus of policy-making power' and therefore 'also the highest policy-making body in China that makes major national policies' (Chan et al. 2008:47, Guo 2013b:129).

331 His increasing political influence was directly linked to his nomination of the chairman of the Central Military Commission on October 21st, 2007.

332 Furthermore, the CCP decided to provide additional funding (0.01 percent of the GDP) for the *Five Guarantees* to tackle the issue of rural poverty.

3.3.6 Welfare Regime with Chinese Characteristics

In the Chinese case, the situation is not quite so different than the Indian one in regard to the unique character of the contemporary welfare regime. As was discussed in the previous chapter, China has undergone distinct periods of development in its social security politics (Gang et al 1998, Information Centre of the SC 2004b, Hu 2005).

In the post-World War II period Mao's communist reign ambitiously tried to build a typical left-totalitarian welfare regime and *classless society*.[333] In 1978 the 'critical juncture' in the form of economic and social grievances supported Deng Xiaoping's political ambitions and offered him the opportunity to initiate radical policy changes under the 'Four Modernizations' reforms (Teiwes 1985, 1995, Yang 2012). Accordingly, the Chinese welfare regime was transformed from a typical left-totalitarian communist regime type into a mixture of a social democratic and liberal welfare regime. Under Deng Xiaoping's market-oriented reforms the CCP remodelled the old 'commune' welfare regime and limited the range and scope of social security and social security politics (Leung and Nann 1995). The underlying logic of social security politics is clearly visible in the strategic choice to promote social and economic output by ensuring the health and constant growth of the urban workforce, which is seen as an essential source of constant cheap labour for the expanding economy (Wong and Ngok 1998).

The development of the Chinese welfare regime illustrates the conceptional flaws of the NIC typology. It is often assumed in country-specific literature that the Chinese welfare system transformed from a left-totalitarian communist regime into a *NIC* welfare regime by providing minimum social security for the urban working-aged population. Such a simplified typology neglects the existing if ill-designed social security schemes for the rural population. Undeniably, the range, scope and benefits of the major social security system discriminate in favour of the urban working-aged population. Still, the existing ambition of universal coverage for the rural and poor segments of society has to be taken into account (Chan et al. 2008:186). Consequently, China's welfare regime can be better associ-

333 The *danwei* system, full employment, and state capitalism are classical features of the left-totalitarian welfare regime (Leung and Nann 1995:57).

ated in various aspects with a liberal welfare regime instead of with the NIC category in the second period (1978 to 2004).

In the third period (2004-2009), the expansion of the social security system seems to bring China closer to the *social-democratic* category.[334] The leadership change in the CCP in 2002 saw the ambition of the newly nominated Hu Jintao[335] (2005) to produce a minimum level social security system for all citizens (Göbel 2010).[336] On the other hand, the traditional objective of providing urban-focused social policies for the working-aged force continued, and China, contrary to the logic of *left-totalitarian* welfare regimes, did not opt for full employment or universal coverage with a high level of benefits. Instead it focused on the older generation and improved the pension system.

A crucial 'critical junture' was the events in 2007. Following the personal changes in the Politburo, the 17th National Party Congress announced structural reforms to the fiscal system (Hu 2005). The new fiscal situation allowed authorities to expand the range and scope of the social security system to improve overall coverage with only minimum benefits (Zhang 2005, SC 2006). Distinctly visible here are the autocratic party-state-society relations in the industrial realm: The implemented authoritarian corporatism affects the state-owned industrial branches as well as the private ones. A permanent feature of the Chinese welfare regime is state capitalism and authoritarian cooperatism.In this aspect China fulfils the classical Leninist left-totalitarian regime structure of a one-party state with central planning and authoritarian corporatism, including a state-controlled central union federation, and overall party control of political and economic processes (Metcalf and Li 2005).[337] Despite the commitment to a market economy and the increasing independence of economic entities in its day-to-day work, the state has ensured the monopoly of the SOEs in the strategically important industrial branches (i.e. telecommunication and energy) (The Economist 2014d).

---

334 See Esping-Andersen's (1990) typology for democratic welfare regimes.

335 Hu Jintao was Deng Xiaoping's favourite candidate and was officially nominated for the party leadership at the National Party Congress in 1994 (Guo 2013b).

336 A major step was made in 2007 with the improvement of social security coverage for the rural population.

337 In his article 'The Political Party Goes to the Countryside' Xu (2007) illustrates the typical hierarchical grassroots organisation, including party and union cadres.

Table 14: Development of Social Security Politics in China (1949-2009)

Era	State's role in development	State's role in social policy	Guiding principle
Mao	High	High	Socialist welfare regime; full employment / danwei system
Deng	High	Low	Cutback of socialistic welfare regime
Liberalisation (1993-2002)	High	Low	Market-orientated and liberal social policy reforms
Jintao (2002-2009)	Medium	Increasing	Combination of liberal and socialistic policy making; universal social security coverage with low benefits

Source: author's own table

As indicated above (table 14), China has embarked on setting up a left-totalitarian welfare regime but under the pressure of economic, institutional and social realities has had to make compromises and cutbacks. In effect, the left-totalitarian welfare regime has transformed into some kind of liberal welfare regime and is ambitiously trying to converge with a socialist welfare regime or postulated '*socialistic capitalism market economy*' (White 1999).

What China has in common with a *social democratic* welfare regime is not '*democracy*' but the commitment of the governing party to set up universal social security. In doing so, China is not following the traditional left-totalitarian path of full employment and generous social security but a market-oriented vision of providing minimum social security to the poor and social insurance to the working-aged population. Also in the ongoing process of shifting the responsibility for social security from the state to the market, the market is becoming the major producer of welfare, social security and employment. In fact, the shifting logic has increased the tendency of the individual level of welfare to be based on employment status (Zhang 2005, Chan et al. 2008:66-68, 81, D. Liu 2011:122, 167-9).

As a consequence the success of Chinese experience, as compared to other socialist regimes, such as the former USSR or GDR,[338] lies in the fact that the Chinese government has not overburdened its financial and administrative resources to provide a high level of social welfare. Thus, in

338 See Klaus von Beyme (1988, 1995) for the USSR and for the GDR see Manfred G. Schmidt (1999b, 2012).

the course of pursuing its ongoing adjustment strategy since the late 1970s, Chinese decisionmakers have cancelled the classical socialist policy ambition to provide egalitarian social security, guarantee employment and support demographic growth[339]. Compared to typical left-totalitarian regimes, China's *decommodification* has always been low in all periods due to the market-oriented reconstruction of the social security system in 1990s. Another difference from the left-totalitarian as well as liberal stereotype is China's population reduction. China's one-child policy runs contrary to classical *fecundism* or the willful increase of birth rates. Interestingly the CPR abandoned the typical full-employment scheme of *socialist* or *communist* countries (Zhang 2005).

Contrary to the *typical left-totalitarian* regime, China has implemented social schemes and programs that have a discriminating character based on individual residency[340] and employment[341]. Non-egalitarian modalities, birth control policies, a strong emphasis on pension, and the overall discriminating character of social security schemes run counter to typical left-totalitarian policymaking. Universal social security with minimum benefits excludes China from being categorised as a typical NIC. To sum up, the Chinese welfare regime is a unique one which cannot be easily categorised.

---

339 The major determinant of China's success is its trade openness and integration into the world market since 1978. Contrary to the typical closed economies of other autocracies, such as the GDR and Hungarian or Czech Republics, China's open market has produced economic prosperity, including employment, international investment and higher level of productivity, as well as offered financial means for the government to satisfy the domestic need for imports.

340 In other *left-totalitarian* regimes the access to services and benefits also varies for a range of reasons; however, in theory the access is not discriminating.

341 Income disparity for salaries varies according to the status of employment. Urban employees are paid better and gain better access to medical and pension schemes than rural employees. The disparity also varies between urban employment in private and public jobs. Employees in public administration or state-owned enterprises (SOE) have access to higher wages and social security schemes than workers in private firms or in agriculture. An average 85 percent of medical services are reserved for public employees. Status of employment also determines access to social security and welfare schemes. In 2004 the pension of a retired private employee was around 6,830 Yuan lower compared to the pension in the SOE and even 8,451 Yuan lower than the pension granted for retirement from public administration (Chan et al 2008: 280-284).

3.3.7 Comments on Social Security Provision in China

The 'structured' and 'focused' investigation of China as crudely presented here does not allow us to draw any significant and detailed conclusions regarding the role and function of its distinct institutions for the provision of social security. At the same time the basic data covering all periods suggest that social security trajectories are distinctly visible. However, the stronger the path dependency of social security schemes (i.e. the sequ system), the more likely are sub-optimal outcomes in regard to the adoption potential of the schemes. In particular, social security in China is characterized by various shortcomings. On a national level the lack of a coherent policy strategy, low central funding, and low priority of social security has been an issue since 1978. Moreover, the decentralisation process and national differences in socio-economic conditions accelerated the discriminating character of social security not only in terms of employment but also locality. The classical deficit of decentralisation was signalled by the overburdened administration and its gatekeeper function in providing access as well as the provision of social security. At the same time the constant economic transformation process has focused government attention on local and national levels by addressing economic growth and social security provision 'step by step'.

In contrast to earlier periods, the period from 2004 to 2010 has proven different in regard to the new social policy objectives, backed up by structural reforms, in pursuit of universal coverage with low benefits. At the same time, the central government has seemed more open to structural and financial reforms than has been the case since 1978. What could be diagnosed is the positive impact of national financial contributions to social security in 2007. Furthermore, the ability of the Chinese government to pursue long-term planning and fast-paced reforms by ministries without consulting other institutions appears to fit quite well with its high institutional performance. Another dimension here is the pilot projects, as evidenced by the success of the recent national social security schemes. Accordingly, the improving scores in social security are closely related to the ongoing modernization of administration, the improvement of funding, as well as the higher commitment of the central government. But the old issues cannot be rooted out.

3.4 Same Goal, different Paths: Evolution of the Indian case

Historical studies (Kohli 1989, 2012, Chibber 2012, Mitra 2013) have accumulated evidence of the view that contemporary social security politics and related socio-economic conditions and demographic tendencies are products of policy choices dating back to the first years of independence. The best example is founded in the legislature, where the formal employment-related social insurance with its schemes, programmes and services are still legally grounded today. Furthermore, low coverage of informal and rural employees, mass poverty, and illiteracy have been constant features of Indian democracy.[342]

Accordingly, the economic stagnation of the 1970s and 1980s, which resulted in the so-called 'Hindu rate of growth'[343] of 4 percent, significantly reduced the overall financial revenues of the state and produced concern about the deeply structural radical reforms (Nagraj 2000, Rodrik and Subramanian. 2004). However, the commitment to the 'closed door' economic policy and state capitalism did not change much over time: state capitalism survived the partial liberalization, and despite the closure of 'sick industries' the overall low performance of state-owned entities is challenging the future of India's economy.[344] Stability and persistence have been the main objectives of the INC government, even if they exacted a heavy toll on the financial budget to fund the so-called 'sick' state-owned industries (Rothermund 1995c:537, Jenkins 1999). As a result, social security politics is a prominent topic but the worsening situation has discouraged the government from pursuing the radical reformation of existing social security strategies. The flourishing of the domestic economy in the 1980s[345] and the corresponding increase in human development

342 See various reports (WHO 2000, NCEUS 2006, 2007, ILO 2010a).

343 The prominent term has been coined in response to the constant 4 percent economic growth rate of India's domestic economy; see Rodrik, D. and A. Subramanian (2004) '*From "Hindu Growth" to Productivity Surge: The Mystery of the Indian Growth Transition*'.

344 A perfect example is the domestic energy industry. Despite shortcuts and insufficient infrastructure for electricity, the state has the monopoly on coal production. Despite the large coal reserves, the inefficiency of the state-owned coal production firms has resulted in dependency on foreign coal imports from Australia.

345 In the 1980s economic growth, in combination with structural programs for infrastructure and rural development, especially for small farmers, could achieve

suggested that the synergy effects of the trickle-down effect could be realized (Chamarbagwala 2006, Bardhan 2007, Dev and Ravi 2007).[346]

Table 15: State and Welfare in India (1949-2009)

Era	State's role in development	State's role in social policy	Guiding principle
Nehru (1947-1964)	High	Low	Soviet developing model
Indira Gandhi (1967-1977/1982-1984)	High	Medium	Social democratic orientated welfare regime
Liberalisation (1993-2004)	Low	Low	Market-orientated liberal social policy making
UPA (2004-2014)	Low	Low/Medium	'Indian way': universal social security coverage with low benefits

Source: Author's own table

Shorty after the implementation of partial liberalization[347], mass unemployment, worsening working conditions and increasing income inequality occurred and produced significant public protest by labour federations (Hindu 2007, 2008, 2013). The partial liberalization and shortcuts in social expenditures produced financial difficulties for rural and urban households and affected the average citizen. In the late 1990s the INC paid attention to the socio-economic problems and opted for more social expenditures to tackle persisting mass poverty and low social security (Sülzer 2008:211-212, Chibber 2012:185). The majority of the working-aged population is not covered by social insurance and their well-being is threatened. 75 percent of the population is living below 2 US $ a day and encountering financial difficulties due to the increasing cost of living, low

short-term measurable success in promoting economic and human development (Nagaraj 2012a:46-7).

346 See Dev and Ravi's (2007) historical investigation of the issue of inequality across the Indian union states in the time period of 1983 to 2005.

347 In anticipation of the impending financial crises the Indian government accepted the IMF *Stand-By-Arrangement*. The terms of agreement for financial help included the pursuit of structural reforms and economic liberalization. In addition, the Indian government had to remove the quantitative import restriction and open up the domestic market for private entrepreneurs. The economic success of liberalization can be analysed in terms of the high average growth rates of over 8 percent, including a rapid growth in per capita income (Sen 2003).

wages and insufficient public health (Chamarbagwala 2006:2001-6, Bardhan 2007:3849, ILO 2010a). This sharpening inequality has created public turmoil reflected in the sharp rise of nation-wide labour protests against the worsening living conditions, which have become a constant feature in India's public sphere in the 21st century.[348]

Public dissatisfaction with the ruling government and political parties resulted in the urgent need to adopt an effective nation-wide strategy for tackling the increasing socio-economic challenges of unemployment, deprivation, and poverty. In 2004 the UPA coalition government attempted to address the lack of social security and low living standards. Various social policy schemes and acts were passed by the legislature; however, the overall impact was modest (Sülzer 2008, Chibber 2012:185-7). In 2009 it became clear that the 11th Five Year Plan (2008) and the UPA could improve economic growth but achieve neither socio-economic development nor social security coverage (Nagaraj 2012a:50-51, Kohli 2012:210-12).

3.4.1 Following a socialist Vision, 1949-1977

Independence, besides the tragedies of partition[349], clearly marked the first critical juncture in the development of the modern state and public policy-making in India. The post-independent period in India is closely associated with the one-party dominance of the INC on the national level under the leadership of Jawaharlal Nehru. A political majority in both chambers expanded Prime Minister Nehru's '*room to manoeuvre*' for realizing his vision of a modern and democratic Indian nation. To achieve the goal the Indian state reverted to the classical *Soviet development model* under the

348 See *The Hindu* (2007, 2008, 2013)

349 'It has proven much more difficult to arrive at a consensus figure on the numbers of persons who died as a consequence of violence that occurred during the impending partition, the partition itself, and after it in the misery of the refugee camps. Estimates range from around 200,000 at the low end to a million and a half at the high end. A consensus figure of 500,000 is often used, but the sources that are most likely closer to the truth give figures that range between 200,000 and 360,000 dead' (Brass 2003:75). See Paul Brass. 2003. *'The partition of India and retributive genocide in the Punjab, 1946–47: means, methods, and purposes'*, *Journal of Genocide Research*, vol. 5, no.1: 71–101.

mixed economy[350]by relying on a closed economy, state capitalism, and centrally administrated Five Year Plans[351] in which it dictated development. Industrialization and the working class were seen as the keys to achieving progress and socio-economic equality.[352]

Two areas where party priorities affected the government targets were labour law and industrial relations. The pro-labour attitude of the legislature was funded by the commitment to democratisation and state-controlled industrialization (Rothermund 1993, 1995c, Sharma 2006). In the environment of a mixed economy, state capitalism and central planning, the INC legislature improved the rights and relevance of labour organisations, which resulted in a pluralistic setting, or as Rudolph and Rudolph (1987) call it, '*state-controlled pluralism*'. The national politics of the INC government relied on an ideological and pragmatic perspective to support the growth of a healthy urban working class. Industrial peace and cheap labour were seen as the pillars of economic productivity (Nayar 1989). A side effect of the pro-labour legislature was the ironic weakening of the labour movement in two ways. First, the low criteria to found a union, the labour friendliness of the state, and the unlimited co-existence of unions in a single enterprise motivated the burgeoning of new unions without significant increases in overall membership. Second, the strong bargaining position of every labour union has the right to take their dis-

350 To do so, the central government embarked on the Soviet planning model and adapted it to the domestic concept of the *mixed economy* in 1951. In addition, the National Development Council was constituted and put into practice by the state's chief minister. The main body of the council was made up of experts and technocrats to provide expertise on the central government's policymaking aimed at guaranteeing economic growth and modernization (Nayar 1989, Mitra 2009:140).

351 Therefore, the early, centralised Five Year Plans included the goals and funds for economic programmes as well as social and political programmes, schemes and services. The Indian government continues to implement the Five Year Plans today to achieve its overall development goals and related financial aspirations.

352 In keeping with the country's adoption of the Soviet model, in India as in China, labour played a supportive though not constitutive role in political parties and the economic success of the structural reforms aimed at modernization. As in China, in India the government committed to industrial modernization under a Soviet centralized planning model that included the implementation of social security to guarantee the well-being of the urban labour force.

pute to a state tribunal resulted in the manipulation of labour organisations by political individuals or parties for selfish ambitions (Nayar 1989).[353].

Table 16: Early Social Security Legislation in India

Act	Year	Scope
Workmen's Compensation Act 1923	1923	Formal sector
Workmen's Compensation Rules 1924	1924	Formal sector
Employees' State Insurance Act 1948	1948	Formal sector
Employees' Provident Funds and Miscellaneous Provisions Act 1952	1952	Formal sector
Maternity Benefit Act 1961	1961	Formal sector

Source: Author's own table

As a result of the constitutional and political commitment to the industrial working-aged population the legislature enacted various laws concerning the welfare of workers in the formal sector. These enactments represent the blueprint of today's social insurance system in regard to illness, pension, compensation for employment-related accidents, disability and death (Nagarah 2012a:26-27). Four of the five main social security acts that were drafted were put into practice:

3.4.1.1 Continuity and Departure of Social Security Provision in the 1960s

Public policy and social security legislation in the formal sector does not change much over time and continuity is their main characteristic. This continuity has to be understood in regard to the British colonial legacy. In 1923 the British imposed various pieces of social security legislation concerning trade unions, industrial disputes and working conditions (Austin 1966, Conrad 1995). These laws and regulations were mostly adopted by the new government in its attempt to follow the European model of industrialization. However, the lack of social security schemes and programmes for the workforce under colonial rule produced a broad commitment of the

353 After the prominent dispute between Congress and communists and the resulting split of the AFTUC labour organisations more and more unions were used as party instruments for mass mobilization, protests and a source of government pressure. In addition, it is not surprising that the multiplication of union organisations resulted in the internal fragmentation of the labour movement (Duta 2007).

founding fathers to assure democratic rights and human well-being for the workforce of modern India (Nagaraj 2012a:51-52, Chibber 2012:174-175).

As a consequence, the Indian constitution under the guiding hand of Sardar Patel[354] included rights not only for minorities specifically but also for male and especially female citizens more broadly. While the central government achieved relatively significant outcomes for social security in the organised sector, the situation in the unorganised sector was neglected because of the underlying logic that industrialisation and modernization are inextricably interrelated (Argarwal and Khan 2002 and Nagaraj 2012a: 53).

Under the banner of the '*mixed economy*', the development strategy was relatively simple and sound, based as it was on the Soviet model and its postulated success (Nayar 1989, Nagaraj 2000). Politicians and technocrats trusted in the positive side-effects of the industrialisation, urbanisation and modernization processes for improving overall human development (Mihra and Raveendran 2011, Sen and Rajsekhar 2012:104, Kohli 2012:201-2).[355] In the first stage, the increasing productivity of India's manufacturing sector would produce significant growth, employment, wage increases, and welfare. In the second stage, the growing economic prosperity would produce synergy effects and lead to more distribution, employment for the poor, and hence less socio-economic inequality, higher living standards and less poverty. Instead, the synergy effects failed to appear and the financial deficits and low industrial and agricultural productivity tested India's future prospects (Chibber 2012:174).

The Workmen's Compensation Act, 1923: Relics of Colonial Rule

The *Workmen's Compensation Act, 1923* and the related *Workmen's Compensation Rules, 1924* illustrate the adaptation process of colonial legisla-

---

354 Chopra (1997) remarks that Sardar Patel was the 'Iron Man [that] so dominated the assembly that the Constitution which emerged from it bore his stamp and could be aptly called the Patel Constitution'. Patel took a firm stance on issues of civil rights and the division of power. See P. M. Chopra (ed.) 1997. *Collected Works of Sardar Vallabhbhai Patel, Volume XI*. Delhi. Konark Publishers.

355 The assumed causal sequence of economic growth as a precondition for high levels of social development and the reduction of poverty is often referred to as the 'trickle-down effect' or 'inclusive growth'.

tion as well as the party priorities of a left-leaning government in the 1920s. The act is one of the earliest laws concerning welfare and social security for industrial workers[356] in India. In 1923 the electoral victory of the left-wing government and the experience with industrialization in the British homeland affected policymaking for the colonies. In effect, the British parliament approved the enactment of the *Workmen's Compensation Act, 1923* to provide at least minimum employment-related compensation for industrial workers in cases of injury, partial or total disability or death (Rao 2007, Sülzer 2008:220-21). After Independence the Act was taken over by the Indian legislature for industrial workers who are '*more or less organized*' and/or work in a hazardous environment to:'1) Provide workmen and/or their dependents some relief or to consider compensation payable by an employer to his workmen in case of accidents arising out of and in the course of employment and causing either death or disablement of workmen as a measure of relief and social security. 2) Provide for payment by certain classes of employers to their workmen compensation for injury by accident. 3) To enable a workmen to get compensation irrespective of his negligence. 4) It lays down the various amounts payable in case of an accident, depending upon the type and extent of injury. The employer now knows the amount of compensation he has to pay and is saved of many uncertainties to which he was subject before the Act came into force.'

These benefits have to be paid by the employer in the case of accidents related to employment. In cases of temporary disability the employee is theoretically entitled to receive a percentage of compensation proportionate to the loss of earning capacity permanently caused by the incurred injury; in cases of total disability the workman is entitled to 60 percent of monthly wages or at least Rs. 90,000. In the case of death during employment a lump sum has to be paid by the employer equal to 50 percent of the

---

356 Workmen are defined thus: 'A railway servant as defined in section 3 of the Indian Railways Act 1890 not permanently employed in any administrative district or sub-divisional office of a railway and not employed in any such capacity as is specified in Schedule II, or a) A master seaman or other member of the crew of a ship. b) A captain or other member of the crew of an aircraft. c) A person recruited as driver, helper, mechanic, cleaner, or in any other capacity in connection with a motor vehicle d) A person recruited for work abroad by a company and who is employed outside India in any such capacity as is specified in Schedule II and the ship aircraft or motor vehicle or company as the case may be is registered in India' (*Workmen's Compensation Act*, 1923).

monthly wages or Rs. 85,000. A common problem is that in most cases the employers cannot or do not want to pay the compensation. In such cases the family of the survivor can appeal to the state labour department (Sülzer 2008:226-29, Rao 2011, SSA 2010:83).[357]

The Act aimed to provide compensation for industrial workers who are not insured under the Employees' State Insurance Act of 1948.[358] The clerical employment in public administration is covered under the ESI scheme (Sen and Raj 2012:100-101) but the majority of workers (roughly 90 percent) in the '*more or less organised*' sector are not covered (NCEUS 2006, 2007).

The Employees' State Insurance Act, 1948

The *Employees' State Insurance Act, 1948* (ESI) includes the *Central Government Health Services* (CGHS) which represents the primary health care insurance. It is administered by the Employees' State Insurance Corporation under the authority of the Ministry of Labour and Employment (SSA 2006:83). The ESI is available for workers in the formal sector but also for economic entities with 20 or more employees in the informal sector, including factories without electricity, restaurants, shops, hotels, cinemas, newspaper and road-motor establishments. The scheme is financed by employees and employers. Employees have to contribute 1.75 percent of their wages if they earn more than Rs. 50 per day. Employers contribute 4.75 percent of the wages to finance the scheme and the state government provides 12.5 percent of the total costs for medical care (Rao 2007, 2011).

Where the ESI diverges from other schemes is in its administration. The ESI is monitored by a corporate body, the Employees' Insurance Corporation, which includes representatives of the central and federal states, members of parliament, employees and employers, as well as medical experts (Sen & Rajasekar 2012:99). The scheme's dispensary level has a broad

357 See the '*Workmen's Compensation Act, 1923*' (2009-04-03).

358 'An insured person or his dependents shall not be entitled to receive or recover whether from the employer of the insured person or from any other person any compensation or damages under the Workmen's Compensation Act 1923 or any other law for the time being in force or otherwise in respect of an employment injury sustained by the insured person as an employee under this Act' (Employees' State Insurance Act 1948:Section 53).

range, offering cash benefits for sickness, maternity, temporary disablement, as well as medical services which are provided by a network of medical institutions such as state-owned dispensaries, diagnostic centres, and hospitals, or in limited cooperation with private medical facilities. Compared to the CGHS the range and scope of the ESI is limited in providing adequate medical care. It is estimated by the World Bank (2007, 2008, 2009) that roughly 92 percent of the health care in India is paid out-of-pocket by individuals due to a lack of health insurance coverage for the majority of society's members (Sülzer 2008:220-21).

The Employees' Provident Funds and Miscellaneous Provisions Act, 1952

The *Employees' Provident Funds and Miscellaneous Provisions Act, 1952* (EPF) consists of a broad package of various social security programmes that provides for the implementation of the provident fund, the family pension fund, and a deposit-linked insurance fund for employees in factories and other establishments in times of financial and physical distress. The EPF has to be understood as a complement to the *Employees' State Insurance Act* (Rao 2011:72 sp).

The EPF constantly expanded its scope and range over time to achieve comprehensive coverage. The core component was the *Employees' Provident Fund Scheme, 1952*. In the following decades the *Employees' Deposit-Linked Insurance, 1976*, and the *Employees' Pension Scheme, 1995* or the so-called *Employees' Family Pension Scheme and Employees' Pension Scheme* were included as preambles in the EPF (Nagaraj 2012a: 51-52):

The *Employees' Deposit-Linked Insurance, 1976*[359] and the *Employees' Family Pension Scheme* are for the purpose of providing family pension and life insurance benefits to employees (Section 6A). To guarantee financial funding of the scheme the available cash benefits are financed by em-

359 *Employees' Deposit-Linked Insurance Scheme, 1976* is designed for life insurance for the money-earning member of a household. Contrary to the other funds the scheme is funded by the contribution of the employer, which has to contribute 1 percent of the average payroll. The employee only needs to contribute no more than one fourth of the sum contributed by the employer to cover the expense of administration. In cases of death the survivor is entitled to the benefits (Section 6a of the Act).

ployees and employers.[360] The collected contributions are transferred to EPF funds which are invested in government bonds to guarantee secured but also low interest rates. The investment, monitoring and other administrative functions fall under the responsibility of the Central Board (Seventh Five Year Plan 2008, Rao 2011:122-24).[361]

The programmes of the EPF grant time-limited financial benefits to beneficiaries in cases of disability, old age, early death of the primary income earner, and other contingencies. The benefits are calculated from the years of employment, salary and individual contributions over time. Similar to the other legislation the scheme is discriminating and the target group is restricted to official employees in the organised sector and their households.[362]

Concerning the scope of the Act, section one of the EPF states that it covers all of India, except the states of Jammu and Kashmir and their inhabitants. This suggests broad coverage, but in paragraph 2 the scope is limited to employees working in economic entities under the *Indian Factories Act, 1948*[363] (Rao 2007:9, Chibber 2012).

---

360 As stated in Section 6 of the EFP 'the contribution paid to the Fund by the employer shall be 10% of the basic wages and the dearness allowance and retaining allowance and the contribution payable by the employee shall be equal to the employer's contribution. Employees, if they desire, may make a higher contribution'.

361 The Central Board is appointed by the Central Government according to the proportional representation defined in Section 5 of the EPF: '*As a Chairman and a Vice-Chairman to be appointed by the Central Government; a) The Central Provident Fund Commissioner ex officio; 2) Not more than five persons appointed by the Central Government from amongst its officials; 3) Not more than fifteen persons representing Government of such States as the Central Government may specify in this behalf, appointed by the Central Government; 4) Ten persons representing employers, or the establishment to which the Scheme applies appointed by the Central Government after consultation with such organizations of employers as may be recognized by the Central Government in this behalf; and 5) Ten persons representing employees in the establishment to which the Scheme applies appointed by the Central Government after consultation with such organizations of employees as may be recognized by the Central Government in this behalf.*'

362 Furthermore, a feature of the schemes is that they allow beneficiaries to withdraw sums from the life insurance, pension and retirement funds in cases of financial hardship (Rao 2007:52ff, 193).

363 As mentioned before, *The Factories Act, 1948* applies to all economic entities employing either at least 20 persons or at least 10 persons and using electricity. Still, a majority of small firms and workshops are either operating under the radar

The Maternity Benefit Act, 1961

The Maternity Benefit Act, 1961 'regulates employment of women in certain establishments for certain periods before and after child-birth and to provide for maternity benefit and certain other benefits' (GoI 1961:1). According to Article 42 the Act grants cash benefits, regulates maternity leave, and ensures job protection for pregnant women employed in the formal sector. Under the Act every pregnant woman is entitled to cash benefits and wage compensation during the time of pregnancy for 12 weeks. The maternity leave is limited to six weeks before delivery and six weeks afterwards. In this time the employer cannot terminate the employment contract. The employer has to pay the pregnant woman an average daily wage during maternity as well as provide a medical bonus of 250 Rupees[364] 'if no pre-natal confinement and post-natal care is provided free of charge by the employer' (Yadav 20008:198).[365] The Amendment Bill passed in 2007 aimed to increase the financial benefits because in 'the present economic scenario, it is felt that the medical bonus, which is presently Rs. 250/-, is inadequate. Therefore, it is proposed— (i) to raise the medical bonus payable under the Maternity Benefit Act, 1961 from Rs. 250/- to Rs. 1000/-; and (ii) to give powers to the Central Government to revise the medical bonus from time to time subject to a maximum of Rs. 20,000/-.6. The Bill seeks to achieve the above objects.' (GoI 2007:3).

Before 2001 the Act only covered factories, mines, plantations and/or establishments run by the state or central government (GoI 1961: Section 2). In 2001 its responsibility was transferred under the authority of the Department for Family and Health. Also the amendment in 2001 extended

---

by employing less workers or are registered but have no official employment contracts with their workers. Therefore the coverage of the Act is heavily limited by the informal character of employment which is considered to be above 754 percent of the total employment in India (ILO 2010).

364 In 2007 an amendment to the Act was issued for a financial bonus of one thousand Rupees to be given to pregnant women by their employers if no pre-natal or post-natal care is provided by the employer at no cost to the employee. The bill was passed and enacted in 2008.

365 Concerning the medical bonus for maternity leave the Act (GoI 1962: Section 8) states that every 'woman entitled to maternity benefit under this Act shall also be entitled to receive from her employer a medical bonus of 1*[two hundred and fifty rupees], if no pre-natal confinement and post-natal care is provided for by the employer free of charge.'

the coverage of the scheme and included female workers in shops, hotels, restaurants, movie theatres/cinemas and other similar establishments with 20 or more employees. In 1995 roughly 6.5 lakh women were entitled to maternity benefits until 2002 (Sen and Rajasekhar 2012:100).

Government and Public Enterprise Schemes

Under the umbrella of the ESI Act another scheme is included for the welfare of government employees: the Government and public enterprise schemes (CGHS). The CGHS is a special programme limited in its access to active and retired government employees and their families. The CGHS offers wide range of medical services and was introduced, like nearly all other policy schemes, in the immediate post-independence period, in 1954. The scheme is financed by a contribution between Rs. 15 and 150 per month depending on the individual salary of the state employee (Rao 2011, MoL 2014).[366]

A degree of coordination was achieved in certain localities, including 23 cities and about 500 hospitals in 17 cities. Compared to the normal ESI the CGHS recipients can access modern medical facilities and treatments[367] which are not available at the dispensary level. Furthermore, the medical costs for treatment are reimbursed. The scheme covers one million cardholders and roughly 4.3 million of beneficiaries. Although relatively successful in terms of demand, the high level of utilisation has undermined the administrative and financial capacity to provide high-quality medical assistance. In addition, the Sixth Pay Commission encouraged the government to replace the CGHS with a voluntary scheme for government employees, excluding defence and railway employees, either currently in service or retired. Furthermore, the new schemes should be mandatory for newly recruited employees to alleviate the increasing pressure on the CGHS (Sen and Rajasekhar 2012: 99-101).

---

366 MoL's homepage: http://labour.gov.in/content/division/social-security.php (2014-07-01).

367 See also the revision of the '*Employees' Provident Funds and Miscellaneous Provisions Act, 1952*' and the subsection concerning additional health services for beneficiaries.

Payment of Gratuity Act, 1972: the Eve of Paradigm Change

In 1972 the Parliament announced the last social security legislation for the formal sector, the *Payment of Gratuity Act, 1972*, which in some way marked the political paradigm of India.

Nehru's death in the mid-1960s initiated a new political era, not only but primarily in social security politics. Two main critical events mark the paradigm change in social security provision in India: the monsoon failure of 1966–1967 and political generation change. The monsoon failure and resulting decline of agrarian productivity[368] slowly opened the eyes of decision-makers to the limitations of the old 'industrial-focused' development strategy of the mixed economy.[369] The scope of social security provision was limited to workers in the formal sector and marked by a '*near-absence of any real welfare policy*' except for the small part of the workforce in the organised sector (NCEUS 2006, 2007, Sen and Rajasekhar 2012:106-108, Chibber 2012:172-173).

On the political floor Indira Gandhi, Nehru's daughter, struggled to assume her heritage in form of the party leadership and initiated a split of the INC to purge the party. Two new parties emerged: the INC (R) under Gandhi and the INC (O) (Wagner 2006:119-20). To maintain electoral success Gandhi initiated harsh programmatic change under the election slogan *Garibi Hatao* ('abolish poverty'). In the election of 1971 Gandhi's INC (R) achieved 44 percent of the votes and a total of 352 seats.[370] The slogan marked not only an organisational and ideological shift for the INC but more importantly a logic of social security provision that prevails today (Rothermund 1993:57-59, Mitra 1994a, Wagner 2006:119-20).

Against the background of the increasingly visible limitations of the 'closed door' policy, which produced more than 4 percent economic growth, in the post-Nehru period the former Prime Minister's daughter achieved electoral victory and her father's previous postion (Wagner 2006). Although Gandhi followed a different logic of social security pro-

---

368 See Appu (1996) for the resulting retreat of INC from the planned land reforms,

369 The central government focused on the agrarian sector and announced the 'Green Revolution' in 1970, which attempted to modernize production methods and improve productivity by relying on modern genetic crops, chemical fertilisers, and subsidized water and electricity for farmers (Kohli 1990).

370 The INC (O) lost the election by a wide margin, gaining only 10 percent of the total votes and 16 seats (Wagner 2006:118).

vision, her policymaking can be best associated with social-democratic impulses in its attempt to improve social security for the total population.

The *Payment of Gratuity Act, 1972* established the compulsory payment of gratuity for employees in factories, mines, oil fields, plantations, ports, railway companies, motor transport undertakings, shops and other establishments (GoI 1972:1). Hence, every employee could receive gratuity payments upon the termination of employment after at least five years of regular employment or death (GoI 1972: Section 4).[371] Similar to the CGHS the *Payment of Gratuity Act, 1972* elicited harsh critiques for its limited range and scope. A major concern was increasing life expectancies and years of service compared to the 1950s when the Act was originally designed. Another problem was poor accumulation of the funds. Most of the recipients withdraw their cash benefits immediately instead of waiting for retirement. Furthermore, the funds generate a low rate of return based on their safe investment strategy of minimizing risks and providing secure rates of return (Chakravarty 1990: 133, Nagaraj 2000). Yet demographic changes, longer life expectancies, and adjustment of pension benefits tested the self-financing of the pension funds to provide the needed rates of return in the long run to generate increasing costs for gratuity payments in the future (Chibber 2012:174 sp).

3.4.2 The First Period: Blueprint for the modern Welfare Regime, 1978 to 1992

From 1967 to 1977[372] the government of Indira Gandhi came close to setting up a social democratic welfare system using her electoral support to wield any available state instrument, even declaring the 'emergency' in establishing her political power (Kohli 1987, 1989, and 2012:203-4). The

371 '*Provided that the completion of continuous service of five years shall not be necessary where the termination of the employment of any employee is due to death or disablement*' (GoI 1972: Section 4). Cash benefits are calculated based on 15 days' wages for every completed year of service and based on the last salary. Gratuity benefits are limited to Rs. 350,000 for an individual employee. Gratuity is normally paid at the time of retirement, death, or resignation, but a common practice is for employees to gain the cash-benefits earlier.

372 In 1977 Indira Gandhi lost the election but was re-elected in the elections in 1980 and regained the political majority as well as the position as prime minister until her assassination in 1984 (Rothermund 1995b).

early 1970s witnessed a critical juncture marked by the oil crises of 1973–1974, the failure of crops, and the intense public protest led by J.P. Narayan in his stance for civil rights and democratic virtues. In 1975 the High Court in Allahabad declared Gandhi's electoral win in 1971 illegitimate, inciting the Prime Minister to declare emergency rule which empowered her to take complete political control of India (Wagner 2006:119).

Under her strong, nearly authoritarian leadership public policy shifted towards poverty reduction[373] and improvement of agricultural production to ensure the self-reliance of the Indian state[374]. In 1975 she insisted on declaring emergency rule and accelerated the centralisation process. In the late 1970s the central state in India was at its peak. Although the centralisation process concentrated power in Delhi, the weaknesses of the central planning in administering such a vast and diversw territory became clearly visible. The central objective was to provide '*Growth with Redistribution*'[375]. Indira Gandhi expanded the *Nehruvian* policy strategy and added her own populist policies to achieve redistribution and political support with left-leaning policies, such as taxes for the rich, anti-monopoly laws, the nationalisation of banks, expansion of access to credit for the poor, and land reforms (Kohli 2012:203). In addition, the major focus of public policies in the 1970s was to grant subventions for agrarian production and

373 Fourth Five Year Plan 1969-74 increased the available resources with a significant larger allocation of 76.81 crores Rupees for social schemes. The schemes aimed to improve the socio-economical conditions for poor women and their children in increasing the women overall wages and access to education for mother and children (Yadav 2008: 65-6).

374 Self-reliance has always been an important aspect of foreign and domestic politics since the 1950s and Nehru's '*Five Principles of Peaceful Coexistence*' or '*Pancha Sila*' to establish India as independent international actors which coexist and has not to rely on the established international actors (Mitra 2001, 2011).

375 The policy strategy of the '*Growth with Redistribution*' '*was based on an assessment of the progress mad till then. It believed that 'growth with retribution' had actually led to a reduction in poverty and even cited the following numbers: There was growth in real per capita consumption. There was an improvement in distribution too. Between 1960-1 and 1977-8, consumption share of the bottom half of the population increased by 0.28 per cent annum in rural areas and 0.44 per cent per annum in urban areas while that for upper half of the population declined by 0.12 per cent per annum and 0.17 per cent per annum in rural and urban areas, respectively. Estimates of summary measures like the Lorenz ratios based on grouped consumption data at current prices declined by 0.38 per cent per annum in rural and 0.59 per cent per annum in urban areas* (GoI 1981:82).'

fixed prices for food to realize food security. Improving poverty reduction instruments and social assistance schemes was an essential feature of the social security provision; however, most of the approved social assistance schemes and programs were ad hoc measurements and could not produce significant outcomes or longitude[376].

It is worth noting that in the formulation of Five Year Plan the *Garibi Hatao* was of secondary importance, resulting in low funding and ad hoc social security and assistance schemes to tackle the socio-economic realities of mass poverty (Suryanarayana 2012:70-71). Indeed, the central and local governments paid serious attention to the issue and various redistribution schemes in rural and urban areas were passed: old age, widow and disability pension, and maternity and family benefits, including the *Minimum Needs Program*[377]. Still, the socialist rhetoric and ad hoc social security scheme could not produce significant short- or long-term effects for the poorer segments of society. The inefficiency of the public policies was related to a lack of funding, misconceptions and an administration overburdened by the extreme centralisation of power. Contrary to plan, the centralisation tendency had negative effects on bureaucratic efficiency and overall policy performance (Kohli 2012:203). Despite stronger centralisation of the social security administration, the IAS struggled to implement, manage and administer the various social security schemes due to the fact that, in addition to the inflexibility of the bureaucracy, the fourth Five Year Plan (1970-1975), launched in 1969, did not include financial resources for the designed projects (Potter 1996). As a consequence, the programmes had limited financial resources and the initiatives could not produce significant outcomes. But more importantly, the centralisation, financial constraints of the Five Year Plan, and ambitious policymaking overstretched the administrative and financial capacity of the central government and illustrated the clear limitations of the centralisation attempt (Kohli 1989, Potter 1996, Chibber 2012: 174-76).

376 In the fifth central plan, 1974–1979, the government increased the budget to 86.12 crores Rupees and included preventive programs for the handicapped, minimum needs programmes, as well as a national policy for children in 1974, and the ambition to strengthen the welfare administration (Yadav 2008:66-7).

377 The central government sponsors the old age pension, as well as maternity and family benefits schemes. The other two schemes are supported by the union state governments.

The Relevance of Party Differences, 1977 to 1992

Yet in March 1977 Indira Gandhi attempted to legitimate her rule and allowed elections to be held. Contrary to her perceptions and despite the political oppression of any opposition she lost the election to joint opposition under the banner of the newly formed Janata Party (Wagner 2006:140-141. The event marked not only the end of emergency rule but also the first national electoral defeat for the INC (Mitra 1994a). In the aftermath of Gandhi's emergency rule[378] the Congress government lost the national election in 1977 and ended the era of one-party dominance (Rothermund 1995b).[379] The newly elected Janata Party government (1977-1980) felt the pressure of financial and economic deficits as well as the insufficient outcomes of the poverty reduction policies.[380] Without a coherent nation-wide strategy or financial backup for social security political objectives, even the reform ambitious and newly elected Janata Party government could not produce any significant changes (Wagner 2006:140-141). In fact, the elected government expanded social policy to include education. Various schemes and positive discrimination mechanisms were instantiated to increase the available education for poor people. However, the programs targeting food and financial insecurity, education and employment for the poor, especially in rural areas, in the 1970s and 1980s produced only modest results in poverty reduction. In the late 1970s it became clear that neither of the Five Year plans could achieve significant outcomes in terms of poverty reduction (Kohli 1987, Nagaraj 2000: 2831, Patnaik and Patnaik 2001).

Without available financial revenue the state budget became tight and the central government urged local authorities to provide their own social assistance programmes (Rothermund 1993:69-71, Sen 2000, Sen and Rajasekhar 2012:115-117). The financial constraints in the central planning

378 For a detailed elaboration of Indira Gandhi's 'emergency regime' see Dhar (2000) '*Inidra Gandhi, the 'Emergency' and Indian Democracy*' cit op.

379 It is worth noting, as Subrata K. Mitra stresses (2002), that the electoral success and resulting political majority of the Congress was limited to the national level, the 'Lok Sabha' and 'Lok Rajya', even before the electoral national defeat in 1977.

380 The Sixth Plan (1980-85) sharply increased the social budget up to 271.97 crores. The main concern of the Plans did not shift and involved reducing unemployment with the Minimum Needs Program for rural and urban handicapped groups, as well as supplying drinking water, elementary education, housing, electricity and nutrition programs (Yadav 2008:68).

became evident and the fifth Five Year Plan (1975-1980) only slightly increased in social budget but the programmes produced significant restrictions on the state budget and even sharpened the intercountry inequalities.[381]

Interestingly, the main purpose of the Sixth Five Year Plan (1980-1985) under the newly elected government followed Indira Gandhi's poverty reduction scheme. Accordingly, the technocrats significantly increased the available budget for social assistance programs to Rs. 271.97 crores (Yadav 2008:67). The new financial impetus of the Five Year Plan granted the administration more capacity to build and expand the national security net for the urban and rural population. Over the following five years public policymaking achieved the reduction of rural inequality by 27.42 percent and urban inequality by 8.93 percent (Suryanarayana 1983)[382].

Although Gandhi would reclaim her political majority in the election of 1980, the electoral defeat seemed to have a positive effect on the commitment of the INC and the other political parties to following the new and popular agenda of poverty reduction. In the accelerated modernization process societal groups gained more attention, particularly the poor segment of society which represents more than 75 percent of the population (Kohli 1989, Mitra and Singh 1999). Consequently, a change in the underlying rationality[383] and resulting policy choices of office-seeking politicians in favour of social security political objectives and poverty reduction was distinctly visible during the 1970s—at least on paper (Chibber 2012:174). In the 1980s the economic sitatuion worsened and governments faced serious administrative burdens as well as financial deficits (Nagaraj 2000, Rothermund 1995b).

381 The modernisation of agrarian cultivation methods sharpened the local inequalities between rich and poor states as well as the poverty of landless peasants due to the shift from labour to capital and water-intensive production.

382 From 1985 to 1986 the Indira Awas Yojana program was introduced to tackle the poverty problem. The program was designed to provide housing for poor widows and unmarried women. Under the scheme 7.9 million houses were built (Yadav 2008:198).

383 Perception is seen as a combination of 'zwecks-' and 'value' rationality (Böcher and Töller 2012).

3.4.3 The Second Period: Performance has Priority, 1993 to 2004

In the 1990s one event – partial liberalization – shaped India's future political, economic and social development. In the late 1980s the Indian state faced a critical juncture in which it came close to bankruptcy. Desperately in need of credit the Indian government approved the conditions of financial support as set out by international agencies, including partial liberalization and the opening of its 'closed' economy to the international market (Jenkins 1999; Kohli 2006a:1251-54).

In the first legislative period during the 1990s the newly elected INC coalition government under Prime Minister Narasimhao Rao and Finance Minister Manmohan Singh transformed India's closed economy into a liberal market economy. The financial crisis and external pressure on the political system and policymaking process offered the government the ability to implement a range of structural changes (Wagner 2006:125). Contrary to Rajiv Gandhi's failed liberalization attempts in the mid-1980s, the party government's reforms were enacted relatively easily due to the INC majority in Parliament and external pressure for reform by international money lenders (Rothermund 1993, 1995b, Wagner 2006:125).[384] More importantly, in the new liberal climate a number of important changes for social security politics were introduced (Nagaraj 2000). The overall objective of the Eighth Five Year Plan (1992-1997) concentrated on economic structural reforms. The shifting focus on an *inclusive growth* strategy explicitly affected social security politics in two ways (Rao 2007, Chibber 2012:173, Kohli 2012).

First, in the 1990s the central government implemented a typical reduction of financial resources for social security and assistance programs and schemes[385]. Second, the INC party coalition government narrowed the scope of the 'universal' schemes in favour of a more target group-based approach focusing on *human development*. In the following year the government reduced social expenditures to unburden the state budget and free

384 The international money lender institutions, such as the World Bank and International Monetary Fund, operate under a strict policy. Financial support is only granted in exchange for the commitment for reforms.

385 Social expenditure in the reform decade was noticeably lower than in the 1980s. In the 1980s the average social expenditure accounted for eight percent of the GDP and in the late 1990s it decreased to roughly seven percent (MoF 1993, 2009, World Bank 1995)

up more resources for economic development. Therefore, the agenda setting of the Ninth Five Year Plan (1997-2002) can be best associated with the concept of *inclusive growth*. The main objective of the central planning was a stable economic growth ratio and structural adjustments of the existing policies as a response to the new realities (Jenkins 1999, Chamarbagwala 2006). In the following decade, the liberal political decision-making and resulting privatisation of the economy would produce an enormous growth rate but economic prosperity would not significantly improve the socio-economic situation of employers or reduce the overall low living standards and inequality (ILO 2010a).[386] Recent studies on income distribution indicate a further worsening of income distribution during the mid-2000s (Rao, Shand and Kalirajan 1999, Mazumdar and Sarkar 2007).[387] In effect, even with a political majority favouring economic reforms, privatization and retrenchment of social expenditures in the early 1990s, growing public disagreement and intensification of public protests led by labour union federations pressured the INC coalition government to increase public spending to seven percent in the mid-1990s as well as resulted in a decline of electoral support for the INC coalition government (Chibber 2012:187, Kohli 2012).

Following liberal policymaking, the government trusted in '*market-led growth dynamics*' to permit and equalize income distribution (Suryanarayana 2012:71). Moreover, the Eight Five Year Plans (1992-1997) lacked significant operational content to realize the ambitious goal. In this context the Ninth Five Year target based-group programs for the relative and absolute poor were seen as crucial elements of the national anti-poverty strategy (Nagaraj 2000, 2012a:32-35). The purpose of the newly elected BJP coalition government was to satisfy the public demands, fulfill electoral promises, and generate public policy outputs. Various social assistance programs were designed and introduced to tackle rural as well as urban poverty, such as the national Swaranjayanti Gram Swarozgar Yojana (SGSY), Swaranjayanti Jayanti Shahri Rozgat Yojana (SJSRY) and Urban Self-Employment Programme. In particular, these three programmes

386 In times of increasing profit sharing real wages rose only marginally and even slower between 1995 and 2005 compared to the period of 1983 to 1994, with less economic growth and surplus (Nagaraj 2000, 2012a:54).

387 Mazumdar and Sarkar (2007) have found that a progressive shift is taking place in the sectoral origin of income to the tertiary sector and its high dualism, which seems to prove worsening income distribution.

played an important role in the social security political trajectory during the 2000s (Yadav 2008:197-198, Sen and Rajasekhar 2012:113). One of the most popular was the SGSY. In 1999 the SGSY was introduced as a target group-based program for households above the poverty line. The program granted a compact package of cash benefits and available bank benefits for beneficiaries. Until 2002 roughly 4.3 million poor households participated in the poverty allocation project (Yadav 2008, Sen and Rajasekhar 2012).[388] Similar to the SGSY, the SJSRY was designed to generate paid employment opportunities. The SJSRY was put into practice in 1997 (Yadav 2008:197-198). A component of the SJSRY was the Urban Self-Employment Programme (USEP) to cover the urban poor self-employed, particularly women (Yadav 2008:198).[389] Critical evaluation of the success of the programs has emphasised that the social policy strategy of the government is 'characterised by much hype on theoretical reasoning, with little empirical understanding/operational content' (Suryanarayana 2012:71). A historical case of misconception was the land reforms under Nehru which could neither reduce the rural poverty nor the structural problems of the agrarian sector in the poorer union states[390]. Public policy performance has suffered since the 1970s as a result of the inefficiency of various transfer payment programs which fall prey to fraud and can neither identify their target groups nor provide the range and scope (Nagaraj 2000, 2012a:46). The main misconception of social security provision in India has been and still is the gap between the well-funded and well-designed schemes for the marginal number of employees in the organised sector and the mostly ad hoc and under-financed social security schemes for the rest of the population. In effect, the historical exclusion of the unorganised and rural population has produced significant constraints

388 http://www.archive.india.gov.in/sectors/commerce/insurance.php (2014-09-01)

389 Under the program a scheme was introduced for the Development of Women and Children in the Urban Areas (DWUCA). The scheme was designed to provide cash benefits for women to set up their own self-employment ventures. In the first year the DWUCA covered 33,875 women establishing their own joint self-employment ventures (Yadav 2008:199).

390 In 1971 Dandekar and Rath (1971) criticised the land reforms and argued for the need of wage employment programs to tackle the increasing income inequality between rich and poor farmers. Their assumption seems to be valid in taking the increasing agrarian distress since 1990s, evident in the Maoist uprisings and suicide rates, into account.

for the human development and socio-economic situation of India (NCEUS 2006, Kohli 2012:197).

PDS: Policy Trajectories, changed Scope and the BPL Target Group

Generally speaking, India offers a good example of the institutional transition from a colony to an independent state. Most of the legislation concerning national security were either taken over by the independent state or passed to fill the existing gap of the colonial legislature (Suryanarayana 1995). A crucial variable that mattered for public policymaking in post-independent India is path dependency and its sub-optimal outcomes for the goal, scope and range of social security provision.

The *Public Distribution System* (PDS) embodies the first category and was enacted under colonial rule to provide food security for the working-aged population in war times.[391] Food security for urban areas of high population density has always been an important concern in India. In 1942 under colonial rule the PDS evolved out of the fair price system to regulate food prices and food supply for the urban workforce and to reduce the negative effects of speculative food trade on a nation-wide level. The discriminating scope of the PDS in generating food security only for urban industrial areas[392] has opened it to criticism for its 'urban bias' (Surynarayan 1995, Nagaraj 2012b, Sen and Rajasekhar 2012:115-20, Chibber 2012:184-85).[393] Over the course of 60 years the PDS has been modified and adapted to the broader socio-economic realities of independent India (Suryanarayana 1995, 2012). The agrarian crises and near famine in the mid-1960s accelerated the demand for modern production methods in the outdated agrarian sector. The so-called '*Green Revolution*' modernised agrarian production methods but due to the high costs of modern production methods, any measurable increase in agrarian production was limited to richer states such as Bengal. Interestingly, in the course of the massive state-sponsored modernization process the traditionally high state subven-

391 The famine in 1943 could not be prevented by the PDS.

392 In the 1940s the PDS guaranteed food security for workers engaged in the warfare industry.

393 See the introductory section presented by Nagraj (2012b:18) in which he tackles the misconceptions of the PDS. See also in the same volume Sen and Rajasekhar's account (2012:115-117) on the PDS.

tions for the agrarian sectors, such as lower costs for fuel and flat rates for water and electricity, have been untouched.[394]

Despite these obstacles the central government, under the guiding leadership of the INC coalition government, transformed the PDS into a universal scheme to address growing regional disparity, but without success. In the process of the sixth Five Year Plan (1980-1985)[395] the PDS was announced as a universal social assistance program to cover all of India including inaccessible and remote areas. In the seventh Five Year Plan the PDS was included in the *Minimum Needs Program* in an attempt to realize the ambitious plan of ensuring nation-wide food security. Thus, the objective of the PDS to smooth inequalities and improve overall low living conditions could not be realized (Suryanarayana 1983, 1995).

The PDS has been a constant victim of inefficiency, corruption, exploding financial costs and administrative complexity. Similar to all other social security schemes, the PDS has not been able to overcome administrative flaws, ineffectiveness and expanding transaction costs. As Swaminathan (2008) concludes, based on the outcomes of the 61st National Sample Survey, 'targeting has led to high rates of exclusion of needy households' and furthermore there is 'a clear deterioration of coverage in states like Kerala where the universal PDS was most effective.' The PDS has come under serious critique concerning the inclusion of 'excess coverage of ineligible non-poor households,' limited coverage, and expanding transaction costs (Sen and Rajasekhar 2012:117, Suryanarayana and Silva 2007). The limited coverage and target errors of the system resulted in the fact that so-called 'needy' households and localities were excluded by the PDS.

As the Planning Commission (2005) concludes in their official report, the limited range and scope of the PDS has negatively affected its efficiency. Various grievance-causing errors were evaluated in the report of the Commission. It is not surprising that the PDS achieved only a limited cov-

---

394 The rational choice approach and the assumed rationality of office-seeking politicians can be used to explain the policy even in times of budget restrictions. On the one hand, there is the majority of India's population engaged in agrarian production. On the other hand, there is the political rise of rich farmers, which has produced important pressure groups at the local and national levels (Sen and Rajasekhar 2012).

395 See Suryanarayana's (1983) article 'Treatment of Poverty in the Sixth Plan' for an elaboration of the overall poverty reduction goals of the sixth Five Year Plan.

erage of 57 percent of the *below poverty line* (BPL) households.[396] Another major, basic problem is fraud: it is estimated that 20 million ghost card users exist and in addition 20 million entitled households do not gain any benefits due to the overburdening of the system by fraud. Furthermore, only 42 percent of the subsidized grain is issued to households and a large amount is sold illegally. Also the Commission criticised the fair price ships established under the PDS to provide food security on the grounds of their low turnover. The concluding remark of the Commission was that the target PDS costs are much higher than the costs for similar programs (Suryanarayana 1995, 2012). The increasing financial pressure on the state budget and the expanding costs of the PDS, in combination with the inefficient coverage of the universal character of the PDS, made reform necessary in the late 1980s. To take advantage of the situation the INC party coalition redesigned the PDS[397] once again in 1997 with a view toward designing a targeted program for the poor and vulnerable.[398] In 1997 the scope of the PDS was transformed from a universal into a target group-based program for BPL households only (Suryanarayana 1983, 2012:71-72).[399]

In line with the path-dependency argument and the resulting current social security provisions in India, the present shape of these laws and programs, such as the PDS, emphasises the fact that the 'processes responsible for the genesis of an institution are different from the processes responsible for the reproduction of the institution' (Mahoney 2000:4). The PDS has been transformed multiple times, first from an urban-focused program into a universal scheme and lately into a target group-based program for urban and rural poor households.

---

396 See appendix I for the concept and category of BPL households.

397 Due to the transformation the PDS is sometimes referred to as the target PDS or TPDS. In the following section the target version of the program will be explicitly referred to as the target PDS.

398 The government divided the population into two groups based on economic situation. The target group category is defined based on the Planning Commission's poverty level for the year 1993 to 1994.

399 Under the PDS fair price shops are managed to provide certain kinds of grains, legumes and sugar for BPL households. The products are subsidised by the government to be affordable for poor families and to cover their daily nutrition demands. Thus, the ambition was to reduce the related cost of the program and tackle the problem of economic deprivation (Suryanarayana 2012:71, 87 sp).

3.4.3.1 Social Security Provision in the late 1990s and early 2000s

Social security provision and legislation in India has to be understood with respect to the changing attitude of the INC in its social policy guidelines. As indicated in the previous section, as well as in table 17, social security legislation was the focus of the formal sector until 2007. Against the background of Indira Gandhi's social policy focus on limited social security for the 'poorer' population, social security provision was unfit to realize a higher level of coverage in cases of socio-economic uncertainty, such as old age, illness or other related problems. It took until the mid-2000s, over half a century later, for the central government to address the socio-economic problems of roughly 90 percent of the total population.

Table 17: Major social Security Legislation in India

Year	Act	Target Group
1923	Workmen's Compensation Act 1923	Organised sector
1948	Employees' State Insurance Act 1948	Organised sector
1952	Employees' Provident Fund and Miscellaneous Provision Act, 1952	Organised sector
1961	Maternity Benefit Act 1961/1995	Organised sector
1972	Payment of Gratuity Act 1972	Organised sector
2005	National Rural Employment Guarantee Act, 2005	Rural BPL households
2007	Unorganized Sector Workers Social Security Bill, 2007	Unorganised sector

Source: Author's own summary

In 2005 the NREGA attempted to provide an active labour market program for the rural poor population and in the same legislative period the UPA also published the Unorganized Sector Workers' Social Security Bill dealing with the issue of missing social security for the employees in the informal sector. Against the legislative initiative, the UPA backed up various social security schemes for BPL households. Social security provisions in India have improved, but not overcome the structural problems of inadequate financing, program concurrency[400], corruption, as well as ad-

400 Social security schemes such as the PDS have lacked adequate planning, finances and long-term administrative commitment. The often ad hoc programmes have produced inadequate coverage. Their scope and range have varied extremely from locality to locality and their overall inefficiency has reduced the potential to produce significant outcomes (Nagaraj 2012a, Kohli 2012).

ministrative inefficiency and the lack of a national policy strategy to coordinate social security in a highly pluralised context. Interestingly, the phenomena are not restricted to social security provisions but also distinctly visible in other policy fields also suffering the effects of traditional structural constraints, such as education[401] and health[402].

3.4.3.2 India's Social Security and typical Deficits, 1991-2004

In 1991 the partial liberalization and privatization of a large amount of former state-owned industries resulted in a rapid increase of unemployment and wage inequality (Chamarbagwala 2006:1998-99, Bardhan 2007). In the new liberal climate the INC coalition government opted for liberal economic policies to realise the *inclusive growth* strategy and trusted in the 'trickle down' effect of economic growth (Nagaraj 2012a:36). In the late 1990s socio-economic problems, such as increasing food and fuel costs, increased despite the background of economic growth in the wake of the electoral defeat of the INC coalition government (Wagner 2006). At the end of 1990s the BJP used public dissatisfaction with increasing socio-economic problems to muster a government-forming coalition. Their electoral success was grounded in the electoral promise to unburden the 'poorer' segments of society. Shortly after election the government instantiated two concrete social assistance schemes to guarantee employment for the BPL (Rao, Rajasekhar and Suchitra 2006). However, economic performance had top priority and the social security initiative suffered the traditional problem of insufficient funding, uncoordinated planning and administration (Sen and Rajasekhar 2012:112-114).

---

401 Compared to the more equal East Asian and more unequal South American countries, India has a moderate level of inequality. Bardan (2007) has accumulated evidence that educational inequality in India is even worse than in South America due its entrenched social hierarchy.

402 The focus on improving health has also produced only modest outcomes due to the fact that the core problems of public health and access to sanitation, electricity and drinking water have gained less attention due to the historical focus on setting up health care centres to treat infectious diseases caused by the lack of drinking water and sanitation. India spends only 17.3 percent of its health expenditures on public health, whereas China spends 24.9 and Sri Lanka 45.4 in 2002 (National Health Policy 2002). In 2008 only 11 percent of the rural and 22 percent of urban population had access to drinking water (WHO 2010).

3.4.3.3 Expanding the Safety Net for elderly people

In the last decade, the social pension system in India has gained more attention by policymakers as well as academics (Rao 2007, 2011, ILO 2015). Three groups of pension schemes can be distinguished in terms of their target groups, which also illustrate the changing scope of social security provision. The first group, including the *Civil Service Pensions*, *Statutory Pension Scheme, and Provident Fund Scheme for the Organized Sector*, as well as *Superannuation*, is designed for the formal sector under the EPF.

The second category includes only one scheme, the *Small Savings Scheme*. However, the range and scope of the scheme illustrate the modest impact of liberal reasoning on social policymaking. The *Small Savings Scheme* was designed to encourage private households to save and invest money[403] by taking advantage of the very low private savings rate in India, and to improve the economic situation as well as individual benefits of private households.[404]

The third category of pension schemes reflects the policy trajectory for target group-based and means-tested schemes[405]. In particular, these

---

403 India's private households are characterised by a low saving and investment approach which has had a negative effect on the domestic economy (World Bank 2007, 2008, 2009)

404 The *Small Savings Scheme* should be seen as an initiative to encourage less fortunate citizens to trust banks and save money to gain interest and not as a typical social security instrument. Furthermore, the variations in the tax advantages and interest rates problematize comparisons of the scheme. It will therefore not be analysed in following section (Mishra and Raveendran 2011).

405 Means-tested, or target group-based, programs are designed and limited to specific groups fulfilling the characteristics. In addition, these policies are instruments advocated by the state to provide eligibility for benefits. To some extent these social security schemes require certain conditions of their beneficiaries. In most cases the applicants have to fulfil the requirements of an official means test (i.e. daily low income) to apply for the specific schemes. Traditionally such schemes are designed for the absolute poor, offering "social pensions or equalization payments" which "are financed primarily from general revenues" (ISSA 2012:3). Commonly, the means test is applied to the economic situation of the individual or the household in reference to the used calculated standard—in most cases either the local or national poverty line and/or minimum wages. In most countries the local authorities have the responsibility to set the criteria and benefits; therefore, means-tested or target group-based programs are commonly locally administered and adapted.

schemes aim for poverty reduction and expand the coverage of old age insurance for poor people outside the formal sector who lack access to the schemes of the first category. Since 2000 the commitment of the central government to addressing old age poverty has resulted in a variation of sponsored target pension schemes for unorganised poor workers[406]: the *Indira Gandhi National Old Age Pension Scheme*, *Varishtha Pension Bima,* the *Micro Pension Scheme and the National Social Assistance Program* (Rao 2005, 2011).

3.4.3.4 Three Categories: the Range, Ccope and Deficits of typical pension schemes

In the following section, the most recent pension schemes will be briefly discussed—that is, the National Pension Scheme, the National Social Assistance Program, the Indira Gandhi National Old Age Pension Scheme, Varishtha Pension Bima and the Micro Pension Scheme—to illustrate the above mentioned policy trajectories (1991 to 2004) as well as the overall issues facing the pension system in India (Vaidyanathan 2006).

Another issue that confronts social security schemes in general is the modest coverage of these programmes against the background of a broad range of state-subsidised pension schemes. In 2007, even after the implementation of various additional pension schemes, only 9.1 percent of the labour force and 5.7 percent of the population for the age group of 15 to 65[407] was covered by any kind of old age security scheme (Rao 2007). Correspondingly, it is not surprising that pensions and old age security have to be covered by other means. Often the only available institution for a large segment of India's poor society to meet the demands of old age is the family system, especially in rural areas or with private pension schemes (Mishra and Raveendran 2012). A reason for the tendency is that most of the pensions are relatively young because pension funds have not

---

406 The *Informal Sector Workers Social Security Scheme* will not be discussed. It was adopted as a pilot project in 50 districts betwen 2002 and 2005. In 2005 the scheme was closed because of its unpopularity. Only a few thousand participated in the pension scheme until 2005 (SSA 2008, 2012).

407 In the OECD countries the average coverage of the workforce is 80.3 percent and for the age group of 15 to 65 an average of 60.4 percent has been realized (OECD 2007).

been very popular in political decision-making, have not gained financial professionalism and diversification, and have been treated as assets (Vaidyanathan 2006).

The National Pension Scheme[408]

The National Pension Scheme (NPS) under the EPF belongs to the first category of pension systems for the formal sector. On January 1st, 2004 the NPS was imposed as a modern contribution pension scheme and replaced the EPS for any newly recruited government employees[409] and/or employees in the public sector in the majority of union states. The NPS is a modern pension scheme for the formal sector. It is designed to grant its beneficiaries pension entitlement with an extremely high cost-benefit assessment[410] compared to other developing countries. The attractiveness of the NPS lies in its low fee of only 5 percent of the total flow a year, making it 'the lowest cost contribution pension plan anywhere in the world' (SSA 2006:92).[411]

Another new feature of the NPS concerns the management of the uncommitted capital reserve of the pension fund, which consists of individual accounts[412]. The new investment fund system is a major step forward. Funds are not limited to government security bonds, as is the case in China, but are split among various investment funds to assure stable invest-

408 In 2009 the scheme was renamed the *New Pension Scheme* by the Government.

409 Military and railway service employees were not included in the reform of the social security scheme.

410 At the age of retirement the beneficiaries are entitled to the cash benefits of the NPS. The majority of the account will be paid as a lump sum and the rest of the individual account will be paid as a monthly pension. To be entitled to the cash benefits the beneficiary has to pay at least Rs. 500 a month for at least four years. In a normal contribution of Rs. 6,000 (US $140) the fee is only Rs. 300 a year. If the beneficiary contributes above US $1,000 per year the fee will be reduced to only one percent (SSA 2006:92).

411 In Mexico contributions to the pension scheme have a yearly fee of 20 percent (ISSA 2008).

412 Taking part in the scheme also requires the beneficiary to open a non-withdrawable account. This account is mandatory for the monthly contributions. Furthermore, the beneficiary has the option of a voluntary savings facility which provides additional liquidity to the affiliates in the future.

ment rates, with other bonds regulated by the *Securities and Exchange Board of India*.[413]

To sum up, the NPS is a modern-designed and -funded pension scheme for formal employees set up by the central government, which illustrates its strong and enduring commitment to the well-being of the public administration and formal sectors.

The Pension Scheme under the National Social Assistance Program

An overall objective of social security politics is the implementation of a safety net for elderly people, particularly those with low incomes. In August 1995 the central government approved the establishment of the *National Social Assistance Program (NSAP)* The NSAP is best described as a package of employment-oriented social security schemes, including a pension scheme, for unorganised workers aimed at closing the existing gap.[414]

The sponsored pension scheme could not achieve the hoped-for participation. Participation heavily declined in 1997 due to the financial limitations of the government's budget for the pension scheme and the restriction of the program to BPL households exclusively. The construction of the national pension scheme was premised partly on the overall budget allotment for social expenditures.[415]

The second scheme under the umbrella of the NASP is the Family Benefits Scheme. In cases of the natural or accidental death of the principal earning member, the family is entitled to Rs 10,000. In 2005 the program had 2.11 million beneficiaries (Sülzer 2008: 222)

Third, the Maternity Benefit Scheme grants pregnant women Rs. 500 per live birth and is limited to two live births.[416]

The Maternity Benefit Scheme has been criticised on various levels (NCEUS 2006, Sen and Rajasekhar 2012, Varma 2004). In particular, it has been argued that institutional delivery is not easily available in terms

413 For example, liquid funds of asset management companies.

414 See http://nsap.nic.in/ (2010-09-12)

415 In effect, the pension benefits have nearly tripled from only Rs 75 to Rs 200 per month in 2006 to 2007. A revenue of Rs 200 per month is still very low for elderly people in urban areas (Sülzer 2008: 220 sp).

416 See http://nsap.nic.in/ (2010-09-12)

of costs and nearby medical facilities for poor women. In addition, pregnant women depend on the permission and the support of their husbands or other male household members. These women cannot normally afford to leave their families for the time of institutional delivery (Sen and Rajasekhar 2012:119). Furthermore, the NCEUS recommended a necessary increase in the cash benefits of the national scheme to encourage participation. The most important deficit of the national Maternity Benefit Scheme is the lack of a coordinated social security policy. Various state governments have created maternity schemes and the competition and lack of information has resulted in the low participation of pregnant women[417] in the national program (Rajasekhar and Manjula 2005, Sen and Rajasekhar 2012:98, 100, 119).

The central government has handed the responsibility for providing the Disability and Widow Pension to the states. The state-sponsored widow pension schemes, similar to the old age pension, have been relatively unpopular due to the low state contributions and resulting marginal revenue of only Rs. 75 per month. With the aim of redressing the modest coverage, the steadily increasing demand, as well as the financial costs, the eleventh Five Year Plan increased the budget for the NASP to Rs. 1663.31 crores (Planning Commission 2008).

However, the overall coverage of the NASP has been modest. The special report 'Social Protection for a Changing India: Main Report' conducted by the World Bank (2011) on India's social security scheme concluded that the old age pension scheme covers roughly 8.3 percent of elderly households. The *Widow Pension Scheme* accounts for 6.2 percent of widow households, and the *Disability Pension Scheme* reaches 14.1 percent of disabled households.

---

417 On the issue of missing participation and the problem of social security administration identifying the target groups, see P. Madhava Rao's study (2001) '*Social Security Administration in India*'.

Indira Gandhi's National Old Age Pension Scheme[418]

Without a doubt the *Indira Gandhi National Old Age Pension Scheme* (IGNOAPS) represents the flagship in providing non-contribution benefits for elderly poor people in India. In 1995 the central government imposed the scheme, which is estimated to cover 17 million elderly beneficiaries above the age of 65. The ambitious social security scheme was designed as a group-based target program for elderly citizens above the age of 65 below the poverty line.[419] All beneficiaries[420] who fulfil the requirements can apply for the scheme and gain approximately Rs 75 (US $ 2) per month.[421] The central government contributes half of the total pension and half is provided by the state government. However, the individual benefits vary from state to state due to the fact that the state governments, and particularly the local branch of the Department of Social Welfare, can either increase or decrease the monthly benefits (Varinder 2010:13).

The demand for the IGNOAPS has been underestimated and consequently the program barely reached its financial and administrative objectives (Varinder 2010). Its ambitious and broad coverage overburdened the administrative as well as financial capacity and greatly reduced the effectiveness of the program. In 2000 at least 20 percent of the entitled rural beneficiaries did not receive any pension benefits. As a direct reaction in the same year the Ministry of Rural Development set up the ad hoc *Annapurna* social assistance scheme which granted cash benefits to these claimants (SSA 2008). A major problem for the administrative body has been the identification and verification of the target groups. The task of verifying that recipients earn less than US $ 7 is nearly impossible to meet. Furthermore, the determination of age is also an obstacle for the administration due to the fact that in India most of the elderly people do not have official birth certificates and fraud is common (Varinder 2010:14-18,

418 In 2000 the existing *National Old Age Pension Scheme (NOAPS)* was renamed the *Indira Gandhi National Old Age Pension Scheme* in honour of former Prime Minister Indira Gandhi's ambitious struggle against poverty.

419 Elderly people with a monthly income of less than Rs 300 (US $ 7) who are below the official poverty line gain access.

420 Applications are administrated by the local government and have to be approved by local members of the Legislative Assembly.

421 For details see the official database for the IGNOPAS provided by the central government of India, available at http://data.gov.in/keywords/ignoaps (2014-01-12).

The Economist 2014m).[422] Above all, the IGNOPAS illustrates the increasing challenges for the central government's budget and the states' financial and administrative resources to provide adequate and subsidised pensions for the growing segment of elderly people below the poverty line.[423]

Varishtha Pension Bima: A 'fill-in' for the IGNOPAS

A major reform step taken in 2003 was the implementation of an additional pension scheme to overcome the missing coverage and problems of the IGNOPAS to deliver a safety net for elderly people. In 2003 the central government announced the *Varishtha Pension Bima (VPB)*. The pension scheme is an attempt to produce an immediate solution to old age poverty in the unorganised sector. In addition, the scheme involves a group-based target for old people 55 years of age or older (in 2003) who were employed in the unorganised sector. Moreover, the pension scheme is interesting because the participants only have to pay one premium in one lump sum of at least Rs 33.335 (US $ 5,300) and not more than Rs. 266.665 (Us $ 670) to be entitled to lifetime pension benefits. In cases of death the pension will be paid to the survivor of the beneficiary.[424] Similar to the other pension schemes of the third category, these schemes are heavily subsidised by central government. At the moment the participation rate of these schemes, such as the VPB, are still relatively low due to the lack of information. But taking into account the increasing financial burdens of the IGNOPAS, the question arises: Can the government continue to provide social security in the future?

422 In most cases the beneficiary only needs certification by a government-certified medical officer, who is often amenable to bribes for his service (The Economist 2014m:22).

423 In 2009 the government noted increasing demand with an estimated 7.1 million beneficiaries (ISSA 2008).

424 Benefit rates vary between a minimum of Rs. 250 (US $ 5) and a maximum of Rs. 2000 per month depending on the premium paid (SSA 2004, 2008:78-79).

The Micro Pension Scheme: Empowering Women

The *Micro Pension Scheme* has to be highlighted due to its unique character in aiming to empower women as well as close cooperation between state and private institutions. It was launched in 2006 by the central government in cooperation with the UTI Asset Management Company and Employed Women's Association Bank to provide a national pension scheme for rural and urban women. The scheme was an initiative to promote the empowerment of women and give them the opportunity to meet their financial needs in old age[425]. The idea behind the *Micro Pension Scheme* is to provide 'long-term savings by relatively low-income informal-sector workers, with the objective of obtaining income security during old age' (Shankar and Asher 2011).[426]

3.4.3.5 Social Security and Health insurance in the unorganised sector

Unlike the formal sector which has a series of well-defined programmes for employment-related health care, such as the ESI and the CGHS, the informal sector has inadequate employment-related health care schemes. The lack of an adequate national social insurance system for unorganised workers and their households reflected the ad hoc character of social policymaking in former periods. In recent decades the government has been engaged in efforts to provide affordable health insurance, with the launch of the *Janashree Bhima Yojana (JBY), Universal Health Insurance (UHI) and the Rashtriya Swasthaya Bima Yojana (RSBY).*

The strong cooperation in the design process of the net scheme between NGOs, communities, and public as well as private organizations reflects the partnership that has evolved in the implementation of social insurance, with the state and insurance companies working together to substantially

425 In social policymaking micro credits for women have become a tool for coping with existing inequality and the gender gap (Yelne 2007).

426 In particular, the *Micro Pension Scheme* was designed on the basis of low monthly contributions between Rs. 50 and 200 until the age of 55. Pension benefits are paid monthly from the age of 58 onwards and administrated by the UTI Asset Management Company (Shankar and Asher 2011, SSA 2008:89).

advance the range, scope, benefits and administration of the existing programmes in India (Radermacher et al. 2006).[427]

Janashree Bhima Yojana: The modern Health Care Scheme

In 2000 the BJP government had to deal with the inefficiency of the former social security administration and ambitiously tried to increase its policy output. To do so the government approved the *Janashree Bhima Yojana (JBY),* a group-based social insurance plan for 18 to 60 year olds belonging to BPL households (Sen and Rajasekhar 2012:119). The JBY has taken a major step forward in regard to the modern administration of such programmes. All the beneficiaries are provided with a Smart Card for identification and constant monitoring. As mentioned before, the insurance is the result of public-private cooperation and administrated by the Life Insurance Corporation of India (Varinder 2010:22, Ministry of Finances 2014).[428]

A cooperative network of roughly 2,000 hospitals and 1,500 private clinics all over India has been utilized to ensure the medical treatment of clients. Medical providers are paid on a fee-for-service basis. Under the JBY medical costs for treatment are covered for up to Rs. 30,000 (US $ 700). The premium during hospitalization ranges from Rs. 400 to Rs. 600 with an option to gain Rs. 100 (no more than Rs. 1000 per year) as financial compensation for transportation costs in cases of visitation by family

---

427 A relevant point in India's pluralistic social security system is information. According to Ruchismita and Churchill (2012) in the state-funded micro insurances the numbers of recipients increased from only 75 million in 2007 to roughly 302 million who use any kind of mirco insurance. Demand for national social security and assistance programs, such as the UHI, is determined not only by the available information, modalities and benefits but also by the competition with local schemes. The pluralistic context in social politics has promoted a flourishing number of policies designed by state governments for the needs of local target groups: to mention only the most popular ones, the *Yeshasvini Health Insurance Scheme for rural farmers and peasants* in Karnataka covering 2.2 million farmers, the *Aarogyasri* in Andhra Pradesh, and the *Kalaignar* in Tamil Nadu (Government of Andra Pradesh 1997, Ruchismita and Churchill 2012).

428 See also the Indian government's Ministry of Finances' (2014) homepage for detailed information on the JBY scheme, funding and benefits. http://financialservices.gov.in/insurance/gssois/jby.asp (2014-05-01).

members. Furthermore, transportation for beneficiaries to the hospital is cashless and covered by insurance (Ruchismita et al. 2012).

Another important component of the JBY includes the additional promotion of education. Thus, the scheme tackles one of the major problems of poor unorganised households: the medical coverage and education of the children. Up to two school-going children of insurers gain a monthly scholarship of Rs. 100 each. The combination of life and disability insurance and the additional financial benefit of Rs. 100 per school-going child have produced an increasing demand on the part of the target group of poor people.[429]

Half of the annual premium of the insurance is financed by the central government. Similar to other insurance, it provides Rs. 20,000 in case of natural death, Rs. 50,000 in case of accidental death or permanent disability, and Rs. 25,000 in case of temporary disability.

As regards participation and coverage, the JBY still has very low coverage due to its restriction to BPL households[430] and potential clients' lack of knowledge about the scheme (Rajasekhar and Manjula 2005).[431] Also Sen and Rajasekhar (2012) note that the 'poor are sceptical of contributing to a scheme wherein they realise that they will not get any returns unless the eventuality that they have taken the insurance occurs.' Hence, the target group of poor people have to struggle to survive from day to day and mostly take the risk of paying for something without gaining any benefits.

The Universal Health Insurance Scheme

Contrary to the JBY, the *Universal Health Insurance Scheme (UHI)* is designed as health insurance for the earning member of the household who is employed in the unorganised sector and lacks any employment-based health insurance. The construction of Indian health care insurance was premised in part on the organised sector in former periods, which had a significantly negative effect on the coverage of unorganised workers. In

429 See the official online data published by the Ministry of Finance (2014), cit op.

430 The BPL household criterion has been under critique for its minimalist and inappropriate approach to needy households (Rao, Rajasekhar and Suchitr 2006).

431 Rajasekhar and Manjula (2005) found in their sample that in Karnataka alone only five percent of the surveyed unorganised workers had knowledge of the existence of the available programmes.

the 1970s, the government attempted to increase the social security of unorganised workers but did not achieve significant results in health care. Traditionally health expenditure is out-of-pocket for all citizens due to low government benefits and insurance (NCMH 2005).

Neither the social security legislation of the 1990s nor the so-called reform period improved the access of unorganised workers to health care in times of economic hardship. The National Sample Survey in the 1990s gave clear evidence of the increasing challenge of health inequality and the rising costs of treatment for unorganised workers, which worsened the available access of these vulnerable groups (Sen, Iyer and George 2002:1351-54).

However, unorganised workers have become an important electoral group and public pressure for further health care legislation continued. The result was the introduction of a group-based programme, the *Universal Health Insurance Scheme*, by the central government in 2004 (Sen and Rajsekhar 2012, OECD 2010c:191).

The scheme can cover either an individual or a household up to seven people. It covers health care costs up to Rs. 30,000. Furthermore, the scheme provides compensation of Rs. 50 for 15 days if the income earner of the household falls sick. Concerning the coverage, the UHIS, similar to the JBY, is only accessible for BPL households. From the beginning the UHIS was designed as universal health insurance; however, the scope of the scheme has been limited to BPL households in an attempt to produce a target group-based program for unorganised workers. The limitation has significantly reduced the potential of the health insurance scheme to reduce overall health care inequality and limited access of vulnerable households and individuals (Sen and Rajsekhar 2012:122-23).[432]

As a result, the UHIS could not meet the expected demand of ten million individuals. By the end of 2004 around 417,000 households or 1.16 million people had obtained health insurance across India (Ahuja 2004, Ahuja and De 2004). However, similar to other social security schemes, the UHIS coverage varies extremely from locality to locality. Half the

432 Upon closer look at the insurance policies, one sees that only 11,408 of the total 1.16 million recipients belong to BPL households, which undermines the scope and regulatory mechanism of the scheme (Sen and Rajsekhar 2012:122).

clients of the UHIS are located in only four states: Maharashtra, Andhra Pradesh, Tamil Nadu and Gujarat (Chidambaram 2004).[433]

Finally, to broaden the programme's reach, the central government increased the subsidy of Rs. 100 over time. In 2004 the subsidies were increased from Rs. 100 to Rs. 200, then Rs. 300, and then to Rs. 400 by the end of 2005. The positive effect could be easily measured in the sharp increase in participation from 1.16 million to 100 million in only 2 years, though at the cost of increasing financial commitment on the part of the central government (OECD 2010c, Sen and Rajsekhar 2012:121-122).[434]

SEWA Health Insurance - A Non governmental Initiative

An outstanding initiative is the health insurance provided by the *Self-Employed Women's Association of India (SEWA)*. The SEWA is a trade union for poor, self-employed women workers founded in 1972. Beginning in 1984 the SEWA offered health insurance to its members. In the 1990s the initiative gained the public attention of the *Deutsche Gesellschaft für internationale Zusammenarbeit* and central government. Thus, in 1992 health insurance became a financially supported pioneering approach to providing social security for self-employed women workers in the informal sector. In cooperation with the GTZ, the SEWA was entitled to government funding to administer health insurance. The scheme is financed by three different sources: beneficiaries (50 percent), the Indian Insurance Company of the central government (25 percent), and interest paid on a grant by the GTZ (25 percent) (Venkatesh 2005).

What is not typical for the Indian context is that the SEWA is administered by the stakeholders themselves and government involvement is limited to providing financial subsidies. The scheme provides benefits in cases of maternity, natural and accidental death, disability, and loss of either housing or work equipment. Above all, the individual contribution rate, for the recipient to be entitled to all benefits, is only Rs. 60 (US $ 1.50)

433 See the official speech of the Finance Minister, P. Chidambaram, delivered on July 8 (2004).

434 The Ministry of Finance (2014) homepage, available at http://financialservices.gov.in/insurance/gssois/uhis.asp (2014-04-05).

per year. Until 2000 the scheme was the largest existing scheme for over 25,000 female workers in the unorganised sector.[435]

3.4.3.6 Social Security Schemes for the unorganised Sector

In 2000 the BJP coalition government launched two social insurance schemes for the unorganised sector. The Janashree Bima Yojana (JBY) was introduced in 2000 to replace the former ad hoc social security insurance and one year later the Krishi Samajik Suraksha Yojana was introduced to expand insurance coverage to rural workers in particular (Varinder 2010:21-22, Sen and Rajsekhar 2012:119)

The Janashree Bima Yojana[436] Life Insurance

Janashree Bima Yojana (JBY) was launched on August 10th, 2000 and merged two life insurance schemes, the *Social Security Group Insurance Scheme* (SSGIS) and the *Rural Group Life Insurance Scheme* (RGLIS), together. The JBY is designed as a target group program for approximately 45 groups of workers, which were identified in the national survey as members of unorganized sector, such as beedi (cigarette) workers, construction workers, firecracker workers, fishermen, and also the rural poor. [437] Although the premium is set at Rs. 200 per year, the premium contribution is heavily subsidised. Of the Rs. 200 half are funded by the LIC's Social Securiy Fund, and Rs. 60 by the central government; therefore the beneficiary only has to contribute Rs. 40. In cases of natural death the scheme provides a lump sum of Rs. 30,000, or Rs. 75,000 in cases of accidental death or permanent disability. Furthermore, similar to the JBY health insurance, a scholarship of Rs. 1,200 per year is provided for the re-

---

435 See the official homepage, available at http://www.sewa.org/ for detailed information (2014-04-05).

436 Concerning the similar names, the health as well as life insurance were named after Janashree Bima Yojana but are two separate programs.

437 The requirement conditions to participate include belonging to one of the 45 occupational groups; according to the definition of the category, a member of the 'rural poor' is any person between the ages of 18 and 59 below or marginally above the poverty line (OECD 2010c:190-192) http://www.archive.india.gov.in/sectors/commerce/insurance.php (2014-09-01)

cipient's children (Eleventh Five Year Plan 2008, Sen and Rajsekhar 2012:120-121).[438] To sum up, the JBY aimed for an ambitious goal, but suffers from a low participation rate (typical of most of the national social schemes), missing coverage for additional health care, as well as low benefits.

The Krishi Samajik Suraksha Yojana – just a policy

In its short time of providing services (2001–2004), Krishi Samajik Suraksha Yojana offered a classic example of the fiscal constraints as well as party government concurrency on social security provision. It was set into motion in 2001 by the BJP coalition government and was designed as life protection insurance for BPL households.[439] However, as illustrated before, not every social security scheme is well-designed and well-funded. The Krishi Samajik Suraksha Yojana overlapped with various other local schemes. Shortly after its implementation in 2001 the Krishi Samajik Suraksha Yojana ran into serious funding problems to cover the liabilities of its recipients. Accordingly, similar to other ad-hoc programs, the newly elected UPA government had neither the patience to deal with the initiatives of the former rival government nor the resources for structural remodelling; it shut down the scheme in 2004 (OECD 2010c:191-92).[440]

---

438 See the official document published by the Life Insurance Company of India (Mumbai) (2014) concerning the benefits for the scheme, available at http://nrega.nic.in/circular/Janashri_Yojana.pdf (2014-05-01). Another official source is provided by the Indian Government's Ministry of Finance (2014) homepage. http://financialservices.gov.in/insurance/gssois/jby.asp (2014-01-14).

439 The program was a target group-based social assistance program for rural agricultural workers between the ages of 18 to 50 in 50 districts. All beneficiaries paid Rs. 1 per day and the government contributed Rs. 2 into the fund. In cases of permanent disability Rs. 75,000 were available; in cases of death due to accident Rs. 75,000 were also available; and in cases of the loss of one or both eyes Rs. 37,500 and 75,000 respectively were available.

440 http://www.archive.india.gov.in/sectors/commerce/insurance.php (2014-09-01).

3.4.4 The Third Period: Balanced economic and social Development, 2004 to 2009

In 2004 the United Progressive Alliance under the chairperson Sonja Gandhi (INC) achieved electoral success (Rao, Rajasekhar and Suchitra 2006). During its rule from 2004 to 2009, the UPA pledged to economic as well as human development.[441] The central government therefore designed various social security schemes and programmes, as well as passed social security legislation to improve the inadequate social security net for the 'poorer' segments of India's population (NCEUS 2006, 2007). The UPA coalition government passed a bill concerning social security for the unorganised sector in 2007 as well as introduced two decent social assistance programs to realize its ambitious electoral promise. Despite the increase in the economic growth rate and the rhetoric, the outcomes in 2009 for providing human development and substantially increased social security were less than modest. A main problem was the focus of decision makers and the planning committee on economic growth and public health instead of on social security and assistance, which was guided by the still-dominant *inclusive growth* concept and the hope of a trickle-down effect (Nagaraj 2000, 2012a:36).

Consequently, the '*Eleventh Five Year Plan, 2007-2012*' (2008) successfully opted for overall objectives to improve economic performance in the urban and rural sectors.[442] Although the economic growth objective for state industries could not achieve the aspired 9 percent growth rate, a fair-

441 See the UPA's Common Minimum Programme (quoted in the Hindu May 28 2004): 'To preserve, protect and promote social harmony and to enforce the law without fear or favour to deal with all obscurantist and fundamentalist elements who seek to disturb social amity and peace. To ensure that the economy grows at least 7-8% per year in a sustained manner over a decade and in a manner that generates employment so that each family is assured of a safe and viable livelihood. To enhance the welfare and well-being of farmers, farm labourers and workers, particularly those in the unorganised sector, and assure a secure future for their families in every respect. To fully empower women politically, educationally, economically and legally. To provide for full equality of opportunity, particularly in education and employment for the Scheduled Castes, Scheduled Tribes, OBCs and religious minorities. To unleash the creative energies of our entrepreneurs, businessmen, scientists, engineers and all other professionals and productive forces of society.'

442 Rs. 10401.86 cores were invested as part of the eleventh Five Year Plan to promote agricultural production (Planning Commission 2008)

ly good result with an average 8.33 percent Gross State Domestic Product growth[443] was realized, and the coalition party government focused on the low level of human development, particularly rural mass poverty and low public health. In effect, the UPA and the eleventh Five Year Plan changed the scope of public policy and dramatically increased the funding for public health (Rs. 6288.27 crores); however, other social assistance and insurance programmes – beside the NEGRA – were not the top priority of decision-makers (GoI 2006, Planning Commission 2008, Kohli 2012).

What was new is that the legislation under the '*Unorganized Sector Workers' Social Security Bill, 2007*' granted an unofficially employed worker the opportunity to obtain voluntary social insurance. Subsidies were provided by the central government, which contributes an additional sum for funding the insurance schemes. Furthermore, the central government issued two major social insurance schemes, namely the Aam Admi Bima Yojana (AABY) and the Health Insurance Scheme for Unorganized Sector BPL workers, 2007, which assured broader coverage of social security (Eleventh Five Year Plan 2008:152-53).

3.4.4.1 The NREGA and Social Assistance in India

An atypical tool for democratic developing countries is active labour market programmes to guarantee employment. In the 1970s the central government attempted to tackle the problem of insufficient social security coverage for unorganised workers in the Five Year Plans. Hundreds of ad hoc social security schemes and programs have been introduced since then. Nonetheless, the central government has 'failed to provide a comprehensive national scheme in order to protect 93% of its workforce' (Mridula Ghai 2007).[444] The roughly 370 million-strong labour force of unorganised workers contributes about 60 percent of the country's gross domestic product, yet the government has not designed an adequate national policy to provide social security to the majority of its labour force (Sakthivel and Joddar 2006, NCEUS 2007).

443 The Gross State Domestic Product growth surpassed the All India's GDP growth of 7.94 percent as well as the results of the former Five Year Plans (Plans Planning Commission 2008).

444 Sakthivel and Jodda (2006) estimate that up to 98 per cent of the unorganised workforce has not been covered by the national social security schemes.

In 1995 the government, despite changes to party coalitions, hastened the pace of public policy and expanded the overall objectives of the national security net. Various components of the national security net were designed and/or remodelled to tackle existing socio-economic realities. Although the output performance of the social security and assistance programs increased in terms of range and scope, the outcomes were modest. In response to the modest performance, the newly elected UPA focused on the low human development in the late 1990s and early 2000s. The UPA engaged in realizing the constitutional preamble and merged the existing social assistance programs to provide the *right to work*. At the same time, these developments and the inefficiency of the programmes[445] set in motion a critical evaluation in which the government appointed a commission to report on the situation of the working population in the unorganised sector (Nagaraj 2012a:36, Kohli 2012).

The Active Labour Market Programme or the 'Right to work'

In the last three decades the social security legislation has addressed the lack of social security, low human development, and unemployment, particularly youth unemployment in rural areas. In 1970 the legislature extended its formal objectives to reducing the economic deprivation of unorganised workers, especially in rural communities. Meeting the objective of producing adequate services and schemes to reduce economic vulnerability has been a constant challenge for every newly elected government.

Before the 1990s the majority of social assistance programs had an ad-hoc character and suffered insufficient financial and administrative resources. The mid- to late-1990s, when the government formulated, approved and implemented various national social security and assistance programs for the poor population, were groundbreaking for the field of social security.

In the early and mid 2000s the main objective did not transpire into reality. Both coalition governments, the BJP and the UPA, engaged in a constant remodelling and merging of existing social security programs and schemes to achieve the goal of a sharp increase in coverage. Consequent-

445 The issue of administrative inefficiency, missing target-group identification, corruption, as well as fraud was discussed throughout the study (Kohli 2012).

ly, in the 2000s the legislature announced various new programs which were either renamed or combined former schemes under a new name (Sülzer 2008, Sen and Rajasekhar 2012: 113, Mitra 2014).

The attempt to provide security for the rural poor population was also an objective. In 1999 the legislature passed the Sampoorna Grameen Rozgar Yojana (SGRY)—the Universal Rural Employment Programme in English—which was set up on nation-wide level in 2001. What is interesting is that the SGRY marks a new era of social security policymaking and was a combination of two former programs: the Employment Assurance Scheme (EAS) and Jawahar Gram Samridhi Yojana (JGSY).

National-level coordination and consolidation of the various programs and schemes continued and in December 2004 the legislature passed the *National Rural Employment Bill* and the resulting Act (NREGA). Under the umbrella of the NREGA the *National Rural Employment Guarantee Scheme* (NREGS) was instantiated in November 2005 and available to recipients in February 2006.[446] The NREGS attempts to realize the constitutional social rights of the citizen and the stated 'right to work' (article 41; see subsection 6.7.2.2). The state has assumed the legal responsibility to guarantee 125 days (100 days until 2007) of unskilled manual work per rural household and job seeker. Therefore the Act represents a typical social assistance program in its range and focus on BPL households.[447] Moreover, the second component of the NREGA is a watershed for social security politics in India. It is the major consolidation of the various former ad hoc versions of the nation-wide wage employment schemes of the last three decades (Nagaraj 2012a:55-59).

In addition, the ambition of the program is to cope with the traditional problem of rural poverty, unemployment and livelihood security of vulnerable households. In the period of the eleventh Five Year Plan (2008:192) the wage rate was raised to Rs. 121 per day and the programme created 143.65 crore paid days of employment. In the formulation of the eleventh Five Year Plan the decision-makers funded Rs.17342.40 crores for the NEGRA to improve the number of beneficiaries, paid benefits and length of the service. 'The unprecedented commitment of financial resources is matched only by its imaginative architecture that promises a

446 Beginning with the 200 poorest rural districts the scheme was constantly expanded to cover nearly all rural areas until 2008 (Nagaraj 2012a:47-49).

447 The NREGA, accordingly to the WTO (2010), ranks among the most powerful initiatives ever undertaken to transform rural livelihoods in India.

radically fresh programme of rural development' (Ambasta, Shankar and Shah 2008a:49).

3.4.4.2 Initiatives to improve the Social Security of unorganised Workers

Another element of the battle against deprivation is the attempt to improve social security coverage for unorganised workers. The central government issued two major programs to achieve such coverage. In the following section, the features and characteristics of these two schemes are presented.

Bima Yojana – the flagship scheme and its problems

The *Rashtriya Swasthaya Bima Yojana* (RSBY), or officially the '*Health Insurance Scheme for Unorganized Sector BPL Workers, 2007*' was hailed as 'one of the best health insurance schemes around the globe' by the World Bank and the United Nations (Hindu 2014b). The RSBY was proclaimed as the flagship of the UPA's social security provision program in response to the lack of social insurance in cases of illness for BPL households that earn only Rs. 30,000 per family per year. RSBY's benefits cover '(i) cashless attendance to all covered ailments; (ii) hospitalization expenses, taking care of most common illnesses; (iii) all pre-existing diseases to be covered; (iv) transportation costs subject to prescribed limits payable to the beneficiary. Flexibility is provided to the States to add to the benefits by meeting the additional premium requirements from their own resources. State governments would decide the Implementing Agency and also bear the administrative costs' (Planning Commission 2008:153-154).

It is worth noting that the RSBY is a pioneering project in the sense that it relys on digital smart cards to cover the out-of-pocket health care costs of its recipients.[448] Despite the introduction of biometrical smart cards to

---

448 Entitlements are administered through smart cards issued by the implementing agency covering the out-of-pocket health costs. The cost of a smart card is subsidised by the central government and the beneficiary is only required to pay Rs. 30 per annum as a registration and/or renewal fee. The prescribed premium of Rs. 750 per member/family is split between the central and the state government to a ratio of 75:25.

tackle the issue of fraud, the problems of the RSBY are linked to slow administration, technical issues and the missing cooperation of state and private institutions. Smart card technology is producing its own problems despite solving others. Distribution of the smart card is lagging behind schedule (e.g. in Maharashtra only 38 percent of recipients have been handed a smart card) (Hindu 2011, Rajasekhar et al. 2011). Another issue is the fact the hospitals are ill-equipped to manage the new technology as well as the administrative issues of reimbursing the out-of-pocket costs (Rajasekhar et al. 2011:63). Another structural issue is that most private or even state-funded health care facilities do not accept the smart card (Hindu 2011, Rajasekhar et al. 2011:61-62).[449]

What should be kept in mind is that the RSBY's success comes with a high price or a specific financial burden for the central government, which absorbs over 75 percent of the costs (Rajasekhar et al. 2011). Although in the eleventh Five Year Plan the costs for the scheme are said to be at least Rs. 7078.25 crore, the estimated budget far from covers the actual costs of the scheme. The RSBY was designed to overcome the typical low coverage and funding problems of former programs and attempts to address the medical demands of BPL households of 6 crore families over the five years (1.2 crore per annum) (Planning Commission 2008, Eleventh Five Year Plan 2008).[450] Shortly after the introduction of the scheme in 2008 the UPA as well as non-UPA governed union states took it over. Four union states have achieved coverage for 75 percent of their BPL households and another six union states reached at least 60 percent coverage (Hindu 201). The miscalculation was a result of a failure to correctly estimate demand and costs (Hindu 2011, Rajasekhar et al. 2011:63).

The RSBY has the theoretical potential to be the flagship of social security provision in India in its attempt to reduce the economic uncertainties of the 'poor'. However, at the moment the potential of the RSBY is limited by various problems prevalent in Indian social security programs: inefficient administration, fraud problems, missing cooperation between private and state institutions, as well as the 'childhood disease' of modern smart card technology (Rajasekhar et al. 2011:60-62).

---

449 In a survey of 39 hospitals in Karnataka, nine did not treat any RSBY recipient at all and the other 20 did not treat more than 10 each (Rajasekhar et al. 2011:61).

450 In 2011 the government announced that the RSBY aims to reach 60 million families, amounting to 300 million individuals by 2013.

Aam Admi Bima Yojana

The *Aam Admi Bima Yojana* (AABY) is a target group social life insurance scheme under the umbrella of the new legislation for unorganised rural workers who are occupationally employed—such as *beedi* workers, fishermen, and plantation workers—as well as for rural households (Eleventh Five Year Plan 2008:153-154, MoF 2013).[451]

Following the commitment to more social security the UPA designed the AABY as a heavily subsidised scheme which requires no contribution by the beneficiary.[452] Contrary to the RSBY, the AABY's 'bottom-down approach' could not overcome the typical problem of low participation due to missing information on potential recipients (MoF 2013).[453]

What stands out in the 'bottom-up' approach is that the enrolment of beneficiaries was handed to NGOs and local state government entities with the introduction of a BPL card for recipients, similar to the RSBY. Contemporary social security pluralism is generally to expected to enhance the effectiveness of the schemes; however, social security provision in India and participation in national schemes have not been very well coordinated and marketed, and have suffered low participation rates. Accordingly, the AABY illustrates the drastic attempt of the government to pass the responsibility for administration to the LIC and the responsibility for enrolment to NGOs and state entities,[454] which has a positive effect on

451 AABY insures the head of the family or an earning member of the family for rural landless households whose earners are working-aged (18 to 59 years). The insurance grants Rs. 75,000 in cases of employment-related death or permanent disability. For partial disability due to employment-related accidents the beneficiary gains a lump sum of Rs. 37,500 and survivors earn Rs. 30,000 in cases of natural death. Also the scheme has a provision for the payment of a scholarship of Rs. 300 per quarter per child and up to two children studying from 9th to 12th standard (Eleventh Five Year Plan 2008:153).

452 50 percent of the premium cost of Rs. 200 per annum per person is contributed by the central and the state governments in a ratio of 50:50

453 Officially it is expected 'that in the first year approx. 70 to 80 lakh of rural landless households would be covered under the scheme requiring an expenditure of Rs 70–80 crore by the Central government towards its share of 50% premium. With an 8% per annum return expected on the Rs 1000 crore fund, the amount would be sufficient to meet the liability of premium payment' (Planning Commission 2008:153).

454 The LIC has the responsibility of managing both of the funds, the first one of Rs. 1000 crore for meeting the liability and a second one of Rs. 40 crore to cover

the financial costs of the day-to-day administration of the scheme (MoF 2013:12).

3.4.5 Welfare Regime with Indian Characteristics

India has produced a unique welfare system in recent decades and thus cannot be easily categorized using the common ideal types. Since independence India has witnessed various 'critical junctures' and has adapted its social security provisions to political, social and economic realities (Rothermund 1993:30-34, Nagaraj 2012a:32-33). In effect, the welfare regime and social security provision in India has not followed a straightforward policy trajectory but a unique path shaped by political, economic and demographic experiences (Sen and Rajasekhar 2012: 97, Kohli 2012:198).[455]

In the first period (1947-1977) India embarked on what was, for a South Asian autocracy, a typical welfare regime in which the state mainly focused on providing welfare to the urban working-aged population. The INC government under the leadership of Nehru strategically used the *mixed economy* policy, central planning and urban-focused public policy to accelerate industrialization, modernization and urbanisation processes (Swamy 2010).[456]

Table 18: India's welfare categorisation

Dominating welfare regime characteristic	State's role in welfare	Dominant locus of solidartiy	Dominant mode of solidarity	Degree of decommodifications
NIC/conservative	Low/subsidary	Family	corporatism, formal workers, family	low
social-democratic	Medium	Family/State	universal	low

the costs for the additional scholarships (Planning Commission 2008:152-153). The fund can cover up to 333000 children of the beneficiaries (Planning Commission 2008:153)

455 In the following section, only a short overview of the social security periods is provided. An indepth investigation of the time periods, policy changes, and social security provisions is conducted later.

456 The '*mixed economy*' as a feature of the so-called '*Nehruism*' (1947-1961) has been discussed by numerous scholars (Brass 1994, Kohli 1999).

Liberal	Low	Family/Market	individual	low
conservative/ social-democrat-ic	Medium/ subsidary	Family/State	universal, family, kinship	low

Source: Author's own table[457]

Accordingly, the overall engagement of the state in welfare has been low and the *dominant locus of solidarity* for the majority of the Indian population outside the formal sector has been the family and kinship (Nagaraja 2000, Kohli 2012). India's welfare regime and clear commitment, by Prime Minister Nehru to employees in the formal urban industrialized sector, has produced a slightly 'discriminating' welfare regime in favour of the urban working-aged population and a low degree of *decommodificaton* (Nayar 1989).[458] In the second period (1977-1991), Indira Gandhi initiated radical policy changes in an attempt to provide universal undiscriminating social security for all segments of society.[459] In the changing political climate the state increased its role as the *dominant locus of solidarity* (Kothari 1970, Rudolph and Rudolph 1987).[460] Under Gandhi's leadership the re-elected INC government paid attention to the stagnating economic growth and missing social security for the poorer segment of society. The Indian government opted for a *social democratic* welfare regime by expanding existing social assistance programmes for poor people. But the limited state capacity could not close the gap between policy objectives and outcomes. The degree of *decommodification* remained low and the family remained the main contributor of welfare for the individual (Esping Andersen 1990:85). In the following years, the assumed economic growth rate and trickle-down effect could not be realized and the social security politics initiative could not achieve the rapid improvement of social coverage or overcome the problems of the ad hoc character of the social policy

457 Categories taken over by Kersbergen and Becker's (2002:197) and Esping-Andersen (1999:85) based upon Esping-Andersen's cluster analysis (1990).

458 For a critical review of Nehru's one-sighted social policy making and missing reforms see Sen and Rajasekhar (2012) article and critical evaluation of policy trajectories.

459 See also N.P. Dhar, cit. op.

460 Indira Gandhi's ambition to build a typical social democratic welfare regime with universal social security and socialization of risks (Esping-Andersen 1999:79, Wagner 2006:119-120).

schemes and overburdened administrative capacity (Kothari 1970, Kohli 1987, 1989).

The third period (1991–2004) is closely linked to partial liberalization and its socio-economic as well as political implications, which marked a new era for India's overall development. The changing party coalition governments[461] began to design and reconfigure the existing social policies to explicitly target the BPL households, but economic reforms[462] had priority (Sülzer 2008:214-17). In the early and mid 1990s the political weight and fate of the '*inclusive growth*' or '*invisible hand of the market*' limited the range and scope of poverty reduction measurements and resulted in a low degree of *decommodification* (Kohli 1999, Nagaraj 2000, 2012a:36).

Consequently, the state reduced its role as contributor of welfare, with the *dominant locus of solidarity* remaining in the hands of the family as well as shifting to the market due to increasing urbanisation and the slow break-up of the traditional family system (Sülzer 2008, Chibber 2012). In the early 2000s it became obvious that the *inclusive growth* strategy could improve low human development and inequality (Suryanarayana 1995).

The last period (2004–2009) is dominated by the legislation of the UPA and the enactment of the eleventh Five Year Plan to carry through the 'discriminating' universal social security system with minimal benefits (Planning Commission 2008). Undeniably, the state increased its role as a contributor of welfare by enacting various newly designed social security schemes, programmes, and legislation. In addition to the political commitment, an impetus for the increasing attention was the report of the NCEUS[463], founded in 2004, with the policy advice by the Labour Ministry on grievance-limited coverage of social security producing a general understanding of the necessity of deep reforms to expand limited coverage for the rural population and those employed in the informal sector

461 Since 1989 the BJP government has been consistently re-elected. The main reason for its enjoyment of electoral support has been the military success against Pakistan in Kargil (Wagner 2006:114).

462 In the late 1980s India experienced significant economic and financial challenges. The low productivity, stagnating growth, inefficiency of central planning, and financial debts produced significant external and domestic pressure for economic structural reforms in the 1990s.

463 The official report was published in 2007 and gave concrete policy suggestions for addressing the lack of social security and poor working conditions in the *unorganized sector* (NCEUS 2007).

(NCEUS 2006, 2007, Planning Commission 2007). Following the new agenda the UPA enacted the *National Rural Employment Guarantee Act* in 2004 and the *Unorganized Sector Workers Social Security Bill* in 2007, which marked a new era in social policymaking in India. For the first time the central government carried through social security legislation which focused on the 'unorganised' sector's employees and rural population (Chibber 2012).

The unique development of India's welfare regime[464] illustrates the limitation of typologies and highlights the relevance of an indepth descriptive perspective for capturing the country-specific features of social security provision over time. In the twenty-first century the Indian state attempted a 'socialization' of socio-economic uncertainties by providing tax-financed social pensions (Sülzer 2008, ILO 2015). These introduced discriminating target-grouped schemes aimed at providing coverage for the roughly 75 percent of the population living below 2 US $ a day.[465] The socio-economic-related outcomes of the legislation are moderate and the family represents the main pillar of social and economic support for most elderly people in India (Ambrasta 2008b).

Characteristic of the mixed character of the Indian welfare regime is the paradoxical relationship between the formal and informal sectors and employment-related social security. On the one hand formal employees can rely on well-designed and well-funded social security schemes and programmes. Even the decline of the state's former role as dominant employer in the industrial sector given the liberal political context that has prevailed since the early 1990s has not altered the traditional state's function as the main contributor to welfare, health and pension schemes (Rothermund 1993:72, Jenkins 1999, Wagner 2006).[466] The ambitious legislation represented by the *Unorganized Sector Workers Social Security Bill, 2007* represents a milestone in improving social security in the unformal sector, but the outcomes have been modest (ILO 2015).

---

464 For the categorisation of welfare regimes and their specific features see Esping-Anderson's (1990) cluster analysis and narrow definition, which were discussed earlier.

465 See the descriptive introductory section of the chapter (table 1, 2 and 3).

466 The continuity of social security politics was discussed in the historical-descriptive case studies in Chapter 3 of the study, which offered more indepth insight into policymaking.

By 1991, the liberal policy commitment of the central government had produced business-friendly conditions for the growth of private-owned enterprises (Masilamani 1995, Jenkins 1999). At the national level the liberal reforms to the labour market accelerated a partial decentralization of wage-bargaining mechanisms. New labour contracts, decentralisation of the labour market, and skyrocketing numbers of low-wage employment were accomplished through a low degree of *decommodification.*[467] Rather than place the state in charge of the labour market, the deep structural reforms and passive union federations accelerated the ongoing decentralisation of industrial relations in the private sector (Sharma 2006, Das 2011). Industrial relations in India reflect the hybrid character of the production regime by combining liberal and conservative features.[468] Although India's private economy the bargaining mechanisms are highly decentralised —combining low union coverage with the existence of independent enterprise unions in the private sector—the remaining state-owned enterprises and traditional manufacturing branches opposed any attempts at decentralisation (Swamy 2011). Traditional, strong-rooted unionism in the formal sector is not exclusively limited to state-owned entities but can also be found in various traditional manufacturing industries; the most prominent exceptions are the Tata enterprise group and cigarette production (Masilamani 1995, Verma et al 1999, Das 2011).

3.5 Comments on the historical descriptive Perspective

Taken together, the various aspects of the historical-descriptive investigation suggest that similar historical periods of social security politics can be curved out in China and India during the time period in question. Undeniably the policymaking in both countries during these periods are marked by differences in the range, scope and goals of social security politics. What both share in common are similar challenges concerning institutional performance and state capacity to provide adequate social security for rural and urban populations in times of rapid socio-economic change. The Indian case is instructive for the relevance of policy trajectories. Similar to the Chinese case, evidence seem to suggest that strong path dependency

467 Liberal welfare regimes tend to exercise low levels of decommodification (Esping-Andersen 1990).

468 This topic will be discussed later in detail.

has sub-optimal outcomes in terms of adapation potential. Long-term social security schemes (e.g. the PDS) have been plagued by limited scope, range and target-group identification as well as by internal and external program deficits concerning access and/or fraud. Another similarity to the Chinese case is the issue of decentralisation, low priority for social security, as well as a missing coherent national strategy. In particular, program concurrency with other social security schemes due to limited cooperation of national and state administration has negatively affected policy performance. Furthermore, the decentralisation of social security provision has widened intercountry differences and produced a discriminating character with respect to the position of the beneficiary.

Yet, parallel to China, in 2004 the political appetite for providing social security increased. The UPD government coalition continued and even improved the provision of social pensions for the elderly as well as 'right to work' legislation and the NEGRA. The NEGRA alone consumes one percent of the GDP. But the overall low priority of social security, the persistently inadequate funding in the Five Year plans, as well as the lack of a coherent strategy signal that India has a long way to go.

IV. Economical-descriptive Approach

The classic socio-economic and socio-cultural approaches explore the social, cultural and economic determination for policy outcomes and state performance. Similar to the path-dependent approach, the empirical-descriptive approach[469] focuses on the economic development of a country and its implications for policy output. Contrary to actor-oriented approaches, the main factor for the development of the welfare state is not linked to involved actors but to necessary economic conditions. One of the most popular students of deterministic reasoning is Adolph Wagner. In his so-called Wagner's law (1911), or more correctly, the '*law of increasing state activity*,' he explains variations in policymaking accordingly to the macro-economic and socio-economic conditions of a country. According to Wagner, economic development increases state revenues but at the same time requires the state to react to increasing societal demands for public goods.[470] The persisting relevance of Wagner's law has been empirically validated by various recent studies (Wilensky 1975, 1985, Barr 1993, Wagschal 1996, Schmidt 2000a).[471] In effect, his postulated law—grounded in empirical evidence on the industrialization process in Britain—links expanding state spending to the ongoing industrialisation and ur-

469 It is not surprisingly that in the 1960s and 1970s the economic-descriptive theoretical approach was often directly associated with Marxist theories related to Marx and Engels; however, historical-materialistic and other non-Marxist theoretical schools are engaged in the same theoretical line of reasoning (Schmidt 1993b:373). In these approaches state policymaking is directly related to social, economic or cultural processes (Schmidt 1993a:372). Structural economic processes such as industrialisation are seen as the main determinants, in addition to the economic growth and welfare level of a nation.

470 The assumption follows the theoretical logic of functional approaches to industrialisation and modernisation.

471 Accordingly, it is useful to distinguish between a 'hard' and 'soft' version of Wagner's law or the causal relationship between the two indicators. While the 'hard' version, in the context of this study, is defined as positively associated increase of economic growth and public expenditure, the 'soft' version is only an increase of public expenditure in the case of increasing economic growth rates.

banisation processes in the modern nations which produce the demand for state-provided welfare (Schmidt 2000a:24).[472].

Evidence strongly suggests the fact that higher economic productivity and living standards tend to produce a growing demand for collective goods and services (Scharpf 1976:13). Wilensky (1975) and other prominent scholars (Schmidt and Ostheim 2007:33) have identified a causal link between the economic development and welfare level of a country, resulting in the general thesis that the higher GDP per capita, the higher public policy expenditures (Wilensky and Turner 1987:384, Castles 1989:436-38).

Hypothesis 2a: *An increasing GDP has a positive effect on social security-related outputs and outcomes.*

Accordingly low levels of economic growth and a decline in national economic prosperity reduce the state's welfare expenditures. Lower taxes, demands for fiscal discipline, and expensive economic reforms have a direct impact on the state's fiscal resources, the level of welfare expenditures, and policy output legitimacy[473]. It should be noted that the implications of the assumed causal relationship between increasing economic growth and social expenditure has to be elaborated from a cross-national and historical perspective. As argued before, the USSR was an example of exploding social expenditure without the economic growth that is assumed to be necessary (Beyme 1980, Fukuyama 1992).

472 A point of departure is given by the functionalistic approaches in explaining the erosion of the traditional social security system, such as family and church, due to urbanisation. In addition, the state has taken over the role by responding to the growing societal demand of social security (Kerr 1960, Cutright 1965).

473 Low policy performance can result in social protests and uprisings (Huntington 1968, 1991). A prominent example of the interaction of low economic performance and political instability is the former USSR, as due to the financial deficit, low economic performance and high military spending the central government was unable to satisfy public demands for collective goods and social services, which resulted in social protests and a decline in the state's public support (Fukuyama 1992, Schmidt 1999b).

4.1 Elaboration of Wagner's Law in times of austerity

Nowadays there is little dispute that the balance of the state budget is an important variable when it comes to social expenditures, policy choices and the available liquidity of any state in the long run. The importance of economic resources and growth for the long-term social policy outputs of young democratic as well as autocratic regimes cannot be denied (Barr 1993, Beyme 1994, Wagschal 1996, Schmidt 2005).[474] It is undeniable that financial resources strongly affect the state budget in general and the available funds for social expenditure specifically. For this reason, Pierson has repeatedly stressed (1994, 1998 and 2001) the importance of financial resources for the modern welfare state. In his study '*Dismantling the Welfare State?*' (1994), he evaluated the increasing financial pressure of social services on state budgets. In effect, Pierson's (1996: 4-6, 164-65) '*new politics*' argument has a logical implication for variations in public policy outcomes: the state budget in times of austerity places constantly increasing financial burdens on existing social policies.[475]

The general character of the hypothesis has been criticised on theoretical and empirical levels (Siegel 2002). Siegel's (2002:91) demand for a modification of the argument has been fulfiled by Kittel and Obinger (2003). Kittel and Obinger stress the importance of the 1990s for supporting Pierson's hypothesis: 'In total, the evidence first suggests that the effect of politics on social expenditure is rather limited, and, second, tends to support the 'growth-to-limits' and new politics' perspectives more' (Kittel and Obinger 2003:20). Concerning both arguments, a 'soft' version of Wagner's law is assumed for India and China in regard to the financial pressure of not only existing social policy but also other policy fields, such as defence, security or economic reforms.[476] For India and China, a

474 Comparative studies of the variations in social policymaking and the relevance of economic performance can be found in Schmidt's comparative historical study of the former East and West Germany (1999, 2012).

475 It is argued that the ongoing expansion and increasing numbers of recipients of social welfare programs and schemes overburden state financial capacity and threaten overall liquidity. As a consequence austerity policymaking is indispensable for most governments and can no longer be attributed to the ruling dominant party (Pierson 1996:4 sp, 2001).

476 Moreover, as discussed before, ideology and path dependency also have a part to play in social security provision. Party lines, ideology, election promises, and lobbying by organised interests and coalition forces represent a dominant factor

soft version of the causal relationship is expected in regard to the traditionally limited link between national policy objectives and budget restrictions as well as the increasing '*problem*' pressure on left-leaning party governments for structural reforms in other policy fields, such as defence, infrastructure, energy and/or environment (Schmidt 1999a, 2005), particularly in the developing countries of China and India (The Economist 2014f/k/l/m).

A short sidenote on the methodological issue is required here. To test the hypothesis of austerity the time period since 2000 will be analysed due to the pragmatic shift in social/political behaviour in the late 1990s in both countries. Taking a limited timeframe into account is not as problematic as may be assumed by traditional studies on policy expenditure (Castles 1989, 1989, 2002). A short timeframe can also reveal relevant tendencies in public policy. Paul Pierson (1994:2-6), for example, has analysed selected periods such as the worldwide oil crisis in 1973 or the ruling period of a specific government in Britain and the USA[477]. Moreover, Kittel and Obinger (2003) have also stressed the relevance of the late 1990s and its changing dynamics, arguing that the 'most remarkable finding is that the effect of parties and institutional constraints break down in the 1990s' (Kittel and Obinger 2003:32).[478]

4.2 Economic Growth and institutional Causality

In his widely cited work on welfare states Wilensky (1975:56) announces that rapid 'rates of growth together with high revenue elasticity greatly in-

---

which shapes the decision-making, polity guidelines and the room to manoeuvre for ruling elites. Due to programmatic and ideological pressure the state has to maintain or expand high levels of public expenditure even in times of financial hardship. These attempts have not been restricted to former left-totalitarian regimes, such as the GDR, Czechoslovakia, Peru, Argentina or Cuba, but have also been witnessed in Britain and the USA in the 1980s (Schmidt 1998, Pierson 2001). Pierson's basic claim is underlined by Kirchgässner and Pommerehne (1997:20)—that financial resources are an explanatory variable to help us understand variations in policy outputs, which are often neglected in the analytic frameworks of comparative studies.

477 Pierson (1994) explores two cases: the non-conservative government under Margaret Thatcher in Britain and the Reaghan presidential period in the USA.

478 The assumed declining partisan effect on social policymaking will be discussed in Chapter 7.

crease the capacity of committed elites to collect and spend for welfare purposes.' The failure of the former Eastern European communist countries verifies his claim. As Wagner (1911) has pointed out, higher levels of economic development can be positively associated with higher levels of social expenditures.[479] Accordingly, economic growth can also compensate for the positive regime effect of democracies on social expenditure due to increasing state revenues and larger available financial resources for social expenditure in non-democracies (Wagschal 1996, Schmidt 2013:423). As mentioned before, democracies foster positive institutional effects, such as election cycles and participation, for the steady increase of social expenditure. But economic growth is not restricted to democracies per se. What is significant is that taking control variables into account, the regime effect is not distinctly visible any more (Schmidt 2005, Wurster 2011).[480]

Hypothesis 2b: *India's democracy has no comparative advantage in providing higher levels of economic growth.*

There may be no better evidence than using control variables for a closer look at the effects of regime types, such as the level of the state budget deficit. In his comparative study of 122 autocracies and democracies in 2009 Wurster (2011) empirically validated the fact that the level of the budget deficit is not restricted to democracies.

Last but not least, it is worth noting that the financial pressure of social security, social assistance and labour market schemes can also be outsourced by the state towards the individual and the market—i.e. by relying on public funding from individuals and employers (Bloom et al. 2002, M. Liu 2011). Liberal governments tend to promote the shift of responsibility for social security from the state towards the market/individual (Esping-Andersen 1990). Market-oriented social security schemes contributed entirely or mostly by the beneficiaries and employers significantly reduce constraints on the state budget. Publicly funded programmes and schemes can be realized without the state financial or even administrative contribu-

479 See Wilensky (1975) and/or Wagschal (1996).

480 Stephan Wurster's (2011) comparative study on the state budget deficit in 122 democracies and autocracies emphasises that the level of the budget deficit does not correspond to regime type, as the United States of America and Britain as well as the autocratic Egypt both had high budget deficits in 2009.

tion and expand the coverage of the market provided by social protection.[481]

4.3 Explanatory Power of the demographic Growth

Socio-cultural approaches emphasise demographic growth as a major determinant of the level of social welfare (Wilensky 1975, 1981). 'For this sixty-country sample, the primacy of economic level and its demographic and bureaucratic correlates is support for a convergence hypothesis; economic growth makes countries with contrasting cultural and political traditions more alike in their strategy of constructing the floor beneath which no one sinks' (Wilensky 1975:27).

Hypothesis 2c: *Rapid changes in demographic growth produce additional pressure on social security reforms and on social security provisions to adapt to new realities.*

Although the argument fits very well in comparing advanced and developing countries, the variations among similar 'advanced' countries cannot be adequately explored by relying solely on the demographic process as an explanatory variable (Schmidt 1993:374). Comparative studies have produced a critical evaluation of demographic growth as a causal determinant of the welfare level (Castles 1989, 1998)[482]. Furthermore, various comparative studies on left-totalitarian systems have produced the consensus that in *left-totalitarian* countries demographic pressure has a lower impact on policy choices (e.g. pension system) than it does in their democratic counterparts or so-called 'paradise for pensioners' (Beyme 1988, 1994, Pierson 1996, Schmidt 1999a/b, 2000a, Castles 2002).[483] It seems that in regard to

481 For instance the worsening environmental pollution of Chinese cities (The Economist 2014d) and India's own shortcomings in ensuring the energy supply (The Economist 2014a) are consuming a good share of the budget. Another lion's share is consumed by the expenditure for the defence and security forces of both countries (ADB 2012a/b and World Bank 2014).

482 In his study on the educational expenditures of the OECD countries, Castles rejects the postulated causality of demographic growth and welfare expenditures as a universal explanatory variable (Castles 1998:193 sp, 1999, 2002).

483 The positive regime effects of democratic constitutions, free and fair elections, as well as interest mediation systems for an increased participation of the 'aging'

the stated problem and the institutional-oriented approach, demographic growth needs to be handled as a control variable.

4.3.1 Economic Constraints on Social Security Policy Performance

In the last two decades India and China have achieved enormous economic growth rates. Since 2000 both countries represent the dominant economies in Asia and are labelled as BRIC states by the World Bank. The category includes four nations—Brazil, Russia, India and China—which have achieved the transformation of their domestic economies into so-called '*emerging markets*' (World Bank 2006, 2007, 2014). Undeniably, the lasting economic growth rate of India and China is closely related to the economic transformation spurred by partial liberalization. Compared to other developing countries which have undertaken full liberalization, India and China have achieved higher and more stable economic growth rates World Bank 2014, The Economist 2014d/l). In comparison India's modest structural reforms, excessive regulation, licensing system, missing structural reforms as well as administrative hurdles for foreign investors have taken their toll on long-term growth (Jenkins 1999, Kohli 2012, World Bank 2014, The Economist 2014d/k/l).[484]

segment of society in party politics has been previously discussed in the 'party-do-matter' section.

484 See '*doing business*' indicator (World Bank 2014), cit op.

Diagram 4: Gross Domestic Product per Capita

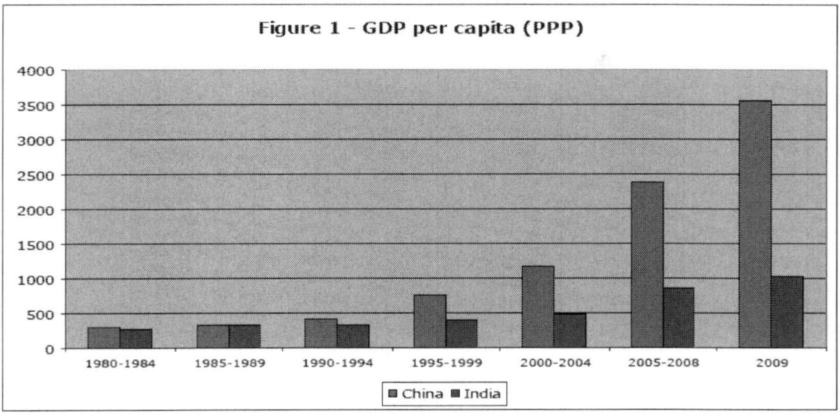

Source: IMF Database (2014)[486]

As a result, the Chinese and Indian growth rates of the real GDP per capita gradually caught up with the OECD countries in the period from 2000 to 2008; however, it is still roughly 20 percent below the average GDP per capita of the OECD (OECD 2007, 2010).

Table 19: Economical Data

Year	1990	2000	2004	2005	2006	2007	2008	2009
GDP growth (annual %)								
India	5.5	3.8	7.9	9.3	9.3	9.8	3.9	8.5
China	4.1	7.6	10.1	11.3	12.7	14.2	9.6	9.2
GDP per capita (constant 2005 US$)								
India	403.1	578.2	687.3	740.1	797.3	863.5	885.2	947.7
China	483.2	1,122.3	1,564.4	1,731.1	1,939.7	2,202.9	2,402.8	2,611.2
GDP per capita growth (annual %)								
India	3.4	2.1	6.3	7.7	7.7	8.3	2.5	7.1
China	2.5	6.8	9.4	10.7	12	13.6	9.1	8.7
GDP per capita, PPP (current international US$)								
India	1,173.9	2,063.0	2,669.0	2,966.3	3,293.5	3,661.7	3,827.1	4,129.2
China	1,006.6	2,864.1	4,345.5	4,962.9	5,731.8	6,682.2	7,431.0	8,137.6

Source: World Bank Database (2014)

486 www.imf.org/external/data.htm (2014-07-15)

As indicated in table 19 (see also table 46 and diagram 9), the constant and relatively high economic growth had an only marginal effect on the increase of public expenditures for social security and welfare in India and China. In the 2004 to 2009 the constant economic growth rates in excess of 8 percent resulted in a slow but also steady increase in social expenditures and the overall commitment of both central governments to improve their social security systems, particularly for the rural and poorer segments of society. In the following years, until 2008, India's economic growth rate jumped to 8.5 percent and even caught up with China's 8.7 percent in the same period (IMF 2014, World Bank 2007, 2008, 2014).[487] Interestingly, both governments, in opting to improve social security coverage, did not raise public expenditure proportional to the increase in government revenues (see table 46). The positive but relatively disproportionate growth of social security expenditures compared to the growth rate of the GDP and total government revenues—a soft version of Wagner's (1911) laws—can be diagnosed for India and China in recent decades, which illustrates the argument that policy- and budget-making are largely independent.

4.3.2 Budget Restrictions: Debts and Revenues

Certain conclusions can be drawn from the patterns indicated in the presentation of the data in the table '*GDP, expenditures, social security and debts*' (see table 46). The first indicator to be dealt with here concerns levels of debt. Following the conclusions of cross-national studies (Wurster 2013) the autocratic CRP has a tight fiscal policy and relatively low levels of foreign debt. In contrast, India has accumulated increasingly high levels of foreign debt. A consequence of increasing debt is often strict fiscal discipline, which both countries have witnessed—China in the late 1970s and India in the late 1980s. In both cases there seems to be no direct causality between fiscal debt and social expenditure in terms of percentage of the state budget.

487 India's labour market is steadily growing but the majority of workers are unskilled. At the moment India is compensating for the lack of innovation and technology, which will become an increasingly crucial challenge for the manufacturing sector in the coming years (The Economist 2013).

4.3.3 Budget Restrictions: Programm Concurrency

Another and related constraint on the percental expenditure of the state budget for social security is program concurrency with other policy fields. The funding of other state relevant policy fields reduces overall financial resources. In addition to education, public health, and infrastructure, another item of expense for the state budget is 'physical' security, including the military budget as well as the budget for internal security and law enforcement. High military expenditures limit the state's available resources for social expenditures and other policy fields (e.g. health, education, social security, and infrastructure).

A core function of the state is to protect its citizens. Regional concerns, historical experience, as well as state ambitions, size, and conflicts are all strong potential determinants of the state's internal and external security.[488] The military clashes and recent border skirmishes between India and Pakistan as well as India's high military spending to secure the vast territory and its borders undermine the common assumptions of the *democratic peace theory* for democracies. Schmidt suggests (1999a, 2000, 2005) that the *democratic peace theory* should be critically questioned in terms of the postulated 'peacefulness' of foreign politics and low military spending in Western democracies. Democracy, 'checks and balances' on the executive, and electoral pressure produce constraints on the ability and willingness of politicians to go to war; however, there are also other relevant factors, such as collective experiences as well as mutual and multilateral peace agreements. In particular the multilateral peace treaties, membership in the *North Atlantic Treaty Organization* (NATO), public condemnation of warfare, as well as the collective historical experience of Europe have virtually nullified the likelihood of an official military conflict between NATO members (Schmidt 1983, 1999a, 2003). This is not the case for all democratic nations. The military clashes between India and Pakistan as well as India and China in 1962[489], together with India's ambition to be-

488 Paul Pierson reminds the reader that the path-dependency approach can explain state expenditures generally—both in the sense of social *and* military expenditure (Pierson 2000).

489 The border issue of 1962 remains unresolved to this day. Despite the military defeat the Indian government has not officially given up its claim on the territory occupied by the Chinese military. Both governments have ignored the issue in foreign politics and focused on peaceful trade relations.

come a hegemonic power[490] and continuing member of the United Nations Security Council, promote a high level of military spending. India spends around 18 percent of the state's expenditures a year on military-related costs, including its nuclear weapons program[491]. In a comparative perspective the amount is relatively high compared to Western democracies such as France and Germany with only 4 to 5 percent. The United States of America also spends approximately 18 percent of its budget on military spending (World Bank 2014).[492]

4.4 Social Security Provision in Times of Global Economies

Although the students of Wagner's law mainly focus on domestic socio-economic variables, various scholars (Scharpf 1999a/b, Kurzer 1999) offer a more 'global' explanation of cross-national variations. Several characteristics mark the common understanding of globalisation in academic debates. It is worth mentioning at the outset that 'globalisation' is in most cases defined as economic globalisation. In her widely cited article on globalisation Ina Kerner (2004)[493] immediately turns to the economic aspects of globalisation and related theoretical assumptions before taking a look at its political and social dimensions. Classic studies on globalisation and welfare regimes have been conducted by David Cameron (1978) and Peter Katzenstein (1985). David Cameron (1978) has offered evidence of the causal linkage between increased economic openness and a growing public sector. Katzenstein's (1985:200) analysis arrives at the conclusion that smaller countries tend to set up corporate arrangements to compensate

---

490 The issue of naval security has recently gained new attention by the Indian government, which seeks to modernize its navy (Shöttli 2014).

491 The Indian nuclear weapons program has a long tradition dating back to the 1970s and the first testing in 1974. In 1998 India successfully tested its own prototype – code named Operation *Shakti* – which was shortly followed by Pakistan's nuclear weapons test. In subsequent years Indian scientists developed and improved the intercontinental ballistic missile (Rothermund 1993:103-106). In 2013 the newest developed and successfully tested Agni-7 missile expanded the operational range of India's nuclear weapons to reach as far as Beijing.

492 For an investigation of the public expenditure of the OECD countries, the online database of the World Bank (2014) has been used (2014-04-03).

493 Kerner, Ina. 2004. 'Globalisierung', in Gerhard Göhler, Mattias Iser and ibid (eds.), *Politische Theorie. 22 umkämpfte Begriffe zur Einführung*, 190-208. Wiesbaden: VS Verlag für Sozialwissenschaften / UTB.

for the global effects on their domestic economies, which these countries cannot affect in turn due to their minimal influence on the global market. Still, Katzenstein (1985: 207) himself remarks that his findings cannot be generalised and 'cannot apply the 'lessons' of the small European states for the simple reason that we cannot remake our history.' Paul Pierson (1996) touches on the controversial topic and argues that 'it is important to recognize the linkages between international and domestic developments… such links are likely to be more modest, complex and bi-directional than is commonly suggested.'[494]

What can be learned from the globalisation debate? A major contribution is provided by Gourevitch's (1978) '*The Second Image Reversed: The International Sources of Domestic Politics*' in which he articulates the two dominant questions of how far globalisation is affecting the international system and domestic decision-making or policies. Concerning the international system Gourevitch (1978:911) remarks that it is 'not only a consequence of domestic politics and structures but a cause of them. Economic relations and military pressures constrain an entire range of domestic behaviors, from policy decisions to political forms.' Of the second, and for the study more interesting, question of the impact of globalisation on domestic policymaking, he writes that 'however compelling external pressures may be, they are unlikely to be fully determining, save for the case of outright occupation. Some leeway of response to pressure is always possible, at least conceptually. The choice of response therefore requires explanation' (Gourevitch 1978: 911). To sum up, Gourevitch (1978:883f and 896) comes to the conclusion—which is mainly supported by a cohesive body of literature (Swank 2001, 2002 Schwarz 2001)—that the globalisation and its implications cannot really be measured.

Hypothesis 2d: *A higher level of trade openness has no measureable effects on social security performance.*

Moreover, the popular thesis that trade openness promotes the expansion of the welfare state (Garret et al. 1998) has recently been critically evaluated in the empirical studies conducted by Herman Schwartz (2001) and

494 It is worth noting that the degree of trade openness as well as the resulting liability for external shocks of the domestic economy are taken into account as a control variable.

Torben Iversen (2001).[495] Meanwhile, a broad consensus in the recent welfare literature argues that the effects of globalisation have only a limited impact on social policy because, it is argued, the effect is mediated by national arrangements (Garret and Lange 1995, Kitschelt et al. 1999) or the attributed pressure on the welfare state are not effects of globalisation in the first place (Pierson 2001, Iversen 2001).

Changes in the global market economy are important to explain variations in the domestic economy: external shocks, interdependent relations, as well as global players can affect the domestic labour market and economic conditions.

Diagram 5: Degree of Trade Openness

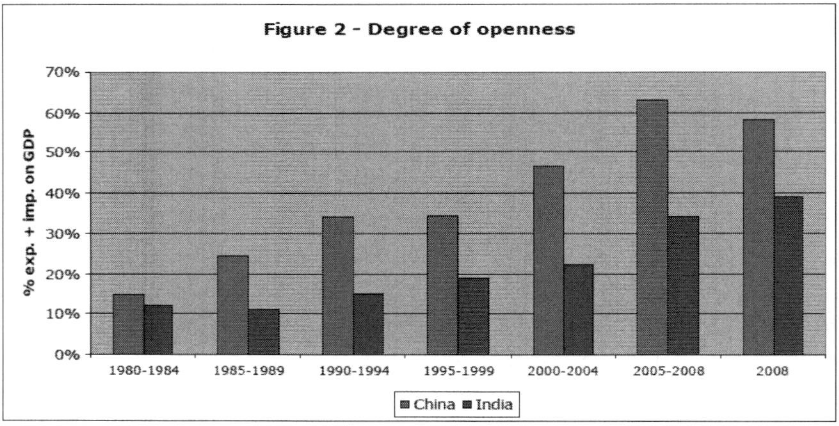

Source: IMF Database (2014)

With regard to the export/import ratio India has been ranked 139 of 175 countries in 2007/2008[496]. China has managed to be 38th worldwide. (OECD 2010b, Swamy 2010:280). India's low ranking has to do with the

495 In his empirical research on 18 OECD countries Schwartz concludes that 'trade has no statistically significant effect on [welfare] spending' (2001:64). Iversen's (2001) empirical findings seem to validate the assumptions of Schwartz.

496 Despite the annual GDP growth rate decline from 2007 to 2008 from 9.3 to 6.7 in India and from 14.2 to 9.6 in China, the effects on the total expenditure and spending for social security are marginal due to the fact, as argued throughout the study, public expenditure and budget issues are treated separately during decision-making processes (Appendix, table 46).

focus of its industry on the domestic market, which is a legacy of the pre-liberalization era. In contrast China successfully implemented market-oriented reforms in 1978, which produced a healthy international trade relationship with foreign nations. India's export/import ratio also suffers from the inability to enforce contracts effectively. Of 175 countries India was ranked 174 in 2006 regarding the juridical chances of economic actors enforcing contracts and services. China was ranked 63rd worldwide (World Bank 2011b).

Table 20: KOF (1980-2009)

	1980	1985	1990	1995	2000	2004	2005	2006	2007	2008	2009
China	20.0	23.28	34.24	41.87	52.18	59.13	61.32	60.42	61.34	60.36	60.77
India	25.96	26.72	29.67	36.93	43.98	46.82	48.59	49.71	50.9	50.39	50.34

Source: KOF (2014)[497]

As indicated by the KOF index, China has achieved relatively higher trade openness than India. The empirical results validate the general hypothesis that *trade openness* positively affects economic growth (Frankel and Romer 1999, Bensidoun et al. 2009). China's higher level of economic growth seems to correlate with its increased trade openness compared to India.[498]

India and China are no exceptions, as indicated in table 20 (and diagram 4); the global crisis and recession in 2007/2008 has taken its toll on the export/import ratio and the GDP. However, a high degree of trade openness also implies a risk of high vulnerability from external shocks, such global financial crises or recessions. As the IMF Report (2009) argues, the spill-over effects from the global crisis have taken a toll on the performance of Asian economies due to their increased integration into the global market. The same point has been stressed by the Chinese state council adviser Quansheng (cited by Swamy 2010:156), who mentioned at a forum in Beijing in December 2008 that the loss of roughly 6.8 million

497 See the online data base provided at http://www.kof.ethz.ch/de (2014-07-15).

498 As it is generally agreed that both variables are positively associated with each other, the role and effect of institutions on long-term economic development and trade openness is far more complex (Alcalà, F. and Ciccone, A. 2004. 'Trade and Productivity', *Quarterly Journal of Economics*, May 2004).

jobs can be attributed to the effects of the international financial crisis in 2007 on the domestic economy.

4.4.1 Changing Employment Situation, Trade Openness and Social Security

Economic transition and increasing trade openness have constantly shifted labour demand structures. It becomes distinctly visible in the decline of the traditional agrarian sector in both developing countries.

Table 21A: Sectoral composition of GDP (1980-2006)

	Year	1980	1990	2000	2006
Agriculture					
	China	30.1	27	14.8	12.5
	India	40	32	24	17
Industry					
	China	48.5	41.6	45.9	47.3
	India	24	27	27	28
Service					
	China	21.4	31.3	39.3	40.3
	India	37	44	49	55

Source: various sources[499]

Table 21B: Employment structure and sectors

		2000	2005	2009
India				
	Labour force (million)	345.9	380.8	438.9
	Agriculture	201.8	207.1	227.6
	Industry	54.9	69.4	92
	Services	79.9	92.4	108.3
China				
	Labour force (million)	739.8	761.2	775.1

499 Marelli, E. and Signorelli, M.2011. 'China and India: Openness, Trade and Effects on Economic Growth', *The European Journal of Comparative Economics*, vol. 8, no. 1: 129-154 and Amighini, A. and Chiarlone, S. 2007. 'La trasformazione dell'economia cinese: proprietà delle imprese e modello di specializzazione', *Economia e Politica Industriale*, (3):185-200.

	2000	2005	2009
Agriculture	360.4	334.4	288.9
Industry	162.2	177.7	210.8
Services	198.2	234.4	258.6

Source: Asian Development Bank (2012a, b)

The major changes occurred in the agrarian sector (see table 21a/b), with its decreasing demand for low-skilled and cheap workers. In both countries the sectoral composition of the GDP dropped in the agrarian sector from 40 percent in India and 30 percent in China to only 17 percent in India and 12 percent in China in the period from 1980 to 2005.[500]

A consequence is the migration of the rural population into urban areas in China and India and the employment shift from the agrarian to the service sector, as indicated by the increasing composition of the sectoral GDP (Valli and Saccone 2009).[501]. In contrast to most developed countries India and China still rely on a strong industrial sector, which is a reason why labour unions have to be taken seriously (Iversen and Wren 1998). As a consequence, the shift in employment has direct implications for the requirement to adjust the traditional employment-related social security to the new contract and employment situation (Sharma 2006, Xiahua News Agency 2006a).

4.5 Economical, Social and Demographic Factors

Generally speaking, economic performance matters for social policy outcomes and the relative size of the state budget. Widely cited is Adolph Wagner's (1911) observation on the correlation of increasing economic growth and expanding social expenditures, which became known as Wagner's law in the literature.

In the 1960s North American scholars took up the issue to explain interstate differences of social politics and policy outcomes across North American states. The vast literature on the issue produced evidence of the

500 See also the table 46 on the expenditures in the Appendix II.

501 Valli and Saccone (2009) investigated the economic development of India and China as well as the implications for the sectoral shift in labour according to a "*Fordian perspective.*"

relevance of economic performance and dismissed the partisan effect (Dawson and Robinson 1963, Dye 1966).[502]

An internationally influential account has been Wilensky's landmark study '*The Welfare State and Equality*' in which he concludes, based on the data of sixty countries, that 'the primacy of economic level and its demographic and bureaucratic correlates is support for a convergence hypothesis; economic growth make countries … more alike in their strategy of constructing the floor beneath which no one sinks.'[503] In this line of reasoning, the decline of the Golden Age of welfare states in Western countries seems to prove the missing autonomy of political actors and the constraints of economic growth on social politics (Boix 1998, Scharpf 1997, Rhodes 1997).[504] The austerity politics of modern industrial countries in the 1990s seem to validate the assumption of the economic growth as a main determinant in most countries and has encouraged the debate on the 'new politics of the welfare state' (Pierson 1994, 1998, 2001). As a consequence, in the 1990s most of the 'old' welfare states struggled to finance increasing public expenditures and attempted to some extend fiscal discipline in battling such expenditures. Moreover, the situation of modern states reflects decision-makers' dilemma of choosing between public demand for public goods and unpopular fiscal discipline. As illustrated, cutbacks in social expenditure are unpopular measures that can easily erode electoral or political support; even for the Chinese *ideocracy*[505] the legitimacy of social policy output is an issue. Accordingly, one needs to consider that decision makers are driven by personal and ideological ambitions than rational reasoning. Another issue is the potential cost explosion of expenditures for policy schemes, such as pension programmes.

---

502 Early comparative studies in which the authors compared democratic and communist countries in terms of social policy performance came to the same conclusion (Pryor 1968).

503 A crucial aspect for the development of the welfare state, especially for authors such as Wilensky (1975), is population aging. An aging population increases the political demand for expansion of the welfare state. But these demands are more "relevant in democratic than in communistic systems" (Castles 2002:220). In addition, the primary focus will be on the economic variable to explain cross-national variations between China and India.

504 In his case study Boix (1998) provides empirical evidence of the decline of the assumed partisan effect of left-leaning governments on taxes and social spending.

505 See appendix I for a discussion on the concept of *ideocracy* by Kailitz (2009).

Kirchgässner and Pommerehne (1997:20) criticise the lack of most analytic frameworks to include budget restrictions to explain variations of public expenditure, because various countries have become victims of their own overambitious social policymaking and cost explosion.[506] Undeniably, economic considerations produce significant constraints on long-term social policymaking. Still, the 1990s and the fall of the USSR provide empirical evidence of the fact that economic performance matters and that social politics are not always sensitive to economic determinants. Comparative political scholars have repeatedly stressed the relevance of economic factors but at the same time a majority of these authors point out that the economic conditions are insufficient as a sole explanatory variable of cross-national variations (Castles 1987, Esping-Andersen 1985, 1990, Kersbergen and Becker 2002).

4.5.1 Demographic Change and Public Policy

A common accepted argument made by various prominent scholars, such as Wilensky (1975) and Pierson (1996, 2001), is that rather than globalization the expansion of living standards and life expediency increased the cost of public policy. The 'greying of the population' challenges the existing social security system and, as argued by Pierson (1998), produces powerful interest groups of pensioners. Not without reason are democratic countries often described as the 'paradise for pensioners' (Kersbergen 2002).

Socio-economic and socio-cultural approaches strongly suggest the importance of economic and demographic processes for policy choices, decisions and outcomes in addition to the variations in the political system.[507] A central premise of socio-cultural and socio-economic approaches is that demographic change reflects a crucial determinant of public policy.

---

506 The financial burdens of expanding social programs and schemes are limiting economic and policy performance in Venezuela and Cuba.

507 In modern states the GDP level is not an only indicator of the level of welfare spending. While social-democratic and Christian governments tend to increase welfare, other elected governments such as liberal ones believe in the free market and tend to provide minimal state welfare. The best example is the liberal welfare regime in the United States of America with a high GDP and relatively low level of welfare spending (Titmuss 1974:62, Pierson 1994:147).

In economic as well as demographic terms China and India are two of the most important countries in the world (Rustow 1960, The Economist 2014d). In 1975 the dependency ratio in China and India was around 1.3, which means that the actual working-age population (age 15 to 64) has been only modestly larger (0.3) than the non-working-age population or dependents. The United Nations Report (2005: xlv-xlvii)[508] predicted that in China the percentage of people over aged 60, which has been 10 percent of the total population, will be doubled by 2025. According to the projected demographic tendencies population growth will be negative in 2020. As a consequence, the working-age population will decline from 65 percent in 2000 to 62 percent in 2025 and 53 percent in 2050 with over 400 million elderly Chinese. Recent demographic developments and the one-child policy has sparked criticism by Chinese and international experts due to the fact that the ongoing process will lead to significant pressure on economic performance and the social security system (Bloom et al. 2005, Xinhuanet 2005).

Table 22: Population Aging

	Population 65+ (%)		**Proportion of population 65+ in total population (%)**		**Proportion of women 65+(%)**	
Year	2010	2050	2010	2050	2010	2050
World	100	100	8	16	56	55
More developed regions	37	22	16	26	59	55
Less developed ones	63	78	6	15	55	55
Asia	54	62	7	18	54	55
China	**21**	**22**	**8**	**24**	**52**	**54**
India	**12**	**16**	**5**	**14**	**53**	**54**
Europe	22	12	16	28	61	58
Africa	7	9	3	7	56	54

Source: ILO Report (2010a:55)

The majority of high-income countries have challenged by the pressure from demographic change (table 22). Overall percentage of older people

508 A revision of the 2004 published United Nation's report.

rose significantly in India and China in the last decades due to better living conditions. In particular, in China but also in India the increasing number of elderly people has resulted in an increasing attention for elderly protection in both countries. Contrary to China, India could rely on a higher proportion of younger people as a subset of the total population. The percentage of older people above the age of 60 was only 7.5 in 2000 and is estimated to rise much more slowly than in China. It is assumed that on the basis of the current tendencies only 12 percent of the total population in 2025 and 21 percent in 2050 will be above the age 60 (ILO 2010a). Another factor that has to be considered is the fertility ratio. Padmadas et al. (2005) stress the relevance of the fertility rate as a key indicator of demographic growth. India's population is still growing despite the policy attempts of the central government in the direction of family planning in the 1970s and 1990s (Padmadas et al., 2005).[509] However, the fertilisation ratio has constantly declined over the years from 5.4 between 1970 and 1980, 4.2 between 1985 and 1990, and to 3.1 between 2000 and 2005 (United Nations 2005). In 2005 the population growth was still positive and above the average replacement level of 2.1 births per woman.

In the 1970s the Chinese government launched the '*later, longer, fewer*' campaign which restricted family planning. Urban families are allowed to have two and rural families up to three children.[510]

509 The sterilisation program during the Emergency regime of Indira Gandhi (1975-77) could not produce any significant outcomes in its attempt to reduce the fertility rate. In 1996 the government followed another strategy in improving female education and health as well as family planning (Padmadas et al. 2005).

510 Exceptions were made for minorities or other cases.

Diagram 6: Fertility Rate

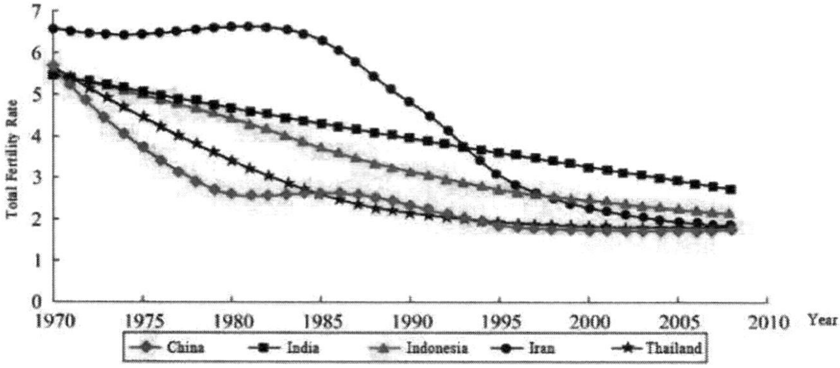

Source: Feng Wang. [2011] 2012. 'China's Demographic Transition in Comparison with Other Countries and the Gain and Loss of Demographic Dividend Background', in *China Development Report 2011/12: Demographic Changes and Policy Adjustment*, CDRF.

Compared to India, China's 'one-child policy' has been an effective (perhaps too effective) instrument for state-controlled fertility reduction (Xinhuanet 2005).[511] In effect, in 2000 the fertility rate dropped to 1.8 births per woman, below the replacement level of 2.1 births per woman (Sharping 2003).[512] In 1997 a special report in China conducted by the World Bank took up the issue and criticised the missing adaptation of the retirement age to increased life expectancy. The retirement age for males and females (see table 22) dates back to the time when the average life expectancy was only 50 years. In effect, the decline of the working-age population and increasing numbers of pensioners will challenge the public and economic policy performance in the next decade (World Bank 1997, WHO 2000).

Interestingly, while India can rely on a higher fertility ratio and a younger average population the same issues of retirement age as well as

511 At a forum on China's population and economy at Beijing University a general consensus was achieved on the necessity of relaxing the family planning policy as well as addressing the gender issue (Xinhuanet 2005).

512 Official figures published by the National Bureau of Statistics reported 1.22 births per woman; however, as Sharping notes, the number is relatively low because of the unreported cases of birth (2003).

missing pension coverage also challenge the Indian government in its performance (Heller 2006).[513] In her prominent article on the issue of pension schemes in Asia, Heller (2006) emphasised that both India and China are 'lagging' behind other Asian countries in providing adequate pensions, health insurance, and labour policies.

4.6 Comments on socio-economical Determinants

Let's return to the core question of the chapter: do the differences between India and China in the economic domain matter for institutional performance? In both cases a relative increase of social expenditure to the level of economic performance stated by Wagner's'soft' law can be validated in the period between 2001 and 2009. As argued by the Zöllner model, economic and demographic conditions seem to determine the state capacity to a decent degree. A major trend is the '*greying of the population*' and the provision of pensions in both contemporary welfare regimes. It seems that another key issue is programme concurrency (e.g. with defence and security). Traditionally, high expenditures limit the available resources for other policy subjects, such as social security. Last but not least, contrary to the earlier argument, the inquiry into the relationship between trade openness and social security provision seems to be valid. An increasing level of trade openness is a relevant factor for social security provision in various ways and has a positive effect on stuructral reforms and increasing expenditures.

513 Demographic changes are also challenging China and India. Lower birth rates and growing numbers of retiring people are challenging the pension and social insurance systems. Better living and health conditions as well as the one-child policy enhanced the age-related imbalance in the Chinese case. India is also affected by demographic changes and as a consequence the financial burdens of both nations of maintaining the welfare system are constantly increasing from year to year. For instance, at the end of the 1990s the average OECD country dedicated 70 to 80 percent of total social spending to pension and health (Kersberg and Becker 2002).

V. Social Security Provision, State Capacity and Regime Type

Does institutional performance involve institutional *causality*? In investigating the impact of institutional causalities on state capacity and institutional performance, a first step is to discern the difference that democracy (and non-democracy) makes for outcomes. To do so, the study uses Tocqueville's model on the assumed institutional causalities of public policy in democracies.

In his widely cited work '*Democracy in America*' Alexis de Tocqueville (1990) argues for the *positive advantages* of democracy based on his empirical and theoretical examination of the experiences of the young North American democracy. In his perspective the comparative advantage of democracy is mainly grounded in the fact that it tends to produce higher levels of *égalité des conditions* (egalitarian political and socio-economic conditions) for all citizens regardless social status, class and gender.[514] In his work Tocqueville (1990) implies that democratic governments tend to expand their public sector to provide higher levels of socio-economic equality for all citizens - regardless social status, class or gender.[515]

5.1 In Pursuit of Regime Type: General reflection

The development of the typology of regime types in political science dates back to ancient Greek. Most of scholars have turned their full attention to the typology of democracies[516] (Dahl 1971, 1989, 1998, Schumpeter 1972, Schmidt 2000a:404-6), leaving autocracies aside in their theoretical definitions and analyses. As mentioned earlier, regime type is used as the independent varable. Undeniably, regime type shapes the relationship of the

514 A sidenote is needed concerning Tocqueville's (1990) political attitude, which is not in favour of socialism or socialist democracy.

515 The logical assumption is based on the responsiveness of elected politicians. It should be mentioned that Toqueville does not argue for a '*classless*' society as a condition or goal of democracy (Daalder 2002).

516 See in particular Manfred G. Schmidt's chapter (2000a:404-8) which deals exclusively with the implications of democracy for a more sophisticated investigation of the different types of democracies.

legislature, executive, judiciary and the party-state-society, which produces constitutional constraints on the ability of policymakers to carry through their policies. Furthermore, regime type has a clear impact on overall social policy choices and the arsenal and character of state instruments. In the following section, a minimum definition of democracy[517] is provided as well as a '*ex negativo*' of the autocratic version (Schumpeter 1976, Sartori 1987)[518] in order to distinguish these two regime types from each other.

5.1.1 Defining Regime Types

Given the stated problem, a major challenge for the study is to produce an autocracy-democracy dichotomy for the comparative analysis and definition of both regime types. Phrased as a question, how do we compare and distinguish oranges and apples? Adam Prezworski and Henry Teune (1970:25) have tackled the sensitive topic and emphasised the need to move to a higher level of analysis to compare and distinguish both types. To accomplish this, the study uses a simplified definition of democracies not for the purpose of categorising and comparing different similar regime types to each other but in order to give an adequate working definition to examine the authoritarian Chinese system and the democratic Indian one together.

An investigation of the academic discussion of the nature of democracies and the existing diversity of various definitions is a useful starting point for formulating a simple working definition of democracy. Rather

---

517 In the tradition of Dahl (1971, 1998) and Schumpeter (1972) a substantial definition of democracy is used. It is worth noting that in the academic political literature there is a wide range of existing definitions from minimal to middle (Magaloni et al. 2013), and even broad ones (Freedom House 2014). Definitions and concepts of democracy are discussed at length in the methodological section of the study. For a start Robert Dahl's (1971, 1989, and 1998) minimum definition of democracy is used here. A democracy, accordingly to Dahl, demands universal suffrage and the right to run for public office; free and fair elections; observance of the right to free speech and protection to do so; the existence of and free access to alternative information; the undisputed right to form and to join relatively autonomous organizations, in particular political parties; responsiveness of the government to voters and government accountability regarding election outcomes and parliament (1998:38sp).

518 See the next paragraph.

than engaging in a full review of the literature (Huntington 1990, Dahl 1989, Daalder 2002), the study is restricted in scope to producing a simplified definition based on the dimension of political participation and competitive elections in which democracies stand out from all other regime types. As Wolfgang Merkel (2004:36-38) and colleagues (Collier and Adcock 1999:559, Møller, Muni and Skanning 2013:93) note, competitive elections are the '*condition sine qua non*' of democracies. Referring to the minimal definition of democracies [519] (1986, 1991), Przeworski offers the view that electoral competition offers an unpredictable variable for political parties; in democracies the 'outcomes are not known ex ante: each party does the best it can, then rolls the dice to see who will win. Democratization is an act of subjecting all interests to competition, of institutionalizing uncertainty' (Przeworksi 1991:14).

Giovanni Sartori (1987:205-206) maps one simple road to solving the autocracy-democracy dichotomy and defines autocracy as a political system vis-à-vis democracy. In his notion autocracy is 'an undisputed and hardly disputable good opposite of democracy' and 'democracy is non-autocracy, the exact contrary and indeed the precise contradictory of autocracy'[520].

Referring to the above stated minimal definition of democracy, Schumpeter points out in his widely cited work (1974:269) that the one crucial criterion for democracies compared to autocracies is the existence of the '*competitive struggle for people's vote*'. According to Møller, Muni and Skanning (2013:93) and Lauth (2002) the provided '*ex negativo*' definition has the strength of offering a clear dichotomy and also overcomes the common '*threshold*' problem of gradualist definitions. In this sense, the operationalized minimal definition of political system is a useful beginning for distinguishing the political regime types of both cases.

---

519 Three dimension of Przeworski's (1991:50-51) minimal definition are '*ex ante uncertainty*', '*ex post irreversibility*' and '*regularity*'.

520 See Møller and Skaning (2010:261sp) and Møllner, Muno and Skanning (2013:93) or to quote Friedrich and Brzezinski (1965: 5), an autocracy is 'any political system in which the rulers are insufficiently, or not at all, subject to antecedent and enforceable rules of law – enforceable, that is, by other authorities who share in the government and who have sufficient power to compel the law-breaking rulers to submit to the law.' In contrast to democracy 'an autocracy is by definition a society where one person (or clique) is above the law' (McGuire und Olson 1996:. 93-94). The provided definition illustrates perfectly the Chinese case and its ongoing struggle to establish rule of law (NZZ 2014d).

Table 23: Regime Types in India and China over time

country	time-series	regimeny[521]	regime1ny[522]	regime1nyro-bust[523]	regimero-bust[524]
India	1974	Democracy	Democracy	100	100
India	1975-1976[525]	Democracy	Democracy	4	1
India	1977-2012	Democracy	Democracy	100	100
China	1974-2012	One-party	One-party	3	8

Source:Authoritarian Regimes Dataset (2014)[526]

As indicated in table 23, the Authoritarian Regimes Dataset distinguishes between different regime types, previous regime types, and their 'robust' designs over time (Teorell and Hadenius 2007, Wahman; Teorell and Hadenius 2013). To conduct an indepth analysis of the country-specific sub-type Axel Hadenius and Jan Teorell (2007) have set up a comprehensive dataset on 195 countries and their regimes between 1972 and 2012.[527] The dataset is constructed based on various variables, indicators, and indexes, such as the prominent Polity IV[528] as well as the Freedom House

521 Regime1ny indicates the current regimes' previous regime type

522 Regimeny indicates the current regime type

523 Regime1nyrobust indicates the current regime type(1 Monarchy, 2 Military, 3 One party, 4 Multi party, 9 No party, 99 other, 1000 Democracy)

524 regimerobust ondicates the current regimes' previous regime type (1 Limited Multi-Party, 8 One-party, 1000 Democracy)

525 Exception has been the short time of 'authoritarian rule' by Indira Gandhi (1975-1977). Although the 'emergence' reduced the civil and political rights (from democracy to limited multi-party), but did not change the regime type (democracy) as well as bounced back to the normality in 1977. The reason is that Indira Gandhi detained the displaced elections in 1977, repealed the 'emergency' and accepted her electoral defeat. Furthermore, the announcement of the national 'emergency' rule is a legitimate mechanism grounded in the Indian constitution. The fact that Indira Gandhi abused the instrument to establish her power is not of relevancy here (Wagner 2006, Authoritarian Regimes Dataset 2014)

526 For detailed information see the database and codebook, Authoritarian Regimes Dataset (2014), cit op.

527 See the Authoritarian Regimes Dataset, available at http://www.svet.lu.se/ARD/ (2014-09-05).

528 Polity IV and its 21-point scale distinguishes between '*fully institutionalized autocracy*' (-10) and '*fully institutionalized democracy*' (+10); in the middle are '*mixed, or incoherent, authority regimes*'. The scale points are as follows: autocracies, -10 to -6; anocracies, -5 to +5; and democracies, +6 to +10. The polity IV index uses five aggregated indicators for the specific categorisation.

(2014) index, granting the *Authoritarian Regimes Dataset* a broad range and reliability. The accumulated data clearly illustrate the continuity of both regimes in time.[529]

5.2 Assumed institutional Causalities and Social Security

Generally speaking, in terms of policy output performance democracies tend to be superior to non-democratic regimes or to be specific in an aggregated comparison in which the relatively high number of established and well-performing democracies have traditionally comparative advantages for the levels of political and economic performance as well as the resulting socio-economic conditions (Schmidt 1998:283). It is worth noting that the age of democracies has been singled out as a major explanatory variable for the comparative advantage in public policy performance[530]. Why is that so? Four major institutional mechanisms[531]—participation, constitution, civil society and corporatism—can be clearly singled as promoting increased public spending over time in democratic settings (Keman 1999, Pennings et al. 1999, Schmidt 2002:167)[532]:

First, mechanisms are *rule by the people* or the existence of electoral cycles. Voting participation and elections are mainly shaped by institutional settings and the political system (Budge and Farlie 1976, Franklin 1996, Scharpf 2000). Consequently, it has been argued by theorists of democracy that electoral pressure produces a so-called political market in which political parties act as political entrepreneurs to gain electoral support (Downs 1957). With some modifications, the theoretical assumption can be upheld for most established democracies; however, in non-democratic settings elections are often only '*window dressing*' if they exist at

529 See appendix I on the sub regime type as well as previous footnotes.

530 See Manfred G. Schmidt's articles (1998, 2002) on the age of democracies as an explanatory variable.

531 These four most important mechanisms have been singled out in addition to other features of democracy, such as political competitiveness.

532 It is an abstract analysis and of course the postulated positive effect of these four mechanisms on public spending has to be approached with caution. The '*Nixon goes to China*' phenomena and related policymaking of Margaret Thatcher illustrate that politicians can carry through austerity policies (Moon 1993, 1995).

all; free, fair and regularly held elections[533] are seen as pillars for modern states that foster political competition, accountability, democratic virtues, and egalitarian conditions. Therefore, crucial for every functioning democracy are fair and free elections in which the political participation of all citizens, particularly minorities, is guaranteed and instruments exist through which to hold elected political leaders accountable (Dahl 1966, Lane and Ersson 2002). A second effect of regular, fair, and free elections is the tendency toward increased public spending. Political competition and elections of political leaders tend to promote the rational behaviour of office-seeking politicians,[534] who attempt to gain electoral support by taking public demands seriously. As Paul Pierson (1994, 2001) stresses, in the democratic system public policies tend to create their own support groups, such as pensioners, which represent potential voters for rational politicians. Empirical evidence has demonstrated that the electoral cycle and age of democracy have positive effects for increased public spending as a result of the need to gain electoral support.

Second, a democratic constitution or at least rule of law[535] is essential to providing 'checks and balances' on the executive (Scharpf 1991, Fukuyama 1992 and Schmidt 2000). For established democracies, effective power-sharing mechanisms are crucial to guaranteeing 'rule by the people' and trust in the political system.[536] Concerning the first argument,

---

533 However, the existence of elections does not guarantee political participation. Various studies on the abuse of elections in autocracies and anocracies by ruling elites to legitimate their rule emphasise that elections do not guarantee free and fair political competition (Gandhi and Prezworski 2007). As Manfred G. Schmidt (1998:284) notes, such mechanisms 'do not prevent politics and policy making behind closed doors, but it guarantees a much more viable and responsive link between the rulers and the ruled.'

534 From a rational point of view, it is assumed that politicians opt to be elected for an office that demands electoral support. To maximize potential votes elected politicians are cooperative and interested in consensual decision-making to achieve policy output performance (Størm 1990). A classic example of the process, which Subrata K. Mitra (2010) describes as '*from rebels to stakeholders*', is given in the Indian context; after their successful election the local ethnic parties, in Bengal and Tamil Nadu, cooperated and carried through consensual policies despite previous political conflicts.

535 The prominent argument that a constitution is not a necessary condition for an established democracy is given by Britain, which, however, represents a historically unique case.

536 The overall trust of Indian society in the political system is evidence of the assumption. In 1999 Mitra and Singh conducted a survey and interviewed 9.475

it is worth noting that orderly rule and accountability are not restricted to democracies.[537] Autocracies and non-democracies can also establish stable institutional settings, policy outcomes, and policymaking accountability.[538] It is worth mentioning that cross-national studies have provided evidence that in established democracies the constitution tends to promote increased levels of welfare and public spending due to constitutionally-enshrined individual rights, institutional veto points, as well as electoral mechanisms (Schmidt 1999a, 2000a, 2012).[539] Rule of law is relevant for guaranteeing civil liberties; however, for orderly rule and political stability it is not a pre-condition. Other instruments, such as oppression, can be used by the state to guarantee orderly rule.

Third, the existence of a free civil society is a crucial pillar for democratic virtues and civil liberties. Accordingly *civil society organisations* (CSOs) or so-called non-governmental organisations and free mass media are crucial for providing a public sphere in which citizens can discuss politics outside political institutions. CSOs fulfil an important role in aggregating, articulating and formulating collective interests and providing the party government with an essential feedback function, even in non-democratic systems with a limited input dimension (Easton 1965). Nowadays there is little dispute that civil society and interest groups are relevant for positive feedback, and to what Lehmbruch (1984, 1999) refers to as the '*social partnership*' between the state and CSOs.[540] However, as dis-

---

persons; their conclusion was that the majority of citizens have significant trust in democracy but mistrust individual politicians (Mitra and Singh 1999). In particular, the socially and economically disadvantaged segments of society are assured that their vote matters and muster a slightly higher election participation rate of 60 percent compared to more affluent voters (ibid 1999:140 sp).

537 In democratic institutional settings with a proper division of power the '*rules of the game*' guarantee political accountability. Citizens can rely on the rule of law, civil rights, as well as an independent judiciary to enforce their demands against the state if necessary (Scharpf 1991).

538 As indicated by the *Doing Business Index* published by the World Bank, China has a much higher rating than India, particularly in terms of the enforceability of business contracts (World Bank 2010, 2014).

539 Furthermore, democratic constitutions grant not only civil rights but also the protection of the individual and his/her liberty from state oppression. Another aspect of rule of law is the ability of citizens to take action against misbehaviour or discrimination by the law or state administration (Dahrendorf 1977, Deva 2010).

540 Lehmbruch (1984, 1999) has put forward an explanation for the evolution of cooperative exchange patterns. He argues that '*social partnership*' relations tend to

cussed before, in autocracies, similar to democracies, political parties and politicians are in demand of support. Although the pattern and access of interest mediation in the non-democratic system is limited and mainly dominated by informal interaction patterns, the regimes tend to set up relations of strategic cooptation with economic or social elites.[541]

Fourth, mechanisms are related to the degree of centralised industrial bargaining mechanisms, or corporatism, which offer the organized interests participation opportunities in various ways. However, corporatism is not a feature of democracy per se. *Consocietal* democracies,[542] such as Austria and Netherlands[543], tend to promote corporate arrangements, and Westminster democracies, such as Britain and the USA, tend not to (Lijphart and Crepaz 1991). Both of the interest mediation systems, as Armingeon (1994, 2002:143) remarks, 'share the element that decisions are usually not reached by plurality of votes or other power resources.' In one of his widely cited works on corporatism, Gerhard Lehmbruch (1979:150) observes that corporate settings are 'institutionalized patterns of policy formation in which large interest organizations co-operate with each other and with public authorities (…) in the authoritative allocation of values and in the implementation of such policies.'[544]

---

flourish in contexts in which political elites have experience with techniques and strategies for compromise.

541 That said, the strong informality suggests that the influence of collective actors on the policy process and party politics has to be qualified for every case and varies from country to country.

542 Longitude analyses by Lijphart (1999:255) point to the resilience of *consocietal* democracies.

543 For a detailed description of the Netherland case see Arendt Lijphart's (1986). '*The Politics of Accommodation: Pluralism and Democracy in Netherlands*' and for the Austrian case see Gerhard Lehmbruch's work (1967) '*Proporzdemokratie. Politische System und politische Kultur in der Schweiz und Österreich*' in which he also discusses the concept of '*Proporzdemokratie*'.

544 In his introduction to '*Einleitung. Korporatismus, Pluralismus und Demokratie*' Werner Reutter (2001) offers a sophisticated insight into the corporatism debate, as well as the literature and theoretical discourse on concepts of pluralism and corporatism. Empirical studies have shown that corporate settings tend to promote the nature of the welfare regime and social security for employees. It has been argued that the decline of the welfare states in Western Europe in the mid-1970s is directly associated with the decline of corporatism in countries such as Britain (Armingeon 1997, Schmitter and Grote 1997).

5.3 Social Expenditure: Assumed Effects and the Reality

Without a doubt, democratic systems and their institutional features, such as constitutions, political competition, and elections, have a positive effect in most cases on the expansion of welfare spending, political participation, as well as the responsiveness of policy makers. Consequently, democracy has been analysed in terms of its pre- or resulting conditions for economic and human development (Dahl 1971, 1998, Lane and Ersson 2002, Halperin et al 2010).[545] Although democracies tend to have significant comparative advantages for political participation, rule of law and various fields of policymaking (e.g. environmental protection), the general comparative advantages cannot be applied to all fields and/or cases (Schmidt 2000a, Wurster 2011).[546]

Diagram 7: Public Social Expenditures since 2000

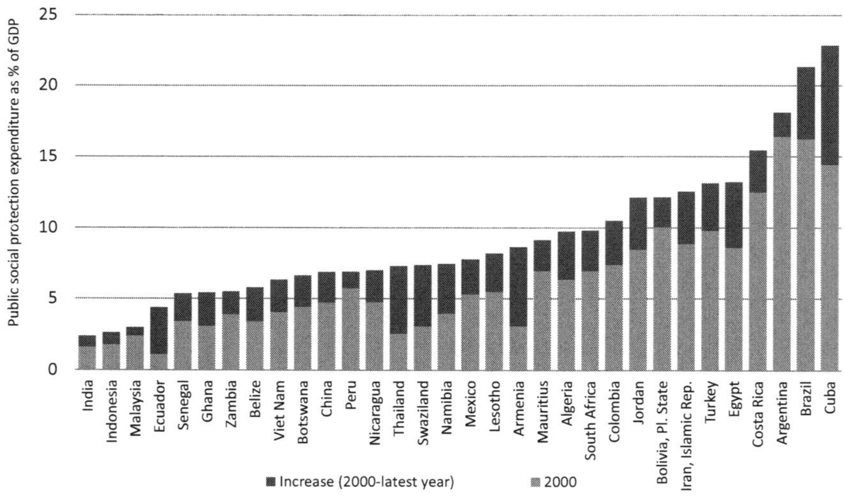

Source[547]

545 For a close investigation of the positive effect of political competition, electoral cycles and democratic constitutions, see Manfred G. Schmidt (1999 and 2002).

546 See Manfred G. Schmidt's textbook (2010) for a sophisticated review of theoretical and practical issues and the relevance of country-specific constitutional and institutional constraints on policymaking.

547 http://www.social-protection.org/gimi/gess/RessourceDownload.action?ressource.ressourceId=43537 (2015-05-01).

The empirical evaluation of the ILO Report (2015, Diagram 7) credits China with higher social expenditure (in percentage of the GDP) compared to India. It is worth noting the fact that 'poor democracies perform poorly' (Keman 2002) or, to be more precise, 'poor states perform poorly'.[548] Since 2000 the CCP the increasing economical growth positively affected the overall state budget and the avaialbale funding for social security.

Table 24: Social Expenditures in percentage of the GDP

country	Public social protection expenditure for the working age	Public social protection expenditure for children	Non-health public social protection expenditure on pensions and other benefits for older persons
China	1.899	0.22	2.89
India	0.6	0.057	0.75

Source: various scources (SSA 2008, 2012, ILO 2015)

Deprived from table 23, the evidences correspond to the assumed Zöllner model and correlation between the higher economical performance and social expenditures. China sacrifices more financial resources for social security than India. The latest ILO Report (2015:27) states that worldwide '*about one-third of total non-health public social protection expenditure, amounting to 2.3 per cent of GDP, is spent on benefits for people of working age*', this seems to be true for China but not for India's still low budget.

548 Various cross-national comparative analyses and the prominent examples given by non-democracies, such as Singapore, Saudi Arab and China, have provided empirical evidence that democracies are not necessarily superior in all policy fields compared to non-democracies.

Diagram 8A/B: Trends in Social Expenditures

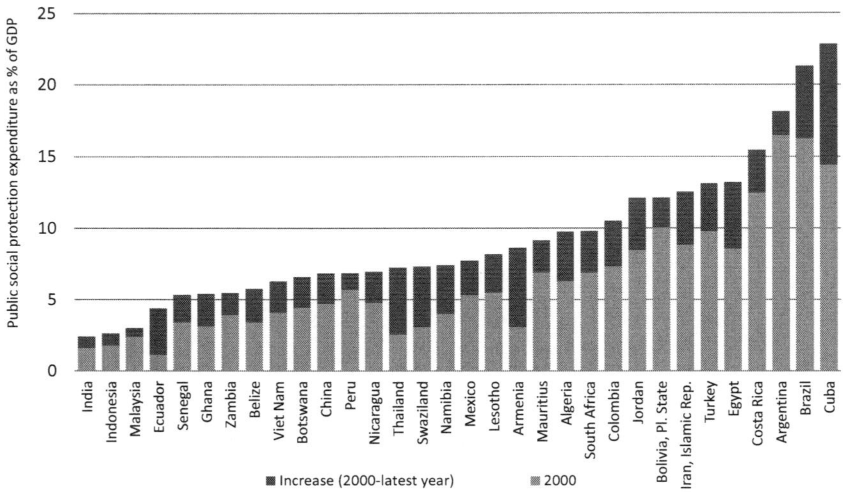

Note A = 2007-2009 / B = 2009-2011

Source: ILO (2015:127)

In diagram 8 a/b, the overall correlation of the state budget and percentage spent for social security. In 2007 to 2009 (see diagram 8a) both governments have used the fiscal stimulus and consolidation for improving the funding for social security. In 2009 onwards, the trend drawn by diagram 8b significantly illustrates the decline in the financial commitment for expanding the social security of the Indian UPA for social security. Rather than targeting and scaling down social security in terms of funding, China has stepped up since 2007.

5.4 Remark on the Regime Type and Social Security

The data on social expenditure crudely presented here does not allow us to draw any fast conclusions regarding regime type. However, the recently conducted macro-level studies on cross-national variations in social politics in democracies and autocracies seem to support the conclusion (World Bank 2007, 2008, Swamy 2011, Wurster 2011). In brief, the evidence illustrates the limitations of the 'comparative advantage' of democracies in terms of higher social security expenditures and policy performance. Accordingly a more nuanced country-by-country analysis of state capacity is required for understanding, in the cases of China and India, the differences in institutional performance in providing social security.

Overall this chapter has served its purpose of demonstrating the requirement of empirical and theoretical analysis with respect to the interactions between state capacity, social security policy performance, and institutional and non-institutional determinants, in addition to regime type.

VI. State format and Social Security Provision

One question attracts the most attention of political scholars and is formulated by Harold Lasswell (1950): '*Who get what, when and how?*'[549] This crucial question has been used to explain new institutional-oriented approaches.

6.1 Institutional Constrains on Policy Making

Another question in regard to the causal relationship between institutional design, political regime, and performance concerns the reasons why governments either follow or leave policy trajectories. In academic discourse controversy on the reasons for policy continuity or changes continues, and the issue is fiercely debated.

Although the institutional argument for the relevance of formal institutional patterns has not gone without criticism, liberal traditional reasoning implies negative aspects of the process of institutionalisation for the state, as mentioned by Hobbes, and also for individual citizens, as argued by Rosseau. In contrast, Max Weber (1976:201,662) as well as Edmund Burke point to the relevance of formal institutions in guaranteeing political and economic stability and efficiency, and in providing firm rules to reduce the potential for conflict between actors.[550] A persisting and fiercely debated question in comparative political science discourse regards the existence and relevance of institutional causalities. Inspired by early institutionalism, most students of classical institutionalism define formal institutions as relevant variables in the political realm which determine policy processes, structures, and outcomes.

Given this perception, formal institutions have long been considered as the only relevant variable; however, in the meantime the turn to institutionalism has begun to paint a sophisticated picture of the importance of institutional design, role of actors, and informal institutions for political

549 Harold D. Lasswell. 1950. *Politics. who gets what, when, how*. New York: Smith.

550 Katz and Crotty (2010) and Eisenstadt (1968:410) emphasise the high value of the '*rules of the game*'.

legitimacy and institutional performance (MacIntyre 2003, Ostrom 2005, Köllner 2006, Radnitz 2011). Formal and informal institutions can be best described as the *institutional set* and do not exclude each other in their existence; in fact, the opposite is the case (Przeworksi 1991:14).

In addition to other explanatory approaches, an answer to the question has been given by the widely cited work of Tsebilis (1990, 1995, and 1999) on the relevance of institutional veto players in limiting the '*room to manoeuvre*' and thus the chance of radical policy change.[551] It is worth noting that the number of formal veto players significantly varies across democracies. Country-specific institutional features, such as federalism/centralism or bicameralism, affect the number of individual institutional veto points (Schmidt 2000a). Accordingly a veto player is 'an individual or collective actor whose agreement is required for a change in policy' (Tsebelis 1995:301). As a consequence, the higher the number of veto points or players in the decision-making process, the less likely are radical policy changes (Tsebellis 1995, Immergut 1992). Although the veto player theorem has been validated as an important variable for explaining cross-national differences in public policy outcomes under similar conditions (Tsebelis 1995, 1999)[552], it is limited to strongly formalized institutional settings. In institutional settings with strong informal regulatory mechanisms—typically found in autocracies, fragile democracies, or hybrid regimes—the formal analysis cannot fully grasp the existing numbers of veto points, their potential veto power, as well as the interaction patterns (Gandhi 2007a/b, Scott 2011).

---

551 Similar to several of his colleagues (Greif 1995, Crépaz 1996, Schedler 2009) he argues for the relevance of existing formal institutional veto players. The veto players, also referred to as veto points (Immergut 1992), shape the room to manoeuvre for decisionmakers. Consequently, empirical evidence demonstrates that in established democracies a high number of veto points guarantees stable continuity of policymaking in most cases (Keman 1998, 2002).

552 See Immergut (1992) for a similar line of argument.

6.1.2 Autocracies, Democracies in Developing Countries, and institutional Veto Points

Institutions, such as parliaments and judiciaries in autocracies,[553] do not have the same function, and consequently the assumed veto competency, of their counterparts in established democracies. Furthermore, the balance of power, existing institutions, and related veto ability of these actors are determined by country-specific institutional settings and existing formal and informal institutional patterns (Chalmers 1979, Gandhi 2008a, Schedler 2009, Scott 2011). This calls for an elaboration of the country-specific institutional arrangement to identify the existing veto players and *co-regents*[554]. Consequently, the recent turn in academic discourse on autocracies points to what in most autocracies, as well as hybrid and some democratic countries, are 'weak' formal institutional veto players (Tsebelis 1990) that lack the function and competency of their democratic counterparts (Levitsky and Way 2002, Gandhi and Prezworski 2007a/b, Schedler 2009, Köllner 2013:272-273).[555]

Returning to the given problem of identifying the underlying patterns of policy processes, it is argued that the informal dimension matters in structuring political behaviour, patterns of exchange, and power (Radnitz 2011, Scott 2011, Köllner 2013:274-76). Though there is consensus that the relevance of informal institutions tends to dominate more in autocratic and less formalized institutional settings, it is not restricted to autocracies and can also be found in hybrid and democratic systems. In particular, clientelism, as Allen Hicken (2011) notes, represents a typical informal mechanism that shapes political reality, opening new space for political actors to use informal patterns of exchange to affect allocation, policy processes, and structures in China as well as in India (Dittmer and Wu 1995, Kohli 1987, Wang 2002, Chandra 2004). Consequently, the veto player theorem offers a causal explanation of the likelihood of radical policy change in es-

553 Evidence has been provided demonstrating that the functioning of institutions varies across regimes types, including in cases of 'hybrid' states.

554 Co-regents are defined as institutional or non-institutional actors who can effectively modify policy decisions by relying on formal or informal institutional elements (Schmidt 2000a).

555 For instance, parliaments or elections in autocratic regimes are more or less '*window dressing*' and have no real competency of impact on the decision-making of the ruling party and/or elites (Kailitz and Köllner 2013a).

tablished democracies; however, it is limited in its range and scope for the comparative task ahead for two main reasons:

(i) India and China, typical for developing countries, have evolved strong informal institutional patterns through which actors can modify policy choices and allocation processes (Bardhan 1984, 1997, 2008). These informal patterns cannot be adequately captured by the veto player theorem.

(ii) The Chinese autocratic system has only one dominant veto player, the CCP. Interestingly, contrary to the assumption of the veto player theorem, the historical development illustrates that radical policy changes are not typical events in the policymaking of the CCP (Guo 2000, Chan et al. 2008).

6.1.3 MDCD and the Issue of Comparison

New institutionalism[556] has recently been used in various comparative studies to explain cross-national differences in politics and policy outcomes (Schmidt 1999, Czada et al. 1998, Keman 1998, Kersbergen and Becker 2002) and illustrate the importance of informal rules that make the formal ones work (Gandhi and Przeworski 2006, 2007 a/b, Hicken 2011). Following an analysis of the new-institutional perspective, institutions will be used as variables to explain national differences. Institutions are seen as intervening variables that link political inputs to policy outcomes across polities and over time (Putnam 1993:8-9), and which can be empirically evaluated to compare and explain cross-national and/or inter-temporary variations (Scharpf 1991, 2006).

During the 1990s, studies of autocracies tended to neglect the importance of institutions such as parliaments, elections, or parties.[557] Thus,

---

556 In his widely cited studies (1981, 1990a) Douglass North identifies the relevance of and relationship between state institutions and political, economic and social determinants for the development of the country. North's studies in the field of historical institutionalism and his ambition to explain institutional change and its relevance to the rise and fall of nations have reshaped the field of political science. His interdisciplinary macro approach emphasises the relevance of subfields of policymaking.

557 Classic studies of autocratic totalitarian regimes such as military dictatorships have mostly focused on key institutions, such as the state party or Junta (Chalmers 1979).

country-specific institutions did not gain much attention and hardly mattered because they were assumed to be '*window dressing*' for autocratic systems—assumptions that were made without exploring underlying institutional political patterns (Gandhi 2008: XXI). Typically institutional features of autocracies tended to be neglected due to the general assumption that these systems tend to be '*weakly*' institutionalised (Acemoglu, Egorov and Sonin 2007).[558]

All this has dramatically changed. The recent turn in the autocracy debate towards new institutionalism has exposed the relevance of institutions for the performance, effectiveness and function of these systems (Schedler 2009, Gandhi and Prezworski 2007 a/b, Gandhi 2008). The last decade has witnessed an outpouring of cross-national studies critically investigating the role and function of institutions in autocratic systems, such as electoral institutions (Levitsky u. Way 2002), parliament (Gandhi and Prezworski 2006), the judiciary (Barros 2002) and civil society (Wischermann 2013). These studies have enhanced the knowledge of autocratic regimes, political processes, and structures (Schedler 2009). All these studies argue that institutions in autocracies cannot be compared to their democratic counterparts. Despite missing democratic functions, institutions in autocracies can be compared in their core functions to institutions in democratic settings in terms of facilitating formal as well as informal arrangements to enhance political order, conflict resolution, and the functioning of government (Keman 1999, 2002, Schmidt 2000a, Kersbergen and Becker 2002).[559] Accordingly, the argument by Guy Peter et al. (1977) that variations in the institutional arrangements and composition of the government (Hibbs 1977, 1994, Schmidt 1983) affect policy 'style' seems to be valid even for non-democratic systems (Schmidt 1999b, 2005, Kailitz 2010a, Kailitz and Köllner 2013b).

In many cases the recent new institutional turn in comparative discourse on autocracies expands the limited focus of the field of research. One obvious way to overcome the limitations of this discourse involves taking

558 Acemoglu, Daron, Georgy Egorov, and Konstantin Sonin, 2010. 'Political Selection and Persistence of Bad Governments,' *Quarterly Journal of Economics*, vol 125, no. 4: 1511–1576.

559 In their works Jennifer Gandhi and Adam Przeworski (2006, 2007, and 2008) elaborate the importance of parliaments in totalitarian regimes as arenas in which to formulate, implement and legitimize policy choices and include the opposition in the process to some degree.

over the research categories and fields of inquiry of democratic discourse. The success of the theoretical shift can be observed in the pioneering work on elections (Schedler 2009) and parliaments (Gandhi and Przeworski 2006, 2007). However, Jennifer Gandhi and Adam Przeworski (2008:xv) remind us that parliament, elections and civil society should not be misunderstood as equal to their counterparts in democratic settings (Wischermann and Nguyen 2003, Wischermann 2013:324).[560]

In effect, institutions have to be analysed as entities in their country-specific settings. Following this line of argument, the combination of formal and informal institutions is seen as the lens through which to explain the ability of political regimes to structure interests, participation, allocation processes and define the '*room to manoeuvre*' for actors (Mitra 1991, Colomer 1996, Shepsle 1997, Scharpf 1998, Scott 2011). As Patrick Köllner points out (2013:275), formal and informal institutions provide orientation and order for political actors and can be applied to regulate and control political interaction (Hicken 2011). According to Subrata Mitra (1994a/b, 1999b), institutions set the '*rules of the game*' and structure the '*room to manoeuvre*' for involved actors to modify policy processes and outcomes in their favour.[561]

Hypothesis 3a: *The higher the number of veto players, the less likely deep structural reforms and policy changes.*

Institutions structure the interaction patterns, strategies, and behaviour of involved collective actors—the state, political actors and unions. The students of *new institutionalism* (Williamson 1985, March and Olsen 1989, Steinmo and Thelen 1992) link structures and configurations to agency and action. 'Political institutions are the building blocks of political life. They influence available options for policy-making and for institutional

560 In this context, Schedler conducted various indepth studies on the functioning of institutions and manipulative methods of ruling elites in elections (2006, 2007), parliament, the judiciary and media (2009). Shedler (2009:9) concludes that the ruling elites 'will always try to make sure that the *nominally democratic* institutions they set up remain *substantively authoritarian*. Political institutions that are created by and embedded in an authoritarian regime are never, except by a slip of language, 'democratic institutions' [emphasised by authors].'

561 The class conflict in modern states is solved by '*means of those institutions that facilitate the formation of acceptable and feasible agreements*' (Keman 2002:7) between the state and the organisational representative of labour as well as capital. The bargained solutions are considered as '*an optimum*' (ibid:7).

change. They also influence the choices made among available options' (Olsen 1998:95). Thus, bureaucratic institutions are important for mediation and aggregation (Budge 1993)[562]. As Max Weber (1976) notes, institutions inherit authority to produce regularized decisions and rules which structure the behavioural patterns of the involved actors (Shepsle 1997).[563] Although formal and informal institutions tend to produce stable outcomes, norms and rules (Gibbson 1992, Scott 2011), in the case of weak formal institutions, informal institutions can also have negative effects on the political system, legitimacy and institutional performance (Colomer 1996, Schmidt 1999, Helmke and Levistsky 2006).

Hypothesis 3b: *A higher degree of joint decision-making (so-called 'Politikverflechtung') and decentralised provision of social security tends to result in sub-optimal solutions.*

A good number of studies on democracies have repeatedly argued for the positive or comparative advantage of formal institutions, such as the constitution, federalism and judiciary, and their constraints or veto ability on the executive in the democratic system (Dahl 1971, 1989, and 1998, Schmidt 2005, Halperin et al 2010). In particular, in most established democracies the 'egalitarian character' of the constitution, which guarantees political and social rights to its citizens, as well as political competition, tends to promote steadily increasing social expenditures even under changing party coalition governments (Schmidt 1998, 1999a).

A negative side effect of the electoral cycle, political competition, and government responsiveness to current socio-economic problems is the often-diagnosed short-term policymaking. Tocqueville (1990) has proclaimed the danger of democracies falling prey to this shortsightedness. In '*Advocacy and Pluralism in Planning*,' a study of the planning process of social development in democracies, Paul Davidoff (1965) offers evidence of Tocqueville's assumption that policy planners become advocates of specific societal demands and interests.[564]

562 The interests and preferences of the collective actors represent exogenous variables. Institutions are seen as formalized interaction patterns to reduce transaction costs and conflicts (North 1990, Scharpf 1987).

563 In a sense, information asymmetries and social relations have an impact on the behaviour and perceptions of the involved actors (Mitra 2009).

564 Down's *political market* concept (1968) defines political parties as rational actors which are office seekers that have to balance, adapt, and react to current public

Hypothesis 3c: *A low regulatory competency of bureaucracy has a negative effect on social security performance.*

Accordingly, higher responsiveness to inputs, electoral constraints on decision makers, and changes in government composition tend to reduce the long-term regulatory competency of the bureaucracies in democracies (Strøm 1990, Budge et al. 2002:81-82).[565] Also autocracies can issue an increasing number of legal and traceable regulations on the modalities, scope, range and access of social policy schemes to produce transparency and pressure on the local administration for implementation (SC 2000, 2006, Tao and Qin 2007, D. Liu 2011).[566]

6.2 Descriptive Perspective: Constitutional and institutional Constrains

The historical comparison has offered evidence of the measurable effect of institutional and constitutional constraints on the ability of the party government to carry through their policy plans.[567] Accordingly, the institutional and constitutional constraints as well as involved actors have an impact on social security politics, policy trajectories and social security-related outputs in both political regimes (Mitra 2013, 2014, Guo 2013b). In the tradition of institutional-oriented approaches, the question of the existence and relevance of regime and/or country-specific institutional effects for social security politics is discussed here. In his widely cited article (2011) Francis Fukuyama transforms his earlier thesis of the *end of history*

demands in safeguarding their electoral support in order to guarantee re-election. See also Paul Pierson's argument for the relevance of demand groups, such as pensioners (1994, 1996).

565 See the World Government Indicators (WGI 2014)

566 The Chinese case provides a range of examples of social security laws, regulations, as well as constitutional amendments through which the autocratic system regulates and coordinates the functioning of social security provision, including the modalities, funding and benefits of social security (D. Liu 2011: 55 sp).

567 Even in the CPR formal and informal institutions produce constraints on the *'room to manoeuvre'*. In particular, the sole but central formal veto point, the Politburo, combined with the informal power of the leading party elites—for instance, Deng Xiaoping's lasting political impact even after his 'official retirement' or Zhou Yongkang's dominating position in the CCP (see footnote 607)—placed measurable constraints on the current *'room to manouvre'* of the party leadership.

(1989)[568] into a more modest version of the *return of history* in regard to the flourishing of autocracies and anocracies. Is Fukuyama (2011) right in his assumption that democracies, such as the USA, can learn from China's policy performance and economic outcomes? In the realm of the conducted study, the question arises: *Do their institutional effects explain the superior performance of China?*

6.2.1 Institutional veto points in China and India

In the following section the institutional design is the subject of inquiry, as is its implications for the '*room to manoeuvre'* for decision-making and public policy choices in the countries of both case studies. Political systems not only differ in their party systems[569]—in the existing political spectrum of leftist, liberal, conservative or centrist parties (Hadenius and Teorell 2007)—but also in their constitutional structures and the extent of major veto players which vary from country to country. These institutional veto players—a term coined by Tsebelis (1995)—can produce significant constraints on decision makers:

Table 25: Constitutional Structure and Veto Players, 2000-2009

Country	Type/Character of Decision-making	Federalism vs. Unitary state	Veto Player Index[570]
China	Authorian - unitary	Decentralised / unitary state	0-1*
India	Consensus - federal	Decentralised / federalism	7**

* Only existing major veto player is the CCP (the Politburo can be seen as the embodiment of the CCP's veto capacity); **1. Federalism, 2. Independent judiciary, 3. Independent Central Bank, 4. Bicameral, 5. Protection of minorities, 6. Coalition government, 7. Consocietal democracy (Schmidt 2000a)

Source: various sources

568 Fukuyama (1989), cit op.

569 For a comprehensive textbook on party systems see Waren (2007) '*Political Parties and Party System*' or Nohlen (2004) '*Wahlrecht und Parteisystem*'.

570 Veto player Index is based upon Schmidt (2000a). The veto player index reflects the number of major veto players and is based on 10 dummy variables including: 1. Consociational democracy, 2. Federalism, 3. independent judiciary, 4. independent central bank, 5. bicameral, 6. protection of minorities, 7. coalition government, 8. Eu Membership or comparable Membership in another international body, 9. self administration in social policy, 10. degree of the direct democracy.

A descriptive look at the government indicators provided by the World Bank offers a glimpse at the review of the '*quality of governance*' in various sub-fields which affect policy processes, structures, and overall performance.

Table 26: World Governance Indicators (2000-2009)

	2000	2002	2003	2004	2005	2006	2007	2008	2009
Voice and Accountability									
China	-1.29	-1.57	-1.54	-1.46	-1.50	-1.68	-1.66	-1.64	-1.66
India	0.26	0.36	0.39	0.38	0.39	0.42	0.43	0.44	0.45
Political Stability									
China	-0.27	-0.36	-0.57	-0.36	-0.48	-0.54	-0.49	-0.48	-0.43
India	-0.99	-1.24	-1.53	-1.22	-0.99	-1.06	-1.15	-1.10	-1.33
Government Effectiveness									
China	-0.09	-0.05	-0.04	0.00	-0.09	0.08	0.19	0.15	0.11
India	-0.14	-0.13	-0.07	-0.10	-0.08	-0.05	0.11	-0.03	-0.01
Rule of Law									
China	-0.48	-0.41	-0.47	-0.43	-0.49	-0.55	-0.45	-0.34	-0.32
India	0.28	-0.04	0.10	0.04	0.16	0.19	0.11	0.09	0.02
Regulatory Quality									
China	-0.33	-0.53	-0.34	-0.28	-0.13	-0.18	-0.15	-0.13	-0.20
India	-0.14	-0.13	-0.07	-0.10	-0.08	-0.05	0.11	-0.03	-0.01
Control of Corruption									
China	-0.24	-0.65	-0.41	-0.56	-0.64	-0.51	-0.59	-0.54	-0.54
India	-0.37	-0.50	-0.44	-0.41	-0.40	-0.30	-0.42	-0.36	-0.48

Source: Kaufmann et al. (2008, 2010, 2014)

The findings in table 26 regarding institutional effects on performance seem to indicate that institutional effects other than those listed matter for social security politics. Obviously India is doing slightly better than China in all categories. The only exception is political stability, which is hardly causally related to comparative divergence in the realization of social security politics.

What the findings illustrate is that India's democracy lacks the hoped-for comparative advantages due to its regime type. As discussed before, Toquevillian assumptions are causal observations but not universal ones—even for an established democracy such as India. In other words, we would have expected that India performed better in all sub-fields of governance quality compared to China. Interestingly, both systems are relatively close to each other, except in the area of *rule of law*. In accordance with the above stated facts, it is argued that regime type cannot fully explain the variations as well as simultaneous developments in social security provision.[572]

Judging by the table it appears that, as argued by Tilly (1975) in '*The Formation of National States in Western Europe*,' the country-specific historical development of economic and political conditions shapes the current state format and institutional arrangement of modern states.[573] As argued in the previous chapter, social security provision and outcomes are assumed to be determined by the formal and informal features of the party-state-society relationship, including institutional determinants as well as socio-economic conditions, which shape the objectives and outcomes of social security provision.

6.3 State Format: National Level and Decision Making

In addition to the extant party system, the state format (Tilly 1975) imposes various institutional constraints on the policy performance of modern states. In particular, the format of the state (unitary-federal) has a significant impact on the existing number and relevance of veto players, social security policymaking, as well as the provision of public goods across the state (Lijphart 1999).

6.3.1 India's resilient Democracy

India did not start out with similar starting conditions or experience as its democratic[574] Western counterparts but it has still achieved a strong re-

---

572 As argued in the two previous chapters, India and China have witnessed comparable periods of social security development over recent decades, despite different policy objectives.

573 In his work Tilly (1975) put together nine essays which all argue for the relevance of path dependency and historical, economic, and political processes for the evolution of the current state format in Western European countries between 1500 and 1990.

574 For Dahl (1984:237), democracy is a set of institutions and a 'kind of regime for governing nation-states in which power and authority over public matters are distributed among a plurality of organizations and associations that are relatively autonomous in relation to one another and in many cases to the government of the

silient democracy which can be compared to its democratic Western counterparts in its persistence (Mitra 2013).[575] Without a doubt, the Indian path to democracy has been a unique and challenging one in the context of a vast territory inhabited by a deeply fragmented society. In the 1950s, India was directly in the middle of its peaceful transformation from the colonial *British Raj* into the independent Democratic Republic of India. Despite low levels of economic growth, a deeply fragmented society, mass poverty, and illiteracy, India succeeded in establishing resilient democratic institutions, civil virtues and democratic patterns as well as in guaranteeing political stability without falling prey to the *Huntington-Gurr* scenario.[576] India's resilient democratic system was able to deal with these challenges without falling prey to political instability and regime changes, in contrast to its neighbouring countries. In Pakistan and Bangladesh coups replaced the democratic elected governments, a Maoist civil war raged across Nepal, and Sri Lanka's ethnic exclusion of Tamils continued even after the dreadful experiences and ceasefire of the civil war (Mitra 2013:229).

It is argued that the key to India's success is the flexibility of the democratic system in producing '*political capital*' and transforming '*rebels into stakeholders*', as Subrata K. Mitra (2013:227-29) has described the process. As a result of resilient democratic institutions, minorities as well as local groups have been successfully integrated into the policymaking process on local as well as national levels; the importance of existing institutional and constitutional mechanisms[577], such as the bi-cameral system,

---

state as well.' Accordingly, even modern definitions, such as those provided by Magaloni, Chu and Min (2013:6), underline that '(1) A civilian government (as opposed to military or royal court) provides the main source of policy making; (2) Political leaders form multiple and competitive parties, and the parties interact and run the government through a legislature; (3) The executive is institutionally constrained or checked by other parts of the government; (4) Elections are used to select the political leadership, and they are largely open, competitive, and free and fair.' Magaloni, B., Chu, J. and Min, E. 2013. '*Autocracies of the world, 1950-2012*', available at http://cddrl.stanford.edu/research/autocracies_of_the_world_dataset (2014-06-04).

575 'Persistence' of a democratic regime is measured in terms of the age of democracy.

576 As discussed earlier in Chapter 2.

577 Lipset and Lakin (2004) emphasise the relevance of democratic constitutional features to guarantee civil rights, freedom of the press, freedom of speech and the possibility of electoral 'losers' running as independent candidates in the next election.

minority representation, political participation, and elections cannot be overestimated here.

6.3.1.1 Constitutional and institutional Features of India's Political Regime

As highlighted in the definition by Magaloni et al. (2013), at least three power-sharing mechanisms are essential features of any democracy. It is worth noting that the concentration of power varies among democracies, ranging from a relatively high concentration of power in the Anglo-Saxon "*Westminster democracy*" and the dispersion of powers in the "*continental democracy*," such as Germany.[578] The argument by Paul Pierson (1996) for the relevance of historical development seems to be valid for India's "*Westminster democracy*" which embodies strong federalism and has cultivated a multi-party system on the national level.[579]

As a consequence, governments in the bi-cameral system and with a highly fragmented political party system are challenged to find a majority for coalition building as well as political support to pass policy initiatives in both chambers (Schmidt 2008:209).

India's political system represents a 'unique' modification of the Westminster model (Morris-Jones 1968, Brass 1994, Kohli 1999). While India has a similar institutional design, including an asymmetrical bi-cameral system and a flexible constitution, the established democracy is an example of parliamentary federalism (Lijphart 1999, Morris-Jones 1968). As

---

578 German democracy has established a number of veto points, such as the demand for coalition governments, a federal chamber, an active constitutional court, as well as an independent central bank (Schmidt 2012).

579 In the long run, India's national party system has undergone three major stages, changing from 'one-party dominance' (1947 to 1967), to a two-parties-and-a-half dominance (1977-1991), and ending up with a multi-party system (1991-2015). The last phase (1991-2015) witnessed the transformation of the national party system into a multi-party system and is closely linked to the 'ascendency of Hindu nationalism and retreat of the state, following liberalization of the economy in the early 1990s' (Mitra 2013:230). Although the diversity and multiplicity has made political discourse healthier on a national level, in terms of the direct participation of smaller regional parties, it has also complicated the consolidation process, coalition building, and the ability of party governments to carry through their policy choices in the bi-cameral system (Brass 1994:84sp, Mitra 1999, 2013)

Budge and colleagues (2002:66) note, democracy is 'considered here as a set of institutional and political processes operating in similar ways across different countries.'

Figure 7: Paths to Public Policy Formation

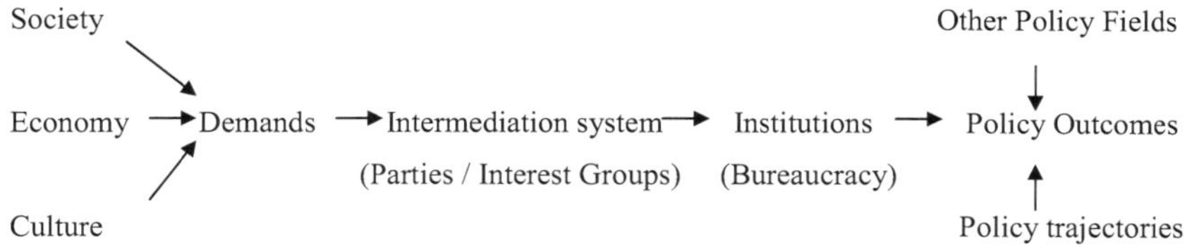

Source: Author's adaptation (Penning et al. 1999)

The simplified model gives a clear overview of the involved actors and policymaking processes. However, the country-specific institutional design, political parties and patterns of interaction vary across countries; therefore the uniqueness of India's democracy will be taken into account for further analysis. Besides the constitutional and institutional features which determine the *'room to manoeuvre'* for the elected party government, the crucial democratic chain of command in India is comparable on an abstract level to other established democracies (Keman 2002). The core actors (figure 7) are political parties that have two kinds of motivations. The first motivation is to gain electoral victory. In the office-seeking process parties will try to rally as much support as possible; to do so they will include various societal demands in their electoral agenda. The second motivation after being elected into office is determined by policy-seeking motives and the ambition to carry through the policy guidelines (Strøm 1990, Scharpf 1997, Pennings et al. 1999).

6.3.1.2 Lok Sabha and Raj Sabha: Social Policy Making

The Indian Parliament is bicameral. It comprises the Lok Sabha (lower house) and the Rajya Sabha (upper house). The Lok Sabha has the authority to pass bills concerning the so-called 'collective responsibility' of the government and particularly financial matters, such as the state budget and financial resources for ministries.

Figure 8: Check and Balances in India

Executive Activity	Remarks
Power to convene Parliament	
The President, on the advice of the Cabinet, summons the sessions of Parliament. The Constitution specifies that there should not be a gap of more than six months between two sessions.	The government (and not MPs) decides the dates of Parliament sessions, provided it abides by the six-month rule. In 2008, Parliament met for just 46 days (the lowest ever in a year), and had only two sessions, instead of the customary three sessions.
Power to dissolve Lok Sabha	
The Prime Minister may recommend to the President that Lok Sabha be dissolved.	The President has to act on the advice of the Prime Minister. This power is usually used either when the government wants a mid-term poll which it believes it will win, or is likely to lose a confidence vote.
Legislation	
Government may introduce bills, which are then considered by Parliament. Bills also contain an explanatory memorandum on various clauses, and a financial memorandum detailing the expected financialimplications.	Most govt Bills are passed because MPs are required to vote on party lines. Explanatory memorandum rarely detail the purpose of each clause and the overall structure of the legislation. In some cases, the financial implications are not provided.
Many Acts authorise the government to formulate rules and regulations. These are tabled in parliament and usually MPs may raise objections within 30 days.	In the 14th Lok Sabha, there was not even a single instance when these rules were discussed in Parliament.
Many Acts permit the government to announce the date when particular sections of the Acts come into effect.	In some cases, these Acts, or parts of Acts have not been notified for a long time. For example, the Delhi Rent Act was passed in 1995 but has not yet been notified.
Ordninances	
When Parliament is not in session, the President can, on the advice of the Prime Minister, promulgate an Ordinance. They are valid for six months, or for six weeks after the commencement of the next session of Parliament, whichever is earlier.	Use of ordinances increase during times of governmental instability. Between 1990-1999, an average of 20 Ordinances were promulgated per year. It came down to 7 per year between 2000-2007.

Source: PRS (2009:3)[581]

Any party government is limited in its ability to carry through its policy choices by institutional and constitutional constraints. Accordingly, the In-

581 PRS Legislative Research. 2009.'The Executive versus the Legislature Background Note for the Conference on Effective Legislatures', available at http://www.prsindia.org/administrator/uploads/general/1370582764_Executive%20vs%20Legislature.pdf (2015-01-01).

dian party government in charge requires electoral success to gain a nominal as well as a political majority in the parliament – the '*Raj Sabbah'* – and in the second chamber – the '*Raj Lok*' – and thus carry through its policy choices (Mitra 1994b, 1999a/b, 2005, Wagner 2006:44, 48, 69).[582]

The Rajya Sabha

The Rajya Sabha or Upper House is a federal chamber that enjoys certain special powers under the Constitution. Its history dates back to colonial times; the former Council of States, as it was called, was founded in 1919 under the Government of India Act, 1919. In 1954 the Council of States was renamed the Rajya Sabha. It represents the upper house and consists of 250 seats. 238 of these seats are granted to representatives of the Union States and Union Territories. At the state level public elections select candidates for the State Legislative Assembly (MLA). In the MLA the nominated persons select the members[583] of the Rajya Sabha for a six-year term. The missing 12 seats are nominated by the President to guarantee the representation as well as rights of minorities (Wagner 2006:48-50, Mitra 2011).

The Lok Sabha

The Lok Sabha is the Upper House of the Indian Parliament. It consists of representatives elected by the people on the basis of universal adult franchise through secret ballot. The constitution prescribes a membership of not more than 530 representatives and further limits the number of represenatives for each Union State to no more than 20.[584] In addition, the President nominates more than two members of the Anglo-Indian community for the Lok Sabha. The representatives are elected for a five-year term.

Another relevant fact is the weakness of the legislature related to the standing committees. The members of the standing committees, including

582 For a general inquiry into the 'veto point theorem' see Tsebelis (1990, 1995), Immergut (1992), Keman (1999) and Schmidt (2000a).

583 Article 84 of the Indian constitution states the qualifications for membership.

584 It is worth noting that the Constitution empowers the Parliament to readjust the number of seats for each union state according to demographic tendencies.

the Public Undertaking Committee, Estimates Committee as well as the Public Accounts Committee, are nominated by proportional representation. In addition, the political dominance of a party or party coalition enables it to take the key position in decision-making as well as control of the committees (Morris-Jones 1968, Wagner 2008:52-54, Mitra 2011).

The two Houses and the Law Making Process

The balance of power in the Indian system is in favour of the executive.[585] In general, the law-making process is clearly defined. In the Indian sytem all subjects or areas of legislation are divided into three so-called lists: the *Union List,* the *State List* and the *Concurrent List*. These lists divide legislative authority between the Union and the States. The *Union List* consists of 99 items and grants the Lok Sabha exclusive authority in the legislature and law-making ability for the listed subjects—that is, foreign affairs, defence, armed forces, communications, postal service, and foreign trade. As discussed earlier, party dominance in the Lok Sabha enables the party/ coalition to take key committees. Also with respect to lawmaking the Lok Sabha has a numerical advantage over the Rajya Sabha. This fact is crucial in 'joint sittings,' which are seldom events; the last was the passing of the Anti-Terrorism Law in 2001.

The *State List* determines the sphere of authority for the Rajya Sabha and consists of 61 subjects on which the States alone can ordinarily issue laws—that is, public order, the police system, administration of justice, the prison system, and local governments.

The Constitution and the Indian system contain a number of unitary features. Article 75(3) of the Constitution emphasises that the Council of Ministers is collectively responsible to the Lok Sabha. Concerning the legislature this relationship is expressed in the *Concurrent List* which comprises of 52 items—for example, criminal and civil procedures, marriage and divorce, economic and special trade planning unions, electricity, newspapers, books, education, population control, and family planning. If both chambers approve an introduced bill, the President has a veto right.

585 The government can issue so-called 'ordinances'. These ordinances are only temporary laws for addressing immediate issues and have to be ratified by the upper and lower house within six months.

Although the States can enact laws concerning these subjects, the Lok Sabha has the ability to override the States in cases of conflict between state and union. Another unitary feature concerns the limited authority of the Rajya Sabha with respect to financial or monetary issues as well as its confidence or no-confidence motion. These bills concern taxation or loans and can be exclusively introduced by the President in the Lok Sabha. The Rajya Sabha can only add comments but has no ability to reject currency. Such financial issues can be exclusively introduced in the Lok Sabha. If the Lok Sabha passes a bill, it is handed down to the Rajya Sabha for concurrence or recommendation. Social security bills have to be ratified by both chambers by majority vote.

6.3.1.3 Social Policy Making: Involvement of Legislative and Executive

Concerning the second ambition, India's bicameral parliament system, fragmented party system and constitutional veto produces significant constraints on the ability of politicians and parties to carry through their policies. Since the early 1990s the regional fragmentation of the political sphere has spread to the national level. In effect, the ruling party governments are grand coalitions desperately in need of direct or indirect political support of either the INC or the BJP.[586]

Another constraint is that the temporary majority's formation of a party coalition government does not imply the willingness of the parliaments and its members to support the government at all times; examples are given by the short-term minority coalition governments in 1990 and 1996.[587] Although the executive, the prime minister, and his cabinet have state institutions under their direct authority, they are formally responsible to the parliament[588] and depend on the cooperation of a majority in both cham-

586 However, neither the BJP nor the INC could achieve a majority and both were in need of coalition partners to carry through or blockade bills and legislatures. In particular, public policy bills have always been controversial due to their character as well as financial and administrative costs (Wagner 2006).

587 The previous section discussed Janata Dal's '*INC towards a catch-all party*' (1990-1991) and the United Front (1996-1997) coalition governments and their dependency on the INC to back them up.

588 The parliament has the constitutionally-given right to pass a mistrust vote against the prime minister and current government, in which case the government has to step aside. For instance, in 2008 a broad coalition of left and communist parties

bers of the legislature to pass bills and laws concerning their policy choices. In addition, the relatively regular and strong electoral turnouts have granted the INC a leading role in political decision-making on the national level in recent decades (Mitra 1994a, 2005, 2013).

6.3.1.4 The Indian Social Security Administration

Another thrust of the study is the argument in public administration literature that the administrative body is relevant to policymaking, policy implementation, and the provision process (Wildavsky 1968, Kaufman et al. 2010). In India responsiblity for the administration, monitoring and implementation of social security and the key department for the day-to-day administration of social security is horizontal and vertical, divided between ministries and commissions on national and union state levels. Accordingly, it operates on all four administrative tiers: national, provincial, municipal and county (Sülzer 2007, Rao 2007). At the national level the two key actors are the Ministry of Labour and Employment as well as the Department for Social Welfare, which coordinate, implement and pass down the responsibility for social security policy schemes, services and programs. The responsibility and authority for social security administration in the formal sector lies with the Ministry for Labour. The history of the Ministry has shown that the development of administration is one in which old patterns are constantly adapted to the pace of time.[589]

were able to achieve the necessary majority in parliament to initiate a mistrust vote against the acting Prime Minister Singh. The reason was Singh's nuclear deal with the USA; however, the UPA and Singh could muster enough votes to block the veto (Handelsblatt. 2008. '*Indiens Regierung bleibt an der Macht*', 2008-07-22)

589 See http://delhi.gov.in/wps/wcm/connect/doit_socialwelfare/SocialWelfare/Home/(2014-09-01).

Figure 9: India's central Social Security Administrational Bodies

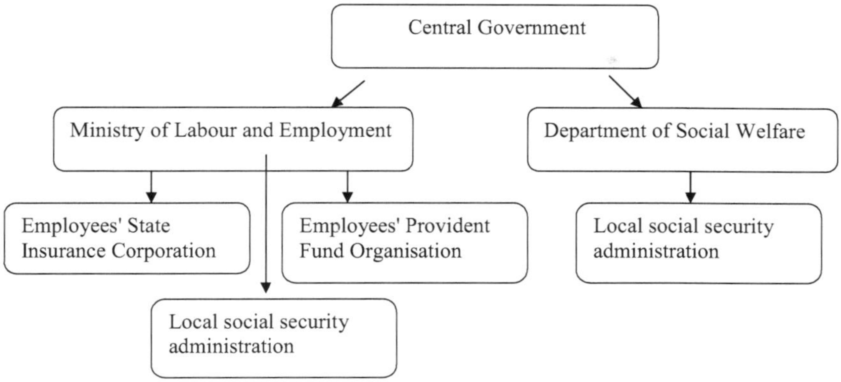

Source: Author's own model

Both national bodies have established local agencies at all levels of the institutional setting and also cooperated in the third tier (village council or PRIs).[590] But the *de facto* power of these national institutions is limited in various ways.

There is no coherent national social security law but a division of labour in the social security administration among the state institutions (ILO 2013). Thus, despite one responsible ministry for a specific social security programme, the provision of the schemes is often in the hands of sub-branches and/or in cooperation with union state institutions. Furthermore, the missing coherent legal framework for the social security system and federal character has promoted intra-country differences in the availability and modalities of access of local 'target groups', (e.g. BPL household criteria).

The complexity of social security administration and joint ventures between the national and state union level makes it hard for state authorities to effectively address current problems. Another issue, as argued earlier, is the financially and administratively overburdened local governments, which struggle to provide social security (Vijay Shankar and Shah 2012). In the following section, the main institutions responsible for social securi-

590 The third tier or PRIs, implemented in 1992, will be discussed at length in the 'state format' section.

ty administration are briefly presented and discussed to give an overview of the complexity of their organization.

Ministry of Labour and Employment

The Ministry of Labour and Employment in India (MoLE) is one of the oldest ministries and the central body responsible for labour-related matters, such as monitoring and managing social security, labour relations, minimum wage, labour conditions, education and so on. As in the case of the MoLE, issues of administration have produced autonomous bodies to monitor, safeguard, and guarantee the provision of social security, labour protection, minimum wages and other related services (e.g. education for workers). Social security is an important focal point and two of the six autonomous bodies, namely the Employees' Provident Fund Organisation and Employees' State Insurance Corporation are responsible for surveying related social security schemes.[591] Besides the autonomous board the MoLE has set up a subordinate Employees' State Insurance Corporation to supervise the ESIC and the Labour Welfare Organisation in administering the 2007 *Rasthriya Swasthya Bima Yojana* (RSBY), an explicit social security scheme for the unorganised sector (ILO 2011:74). Among the responsibilities of the MoLE to safeguard labour-related manners is the obigation to enact labour-related statutes on the national level on matters related to the minimum wage, accidental and social security benefits, occupational safety and health, employment conditions, disciplinary action, and the formation of trade unions, industrial relations and other labour-related issues (Rao 2011).[592]

Employees' Provident Fund Organisation

The Employees' Provident Fund Organisation (EPFO) is a statutory body under the authority of the MoLE. On a national level, the EPFO is managed by a tripartite board, a so-called Central Board of Trustees of the

591 The other autonomous bodies are the Central Board For Workers' Education, the V.V. Giri National Labour Institute, the National Instructional Media Institute, and the National Safety Council (ILO 2013:74).

592 See the official website, http://labour.gov.in (2014-09-05), for more information.

Employees' Provident Fund consisting of representatives of the central and state governments, employers and employees. Under the supervision of the tri-party board and the MoLE the EPFO has set up 120 agencies operating on various administrative levels to ensure the administration of the EPF scheme (Rao 2007:85-86).[593]

Employees' State Insurance Corporation

The Employees' State Insurance Corporation (ESIC) is also under the control of the MoLE. ESIC has been designed to manage the provision and funds of the ESI since 1948. To do so the ESIC has set up regional and local offices for the registration, monitoring and provision of social security benefits under the ESI Act. Furthermore, in some cases the ESIC grants reimbursement of medical benefits granted by state governments if the service is covered under the ESI scheme.[594]

Department of Social Welfare

Contrary to the MoLE, the Department of Social Welfare focuses on social security for the unorganised workers and elderly people not covered by the official employment-related social security schemes for the organised sector. The Department of Social Welfare is a highly decentralised institution and has administered social security schemes for the elderly, disabled, and vulnerable since 1959.[595] Under its responsibility is the IGNOAPS and another state-provided scheme, the *Bombay Prevention of Begging Act*, for the target group. The department reflects the pluralistic character of social security in India. Its agencies are operated individually on the state level under the official supervision of the national department. As a consequence, the granted benefits and schemes are determined by the

593 Detailed information is available at http://www.epfindia.com (2014-09-05).

594 See http://www.esic.nic.in (2014-09-05).

595 The MoLE has set up 10 district units all over India to provide as well as inform social security schemes, avenues and benefits for beneficiaries.

locality and social security politics of the state due to a missing national policy strategy.[596]

Ministries and Social Security Administration

Counting on decades of service dating back to colonial times the Ministry has established a complex network of subordinated agencies on national, state, regional and sub-regional levels,[597] including various committees on the national level for specific social security funds (Rao 2011:123-25). In the decentralisation of responsibility for social security the central government finances all national social security schemes to a decent degree; in most cases 50 percent of the premium sums. In particular, since the introduction of the third tier, the PRIs, in 1993, the administrative responsibility for providing social security benefits has moved to the local and village administrations (Besley, Pande and Rao 2005). Although employment-related social security in the formal sector is well funded and formulated, the administrative capacity on lower tiers, the refusal to cover the whole country, the large number of recipients, and the complexity of the rapidly growing and constantly changing labour market is taking its toll on the efficiency of the administration.

596 A major issue has been the variations in the benefits granted by the social security and assistance programs all over India. Even the nationally administered schemes, such as the IGNOAPS, vary from locality to locality in terms of coverage, benefits and accessibility.

597 Regional, sub-regional and sub-account offices throughout India mainly engage in providing the cash benefits, registration, and other administration-related services for the beneficiaries of the social security schemes administered by the central government.

6.3.2 Political Chain of Command and Control in China

China's 'ideocracy' is representative of a typical authoritarian[598] party state. In the one-party system[599] the locus of political power is concentrated in the CCP (Wang 2002). Even the structural reforms in 1978 and the resulting transformation of the CCP's character from a totalitarian to an administrative party have not eroded its dominant ideological or political role as the locus of political, economic and social authority (Zheng 2004). In contrast to India's democratic system, in an autocratic state such as China democratic institutions, such as the parliament (NPC), tend to be 'window dressing' and thus do not really provide democratic mechanisms (Kailitz 2009a, Gandhi and Przeworski 2008). Having a parliament or elections in the National Congress and a number of political parties are no determinants of democracy. In most cases these institutions are only instruments to legitimate decisions and lack any democratic mechanisms (Gandhi and Prezworski 2007 a/b, Kailitz 2013).[600] Thus, participation is clearly limited by preventing voters from selecting alternative candidates or providing feedback on policy processes (Heilmann 2002).

6.3.2.1 CCP the Locus of Political Life

The CCP hosts its National Congress every five years, representing on paper the highest party institution to set the policy direction and formally elect or confirm party leadership. The National Congress officially appoints the 150 members of the *CCP Central Committee*, the *Military Central Committee* and the *Central Commission for Discipline Inspections* (Chan et al. 2008:46-47). Although the National Congress seems to wield enormous power in electing party leaders and dictating policy choices for the subsequent five years, in reality the decisions are made by party elites and the broadly formulated policy guidelines are mere parameters for the

---

598 The authoritarian character of the Chinese party state or 'ideocracy', to quote Kailitz (2009a, 2010), has been defined by the Polity IV as a 'fully institutionalized autocracy' (rating of -10).

599 Hadenius and Teorell (2007) reviewed the political system in China, which has accordingly been defined as one-party system (Brooker 2000:40, 2009).

600 Altered functions of institutions or so-called '*window dressing*' (Wintrobe 1998) in autocracies as well as the resulting implications for political analysis were discussed in Chapter 2.

day-to-day work of the Politburo and the state institutions. Similar to the NPC, the Chinese parliament, or the National Congress, is a so-called '*rubber stamp*' to legitimatise the CCP and its policymaking every five years (Lieberthal 1995, Saich 2001).

The choices of the National Congress are binding and every six months the legislature, embodied by the NPC, formally passes the policy choices in its plenary session. Thus, the *rubber stamp* function of the NPC emphasises the interlocking relationship of party and state institutions as well as the missing independence of the legislature (Guo 2013b:143).

Figure 10: CCP's Central Organisation and Institutions

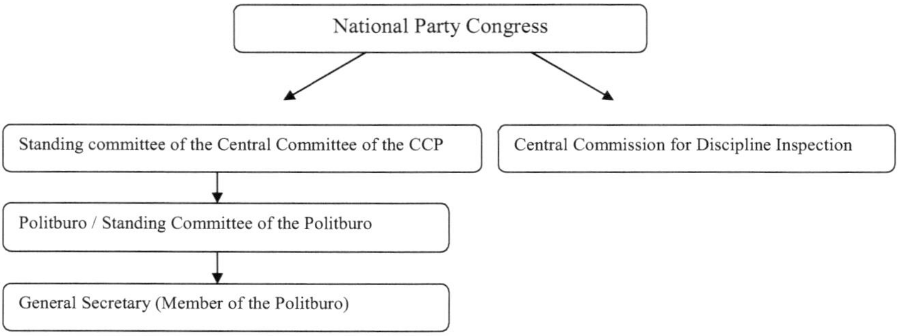

Source: Author's own figure[601]

The presented system-model of the CCP's central organisation (shown in Figure 10) illustrates the key actors of the 'political chain of command and control' in China. The two key actors for policymaking are both found in the central committee of the CCP. The general secretary is the highest ranking official as well as the political leader of the CCP (Falk 2009). He dictates the main political strategy of the CCP and therefore the Chinese state. The second actor under his direct control is the Politburo. In the five years until the next National Congress the Politburo takes over the responsibility for realizing the announced policy directions. As mentioned be-

601 For details on the internal organisation of the CCP see the officially published '*Constitution of the CCP*' http://www.china.org.cn/china/18th_cpc_congress/2012-11/16/content_27138030.htm (2014-07-16). For an elaboration of the historical evolution of the CCP's internal organisational structures see Sujian Guo's works (2000, 2013b:143-44).

fore, the Politburo is the highest policymaking body and the members of its standing committee also hold the key positions of the president, premier and chairperson of the NPC and other state ministries (Saich 2001, Heilmann 2002). Consequently, social security politics is in the hands of the Politburo and the day-to-day work of the SC and the ministries in which they formulate the issues concerning the administration, monitoring and implementation of the social security schemes, programs and services (Chan et al. 2008:48-51, D: Liu 0211).

Figure 11: Structure of the Chinese State - *中国的民主政治建设白皮书*

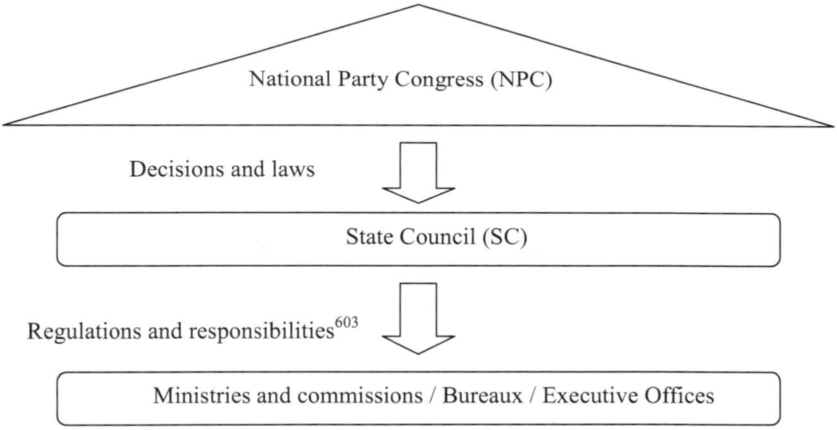

Source: Guo (2013b:136-137), Chan et al (2008:49) [603]

All major functions of the government and state institutions are either personal, as chairmen of the involved institutions or their behaviour are directly controlled by members of the Politburo (Chan et al. 2008, Guo 2013b). In addition, the key positions in the state, such as president, premier and chairperson of the NPC, are appointed by the Politburo standing committee (Lieberthal 1995, Guo 2013b:138). Hence, the Politburo's

603 Officially the NPC is the highest organ, however, in the current institutional setting the NPC is only a 'rubber stamp' for the CCP and the SC and the ministries can enact law-like regulations and decisions without the approval of the NPC, i.e. regulations passed by the SC concerning old age and unemployment insurances (1986, 1991, 1993 and 2006). For the day-to-day business of the CPR the NPC plays only a symbolic role.

standing committee determines the course of policy formation including social policies.[604] Concerning the official hierarchy, a side note is needed to say that the 'day-to-day' business is in the hands of the SC, ministries, and local authorities. The superiority of the NPC and its lawmaking ability are less relevant in a decentralised environment:

Table 27: Law Initiatives

Year	Laws	Administrative regulations	Local regulations	Amount (total)
1991	27	111	1.601	3.879
2000	31	171	5.628	8.846
2005	36	164	14.124	18.121

Source: World Bank Legal Review (2013:185)[605]

As indicated in table 27, the number of national laws has been traditionally low compared to the administrative regulations published by the SC and ministries as well as the increasing relevance of local regulations. In particular, the local regulations have heavily increased due to a missing coherent national policy, including strategies and guidelines for the local authorities (Wong 1998, D. Liu 2011).

Since the 1980s social policymaking is mainly in the hands of the standing committee of the SC. It represents the highest official institution and is granted administrative and executive power over all other state institutions. The SC represents the main executive power including all governmental departments involved in the provision, monitoring and adjustment of social welfare policies and services. These are the Ministries of Labour and Social Security (MLSS), Civil Affairs (MCA), Health (MH), Education (ME), and Construction (MC). Furthermore, actual social policymaking in China is determined by the administrative bodies under the discretion of the SC (Chan et al. 2008:50-52). The Ministries and the SC have the authority to publish their own law-like decisions without the re-

604 Similar to the Politburo in the USSR, the Chinese counterpart exercises authoritarian and unchallenged political, ideological and organisational control (Guo 2013b:131 sp).

605 World Bank. 2013. *World Bank Legal Review: Volume 4. Legal Innovation and Empowerment for Development* .Washington, D.C.: World Bank.

quired approval of the NPC.[606] Therefore the NPC is only superior on paper. All social security schemes and programs, such as insurance and pension schemes, are formulated by the central government's executive bodies. However, the funding, administration and implementation are the responsibility of the local authorities (D. Liu 2011:133-134).

Undeniably, the administrative superiority of the executive regarding law in social policymaking has positive effects on welfare politics (Chan et al 2008:49-50). In an institutional environment without checks and balances the executive has '*room to manoeuvre*' (Mitra 1991, 2002) as well as control over various state policy instruments to react to socio-economic realities and critical junctures. Another reason is the limited party constraints on policy makers due to the fact that the lack of internal party debate on policy issues and non-existing factionalism grant party leaders flexibility in their decision-making. The classical left-right conflict, or to be correct the conflict between pragmatists and ideologists, in the party itself has been limited due to hierarchical structures (Guo 2013b:144). Although factions do not play a crucial role in the internal decision-making of the CCP and the hierarchy fosters the independence of party leaders, strong personalities[607] as well as the composition of the Standing Committee of the Politburo represent considerable constraints on the '*room to manoeuvre*' even for party leaders.[608]

606 The issue of limited de-facto power sharing will be discussed in the following section, both generally and in terms of specific institutions.

607 The most prominent example is given by Deng Xiaoping, who after his official retirement directly nominated the next party leader, Hu Jintao, in 1994. Another prominent example is the former Minister of Security, Zhou Yongkang, who was proclaimed to be the second most powerful man in China. After his retirement the acting president Xi Jinping, in 'a show of power,' announced an investigation of Zhou Yongkang on charges of corruption (Xinhuanet. 2014. '*Zhou Yongkang investigated for serious disciplinary violation*', 2014-07-29, http:// http:// news.xinhuanet.com/english/china/2014-07/29/c_133518450.htm (2014-07-29)).

608 In particular Hu Jintao had to wait until 2007 to nominate his own trusted politicians in the Politburo at the 17th National Party Congress in order to solidify his political power and set into motion his 'harmonious society' agenda to improve overall social security coverage for rural people (Hu 2005, MoC 2005, China Daily Online 2006, People Daily's Online 2006b).

6.3.2.2 The Politburo: A key actor

A fundamental aspect of the Chinese political regime is the continuity of the sovereignty of the CCP. As Chalmers Johnson (1970:7) puts it, 'communist regimes are the product of revolutionary movements, not rebellious ones. They seek not merely to correct certain wrongs or to restore an old, betrayed society, nor to build a new society and a new man.' Accordingly, the communistic revolution aimed to establish the CCP as the sole party and in the process the CCP inherited total control of all political institutions, policy processes and even the law. Generally speaking, the CCP dominates all aspects of politics in China (Saich 2001, Guo 2013b). The CCP has established a complex network of party cell organisations on national, provincial, municipal and village levels. In addition to the national level the constitution of the CCP appoints the National Congress and its standing committee, the Central Committee of the CCP, to the highest party institutions; it is the executive organ that formulates the political strategy of the CCP, the Chinese state, and the Chinese people for five years. To meet its objectives, every five years the National Congress convenes to discuss, articulate and formulate the policy choices for the next five years (Falk 2009). Also the National Congress appoints roughly 150 members of the Central Committee to articulate and formulate the overall policy guidelines and provide 'suggestions' to the state authorities.[609] In the power of the Central Committee is the appointment of key positions in the CCP's departments, such as the Politburo, but only if former members have retired.[610] For example, in 2004 the newly elected political leaders of the CCP and their subordinated Central Committee had to wait until 2007 to replace the former Politburo members with their nominated candidates (Falk 2009, Bo 2013).

The Central Committee can appoint all twenty members of the Politburo and chooses nine of these members to represent the Politburo Standing Committee. Furthermore, the Central Committee also sets up all other CCP departments, including the General Secretary and the Central Secretary, which manage the day-to day work of the Politburo (Chan et al. 2008:47).

---

609 The decisions or suggestions of the Central Committee are binding for the state government and its institutions (Heilmann 2002).

610 Retirement patterns have been standardized nationwide by Deng Xiaoping's administration (ISSA 2010).

In addition, the Politburo represents the 'central locus of policy-making power' for the CCP to realize the policy strategies issued by its Central Committee (Guo 2013b:136-37). In the same way as its whole governing hierarchical structure, the Politburo combines the *de facto* supreme power over policymaking through its institutional and direct influence on all important state institutions, ministries, and law enforcement (Lieberthal 1995).[611] Consequently, party-state-institutions relations, including the National People Congress, can be best characterized, in Sujian Guo's (2000:85) words, as '*master-servant*' relations.[612]

6.3.2.3 The Chinese State, Social Security and Administration

The Bureau of Social Insurance Management (BSIM) or '社会保险经办机构' ('*shèhuì bǎoxiǎn jīngbàn jīgòu*') is responsible for the administration, monitoring and implementation of social security and is the key department for the day-to-day administration of social security in China. It operates on all four administrative tiers: national, provincial, municipal and county/township (Chan et al 2008:49-50, D. Liu 2011). At the national level the BSIM coordinates, implements and is responsible for social security policy schemes and programs; in reality the institutions mainly monitor and indirectly control them. The central government has been granted its own lawmaking ability regarding the administrative regulation of social security. In particular, since the introduction of public funding in 1999 the administrative body has issued various regulations concerning public and personal funds.[613] The BSIM has established local agencies at all levels of the institutional setting, such as departments at the second tier

611 All key positions in the government, court, procurator and public security are for members of the Politburo or deputy secretaries of the CCP's party committee (Guo 2013b).

612 This is important for the balance of power. Officially state institutions are subordinate to the people and elected by the National's Congress but due to the fact that all heads of state institutions outrank the National People's Congress, its formal political influence is non-existent (Guo 2000:85, 2013b).

613 In 1999 the social security administration issued various regulations concerning the financial regulation of social funding—i.e. § 6, 16, 29 and so of the '社会保险基金财务制度 ('*Financial Regulation of Social Funds*')' (D. Liu 2011:135).

(the provinces), the third tier (the municipalities)[614] and the fourth tier (the counties). These local agencies are integrated and under the authority of the local administration. Therefore the *de facto* power of the BSIM is limited (Loo and Chow 2006). [615]

The BSIM has the responsibility to ensure the four categories of social security schemes: the pension scheme (including old age, disability, supplementary benefits, survivor pension schemes), health insurance, employment injury insurance, and maternity insurance. But the day-to-day operation of the four social security schemes generate various administrative functions for the BSMI. The BSMI registers employers and employees[616], collects contributions, pays and controls entitlement demands, manages funding and social pooling of the schemes, and monitors the progress of the programs in statistical reports (Wong 1998).

The social security administration is located on various levels on all four administrative levels. There is no national social security law and no division of labour among the state institutions in the social security administration (ILO 2006:38, White 2006). Thus, although there is one ministry responsible for each specific social security programme, it is a common phenomenon that social security schemes are managed by two or even more ministries at the same time.[617] For example, the Ministry of Labour and Social Security (Ministry of Personal and Social Security) manages the employment-related health insurance of urban employees but the Ministry of Health covers the related medical costs for treatment under the schemes as well as finances the government health facilities providing the medical treatments (Bloom and Tang 2004:15, Chan et al 2008:10).

---

614 Some large counties have been granted the administrative status of cities by the state government.

615 Another issue is the financial resources available for the administration. The lower the levels of administration, the lower and the tighter are the budget restrictions due to tax reform (Loo and Chow 2006). For instance, as Ding (2004) reports, roughly 60 percent of the county governments and even 75 percent of the township governments struggle to cover their salaries.

616 Employers and employees have to register separately for each social security scheme at the responsible ministry. Registration at the BSIM only accounts for the pension schemes. As mentioned before, the BSIM is only responsible for fulfiling the day-to-day operations, not including registration or the design of the schemes.

617 See Gongcheng Zheng's (2002:249sp) work '郑功成, 社会保障学' (*'Social Security'*) for an overview of the various ministries responsible for social security.

Furthermore, the missing legal framework for the social security system emphasises the fact that social security is not regulated by law but by the decisions, directives, circulars and proposals issued by the SC, ministries and/or regulations of the BSIM. Contrary to law, these directives do not have to be approved by the NPC but have similar power as laws (White 2006, Chan et al. 2008:9-10). Also, the complexity of the social security administration and simultaneous responsibility of various ministries for one scheme make it hard for state authorities to effectively address current problems or enforce the implementation of these schemes on the local level due to the fact that the short-term regulations on social security issued by different ministries often overburden the financial and administrative abilities of local governments to implement the regulations (Bloom and Tang 2004:5). In the following section, the main institutions involved in social security administration are briefly presented and discussed to give an overview of the complexity involved.

The Chinese State Council

The State Council represents the Chinese government and is the highest executive body. In its function as the principal policymaker it formulates administrative regulations, monitors and implements policies, and drafts legislative bills that have to be passed by the NPC (Chan et al. 2008: 47-48). The SC is directly under the authority of the premier who is also the acting chairman of the SC.[618] Moreover, the SC is granted authority over 29 ministries and state commissions through which it administers, controls and monitors the functioning of the state government and day-to-day business. Accordingly, the SC supervises a wide range of state departments and agencies which can broadly categorised into four groups (Luo 1998:8-9, Chan et al. 2008:48): (i) *ministries and commissions*, which are responsible for managing, monitoring and administering macro-economic processes; (ii) *bureaus that are directly under its authority*, such as the specialised economic departments concerned with taking care of the specific economic and industrial sectors and zones in China; (iii) *executive offices*, which are responsible for administering Personnel, Labour and So-

618 The premier and his selected cabinet are officially nominated by the NPC to carry through the policy guidelines announced by the National Congress (Falk 2009).

cial Security, and Education; (iv) law and order departments and ministries, which are responsible for providing and enforcing law and order, as well as public and state security (Luo 1998:8-17).[619]

To compare the NPC and the SC in terms of responsibility and political power, the SC concentrates much more power due to its policymaking ability and the various key ministries and departments under its direct authority. In the particular sub-field of social security politics but also in foreign policy the SC wields real power by controlling the agencies responsible for the actual implementation of the policy choices of the CCP which have been approved by the NPC (Guo 2013b:143-47).[620]

The National People's Congress: The 'rubber stamp'

According to the Constitution the NPC represents the highest organ of the state and has superiority over all state institutions as well as final responsibility for every passed law. Theoretically the NPC holds all government power (Guo 2000:83, 2013b:141-42). In its function the NPC has the authority to pass all laws but basic ones. Furthermore the NPC announces the leader of the government. Its legislative power is based on the membership of 3,000 elected deputies who represent the provinces, autonomous regions and municipalities as well as the army. Elections are held every five years and sessions are held in the early quarter of every year. The NPC deputies are elected for five years and meet once a year. For the day-to-day business of passing and formulating laws the NPC has a constant standing committee. However, the power of the NPC is extremely limited compared to the CCP and State Council. The reasons can be found in the personal recruitment patterns of the chairman. The acting chairman of the NPC Standing Committee is a member of the Politburo (Luo 1998).

Another institutional constraint is grounded in the fact that, as mentioned before, the NPC has only theoretical superiority over all state institutions. On the one hand the appointed heads of the departments, such as

619 For a detailed account see Luo's report (1998) '*Explanatory note of the program for restructuring the State Council*' delivered at the 1st Session of the Ninth National People's Congress on 6th March.

620 See Harmin and Zaho's (1995) '*Decision-making in Deng's China: Perspective from Insiders*' for a look behind the curtain of policymaking.

the Politburo, hold higher positions in the CCP and therefore outrank the NPC; on the other hand the ministries have additional independence in their day-to-day work. Consequently, the NPC is often referred to as the '*rubber stamp*' due to its symbolic function in legitimizing the laws handed down by the SC (O'Brien 1990, Saich).

The Ministry of Labour and Social Security

The Ministry of Labour and Social Security (MLSS)[621] together with the Ministry of Civil Affairs are jointly responsible for the functioning, provision and implementation of the social security system and related services. In its current form the MLSS was founded in 1998 and is directly under the authority of the SC. The MLSS deals with all issues concerning unemployment, rural pension schemes, re-employment programs and centres for laid-off workers. Furthermore, in addition to its executive function of implementing the policies, the MLSS is the main actor in producing proposals for labour and re-employment policies and programs (Ngok and Zhu 2003).

The ACFTU: Quasi Law Making Power

The ACFTU[622] is considered as a 'transmission belt'[623] to grant two-way communication between the CCP and the workforce (Chan 1993:26, Metcalf and Li 2005, Qi 2011). The ACFTU has no constitutionally granted power but quasi lawmaking power (Chan et al 2008:50-53). Hence, the ACFTU 'is assigned two functions: by top-down transmission, mobilization of workers for labour production on behalf of the nation's collective

621 The ministry has lately (2008) merged together with the *Ministry of Personnel* and has been renamed the *Ministry of Human Resources and Social Security.*

622 The ACFTU will be discussed in detail later.

623 In 1921 in Pravda, Lenin announced the famous dictum that labour unions have to act as a 'transmission belt between the Communistic Party to the masses.' For Lenin the unions had a dual character in helping the party to achieve its goals as well as the workers in protecting their interests and rights (Ruble 1981:10-12). See Ruble, B. 1981. *Soviet Trade Unions: Their Development in the 1970s*. Cambridge, Cambridge University Press.

good; and bottom-up transmission, protecting workers' rights and interests' (Chan 1993:36, Metcalf and Li 2005).[624]

The Ministry of Civil Affairs

The Ministry of Civil Affairs (MCA) has been correctly described as the '*key department*' besides the MLSS for dealing with social security issues concerning social assistance for poor, old, ill and disabled people. The MCA fulfils a wide range of services which have expanded since the 1980s. At the beginning the MCA only conducted funeral and marriage registrations and services but since the 1980s it is also concerned with poverty reduction in urban areas and since 1997 nation-wide. In addition, the MCA is concerned with social assistance for marginal groups. Hence, it is the authority on the *Minimum Income Guarantee* scheme (Wong 1998, D. Liu 2011:147-48).

The Ministry of Health

The Ministry of Health (MH) is concerned with the functioning and quality of the education and health systems. The MH has the power to draft health policies for the necessary allocation of health resources and/or creation of health programmes to ensure the quality of both services (Chan 2008:51-52, D. Liu 2011:134).[625]

The National Fund of Social Security Funds

Before concluding the section on social security administration and the involved institutions the *National Social Fund* (NSF) should also be taken into account. In 2000 the SC introduced the NSF as a committee to control

---

624 In section 6.8 the study conducts, in the tradition of the power theorem approach, a closer analysis of organised labour and its political impact or 'organisational power' to modify political allocation, policymaking and policy provision processes in China as well as in India.

625 Although health care is not the focus of the study, the BHIS (4.2.4.2), which is under the authority and supervision of the MH, is a crucial part of the social security system in China.

the investment of social funds (D. Liu 2011:136-37). The NSF is an independent institution on paper but under the direct authority of the SC. The NSF has the duty to administer, invest and ensure the interest rates of the newly founded public funds, the individual funds of the introduced social security schemes, as well as older pension funds which are still operating.[626] The NSF has been granted the authority to select investment opportunities, nominate trustees, and invest in trustee funds; it also bears the responsibility for coordinating bookkeeping and issuing reports on development.[627] In 2006 the NSF accumulated 282.8 billion RMB which have been, according to the regulations, invested mostly in the national capital market, such as state funds and saving deposits.[628]

6.4 The State Format: Federalism and Decentralisation

A common agreement in the comparative literature is that federalism tends to set up multiple veto points and restrict the ability of party governments to carry through radical policy changes as well as expand the social budget (Tsebelis 1990, 1995, Immergut 1992, Schmidt 2000a). [629] In contrast to unitary states, federalism extends the number of veto players and constrains decision-making (Wilsensky 1975, Cameron 1978, Lane and Errson 1998, Braun 2000).

The related assumptions as well as their implications for policymaking with respect to the type or format of the state should be noted carefully. Multiple veto points are not restricted to federalism. Unitary centralised

626 Due to low interest rates the Central Committee issued decision no.9 in 2003 in which the National Fund gained additional financial subsidies.

627 See, for instance, for the year 2006 the 年全国社会保障基金年度报告 *('Yearly Report of the National Fund for Social Security')*, http://www.ssf.gov.cn/xxgk/tzycb/cwbg/200904/t20090427_905.html (15. 07. 2014).

628 Huaicheng Xiang's (2006:10sp) article '项怀诚, 关于全国社会保障基金的几个问题' ('*Question on the National Fund for Social Security*') evaluates the investment patterns of the National Funds at length.

629 It is assumed and generally validated that the more veto players are involved in the policy process, the less likely are radical changes to the status quo. Each of the veto players adds an obstacle for decision-making and the opposition of veto players can produce political as well as public defiance of the government (Immergut 1992, Tsebelis 1995)

states can have an institutional equivalent similar to the institutions of federal decentralised states.

Table 28: State Format and Policy Performance

	Policy Performance			
	General Govenrment		*Social Policy*	
Intercept	13.33		22.91	
Federalism	-0.45	(-2.48)	-0.71	(-2.52)
Decentralization	0.49	-3.46	0.75	-2.7
Bicameralism	-0.35	(-2.27)	0.02	-0.13
Adj. R2	13.70%		15.40%	

Source: Lane and Errson (2002:277)[630]

As indicated by the correlation analysis in table 28, decentralisation is a main but malleable force for positive social policy performance, in contrast to federalism, which explains why Indian federalism has no advantage in the field of social policy performance compared to the *de-facto* decentralised CPR (Guo 2013b). Summing up, the features of the state format have a considerable effect on policy formation and performance (Scharpf 1991, Colomer 1996).

6.4.1 State Format and Social Security in India and China

One major insight of the institutional debate is that state design matters for politics, policy outcomes and outputs, or as Brennan and Buchanan (1980:181) note, the 'dispersal of fiscal authority among different levels of government' restrict the 'Leviathan's overall fiscal appetite.'

India and China represent two of the largest countries in the world. It should be taken into consideration that the 'impact of governmental structure is not restricted to the size of the state' (Castles 2002:231). Under such geographic circumstances, decentralisation seems to be a necessarily feature. As Steffen Kailitz and Patrick Köllner point out (2013a:18), such large territorial states, even under the firm grip of autocratic rule, cannot

630 The data is based on OLS-regression technique with t-values in parentheses and standardized coefficients values. For a detailed explanation of the operationalized variables see Lane and Errson (2002:275-277).

avoid decentralisation processes but also produce positive effects on political legitimacy and bureaucracy. Consequently, federalism and decentralisation can come in handy for the central government in shifting responsibility to the local authorities, increasing the cooperation and support of the local elites in empowering them, and at the same time unburdening the central bureaucracy. Although the process of decentralisation is typical for larger states, such as the USA, India or Canada, and their non-democratic counterparts of Russia, China and Mexico, the degree of autonomy varies immensely from country to country and particularly from democracies to non-democracies (Mitra 2005, Landry 2008)[631].

6.4.1.1 Chinese-Style Federalism

Chinese scholars from the Central Compilation and Translation Bureau of the CCP issued the term 'commanding control system'[632] to describe the growing tension between the local and central governments in the 1990s. The federal character of the commanding control system relies on a 'forceful bureaucratic hierarchy, the localities are spurred by the administrative orders from the upper level rather than the stimulus from the bottom' (Yang and Li 2013:79).

Although the central government dictates the economic strategies and provision of public services for the local tiers, the local governments can rely on a decent degree of autonomy. The relationship is best associated with a political 'contract system' and the local governments are either financially rewarded for fulfilling the goals or punished if they cannot deliver (Dai 2004).[633]

---

631 India has learned of the importance of decentralisation in achieving the cooperation of local elites from its separation attempts in the Punjab in the 1980s. See Subrata Mitra (2002, 2009) for a detailed analysis of India's successful integration strategies concerning regional elites and regional ethnic groups.

632 The 'commanding control system' has been developed as a theoretical approach to explain the contemporary situation; however, the analytic concept is underdeveloped and used, as Yong Xu (2006) points out, as a description of the local-centre relationship rather than as an analytic framework.

633 World Bank report (2002:2-6) '*China National Development and Sub-National Finance*'.

Figure 12: Governmental Administrative Structure in the CPR

I. Central Government

↓

II. Province Government (34 units including 23 Provinces, 5 autonomous regions, 4 municipal government of centrally administered cities, 2 Special Administration Regions Hong Kong and Macau)

↓

III. District government (333 units including prefecture administrative office, autonomous prefecture government, municipal government of large cities with districts)

↓

IV. County government (2862 units including District -, city -, county governments and autonomous counties)

↓

V. Township/town government (41636 units)

Source: Ministry for Civil Affairs (2014) [634]

In 1988 the Central Committee of the CCP announced a fundamental tax reform in favour of the central government's revenue—a reform that was fully realized in 1994[635] against broad opposition from the local administration.[636] Despite fierce protests, the tax reform was successfully implemented. It has produced a massive loss of revenue for the local governments and negatively affected their ability to fund the less prioritized social security scheme (Yang and Li 2013:79).

634 Ministry for Civil Affairs (2014) '民政部, 中华人民共和国行政区划统计表 ('*Governmental administrative structure of the CPR*')', http://qhs.mca.gov.cn/article/zlzx/qhtj/200711/20071100003177.shtml (25. 07. 2014).

635 On the 28.01.1994 the SC issued law No. 142 '*Individual Tax Law of the Chinese Peoples' Republic Regulations for its implementation*'.

636 In 28.07.1988 the State Council initiated the tax reformation and issued document No. 50 named '国务院关于地方实行财政包干办法的决定' ('*Decision of the State Council on the full fiscal responsibility of local governments*') concerning the regulation of the fiscal system.

Table 29: Revenue ration of the Central Government (1980-2004)

Year	Total Revenue (billion RMB)	Central Govenrment's revenue ratio (%)
1980	115.99	24.5
1985	200.48	38.4
1990	293.71	33.8
1995	624.22	52.2
2000	1339.52	52.2
2004	2639.65	54.9

Source: 中国统计年鉴 2005 (China Statistical Yearbook 2005)

As indicated above, the new taxation system increased the overall revenue of the central government from 38.4 percent in 1985 to 52.2 percent in 1995. Consequently, the local bureaucracy, particularly in rural provinces, has been challenged in attempting to meet the increasing economic expectations of the central government.[637] The local authorities have either had to exploit other sources of revenue or reduce their existing costs to safeguard a business-friendly environment and foster constant economic growth (Dai 2004). A negative effect of the increasing financial pressure on policymaking is noted in Kevin O'Brien and Lianjiang Li's research (1999) on policy implementation in rural China. Local authorities have begun to either strategically use policies to promote their innovation and flexibility or exploit them to serve the demands of the local bureaucracy. An example of the abuse of policies is the constant increases in local taxes for farmers in order to gain more revenue (Dai 2004). As a consequence of the commanding control system and related policy contract the local authorities lost much of their autonomy and now measure their success mainly in terms of socio-economic development targets and indices. The central government's control of policy implementation, lawmaking, and local conditions was heavily limited until the reform in 2007 (Yang and Li 2013). As O'Brien and Li (1999) point out, through 'readily measurable policies the center has established effective controls that lead implementers to define their tasks as policymakers wish. Enough feedback

637 In their article '*政府间财政转移支付: 问题及政策建议*' ('*Chinese Intergovernmental Fiscal Transfer System: Problems and Policy Suggestions*') Zhaohui Long and Jianxin Deng (2005) provide an indepth analysis of the tax reform as well as its implications for the transfer of financial revenues and resulting limited income for 'poorer' provinces and regions.

reaches higher levels, and well-designed inducements and sanctions encourage most ground-level officials to execute even remarkably unpopular measures. On other policies, for which success or failure cannot be assessed without increased popular input, top-down controls have been largely ineffective, and grassroots officials have easily frustrated efforts to monitor them. In these cases, the center has not been able to prevent implementers from ignoring or even sabotaging central plans.' In effect, the tight fiscal situation has given way to the tendency for the provision of social services to fall prey to local financial cutbacks due to the fact that the number of recipients can easily be falsified by the local administration (Xinhua News Agency 2006c).

Under the banner of the policy of a '*Socialist Harmonious Society*'[638] the central government resolved in 2007 to improve social security coverage and unburden the local authorities by splitting the costs for social schemes among various tiers, as the institutions assume responsibility for collecting the revenues for industry, trade and land. Correspondingly, the central government reduced the autonomy of local governments in issuing laws, particularly concerning taxation (Xi 2007, D. Liu 2011).[639] Deregulation has not occurred but the central government has forced all local authorities to work out and include the expenditures for social assistance schemes in their budgets. Furthermore to reduce the financial pressure and extend coverage the central government has given financial support to poor regions in letting the *collective village enterprises* (TVEs) take a part in providing additional funds for the local *Five Guarantees* (SC 2006).

6.4.1.2 India's unusual Federalism: a Balance of self and shared Rule

In the transition from colonial to democratic rule, the concrete question for the political elite became how to design and adapt the federal institution to the Indian context. Article no. 1 of the Indian constitution states that '*India, that is Bharat, shall be a Union of states*' and emphasises the unusual

---

638 See the decision of the Central Committee of the CCP under Hu Jintao's leadership in 2006 for the construction of a '*Socialist Harmonious Society*', cit op.

639 See Zhaohui Long and Jianxin Dengs' (2005:39-44) article '政府间财政转移支付：问题及政策建议' ('*Chinese Intergovernmental Fiscal Transfer System: Problems and Policy Suggestions*') on the issue of the taxation system, problems and suggestions for reforms.

federal design.[640] Out of fear of another case of '*Balkanization*', India's political leaders were extremely resourceful in adapting the federal institutions to the Indian context and achieving a resilient institutional framework to balance regional and national interests (Rothermund 1995b, Mitra 2005:87-88). In contrast to other countries, such as the USA, the Indian federal system is not the mutual coming-together of pre-existing states but a product of the forceful participation of India and Pakistan and the administrative reorganisation of the union states along linguistic criteria in 1957[641]. As a consequence of the brutal division of territory, civil riots, and violent conflict in 1947, the INC's first and overall objective was to ensure the unity of India. What is particularly notable about the constitution is that the term '*union*' refers directly to the territorial unity and superiority of the central state instead of federalism (Mitra 1999b, Bhattacharyya 2002).[642] The fathers of the Indian Constitution, particularly Ambedkar, issued the strict definition in the drafts of the constitution on November 4th, 1948 to empower the position of the central government and repress any secession attempts: 'Though the country and the people may be divided into different States for convenience of administration, the country is one integral whole, its people a single source living under a single imperium derived from a single source.'[643]

Since independence, local-central relations in India have become a prominent area of research for specialists of federal theory (Thakur 1995, Wagner 2006). Today's federalism has to be understood as an attempt to safeguard regional and sectional identity while ensuring a decent degree of central control over the union states, or to quote Watts (2008:7), to '*combin[e] self-rule and shared rule*'.

Although the founding father advocated a strong normative sense of democratic self-determination, the regional violence fuelled by religious separatist tendencies and the trust in central planning jeopardized the full autonomy of union states. As pointed out by Subrata Mitra (2002, 2005),

---

640 H. Bhattacharyya. 2001. *India as a Multicultural Federation: Asian Values, Democracy and Decentralisation*. Fribourg: Instiut du Federalisme.

641 Regional identity has always been a prominent issue in politics. In the 1920s the INC organised its provincial committees mainly on the basis of linguistic criteria (Mitra 2005:90-91).

642 See Bhattacharyya (2001), cit op.

643 Ambedkar cited by P. Singh (2008:63) in his book '*Federalism, Nationalism and Development: India and the Punjab Economy*' which also offers a close examination of the Constituent Assembly Debates in 1949.

India set up a 'corporate federalism'. The high degree of centralisation and the implications of the local-central relationship are obvious in two major respects. First, the central government controls the financial revenues of the states as well as the benefits of the majority of tax incomes (Mitra 2002). The financial dependence of the union states empowers the centre in Delhi – which has its own status as national capital – and gives it additional leverage in the political bargaining between the centre and the elected local governments.[644] Second, there is only one constitution in India. The union states do not have their own constitution – with the exception of the union states Jammu and Kashmir, which have to be treated separately due to their individual history.[645] In fact, the constitution grants the centre exclusive authority in matters of defence, foreign affairs, currency, banking and income tax. In the Union List the 97 items under the authority of the centre have been issued to empower the centre with special powers in order to guarantee the political, economic, territorial and social stability of India as a whole (Mitra 2005:91, Wagner 2006:89).

Furthermore, the constitution allows the central government to take control of the union states under certain circumstances. [646] According to Subrata K. Mitra (1994b, 1999b, 2005), the resilience and recommended policy of the central government can be best described in the phrase '*hit them on the head and teach them how to play the piano*'.[647] India's federalism has been historically questioned by various separatist movements and local violent outbreaks on a large scale that have polarized parts of In-

---

644 See Bhattacharyya (2001), cit op.

645 Article 370 of the Indian constitution grants Jammu and Kashmir a separate constitution (Thakur 1995:93, Rothermund 202:24f, Wagner 2006:89)

646 The Central state declared an emergency under Articles 256, 352, and 360 and took over executive power under Article 256, 257 and 360 and legislative power under Article 249 (Rothermund 1995b:392, Mitra 2005:91).

647 One of the most famous cases is represented by the violent sub-national separatist movement of Sikhs in the 1970s and 1980s. The insurgency of some parts of the Sikh community in the Punjab escalated into a military dispute and peaked with the assassination of Prime Minister Indira Gandhi in 1984. Despite fierce fighting between the Indian military and Sikh separatists – who took their last stand in the Golden Temple – the ethnic majority of Sikhs were once more successfully integrated into the Indian union and democratic system. In the following years, the local party representing the majority of the Sikhs became the ruling political party and ensures the political stability, political influence on national decision-making, and economic success of the union state of Punjab (Rothermund 1990:27, 53, 1995a, Thakur 1995).

dia.[648] In particular, the resilience of India in managing separatism in the long term is grounded in the overriding authority of the Central State and its commitment to take all necessary measures to protect India's territorial unity and democracy.[649] Although violent or militant outbreaks erode the rule of law and result in brutal clashes between rebels and state authorities, the use of legitimate power has always been a means to the end of re-establishing democratic and orderly rule by transforming '*rebels into stakeholders*'.[650] Although the centre has exclusive authority in cases of national importance, the constitution grants the union states their own independence in the field of legislation, granting them independence in decision-making for 66 items.[651]

Another relevant landmark for the decentralisation of Indian federalism and social security provision was the implementation of the third tier – the PRIs or village governments – in 1993 (Gosh and Kumar 2003, Besley et al. 2005). Under Prime Minister Vajpayee the local village governments gained additional independence in becoming the locus for regulating, implementing and monitoring economic, social and other kinds of policies. The roots of self-administration can be traced back to the first experiments in 1870 and the official Government of India Acts in 1919 and 1935 in which the extent of local self-administration and minority representation was issued. Although the political elites favoured democratization and to a

---

648 A prominent example of religiously fuelled riots is the incident involving the destruction of the Babri mosque or mosque of Babur in Ayodhya (Uttar Pradesh) in 1992. The violent destruction of the ancient Muslim mosque by Hindus ignited a wildfire of religiously fuelled violence against the Muslim minority all over Uttar Pradesh that spread to other parts of India (Mitra 2009,Jürgenmeyer, cit op.).

649 In the early decades after independence, the central government used its overriding authority to re-establish political order in the union states on several occasions. The most prominent and still relevant example is the special status of Jammu and Kashmir (Rothermund 2002:24 sp).

650 See Subrate K. Mitra and V.B. Singhs' (2009) work '*When Rebels become stakeholders*' on the issue, process and historical examples in which the Indian state either achieved or failed to integrate regional ethnic and religious groups as well as separatist movements (e.g. Sikhs or Naxalites).

651 In particular, 66 items of regional importance – defined in the concurrent list – give the union state legislative authority in matters concerning public order, police, welfare, health, education, industry, agriculture and local administration (Thakur 1995). However, a key bias is clear in the fact that in cases of conflict (e.g. in the fields of civil or criminal law and/or economic and social planning), the central law prevails (Wagner 2006:89).

decent degree the independence of local governments, in the early years of independence the nation-wide implementation of the PRI was suspended until 1993 because the pilot project in three union states in 1959 could not produce any significant outcomes (Wagner 2006:98 sp, Watts 2008). Today the PRIs have gained additional regulative competency and are partly responsible for the local distribution and monitoring of social security (e.g. for the NREGA) (Gosh and Kumar 2003, Rao 2011).

6.4.1.3 Pluralism: Performance differences on Local Levels

Variations in the range and expenditures of welfare programs and service occur not only on a local level in the countries themselves but also on a cross-national level. This phenomenon is not restricted to the political system or the development of countries. In OECD countries, social expenditures range at the state level and across time (Schmidt 1983, 2012, Castles 1998:312-14).[652] Similarly, in India and China social expenditures and access to social services are heavily influenced by the local governments' policy choices, objectives and administrative as well as financial capacities to back them up. As pointed out by Lynn, some of the 'Social Security institutions particularly in developing countries had been for bad management, lack of modern techniques, training and other deficiencies which resulted in complaints from the beneficiaries. In some regions Social Security had acquired a bad name because of these deficiencies' (1994: 32-42). For instance, the richer states and provinces, such as Shanghai or Gujarat, offer higher levels of welfare for their citizens than their poorer counterparts (Singh 1994, Rothermund 1993: 83, Chan et al. 2008:67,132, Wang et al. 2012, Nagaraj 2012a:42)

India's Pluralism and Social Security Provision

In India the administrative authorities on social policies are split between the national and state governments. The central government sponsors the old age pension, as well as maternity and family benefits schemes. The other two schemes are under the authority of the state governments. How-

652 For a historical source on the development of expenditures from 1960 to 1997, see the OECD Report (1999) '*OECD Historical Statistics 1960–1997*'.

ever, federalism has an asymmetrical character due to the union states' dependency on the central government's institutions[653] for their financial revenues and development strategies (Watts 2008).

The main contributor to social security schemes, except for insurance, is the state government. Many, though not all, of the existing schemes are either directly managed by the government or at least subsidised (Rao 2007, 2011). The commitment to regulate, monitor, control and coordinate these programmes, schemes and services produces significant administrative pressure on the capacity of local authorities. The government of Karnataka alone has set up more than twenty boards to fulfil the various administrative tasks. The state of Kerala has created an additional apex body to assure the functioning and cooperation of the various boards (Sülzer 2008:221). Furthermore, the union states also depend on the central *Indian Administrative Service (IAS)* in producing policy outcomes. In addition, the efficiency and access to welfare schemes and programs depends on three key determinants (Wildavsky 1980, Potter 1996):

Nowadays there is little dispute that the financial condition of the union state determines the quality of welfare system (see table 2). Richer or economically better performing states tend to have higher human development than poorer states. Also, richer union states, such as Tamil Nadu (Guhan 1992b, Kohli 2012:209-210), have produced additional and effective social programs; some of these schemes have even been introduced nation-wide.[654]

Second, the institutional capacity to implement social policies is directly linked to the capacity of the local administration under the command of the IAS. The administrative body is 'poorly motivated, sometimes corrupt, and has its hands full with a host of other responsibilities. The individual requests have less priority for the administration than their duty to permit the functioning of the institutions and implementation of structural adjustment projects' (Sen and Rajasekhr 2012:114). Accordingly, '*incrementalism*' can occur if the bureaucracy 'sometimes actively sabotages' (Sen and Rajasekhr 2012:114) but there is a fine line between active opposition and an overcharged administration. In most cases the administration is 'over-

---

653 Against the background of federalism, the Finance and Planning Commission on a national level is responsible for the allocation of financial revenues as well as for the planning of national development projects in the different union states.

654 The local Maharashtra Employment Guarantee Scheme (EGS) in 1973 (Nagaraj 2012a:59).

charged' and/or ill equipped in terms of time, manpower and financial resources as well as competency to handle social security provision. [655] Accordingly, it is not surprising that in the big picture, the 'poorer' rural union states, such as Andra Pradesh, combine both low resources as well as ineffective social security provision (Government of Andra Pradesh 1997, Desphande 2007:32-35)[656]. Hence, it seems that the lack of competent administrative and financial resources seems to be the main determinant for explaining 'harsh' intra-country differences in the level of social security coverage.

Third, in the early 1990s the central government attempted to solve the regulation problem by creating the local self-governing bodies, the so-called *Panchayat Raj Institutions* (PRIs) to reduce the expanding costs of the administration of the various social security schemes and services. In 1992 the parliament passed the Enactment of the 73rd Constitutional Amendment, which officially introduced a third tier on the local level in the federal system, the so-called *PRI*s[657]. However, the PRIs could not fulfil their role as a major contributor of social security. Hence, the PRIs lacked the competence, information and administrative ability to effectively contribute to the social security schemes. Therefore the success of most programmes coordinated by PRIs lacked either '*people's participation*' or '*beneficiary control*' (Vijay Shankar and Shah 2012:139). Vijay Shankar and Shah (2012:140) described the recent trend of entrusting social services to overburdened local communities as 'universalisation without quality'.

655 The Comptroller and Auditor General found that only an all-India average of 33 instead of the promised 100 paid days of employment has been realized for roughly 25.5 million households. Moreover, the number of registered job cards is higher than the actual number of people attending work (Sen and Rajasekhar 2012:14-15).

656 For instance, the Universal Health Insurance Scheme (UHIS) launched in 2004 should cover 10 million recipients in its first year, but could only achieve around 1.16 million. Furthermore, 48 percent of all policies are limited to four states alone (Bhat and Saha 2004, Ahuja and De 2004).

657 In the administrative body of the PRIs roughly 3.2 million local men and women are officially enlisted (Sülzer2008: 223)

Chinese Pluralism and Fiscal Constraints on Social Security Provision

The same causality can be observed in the Chinese case. China has a traditionally high level of socio-economic inequalities between rich coastal and poor rural provinces. The central government of the Chinese unitary state determines the financial revenues, administrative staff, and economic as well as social development. As a consequence of low financial distributions for the poorer provinces, the local governments, including administrative units, villages, and town authorities have been tested in their ability to deliver the *Five Guarantees* due to their financial burdens and insufficient administration (Chung 1995, Leung 2005, Yang 2006). Since the abolishment of the Agricultural Tax in 2005 the financial situation has worsened, especially for the lower tier administrations (Ding 2004).[658]. In response, the provinces have begun to report lower numbers of recipients to the central government to reduce their social expenditures (Yang 2006). According to the MCA, only 2.97 million people are officially reported of an estimated 5.7 million recipients who should have access to social support (Hong et al. 2004). Richer urbanised provinces or municipalities have much more financial resources and employment opportunities due to urbanisation and political patronage.

Table 30: Regional differences in the monthly benefits of the MSLS

City name	Monthly MSLS rate per person (in Yuan)	City name	Monthly MSLS rate per person (in Yuan)
Guangzhou	330	Fuzhou	200-220
Shenzhen	290-344	Kunming	210
Dailan	240-363	Nanning	210
Ningbo	300	Changsha	200
Hangzhou	280-320	Herbin	200
Beijing	290	Lhasa	200
Shanghai	290	Xian	200
Xiamen	265-315	Zhengzhou	200

658 In 1994 the reform of taxation by the central government had a significant effect on the financial budget. While the central government could increase its revenues, the reform shortens the local authorities' financial incomes and about 50 to 60 percent of them are heavily in debt (Bernstein and Lü 2008), reducing their ability to implement social policies or expand their administrative staff. In most cases, the local administrative body has not been trained to provide access to welfare services for recipients.

City name	Monthly MSLS rate per person (in Yuan)	City name	Monthly MSLS rate per person (in Yuan)
Tianjin	265	Chongqing	195
Nanjing	240	Huhlot	190
Jinan	230	Lanzhou	190
Qingdao	230	Nanchang	190
Hiakou	221	Taiyuan	183
Shenyang	220	Yinchuan	180
Shijazhuang	220	Guiyang	170
Wuhan	220	Changchun	169
Chengdu	210	Xining	165
Hefei	210	Urumqi	161

Source: Secretary of Chinese Social Security Forum (2006)[659]

As indicated in the table 30 above, it is worth noting that the level of social security heavily varies from location to location. Rural and poorer provinces have neither the financial resources to realize a wide range of social programs and schemes nor the available welfare programs for the rural poor. Social policy, as mentioned in the previous chapters, focuses on urban working force in the urban regions. In addition, the national welfare system produces regional and social inequality.

Another problem of implementation is the limits of administrative competence as well as the Hukou system.[660] China's social security administration lacks the skills, training and knowledge to tender the services.[661] Local social security administration is often not trained in providing the programs and has only limited financial resources available. In effect, even the access to the MSLS-financed additional schemes tended to be restricted until 2007 (Chan et al. 2008:84-85). As a reaction, in 2007 the central government not only reworked the balancing of costs but also attempted to professionalize the social security administration (BMIS) on all tiers (Yang 2006). Without going into further detail on the institutional differences between the two, the argument is plausible that China's strong-

659 Secretary of China Social Security Forum (2006) '*The standard rate of the Minimum Standard of Living Scheme in 36 cities*', www.cnss.cn/zlzx/sjtj/qttj/200609/t20060914_30898.html (2012-05-05).

660 For the relevance of the Houku system in determining the access of citizens to welfare, see section 2.7.6.

661 In his popular study on *Henan* and the North-Central region Feng Chen points out the higher level of corruption in the rural and north-central regions compared to the urban coastal provinces (2000).

ly decentralised unitary state seems to have a more positive effect on social security politics, provision and delivery than India's modestly decentralised federalism (Watts 2008). In fact, decentralisation offers 'richer' states and provinces more flexibility in social security provision but 'poorer' states and rural provinces struggle to offer the minimum level of social security (World Bank 2002, Yang 2006).[662] Consequently, the degree of decentralisation, particularly of financial revenues, heavily affects the policy performance of lower administrative bodies.[663]

6.4.2 Comments on the State Format

India's *soft state*[664] exercises a moderately decentralised system, in which social security and expenditure regime are the perfect examples. The central government still announces Five Year Plans, including budgets for the schemes and programs set into practice by the central government. Despite centralised structures[665], the union states have additional independence in the public policy field. One reason is that the Indian central government has 'a bureaucracy that is professional at the apex but not so in the periphery' (Potter 1996, Kohli 2012:197); thus, local governments can determine the range and scope of their policy outcomes. In addition, the welfare regime and social security politics in general and the provided level of welfare as well as public goods specifically varies from union state to union state (Sen and Rajasekhr 2012:114, Desphande 2007:32 sp)[666].

---

662 The World Bank report (2002) '*China National Development and Sub-National Finance*' provides an investigation into the sub-finances which illustrates the regional budget differences all over China.

663 Financial constraints on policymaking has been discussed in chapter VI..

664 Atul Kohli's (1987, 2012) accounts provide evidence of the process.

665 On the one hand, the central government exercises power over the financial resources for the states, which determines the overall financial budget especially for the poorer union states. On the other hand, the administrative body is mainly represented by the ICS. The ICS, or so-called the '*steel frame*,' represents the higher echelon of the administrative carter and is managed by the central government. In addition, the administrative competency of the union states is also influenced by the central governments' personal policy and the resulting bureaucrats of the union states' day-to-day business.

666 The Universal Health Insurance Scheme (UHIS) is one example of the variation. The program was launched in 2004 and should have covered 10 million recipients all over India in its first year, but could only achieve around 1.16 million.

Similar to India, the Chinese state is even more decentralised on all tiers in terms of social security administration and expenditure regime; however, as mentioned before the provincial, municipal and local authorities have no real autonomy. Consequently, the decentralization process in China has often been called '*federalism: Chinese-style*' which implies a high degree of decentralisation of administrative responsibility without giving the lower tiers more autonomy. In particular, as part of the ongoing decentralisation process starting in the late 1980s the tax reform in 1994 was an instrument of the central government to ensure the dependency of the local tiers (Montinola, Qian and Weingast 1995, Laundry 2008). Although the central government determines the financial revenues, administrative staff, and main objectives of economic as well as social development for all provinces[667], the resources are not equally divided, resulting in the traditionally high policy performance gap between the rich coastal and poor rural provinces. In theory the local governments have to grant access for recipients regardless of their own limited financial and administrative resources; but in reality the provincial, municipal, and local governments in poorer regions struggle to provide the necessary scope and range of benefits and coverage when it comes to existing schemes and programs (Ding 2004, Yang 2006a/b, Kennedy 2007).[668]

In comparing India and China, the assumed negative effect of the Indian bicameral system on public expenditures cannot be validated and the Chinese 'unitary' state[669] seems to follow the same strict budget strategy

---

Furthermore 48 percent of the scheme is limited to only four union states (Bhat and Saha 2004, Ahuja and De 2004).

667 Since the 1970s and the success of pioneer projects in improving local socio-economic conditions, the province and local authorities can also initiate compulsory schemes or programs (Chan et al. 2008:Chapter 5)

668 Recent academic and public debate on the welfare states emphasises the constant struggle of balancing their social policies, state expenditures as well as economic competitiveness (Pierson 2001). Welfare regimes are no longer restricted to the advanced industrial nations. Developing countries and emerging markets are trying to promote economic growth as well as social welfare for their citizens (Kersbergen 1995, Zacher 2001:404-8). *Old* and *younger* welfare states alike are both challenged in similar ways to address socio-economic realities on the one hand and to balance financial resources on the other hand (Cable 1995). Higher welfare levels also mean higher state expenditures, which compete with other government projects on, for example, infrastructure or the military.

669 On paper China is a 'unitary' state; however, the reality is that China has developed a strong pluralism (Guo 2013b).

for social security provision during recent years (diagram 7, 8 a/b and table 46). Contrary to the commonly assumed relevance of financial resources the budget issue is not as relevant on the national planning level as it is on the local level for policy outputs (Ma and Hou 2005, Nagaraj 2012a:56-57). As previously indicated (see Table 2) human development as well as the provision of social security seems to correlate directly with the economic performance of the region and the resulting financial capacity of the local authority. National social security politics and the central Five Year plans have been less responsible for income disparity between the rich and poor states which, however, produce significant constraints on the access and coverage of social security all over India, particularly in the poorer regions (Ministry of Finance 1993, 2000, 2009, World Bank 2002, Wagner 2006:87-89).

6.5 Bureaucracy and Longitude of Policy Making

Public administration literature as well as cross-national studies have demonstrated evidence of the enormous role of bureaucracy or the '*machine'* in formulating policy goals, regulations and laws as well as providing public goods, services and social security schemes (March and Olsen 1989, Scharpf 1991, Potter 1996, Kaufmann et al. 2005).

In regard to the earlier discussed assumed 'comparative advantage' of democracies in inheriting higher levels of political performance vis-à-vis higher levels of administrative performance, the data accumulated by the WGI (table 26) for India and China does not allow us to derive such a conclusion. India is doing only marginal better in terms of regulatory quality (-0.05 for India and -0.18 for China in 2006) but in terms of government efficiency China is scoring much higher (0.08 for China and -0.05 for India). A common argument derived from the electoral cycle in democracies is that autocracies have an advantage in terms of long-term planning capacity of social security programs. Without denying the fact, the earlier discussed strong path-dependency of social security programs, central planning and Five Year plans in India seem to provide a counterexample.

6.5.1 Chinese Bureaucracy and Long-term Planning

Undoubtedly, the Chinese case clearly illustrates the merits of authoritarian rule for longitude in social security provision (e.g. the life cycle of most national social security schemes which started out as pilot projects) (Chan et al. 2008). Central planning and longitude are common features of Chinese socials security politics. Every five years the National Party Congress decides on the major policy guidelines (Guo 2000, 2013b). The implementation of the guidelines is overseen by the standing committee of the Central Committee of the CCP which issues decisions and suggestions for policymaking (Meisner 1995, Guo 2013b:140-144).

6.5.1.1 Qualitative Constraints on Chinese Bureaucracy

Taking a closer look at the relationship of business and politics, China has an extremely high level of connection between both kinds of actors. In cross-national measurements of business connections with parliament, China scores 12.25 percent, similar to Russia (12 percent) and higher than any other developing country, including India.[670]

It is common for Chinese economic actors to rely on various types of political connections with high-ranking party members or officials on various levels of administration. Wang (2013:11) estimates that 2,154 (87.7 percent) out of 2.465 enterprises had some kind of political connection. Of these firms the overwhelming majority had a direct connection with the party state (78 percent) rather than the Chinese parliament (SC). Furthermore, the local government is also extremely important. At least 28.15 percent of the firms have established ties to local authorities.

670 According to Faccio's measurements (2006), China has an extremely high level of connection compared to other countries. Surprisingly it is estimated that only 2.28 percent of the firms in India have long-term connections with ministers or members of the parliament. The other BRICS states, Brazil and South Africa, scored zero percent. Compared to other countries—Italy (10.3), Indonesia (7.79) and Thailand (8.42)—the value and resulting tight business connections with politicians is extremely high (Faccio 2006).

Red capitalists and the CCP

As Dickens (2003) notes '*wealth to power*' has been a common strategy of cooperating with business interest groups and demands in autocratic systems. The government and ruling elites demand economic growth, foreign investment, and international trade to legitimate their political reign as well as accumulate state or private financial funds (Gandhi and Przeworski 2007). Such a strategy has also been 'aggressively' used by the CCP to 'involve private entrepreneurs in politics via making them Party members or people's congress representatives' (Wang 2013:8-9). The increasing numbers of party members recruited among private entrepreneurs are commonly referred to '*red capitalists*'. Furthermore, the recruitment patterns have constantly increased the internal power of the liberal faction.

Administrative Brain Drain

A common phenomenon in China is the administrative *brain drain* which is empirically hard to measure. Still, a number of qualitative studies have produced strong evidence of the problem (Wedemann 2004, 2012, Bardhan 2007, Wang 2013). An increasing number of officials resign from public office in favour of employment in the private sector. The demand for such people in the private sector is extremely high. Private entrepreneurs have to '*grease the wheels*' which is needed for the cooperation of the state and local authorities in order to safeguard a business-friendly environment (Bardhan 2007, 2008). Promotion patterns and available top positions in the Chinese bureaucracy are limited[671] and recruitment policy is not only based on skills but also heavily affected by personal ties (Landry 2008, Shih, Adolph and Liu 2012).[672] In addition, the brain drain is not restricted to the lower administrative body; higher cadre members have taken other employment opportunities, either resigning early or

---

671 The probability of a civil servant being promoted to the ministerial level is only 0.04 percent (Wang 2013:8).

672 See Shih, Adolph and Lius' article (2012) '*Getting Ahead in the Communist Party: Explaining the Advancement of Central Committee Members in China*' for an investigation of the issue of political carries.

after they reach their sixties[673] (Wang 2013). As mentioned before, the Chinese system is a highly decentralised system and can be described as '*local protectionism*' (Wedemann 2004, 2012). As a consequence, the brain drain of officials—including their administrative skills, experiences, and contacts—empowers the overall ability of business interests to modify political decision-making, especially on the provincial and local levels.

6.5.2 India's Bureaucracy and Long-term Planning

In democratic settings the electoral cycle produces constraints on the longitude of policymaking either by changing the composition of the government or the requirement of the elected government to be responsible for the current demands of the majority to ensure re-election.[674] In the Indian case, and with respect to social security provision, the picture is not so clear. On the one hand, the constant introduction or remodelling of social security schemes for poverty reduction in India seems to validate the assumption of the short-term policymaking of democracies.[675] But on the other hand, taking a closer look reveals that the changes are marginal in order to modify the funding of existing programmes, expand the social security net, or remodel the scope and range of social security programmes, such as the constant adaptation of the PDS. Furthermore, the social security legislation for the formal sector has been untouched even in times of increasing financial pressure and liberal-oriented policymaking (Nagaraj 2000, 2012a). Despite a context of regular electoral cycles and constant remodelling of the composition of coalition governments (Wagner 2006, Election Commission of India 2014) India has advocated longitude in so-

---

673 Deng Xiaoping announced sixty as the officially retirement age to reduce the number and influence of old cadre members in key positions (Manion 1993).

674 It is worth mentioning that the short-termed nature and responsiveness of policymaking is not generally seen as a negative tendency. Responsiveness and political participation grant the government postive feedback in order to react to actual problems, such as environmental pollution (Easton 1965, 1970).

675 Since the 1990s the electoral changes in the government also had a significant effect on reconstructing the social security policy scheme, as well as responsibility and administration of the unorganised sector. Every government reformulated the range, scope, target groups and even the social security programmes (e.g. the introduction of the *NREGA*, *Indira Gandhi National Old Age Pension Scheme* and *Varishtha Pension Bima*) (Ambasta et al. 2008a/b, Chibber 2012:173.175).

cial policymaking. The major reasons include the ongoing Five Year Plans determining the financial resources and social security objectives for the next five years. The planning and approval of the Five Year Plans are often performed by the former legislature and affect the subsequent elected government's policy choices (Seventh Five Year Plan 2008). Consequently, India's policymaking has adapted a decent degree of longitude.

6.5.2.1 Qualitative Constraints on India's Bureaucracy

India's administration is plagued by corruption (see table 26), a complicated licensing and tax system, as well as excessive regulations on the national and local level (Potter 1996, Kohli 2012:214). In particular, the social security administration is mostly overburdened by the day-to-day business of implementing, registering and administering the social security programmes as well as processing the numerous applications for social services and benefits by citizens (Potter 1996, Rao 2007:60-63). In this context, Lant Pritchett of Harvard University describes India as a 'failing state' in regard to its incompetent and incapable administration, which is not up to the task of providing modern and effective administration (The Economist 2014f:49).

Excessive Regulations and Red Tape Bureaucracy

The complexity of the Indian administration system is perfectly reflected in the complicated and inefficient licensing and taxation system, which dramatically reduces India's 'doing business' attractiveness (World Bank 2014). Furthermore, the same administrative hurdles and excessive regulations are slowing down the access to social security services and benefits. The complexity of the registration formula and the necessary official documents, such as an ID card or birth certificates, are challenging, to say the least, for most of the applicants, who have neither the expertise, money, time or the official documents to gain access to the available programmes (Sülzer 2008).

The Challenge of Corruption and Fraud

As indicated in the corruption index (table 26), the culprit of public civil services, including law enforcement and administration, is deeply rooted corruption. India's civil administration is overburdened by numerous demands, overstretched resources, as well as complex regulations. Accordingly, it has become a common practise for applicants to pay bribes for the services of the administration.[676] As argued before, most of the applicants of social security programmes lack the needed official documents as well as the expertise for the complex registration processes. However, the corruption is also taking its toll on administration efficiency as well as on the coverage of social security. For instance, the social administration employs local Provident Fund Commissioners for the task of administering and guaranteeing the registration and coverage of any economic entities under the Factory Act. But in reality the registration for the Provident Fund and Pension Scheme is in most cases up to the employers and consequently huge '*blacklogs*' appear in the issuing of annual statements as well as in payments (Rao 2011:263-4). Another issue is that fraud has become a common phenomenon of social security provision in India (Sülzer 2008, Ambasta et al 2008a).

6.5.3 Comments on bureaucratic Efficiency

Another relevant and often unaccounted variable of cross-national variations in policy performance is the bureaucracy or so-called '*machinery*' (table 26). A common consensus agrees on the relevance of bureaucracy for policy outcomes; however, most comparative political studies do not integrate the bureaucracy as a variable to explain cross-national variations between or within countries.[677] Social security programmes have to be planned, funded, monitored and administered and cross-national differences of similar social schemes are often directly related to administrative competency (table 2 and 13).

676 A nation-wide initiative under the name 'I paid a bribe' was founded in the mid 2000s to register paid bribes for civil servants in an attempt to tackle the corruption problem. Information is available at http://www.ipaidabribe.com (2014-01-12).

677 For the variations in the HDI in India and China see table 2.

A closer investigation of the regulative performance of governmental administration in both cases reveals a strikingly similar low profile of bureaucracy due to overstretched administrative capacity, insufficient training or competency, as well as other deficits. In India as well as China the bureaucracy could only achieve low scoring of the administration in regulatory competency, as well as government effectiveness and corruption, which is verified by various examples of miss-management, fraud and limited coverage of social security schemes on the local level (Xinhua News Agency 2006c, table 26). Accordingly, evidence demonstrates the relevance of bureaucracy; however, China has better administrative competency but at the same time India provides a higher value of regular quality.

VII. Political Parties and Social Seucirty Provison

How to explain policy variations under similar political conditions? A prominent point of departure is the 'parties-do-matter' hypothesis or the so-called partisan theory which argues for the crucial function of political parties (Hibbs 1977, 1994, Castles 1982, Schmidt 1983, Mitra 1994a, Mitra et al. 2004).[678] Naturally, comparing an autocracy one-party state with a multi-party democracy is a problematic enterprise. Accordingly, in the following chapter the INC will be singled out in regard to its legacy as the dominant party in India until 2014. Neither are compared to each other (Gandhi and Prezworski 2007a/b, Kailitz 2009a, Köllner and Kailitz 2013a).[679] However, the changing political commitment for carrying through social security policies is compared. For such an investigation as this, the differences in political context will be elaborated.

A point of departure in political science is the 'party effect' or 'partisan effect,' which has gained intense attention in comparative political research on welfare regimes in democratic settings (Schmidt 2002). According to Seymour Martin Lipset (1959), the class conflict of the early 20th century has been transformed into a '*democratic class struggle*' which is fought by the political parties in parliament and at the vote polls. Lipset (1959:229) argues that 'leftist parties represent themselves as instruments of social change in the direction of equality; the lower-income groups support them in order to become economically better off, while the higher-income groups oppose them in order to maintain their economic advantages.'

Empirical evidence has been accumulated by various authors, such as David Cameron (1978, 1984), Hans Keman (1984, 1988) and Jan-Erik Lane and Svante Errson (1998). What all these authors have in common is that they have evaluated the leftist governments as the major determinants of the nature of welfare regimes and big governments. Moreover, the prominent cases—on the one hand the experiences with Social-Democrat-

678 Mitra, S. K. et al. (eds.) 2004. *Political Parties in South Asia*. London: Praeger.

679 In particular, the missing institutional and constitutional veto points as well as the oppression of any political or civil opposition strengthen the party's status quo as sole decision maker (Köllner and Kailitz 2013).

ic rule in Sweden, and on the other hand the policymaking of the liberal market-oriented party government in the USA—seem to validate the assumption of the partisan effect and the relevance of party government composition for policy outcomes in a cross-national perspective (Castles 1989, 1998, Gould 1993, OECD 1999).

7.1 Political Parties, Party Effect and Policy Outcomes

Douglas Hibbs (1977, 1994) and others (Castles 1987, 1993, 1999, Gould 1993, Cusack 1995)[680] have repeatedly argued for the empirical measurable effect of left-winged parties on policy making and *big governments*. Political parties are *vote seekers* and have to realize their electoral promises to gain electoral support in the future (Strøm 1990, Cukierman and Tommasi 1998, Müller 2010).[681]

Hypothesis 4a: *A higher level of left-oriented parties in government has a positive effect on social security expenditures.*

A more critical point of departure is given by Pierson's argument (1994, 1996, 2000) for the '*New Politics of the Welfare State*' and the decline of the party in times of austerity. In constrast to the '*politics and parties do matter*' argument, other scholars (Kittel and Obinger 2003) argue that the 'classical' party effect has faded. According to the empirical evidence of studies on electoral turnout, the composition of the party in government has a lack of effect on state expenditures. The decline of party effects on expenditures is labelled the '*new politics*' of the welfare states (1994, 1996, and 2001) by Paul Pierson. In controversial articles he (1994, 1996) argues for the decline of 'classical' party effects under the trend toward tightening fiscal resources, pointing to the electoral impact of beneficiaries

---

680 See also other authors' accounts of the 'party-do-matter' hypothesis (Schmidt 1983, 1999a, 2002, Mitra 1994a, 2002 and 2013).

681 Otto Kirchheimer (1964, 1966b) elaborates the transformative process of modern political parties in terms of party polity as well as electoral support. Compared to the classical political organisations of the late eighteenth and early nineteenth centuries, modern political parties are so-called '*catch-all*' parties; the term is coined by Krichheimer (1964), which he defines as presenting broader demands to attract electoral support above class cleavages.

of welfare schemes as new pressure groups[682] in determining the development of the modern welfare state. His articles have given rise to various accounts of the implications of austerity politics for political, economic and social development. At the same time, many scholars have been inspired by his argument and critically tested its assumptions. The empirical evidence mostly resonates with Pierson's analysis (1998, 2002), suggesting that the '*the evidence (...) tends to support the 'growth-to-limits' and new politics' perspectives more'* (Kittel and Obinger 2003:20).[683]

Hypothesis 4b: *If the political conflict potential of social security reforms is relatively high, the likelihood that they will be carried through is lower.*

It is worth noting that Paul Pierson's argument on the decline of 'classical' party effects is nothing new. Students of partisan theory emphasise the fact that every political system or so-called political market varies because of the different institutions of the democratic process (Schmidt 2002:168). In the past the outcomes of the partisan theoretical approach, such as the Social-Democratic model, have been under criticism because of their incoherent empirical data (Daalder 2002). Taking the criticism of the statistical techniques seriously, later studies have taken into account various control variables to evaluate the partisan effect of left-wing parties on social expenditures based on various time periods in various countries (Hicks and Swank 1984, Korpi 1983, Huber et al. 1993, Schmidt 1996a). Other output-oriented studies have gathered data that the left-right differences in expenditures have converged in most policy fields and demonstrated the rel-

682 Pierson also argues for the concept of positive feedback. His point of view stresses the fact that welfare policies create their own public supporters and therefore ensure their survival (Pierson 1996, 2002).

683 Various scholars have provided theoretical and empirical evidence of the persisting impact of political parties (Schmidt 1996a, 2000, and 2007, Mitra 1996, 1998 and 2005), state format (Budge et al. 2002), interest mediation systems and institutions in general (Castles 1998, 2002, Mitra 2013) on the development of welfare regimes and social expenditures, demonstrating evidence of the limitations of Pierson's argument regarding the dominating effect of 'austerity' measures on policymaking. For instance, Kirchgässner and Pommerehne (1996) demonstrate that the Swiss welfare state did not break down under the threat of fiscal competition.

evance of economic and demographic processes (Hofferbert 1966, Wilensky 1975, 1981, 1987).[684]

In recent decades a coherent body of empirical evidence has accumulated in favour of partisan theory[685], strongly suggesting that the composition of the party government has directly affected policy choices, outputs and outcomes. It is worth noting that in recent times the 'old' or 'classic' left-right partisan effect on taxes and social expenditures is no longer so visible in the advanced industrial welfare states of Western Europe and needs to be critically elaborated for developing countries (Broix 1998, Kittle and Obinger 2003).[686] Against the background of declining 'classical' party effects, the classical right-left conflicts and resulting party priorities in the policy areas of welfare and defence[687] are still distinctly visible, as are the character of policy instruments (Budge et al. 2002:77).[688]

---

684 In 1955 Raymond Aron foresaw that 'the political categories of the last century – Left and Right, liberal and socialism, traditional and revolutionary – have lost their relevance.' See also Daniell Bell's '*The End of Ideology*' (1960) on the decline of party effects.

685 Some of the authors and accounts include Douglas A. Hibbs (1977) '*Political Parties and Macroeconomic Policy*' and Manfred G. Schmidt (1996a) '*When parties matter: A review of the possibilities and limits of partisan influence on public policy*'.

686 In his widely cited research Broix (1998) has observed that the differences between left-wing and conservative or liberal party politics can no longer be attributed to social expenditures but have to do with the 'instrumentalization' of policies as state intervention instruments. Similarly Kittel and Obinger (2003:40) observed that the 'partisan effects of current decisions are less amenable to quantitative analysis because they have little impact on the aggregate level of social expenditure. More important are qualitative differences and preferred programme foci, which either tend to turn up at the disaggregated level or have little impact in terms of expenditure levels at all.'

687 The reason is grounded in the ideological as well as financial realms: most of the funds in the state budget are directed to those areas which are inflaming political right-left conflict, including internal party debates between right and left factions (Keman 1984).

688 See Birchfeld, V. and Crépaz, M.M.L. 1998. 'The impact of constitutional structures and collective and competitive veto points on income inequality in industrialized democracies', *European Journal of Political Research,* vol. 34, no.2: 175–200. Arendt Lijphart (1999) even suggested that the consensual style of politics tends to be more successful than 'macro-economic' management.

7.2 Political Entrepreneurs in India and China

The historical perspective has illustrated the importance of strong political actors or entrepreneurs[689] which wield enough power to modify policy processes in their favour. In India and China the constitution and role of the one dominant party gave way to strong political leaders which have played a major role in political, social and economic development. A wealth of literature on prominent political leaders has provided evidence of their relevance in determining the overall objectives of policymaking. According to such research, those '*who believe that design choices in social protection programmes...are purely pragmatic technical issues... [are] missing the point...Which choices are made, and for what reasons, reflects the kind of society that policymakers and technocrats with power to direct social policy wish to promote...Social protection is self-evidently about a vision of society*' (Devereux and Sabates-Wheeler 2007:2). In an indepth analysis of the development of social security politics the personal variable has to be included.

Thus, individual actors can determine the course of social policy choices and outcomes (Böder and Töller 2012:190) either on a national or local level in democratic as well as non-democratic systems under specific conditions. Keman (2002:276-77) argues that the 'state format per se is only indirectly relevant for policy performance.' Furthermore 'if the Head of the State, whether or not in a so-called presidential system, is institutionally strong, this affects policy-making' (Keman 2002:277).

According to Scharpf (1997) and others (Rhodes 1997) the ability of politicians to carry through their polity guidelines as well as their '*room to manoeuvre'* in decision-making relies on their ability to overcome institutional and constitutional constraints.[690] In addition, they have to:

(1) muster a political majority, including support of collective actors, or obtain sufficient power to enforce their decisions,
(2) overpower existing institutional veto points, such as majority institutions,

689 See Böder and Töller (2012:190)

690 Veto points, such as federalism or judiciary, are not always obstacles for the party government. For instance in Germany in 2013 the coalition government of SPD and CDU gained a majority in both chambers, in the *Bundestag* and *Bundesrat*, at once.

(3) gain the support of collective veto points (e.g. demand groups), and
(4) pay attention to economic realities.[691]

As mentioned by Devereux and Sabates-Wheeler an important variable is the personal perceptions of elites and existing political leaders who are able to modify allocation and decision-making processes in their favour. Individual actors in leading positions – not only in politics but also in administration or on committees – can significantly alter the perception and strategic thinking of their party and the state.

Hypothesis 4c: *In the context of a dominant political entrepreneur or elite, the party ideology is less relevant.*

Of course even a strong political entrepreneur requires political support to overcome opposition, constitutional and institutional veto points. As indicated by the theoretical inquiry, such enterprises can be successful even in political contexts with a high number of veto points. Another crucial element of success is the 'opportunity window'. Examples are provided by the sweeping social policy changes of Ronald Reagan in the USA, Margaret Thatcher in Britain, Deng Xiaoping in China, and Indira Gandhi in India, who successfully overcame opposition and initiated substantial changes to the status quo.[692]. Also their liberal reforms significantly reduced the organisational power of existing labour movements (Goldthrope 1984, Rothermund 1993:69-72, Metcalf and Li 2005:16). However, far-reaching policy changes and/or slow but steady changes to the status quo do not always require strong political leaders. As Kingdon (1984) repeatedly argued, political entrepreneurs can use '*windows of opportunity*' or combine various '*Politikströme*' to gain a temporary majority for their agenda. This seems to be the case in Indian and Chinese current policy-making.

---

691 It should be mentioned that the room to manoeuvre is limited for individual actors, especially in democratic settings. The decline of the golden age of welfare states in the 1980s is more directly related to the financial constraints on decision-making than to individual politicians' preferences (OECD 1981). Scharpf (1997) correctly observed that pro-welfare governments began to cut the expanding costs of the mature welfare state.

692 Collective actors and interest groups need formal or informal opportunities to affect the drafting process or the preferences of decision-makers. Formal as well as informal rules are made by the institutions and foremost by individual actors in the national, provincial and/or local bureaucracy.

In sum, in Indian and Chinese national politics have the tendency to be directly affected by individual strong political leaders. Taking a closer look at the party system and party politics in India and China, the assumption seems to be only partly true. In the case of China the hierarchical party structure seems to clearly promote strong leadership but the '*Tiananmen Incident*' (Guo 2000), the demand for a structured recruitment system for political leaders, and corruption decreases the ability of even the CCP to generate strong leadership. In India the INC and other political parties certainly have a tendency to function as vehicles to back up the political ambitions of individual leaders but political competition has taken its toll on personal power. Despite the Nehru-Gandhi dynasty, Sonja Gandhi could not be nominated as the Prime Ministerial candidate due to public as well as internal party opposition, which even resulted in the splitting of the INC (Wagner 2006:116-19).[693] However, institutional and collective veto points and internal party factions should not be underestimated in either system (as discussed in the beginning of the chapter). In recent decades policy choices and development in India and China have been directly affected by strong popular leaders. In the following section, the study briefly illustrates the power of individuals to influence social policy choices.

7.2.1 Relevance of Party Politics and Ideology

Let us return to the question: What are the relevant variables determining social security politics and its related components, including the range and scope of social policies in India and China? This study tests an important dimension of the answer. Where the two cases converge – with consequences for state interventions to control and guide human development – is in the dominating role of the leading ideological left-oriented political party in steering and determining the state capacity to shape public policy guidelines.

As illustrated in detail, in India the INC has achieved long-term one-party dominance and could muster a national majority most of the time (Brass 1994). In the one-party system of the CPR the locus of all decision-making has been the CCP (Guo 2013b). Undeniably, the transformation

693 See Wagner's (2006:116sp) sub-chapter on the Congress party and Nehru-Gandhi dynasty.

from 'performance has priority' to '建设小康社会' (*'society with a modest welfare level'*) has been followed by the commitment to a '建设小康社会' (*'harmonious society'*) to improve social security for urban and rural dwellers (Information Office of the SC 2004b, Hu 2005). In India the newly elected UPA under the leadership of the INC announced its decision to take drastic action in the fight against deprivation and issued two landmark pieces of legislation as well as various social pension and social assistance programs for the poorer segments of society (NCEUS 2007).

7.2.2 Leading Political Parties in India and China

The issue at hand has been discussed at various points in the previous pages and thus the following paragraph simply summarizes the analysed role of the CCP and the INC in the political system and social security provision of India and China.

Table 31: Constitutional and institutional Features of India and China

Country	Party System	state format	electoral system	autonomy of central bank	Veto Player
India	multi party system	semi sovereign[694]	Democratic elections	yes	7
China	one party system	souvereign	none/authoritarian	none	1

Sources: Various sources

The type of party system and whether or not there are elections and opportunities for voters to change the party government has to be considered in the inquiry into the political process, structure and party effect.

7.2.2.1 The Asian Case and why parties matter

Following the 'politics matter' hypothesis (Hibbs 1977, 1994), the political realities of both Asian cases and particularly the party politics of social policy development provide evidence that strongly opposes the argument

694 In India's federalism sovereignty is constitutionally divided between a central governing authority and constituent represents of the union states.

on the declining *party effect* and supports the controversy.[695] The controversy on the *party effect* and the decline of 'classical' left-right party effects on public expenditure can also be observed for India (Kohli 1989, Wagner 2006) and China (Falk 2008), in which the public expenditures of the welfare system have not rapidly increased under left-wing party governments and constant economic growth since the 1990s (Nayar 1989, Rothermund 1995, Guo 2000, Mitra 1994b, 2005, Falk 2008).[696]

7.2.2.2 The INC in the Indian political system

The argument of the decline of the *party effect* on public expenditure seems at first look to be true for India; however, an investigation into the nature of the modern INC and party system suggests exactly the opposite. Under the prominent slogan 'mother of Indian parties' the INC was the leading political party in the national parliament until the 1980s (see table above). It is worth noting that the INC can be best described as a left-of-centre *catch-all party*[697] or so-called *shop keeper* (Morris-Jones 1968) due to its traditional ambition of aggregating, articulating and formulating the interests of all regional, ethnic and religious groups in its party polity.

The party has proven its claim to serve the historical mission of transforming India and its traditional society into a modern democracy. As the pivotal participant in the independence movement the INC cultivated its legacy and became the leading political party on the national level. In the following decades the party leadership was in the hands of one family, the so-called Nehru-Gandhi dynasty: Jawaharlal Nehru (1947-1962), his

695 A particular elaboration of the traditionally strong role of political parties and their leaders in South Asia is presented by Subrata K. Mitra et al. (2004) in '*Political Parties in South Asia*', cit op and Kailitz and Steffen (2009a) '*Stand und Perspektiven der Autokratieforschung*' concerning the Chinese case.

696 See Chapter 5, diagram 8A/b and Appendix table 46 for a detailed investigation of the assumed causal link between increasing public expenditures for social security and increasing economic growth rate.

697 Otto Kirchheimer (1964, 1966a) coined the term '*catch-all party*' to refer to the decline of class as a category for party guidelines and the ambition of political parties to integrate cross-class perceptions in their electoral appeal.

daughter Indira Gandhi (1968-1982)[698], and Indira's son Rajiv Gandhi (1982-1991)[699]. Jawaharlal Nehru and Indira Gandhi both nurtured a strong central state and relied on the Soviet adopted central planning model to guide economic growth, democratization, as well as social-economic development (Kohli 1989, Mitra 1999b). In the context of a failed bid for power, ongoing decentralisation in a transforming a political system from one-party-dominance into a multiparty system, and the financial deficits of the late 1980s, the INC and central planning established themselves as permanent assets of the modern Indian state (Kohli 1989, Mitra 1999b, 2005, 2014). Undeniably, the INC's one-party dominance on a national level eroded in the process of transforming the party system but did not fade away. Evidence of the INC's political impact is provided by the coalition governments of Janata Dal (S) (1990-1991)[700] and the United Front coalition (1996-1997)[701] and their dependency on INC support.

Commonly scholars on the Indian party system agree that the peaceful transition of the one-party system to a multiparty system started in 1977 with Indira Gandhi's excessive abuse of Emergency rule giving rise to the first electoral defeat at the national level since independence.[702] The decline of electoral turnout[703] since the 1990s is more the effect of the constant empowerment of local elites and their political parties on the national

698 At the same time, in the years from 1962 to 1972 Indira Gandhi was engaged in a fierce internal power struggle in the INC, leading to the forceful split of the party and Indira Gandhi's electoral success in 1972.

699 In 1997 Sonja Gandhi, the widow of Rajiv Gandhi, entered the political arena and continued the Nehru-Gandhi dynasty in reclaiming the chair of the INC.

700 Janata Dal (S) could only muster 54 seats but took over the government because of the support and resulting dependency on the Congress under Rajiv Gandhi (Dua 1994:43).

701 Similar to the Janata Dal (S), the United Front coalition party government rose and fell by the political support of the Congress (Wagner 2006:121).

702 An analysis of the time period and Indira's 'emergency regime' is provided by P. N. Dhar. 2000. *Indira Gandhi, the 'emergency' and Indian Democracy*. Delhi: OUP.

703 In the national elections the INC could only achieve roughly 141 seats (28.3 percent) in 1999, and 145 seats (26.5 percent) in 2004 compared to 352 seats in 1971. The low electoral turnout accelerated internal factionalism and the decline of the traditionally strong socialist base. In effect, the unpopular topic of social security has gained less attention than popular anti-poverty or business-friendly policymaking (Wagner 2006, Kohli 2011). In the election of 1996 the BJP won more seats (161) than the INC (141) for the first time. It is worth noting that the INC has had to rely on multi-party coalitions because neither the INC nor any

level than the decline of public support for the INC (Mitra 1994b, Kohli 2000 and see table 33).

Table 32: Elections and the INC (1971-2004)

Year	Votes (%)	Seats	Year	Votes (%)	Seats	Year	Votes (%)	Seats
1971	43.7	352	1989	39.5	197	1999	28.3	114
1977	34.5	154	1991	36.4	244	2004	26.5	145
1980	42.7	353	1996	28.8	140	2009	28.55	206
1984	48	414	1998	25.8	141	2014	19.3	44

Source: Eenskat, Mitra and Singh (2001) and Election Commission of India (2009, 2014)

Even the transition from one-party dominance to a multi-party system on the national level and the INC's authoritarian rule from 1975-1977, family dynasty[704], low policy performance in the 1980s, and radical policy changes in the 1990s could not erode the solid popular acceptance of the '*mother of all Indian parties*' and its leading political role in national parliament (Mitra 1994a/b). It has been argued that the changes are connected to the INC's internal factionalism, the decline of strong party leaders, socio-economic demands of social groups, and the party's inability to integrate the interests of the rising urban middle class.[705] But increasing political competition, in particular by the Bharatiya Janata Party (BJP)[706], and

---

other political party have been able to achieve an electoral majority (Election Commission 2014).

704 Still the resilience of the INC was proven by Indira Gandhi's re-election in 1980 against enormous odds in the context of her trial, abuse of emergency rule, and authoritarian oppression of public unrest. Despite clear electoral loss in 1977 Indira Gandhi mustered a left-wing coalition government and a relatively high electoral turnout (352 seats) in 1980. Her assassination resulted not in the end of the Nehru-Gandhi dynasty but in clear public support for the INC and her legacy, which has been taken over by her son Rajiv Gandhi. In the election in 1984 the INC under Rajiv Gandhi achieved the highest electoral turnout of the INC since independence (414 seats). Interestingly, in contrast to his mother, Rajiv Gandhi favoured pragmatic politics and needed structural reforms to overcome the stagnation of the economy, but could not muster a majority in the INC or parliament.

705 For a detailed account of the changes as well as implications for other fields of policymaking, see Mitra (1994a, 2000), Wagner (2006) and others (Rothermund 1995b, Bardhan 2007, 2008).

706 The success of the BJP began in the 1980s. In 1984 the right-leaning BJP formulated its own Hindu-nationalist party program and separated itself from the

resulting electoral voting behaviour has also significantly reduced the INC's electoral support since 1991 (Morris-Jones 1968, Kothari 1998, Mitra 2011).[707] Even the return of the Nehru-Gandhi dynasty in 1997 with the nomination of Sonja Gandhi[708] for the chairman of the INC could not renew the former electoral success (Dua 1998).[709] To sum up, the INC lost its dominant position but could regain electoral support as an important but peripheral actor; its appeal is to various societal groups above ethnical, religious and regional cleavages in national elections (Mitra and Singh 1999).

Concerning the ideological and internal policy guidelines of the INC, there have been no significant changes in recent decades. A careful examination of the guidelines suggests that the pragmatic wing has successfully established itself as a leading faction in determining economic goals since the mid 1980s but party policy is best considered social democratic or even left-leaning. Even under the increasing influence of pragmatic politicians, such as Manmohan Singh[710], the INC's social security policy has

---

Rashtriy Swayamsevak Sang (RSS). The electoral success of the party in 1989 was based on electoral support for the economic reforms by the growing wealthy urban middle class. In particular, this urban and better educated middle class was the political pillar of the success of the BJP because the BJP, in contrast to the INC, eagerly promoted the interests of the new social class and their demands for economic prosperity, cultural values and security (Thakur 1995:238f, Wagner 2006:126-132).

707 Social processes and changes in electoral voting behaviour are of minor concern for the study and have been the topic of other studies.

708 Sonja Gandhi's political engagement in 1997 was seen by the majority as an attempt to establish the old Gandhi dynasty in the INC and therefore resulted in fierce opposition and low electoral support for her candidacy. In 1998 she took over as chair of the INC but could not gather a coalition in 1999 or resolve the problem of declining electoral support for the INC. In declining the position of Prime Minister and taking a firm stand on poverty reduction and socio-economic equality, she mustered a surprising electoral victory in 2004 for the INC and again gained a high electoral turnout in Andhra Pradesh, her home state and the traditional stronghold of the Gandhi dynasty (Wagner 2006). However, her rhetoric of poverty reduction and social welfare has been limited to speeches and the INC focused on economic growth and a trickle-down effect in policymaking.

709 The election of Sonja Gandhi as chair of the INC resulted in the split of party. Sharad Pawar took his followers and founded his own party, the Nationalist Congress Party, in 1999 but contrary to the assumed negative effect the INC even gained votes and seats in 2004 (Dua 1998, Wagner 2006:122-23).

710 Singh's leading role in the implementation of liberalization reforms in 1991 gained him approval by all parties and voters. Still the missing effects of the

been focused on poverty reduction and redistribution. Although the INC has taken some major steps towards instituting business-friendly and liberal policies into its political operation, the ideological and political orientation can be best described either as *left-of-centre* or *social-democratic* (Bardhan 1987, 1994, Wagner 2006).[711]

In effect, the party politics of the INC have been more pragmatic for economicl growth but have not lost their former ideological edge (Chibber 2012).[712] The 'radical' and even undemocratic social security policies[713] have been rejected in favour of heavily state subsidised target group social security schemes opting to protect BPL households and the majority of the 'poor' in times of socio-economic distress (Nagaraj 2000, Chibber 2012, Kohli 2012).

Although social security provision has undergone various policy changes in terms of range, scope and characteristics[714], the central theme of granting adequate social security to all parts of society has not changed (Nagarja 2012a). Consequently, the *social-democratic party effect* has not declined but the institutional, financial, administrative as well as economic conditions have produced heavy constraints on the ability of the INC to carry through its policy goals in times of rapid social and economic change (Mitra 1994a, 1999a, 2005).

'*inclusive growth*' strategy for socio-economic equality are challenging the pragmatic focus and have resulted in the implementation of various poverty reduction instruments, such as the prominent NEGRA, and a constant socialist rhetoric of equality in electoral campaigns (Ambasta et al. 2008:44-46).

711 For a general discussion of party systems and parties see Nohlen (2007) '*Wahlrecht und Parteisystem*'.

712 In her legislature (1975-1977) Indira Gandhi attempted to realize but could not fulfil her prominent campaign slogan '*Garibi Hatao*' (abolish poverty) by her 20-point program and authoritarian rule under the declared national emergency (Kohli 1998, 2011).

713 Nehru and Indira Gandhi as acting prime minister approved social policies with a non-democratic character. For instance, Nehru carried through his land reform, which can be best associated with compulsory expropriation. The main goal of the enactment was to disempower the landlords or '*zamindars*'. Contrary to the proclaimed positive effects of the state intervention the reform worsened agrarian productivity and the socio-economic situation of the landless peasants. Another famous example was Indira Gandhi's 20-point program which included several drastic measurements such as mass sterilization of poorer males as well as the forced relocation of slum dwellers (Wagner 2006).

714 See the previous chapter for a narrative perspective on the evolution of social security provision in India.

India's democracy, the Nehru-Gandhi Dynasty, and Social Security Politics

Party politics in the INC have been directly affected by the Nehru-Gandhi family and their family members: Jawaharla Nehru, Indira Gandi, and Rajiv Gandhi. The Nehru-Gandhi dynasty continued to dominate national politics from 1952 to 1991 by inheriting the position of the Prime Minister for 34 of 39 years.[715] Since 1999, with the election of Sonja Gandhi, the political inheritance has continued; however, starting with Indira Gandhi the tradition of the Prime Minister was relinquished and the Nehru-Gandhi influence 'only' remained dominant in internal party discourse (Wagner 2006).

Table 33: Electoral Success of the INC and the Nehru-Gandhi Dynasty

Year	Votes (%)	Seats	Prime Minister in the hands of the Nehru-Gandhi dynasty
1951/52	45	364	Jawaharlal Nehru
1957	47,8	371	Jawaharlal Nehru
1962	44.7	361	Jawaharlal Nehru until 1964
1967	40.8	283	Indira Gandhi
1971	43.7	352	Indira Gandhi
1977	34.5	154	
1980	42.7	353	Indira Gandhi
1984	48	414	Rajiv Gandhi

Source: Eenskat, Mitra and Singh (2001), Wagner (2006:122)

Consequently, India's politics on the national level is directly interwoven with the Nehru-Gandhi dynasty and its individual preferences; in recent times Sonja Gandhi, as the chairperson of the INC, has re-established the Nehru-Gandhi dynasty at least in the INC since 1998. All evidence suggests that the Nehru-Gandhi dynasty continues, with the nomination of Sonja Gandhi as chairperson of the INC[716] as well as the political involve-

715 See previous table 32.

716 Sonja Gandhi entered politics in 1998 and it seems her legacy will be continued by her son Rahul as well as her daughter Priyanka who are both actively involved in the INC. Despite low popularity on the national level Rahul Gandhi achieved his first electoral success in 2004 by winning a parliament seat for Amethi in Uttar Pradesh (Wagner 2006:126).

ment of her two children in the INC leadership (Mitra 1994a, Wagner 2006).

From Nehru onwards to more Liberalism

It is worth noting that today's social security system for the formal sector is mainly the legacy of Jawaharlal Nehru's *mixed economy* and his ambition to foster a healthy urban workforce.[717] Since the 1950s the well-funded and -designed schemes and programmes have relied on the laws by the INC government under Nehru's political leadership as Prime Minister to regulate and guarantee social security for the formal employed workforce. Furthermore, since the 1950s these enactments have not been followed, even in the times of desperate economic decline and financial crisis toward the end of the 1980s.

Indira Gandhi's radical Policy Changes

Comparing Nehru and Indira Gandhi's policy style and social policy objectives reveals a radical policy change. The process illustrates again the relevance of political entrepreneurs using the majority on the national level as well as the '*window of opportunity*' in terms of political and socio-economic transformation processes.

As is the case for foreign policy the changing logic between Nehru's idealised '*Panch Seela*' and the '*Indira Doctrine*' is distinctly visible.[718] In domestic social security politics a clear left shift can be observed. Indira Gandhi's left-oriented electoral campaign '*Gabri Hato*' ('*Abolish Poverty*') aimed to set up a social democratic welfare regime and opted for the support of the poor segments of Indian society as well as the left-leaning parties in parliament (Chibber 2012: 179-82). The shifting attention towards providing social security not only for official employees is a rational political decision and two-fold: First, social security schemes and pro-

717 See B. R. Nayar (1989)'s work '*India's mixed economy: The Role of Ideology and Interest in Its Development*' for a detailed discussion of the *mixed economy*.

718 In contrast to Nehru's non-alignment policy to establish India as a neutral country, Indira Gandhi took a strong stance in foreign politics and attempted to assure India's status as local hegemonic power.

grammes for formal employees have been well-funded and well-designed in contrast to the ad-hoc and inadequate schemes and programmes for informal and rural employees. Second, the INC has always acted as a '*catch-all*' party and follows an office-seeking strategy. Thus, a minority of society is formally employed and consequently the strategy of poverty reduction opts for more votes (Mitra 2001).

At the end of the third Five Year plan a consensus emerged that the previous Five Year plan did not produce a measurable effect in reducing poverty and low living standards. The social policy shift to rural poverty reduction and the growing political influence of rising rich farmer associations are directly linked to the 1980s but started out in the late 1960s with the *Green Revolution* (Brass 1995). In 1967 Indira Gandhi modified the overall objectives of social security politics and shifted the focus to rural poverty reduction for various reasons, including a political strategy to gain the favour of the political left and strong farmer associations. She adapted the Nehruvian planned development model and included her populist goals, such as taxes for rich, to ensure the political support of the left-winged political parties in parliamentary (Brass 1994, Kohli 2004, 2012). Her appeasement policy was a pragmatic reaction to the split of the former INC which on the one hand ensured her leadership in the newly founded Congress (I) but on the other hand reduced the organisational and political power of the new party.

In the following years Gandhi revived the old PDS food distribution system from colonial times[719], implemented the IRDP (Swaminathan 2000) as well as various distribution schemes, such as the land-to-landless scheme, as well as target group programs for rural poor peasants (Mitra, Singh and Vereny 2003). Yet, there has been a gap between rhetoric and outcomes because even with a majority on her side Indira Gandhi could not overcome the constraints on policymaking progress and policy implementation. In the formulation of the fourth Five Year Plan the financial resources for poverty allocation programs did not adequately fund the social assistance programme or provide a coherent national public policy strategy to overcome the ad hoc character and pluralism (Patnaik and Patnaik 2001). Meanwhile the politicisation of the IAS and centralisation resulted in increasingly powerless and inefficient political institutions (Rudolph

719 The PDS was implemented by the British Raj as a food distribution system to ensure the health of the workforce in wartime (Swaminathan 2000).

and Rudolph 1987, Kohli 1994). Most of the social policymaking (e.g. the 20-point program) lacked redistributive programmes that actually transferred income or assets because such measurements 'required, historically, some genuine pressure on ruling classes and political elites' (Chibber 2012:182).

This was not the case in the early and mid 1970s. More importantly, Indira Gandhi had to rely on the support of the rising and political influential rich farmer lobbies to support her political ambitions (Brass 1995, Kohli 1998).[720] In effect, the ambitious rhetoric could not achieve the postulated outcomes, and most of the social assistance programs lacked sufficient funds or design; thus, any significant gains in poverty reduction took until the late 1970s (Patnaik and Patnaik 2001).

The Party System and its Constraints on Social Security Politics

Another dimension is the constitutional and institutional constraints on the bills themselves by numerous veto players, a fragile coalition government, the Supreme Court, federalism, the national bank and the president, as well as strong informal socio-economic elites, such as business and rich farmers (Brass 1995, Kohli 2004, Bardhan 2007).[721]

Typical for the '*multi-party*' system (Sartori 1970) the political competition and need for coalition partners produces significant and constant pressure on the policymaking of the coalition government in charge. In particular the legislative period from 2004 to 2009 illustrates these constraints for the INC in carrying through articulated social security politics (Mitra 2013). Carrying through any significant bills demands a majority in both chambers, the Lok Sabha (the lower house) and Raj Sabha (the upper house).

720 The Green Revolution initiated a breakdown of rural class relations. In the process a new class of rich farmers evolved which sought to increase its political power and began to turn away from the Congress (Kohli 1990, 2012)

721 As will be discussed at the end of the chapter.

The United Progressive Alliance (2004-2009) and its limited Power

Established democracies such as India have been rightly praised for their political competition, which guarantees to a decent degree the rule of the people (Scharpf 2000). However, the negative effects of multi-party and instable coalitions that have become a permanent feature of India's political system tend to create their own constraints on government policymaking. The United Progressive Alliance was formed directly after the election of the Lok Sabha in 2004. The UPA could muster the majority of 217 seats for a coalition government as well as the external support of the Bahujan Samaj Party, Samajwadi Party, Kerla Congress and the Left Front. Numbers tell part of the story. Although the UPA coalition government could build upon the electoral success of the INC with 44 MPs and 145 seats (roughly 26 percent of all votes) and its external support by the communist *Left Front*[722], the internal conflicts in policy decisions with its coalition partners have more than once changed the composition of the coalition government. In the fourteenth Lok Sabah (2004 to 2009) alone, six direct members of the coalition government announced their withdrawal for political reasons. The main political opposing front, the BJP and its allies, could only muster 185 seats.

Table 34: UPA, multi-party Coalition and Constrains on Policy Making

Election results 2004 : UPA Member	Seats
Indian National Congress	145
Rashtriya Janata Dal	23
Dravida Munnetra Kazhagam	16
Nationalist Congress Party	10
Pattali Makkal Katchi	6
Telangana Rashtra Samithi	5
Jharkhand Mukti Morcha	5
Lok Jan Shakti Party	4
Marumalarchi Dravida Munnetra Kazhagam	4
Kerala Congress	2
Indian Union Muslim League	1

722 The Left-Front is a political coalition of left-wing 'socialist' and 'Marxist' political parties in India; the most prominent members are the Communist Party of India (Marxist) (CPI(M)) and the Revolutionary Socialist Party. The term is commonly used in literature as a categorisation but also as a name for the coalition itself on the national and local level, such as the West Bengal Left-Front.

Election results 2004 : UPA Member	Seats
Jammu & Kashmir Peoples Democratic Party	1
Republican Party of India	0

Source: Election Commission of India (2014)

Although the UPA achieved an electoral victory, the majority of the INC and its coalition partners are restricted to the lower house (Lok Sabbha, see table 34). In the upper house (Raj Sabbha) the UPA has to rely on the support of other regional parties.

The Coalition Government and its Constraints on Decision Making

Another aspect of democratic rule is political consensus. Political negotiations, coalition agreements, and consolidation processes consume time and resources as well as tend to produce sub-optimal outcomes. In particular, the issue of coalition consolidation and the fact that party elites seek a reestablishment of their electoral constituency has been a demanding issue for the multi-party government coalition.

As indicated in the table 35, the UPA has been involved in various internal debates, leading to political disharmony and splits. Interestingly, none of the issues are related to social security.

Table 35: Political Issues of the UPA Coalition

Withdrawal from UPA	Year	Reason/discontent on the issue of
Telangana Rashtra Samithi	2006	Congress decision concerning the official statehood for Telengana[723]
Marumalarchi Dravida Munnetra Kazhagam	2007	various political issues
Bahujan Samaj Party	2008	Congress did not support the local BSM government
Left Front	2008	Nuclear cooperation treaty with the USA
People's Democratic Party	2009	Congress supported political rivals National Conference Government in Jammu & Kashmir[724]
Pattali Makkal Katchi	2009	various political issues

723 http://timesofindia.indiatimes.com/india/TRS-withdraws-support-to-UPA-government/articleshow/2021151.cms?referral=PM (2014-12-12).

724 http://archive.indianexpress.com/news/pdp-withdraws-from-upa-unfortunate-says.../406523/ (2014-12-12).

Withdrawal from UPA	Year	Reason/discontent on the issue of
All India Trinamool Congress and Jharkhand Vikas Morcha	2012	Demanded rollback of reforms, i.e. allowing FDI in retail
Nationalist Congress Party	2014	Electoral defeat in the communal elections 2014
Jharkhand Mukti Morcha	2014	Issue of eat sharing and domestic split ups[725]

Source: various sources

Furthermore, the descriptive investigation of the issues as well as the low profile of the social security legislation emphasises that the UPA focuses most of its attention on other policy fields, such as economic reforms and foreign politics.

The UPA: Social Security Objectives and Policy Outcomes

Shortly after the coalition was built, the newly formed United Progressive Alliance released its Common Minimum Programme in May 27, 2004, in which it announced six main principles for its legislative period (quoted in the Hindu, 2004-04-28): 'To preserve, protect and promote social harmony and to enforce the law without fear or favour to deal with all obscurantist and fundamentalist elements who seek to disturb social amity and peace.

To ensure that the economy grows at least 7-8% per year in a sustained manner over a decade and more and in a manner that generates employment so that each family is assured of a safe and viable livelihood. To enhance the welfare and well-being of farmers, farm labourers and workers, particularly those in the unorganised sector, and assure a secure future for their families in every respect. To fully empower women politically, educationally, economically and legally. To provide for full equality of opportunity, particularly in education and employment for the Scheduled Castes, Scheduled Tribes, OBCs and religious minorities. To unleash the creative energies of our entrepreneurs, businessmen, scientists, engineers and all other professionals and productive forces of society.'

The mid 2000s were different. The UPA did not enact much social security legislation with the exception of two outstanding bills concerning the right to work as well as security for the unorganised sector. Yet the

725 http://www.livemint.com/Politics/BPoyaW6I4ySdwWnFzKCpTJ/Ahead-of-assembly-polls-Cong-JMM-part-ways-over-seat-sharin.html (2014-12-12).

perception has been that the INC party elites seek other policy objectives (e.g. the nuclear energy deal with United States and structural economical reforms). It remains to be seen therefore whether the reasons for the low state capacity in social security politics is related to the complexity of the deicison-making process or the 'chain of command' on a national level (Pennings et al. 1999).

7.2.2.3 The 1990s: The End of Personal Rule and Ideology?

Undeniably, the left-wing party effect on constantly increasing public expenditures has been only modest compared to the GDP in the 1990s and even 2000s. The focus of the CCP on economic performance has not altered (Kailitz 2009a, 2010); however, the twenty-first century and particularly the change in leadership in 2002 marks the end of the 'performance has priority' in favour of a balanced development model of the 'harmonious society' (Hu 2005). The breakpoint was the 15th National Party Congress and its announcement of a new social security policy to realize 'comprehensive' urban and rural social security coverage even if it meant sacrificing additional governmental resources (White 2006).

The CCP and shifting Policy Guidelines (2004-2007)

In the period from 2004 to 2009 the Chinese Central Government pursued improving the coverage of social security in urban and rural areas. In 2005 the fifth plenary session of the 16th Central Committee opted for '*social harmony*' and '*orderly rule*'. In the following plenary session the Central Committee gave priority to the issue of social security.[726] The Central Committee officially revised the political principle of making a 'priority of efficiency' by announcing the 'Decisions by the CCP Central Committee on Building Socialism and Harmonious Society'.[727] In response to the

---

726 See the '中共中央关于制定国民经济和社会发展第 11 个五年规划的建议' ('*Suggestions of the Central Committee for the 11th Five Year Plan*') announced in 11. 10. 2005 and published in the 人民日报 (RMRB) 19.10. 2005.

727 Hu, Jintao's (2007) '在中国共产党第十七次全国代表大会上的报告' (*'Report of the 17th National Party Congress of the CCP'*) provides an insight in the decision issued on the 17th National Party Congress.

policy shift the SC published '*Regulations on the Work of Providing Five Guarantees in Rural Areas*'.[728] The commitment is also distinctly visible in the steady increase of financial resources for social security which added up to 1950 billion Rmb in the period from 2003 to 2007 (D. Liu 2011:119).

Another trend has been the reshuffling of financial responsibility for social security and the improvement of the minimum safety net for the rural population. The central government eased financial pressure for local authorities by including all administrative tiers in the funding of social security schemes. To improve the missing social security for rural areas the central government also put into practice a cooperative medical system which achieved coverage of 94 percent of the rural population until 2009 (D. Liu 2011:119). Also in 2009 the newly designed old age safety net for the rural population was introduced nation-wide to tackle the newly increased poverty risk in cases of old age in cities.[729]

The CCP: from commanding to administrative Party

The Chinese one-party system paints a similar picture of the relevance of party politics. After the revolutionary take-over, the CCP established a one-party system and claimed to assume a historical role as the '*revolutionary vanguard of the proletarian*' in the Leninist sense (Falk 2008). The internal organisation of the CCP bears the stamp of authoritarian rule and cultivates a clear pyramid hierarchy (Saich 2001). Likewise, the party plays a paramount role in China and its party committees and grass-root organisations are present on all levels of the state administration, as well as political, economic and social life in China (Wu 1995).

As mentioned before, authoritarian as opposed to democratic regimes favour strong leadership due to the concentration of power in the executive. Chinese politics have been dominated by strong party leaders, such as Mao Zedong and Deng Xiaoping. The evolution of contemporary social

---

728 '中共中央关于构建社会主义和谐社会若干重大问题的决定 (*'Decisions by the CCP Central Committee on Building Socialism and Harmonious Society'*)', No. 456, published 01. 03. 2006 by the Central Committee.

729 See the official report of the Ministry of Civil Affairs (2002) '民政部, 全国百城万户低保抽查结果' (*'Report on the control sample for the MLSS in urban areas')* in which the gap between localities is illustrated.

security provision can only be understood in regard to the dominant impact of Deng Xiaoping and his *Four Modernizations* in shaping Chinese politics beyond his official retirement[730] (Ngok and Tang 2003). The current (2004-2009) social security provision under the umbrella of the 'harmonious society' concept is directly interlinked with the gradual change of the party itself, from a totalitarian to an administrative entity, as well as with the overall policy changes in the wake of the *Four Modernizations* in 1978.

Although the post-Mao regime and its reforms have not changed the party organisation, the party-state-society relationship and party guidelines were significantly altered in the following years. Contrary to the totalitarian *commanding party* in the post-Mao period the CCP transformed into what has been often referred to as an *administrative party*.[731] The CCP still represents the totalitarian '*single official party*' but the nature of the party-state-society relationship has altered over time (Guo 2013b).[732] As Paul Charles Sondrol (1990:14) correctly observed, contrary to other authoritarian regimes in which the ruling party 'generally lacks the militancy, political and ideological vanguard status reserved only to totalitarian parties and may compete with the state, military and private organisations rather than penetrating and dominating them' is only 'content with taking over the government, not totally transforming and remodelling society and man.' Empirical evidence of party politics and issued documents of the National Party Congresses clearly demonstrates that the party has become an *administrative party*; however, in addition to the rationalization and reforms the CCP continues to be the locus of the political, social and economic life and requires all citizens to be subjected to the decisions and guidelines of the party leadership. In fact, the new political agenda setting has been oriented toward economic growth and administrative efficiency to reduce the burdens of the formerly strong centralized state and tackle

730 At the14th National Congress in 1992 Deng Xiaoping not only officially nominated his favourite candidate for the future leadership of the CCP but also determined the remaining time of the current leaders of the party until the political exchange (Bo 2013:8).

731 Yongnian Zheng (2004) has coined the term '*administrative party*' to describe the CCP's shift away from a '*commanding*' towards an '*administrative*' party since 1978.

732 See Sujian Guo's (2000) book for insight into the attempt of the CCP to set up a party system without political competition.

the economic, social and political challenges of former periods (Guo 2000:92, 2013b, Falk 2008).[733]

7.3 Expanding the Veto Player Theorem

Another reasonable constraint on orderly rule and politics in developing democracies[734] and autocracies is traditionally rooted informal patterns of exchange (Grzymala-Busse 2010, Hicken 2011, Azari and Smith 2012).[735] Nowadays the vast amount of literature on developing countries has produced a consensus on the relevance of these informal patterns of exchange and their political impact on policy structures, processes and agency, such as traditionally high levels of corruption (Wedeman 2004, NZZ 2013) and the strong role of informal institutional patterns (Merkel and Croissant 2000) in democratic and non-democratic developing countries, which has produced pressure for a critical dialogue on the limitations of the concept of formal veto players (Tsebelis 1990) in grasping the complexity of the relationship between formal as well as informal veto points in such environments.[736]

---

733 In effect, an investigation into the nature on post-Mao reforms suggests that they aimed to accelerate economic and administrative modernization, which has been identified by pragmatic party elites as a crucial pillar of the future. Neither Deng nor Jiang attempted to alter the party-state relationship and the dominant character of the CCP as the locus of all political, social and economic processes (Meisner 1996:481). In effect, the post-Mao reforms since the 1980s issued the separation of party and state functions, the decentralisation of the bureaucracy, and the improvement of the legal system to support an institutionalization of the legislature, administration and judiciary. The weak institutionalization has clearly negative effects on party control, as well as on economic and social development (Okabe 1992, Guo 2000:72).

734 In contrast to established Western democracies, autocracies as well as democracies in developing countries tend to have much weaker formal institutional mechanisms and actors rely on informal dimensions to modify policy processes and structures (Grzymala-Busse 2010:331). At the same time, a good deal of evidence has demonstrated that informal institutional patterns matter for politics, particularly in autocracies (Helmke and Levistky 2004:726).

735 See Allen Hicken's (2011) work for a general discussion of the issue of patronage and corruption.

736 For instance see Subramanian (1999), Platteau and Abraham (2002), Chandra (2004) Besley, Pande and Rao (2005a), Bardhan et al. (2008).

To sum up, it is argued that approaches that focus exclusively on the formal dimension fail to fully explain the complex interaction patterns of autocracies as well as some democracies in developing countries (Merkel and Croissant 2000, Grzymala-Busse 2010:726-28). However, what has to be taken into account is that informal institutional patterns and their impact on policymaking cannot be easily measured and therefore the investigation into the informality of politics has to be conducted with care (ibid). Accordingly, informal institutions will be analysed using a qualitative method in order to expand and inform the classic theoretical approaches and their assumptions regarding the Asian cases.

7.3.1 Beyond the Veto Player Theorem – The Asian cases

As mentioned before, the division of power in, and efficiency of, the formal institution can be the direct impetus for – but not pre-condition of – interaction patterns between formal and informal institutions (Grzymala-Busse 2010:331, Scott 2011, Köllner 2013). This is a meaningful step towards accomplishing a specific understanding of the variables determining the policy choices, processes and structures in a country-specific political regime.

In his article on the strategies and institutions of autocracies to safeguard political power Köllner (2013:279) emphasises that, contrary to democracies, formal institutions do not determine the '*room to manoeuvre*' for political actors in autocracies due to the fact that the interaction between formal and informal institutions is affected by endogenous and exogenous factors, such as socio-economic development and/or diffusion, adaptation and localisation processes of norms (Croissant 2002:53-61).

China and India are both unique in combining formal and informal institutional patterns, which determine the political processes, structures, veto players and abilities of actors to modify policy outcomes (Dittmer 1995, Wu 2007). Although India represents an established democracy with a constitution and formal division of power (Mitra 1994a), a classical analysis of the formal veto players in the policy process can give only a limited understanding of the political reality. The historically rooted informal patterns of patronage-clientele networks, social hierarchies, and exchange patterns produce significant constraints on the accountability, internal party democracy and administrative performance of the national, state and local governments, including the third tier of the village or *panachyat* system (Besley et al. 2005).[737]

7.3.2 Political Parties as Engines for Clientelism

Although today political parties are seen as the pillars of democratization, political competition and participation (Dahl 1970, Hibbs 1994, Keman 1999, 2002a), the nature and role of party politics in and for the political system varies across countries and political regimes (Sartori 1970, 1976). Recently the academic discussion on the role of democratic institutions, such as parties, elections and parliament in non-democratic systems incited criticism of and debate on the general understanding of such '*democratic*' institutions (Gandhi and Prezworski 2007a/b). In the traditional discourse two kinds of motivations can be distinguished concerning party politics and their effects on promoting informal ties and 'clientelism'.

The first motivation is to gain legitimacy and support; legitimacy depends on the political and institutional setting. In democratic settings political parties have to rely on electoral victories. In the so-called office-seeking process parties will try to rally as much support as possible in including various societal demands in their electoral agenda. Various studies of Western democracies have validated the positive effect of electoral cycles on increasing social expenditures (Schmidt 2000a, Budge et al 2002). But the electoral cycle, campaign costs and dependency on the goodwill of voters produce significant pressure on political parties and candidates. As a result, in most of the developing countries, political parties and their candidates rely on patronage client networks to gain electoral and financial support.

Second, in addition to the attempt to achieve electoral success, the policy-seeking motives of political actors include realizing their electoral promises and safeguarding their re-election by maintaining the support of strong interest and demand groups (Strøm 1990, Scharpf 1997, Pennings et al. 1999). These collective interest groups tend to produce external in-

737 See Bardhan (1997, 2007)

fluence on political candidates, which affects party politics and policy choices to a decent degree.[738]

Despite the fact that '*anocracies*' or autocracies tend to hold elections, these are not comparable to free, fair and representative ones (Stykow 2013).[739] Similar to their democratic counterparts, the candidates and political elites are in need of public acceptance or support by the society or relevant social groups (ibid:238). Consequently, to understand social security politics in developing countries with less formalized institutions compared to Western democracies these informal ways of modifying policy processes, structures, and agency have to be considered. Undeniably, measuring such informal institutional patterns and their causal effects on decision-making is another theoretical as well as empirical problem (Grzymala-Busse 2010, Hicken 2011, Azari and Smith 2012).

7.3.3 The Case of Patronage-client Networks

Although informal patterns of behaviour, exchange and interaction are universal features of all political regimes, their specific nature and relevance for structuring political competition, cooperation and mechanisms to solve societal conflicts varies from country to country (Scharpf 1998, Keman 1999, Armingeon 2002, Köllner 2013). In many Asian cases, political succession and recruitment patterns are not transparent or formalized (Mitra et al. 2004).[740] Consequently, informal institutional patterns and the clientelism relationship can also be found in democracies and tend to determine the political realities, policy processes, structures and political power of individual actors (Azari and Smith 2012). To sum up, Allen Hicken (2011:297) notes that in 'democracies, clientelism is a tool for

---

738 Lobbyism, corruption, patronage and illegal business transactions involving politicians in the government are neither seldom phenomena nor restricted to non-democratic or fragile democracies in developing countries.

739 Stykow (2013) has analysed over 100 presidency and parliamentary elections in eleven post-communist countries between 1992 and 2012.

740 In South-Asian countries family dynasties, such as the Nehru-Gandhi-dynasty in India, have become normal recruitment patterns for political parties. Typical examples are the common succession of the widow of the former political leader, such as Mrs. Zias taking over the leadership of the National Bangladesh National Party in Bangladesh or Mrs. Bhutto acting as the official leader of the Pakistan Peoples Party in Pakistan (Mitra et al. 2004, cit op.)

building a loyal network of supporters. In autocracies, clientelism also involves creating socio-economic dependence on the regime (...), and as corollary political subservience (...). The nature of the regime can also affect the kinds of benefits offered to voters or the nature of the exchange relationship; for example, clientelism in democratic settings tend to be more transactional and less hierarchical than what we observe in autocratic settings. What drives many of the differences between autocratic and democratic clientelism (...) is the robustness of political competition.'

7.3.3.1 Indian Democracy, Vote Banks and Patronage

Scholars focusing on clientelism and corruption in Indian democracy reveal that it seems to be '*patronage democracy*'[741] (Chandra 2004). Indian scholars generally agree that clientelism has been important for political processes and structures since ancient times (Kumar 1965, Platteau 1995). Similar to the process in other democracies, such as Italy (Graziano 1973), India's democratization has changed not only the political system but also clientelism. In fact the traditional form of '*clientelism of the notables*' changed towards '*political party-directed clientelism*'. Generally speaking, the traditional model of clientelism did not change in the new democratic environment. Local patrons became clients of political parties or '*vote banks*' and exchanged public goods, jobs and subventions for using their influence on local voters (Kohli 1987:62, Bardhan 1997, 2008).[742]

Qualitative studies conducted at the local and village level all over India have produced strong evidence of the existence of political patronage-clientelism but only when the local politicians are part of the ruling party[743] (Subramanian 1999, Platteau and Abraham 2002, Besley, Pande and Rao 2005, Bardhan et al. 2008).

---

741 Although political clientelism tends to be a typical phenomenon in democratic *developing* countries, it is not restricted to these countries. One prominent study by Graziano (1973) on Southern Italy touches on the topic and gives empirical evidence of traditionally strong clientelism in democracies.

742 See Kohli's (1987) book '*The state and poverty in India. The politics of reform*' on the issue of 'vote banks' and the impact of strong interest groups on decision-making.

743 Bardhan et al. (2008) have evaluated the role of party membership as a crucial factor of political patronage-clientelism at the local and village levels.

In their case study for the World Bank on the quality of local government, Besley, Pande and Rao (2005:24) observed that households of *PRIs* politicians are overrepresented as beneficiaries of poverty allocation programmes.[744] Platteau and Abraham (2002:126) seem to observe the same pattern for Kerala and conclude on the basis of their empirical findings that the village 'suffers from an important weakness in that it has become a platform for political favouritism in a country plagued by excessive party politicisation down to the local level.' Another example of Kerala's political clientelism is given by Tharakan (2004) who notes that 'the evolution of modern Kerala society and politics resulted in a process of party-politicisation of associational life, which subjected it to the clientelistic principle of winning support by way of partisan favours.'

The problem is not necessarily limited to one party or region, as Subramanian (1999:67) says of Tamil Nadu and the All India Anna Dravida Munnetra Kazhagam (AIADMK) that 'crucial Dravidianist policies (...) were clientelist as they targeted specific groups which gave the ruling party their support in return,' and as Widlund (2000) observes that 'the members are aware of the patronage potential that comes with belonging to the ruling party and they expect to share the benefits.'

7.3.3.2 Veto Players and Co-regents in China

Chinese political scholars agree that taking the category of formal veto points alone into account cannot explain the mechanisms structuring contemporary Chinese politics. Such a perspective does not automatically grasp the various minority veto points or co-regents even in democratic settings and especially not in contexts governed by informal patterns (Schmidt 2000a). Chinese '*ideocracy*' possesses all the institutional elements of a modern state. On first look the institutional arrangement appears quite similar to democratic settings and is indeed comparable on a higher level of analysis (Prezworski and Teune 1970). Such investigations often require modification of typical methodological approaches developed for democratic settings due to the changing function and logic of these adapted institutional patterns (Gandhi and Prezworski 2007). There

744 Although the relationship is highly interesting, the fact has gained only a footnote in the conducted survey on the quality of government (Besley et al. 2005).

is no doubt that the only real veto player is the CCP whose policy setting is represented by the Politburo (Guo 2000, 2013b)[745]. In addition, there is growing evidence that Chinese domestic politics depends on informal patterns and is highly fragmented on the vertical and horizontal dimension along departments and their 'complex vertical and horizontal responsibility' (Lieberthal 1992, Tsou 1995, Mertha 2009). Chinese scholars (Li 2012b: 136, Wang 2013:6) conclude that in a Chinese system dominated by an informal character the political power of the top leaders is constantly declining 'as power and authority has been diffused among their peers within the leadership.' Therefore, an increasing number of '*co-regents*' or political actors can affect policy processes and structures by relying on informal patterns of exchange and weak formal '*rules of the game'*.

In this context, Lieberthal (2011:65) advises that 'one should never base corporate strategy on a single key personal relationship...individual officials and even groups of officials may move on or fall out of favor as political winds shift. It is always important, therefore, to be in touch with every pertinent tier of the system and each locality in which the company operates and avoid basing the success of an initiative solely on sustaining the effective support of a key individual.'

The classical veto player theorem cannot fully grasp the complexity and informal character of Chinese polity and has to be expanded into a more sophisticated approach to include the increasing number of co-regents (Schmidt 2000a) and the informal dimension of policymaking (Merkel and Croissant. 2000, Köllner 2013). Since the 1970s the party-state relation has declined and the executive has gained additional sovereignty in decision-making. But the sole veto player is still represented by the CCP (Tsou 1995, Cheng Li 2012:2). However, the institutional arrangement has produced various *minority veto points* in the bureaucracy (Shirk 1993:118). These institutional veto points, namely the ministries and their power, have significant effects on the scope and range of social policy schemes and programs. In addition, institutional actors even in an autocracy significantly modify the political agenda and resulting outcomes of the decision-making process to safeguard the status quo as far so possible.

745 Lowell Dittmer and Yu-Shan Wu (1995:474-478) have offered insight into the relevance of non-institutional informal relations in the CCP in their article *'The Modernization of Factionalism in Chinese Politics*'.

The CCP, Politics, and the informal Dimension

The CCP has been a prominent topic of research that has witnessed a wealth of sophisticated literature on the nature of shifting power dynamics inside the party (Dittmer and Wu 1995, Guo 2000, Wang 2002, Kailitz 2009a, Yang and Li 2013). Chinese and Western scholars agree that there is more than one relationship in internal policymaking, which has direct implications for the official politics of the central government. Changjiang Wang (2002) introduced the term of '*political party modernization*' to grasp the continuing process of adaptation by the CCP to the changing internal power struggle between the neoliberals and communist hardliners—a struggle which is a typical feature of an '*ideocracy*' under the dominant rule of an ideologically grounded party (Kailitz 2009a). In his prominent work on the complexity and dynamics of internal party coalitions in the CCP Wang (2004) concludes 'while it may be too arbitrary to assert that the vested interest groups exist within the party, no one could deny such signs that the inter-party interest groups are emerging in some places or departments.'

As Lowell Dittmer and Yu-Shu Wu's (1995:478) account of the CCP stresses, the informal dimension has always been the dominant feature of Chinese politics. However, the Chinese reform period and its aftermath changed not only state-party relations but also the internal informal patterns of the CCP (Yang and Li 2013). The major reason for the dominance of the informal dimension on policy processes and structures is missing or weakened formal '*rules of the game*'. Various scholars emphasise two main reasons for the weak formal dimension of politics. First, traditionally the formal rule of law has been weak in China (Peerenboom 2002, 2006, Yang and Li 2013:74). In this context Frederick Teiwes (1984:98-99)[746] observes that political 'leaders have consistently placed higher value on protecting the revolution than on formal restraints.' Although Mao's personal rule was an impetus for lasting intra-party competition, the attitude of the leaders is also grounded in the traditional concept of political reign in the 'Confucianism sense' and its preference for '君子' ('*jūnzǐ*' or '*noble*

746 In his popular case study Frederick Teiwes (1984) argues that formal institutions (e.g. rule of law) have been neglected by political elites. He elaborates that the reasons are grounded in cultural experiences, Confucianism and Mao's strong personal rule.

men'), or personal leaders instead of trust in the rule of law (Teiwes 1984:55).[747]

Second, the transition of the CCP from Mao's era to the post-Mao era resulted in a shift from the '*commanding*' to the '*administrative party*' (Zheng 2004). In his prominent article Zheng emphasises the changing perception of the CCP elites in attempting to realize economic instead of ideological goals, which also included the decline of ideology and the erosion of the administrative power of the government. In fact, the process generated party-government tension and empowered the independence of state institutions.

7.4 Comments on Party Politics, Ideology and Social Security

Current electoral campaigns in India as well as state propaganda in China demonstate that ideology is still crucial for political parties. In India ideology gives the voters and parties a platform through which to illustrate their policy preferences. In China ideology is closely linked to the constructed historical legacy of former dynasties and Maoism, as well as to current political elites.

In the early 1950s, ideology as well as strong political entrepreneurship played a dominant role in determining the policy choices and preferences of both parties.

The following decades proved to be different. On the one hand the slow erosion of dominant internal party leadership with Deng Xiaoping and Indira Gandhi empowered factionalism and political elites. On the other hand the demand for unpopular liberal reforms affected party ideology and policy preferences. Since the 1990s the INC and CCP have more and more departed from economic goal setting, either by referring to 'inclusive growth' or 'performance has priority'. The process is closely linked to the new political attention to policy output performance instead of ideological means. The transition can be best explained by the *new political economy* argument that the success of modern states is grounded to a decent degree

747 For a sophisticated discussion of Confucianism and its implication for the state, see Guo (2000:79-98)

in responsiveness to changing economic realities during *critical junctures*[748]. It is assumed that capitalist market economies 'tend to exert a constant destabilizing effect on the societies within which they operate, so that their own efficient functioning is thereby threatened and can continue only to the extent that this destabilizing is offset' (Goldthrope 1984:3). Consequently, the party in control has to take action to regulate the negative effects of the free market. The twenty-first century experiences with the free market and increasing socio-economic income disparity have produced pressure on both parties.

In its electoral campaign in 2004 the INC, a left-of-centre party, focused on the electoral promise of liberal economic reforms in combination with social assistance for the poor and succeeded against the former right-of-centre BJP government which could not accomplish their 'India is shining' slogan.

In China the political elites also took drastic action in reformulating their earlier deeply liberal 'performance has priority' slogan as the 'harmonious society' theory, which included a normative impetus for balanced economic and social development.

748 Recently Giovanni Capoccia und Daniel Kelemen (2007:343) pointed out that critical junctures are often related to external shocks in the course of war, environmental catastrophes, and economic and social upheavals which challenge the political regime type in its capacity to deal with resulting socio-economic or political pressures.

VIII. The Constitution, Rule of Law and State Capacity

An essential feature of *representative* democracy is, of course, its the constitution and the rule of law to guarantee civil rights as well as a power balance between the legislature, executive and judiciary. In this part the issue at hand is degree of relevance for the level of rule of law as well as constitutionally given social rights for social security policy performance in democracies and autocracies.

8.1 Rule of Law, Constitution and Social Security

In his popular and widely cited works on state-ness Charles de Montesquieu (1989:315) emphasised the close linkage of rule of law and institutions: 'We have said that the laws were the particular and precise institutions of the legislator, and the mores and manners, the institutions of the nation in general. From this it follows that when one wants to change the mores and manners, one must not change them by the laws, as this would appear too tyrannical; it would be better to change them by other mores and manners.'

Prominent scholars, such as the historian Guido de Ruggiero, pointed out that constitutions and laws are not carved in stone but exchangeable written words. 'The love of rationalistic simplification leads people to think that in the mere technicalities of law they possess the means and the power to effect unlimited changes. [Such an illusion is] cherished by lawyers who imagine that, by drafting new constitutions and laws they can begin the work of history all over again, and know nothing of the force of traditions, habits, associations, and institutions.' Concerning the legal framework and constitutional embedment of social rights, various studies on established democracies have emphasised the theoretical relevance of a high level of rule of law and constitutional principles guiding decision-makers (Dahrendorf 1977, Rui 1983, Rao 1990, Pereira 2008). A functioning democratic system under the rule of law is represented by 'a system in which law is able to impose meaningful restraints on the state and individual members of the ruling elite, as captured in the rhetorically powerful if overly simplistic notion of a government of laws, the supremacy of the law, and equality of all before the law' (Peerenboom 2002:2, 2006).

Hypothesis 5a: *A high value in rule of law and constitutional imperatives for social security provision have a positive effect on social security provision.*

Accordingly, the question arises of the causal relationship between the rule of law and social rights embedded in the constitution as well as in social security provision.[749]

8.1.1 Democracies and Rule of Law

A further finding in support of the 'comparative advantage' of democracy is that democracies have higher levels of *rule of law*[750] than non-democracies, such as autocracies and dictatorships. Autocratic systems are not '*lawless*' per se. It is worth noting that non-democratic systems can establish orderly rule of law but, as Toharia in his pioneering work (1975) emphasised, operate in limited parameters compared to democratic settings. Orderly rule is not restricted to democracies per se.[751] The existence of a formal legal framework, courts, laws and a constitution can create orderly

---

749 Another issue is that political systems with high levels of rule of law, as illustrated by the Indian case, are not immune to administrative inefficiency, corruption and excessive regulation (Singh 2000, NZZ 2013) nor are they causally related to higher levels of public welfare compared to other countries with lower levels of rule of law (World Bank 2007, 2008).

750 ''Rule of Law' deals with the social relationships of power by spelling out the general manner by which governments, the State apparatus that they command, and any actor powerful enough to exercise power arbitrarily over citizens, ought to behave, and how conflicts between citizens ought to be adjudicated. Its core aim is to limit the scope of the arbitrary exercise of power by governmental and non-governmental actors, by regulating legitimate discretion and distinguishing such discretion from arbitrariness, wherever and by whomever such power may be exercised.' (Nicolaidis and Kleinfeld 2012:35-36).

751 Take, for example, the enforceability of economic contracts by law; here the non-democratic China is superior to various old and new democracies including India. China is ranked nineteenth in the top 20 nations, followed by Switzerland, the United Kingdom and Portugal. India has the second worst ranking of 185 nations. Only Timor-Leste is ranked lower than India. Concerning civil rights the Freedom House Index categorises India as partly free (2012).

rule that does not imply a high level of *rule of law*. It would be premature to announce *rule of law* as a constant feature of democracies. As discussed earlier, both concepts and their causal relations have to be separated and defined. The misconception derives from the assumption of the superiority of the *rule of law* in democracies; but established democracies can also become *tyrannies of the majority* or be temporary, especially fragile democracies. Witness the breakdown of the rule of law (Schmidt 1998:286).[752]

8.1.2 The Rule of Law and Constitutions in Autocracies

Several recent studies on the so-called predatory state and developing countries emphasise that weak formal institutions and low levels of rule of law provide the fertile soil for corruption, administrative inefficiency and decline of policy output performance (Peerenboom 2002, Radnitz 2011).[753]

Moreover, courts as institutions play an important role in autocracies. In the last decade a wealth of research on courts and the resulting implications for political legitimacy[754] and the degree of justice in autocracies has been conducted (Ginsburg and Moustafa 2008; Helmke 2005). As emphasised by various case studies, political elites and governments in autocracies and/or fragile democracies rely on laws, courts and constitutions to legitimize their actions; the lack of independence gives way to ruling elites who bend the law in their favour (Ginsburg and Moustafa 2008).

8.1.3 Law, the Constitution and Social Security Provision

Correspondingly, various studies have emphasised that flaws within the social security system are often grounded in the lack of a legal embodi-

752 A prominent example is the transition of the Weimar Republic to the fascist-totalitarian regime of the Third Reich and the continuity of the formal rule of law in which newly announced laws sanction oppression, violence, and crimes conducted by the state (Radbruch 1946:105).

753 For a contribution to the 'dependency' of law enforcement and justice in authoritarian regimes see Anthony Pereira's article (2008) '*Of judges and Generals: Security Courts under Authoritarian Regimes in Argentina, Brazil, and Chile*'.

754 Pereira (2008) argues for the important role of courts in legitimizing instruments of oppression and repression used by the authoritarian state against its citizens.

ment of schemes, programmes and services, which releases the social security administration from the legal obligation to tender social security. Consequently, as the famous constitutionalist Walter Murphy (2007:138) correctly observed, institutions are needed to turn 'sheets of paper into hoops of steel'. In fact, the degree of the embodiment of social security in legislation is assumed to have a positive effect on the availability and quality of existing schemes, programmes and services (Dahrendorf 1977, Dreze and Sen 1991, Scharpf 2004, Perrenboom 2006). In this line of argument, it seems plausible to assume that with an increasing number of laws on social security schemes in which the duration, range, scope, content and modalities are clearly defined, social security can be turned from '*sheets of paper into hoops of steel*' (Murphy 2007:138). In addition to the legal embodiment of social security, a fundamental criterion for the legal claim is a functioning legal system and a decent degree of justness. Obviously, the legal embodiment of social security is a first step but can only be fruitful in a legal system in which citizens' legal claims against authorities are taken seriously.

The legal embodiment of social security generates more than '*sheets of paper*' to refer here to Murphy's (2007) notion. The main contribution of its legal character is to provide legal accountability and a clear definition of the modalities for accessing and gaining social services. This is a meaningful step to accommodating a decent legal claim for citizens and enriches the accountability of social security politics concerning the access, range and scope of the social security scheme. The legal embodiment shores up coverage of social security by giving citizens information on the existing schemes, rights and legal claims of social security.

8.1.4 Comparing China and India

A number of observations can be made about the rule of law, orderly rule and social rights embedded in the constitution. As assumed in regard to the 'rule of law' India is doing quite well compared to China. Yet, it also needs to be borne in mind that both countries have established 'orderly rule' and stable political systems (table 26). Interestingly, China seems to have an advantage in providing political stability compared to India (see table 26). Accordingly, a second indicator concerns the constitution.

Hypothesis 5b: *A higher number of social rights in the constitution has a positive effect on social policy performance.*

A second reason for studying constitutionally embedded social rights is paradoxically normative and moral. The descriptive inquiry can also offer an underlying understanding of the social preferences of decision makers in terms of amendments as well as the following postulated principles.

8.2 The Chinese Case: From '人治' to '法治'

In recent decades China has constantly struggled to transform the'人治' ('rule by man') that was exercised by Mao into '法治' ('rule by law'), but with only moderate success due to the traditional shortcomings of the legal system as well as the 'superiority' of the CCP over the law. Although the CCP leadership has set out to improve the situation, the issue is on the agenda of the CCP (NZZ 2014d).[755] Two main critical junctures have to be distinguished for the development of domestic law enforcement, the court system, and the constitution in China (Rui 1983, Feng and Quipan 2006). The first is the communist seizure of power which clearly changed the logic, institutional patterns and constitutional parameters within which the rule of law, the judiciary and law enforcement agencies operate. The second is the overall objective to improve the 'rule of law' announced by the CCP in the late 1980s, which has gained constant attention (Pei 2005, Horsely 2008). Since 2001 the system has been officially divided into seven fields of law—economic law, civil law, social law, and so on, with three legal levels, the constitution and laws, as well as administrative decisions made by the central government and territorial laws.[756]

Despite the commitment to improvement, a number of problems plague the judicial system in China that can be traced to various factors, many related to the autocratic rule of the CCP.[757] As Mu Rui points out, in the par-

---

755 The process is still in development and the current CCP leadership under President Xi is challenged in balancing the *rule of law* and the CCP's status quo above the law (NZZ 2014d).

756 See the official publication of the People's Republic of China. 2003. *The constitution of the People's Republic of China*. Beijing: People's Press.

757 Peerenboom assumes that the CCP uses weak attempts to establish rule of law as a '*mask for oppression and injustice*' without producing a real threat to its political power (Peerenboom, 2002:2). The dilemma described by Peerenboom (2002)

ty-state system the law 'is considered as a needed tool for achieving economic reform and modernization and it is useful and necessary only inasmuch as it promotes that goal' (1983:62). Since the late 1980s the CCP undertook the task of improving the *rule of law*, and built up its control and leadership in the legislature, executive and judiciary through the party group, committee and *nomenklatura* on all political, social and administrative levels (Guo 2000, Köllner and Basedau 2006). As observed by Keith and Lin (2003:623-624), 'policy, as interpreted by the Party leader, was more important than, and could even substitute for, the comprehensive stipulation of law' and the constitution is not 'treated as the supreme law, nor is it enforced' (Peerenboom, 2006:109).

Social Security Law in China and India

A core business of government is to provide orderly rule. Among other things, law-making, law enforcement, courts and hearings are crucial components for modern states to guarantee orderly rule besides the state monopoly of physical force.[758]

The parameters in which the law operates are significant, as discussed above; however the fundamental understanding of law and underlying concept of civil rights are also crucial for the rule of law and law enforcement.

Social security law, definition of social security law, judiciary system and law enforcement in India have been taken over and implemented by the British Raj. Judges, politicians and lawyers have been educated in British legal traditions, which designed the constitution, wrote laws and operated the judiciary system. Until today, the judiciary system, law making and tradition reflects the strong influence of the British law tradition (Conrad 1995).

In the case of the CPR, politics is superior to law making. Ahl (2006) therefore argues that China has no real juridical system in the Western

---

between the ambition for a higher degree of rule of law and to safeguard the CCP's superiority to the rule of law is an issue even today (NZZ 2014d).

758 Referring here to Max Weber's (1976) notion of the legitimacy of physical force owned by the state.

sense.[759] Chinese law is still equal to the English law in regard to its objective character.[760] The term '*shehuifa*' or social law is a relative new concept, which has been introduced in 1993 alongside the concept of the socialist market economy. Social law includes laws concerning employment conditions, employment-related social security as well as other social security laws concerning maternity, protection of minors and disabled. Chinese scholars agree that the social security law in China is ambivalent in the sense that it tackles public as well as private law. Social security law in China is also overlapping with the labour law and regulations of the relationship between employees and employers (Wang 2003:115, Xiahua News Agency 2006a).[761]

8.2.1 The Constitution and Social Security in China

Social security and the social rights of citizens has always been an issue in the Chinese constitution and related amendments. Typical for an 'ideocracy' (Kailitz 2009a) the CCP has been highly sensitive to officially safeguarding citizens' social rights and even civil rights (amendment in 2004), at least on paper. In particular, the formulation that work is the 'duty' of any citizen illustrates the ideological focus (D. Liu 2011:63-64).

Table 36: Constitution and Social Security in China

Constitution1954	Article 91: Right to work Article 92: Right to rest for working people Article 93: right to material assistance from the state and society when they are old, ill or disabled
Constitution 1975	Article 27, paragraph 2: Employees have the right for work and right to material assistance from the state and society when they are old, ill or disabled

759 See also Harro von Seger (1994:176) '*Einführung in das chinesische Recht*' for principal investigation on the Chinese law, constitutions and related issues of law enforcement.

760 Contrary to the German understanding law '*Recht*' which includes an objective and subjective interpretation, the English and Chinese concept is restricted on the objective dimension (D. Liu 2011:56).

761 For a detailed discussion on the technical issue see Wang, Quanxing and Guan, Bin (2003) '王全兴/管斌, 经济法与社会法关系初探 (*A study on the relationship between economic law and social law*)'.

Constitution 1978	Article 48: Right to work as well as the state responsibility to improve job opportunities, wages, working conditions, security and welfare. Article 49: Right to rest for working people Article 50: Employees have the right for work and right to material assistance from the state and society when they are old, ill or disabled
Constant features	Article 25: State provides pensions to martyrs or their families and gives preferential treatment to the families of military personnel. Article 32: Employment-related social security

Source: PRC (2003), Feng and Qipan (2006), D. Liu (2011:89-90)

Before proceeding to the recent constitution of 1982 (revisions were made in 1988, 1993, 1999 and 2004), a short investigation of the relevance of social security in the previous constitution is useful. In the previous version of the constitution (1954, 1975, and 1978), social rights are more or less limited to the right as well as duty of the citizen to work, the right of working people to rest, and employment-related social security. As summarized in the overview, what the different versions of the constitutions share in common is the preamble that social security is restricted to the working population, soldiers and martyrs (Feng and Qipan 2006:58).[762]

8.2.2 The Constitution of 1982 and Social Security

The revision of the constitution implied a new underlying rationale for social security. Article 42, paragraph 1 dictates that citizens of the CPR have the right as well as the duty to work. Correspondingly, the state assumes the responsibility to provide a socialist labour market.[763] A significant change concerning social security was made in article 45, paragraph 1 in which all citizens are entitled to social security and not only the employed.[764] For the first time, the constitution also grants disabled citizens the right to social security.[765] Another relevant change is the revision of

762 See Feng, Cui and Sun Qipan's (2006) article '从历次制宪与修宪看中国社会保障的发展' (*'A Perspective on the constitutional amendments concerning Chinese social security'*).

763 See article 42, paragraph 3, sentence 3 of the CPR's constitution published 1982.

764 The article was the reason for the state's implementation of unemployment insurance system in the 1980s.

765 See article 45, paragraph 3 of the CPR's constitution published in 1982.

article 33, paragraph 3 in which all citizens are equal before the law and have human rights.[766]

The most important development is the amendment of the constitution in 2004 and article 14 which explicitly emphasises the state's responsibility to establish a sound social security system 'compatible with the level of economic development.' The article is an amendment to existing articles 19, 21, and 22 in which the constitution formulates the state's function to grant education, health care, public transportation, and culture.[767]

> *Article 19*: '*The state develops socialist educational undertakings and works to raise the scientific and cultural level of the whole nation.*'
> *Article 21*: '*The state develops medical and health services.*'
> *Article 42*: '*Citizens of the People's Republic of China have the right as well as the duty to*
> *work.*'
> *Article 43*: '*Working people in the People's Republic of China have the right to rest.*'
> *Article 44*: '*The state prescribes by law the system of retirement for workers and staff in enterprises and undertakings and for functionaries of organs of state.*'
> *Article 45*: '*Citizens of the People's Republic of China have the right to material assistance from the state and society when they are old, ill or disabled.*' Furthermore, the article emphasises the responsibility of the state to implement coherent and functioning social security and assistance systems, in particular for soldiers and survivors of the revolutionary struggle.
> *Article 14*, paragraph 4: The article was revised in 2004 and dictated that the state has the responsibility to complete and set up a functioning social security system: '*The State establishes a sound social security system compatible with the level of economic development.*'
> *Article 33*, paragraph 3: The protection of the human rights of Chinese citizens is emphasised: '*All persons holding the nationality of the People's Republic of China are citizens of the People's Republic of China. All citizens of the People's Republic of China are equal before the law. Every citizen enjoys the rights and at the same time must perform the duties prescribed by the Constitution and the law.*'

What should be taken into consideration is that in the revision of the constitution the CCP clearly assumes official responsibility for offering social security. The constitution opts to include the citizen in the benefits of eco-

766 International scholars, such as Ahl (2006:1381sp), argue that the article was a political symbol to appease the international community and human rights groups.

767 The current CPR's version of the constitution was published and enacted in 1982; the revisions in 1993, 1999 and 2004 included only marginal changes in regard to the social rights of citizens which are discussed.

nomic performance. It is worth noting that the constitution emphasises that the economic prosperity of the nation has priority: Social security has to be '*compatible with the level of economic development*' (constitution of the CPR 2003: Article 14) but overall economic performance has priority (D. Liu 2011:93).[768]

8.2.3 The Constitution: Constraints on Civil Rights

In recent decades the Chinese legal system has produced three major constraints on the constitution and the amendments which strengthen citizen rights for welfare, legal assistance and civil rights. First, Chinese law is marked by considerable complexity which demands expertise, knowledge, and experience. The complexity is illustrated in the law-making process alone in which 'power is dispersed, but the lines of authority for law-making are not clear. In many instances, it is difficult if not impossible to state whether an entity was acting within its authority' (Peerenboom 2002:256).

Second, in the absence of any real division of power the judicial system lacks independence. Consequently, the 'Chinese courts are really a part of state bureaucracy, they typically lack the political authority to enforce decisions' (Pei 2005:8). Briefly put, in the party-state-society relationship the CCP is the sole sovereign. In effect, the party controls not only law-making but also law enforcement. A major means to ensure the loyalty of judges is control of the recruitment process. This process, as scholar Jamie Horsely (2008) points out in his work '*Rule of Law in China: Incremental Progress*', had negative effects because until 'recently, judges were drawn from the ranks of the retired military. Appointments were based more on political correctness than on relevant experience or legal knowledge' (Horsley 2008:102).[769]

Third, a longstanding weakness concerns the availability and quality of legal counselling. In its report on the Chinese juridical system, the CECC

---

768 For a particular investigation see the published version of the constitution, related articles as well as sub-sections (CPR 2003, cit op.)

769 Only 40 per cent of judges hold a university degree. Judges were commonly recruited from retired military personnel or appointed out of political correctness and not for their functional competency. A consequence of the recruitment patterns is the fact that most Chinese judges are not adequately prepared for their new functions (Horsley 2008:102 sp).

(2005) reported on the issue of availability of legal counselling; in China the ratio of lawyers to citizens is dramatically low as is the motivation to take over cases against officials.[770]

Despite these obstacles, the current situation is improving since the introduction of a series of crucial laws, beginning with the draft of the Administrative Legislation Law in 1986 and its implementation in 1989. The *Administrative Procedure Law*[771] represents a landmark in defining, facilitating and encouraging the legal rights of citizens and protecting citizens against 'concrete' violations by authorities (Peerenboom 2006). It grants citizens the unprecedented right to legal protection against so-called 'concrete' actions violating their 'legitimate' rights and interests as citizens. It is worth noting that legal protection is restricted to protection from the misbehaviour of authorities and does not grant citizens any rights to question the legal framework and/or any decisions, regulations or documents issued by the central government.

In the 1990s the general trend of legislation reforms improving the legal rights of citizens continued in the attempt to reduce administrative inefficiency, corruption and misbehaviour on a local level, with the implementation of the *Administrative Penalty Law* (APL) in 1996 granting citizens the ability to sue official authorities for the violation of their constitutional rights.[772] Despite somewhat different motives[773], contemporary political elites attempt to improve the availability of legal aid for citizens and tackle the corruption problem even in the higher echelons of the state bu-

770 In China the average ratio is only one lawyer to every 10,000 people (compared to one lawyer to every 550 citizens in the USA). In fact, the fear of state repression for legal counsel is another significant problem. China's lawyers usually shy away from politically sensitive cases (Shu 2008). In her case study of 130 civil disputes Peerenboom (2002) reported that 27 percent of lawyers remained silent, 43 percent made only brief comments, and only 4 per cent made any references to procedural or substantive law (CECC 2006).

771 Also known as Administrative Litigation Law.

772 The APL defines the legitimate right and interests of citizens and grants citizens accused of crimes or stripped of civil rights by government agencies the prospect of defending their individual case in person and may even require a public hearing of the case (Horsley 2004). The APL offers the possibility of suing civil servants of the Ministry of Security for violating the civil rights of citizens.

773 The anti-corruption campaign beginning in the mid-2000s against former high-ranking politicians, bureaucrats and militaries reflects the internal power struggle of the new political leaders which took over in 2002 but, as mentioned before, had to wait until 2007 to size control of the Politburo.

reaucracy (The Economist 2014c). The relevant introduction of the '*Provision for Legal Aid in Civil Actions*' and '*Regulation of Legal Aid*' promulgated by the Ministry of Justice (MOJ) in 2005 improved the situation. The promulgated provision granted legal assistance even if the citizens could not afford it. Furthermore, the MOJ in cooperation with local governments set up government-sponsored legal aid clinics all over China, especially in the impoverished regions. Also the MOJ created various social funds to cover the costs and assure legal aid for women, minorities and the elderly; since 2005 a dramatic increase in disputes brought to court has been witnessed (Peerenboom 2006, Shu 2008:148).

It is still clear that the ultimate authority rests in the hands of the CCP and its organisational branches. It is worth noting that newly enacted laws have improved the legal situation of citizens but are limited in their ability to tackle deficits in the institutional and political framework or contest the supremacy of the CCP. But the CCP has set out to improve the thickness of the *rule of law* and the rights of the citizens, as well as the quality of legal and social services at the national and local levels.[774]

8.2.4 Laws and Constraints on Social Security in China

China has not enacted a national social security law defining the welfare duties of local governments and/or the legal claims of citizens for social services (ILO 2006:38, White 2006). The descriptive comparison of the existing laws concerning social security between India and China reveals that, in contrast to India, China has no social security legislation.

In China the regulation of social security is conducted by ministries and the SC. Moreover, administration, range and scope of the existing programmes and schemes are directly under the responsibility of the SC and responsible ministries (Guo 2013b:169-70). The state institutions publish directives, decisions, circulars, and proposals to regulate the social security system. These documents, directives, circulars and proposals issued by the central authorities have similar power as laws and can be compared to

774 A recent tendency can be observed whereby lawyers have begun to provide adequate legal aid in 'politically sensitive cases involving criminal defendants, activists, and religious worshippers' (Yang, 2007: 153). Furthermore, since 2000 lawyers have become more and more engaged in political consultative congresses (Kahn 2005b).

social security legislation but have not been approved by the NPC (Chan et al. 2008:9, Guo 2013b:170-72).[775]

In contrast to the theoretical superiority of the NPC, the SC and ministries have their own autonomy in managing social security without requiring the further approval of the NPC. In 1995 the SC, without needing the approval of the NPC, issued the *'Circular on Deepening the Reform of the Old Age Pension System for Enterprise Employees,'* which opted to reform the main features of the old pension system (Saich 2001).

In recent decades, the independence has given the ministries additional administrative flexibility to adapt and reconfigure social security programmes and schemes; however, the missing legal grounding, accountability and the changes without further notice have had a negative effect on the ability of local governments to adjust, particularly if the changes require additional financial resources under tight budgets. The result is variation in the quality of social security provided by local authorities, who are not bound by legal measures to offer standardized and accessible social security for their citizens (ILO 2006:38). Consequently, the legal embodiment of social security law is relatively 'low' compared to India's legislation.

8.3 The Constitution and Social Security Politics in India

Another picture is painted by the Indian case, as it is assumed that the '*highly fragmented society and deep-rooted social discrimination have always been in the focus of the national policy maker and their democratic ambition. Since the independence of India the ruling political elites attempted to establish democratic virtues and rights for the minorities. Also social policy making is highly biased in this perspective and the national social policy making consist of three major components*' (Nagaraj 2012a: 46). Along the lines of modern Western democratic constitutions, the architects of the Indian consitution emphasised the rights of minorities in the democratic society. More importantly, various paragraphs were contributed to include the democratic values of equality for all segments of society regardless of sex, ethnicity, language or religion (Rothermund 1993:

775 A principle investigation is provided by Sujian Guo (2013b: Part VI) in the '*Chinese legal and legislative system*' in which the policymaking process, structure and agency are taken into account.

24-26, Conrad 1995, Singh and Deva 2005:650). Of the various articles, the most important ones are Article 15[776], 39[777] and 46[778], which were formulated to ensure the integration of all parts of society. In particular, the Constitution emphasises the need to empower women and grant them equal employment opportunities, livelihood and income.[779] Concerning working conditions, Article 42 empowers the state to ensure these as well as maternity relief for women. Article 51 (A) (e) encourages every citizen to protect the dignity of women (Austin 1966, Singh 2006:8-11).[780] As Sen and Rajasekhar (2012:98) correctly observe, '*the Indian Constitution provides strength and spirit to social security legislation for organised workers through Directive Principles of state policy*'; however, concerning *de jure* postulated rights of other minorities there seems to be a gap between de jure and de facto social policymaking in India (Singh and Deva 2005, Nagaraj 2012a:55, Sen and Rajasekhar 20012:117-119). Although the constitution serves as the cornerstone of democracy, India has until recently failed to produce coherent social security legislation on a national scale.

8.3.1 The Supreme Court and Social Security

As Austin Granville (1966) pointed out, the cornerstone of the Indian Nation was and still is the constitution. On behalf of the constitution, the Supreme Court, in its function as the highest judicial institution, has repeatedly declared that the rule of law is one of the *basic features* of the

776 Article 15 prohibits discrimination against any citizen on grounds of sex, religion, race and caste and in Article 15 (3) also encourages the state to use positive discrimination in favour of women.

777 Article 39 provides a legal basis for the equality of women as employees in terms of income and job opportunities.

778 Article 46, in the Directive Principles of State Policy, indicates that the weaker segments of society, such as scheduled castes and tribes, have to be protected and supported by the state. The article underlines the state's crucial function of guaranteeing minimum living standards for its citizens.

779 See article 39 of the Indian constitution, cit op.

780 M. P. Singh. 2006. *The Constitution of India*. Delhi: Delhi Law House.

constitution[781] and therefore cannot be taken away even by constitutional amendment (Deva 2010:1-2).

Contrary to the Chinese case, India has established a substantive and formal conception of rule of law or *just-ness* without mentioning the term directly in its constitution. However, the Indian constitution has embedded various articles to safeguard the rights of the citizen, restrict state intervention, assure independence of the courts and equip the state with an arsenal of more or less liberal instruments that can be wielded in the attempt to safeguard the weak, ill and old (Verma and Kusum 2000). By adding an arsenal of various laws[782] the constitution authorizes the state to take active measures of intervention in social life by protecting untouchables (Article 17) and secularism (Article 27-30), and fighting patriarchy (Article 14-15), social exclusion and forced labour (Article 23-24).[783] To the above stated problem, the question arises: what are the differences between China and India in the sense of state intervention?

India's history delivers the vital point that the division of power is guaranteed by the constitution and independence of the judicial system. In setting up various institutional constraints on the power of the executive, the constitution and the judiciary determine the '*room to manoeuvre*' for state intervention (Austin 1966, Singh 2000, Deva 2009). The Supreme Court has been issued the functions to act as a decision-making body in disputes between the union and individual states, assure the civil rights of the citizens and adjudicate decisions. Since the introduction of the *Public Interest Litigation* (PIL) the Supreme Court and High Courts have been encouraged to actively address, without any legal case, deficits in the sub-fields of health, child labour, environment and corruption (Wagner 2006:78-79).

Four important dimensions can be distinguished which support the substantive concept of the *rule of law* in India. First, contrary to China, the independence of the High Court and Supreme Court is grounded in the Constitution in which (see Article 124(2) and 217) the recruitment patterns for judges differ from that in China. In India judges in the higher judicial institutions are nominated by the President in consultation with the

781 See the court-issued statements in the cases *Indira Nehru Gandhi v Raj Narain*, AIR 1975 SC 2295; SP *Gupta v Union of India*, AIR 1982 SC 149 (Deva 2010:1).

782 In the constitution Article 12-35 guarantees equality and human rights of citizens either by restricting or encouraging state intervention (Verma and Kusum 2000).

783 See M.P. Singh (2006:8-9,19-20) cit op.

chief justice and servicing judges of these courts. It should be noted that normally the principle of seniority determines recruitment patterns; however, in the past political parties have announced younger and more politically allied judges to break the cycle and improve their support (Singh and Deva 2005: 673-74).[784]

Since 1969 the decline of the one-party dominance of the INC has changed not only the party system, but also the position of the Supreme Court from a passive to an active guardian of the constitution and division of power. The Supreme Court has steadily reinterpreted the constitution, namely article 21, to expand the responsibility of the state on the issue of social protection. An important – and for the issue of social protection crucial – process has been the amendment of article 21 to define the term '*life*' to include '*livelihood*'. Consequently, the reinterpretation of the social protection of livelihood extended the responsibility of the state to provide education, health care, housing and a clean environment for all citizens.[785]

Second, the federal character grants the federal and national legislature law-making ability on specific matters. The constitution clearly defines the situation, duration and content.[786] In fact, the laws have to correspond to the constitution and fundamental democratic rights of the citizens (Austin 1966, Singh 2006:6-12).[787] If that is not the case the laws issued by the legislature are declared unconstitutional by the courts and expire.[788]

Third, the same holds true for the restrictions on the law-making ability of the executive.[789]

---

784 A prominent example is given by Prime Minister Indira Gandhi in 1973. Gandhi lost a law dispute in the High Court. Consequently, she appointed A.N. Ray to the Supreme Court, willingly ignoring all the senior judges which were involved in her case at the High Court (Noorani 1994:104).

785 See the Report to the Employment and Social Policy Committee of the Governing Body of the International Labour Organization on the issue (ILO 2005).

786 See Article 246 and 248-254 of the Indian constitution on the issue of state design (Austin 1966).

787 For a detailed insight into citizens' rights, see Singh's (2006) second and third chapters, '*Citizenship*' and '*Fundamental Rights*' respectively, cit. op.

788 See the prominent case '*Medical and Educational Charitable Trust v State of Tamil Nadu'* in 1996, cited in Ba.

789 As remarked in Article 123(3): '*If and so far as an Ordinance under this article makes any provision which Parliament would not under this Constitution be competent to enact, it shall be void.*'

Fourth, a substantive concept also entails transparency, freedom of speech and legal counselling. Freedom of speech and freedom of the press are crucial determinants of transparency on state actions, law issues and judgements (Austin 1966, Deva 2009, 2010). Undeniably, the availability and quality of legal counselling is also an essential feature for a substantive concept of rule of law. In British tradition, India, similar to most Commonwealth countries, guarantees any prosecuted person legal counselling (Sathe 2002).

8.3.2 Social Security Laws in India

As mentioned before, India's social security has separated the system and schemes for the formal sector from the ad hoc programmes for unorganised sector. The longstanding weakness of India's social security system is its limited coverage. In terms of the existing social security for the formal sector India's legislation has produced well-defined, -designed and -funded schemes and programmes (Rao 2011:10-13, Chibber 2012:174-76). This cannot be said for the mostly ad hoc programmes for the unorganised sector which lack funding, administration and monitoring. In the process of drafting the Indian constitution the leading politicians of the INC, namely Nehru and Patel, apparently saw the need to guarantee social security for workers, living wages, empowerment of women, and equal treatment of women and men at work by law (ILO 2007:8). To achieve these ambitions the constitution was seen as an instrument to provide the legal basis for a decent social security net for workers and equalize coverage for women and men. The Concurrent List of the Constitution of India (List III in the Seventh Schedule) includes the following items and articles concerning social security and the state responsibility for provision (Singh 2006, ILO 2007):

> *Item No.23: 'Social Security and insurance, employment and unemployment'*
> *Item No.24: 'Welfare of Labour including conditions of work, provident funds, employers' liability, workmen's compensation, invalidity and old age pension and maternity benefits'.*

In Part IV of the constitution the '*Directive Principles of State Policy*' are listed which include the following articles concerning the social rights of the Indian citizens:

> *Article 41: 'Right to work, to education and public assistance in cases of unemployment, old age, sickness and disablement'.* Therefore the constitution

dictates that the '*State shall, within the limits of its economic capacity and development, make effective provision for securing the right to work, to education and to public assistance in cases of unemployment, old age, sickness and disablement, and in other cases of undeserved want.*'
Article 42: '*Provision for just and humane conditions of work and maternity relief*' meaning that the '*State shall make provision for securing just and humane conditions of work and for maternity relief.*'

These issues and the lasting constitutional fingerprint have ensured the continuity of the dual social security strategy and the ambition of the decision makers who constantly make amendments to improve and expand the existing social security net for the formal sector (Debi 2011:4).

What is significant is that the laws related to social security, the *Workmen's Compensation Act 1923,* the *Employees' State Insurance Act 1948,* the *Employees' Provident Fund and Miscellaneous Provision Act, 1952,* the *Maternity Benefit Act 1961,* the *Payment of Gratuity Act 1972* are designed for the formal sector, excluding the informal workforce. Only recently, in the mid 2000s, did the legislature attempt to pass the *National Rural Employment Guarantee Act, 2005* and the *Unorganized Sector Workers' Social Security Bill, 2007.*[790]

Table 37: Social Security Legislation in India (1950-2007)

Year	Act	Target Group
1923	Workmen's Compensation Act 1923	Organised sector
1948	Employees' State Insurance Act 1948	Organised sector
1952	Employees' Provident Fund and Miscellaneous Provision Act, 1952	Organised sector
1961	Maternity Benefit Act 1961/1995	Organised sector
1972	Payment of Gratuity Act 1972	Organised sector
2005	National Rural Employment Guarantee Act, 2005	Rural BPL households
2007	Unorganized Sector Workers Social Security Bill, 2007	Unorganised sector

Source: various Legislature acts

Even in times of left-wing government coalitions under Indira Gandhi and the announced radical policy change of empowering the rural poor and unorganised workers, the coalition government with a clear majority at its disposal did not touch the social security laws for the formal sector or is-

790 See the Ministry of Law and Justice. 2005. *The National Rural Employment Guarantee Act 2005*. New Delhi: Government of India.

sue any amendments to provide a legal framework for their new social security politics. Similarly the current expansion of the social security net since 2000 is mainly restricted to ad hoc schemes and programmes without legal embodiment; the only exception is the NREGA (Ambasta et al 2008a:42-45, Debi 2011). [791] In the context of social security laws another related but important law is the *Right to Information Act* (RIA). It presents a landmark in Indian legislation in providing transparency and information to all citizens on the behalf of the day-to-day work of the national and local bureaucracy, including the provision of financial resources, physical access, benefits and services of social security by the local administration.[792]

Case: The Supreme Court and Promotional Social Security Schemes for Children

The Indian case provides an example of the need for a separation of power as well as evidence of the positive impact of the constitution and law system on social security provision. Despite the praise, it is worth noting that the following case has to be pursued with caution. The constitution has not dictated policy goals but based on the fundamental idea of equal access improved the allocation processes of social security in 2001. In that year the Supreme Court reacted to a court case concerning the regional discrimination of the *Mid Day Meal Scheme* (MDMS)[793] which was sponsored by the central government and was until then only available in Madras. The Supreme Court considered the MDMS to be unfair and dictated that the central government had to expand all over India. The resulting program combined a package of social assistance schemes designed to tackle malnutrition and health as well as problems for children attending school[794] to

791 The NREGA corresponds to Article 41 of the constitutions and the postulated '*Right to work*' for all citizens (Singh 2006).

792 http://righttoinformation.gov.in (2014-09-05)

793 The MDMS dates back to 1923 and was provided by the municipal government of Madras (today Chennai). In the 1980s the local state government expanded the scheme throughout the state of Madras.

794 For a case study on poverty allocation policies, policy tracetories and outcomes in Tamil Nadu as well as the role of the ICDS in the provision of these policies see Harshada Rathod (2007:71-83).

generate additional benefits for households (Rathod 2007, Sen and Rajasekhar 2012:124).[795]

8.4 Comments on the Constitutions and Social Security Laws

Taking the various bits and pieces together, this chapter suggests two conclusions on the relevance of constitution for explaining social security differences between nations. First, the level of rule of law is essential for any democratic system. But in regard to social security provision the causality is too problematic to be proven. It can be argued that higher levels of rule of law grant citizens greater access to social security. Without a doubt, the advanced democratic countries score relatively high in rule of law but the evidence for autocratic and non-democratic countries, such as China, Singapore and Saudi-Arabia, compared to less developed democratic countries with higher levels of rule of law suggests that rule of law is not as essential as would be assumed for economic or human development. Second, the formulation of social rights in the constitution and their impact on policymaking is too 'random' to be profound. One major issue is that social rights, if embedded in the constitution, are formulated as principles and do not dictate measurable policy goals.

As illustrated in the previous chapter, India and China have both enshrined constitutional social rights since their independence. In both cases these principles have had more of a moral impact on decision-making. Also the higher degree of rule of law does not help to overcome deficits in the state capacity to provide social security.

795 http://mdm.nic.in (2014-09-05)

IX. Cooptation, Labour Organisations and Social Security

Following the line of reasoning pursued by students of the *power resource theorem*, collective actors in general and labour organisations in particular affect the economic and political processes and policy outcomes of the welfare state. Despite the central function of labour organisations for the development of most welfare states and the configuration of social policy outcomes in the OECD countries (Lehmbruch 1991, Schmitter and Grote 1997, OECD 1999, Castles 1999:312-336), the focus of political studies is political parties and/or institutional design.[796]

Policy choices, outcomes and outputs are the result of the power balance, cooperation[797] and interaction patterns of political and also societal groups. In addition, evidence strongly suggests that the societal actors and not the parties or economic realities alone determine the policy choices of the party government to a decent degree (Schmidt 1993a:377, 1997:579). The postulated assumptions of the *power resource theorem* correlate with the liberal democratic approach. Whether or not the ruling parties implement their preference and enforce their electoral promises, political actors are necessary for collective actors to support their electoral ambitions and policy choices. Similarly governments in general and the welfare state specifically are in need of public support to legitimize their politics and secure industrial peace. The extension of the welfare state in democratic and non-democratic countries during the post-World War II period drew on affiliated labour organisations to gain either electoral support and/or instruments to safeguard the cooperative behaviour of the workforce as well as effective implementation of welfare services. Furthermore labour organisations have become important institutional actors due to the combination of a coordinated economy and welfare state in many modern states. In fact, the recent growing union participation in cross-class coalitions to reform the welfare regimes in European countries (Stephens 1982, Visser

796 A sophisticated study of the institutional arrangement and the inclusion of unions in Germany was provided by SFB Bremen in '*Staatlichkeit im Wandel*'.

797 In the context of the power theorem approach the involved actors are considered as rational entities. Similar to the rational choice approach, the actors willingly bargain and cooperate with each for second-best solution (Jahn 2006:295).

and Hemerjick 1997, Rhodes 2001) seems to undermine the classical supportive role of unions in the expansion of welfare policies.[798]

9.1 Critical Elaboration of the typical Logic of Inquiry

A premise of the study is that labour organisations are in demand of some degree of independence to aggregate, articulate and formulate the demands of their workers outside political institutions. Although the underlying assumption of the *power resource* argument seems to be causal (Korpi 1978, 1983, 1989), it neglects the relevance of other factors which can have significant constraints on the independence and resulting influence of organized interests on party politics.[799] In particular, the argument neglects another relevant indicator in the form of the 'independence' of labour organisations in their internal decision-making to articulate, formulate and aggregate their collective interests or the individual interests of their members. As argued before, the corporatism debate has a significant impact on the field of study and has cultivated an understanding of the internal conflict between the *logic of influence* and the *logic of membership* (Olson 1965, 1993, Lehmbruch 1984, 1986: 273, 288, Streeck 1995:14).[800] As argued throughout the study, in both developing countries, informal institutional patterns of exchange produce constraints on the '*room to manoeuvre*' for political actors (2.5.3.2); however, the impact of this informal dimension is even more relevant for organised labour and its organisations on the national level (Cameron 1984, Lehmbruch 1984, 1991).[801]

---

798 Visser and Hemerjick (1997) provided evidence of the Dutch case as well as Rhodes for the increased '*social pacts*' between labour and politicians above political cleavages in Italy.

799 In addition to economic and social factors, political opposition, and veto points, the individual policymaking process, factionalism, and the perception of the party leadership heavily affect the success of organized interests in modifying policy choices and party polity (Korpi 1983, Armingeon 1994, 1997, Miller 2008).

800 The dilemma of mass organisations in choosing between the divergent interests of the organisations and members as well as the implications for organised labour in India and China will be analysed in Chapter 6.5.

801 Principal investigations of the asymmetrical relationship between unions and political parties in India and China have been conducted by various scholars (Kennedy 1968, Rothermund 1995a, Metcalf and Li 2005).

As a consequence the classical logic of inquiry for elaborating the 'organisational power' of labour in democratic settings has to be critically reviewed for its usefulness in providing insight into the two cases and the informal character of the labour-union-state relationship (Rothermund 1995c, Metcalf and Li 2005). The union confederations' political bargaining power is affected by three main factors: overall union density, the unity of the union movement, and the features of the institutional bargaining arrangement (Cameron 1984, Scharpf 1991, Iversen 1999). In most cases the two first categories are closely interlinked. The scope of the institutional bargaining processes is in most cases closely related to the unity of the movement, in terms of the number of union confederations (Soskice 1991, Hall and Soskice 2001).[802] Centralised bargaining mechanisms enhance the labour unions' organisational power in two ways. Limited pluralism in centralised settings promotes the existence of a limited number of union confederations—also often referred to as 'encompassing' unions due to their broad membership and strong bargaining position (Streeck and Hussel 2003).[803] Another effect of coordinated bargaining mechanisms is that in these settings the involved and limited actors have cultivated longstanding cooperative interaction patterns, such as the 'so-

802 Similarly, various comparative studies argue that these two distinctions determine the organisational power of unions and their related ability to modify political and economic allocation processes in their favour (Allègre 2008, Andreß and Lohmann 2008, Peña-Casas and Latta 2004).

803 Coordinated and centralized wage bargaining institutions on the national or industrial level, such as in the Scandinavian countries, tend to coexist with encompassing unions. These coordinated arrangements in industrial relations seem to promote the political role of unions. In decentralized arrangements, unions, such as those found in the Anglo-Saxon countries including the USA, Great Britain and New Zealand, are more fragmented and dominated by individual craft unions on the sectoral and workshop level. Decentralized economies, such as what are found in Britain, New Zealand, Ireland and Canada, nourish organisational splits and reduce the overall bargaining unity of the labour movement, resulting in the tendency of smaller unions to follow their egoistic interests. In Scandinavian and European countries, such as Sweden, Switzerland, the Netherlands and Germany, union confederation gains more importance due to the centralised bargaining mechanisms and the resulting ability of the union confederations to bargain arrangements for whole industrial branches. In addition, unions represent important resources for political decision-making due to their veto potential. The resulting inclusion of union organisations in various committees, '*bipartite or tripartite parastate or pararfiscal agencies*' (Streeck 1995, Streeck and Hassel 2004:344) enhances their direct ability to affect the formulation of new policy choices.

cial cooperation' patterns in Germany, in which organised labour has a measurable impact on policy choices, wages and unemployment levels (Andreß and Lohmann 2008).[804] In addition, the organisational power of labour has been defined as followed (Cameron 1984:166):

Organisational power of labour = (organisational unity of labour + collective bargaining power of the confederation(s)) x per cent of labour force unionised

The results of organisational power (Appendix, table 45a/b) underline the limited usefulness of the formal elaboration for non-democratic settings. In particular, the membership figures are less explanatory for both cases. In China, union membership in the ACFTU is mandatory and local authorities have to fulfil national quotas (Metclaf and Li 2005, M. Liu 2011, Qi 2013). In India, union membership is voluntary but the World Bank estimates that roughly 2 percent of the Indian workforce is organised under the umbrella of the national union confederations due to their restriction to the 'formal' sector. However, the strike waves in the 1990s and the recurring national strikes in the 2000s illustrate the relatively high mobilisation power of organised labour in all kinds of industrial sectors, such as finance and service, transport and construction as well as the industrial manufacturing sector.

Hypothesis 6a: *The number of union confederations, the range and scope of bargaining, as well as the party-union-state relationship determine the organisational power of organised labour.*

804 In his comparative article Lohmann (2009) analyses 20 European countries and the country-specific institutional features of the labour market for employment, poverty and social policy choices. It is commonly accepted that in decentralized economies pluralism has a negative effect on the macro-economic agenda and the cooperation of organised labour. On the one hand decentralised mechanisms, mostly restricted to the shop or workshop level, produce heavy constraints on the bargaining potential of organised labour in industrial or national arrangements and tend to accelerate the fragmentation of the labour movement. Another issue is the egoistic attitude of smaller craft unions, which represent only a small number of specific workers. As a consequence these smaller union organisations are only interested in maximizing specific demands and oppose broad demands (Olsen 1965, Streeck and Hussel 2003).

Undeniably, as Hans Daalder (2002:28) remarks, 'by emphasizing the close interaction between public and private actors, the neo-corporatist approach seemed successfully to bridge input and output structures, and to present a more realistic picture of power relations and policy-making than either those who had spoken uncritically of 'the' state, or those who had embraced a naive 'pluralism'.

A common consensus in comparative political science is that the distribution of political power[805] for unions is determined by the opportunity structure (Pizzorno 1978, Armingeon 1994, 1997) as well as *privileged links* between parties and unions (Lehmbruch 1979, 1984, Cameron 1984, Korpi 1989). These links are not restricted to social-democratic parties[806] or even democratic systems. In authoritarian regime types, such as China or the former USSR, the party governments tend to have direct control over the labour organisations (Schmidt 2012)[807]. Accordingly, the theoretical reasoning and implicated variables can be used as indicators but cannot account for the complexity of the traditional asymmetrical party-union-state relationship in China or India.

Hypothesis 6b: *The independence of the union confederations matter for their political impact on social security decision-making.*

Consequently, the premise in both cases is the formal and informal features of the party-union-state relationship determine the 'independence' of organised labour, which is seen as a crucial dimension for its potential to modify political allocation processes and social policy outcomes (Bardhan 1984, 1997, Metcalf and Li 2005, Scott 2011). Accordingly, the formal indicators provided by the corporate approach are expanded by a party-centred approach that takes into account the three dimensions of '*organisational independency*'[808]: membership, financial and organisational inde-

805 Power is defined according to Max Weber (1971).
806 Christian-Democratic parties tend to nurture strong links with the labour movement for support of their policy goals (Schmidt 1998).
807 The impact of concentration between state and unions and the effects on internal decision-making and the organisational power of union organisations are relevant (Lehmbruch 1991).
808 The aggregated indicator for organisational independence combines the dimension of independence in regard to the finances, membership and recruitment of key positions. The value is aggregated up to 100 percent – 20 percent membership, 40 percent finances and 40 percent organisational independence. Each cate-

pendence (Kenis and Schneider 1996, Streeck and Schmitter 1996, Wischermann 2013).[809] Korpi's observation (1983) that the higher the organizational level of the wage-earners is within the social democratic movement, the higher the outcomes of welfare policies for the level of solidarity, redistribution and equality emphasises the relevance of the membership category in two ways: Is union membership voluntary? And is it compulsory to party membership? In particular, the organisational and financial dimensions should gain more attention. In contrast to the advanced industrial nations, in China authoritarian corporatism and in India the asymmetrical patronage-client-relationship have enhanced the reputation of the national union confederation but also crippled its independence – transforming it into a 'transmission belt'.[810] Accordingly, the distribution and access to the 'organisational power' of labour unions in India and China can be attributed to three main dimensions: institutional features of the production regime, unity of the labour movement, and organisational independence (Lehmbruch 1984: 131).

Despite the critical elaboration of the Social Democracy Theorem (Pierson 1996, Kittel and Obinger 2003), various studies on modern welfare regimes and *'social pacts'* between political actors and organised labour above typical cleavages have accumulated empirical evidence of the supportive role of trade unions for left-wing welfare policies from a comparative perspective (Stephens 1979, Rhodes 1998).[811] Consequently, the party-state-union relationship seems to continue to be of high relevance, espe-

gory is elaborated based on aggregated values of the three subcategories: free (100 percent), partly free (50 percent) and not free (0 percent).

809 For a general discussion of the issue see Patrick Kenis and Volker Schneider (eds.) 1996. *Organisation und Netzwerk. Institutionelle Steuerung in Wirtschaft und Politik*. Frankfurt: Campus as well as Wolfgang Streeck and Phillipe C. Schmitter's (1996) article '*Gemeinschaft, Markt, Staat – und Verbände'*, pp. 123-164, in the same volume.

810 Strong organisational or ideological links between parties and union organisations are commonly found across countries regardless of the political system (ILO 2010). However, the degree of dependence and the character of the client-patronage relationship varies across and within specific countries. Students of corporatism, such as Lehmbruch (1974, 1991), Cameron (1984), and Stephens (1979), have distinguished the same conditions in the findings of their comparative research.

811 Various studies have empirically validated the importance of trade union participation for pro-welfare parties in producing significant public policy outcomes (Castles 1998:181, Rhodes 1998, Schmidt 2002:12f).

cially in the Indian and Chinese cases of traditionally strong organisational and party-union relationships (Rothermund 1995c, Metcalf and Li 2005, Sharma 2006, M. Liu 2011).

What most of the conducted research on social organisation[812] has in common is a slightly biased *liberal democratic* perspective on civil society organisations (CSOs)[813] as '*engines for democratization*' (Croissant et al. 2000)[814]. The recent academic discussion in comparative political science on CSOs has mostly ignored three dimensions. First, what many comparative studies have used is *liberal democratic biased* methodology and theories in which a common misconception of the nature of CSOs has limited the research on the positive effects of CSOs in supporting civil virtues and democratization processes in society (Alagappa 2004). Con-

---

812 Almond (1983) distinguished three waves of social scientific research on associations; a recent fourth wave on '*social capital*' as well as a fifth wave on the cooptation approach should be added to complete the picture (Anheier et al. 1997, Reuter 2001 on social capital, Gerschewski 2010a, Kailitz and Köllner 2013a on cooptation). Putnam's recent article '*Bowling alone*' has initiated a lively discourse on the positive effect of civil associations on the democratic virtues of society. His work is influenced by Coleman's article and was followed by numerous social scientific studies on the role and function of civil associations in modern democracies.

813 Generally speaking, CSOs have to be distinguished from mass organisations (labour unions, veteran and/or farmer associations) and other kinds of associations, such as NGOs and/or business organisations (Wischermann and Nguyen 2003:186).

814 CSOs have mostly been evaluated in social and political studies for their positive contributions in democratic settings. Undeniably, a functioning civil society and CSOs can be a major factor of democratization in establishing civil virtues and democratic patterns (Croissant et al. 2000). Classical CSOs can articulate, aggregate and formulate collective demands and represent them by relying on various forms of political participation but also function to establish civil virtues, democratic behaviour and political discussions outside political institutions (Habermas 1973, Croissant et al. 2000). A recent point of departure is offered by liberal democratic theory to explain the positive effect of the inclusion of societal demands on social policy legitimacy (Huntington 1968, 1991, March and Olsen 1989). Peaceful cooperative patterns between state, business and trade union organisations create positive feedback for the adjustment of the state (Pierson 1996, Esping-Andersen 1990). Feedback and participation allow the states to adjust social policies to current demands and challenges (Easton 1965). As Luhman (1981:27) notes, political inclusion of all organized interests can effectively counter the exclusion in education, means of production, consumerism, law, health, and politics by promoting public access to institutions (Hyden 2010).

trary to the widely stated hypothesis, corporate scholars have shown evidence that most labour as well as business confederations tend to be hierarchically structured.[815] As a result of the research on determining the dichotomy of the internal conflict between members' collective and individual interests, students of corporatism offered a theory and problem-driven definition of the conflict between two so-called logics which determine the strategies and actions of collective organisations: the logic of influence and the logic of membership. In his widely-cited research on the internal structure of the German Social Democratic Party, Robert Michels (1911) formulated his '*iron law of oligarchy*' thesis describing the democratic structure inside most modern political parties.

Second, it is worth noting that CSOs are defined as politically neutral multipliers (Berman 2003:20) and it is argued that the country-specific or even local political, economic and social contexts can heavily determine their structure, organisation and function (Roßteutscher 2005:240). CSOs do not need an internal democratic structure nor do they promote civic virtue and the democratization of society to produce positive feedback functions for the political system. The politically neutral factor discussed above should be seen as a structural parameter to analyse the CSOs' positive contribution to the political system in enhancing policy performance and legitimacy on various levels in non-democratic systems (Liverani 2008, Gerschewski 2010a). Undeniably all political systems are in demand of feedback mechanisms to increase policy performance as well as methods for including public demands in the policy process (Zöllner 1963, Mesa-Lago 1985, Schmidt 1998:229-241). In particular, non-democratic systems have a deficit in the input dimensions and need to rely on cooptation with either political and/or socio-economic elites or mass organisations. In recent decades a vast number of studies have provided evidence of the changing role of CSOs in autocracies and 'anocracies' (Gerschewski 2010a).

Third, CSOs in non-democratic systems can also become relevant pillars of political systems; however, in comparative political science CSOs in autocracies have gained less attention (Jamal 2007). The limited scope is reasonable due to the biased *liberal democratic* methodology underlying most research designs and the fact that in most of the autocratic systems

---

815 The reasons and effects of decision-making are discussed in detail in the following pages.

CSOs tend to be either state organisations – representing Lenin's famous concept of 'transmission belts' – or irrelevant for policy processes and decision-making because of restricted political participation. In the course of the renewed academic interest in autocracies various case studies have provided evidence of the changing role of CSOs in transforming from a 'transmission belt' into important actors providing positive feedback for the state (Gerschewski 2010a, Wischermann 2013)[816].

9.2 General Reflections on Unionism and Social Security

Interestingly, in many countries where unions suffered significant membership losses, the welfare state is being cut down.[817] Membership determines the economic as well as political power of unions and determines their influence on social policymaking. Similar to unions, the welfare state is an instrument to protect citizens from economic uncertainties, though its capacity and influence is superior to any collective organisation. However, both are currently under pressure from various sides. On the one hand the welfare state is confronted with increasing social expenditures and the need for austerity. On the other hand labour organisations are suffering membership losses (OECD 1999, 2010). It has been argued that the '*principal forces that build the welfare state seem not to have lost ground—notably trade unions and social democratic parties, but also Christian Democracy*' (Esping-Andersen 1997:224). The retrenchment and adjustment of the welfare state follows a different logic than its expansion phase which also renders the role of classical clients of supporters (Pierson 1994). The welfare state has been under criticism. The increasing financial restrictions on state expenditures and exercised state control of social, political and economic processes have been censured by liberals in particular. Moreover, the political and public debate in the OECD as well as in developing countries is dominated to a huge extent by the topic of the wel-

816 Vietnam offers a perfect example of the fact that CSOs are not automatic '*engines for democratization*' but contrary to assumption can even be essential pillars for legitimizing authoritarian rule (Wischermann 2013).

817 In their comparative study on the variations in European Union movements, Ebbinghaus and Visser (2000) gathered empirical data that showed the decline in membership also affected welfare schemes and programs for the working-aged population.

fare state and social expenditures. The traditional role of supporters and opposing forces in this public discourse cannot be easily defined. Recent increases in the participation of social democrats and/or trade unions in reforms to the welfare state undermine the classical assumption.[818] Thus, to explore and explain the contemporary politics and social policy outcomes of the modern welfare regime in the subfield of social security involves a detailed analysis of the involved actors and institutional variables.

The Party-Union Relationship and three Dimensions of Cooptation

In attempting to evaluate whether differences in the institutional framework or political dependence of union organisations account for the variations in organisational power of labour on social policymaking, the institutional and organisational features of the production regime and labour movement are taken into consideration. The presented conceptional distinction that has developed between the institutional patterns of the production regime, the organisational features, and the party-state-union relationship permits a measurement of all the variables determining the organisational power of unionism in India and China.

First, scholars generally agree that the institutional patterns of the labour market and bargaining mechanisms determine the relative power of organised labour. These institutional patterns are far from uniform. To ascertain the country-specific setting and underlying implications for the organisational power of unions, the conducted research on institutional patterns draws on David Soskice and Peter Hall's typology of production regimes (Soskice 1990, Hall and Soskice 2001). Second, the question of the nature of the party-state-union relationship and its implications for the independence and institutional inclusion of unions is addressed. This observation echoes the point on the relevance of informal institutional patterns in structuring the party-state-union relationship and critically evaluates the specific settings of membership as an explanatory variable.

818 In Italy (Baccaro and Lock 1996), Japan (Ichiyō 1997) and even Sweden (Stephens 1996) trade unions in the private sector have joined forces with business organisations and politicians in opposing the expansion of the welfare state. Also the party effect of Social Democrats or Christian Democrats on the expansion of the welfare state can no longer be empirically measured (Pierson 1994, 2001, Kittel and Obinger 2003).

Third, the presented descriptive perspective on country-specific labour organisations permits a measurement of the traditional variables of bargaining power, the organisational features of membership, and their implications for the contemporary organisational strength of organised labour.

9.3 Production Regimes and organisational Power

For a union a desirable outcome is a high level of employment followed by wage dispersion, compulsory pensions, and other employment-related social security schemes (Palme 1990, Huber and Stephens 2000). In the case of trade unions, a crucial variable in the achievement of these benefits is the degree to which they possess access to stable political exchange in order to modify market realities. By seeing the matter in this way, unions can gain long-term benefits in political exchange if they rely on centralised bargaining patterns and representation monopoly. Thus, strong union organisations that establish stable political exchange patterns can modify social policy choices, such as pension schemes. In theory it is argued that the extension of the welfare state implies more cost for the state and economy alike and therefore should result in a lower level of competiveness.[819] The degree of stable political exchange patterns and the organisational power of unions depend partly on the extent of coordinated institutional arrangement (Lehmburch 1984). Hence, the distinct production regime and degree of concentration is generally regarded as one variable, in addition to representation monopoly, for organisational powers to assess social policymaking (Regini 1984).

9.3.1 Measuring the Level of Organised Interest

The literature on the *varieties of capitalism* or *production regimes* (Soskice 1990, Hollingsworth, Schmitter and Streeck 1997) agrees that the *institutional environment* determines the interaction pattern between the market, the state, and economic actors including unions. Soskice's ap-

819 Taxation, unemployment compensation and social expenditures burden financial resources and non-wage labour costs; however, the competiveness of corporate countries, such as Germany, with strong welfare regimes is seriously undermining the theoretical assumption (Huber and Stephens 2000).

proach (1994) distinguishes between two types of advanced industrial economies: the coordinated market economy (CME) and the liberal market economy (LME):

Coordinated Market Economies (CME) have established formal and informal channels and networks between collective economic actors, such as trade unions and business organisations, to provide public goods. These cooperation patterns offer '*room to manoeuvre*' for all actors to bargain and mediate. Stable institutionalized arrangements foster cooperation and stability. Unions and employers can negotiate long-term agreements which enable the unions to secure employment as well as influence the level of wages. The cooperation allows stable conditions and industrial peace which fosters long-term economic investment. Strikes and protests are less frequent than in other less coordinated economies.[820] Such corporate arrangements often include the corporate provision of educational systems for skill formation (Soskice 1994, Thelen 2004).[821]

In coordinated economies trade union organisations are involved in long-term cooperative processes with the state and and/or employers. Thus, strikes and protests are less frequent than in other less coordinated economies, such as Britain or the USA. Furthermore, the close relationship and often-direct involvement in the institutional arrangement leads to a more cooperative attitude on behalf of the labour organisations. In their strategies labour confederations also include long-term benefits in their rational thinking and often willingly accept short-term negative conditions (such as wage restraints) without an increase in the labour militancy. In CMEs, independent of the political context, these long-term cooperation processes allow stable outcomes.[822] As a consequence both labour and capital organisations agree to strong employment protection and central-

---

820 In Britain the strike activity is measured in working days lost in industrial disputes per 1000 in the total labour force (Hibbs 1978) outnumber the German case by 375 to only 28 days lost per 1000 (Cameron 1984:153). The observation is still valid for most cases (Soskice 1994). Corporate centralised systems tend to offer less strike activities and militant industrial disputes.

821 Typical examples of CMEs are Japan, Germany and the Scandinavian countries.

822 Unions are interested in wage settings and in guaranteeing low levels of unemployment. The willingness of the unions to cooperate with business and state enhance their organisational and bargaining power in the future. Also lower rates of unemployment and wages are traded for short-term benefits. Economic actors tend to prefer long-term investments, innovations and new productivity methods for which they need skilled workers. Hence the firms favour long-term contracts

ized bargaining arrangements as a '*benign constraint*' or punishment for non-cooperating firms (Streeck 2002, 2006).

Labour and business organisations will protect each other's power from restrictions or reforms by the government that can endanger the cooperation. Strong union federations are needed for the economic actors to secure industrial peace at the workshop level. In CME unions are becoming *private interest governments* (Hollingsworth, Streeck and Schmitter 1994). In exchange for public status and privileges union organisations sacrifice some of their independence. The state creates an institutional arrangement of *self-governance*, reducing its needed resources to control and interfere. Union organisation can function like a state institution and offer the parties or the state a body of expert knowledge, an organisation to effectively implement social policies, as well as public support for these policies.

Liberal market economies (LME) are characterised by fragmented decentralised features. Formal and informal patterns of exchange are often restricted to specific short-term arrangements. Strikes and protests at the workshop level are common phenomena and the ultimate weapon for unions in negotiating arrangements (Cameron 1984). These arrangements have short-term, solid, and specific characters due the decentralized features of the exchange patterns. Wages and other collective goods are bargained separately. Such an environment and the unstable industrial peace often reduce the attractiveness of long-term investment in the economy and skill formation systems. The USA, Canada, Britain and also Vietnam and South Korea are typical LMEs (Thelen 2004). However LMEs embody another business concept. The interaction of labour and capital is mostly flexible and does not include long-term cooperation treaties and stable arrangements on the national or industrial level. The flexibility of labour contracts often excludes high-skilled labour or long-term employees in private enterprises due to their importance for the production. Still in various branches, such as the textile manufacturing sector, the unskilled labour force suffers short-term employment and bad working conditions.[823]

---

for their high skilled workers. It is worth noting that centralisation fosters the monopolization of the involved organisations (Lehmbruch 1984, 1991).

823 Fragmentation and decentralization are consequences of union organisations. The individual unions at the enterprise and unit level are pressure groups for specific demands of their clients due to the lack of central bargaining patterns. The decentralised labour market restricts and liberal labour laws weaken the unions'

Another aspect of the decentralised system is the impact of a missing national coherent organised labour policy in the context of strong business associations. Accordingly, business interest groups will use their financial influence to enforce more liberal policy choices. A historical example of such policymaking is Thatcherism in Britain.[824] The government's liberal policies are supported by business organisations that restrict the trade unions' power and ability to implement central bargaining arrangements (Wood 1997).

9.3.2 China's autocratic Cooperatism

The Chinese production regime seems on first look to represent a typical CME with authoritarian corporatism, centralized planning and centrally coordinated market institutions; however, similar to the social security system, the Chinese production regime embodies strong coordinated features on the one hand and liberal characteristics on the other hand. The Chinese hybrid production regime has evolved in the ongoing economic liberalisation since 1968. In the 1990s the increasing pace of the economic reforms, particularly of the SOEs, constantly weakened the centralised characteristics and institutions of the Chinese production regime (Jospeh 1990, Meisner 1995, Chan et al. 2008:30-32).[825]

On the industrial and unit level the committees of the ACFTU represent the workers' interests. Hence, China is assigned the highest score in regard to the organisational structure and unity of the labour movement. Despite the strong union confederation and the communist party government of the CCP, the implementation of the liberal market economy in the early

---

monopoly and the importance of union federations. Wage disputes are not fought on the national or sector level but are restricted to the specific context in every case (Wood 1997). The missing framework of labour organisations produces constraints on the ability of smaller marginal groups, particularly contract employees, to organise and represent themselves. Furthermore the surplus of most firms is based on employment flexibility, low wages and non-wages costs, such as social security taxation. Business organisations will promote deregulation of the labour market and oppose all ambitions to centralise (Soskice 1994).

824 Another prominent case is the austerity policymaking of the American president Richard Nixon which has been often been labelled '*Nixon goes to China*' (Cukierman and Tommasi 1998).

825 See H. K. Jospeh (1990) '*Labour law in China: Choice and responsibility*'.

1990s and liberal reform policies of the central government deeply limited the ACFTU's influence on the political and economic level (Metcalf and Li 2005). Even the relatively pro-labour communist party favoured economic growth and business interests instead of protection and regulation of the labour market. The radical privatization of the SOEs is evidence of the neo-liberal agenda (Harmin and Zhao1995, Gallagher 2002:338-40)

Although the government granted the ACFTU official rights (1990), the benefits expected from the bill largely failed to improve the actual unions' power in the mid 1990s. Yet, the neo-liberal pro-growth attitude of the central government and the competition of local authorities for foreign investment reduced the ACFTU's ability to interfere in economic development (Chan et al. 2008:32-37, Gallagher 2005).

The policy shift toward the end of the 1990s was clearly the product of growing socio-economic challenges, mass unemployment, and the deficits of the welfare system. The increasing difficulties of economic transformation, such as bad working conditions, sharpening socio-economic inequality and growing unemployment put pressure on the CCP. It required the government to elaborately react to the challenges of the labour market and demands for public goods. In addition, the central government released its tight grip on the ACFTU and strengthened its position in relation to the local authorities. Until 2005 nearly all local governments had to establish special agencies for labour and social security inspections to control and guarantee wages, pensions and insurance payments and expand the grip of the ACFTU on the private sector. In addition, the political shift constantly increased organisational power in the 2000s. The ACFTU effectively achieved its labour goals in the legislature by drafting various regulations for the labour market regarding minimum wages and working hour restrictions. Under the umbrella of the CCP the ACFTU also unified the private sector in the mid 2000s and initiated a new labour contract law. In addition, union coverage in China constantly increased from 2006 onwards (Gallagher 2002, 2005, Hurst 2009).

9.3.3 India's State Capitalsim and Organised Labour

The contemporary production regime in India has witnessed a harsh transition in recent decades. Before 1991 the Indian case represented a typical CME; however, the economic reforms in 1991 changed the situation significantly. Liberalisation, privatization and implementation of free market forces have produced a dual trend in the economy. On the one hand the partial liberalization promoted the rapid growth of the private sector and privately owned economic entities which operate in a liberal setting. On the other hand, the liberalization and privatization process did not touch the state-owned sector. A consequence is the duality of the production regime embodying features of liberal and centralised market economies (Jenkins 1999).

In contrast to China, where the partial liberalization and opening of the economy began in the 1978, India witnessed a harsh economic transition in 1991 (Rothermund 1993).[826] Facing a state bankruptcy the Indian Government was desperately in demand of the financial support of international money lenders. The major means through which to gain the needed financial support of the World Bank and International Montary Fund (IMF) was attached to structural reforms, particularly open market reforms. These demands largely coincided with the political shift towards liberalism.[827] In 1991 the structural adjustment programs included policies on trade, resource mobilization, efficient use of resources, institutional reforms, and the 'removal of import quotas, cuts in tariffs, public-sector reforms, support to agriculture and industry, and changes in exchange rates, export incentives, taxes, and interest rates' (Ministry of Finance 1993).[828]

9.3.4 Remarks on Typology and the Hybrid Types

Taking a closer look, the Chinese and Indian cases share many similarities; both countries suffer high levels of inflation and unemployment and an increasing number of strikes (World Bank 2007, 2010, 2011, 2014). The production regime is a handy category to understand the country-specific conditions and structures of the economy, but the political system in general and the degree of direct or indirect state intervention specifically

---

826 Growing financial deficits and demand for external credit produced significant constraint on the independence of the central government.

827 Beginning in the 1980s the growing economic problems and the deficit of the stated-owned industry increased the pressure for structural reforms, which could only be partly realized due to the strong opposition to any deeper structural reforms.

828 For a detailed empirical data set, see the economic survey issued by the Ministry of Finances (1993).

heavily determines the formal and informal rules in the economic sphere and the balance of labour and capital.

9.4 The party-centred Approach for India and China

Investigating the institutional features of both production regimes has provided a necessary understanding of the overall importance of economic as well as political allocation processes of union movements in both cases (Rothermund 1995c, Metcalf and Li 2005). For a detailed analysis of the union confederation's ability to modify policy processes and the resulting social security provision the study focuses on the party-state-union relationship.

9.4.1 The Trinity of Party-State-Union

This section aims at bringing into clearer view the party-state-union relationship by focusing on a broad methodology to analyse three internal crucial dimensions guaranteeing organisational independence: recruitment, finances and membership. While the methodological discourse on the institutional features of the political and production system determines the institutional framework, the subfield on social movements[829] underlines the relevance of the three internal organisational dimensions as determinants of the degree of independence.

Lenin's (1929) account of organisation and labour class representation induced a critical (until recently) discussion of the relevance of organisational features for social movements. Although there are famous studies on the negative effects of organisation on internal democratic structures by Luxemburg (Walter 1970) and Michels (1962)[830], other scholars, such as Max Weber (1976), have emphasised the necessity of organisation and professional bureaucracy for the success, effectiveness and longitude of

829 For a detailed overview of the development of sociological studies on social movements see the introduction by David Snow, Sarah Soule and Hanspeter Kriesi (2005:3 sp).

830 For example, Piven and Cloward (1977) argued in their study on social movements among the poor that tight organisational structures limit mobilization potential.

mass organisations. Modern social science, including political science, certainly started to take social movements, particularly labour organisations, further into account. The trend becomes obvious when looking at the steadily increasing number of publications on social movements and collective action.[831] Against what the students of Luxemburg claim, evidence has shown the relevance of organisation for any social movement to achieve its goals. In recent decades various scholars have argued that the social movement organisation (SMO) is the crucial analytic variable for the successful mobilization of resources and for setting and achieving attempted goals (McCarthy and Zald 1977, Gamson 1990). As McCarthy and Zald (1977) pointed out, the SMO is the crucial analytic unit to understand the structure, processes and success of any modern social movement.[832]

A watershed has been the corporatism debate and the vast number of comparative and case studies on the importance of labour organisations for the different development of modern advanced industrial countries in the post-World War II period. The argument presented in the debate is two-fold. First, it is argued that the institutional setting, as previously discussed and illustrated, affects the organisational features and power of unions, which in turn determines their available opportunity channels to modify policy processes, structures, and actors in their favour.

Second, although students of sociology and corporatism fiercely debate the necessity of organisation and internal democracy, they generally agree on the importance of organisational features as a fundamental analytic unit for understanding social movements. The specific organisational features fundamentally shape the mobilisation potential, internal structures and external ties of social movements.

---

831 In the top four journals – American Sociological Review, American Journal of Sociology, Social Force and Social Problems – the number of published articles steadily increased from 2.23 to 9.45 percent between the 1950s and the 1990s (Snow et al 2005:5).

832 Not surprisingly there are controversial interpretations. More critical views of Luxemburg's argument agree that social movements 'are not organisations, not even of a peculiar kind' but 'networks of interaction between different actors which may either include formal organisations or not' (della Porta and Diani 1999:16).

9.4.2 Social Policy Making and the Party-State-Union Relationship

There is general agreement that social movements are 'collective attempts to promote or resist change in society or groups' (Tuner and Killian 1987:223, Benford et al. 2000:17). Students of the welfare state have narrowed the explanatory variable of social movements' success in promoting or resisting changes to their influence in the political arena, or more specifically, to their political ties to ruling political parties. Social organisations, especially those with political ties, are de facto interest groups even in autocracies such as China (Yang and Li 2013:78). For McAdam and colleagues (2001:5) most of the politically involved social movements are variants of 'contentious politics' or to be correct of the 'collective political struggle' that 'occurs entirely within well-bounded organisations,' and are 'manifestly political' because the government or dominant political parties are directly or passively involved as claimants, supporters, targets and/or mediators.

As argued previously, the informality of political patronage and the party-state-union relationship is seen as a crucial variable for the analytic approach in understanding the success of the dual social policy strategy in India and China. Although labour unions have become more than mere '*transmission belts*' for political parties, the external control and dependent relationship still dominates the union confederations (Qi 2013:287). Why is that the case even in the liberal political climate under governments opting for economic growth and business-friendly conditions?

The corporatist culture based on the special party-state-union relationship has been a ruling force for decades. State corporatism in China and state pluralism in India have produced a framework of formal and informal interaction patterns between unions, political parties and state structures. Consequently, labour confederations have become more and more entangled in the political structure of the state and party as regulatory instruments or 'transmission belts,' to quote Lenin (1929). In the process, unions have mainly relied on their output legitimacy and informal ties to political parties. Within the party-state-union relationship that is based on the patronage of the ruling party, the union organisation is directly limited in its independence by the orders of the political elites rather than by the stimulus of the bottom. According to William Gamson (1990), social movements and interest groups are not two kinds of species but the same.

Both long for political influence to modify allocation processes in their favour and produce output legitimacy.[833]

9.4.3 Patronage in the Political Decision Making Process

As pointed out by Regini (1984:129) for 'a trade union, the *advantage* of a stable political exchange cannot be seen, ... solely in terms of power for the leaders or of organisational gains ... the main benefit is, rather, to be understood as the possibility of modifying market outcomes to labours' advantage [emphasised by the author]'.

Although, as correctly pointed out by Regini, political patronage is favourable for any trade union in modifying political allocation processes and decision-making, the culprit of the close relationship is in most cases a decent degree of external control of the decision-making of mass organisations. In exchange for political influence the union has to give up a decent degree of its independence. In most cases the pay-off is willingly accepted

833 In particular, since the economic juncture in the 1990s the monopoly of labour confederations has come under heavy criticism by common workers. In times that demand more responsiveness to the rapid developments in the labour market, the internal hierarchical structure and authoritarian character reduce the input dimension and the opportunity of organised labour to integrate the demands of clients. Longstanding close organisational ties, informal exchange patterns, and the recruitment of external professionals in key positions have nourished a hierarchical internal structure, in which the input dimension and the stimulus of the bottom have been neglected. Within the old party-union relationship and political patronage, union leadership needed flexibility and independence in their decision making to hold up their part of the bargain. Meanwhile as part of the decentralisation process, political parties opened up to business demands and interests in which process the unions enjoyed more autonomy but lost due to the erosion of state-corporatism. In the last decade, in India and China, the pragmatic wing in politics has gained additional support for promoting the liberal tendency and a business-friendly climate, which weakened the economic and political role of unionism (Sharma 2008).
Consequently, the increasing pressure by the workers due to the negative effects of partial liberalization on the labour market, working conditions, and social security has in fact nourished instead of weakened the party-union relationship. Although the unions have less political influence in the current setting, the limited input dimension and their traditional reliance on output legitimacy is modifying policy processes.

by the labour union and is grounded in a long-standing historically developed party-union relationship.[834]

A sophisticated body of literature has evaluated the puzzle of external influence on internal decision-making. Organisational structure and the resulting logic is determined by the union's executive body.[835] The corporatism debate has produced a common consensus on the conflict potential of two dominating logics—the logic of membership and the logic of influence— through which the strategies, goals, behaviour and inclusiveness of the organisation is heavily influenced. Before proceeding, it is worth discussing the two logics for a broader understanding and resulting implications.[836]

The *logic of membership* has positive payoffs for increasing numbers of clients, mobilisation potential, membership fees and representation legitimacy, though the organisational power and ability to modify economic and political allocation processes also increases. However, evaluating the current preferences of the majority of the members for the course of action produces constraints on flexibility, room to negotiate, institutional acceptance and resulting organisational influence.

The above suggests that increased participation of the rank-and-file reduces the strategic flexibility and room for negotiation of the organisation.[837] Also another conflict point can be the gap between what is best for

834 For example, the political patronage of the INTUC by the INC can be clearly traced back, even before the official separation of the INC affiliated unions and the founding of INTUC in 1948, to colonial times and to the beginning of unionism in India (Rothermund 1993:61f-62,1995b).

835 It should be noted that membership can either be compulsory or based on the individual's ideological perspective. The member or client joins the union, pays his fees, and participates in collective action in exchange for positive pay-offs and the protection of his interests (Strøm 1990). The criterion for membership is goal achievement or the union association's ability to achieve its anticipated output. The dilemma of union organisation is linked to the need for member loyalty. Therefore in settings with competition, unions, similar to parties, have to satisfy the demands and preferences of their clients.

836 As already indicated, the output performance of an organisation is affected by various internal and external conditions, foremost membership (Korpi 1978, Streeck 1995). Unions critically depend on membership to legitimize their representation function and inclusion in institutional bargaining of allocation distribution. Similar to other collective associations, such as political parties, membership in unions is mostly a *rational* client relationship (Streeck 1991, 2006).

837 An increased logic of influence doesn't exclude democratic mechanisms. In most cases members have some influence on the course of the organisation, either via

the organisation and what is best for the members. Decisions in favour of long-term benefits or to establish cooperative arrangements can have negative effects in reducing the individual client's benefits, such as exchanging higher rates of employment for lower wage demands (Streeck 1995:12).

Inclusion in institutional arrangements and long-term cooperation with other collective actors and the state produces direct constraints on the association's ability to achieve its members' desired goals (Streeck 1992: 105-106). A stronger hierarchical structure and increasing *logic of influence* offers an organisation the following payoffs: strategic flexibility, policymaking capacity and monopoly or at least a firm position (Lehmbruch 1995:372-74). The negative pay-offs significantly reduce the ability of clients to participate in the decision-making and lowers the feedback function of these organisations for the state (Lehmbruch 1986: 273, 288).[838]

9.4.4 Constraints on the internal Decision Making Process

Contemporary labour organisations are confronted with the dilemma of balancing organisational and member interests[839] or the so-called *logic of influence* and *membership*. In theory both logics can be combined. However, various case studies have empirically validated the conflict potential between the two. The dominance of the logic of influence is a clear but not causal indicator of external influence and political patronage (Lange 1984:177-8). Generally speaking, regardless of the degree of external in-

---

internal participation opportunities or 'the law of anticipated reaction, i.e. their capacity to withhold vital resources such as their financial and labour contribution' (Müller 2010:191)

838 Central and even decentralised bargaining mechanisms rely on accountability and expert knowledge of the involved actors. Also the complexity of labour laws, long-term arrangements and variations in the employment situations of different industrial branches require expert knowledge and strategic cooperation of the involved bargaining agents of labour and business (Xinhua News Agency 2006a).

839 On the one hand, associations have to include the demands and interests of their clients; on the other hand, they need to ensure their influence and organisational strength to be able to negotiate the demanded benefits for their clients. In their study Schmitter and Streeck (1981:48-50) explore the dilemmas of internal decision-making. Schmitter and Streeck refer to the process as a dilemma of logic for the associations because of the need to balance the logic of membership and logic of influence (Lehmbruch 1978, Streeck 1992:105 sp).

fluence,[840] the '*bigger*' the union organisations and the higher the degree of centralisation of the production regime, the higher the tendency for hierarchal structures. Why is that the case? Three distinctive dimensions can be distinguished which determine the need for a decent degree of hierarchical structures and dominance of the logic of influence for labour organisations.

First, unions need *instruments to control a potential crisis of representation* and solve these obstacles effectively (Regini 1984:133). On the one hand, union confederations have to cooperate and need centralised decision-making which aggregates and summarizes the broad interests of their members. Commonly articulated demands enhance unions' ability to enforce their interests in political and economic bargaining. In the 1970s the three dominant union confederations declared a '*unitary pact*' and significantly enhanced their organisational power to enforce their demands. On the other hand, such centralised mechanisms reduce the responsiveness of decision-making to individual or minority demands of the rank-and-file. In addition, internal struggles, outbreaks of dissent and other conflicts have to be channelled to ensure the unity of the movement and high level of individual membership. India's labour movement has witnessed various organisational splits due to unsolved political and ideological struggles. The most popular event was the split in the AITUC and resulting exit policy of the Congress union organisations and the foundation of the INTUC union confederation in March 1947 (Rothermund 1995c:544-5).

Second, to achieve an *oligopolistic position in political bargaining with the government* the number of union federations has to be limited (Lehmbruch 1982, Streeck 1995:1-7) to enhance their bargaining ability and attribution of public status (Offe 1981). Similar to other cases the stability of concentration depends on the cooperation between the involved actors. Neo-corporatist countries, such as Austria, Sweden, and Germany, offer similar conditions, such as a high degree of centralization, concentration of interest organisations, and representative monopoly. In effect, pluralis-

840 Scholars engaged in research on internal decision-making have agreed that unions should be classified as internal or external depending on the extent of external influence on decision-making (Mathur 1991:6, Ramswamy 2000). In most cases unions do not recruit external individuals for positions in their executive committee but exceptions are made for the key position of the president and/or external advisers, who have significant influence on the decision-making of the union (Ramswamy 2000: 54– 56).

tic countries could produce similar arrangements, as Britain did in the 1970s or Italy in the early 2000s (Lange 1984:177, Visser 1997, Rhodes 2002). China represents a perfect example of a neo-corporatist setting due to the existence of only one labour confederation to represent labour interests in national and centralized bargaining arrangements. In India the pluralistic character of the interest mediation system and the fragmentation of labour organisations reduce the organisational power of labour.[841]

Third, a core function of unions should be the ability to pre-mediate a wide spectrum of interests. The aggregation, formulation and representation of collective interests legitimise representative monopoly. A flaw in the representation system reduces membership and as a consequence the overall representative monopoly of labour organisations. For instance the dominating Italian unions could achieve a *de facto* bargaining position due to their ability to pre-mediate different functional interests of pensioners, and salaried and waged workers in the 1970s (Regini 1984:135).

9.4.5 Organised Labour and the Logic of Influence

Empirical evidence has shown that in most centralised settings, broad labour confederations and business organisations tend toward and require decent flexibility and '*room to manoeuvre'*. Compared to farmer or other associations, unions as well as business associations require '*tight coupling*' in key positions to ensure that they are in control of membership, factions within associations, and reliable and flexible leadership for complex negotiations with each other (Lehmbruch 1995:372-75).

Undeniably, internal democratic structures and the resulting responsibility for decision-making are important and favourable features for any mass organisations to ensure competition and participation. It is worth noting that from a rational point of view democratic patterns tend to produce significant constraints on the accountability, flexibility and longitude of organisational decision-making. Democratic participation often fosters a decent degree of unpredictability and involves additional cost and time, which threatens the organisation's bargaining flexibility and long-term cooperative arrangements (Michels 1911).

---

841 The potential of the centralised bargaining arrangements in state-owned industry is weakened by highly fragmented and several involved labour organisations (Rothermund 1993:61-62).

9.5 Political Patronage and the Party-Union Relationship

What both cases share in common is the lack of an industrial revolution and the 'emancipation' of organised labour as a pressure group for the demands of the working class. In both cases the modern labour confederations flourished under the direct impact of political elites driven by the ideological, whether democratic or communist, ambition to ensure the representation of the workers (Rothermund 1993, Guo 2000). Although India's labour movement operates in a democratic setting it has produced a relatively stable arsenal of instruments[842] to deal with pluralism; undeniably, the clash of political patronage and free competition has, in contrast to the Chinese authoritarian system, resulted in the fragmentation of organised labour along fiercely defended political cleavages. Despite the democratic setting, union organisation in India and China relied on a similar arsenal of instruments to guarantee a degree of unity and hierarchical structures (Metcalf and Li 2005, Sharma 2006, Das 2011).[843]

According to Karen Stenner's (2005) value-neutral analysis, four simultaneous and typically undemocratic characteristics of organised labour can be identified for organised labour in India and China:

First, pluralism and individual perceptions are not tolerated, especially in the authoritarian context (Linz 2000, Steiner 2005). In classical political patronage (by the associated political party) the mass organisations exchange political power for independence. As a result, the leaders of labour unions have to be in charge of their members to fulfil their part of the bargain. Internal democratic structures and mass participation would threaten their flexibility and '*room to manoeuvre'*. In addition, hierarchical structures and party ideology dominate decision-making and internal discussions (Chan et al. 2008, M. Liu 2011, Qi 2013:290-91). Generally speaking, the degree of dependence varies form organisation to organisation and country to country. Although in democracies the organisational ties are often less rigid than in authoritarian regimes, the Indian case demonstrates

842 Stenner describes the country-specific arsenal of instruments as an '*authoritarian dynamic*' (2005:14-18).

843 Hierarchical structures and limited member participation are common features of mass organisations, such as labour unions as well as political parties, even in democracies (Michels 1911, Streeck 2006).

that in democratic systems strong party-union relationships can become a typical phenomena.[844]

Second, in both contexts the leaders of the confederation emphasise the *sameness* of the group as a resource for their legitimate rule (Steiner 2005). The representative monopoly of the administrative and political elite in charge is closely attached to its ability to effectively formulate, articulate and represent the long-term group interests of all its clients, despite the individual short-term demands of a minority (Qi 2013:287). On the national level the union confederations address mainly group interests, such minimum wages, employment and price level; individual problems of industrial branches are not taken into account. Local bargaining and peaceful protests for their individual demands are, to decent degree, accepted and tolerated by the confederation (M. Liu 2011).[845]

Third, equalization of social status through the postulated sameness of all workers involves the elimination of the '*other*' or political, ethnic and moral differences which threaten the representative monopoly and legitimacy of the ruling elites (Steiner 2005). Consequently, the national union confederations opt for broad objectives which benefit the majority of workers, such as high levels of employment, decent wages, and social security (Wischermann 2013:333).[846]

Fourth, as a result of hierarchical structures and external influences labour organisations either directly rely on or accept the internal patterns

844 As mentioned before, the degree of dependence varies not only across countries but also over time. In particular critical junctures can – in most cases temporarily – erode the relationship. For example, the crucial economic juncture in 1991 produced significant external and internal pressure on the INTUC to join the protest wave of the united labour movement against the liberalisation reforms of the INC coalition government.

845 It is worth mentioning that these protests and strikes are mostly wildfire attacks without the official acknowledgement of the grass-root branches. In China the grass-root union branches face the classical dilemma between the ACTFU's and central government's encouragement to ensure official minimum work conditions and local authorities' pressure to safeguard a business-friendly environment and social harmony (Metcalf and Li 2005, Qi 2013)

846 For example, although ethnic and religious fault lines still determine the social status of the individual in the deeply fragmented society, for the national labour unions political ideology has always overpowered any other cleavages. Despite its relevance in society, ethnic, religious or even class status has been of no concern for the majority of national union confederations (Rothermund 1995c, Sharma 2006)

and processes which oppress individual demands, criticism, and democratic participation (Steiner 2005). Contrary to the assumed pre-condition CSOs have to be considered politically neutral and adapt themselves to the political, social, and historical context. In Indian democracy the long-standing and deeply rooted patronage-client relationship and hierarchical social structure have produced significant constraints on the internal democratic patterns of the labour confederations (Kennedy 1968, Rothermund 1995c).[847]

9.5.1 India: Evaluating the Independence of Labour

Organisational body. The Bombay case exhibits the core problem of the labour movement in India in which failed progress in the overall problem of external leadership in the Indian labour movement has been painfully illustrated.[848] A consequence of traditional recruitment patterns is that political elites or other external persons have taken over the key positions in the organisational administration. Consequently the higher administrative key positions and the leadership of the unions are in the hands of external personnel. The recruitment patterns can be found on all levels of the union movement.[849] Union leaders are in most cases popular personalities with a political or legal background. Recruitment from political elites is granted on the grounds that such persons have acquired the necessary skills to lead, represent and mobilise people as well as to negotiate with entrepreneurs or political authorities. The second category of recruits is assembled due to their ability to represent the unions and their members in court disputes, which is not an easy task in the Indian context due to the complexity of labour law on the national, state and local levels (Rothermund 1995c, Sinha et al. 2006:130).

The legislature has also been concerned with external leadership, especially since the wave of protests against left-oriented unions in reaction to the government's liberalization reforms in the 1990s. In 2001 the amendment of the Trade Union Act (1926) officially prescribed the numbers of

847 Similar to Chinese case the ruling administrative and political elites in the key position of the union organisation rely on a stable arsenal of instruments to legitimize their monopoly and ambitiously try to repress any significant changes in the power balance (Sharma 2006).

848 Even the smaller independent unions on the local or entrepreneurial level tend to be under the leadership of middle-class elites (Sinha et al. 2013).

849 See the previous discussion of Bombay's grand strike as an illustration of the dilemma.

outside leadership: 'Not less than one-half of the total number of the office-bearers of every registered trade union shall be persons actually engaged or employed in an industry with which the trade union is connected' (GoI 2001). Interestingly, the prescription has not changed the core problem of external leadership. In most unions external personnel is a minority of 10 percent but this minority has key positions in union organisations (Sinha et al. 2006:129-30). Consequently, the recruitment patterns in most cases result in the external control of labour confederations by political parties or ambitious individuals[850] (Bakshii 1986, Rothermund 1995c: 543-547, Sinha 2006:129-31). Hence, the organisation has to be rated partly free due to its close ties to political parties on an organisational and ideological level and the influence of external leaders and experts in key positions.

Membership. Party membership is not compulsory for union members. However, the close connection of unions and political parties and internal cleavages along political ideologies in the union movement emphasises the overlapping membership of union members in the affiliated political parties. But there is no compulsory party membership or restriction such as religion or ethnicity to become a union member in most cases.[851] Membership is therefore rated as free.

Finances. The lion's share of income is membership fees, roughly 60 percent of overall income.[852] The second income resource is donations, at an average of 20 percent, followed by only marginal profits from the interests of investments, the sale of periodicals, and various other miscella-

850 There are also a large number of unaffiliated smaller union organisations. These organisations are either company unions or the vehicle of political ambition for middle-class leaders. In the case of the company unions (e.g. in the coal mining sector), the unions are limited in their bargaining ability due to their dependence on employers. The second category or the unaffiliated union under the leadership of ambitious start-ups are mostly used to ensure the political career of their leaders. Both types are much more independent but isolated in the union movement (Sinha et al. 2006:130-1).

851 There are exceptions in India. While the state unions and confederations do not refer to such categories for membership, there are unions on the lower level which recruit on grounds of religion and/or ethnicity.

852 The Trade Union Act, 1926, introduced a minimum membership fee that every member has to pay. Normally the fees are only 5 or 6 Rupees which is equal to 0.33 per cent of the normal salary in the industrial sector. The fact results in the overall low budget of the unions. In other countries, such as Britain, the membership fee is equal to 1 per cent or more of the salary (Sinha et al. 2006:108-110).

neous sources (Sinha et al. 2006:106-8). Donations are not public. Regarding the relatively high degree of donations in the income distribution, the overall financial independence of unions is moderate.

The Bombay Case: a concrete Example of the All-Indian Experience

The Bombay case can be taken as an example of the *dilemma of logic* in the Indian labour movement. In 1982 the *Bombay Millowner Association* neglected a broad demand for higher wages by the workers. In addition, local textile workers were frustrated and disappointed with their traditional union representation by the *Rashtriya Mill Mazdoor Sangh.*[853] In the following period the workers turned their backs to the RMMS and nominated *Dutta Samta* as their new leader, who saw an opportunity to establish himself in the local labour union movement.[854] January 18th marked the beginning of an overall strike for higher wages under the leadership of Samat in which roughly 220,000 textile workers in Bombay participated (Bakshi 1986, D'Monte 2002). The outbreak of the industrial dispute on a large scale triggered the official involvement of the state as referee. The former central government under Indira Gandhi feared a spread of the strike involving other industrial branches and categorically declined any demands of the workers (Bakshi 1986, Sharma 2006). Instead of reacting to the new situation and the non-negotiable attitude of the central government in favour of business interests Samat used the situation to establish his popularity regardless of the outcomes for the workforce. His firm stand on the unfeasible demands and the unbending attitude of the state as mediator resulted in the continuing strike, and the closing and outflow of more and more textile mills in the surrounding areas of Bombay and other cities. Samat continued the strike until 1983. The result of the strike left 200,000 workers unemployed and led to the decline of the Bombay textile industry (Bakshi 1986).

---

853 Rashtriya Mill Mazdoor Sangh is affiliated with the conservative INTUC and the ruling INC central party government at the time. The INTUC mostly tried to achieve peaceful negotiations for modest demands to ensure industrial peace. In the strike waves in the early 1990s the INTUC was the last central union association to join the protest against the INC coalition government.

854 Samta insisted on abolishing the representative monopoly of the INTUC-affiliated RMMS in Bombay and the Bombay Industrial Act of 1947 to open the way for his own union movement (Bakshi 1986, D'Monte 2002).

As illustrated in the history of the Bombay Strike the British model of external representation[855] granted union members the possibility of gaining outside professional representation but bore the risk of increasing external control whereby decision-making was not in the interests of the workers or the organisations. Bombay is such a case, but no exception. Since the freedom struggle, unions have played a strategic role for political elites and parties to mobilize popular support under the banner of class solidarity (Bakshi 1986). The history of unionism in Bombay reflects the overall tendency of the union movement to rely on political patronage and external leadership in times of crisis (Morris 1965, Rothermund 1995c: 544-547).

9.5.2 China: Evaluating the Independence of Labour

Organisational body. In the course of the trade union laws of 1992 and 2001 the ACFTU function was officially declared as granting 'top-down transmission, mobilization of workers for labour production on behalf of the state; and by bottom-up transmission protection of workers' rights and interests' but in reality 'the Chinese state was so powerful that the top-down transmission of Party directives regularly suppressed any bottom-up transmission relating to workers' interests. The union merely functioned as an arm of the Partystate' (Chan 2000, Qi 2013:287). In effect, neither the organisational structure nor the recruitment policy of the ACFTUC changed significantly. The highest position in the AFTUC is usually taken by a member of the CCP's Central Politburo as well as other officials selected by the CCP.[856] In this context Child (1994) summarizes the relationship whereby Chinese unions 'continue to be subordinated to the authority of the Party.' So organisational independence is non-existing and has to be rated *not free*.

Membership. Union and Party Membership have to be separated and are not compulsory. Taking a look at the increased numbers of the workforce from 95 million in 1978 to 287 million in 2008 and the resulting union membership explosion from roughly 100 million in 2000 up to over 200 million in 2008 the overall representation of ordinary workers in the

855 British external representation is the stepping stone for traditionally strong external leadership in the labour movement. External representation allows unemployed individuals to represent either the interest of the employer or employees in industrial disputes and collective bargaining.

856 Furthermore, union officials are not elected by the members but chosen by the CCP. They are only responsible to state and party authorities (Taylor et al. 2003).

CCP is relatively low by only 9.7 percent (Metcalf and Li 2005, Qi 2013:285). Therefore in regard to membership dimension the ACFTU is rated *free*.

Finances. Normally the main financial source is the union membership fees. In China this is not the case. In theory the unions could charge member fees as union revenue. The levy is 0.5 per cent of the individual workers' salary. Interestingly, the ACFTU decided not to brother their clients. In addition, the bulk of the income revenue depends on the 2 per cent payroll levy contributed by the employers (see Table 38):

Table 38: Revenue of the ACFTU

Sources for Revenues	Elements/Modalities
Wage bill	2 % of wage bill paid either to (i) local government authorities for state employees in non-tradeable occupations or (ii) the City or Provincial branch of ACFTU for the tradeable sector. (0.05 transferred to ACFTU in Beijing; 0.38 transferred to the local, Provincial and industrial union; 0.57 returned to workplace e.g. to pay salary of union officials, for welfare role such as feast at Spring Festival, workers in need, and sports activity)
Membership subscriptions	0.5% of worker's wage paid to union at workplace
Revenue from enterprises owned by the local/provincial ACFTU body	Revenues from cinemas, culture palaces and travel agencies owned by the trade union
Local government	Financial support in times of economical distress

Source: Metcalf and Li (2005:16-7, 44-5)

As indicated by the table (38), the financial independence of the labour organisations is in theory given but the lion's share of income depends on the cooperation and contribution of the state as an employer. The levy is collected by either ACFTU officials or local government authorities.[857] Another income source is revenues of the '*quasi-entrepreneurial activities – owning cinemas and other property, cultural places, and travel agents*' (Metcalf and Li 2005:14-15). Last but not least, the local governments

857 Local authorities, such as the Haikou City Labour and Employment Bureau, are collecting the levy of the employers. The main contribution is made by the state-owned non-trading sector, such as civil services, schools or local administration. Private employers are either not bothered by the administration or do not pay the levy (Metcalf and Li 2005, Qi 2013)

tend to financially support the local union branches in their function of granting social services. The fact that only 0.38 percent of the wage bill revenues are transferred to the local branches often results of the fact that local unions have financial shortcomings and depend on the government (ibid).

Furthermore, local grass-root union organisations are often in demand of state financial support which is granted by the local authorities due to the fact that the unions traditionally take over public services, such as welfare, transportation and caregiving for elderly people (Metcalf and Li 2005, M. Liu 2011). Another relevant point is that the revenues from enterprises, such as cinemas or restaurants, owned by labour organisations are either not producing enough surplus and/or is restricted to cities. Therefore, the ACFTU depends on the government in terms of financial resources and is rated as *not free*.

Chinese paper unions

The Chinese labour movement has been repeatedly criticised. A symbol of the labour movement's failure to represent its clients effectively is the existence of so-called *paper unions* on the enterprise level which are controlled by entrepreneurs and represent the workers only on paper (Metcalf and Li 2005:1, 16-17, M. Liu 2011:160-61). The ACFTU has functioned according to Lenin (1929) as a 'transmission belt' between the party state and the ordinary workers.

9.6 Comments on Organised Labour and its Political Power

What both cases share in common is that their concept of organised labour has been imported and introduced from the top to the bottom. Without a proper industrial revolution, the evolution of the labour movement on the national level has been directly interlinked with the emerging political parties and their peaceful or revolutionary strive for independence. To sum up, the outcomes of the analyses that are presented in table 39 illustrate the historically strong ties of the labour movement with the political parties.

Table 39: Dependence of Labour Confederations

	Recruitment	Membership	Finances	Result
China	Not Free	Free	Not Free	Not Free
India	Not Free	Free	Partly Free	Partly Free

Source: Author's own estimation

The section presented an effort to offer an up-to-date analysis of the political impact as well as role of the established labour confederations as pressure groups of social security. The section focused on the analysis of organised labour in the modern capitalist systems of India and China by discussing the institutional framework of industrial relations and its specific implications for the organisational power of labour. The general overview was expanded by an illustration of the potential for internal conflict between members' and organisation's goals as well as the resulting relevance of labour confederations for the policymaking and implementation process.

In the process, the earlier evidence of the traditionally limited independence of organised labour in both cases could be verified on empirical grounds. In the process of forming the modern states and shaping the party-state-society relations both dominant political parties, the CCP and INC, became directly involved in the foundation of modern labour organizations by supporting the party guidelines in the young states. To sum up, in both modern states the labour confederations are limited in their independence despite the fact that both institutional arrangement offers various formal and informal channels for unions to modify social policymaking, asymmetrical power relations and the dominance of *the logic of influence* which reduces the confederations' organisational power to affect policymaking. But in terms of social security provision the institutional inclusion of the ACTFU in the state apparatus provides additional institutional organ. Still the missing independence and non-existing labour representation is painfully visible in the increasing number of strikes as well as the economic exploitation of Chinese migrant workers.

X. Conclusion

Comparing India and China in terms of social security provision illustrates that autocracies can provide higher levels of public goods, economic growth and human development compared to their 'similar' *developed* democratic counterparts.[858]

A causal explanation for the logic behind the Chinese commitment to employment-related social security can be found in the historical work of Werner Abelshauser (1987) on the early welfare state in Germany. In his work, he argues that social policy is used as a state instrument to ensure a steady supply of human resources for the labour market and at the same time such policy produces output legitimacy and support for the political elites. Continuing the same line of argument, Paul Pierson (1997) asserts that the untypical focus on pensions in a communist system can be best explained by the increasing number of pensioners. Concerning the different range and scope of social security in India, the political actors are in pursuit of a two-fold policy goal. On the one hand the government coalitions are attempting to improve the overall low human development in providing a deeply subsidised social pension and assistance program to the majority of the poor in society. On the other hand democratic governments are also in demand of legitimacy and electoral success. For rational *office-seeking* actors the issue of social assistance offers a popular policy field for electoral support across the political, ethnic and linguistic fault lines. However, to solve the puzzle of how to heighten Chinese policy performance, a short summary is in demand concerning the non-institutional and institutional determinants of state capacity.

Table 40 presented a conclusive presentation of the interaction relations and processes to explain the state capacity. As evident in the investigation, the singled-out institutional bundles involved in social security provision are relevant to the whole process. Throughout the study it is argued on theoretical and empirical grounds that the intra-institutional determinants play the crucial role of acting throughout all three sequences as boundaries in setting the '*rules of the game*' and the '*room to manoeuvre*' for the in-

858 World Bank (2006, 2007, 2014) and Wurster (2011).

Table 40: General assumed institutional Effects

	Sequence I: Policy Formation	Sequence II: Implementation	Sequence III: Monitoring, administration and provision
Determinant			
Regime type	x		
Institutional determinants:			
Political Parties	x	x	
Bureaucracy	x	x	x
Labour organisations	x	x	x
Law/Constitution	x	x	x
Non-institutional determinants			
Demography	x		
Economical situation	x		
State budget / Finances		x	x
Corruption		x	x

Source: authors' own estimation

volved actors in their ambition to modify policy formation (March and Olsen 1989, Mitra 1994a, 1999a/b, Pennings et al. 1999: 224).[859] In the next section based on the outcomes of the comparative findings for India and China an attempt at formulating the theoretically and empirically tested assumptions is conducted. The goal is to formulate the policy field of overlapping findings (on middle-range-theory) in terms of positive as well as sub-optimal arrangements for social security performance and state capacity in India and China.

As indicated in the table above, the socio-economic conditions are most relevant in addition to the institutional constraints. Although social security policymaking in India and China has been separated from the budget in the policy formation, the reality of these conditions deeply affect performance and state capacity.

859 A simplified and generalized model of Penning's (1999:224) '*political chain of command*' theoretical model to analyse policy formation and related performance within established democracies can be adapted to investigate the same processes in India and China to give insight into the relevance of the various sequences of the policy formation process and their determinants of and effects on policy performance. The '*democratic bias*' is taken into account and will be critically evaluated in the empirical investigation.

Table 41: Implications of the institutional and non-institutional Factors

	Socio-economical	social-cultural	power resources	Party-difference	pol. Institutions	Path-dependency	program concurrency
China							
Sequence I	x	--	--	xx	x	xx	xx
Sequence II	xx	-	x		xx	x	x
Sequence III	xx	--	x		xx	x	x
India							
Sequence I	x	--	--	xx	xx	xx	xx
Sequence II	xx	--	--	xx	xx	x	x
Sequence III	xx	x	--	xx	xx	x	x

XX = Strong / X = medium / -- = low explanatory potential

Source: author's own estimation

In accordance with a large part of the political science and economics literature that focuses on the determinants of public policy, this study assumes that economic performance matters.

Thesis 1a: *An increasing GDP has a positive effect on social security-related outputs and outcomes.*

It is immediately clear that the policy performance of government is positively correlated with economic performance. The higher level of Chinese economic growth over recent decades has positive effects on human development as well as social security provision.

Another aspect is the fact that national social security politics is and has separated from the budget in terms of adequate financial funding. The gap between social security objectives and outcomes is closely related to inadequate funding. The NEGRA alone is eating up one percent of the GDP. The lack of adequate financial resources for social security schemes, programs and services resulted in the traditional gap between policy objectives and outcomes varying from locality to locality.

Thesis 1b: *An increasing percentage of the state budget for social security has a positive effect on policy performance.*

It is worth mentioning that both governments have learned their lessons from the past. In the early period the overburdened administrative and financial state capacity put the state on the brink of bankruptcy—a painful experience. In both contexts austerity in social security is clearly visible. However, an existing paradox involves the budget restriction for social security and policy objectives. Budget restrictions seem to be less relevant in policy formation and accordingly both countries have had an issue with the gap between objectives and goals. Yet China sacrifices a measurably higher level of financial resources for social security than India. Closely linked to the restrictions is program concurrency with other policy fields.

Thesis 1c: *Increasing program concurrencies with other policy fields limit the available state capacity for social security provision.*

Defence, security, environmental protection as well as structural economic reforms reduce the overall administrative and financial resources on the national as well as local level. This remains true: the general priorities of economical reform and growth in both countries, in combination with overstretched resources, have sub-optimal effects on social security provision.

Another crucial point is that trade openness seems to matter. The data as presented here does not allow us to draw any general conclusions but for both cases a strong correlation of trade openness, economic growth as well as social security expenditure can be diagnosed.

Thesis 1d: *A higher degree of trade openness has a positive effect on social security performance.*

Yet, trade openness goes hand in hand with shifts in the employment situation and liberalization of the labour market. The close correlation is made to fit quite well with the new political economy argument. Trade openness and the shift in employment produces new realities for the old social security systems and demands a reaction from decision makers. As illustrated in the early 2000s both emerging markets were ill-equipped for the socio-economic transformation processes that challenged their social security systems.

Last but not least, another precise and significant measurable aspect concerning the development of social security provision in democratic settings as well as in the Chinese context is demographic growth, improvement of living conditions and the resulting higher life expectancy of the population (table 8, diagram 6).

Thesis 1e: *Demographic aging of the population affects social security provision and tend to results in sub-optimal policy outcomes.*

In China and India the so-called 'greying' of the population has dramatically amplified the old-aged population as well as increased the pressure on the social security administration to provide adequate funding to guarantee financial benefits and services in the future (diagram 1 and 3, NZZ 2014c/e). A consequence in both settings has been the lack of focus on social security for the younger and future generation. India's social pensions and China's improvement of existing programs demand a higher proportion of available resources.

Of course, non-political factors remain relevant but it appears equally clear that the state capacity, as illustrated throughout the study, as well as the social and strategic preferences of the decision makers matter. 'Economics' and 'financial capacity' are crucial for state capacity, but do not and cannot satisfactorily explain the cross-national variations in institutional performance for India and China. Nowadays there is little dispute that changing economic realities—that is, the economic growth rate, performance and employment situation—have an impact on the range, scope and goals of social security and individual welfare (Wagner 1911). However, such a simplification of the driving forces of contemporary social security is limited in its ability to adapt to the economic forces, leaving out the relevant question of the relationship between institutional causalities and institutional performance.

Another family of theories explains public policy outcomes and continuing decision-making in terms of policy inheritance. Path dependency in social security politics has been a phenomenon across political systems. Various accounts (Guy Peters 1977, Castles 1998) have provided empirical evidence of the effects of static policy inheritance for policy performance.

Thesis 2a: *Static policy inheritance tends to produce sub-optimal solutions.*

The empirical process-tracing of social security development for the two exemplary countries shows a strongly deviating path dependency. As a consequence of static policy inheritance social security schemes and services have been limited in their potential to adapt to either local conditions or socio-economic changes. The flagships of social security in India and China give credit to the thesis. In India the PDS illustrates strong policy inheritance. Typically the classical flagships of social security are challenged in their ability to modify the range, scope and goals to the rapidly changing socio-economic conditions as well as internal system deficits. The same line of argument can be applied to the Chinese welfare system, but Chinese decision makers have been more up to date. Since the early 1980s, social security programs have witnessed a constant evolution towards more market-oriented and modern blueprint. In contrast to the heavily state-funded Indian schemes and services, Chinese social security schemes are characterized by a higher ratio of individual insurance premiums, upgrade options for additional services, and more substantial public funding.

Another precise and significant measurable aspect concerning the development of social security provision in the Chinese context is the adaptation potential. A point of departure is the recent amount of policy analysis (Kittel 2007, Wurster 2010), which offers another relevant insight that seems to be true for the two cases.

Thesis 2b: *Slow adaptation of social security politics to current conditions tends to result in sub-optimal solutions and lower performance.*

Only gradual change in the range, scope and outcomes of social security can be diagnosed. Social security is heavily oriented toward past generations and accordingly the focus of attention is pension schemes. As illustrated in the empirical process tracing, both welfare systems currently focus their attention on providing a safety net for elderly people.

Thesis 3a: *A higher degree of joint decision making (so-called 'Politikverflechtung') and decentralised provision of social security tends to result in sub-optimal solutions.*

India's federalism and the strong decentralisation of social security provision results in sub-optimal solutions and different national levels of social security provision. Although China has followed a similar path in decentralisation towards quasi federalism, the central government has undisputed sovereignty. As a consequence, the ministries at the national level are empowered by quasi law-making abilities. The concentration of power, missing majority veto points, as well as hierarchical administration grants the central government the ability to issue fast-paced reforms. India's bichambered system with the Lok Sabha and Raj Sabha offers checks and balances but at the cost of long-term negotiations and second-best solutions.

Closely linked to the decentralisation and the 'chain of command' of social security provision is the performance of the administration. Yet, although most comparative political science studies have paid less attention to the bureaucracy as a dominant determinant of cross-national differences in policy output performance, in the last decade many case studies on *developing* countries have provided evidence of the relevance of bureaucracy (Wildavsky 1980, Potter 1996, Kaufman et al. 2008). A relevant thrust of the studies is the focus on the 'machinery' or bureaucracy as a major determinant of social security policy in both cases.

Thesis 3b: *Low administrative competence tends to stimulate sub-optimal social security provision.*

Interestingly, both administrations score relatively low in their administrative competency. Comparing the two, Chinese administrative service performs slightly better than its Indian counterpart. The macro-level scoring overlaps with the empirical evidence by conducted case studies on lower administration levels. As indicated earlier, autocracies tend to have an advantage in long-term planning and long-term government periods.

A common consensus in literature emphasises the impact of political parties on policymaking, supporting the claim that 'do parties matter' (Hibbs 1977). Still, empirical evidence demonstrates the decline of the 'old politics of the welfare state', to quote Pierson, or the 'traditional' left-right partisan effect on social expenditure at least in democratic modern welfare states.

Thesis 4: *If the political conflict potential of social security reforms is relative high, the chance that they will be carried through is lower.*

Again, China has an institutional advantage compared to India. Without any veto points, the CCP is the only sovereign. Contrary to the Chinese party state, the Indian elected government has to cope with constitutional and institutional constraints on its ability to carry through needed reforms. As illustrated earlier the electoral promises, coalition arrangements in a multi-party system, and federal system function as 'blocking potential' for any structural reforms. Furthermore, the electoral cycle, collation consolidation and 'office seeking mentality' tend to restrict 'unpopular' decision-making. Concerning the role of organised labour there has been some artificiality in assuming that the same causality of the Western context applies to the Asian cases.

Thesis 5: *The integration of labour representation and organisation in the decision-making process positively affects performance.*

The dominance of leftist political parties in combination with traditional centralised bargaining mechanisms and state capitalism as well as deeply rooted organised labour confederations should be clear indicators of a strong organised labour movement.[860] In India and China the labour unions have been engulfed by political parties which limit their positive feedback function. In particular, the Indian unions have a deficit. In China, the ACFTU is a 'transmission belt' limiting the positive feedback function but offering the party state an additional instrument of social security provision. As indicated in the empirical investigation, the ACFTU has achieved a quasi law-making ability.

On a theoretical level, the thesis has shown the constitutional constraints of decision making in both systems. Against the backdrop of various amendments or reformulations, both states have not touched the imprinted social rights of citizens. Still, in regard to social security performance the constitutionally granted 'social rights' are to be understood more or less as principles or guidelines. Taking a closer look at the causality of constitutional formulations and policy performance, Wurster (2010), Rohm (2014) and others give credit to the assumed thesis derived from the empirical inquiry of both cases.

Thesis 6: *Constitutionally imprinted principles have no measurable impact on social security performance.*

Interestingly, the 'rule of law' in China seems to be of less relevance in the provision of social security. Also the central government has recently been engaged in improving the legal system, social security administration and the legal rights of citizens[861] to report the misconduct of local governments in the provision of welfare, public goods and services.

---

860 See the typical theoretical implications of strong left-wing parties, which can rely on the support of organised labour (Cameron 1984, Korpi 1989, Esping-Andersen 1990).

861 The legal rights of Chinese citizens have been improved; however, not against in a way that diminishes the central state's institutions, repressive instruments,

In pursuit of an answer to the question '*Why is China performing better in providing social security for its citizens*' the inquiry has demonstrated the complexity of social security provision and its multi-dimensional factors, rejecting the over-determinism of the '*comparative advantage of democracies*' based on theoretical and empirical evidence. It is worth mentioning that the macro-level policy analysis has been strictly interested in solving the core question and the puzzle at hand. Concerns regarding democratic and normative implications or policy advice have been left aside.

If one were to ask what social security performance in India and China is about then Piper Norris provides an adequate answer in his work '*Making democracy work?*' by comparing non-democracies and democracies across the world. He argues that the policy performs is a complex product of the state capacity and the commitment of decision makers. It is no coincident that the CPR is doing better in its social policy as well as economical performance compared to India. Another relevant part of the puzzle is the missing constitutional and institutional constraints in the Chinese context. Compared to the resilient Indian democracy, the decision makers, ministries as well as local administration are civil servants. Political consolidation, public discourse and the individual citizen matter. Compared to the resilient Indian democracy, the decision makers, ministries as well as local administration are civil servants. Political consolidation, public discourse and the individual citizen matter. In addition, the authoritarian Chinese state can act more freely and perform slightly better than its Indian counterparts. Another relevant and closely linked part of the puzzle of low social security expenditures in times of economic prosperity is the often underestimated problem pressure as well as program competency with other policy fields, such as defence/security, economic reforms, environmental protection and/or energy security. India is desperately in demand for deep reforms to counter the growing problem pressure of a slowing down economy, decentralised labour market, overburden state administration as well as demographic tendencies. The cross-national empirical evidence suggests that both countries have made huge step forward in providing social security for its citizens in the last decades.

---

or political participation rights. The Chinese legal system and '*rule of law*' is far from being 'independent' (NZZ 2014d, The Economist 2014i).

Bibliography

Abelshauser, Werner. (ed.) 1987. *Die Weimar Republik als Wohlfahrtsstaat.* Wiesbaden: Steiner Franz Verlag.

Åberg, Rune. 1984. 'Market-Independent Income distribution: Efficiency and Legitimacy', in J. H. Goldthrope (ed.), *Order and Conflict in Contemporary Capitalism*, pp. 209-231. Oxford: Oxford University Press.

Acemoglu, D. 2014. 'The world our grandchildren will inherit', in I. Palacios-Huerta (ed.), *In 100 years. Leading The Economists predict the future,* pp. 1–36. Cambridge, Mass: MIT Press.

Acemoglu, D., & Robinson, J. A. 2012. *Why nations fail: The origins of power, prosperity and poverty*. London: Profile.

ACFTU. 1990. *ACFTU Eleventh Congress Documents*. Beijing: Economic Management Publishing House.

Alber, Jens. 1982. *Vom Armenhaus zum Wohlfahrtsstaat. Analysen zur Entwicklung der Sozialversicherung in Westeuropa*. Frankfurt a. M.: Campus.

—. 1989. *Der Sozialstaat in der Bundesrepublik 1950-1983.* Frankfurt a. M.: Campus.

Albrecht, Holger. 2005. 'How can Opposition Support Authoritarianism? Lessons from Egypt', *Democratization,* vol. 12:378-397.

Alemann, Ulrich von and Weßels, B. (eds.) 1997. *Verbände in vergleichender Perspektive*. Berlin: Behnke Buch.

Ahl, Björn. 2006. 'Ein Rechtsstaat chinesischen Typs? Zur Verfassungsentwicklung in der Volksrepublik China', *Blätter für deutsche und internationale Politik*, vol. 11:1381-1388.

Ahmad, E. 1991. 'Social Security and the Poor: Choice for Developing Countries', *The World Bank Research Observer,* vol. 6, no. 1:105-127.

Ahuja, Rajev. 2004. 'Health Insurance for the Poor', *Economic and Political Weekly*, vol. 39, no. 28:3171-3178.

—. and De, I. 2004. 'Health Insurance for the Poor: Need to Strengthen Healthcare Provision', *Economic and Political Weekly*, vol. 39, no. 41: 4491-4493.

Alagappa, M. 1995. 'Introduction', in M. Alagappa (ed.), *Political Legitimacy in Southeast Asia: the Quest for Moral Authority*, pp.1-11. Stanford: Stanford University Press.

Alagappa, Muthiah. (ed.) 2004. *Civil Society and Political Change in Asia.* Stanford: Stanford University Press.

Allègre G. 2008. 'Working poor in the EU: An Exploratory Comparative Analyses', *Document de travail d'OFCE*, no. 35.

Almond, G and Coleman, J. S. (eds.) 1960. *The Politics of the Developing Areas.* Princeton, N.J.: Princeton University Press.

—. and Verba, Sidney. 1963. *Political Culture: Political Attitudes and Democracy in Five Nations*. Princeton, N.J.: Princeton University Press.

Alvarez, R.M. et al. 1996.'Classifying political regimes', *Studies in Comparative International Development*, vol. 31, no. 2: 3–36.

Ambasta, P., Shankar, P.S.V. and Shah, M. 2008a. 'Two Years of NREGA: The Road Ahead', *Economic and Political Weekly,* vol. 43, no. 8: 41-50.

Ambasta, P. et al. 2008b.' Social Security for the Aged', in S. Mahendra Dev et al. (eds.), *Social and Economic Security in India*. New Dehli: Institute for Human Development.

Andreß H.-J. and H. Lohmann. 2008. 'Introduction: The Working Poor in Europe', in ibid (eds.), *The Working Poor in Europe. Employment, Poverty and Globalization*, pp. 1-14. Cheltenham: Edward Elgar.

Anant, T.C.A. et al. 2006. 'Labour Markets in India: Issues and Perspectives' in J. Felipe and R. Hasan (eds.), *Labour Markets in Asia: Issues and Perspectives*, pp. 205-300. Basingstoke: Palgrave Macmillan.

Anderson, B. 1996. *Imagined Communities*. London: Verso.

Anheier, H. K., W. Seibel and Zimmer, A. (eds.) 1997. *Der Dritte Sektor in Deutschland. Organisation zwischen Staat und Markt im gesellschaftlichen Wandel*. Berlin: Sigma.

Appleton, S and Song, L. (2004) *The myth of the 'new urban poverty'? Trends in urban poverty in China 1988-2002*. Mimeo: University of Nottingham, UK.

Apter, D.E. 1965. *The Politics of Modernization.* Chicago: Chicago University Press

Arendt, H. 2005. *Elemente und Ursprünge totaler Herrschaft, Antisemitismus, Imperialismus, Totalitarismus*. München: Piper.

Argarwal, R. and Khan, Z.D. 2002. *Labour Market and Social Insurance Policy in India: A Case of Losing on Both Competitiveness and Caring*. Washington, D.C.: World Bank.

Armingeon, K. 1994. *Staat und Arbeitsbeziehungen. Ein internationaler Vergleich.* Opladen: Westdeutscher Verlag.

—. 1997. 'Swiss corporatism in comparative perspective', *West European Politics,* vol. 20, no. 4: 164–79.

—. 2002. 'Interest Intermediation: The Cases of Consociational Democracy and Corporatism', in Hans Keman (ed.), *Comparative Democratic Politics. A Guide to Contemporary Theory and Research*, pp. 143-166. London: Sage.

Aron, R. 1955 'Fin de l'age idéologique', in T.W. Adorno and W. Dirks (eds.), *Sociologica*. Frankfurt a. M.: Europäische Verlagsanstalt.

Asian Development Bank (ADB). 2008. *Social Protection Index for Committed Poverty Reduction. Volume 2: Asia*. Manila: ADB.

—. 2012a. *Key Indicators for Asia and the Pacific 2012*. Manila: ADB.

—. 2012b. *Key Indicators for Asia and the Pacific 2012*. Manila: ADB.

—. 2013. *The Social Protection Index: Assessing Results for Asia and the Pacific.* Manila: ADB.

Appu, P.S. 1996. *Land Reforms in India: A Survey of Policy, legislation and Implementation*. New Delhi: Vikas Publishing House

Azari, Julia R., and Smith, Jennifer K. 2012. 'Unwritten Rules: Informal Institutions in Established Democracies', *Perspectives on Politics,* vol. 10:37-55.

Babajanian, B. (eds.) *Social Protection for Older People in Asia*. Manila: ADB.

Baccaro, L. 1999. *The Organizational Consequences of Democracy: Labor Unions and Economic Reforms in Contemporary Italy*. Unpublished Ph.D. Dissertation, MIT. Sloan School of Management and Political Science Department.

Banks, A. and Wilson K.A. 2012. *Cross-National Time-Series Data Archive*. Jerusalem: Databanks International.

—. 2004. 'Rents, Cooptation, and Economized Discourse: Three Dimensions of Political Rule in Jordan, Morocco and Syria', *Journal of Mediterranean Studies,* no. 14:155-180.

Bardhan, Pranab 1984. *The Political Economy of Development in India*. Oxford: Basil Blackwell.

—. 1997. 'Corruption and Development: A Review of Issues', *Journal of Economic Literature,* vol. 35, no. 3:1320-1346.

—. 2007 'Poverty and Inequality in China and India', *Economic and Political Weekly*, vol. 42, no. 22:3849-52.

—. S. Mitra, D. Mookherjee, and Sarkar, A. 2008. *Political participation, clientelism and targeting of local government programs: Analysis of survey results from rural West Bengal*. Mimeo: Boston University Press.

Barr, N. (1993) *The Economics of the Welfare State*. Oxford: Oxford University Press.

Barrett, D.B. (ed.) 1982. *World Christian Encyclopaedia: A Comparative Study of Churches and Religions in the Modern World, AD 1900–2000*. Nairobi: Oxford University Press.

Barros, Robert John. 2002. *Constitutionalism and Dictatorship: Pinochet, the Junta, and the 1980 Constitution*. Cambridge: Cambridge University Press.

Bates, Robert H. et al. 1999. *Analytic Narratives*. Princeton, N.J.: Princeton University Press.

Backes, Uwe and Kailitz, Steffen. 2010. *Ideokratien im Vergleich. Legitimation – Kooption – Repression*. Göttingen: V&R.

Bakshi. R. 1986. *The Long Haul: The Bombay Textile Workers Strike of 1982-83*. Calcutta: Oxford University Press.

Beetham, David. 1985. *Max Weber and the theory of modern politics*. Cambridge: Cambridge University Press.

—. 1991. *The Legitimation of power*. Basingstoke: Palgrave Macmillan.

Bell, D. 1960. *The End of Ideology*. Glencoe, Ill. Free Press.

Benjamin, D. et al. 2005. 'Income Inequality During China's Economical Transition', in L.

Brandt et al. (eds.), *China's Great Economic Transformation*. Cambridge: University Press.

Berger, Suzanne, and Dore, Ronald. (eds.) 1996. *National Diversity and Global Capitalism*. Ithaca, NY: Cornell University Press.

Besley, T., R., Pande and Rao, V. 2005. *Political selection and the quality of government, in: World Bank: The political economy of Gram Panchayats in South India. Results and policy conclusions from a research project*. Washington D.C.: World Bank.

—. et al. 2007. 'The Policy Origins of Poverty and Growth in India', in ibid and L. J. Cord (eds.), *Delivering on the Promise of Pro-poor Growth*. Washington D.C.: Palgrave Macmillan.

Besley, T., Pande, R. and Rao, V. 2007. *Just rewards? Local politics and public resource allocation in South India?* Mimeo: STICERD.

Berman, Sheri. 2003. 'Islamism, Revolution, and Civil Society', *www.apsanet.org*, vol. 1, no. 2:11-26.

Bernstein, Thomas P. 2000. *Farmer Discontent and Regime Responses*. In M. Goldman and R. MacFarquhar (eds.), *The Paradox of China's Post Mao Reforms*, pp. 197-219. Cambridge, Mass: Harvard University Press.

—. and Lü, X. 2008. 'Taxation and coercion in Rural China', in O-H. Fjeldlstad (ed.), *Capacity and consent: taxation and state building in developing countries*, pp. 89-113. Cambridge: Cambridge University Press.

Beyer, Jürgen. 2010. 'The Same or Not the Same - On the Variety of Mechanisms of Path Dependence', *International Journal of Social Sciences,* vol. 5:1-11.

Beyme, K. von. 1970. *Die Parlamentarischen Regierungssysteme in Europa*. München: Piper Verlag.

—. 1983. 'Neo-corporatism: a new nut in an old shell?', *International Political Science Review*, vol. 4 no. 2:173-196.

—. 1985. *Political Parties in Western Democracies*. Aldershot: Gower.

—. 1988. *Reformpolitik und sozialer Wandel in der Sowjetunion (1970 - 1988)*. Baden-Baden: Nomos.

—. 1994. *Systemwechsel in Osteuropa*. Frankfurt a. M.: Campus.

Bhagwati, J. and Desai, P. 1970. *India: Planning and Industrialization*. New York: Oxford University Press.

Bhattacharyya, H. 2001. *India as a Multicultural Federation: Asian Values, Democracy and Decentralisation*. Fribourg: Institut du Federalisme.

Bonoli, Giulano, Vic George and Taylor-Gooby, Peter. 2000. *European Welfare Futures*. Cambridge: Polity Press.

Black, C.E. 1966. *The Dynamics of Modernization: A Study in Comparative History*. New York: Harper & Row.

Blondel, J. 1969. *Introduction to Comparative Government.* London: Weidenfeld and Nicholson.

—. 1973. *Comparative Legislatures*. Englewood Cliffs, N.J.: Prentice-Hall.

—. 1990. *Comparative Government: An Introduction*. Hertfordshire: Philip Allan.

Bloom, G. and Tang S. 2004. *Health care transition in urban China.* Aldershot: Ashgate.

—. et al. 2002. 'Financial health care in China's cities: Balancing needs and entitlements during rapid change', *IDS Working Paper 176.* Brighton: Institute of Development Studies.

—. and Canning, David. 2005. 'Global Demographic Change: Dimensions and Economic Significance', in *Global Demographic Change: Economic Impacts and Policy Challenges.* Federal Reserve Bank of Kansas City.

Böcher, M. and Töller, A. E. 2012. *Umweltpolitik in Deutschland. eine politikfeldanalytische Einführung.* Wiesbaden: Springer.

Bo, Zhiyue. 2013. 'China's Fifth Generation Leadership: Characteristics and Policies', in G. Wang and Y. Zheng (eds.), *China: Development and Governance*, pp. 7-15. Singapore: World Scientific Publishing.

Boix, Charles. 1998. *Political Parties, Growth and Equality.* Cambridge: Cambridge University Press.

—. 2003. *Democracy and Redistribution.* Cambridge: Cambridge University Press.

Braun, D. (ed.) 2000. *Public Policy and Federalism.* Aldershot: Ashgate.

Brass, Paul R. 1994. *The politics of India since Independence.* Cambridge: Cambridge University Press.

Brass, Tom. (ed.) 1995. *New Farmers' Movement in India.* Essex: Frank Class.

Brooker, Paul. 2000. *Non-Democratic Regimes. Theory, Government and Politics.* Houndmills: Macmillan.

Brooker, Paul. 2009. *Non-Democratic Regimes.* Basingstoke: Palgrave.

Brownlee, J. 2007. *Authoritarianism in the Age of Democratization.* Cambridge: Cambridge University Press.

Budge, I. 1994. 'A new spatial theory of party competition: uncertainty, ideology and policy equilibria viewed comparatively and temporally', *British Journal of Political Science*, 24: 443–67.

—. and Farlie, D. 1976. 'A comparative analysis of factors related with turnout and voting choice', in I. Budge, I. Crewe and D. Farlie (eds.), *Party Identification and Beyond. Representations of Voting and Party Competition.* London: John Wiley.

—. and Hans Keman. 1998. *Parties and Democracies. Coalition Formation and Government Functioning in 20 States.* Oxford: Oxford University Press.

—. et al. 2002. 'Comparative Government and Democracy' in Hans Keman (ed.), *Comparative Democratic Politics. A Guide to Contemporary Theory and Research*, pp. 65-99. London: Sage.

Bueno de Mesquita, Bruce, James D. Morrow, R. M. Siverson, and Smith, A.2003. *The Logic of Political Survival.* Cambridge: MIT Press.

Büthe, Tim. 2002. 'Taking Temporality Seriously', *American Political Science Review,* 96: 483-493.

Buoye, T., K. Denton, and Dickson, B. 2002. *China, Adapting the Past, Confronting the Future.* Ann Arbor: The University of Michigan Press

Burgess, R. and Stern, N. 1991. 'Social security in developing countries: What, why, who, and how?', in E. Ahmad et al. (eds.), *Social security in developing countries*, pp. 41-80. Oxford: Oxford University Press.

Busemeyer, M. 2006. 'Determinants of public education spending in 21 OECD democracies, 1980–2001', *Journal of European Public Policy,* vol.14, no.4: 582-610.

Cai, H. and Treisman, D. 2006. 'Did government decentralize cause China's economic miracle?', *World Politics,* vol. 54, no. 4:505-535.

Cai, F. and Du, Y. 2011. 'Wage Increases, Wage Convergence, and the Lewis Turning Point in China', *China Economic Review*, vol. 22, no. 4:601-10.

Calderon C and Chong, A. 2009. 'Labour Market Institutions and Income Inequality: An Empirical Exploration', *Public Choice*, vol. 138: 65-81.

Calmford, L. 1983. *Stabilization Policy and Wage Formation in the Smaller European Economies.* Brussels: Centre for European Studies.

Cameron, D.R. 1978. 'The expansion of the public economy,' *American Political Science Review,* vol. 72: 1243–61.

—. 1984. 'Social democracy, corporatism, labour quiescence, and the representation of economic interest in advanced capitalist society', in J.H. Goldthorpe (ed.), *Order and Conflict in Contemporary Capitalism*, pp. 143-178. Oxford: Oxford University Press.

Capoccia, Giovanni and Kelemen, Daniel R. 2007. 'The Study of Critical Junctures Theory, Narrative, and Counterfactuals in Historical Institutionalism', *World Politics*, vol. 59:341-369.

Carothers, T. 1998. 'The Rule of Law Revival', *Foreign Affairs*, vol. 77, no. 2: 95-106.

Castles, F.G. 1978. *The Social Democratic Image of Society. A Study of the Achievements and Origins of Scandinavian Social Democracy in Comparative Perspective.* London: Routledge and Kegan Paul.

—. 1985. *The Working Class and Welfare: Reflections on the Political Development of the Welfare State in Australia and New Zealand, 1890–1980.* London: Allen and Unwin.

—. (ed.) 1989. *The Comparative History of Public Policy.* Cambridge: Polity Press.

—. 1998. *Comparative Public Policy. Patterns of Post-war Transformation.* Cheltenham: Edgar Elgar.

—. 2000. 'Federalism, fiscal decentralization and economic performance', in U. Wachendorfer-Schmidt (ed.), *Federalism and Political Performance.* London: Routledge.

—. 2002. 'The Policy Performance in the Democratic State: an Emergent Field of Study', in Hans Keman (ed.), *Comparative Democratic Politics. A Guide to Contemporary Theory and Research*, pp. 215-233. London: Sage.

—. and Mitchell, D. 1993. 'Worlds of welfare and families of nations', in F.G. Castles (ed.), *Families of Nations. Patterns of Public Policy in Western Democracies.* Aldershot: Dartmouth.

Chakravarty, S. 1990. 'Development Strategies for Growth with Equity: The South Asian Experience', *Asian Development Review* ,vol. 8:133-59.

Chamarbagwala, R. 2006 'Economic Liberalization and Wage Inequality in India', *World Development,* vol. 34, no. 12:1997-2015.

Chan, A. 2000.'Chinese Trade Unions and Workplace Relations in State-owned and Joint-venture Enterprises', in M. Warner (ed.), *Changing Workplace Relations in the Chinese Economy*, pp. 33-56. Basingstoke: Macmillan Press and St. Martin's Press.

—. 2001. *China's workers Under Assault: Exploitation and Abuse in a Globalizing Economy*. Armonk: Sharpe.

—. 2005. 'Recent Trends in Chinese Labour Issues: Signs of Change', *China Perspective,* vol. 57: 23-31.

Chan, K. W. et al. 1999. Hukou and non-Hukou migrations in China: comparison and contrasts', *International Journal of Population Geography*, vol.5: 425-428.

—. 2003. 'Migration in China in the reform era: characteristics, consequences, and implications', in A. Y. So (ed.), *China's development miracle: Origins, transformations, and challenges*, pp. 11-135. New York: Sharpe.

Chan, K. C. et al. 2008. *Social Policy in China*. Bristol: Policy Press.

Chandra, K. 2004.*Why ethnic parties succeed. Patronage and ethnic head counts in India*.

Cambridge: Cambridge University Press.

Chattterjee, Mirai. et. al. 1994. *Organizing for Social Security- Some experiences of Self Employed Women Workers*. New Delhi: Friedrich Ebert Stiftung.

Chen, Feng. 2003. 'Industrial Restructuring and Workers' Resistance in China', M*odern China*, vol. 29, no. 2: 237– 62

Chen, J. and Barrientos, A. 2006. 'Extending Social Assistance in China: Lessons from the Minimum Living Standard Scheme', *CPRC Working Paper 67*. Brighton: Chronic Poverty Research Centre.

Chen, Z. Y. et al. 2011. 'Foreign Direct Investment and Wage Inequality: Evidence from China', *World Development*, vol. 39, no. 8: 1322-32.

Chidambaram, P. 2004. *Speech of the finance minister*. Delivered on the 8 July. New Delhi: Ministry of Finance. [quoted by Gita and Rajasekhar 2012:122 and133]

Chibber, Vivek. 2003. *Locked in Place: State-Building and Late Industrialization in India*. Princeton, N.J.: Princeton University Press.

—. 2012.'Organised Interests, Development Strategies and Social Policies', in R. Nagaraj (ed.), *Growth, Inequality and Social Development in India. Is Inclusive Growth Possible?,* pp.168-194. Basingstoke: Palgrave Macmillan.

Chow, Nelson W. S. 2000. *Socialist Welfare with Chinese Characteristics: The Reform of the Social Security System in China*. Hong Kong: Centre of Asian Studies, University of Hong Kong.

Christoff, Peter, and Eckersley, Robyn. 2011. 'Comparing State Responses', in John S.

Dryzek, Richard B. Norgaard and David Schlosberg (eds.), *Oxford Handbook of Climate Change and Society*, pp. 431-448. Oxford: Oxford University Press.

Clark, William C. 2000. 'Environmental Globalization', in: Joseph S. Nye and John D.

Donahue (eds.), *Governance in a Globalizing World*, pp. 86-108. Washington, D.C.: Brookings Institution Press.

Congressional-Executive Commission on China (CECC). 2005. *Annual Report 2005*. Washington, D.C.: US Government Printing Press.

—. 2012. *Annual Report 2012*. Washington, D.C.: US Government Printing Press.

Collier, D. and Adcock, R. 1999. 'Democracy and Dichotomies: A Pragmatic Approach to Choices about Concepts', *Annual Review of Political Science*, vol. 2:537-565.

Colomer, Josep Maria. (ed.) 1996. *Political Institutions in Europe*. London: Routledge.

Conrad, Dieter. 1995. *Rechtssystem und Verfassung*. Heidelberg: Dieter Conrad.

Cook, Sarah. 2002. 'From Rice Bowl to Safety Net: Insecurity and Social Protection during China's Transition,' *Development Policy Review,* vol. 20, no. 5: 615– 35.

—. and Jolly, Susie. 2001. *Unemployment, Poverty and Gender in Urban China: Perceptions and Experiences of Laid Off Workers in Three Chinese Cities*. Brighton: Institute of Development Studies

Cook, Linda J. 2007. *Postcommunist Welfare States: Reform Politics in Russia and Eastern Europe*. Ithaca, NY: Cornell University Press.

Corbridge, S. et al. 2003. 'Making Social Science Matter – I', *Economic and Political Weekly*, vol. 38, no. 257:17-38.

Crépaz, M.M.L. 1996. 'Consensus versus Majoritarian Democracy. Political institutions and their impact on macroeconomic performance and industrial disputes in 18industrialized democracies', *Comparative Political Studies,* vol. 29, no. 1: 4–26.

Croissant, Aurel. 2002. 'Einleitung: Demokratische Grauzonen - Konturen und Konzepte eines Forschungszweigs', in Petra Bendel, Aurel Croissant and Friedbert Rüb (eds.), *Zwischen Demokratie und Diktatur: zur Konzeption und Empirie demokratischer Grauzonen*, pp. 9-54. Opladen: Leske & Budrich

—. and Thiery, Peter. 2000. 'Defekte Demokratie. Konzept, Operationalisierung und Messung', in Pickel Lauth and Christian Welzel (eds.), *Demokratiemessung. Konzepte und Befunde im internationalen Vergleich*, pp. 89–111. Opladen: Westdeutscher Verlag.

—. and Stefan Wurster. 2013. 'Performance and Persistence of Autocracies: Introducing Issues and Perspectives', *Contemporary Politics,* vol. 19, no. 1: 1-18.

Crouch, C. 1993. *Industrial Relations and European State Traditions*. Oxford: Clarendon Press.

Cui, Feng and Sun, Qipan. 2006. '从历次制宪与修宪看中国社会保障的发展 [A perspective on the development of social security in China in reference to the constitutional amendments]', *社会保障制度* [*Social Security System*], vol. 2: 56-60.

Cusack, T. 1995. *Politics and Macroeconomic Performance in the OECD Countries during the period 1950 through 1990.* Berlin: Wissenschaftszentrum Berlin für Sozialforschung.

Cukierman, Alex and Tommasi, Mariano, 1998. 'When Does It Take a Nixon to Go to China?', *American Economic Review, American Economic Association,* vol. 88, no. 1: 180-97.

Czada, R.M., Heritier, A. and Keman, H. (eds.) 1998. *Institutions and Political Choice: on the Limits of Rationality*. Amsterdam: VU-University Press.

Daalder, Hans. 2002. 'The Development of the Study of Comparative Politics', in Hans Keman (ed.), *Comparative Democratic Politics. A Guide to Contemporary Theory and Research*, pp. 16-32. London: Sage.

Dahl, Robert. 1961. 'The Behavioural Approach in Political Science: Epitaph for a Movement to a Successful Protest', *American Political Science Review*, vol. 55, no. 4:763-772.

—. 1966. *Political Oppositions in Western Democracies*. New Haven, Conn.: Yale University Press.

—. 1971. *Polyarchy. Participation and Opposition*. New Haven and London: Yale University Press.

—. 1989. *Democracy and its Critics*. New Haven and London: Yale University Press.

—. 1998. *On Democracy*. New Haven and London: Yale University Press.

Dahrendorf, Ralf. 1977. 'A Confusion of Powers: Politics and he rule of Law', *Modern Law Review*, vol. 40:1-15.

Dai, Changzheng. 2004. '国家权威碎裂化：成因、影响及对策分析' [Fragmentation of the state authority: an analysis of its reasons, impacts and coping strategies]', *Chin J Adm* [中国行政管理] vol. 6:75-82.

Dandekar, V.M. and Neelkanth Rath. 1971.'Food and Nutrition in India: Facts and Interpretations', *Economic and Political weekly*, vol.6, no. 2: 28-48 and no. 3:106-46.

Darimont, Barbara. 2004. *Sozialversicherungsrecht der V. R. China*. Baden-Baden: Nomos.

Das, Subesh. 2011. *Managing People at Work. Employment Relations in Globalizing India*. New Delhi: Sage.

Datt, G. and M. Ravallion. 1989. 'Is India's Economic Growth Leaving the Poor Behind?' *Policy Research Working Paper 2846*, Development Research Group Poverty Team, Washington D.C.: World Bank.

Datt, R. 2003. *Lockouts in India*. Delhi: Manohar Publishers and Distributors.

Davala, Sarath. (ed.) 1992. *Employment and Unionisation in Indian Industry*. New Delhi: Friedrich Ebert Stiftung.

Davidoff, Paul. 1965. 'Advocacy and Pluralism in Planning', *Journal of the American Institute of Planners*; vol. 31:331-338.

Davis, O.A., Dempster, A.H. and Wildavsky, A. 1966. 'A theory of the budgetary process', *American Political Science Review,* 60: 529–47.

Dawson, R.E. and Robinson, J.A. 1963.'Inter-party competition, economic variables and welfare politics in the American states', *Journal of Politics*, vol. 25: 265–89.

Debi, S. Sani. 2011. *Social Security Law in India*. Bedfordshire: Kluwer Law International.

Deshpande, V. S. 2007. 'Battle against poverty: Some Reflections on Agrarian Economy', in V. Patel and M Karne (eds.), *The Macro Economic Policies and The Millennium Development Goals,* pp. 29-41. New Delhi: Gyan Publishing House.

Dev, Mahendra S. and Ravi, C. 2007. 'Poverty and Inequality: All-India and States, 1983-2005', *Economic and Political Weekly*, vol. 41, no. 6:509-521.

Deva, Surya. 2009. 'Public Interest Litigation in India: A Critical Review', *Civil Justice Quarterly*, vol. 28: 19-40.

—. 2010.'Rule of Law in India: An Overview', in Matthias Koetter and Gunnar Dicey, Albert Venn. 1985. *Introduction to the Study of the Law of the Constitution*. London: Macmillan.

Deng, Z. and Jing, Y. 1992. 'Building the Chinese Civil Society', *China Soc Sci Q*, vol. 1.

Devereux, S. and R. Sabates-Wheeler. 2007.'Editoril Introduction: Debating Social Protection', *IDS Bulletin (Social Protection)*, vol. 38, no. 3:1-7.

DGB (Bildungswerk e.V Nord – Süd Netz). 2007. *Länderportrait Indien: Absatzmarkt, Konkurrent, Kooperationspartner – Indien im Spannungsfeld von Wirtschaftsboom, Weltmachtstreben und sozialer Misere*. Düsseldorf: DGB Bildungswerk.

Ding, X.H. 2004. 'The challenges faced by Chinese higher education as it expands in scale', *Chinese education and Society*, vol. 37, no. 1: 36-53.

Dittmer, L. 1995. 'Chinese informal politics', *China J*, vol. 34:1-34.

—. and Yu-Shan Wu. 1995. 'The Modernization of Factionalism in Chinese Politics', *World Politics*, vol. 47, no. 4: 467-494.

Dixon, John 1981. *The Chinese Welfare System, 1949– 1979*. New York: Praeger.

Dogan, M. 2001. 'Conception of Legitimacy', in John Paynter et al. (eds.), *Encyclopaedia if Government and Politics*, pp.116-219. London: Routledge.

Dodds, R: F: Jr. 1996: 'State enterprise reform in China: managing the transition to a market economy', *Law and Policy in International Business*, vol. 27: 695-753

Domenach, Jean-Luc. 1995. *The Origin of the Great Leap Forward: The Case of One Chinese Province*. Boulder: Westview.

Dong, W. 2001. 'Health care reform in urban China', *Working Paper 2001/2*, Munk Centre for International Studies: University of Toronto.

O'Donnel, G. and Schmitter, P. C. 1986. Transition from Authoritarian Rule. London: John Hopkins University Press.

Doucouliagos, Hristos and Ulubaşoğlu, Mehmet Ali. 2008. 'Democracy and Economic Growth: A Meta-Analysis', *American Journal of Political Science,* vol. 52:61-83.

Dreze J. and A. K. Sen. 1989. *Hunger and Public Action*. Oxford: Clarendon Press.

—. and A. K. Sen. (eds.)1991. *Public Action for Social Security Foundation and Strategy*. New Delhi: Oxford University Press.

—. and A. K. Sen. 1997. *India: Selected Regional Perspectives*. New Delhi: Oxford University Press.

Dreher, Axel; Noel Gaston and Pim Martens. 2008. *Measuring Globalization – Gauging its Consequences*. New York: Springer.

Drouin, A. and Thompson, L. H. 2006. 'Perspectives on the social security system of China', *ESS Paper No 25*. Geneva: ILO.

Dua, B. D. 1994. 'The Prime Minister and the Federal System', in James Manor (ed.), *Nehru through the Nineties. The Changing Office of Prime Minister in India*, pp. 20-47. London: Sage.

Dustman C., J. Ludsteck and Schönberg, U.. 2009. 'Revisiting the German age Structure', *The Quarterly Journal of Economics*, vol. 124, no. 4: 843-81.

Duta, P. V. 2007. 'Trade Protection and Industrial Wages in India', *Industrial and Labour Relation Review*, vol. 60, no. 2: 268-86.

Dutta, R.C. 1998. 'Public Action, Social Security and Unorganised Sector' , *Economic and Political Weekly*, vol. 33, no. 22: L2-L5.

Dyke, Virgina van. 2007. ''Jumbo Cabinets', Factionalism, and the Impact of Federalism: Comparing Coalition Governments in Kerala, Punjab and Uttar Pradesh', in Ramashray Roy and Paul Wallace (eds.), *India's 2004 Elections: Grass-Roots and Rational Perspectives*, pp.116-147. New Delhi: Sage.

Easton, David. Easton, D. 1953. *The Political System.* New York: Knopf.

—. 1965. *A Systems Analysis of Political Life.* New York: Wiley.

—. 1975. 'A Re-Assessment of the Concept of Political Support', *British Journal of Political*

Science 5:435-457.

—. 1979. A System Analysis of Political Life. New York: John Wiley. Freedom House.

Eckstein, H. 1966. *Division and Cohesion in Democracy: A Study of Norway*. Princeton, N.J.: Princeton University Press.

The Economist. 2006a. 'Special report', *The Economist*, September 16th:11-12.

—. 2006b. 'A question for definition', *The Economist*, September 16th:138.

—. 2014a. 'Doing it their way', *The Economist*, January 25th: 16-18.

—. 2014b.'In three parts', *The Economist*, January 25th: 55-56.

—. 2014c. 'What's gone wrong with democracy', *The Economist*, March 1st:43-48.

—. 2014d. 'Special report on China', *The Economist*, March 1st: 4-16.

—. 2014e. 'Disillusioned Workers. China's losers', *The Economist*, March 1st: 49-50.

—. 2014f. 'Narendra Modi. India's strongman', *The Economist*, May24st: 19-22.

—. 2014g. 'Chinese civil society. Beneath the glacier', *The Economist*, April 12th: 57-60.

—. 2014h. 'Uighur activism. A lone voice silenced', *The Economist*, September 27th: 52-53.

—. 2014i. 'The Party v the people. Hong Kong and the struggle for the future of China',

The Economist, October 4th:13-14.

—. 2014j. 'Yes, prime minister', *The Economist*, October 18th:49-50.

—. 2014k. 'Emerging markets', *The Economist*, November 8h-21st: 65-66.

—. 2014l. 'Tax reform in India', *The Economist*, November 8th:67.

—. 2014m. 'Briefing Financial inclusion', *The Economist*, November 15th: 20-22.

Ehrmann, Henry W. (ed.) 1958. *Interest Groups on Four Continents*. Pittsburgh: Pittsburgh Press.

Esping-Andersen, G. 1985a. *Politics Against Markets. The Social Democratic Road to Power*. Princeton, N.J.: Princeton University Press.

—. 1990 *The Three Worlds of Welfare Capitalism.* Cambridge: Cambridge University Press.

—. 1999. *Social Foundations of Post-Industrial Economies*. Oxford: Oxford University Press.

—. and Korpi, W. 1986. 'From poor relief to institutional welfare states', in R. Erikson, E.J.

Hansen, S. Ringen and H. Uusitalo (eds.), *The Scandinavian Model: Welfare States and Welfare Research*. New York: M.E. Sharpe.

Faccio, Mara. 2006. 'Politically Connected Firms', *American Economic Review,* vol. 96, no. 1: 369-386.

Falk, Hartwig. 2008. *Die Kommunistische Partei Chinas heute. Von der Revolutions- zur Reformpartei*. Frankfurt a. M.: Campus Verlag.

Fearon, James D. 1991. 'Counterfactuals and Hypothesis Testing in Political Science', *World Politics,* vol. 43, no. 2:169-195

Feinermann, James V. 1991. 'Economic and Legal Reforms in China, 1978-1991', *Problems of Communism*, vol. 40 (September – October): 62-75.

Feng, L. R. 1982. *Six questions concerning employment*. Beijing: Institute of Marxism-Leninism-Mao Zedong Thought, Chinese Academy of Social Science.

Fewsmith, J. 2001. *Elite politics in Contemporary China*. Armonk: Sharpe.

Fishman, Robert M. 1990. 'Rethinking State and Regime: Southern Europe's Transition to Democracy', *World Politics*, vol. 42:422-440.

Flora, Peter. (ed.) 1986. *Growth and Limits. The Western European Welfare State Since World War II*, Volume 1,2 and 4. Ashgate: Adlershot.

Fortin, N. and T. Lemieux. 1997. 'Institutional Change and Rising age Inequality: Is There A Linkage?', *Journal of Economic Perspective*, vol. 11, no.2:75-96.

Fogel, R. and Elton, G. R. 1983. *Which Road to the Past*. New Haven, Conn.: Yale University Press.

Foster, K. W. 2001. 'Associations in the Embrace of an Authoritarian State: State Domination of Society?', *Studies in Comparative International Development*, vol. 35:84-109.

Frankel F. 2005. *India's political Economy 1947-2004: The Gradual Revolution*. Princeton, N.J.: Princeton University Press.

Franklin, M.N., Mackie, T.T. and Valen, H. 1992. *Electoral Change: Responses to Social and Attitudinal Structures in Western Countries.* Cambridge: Cambridge University Press.

Freedom House. 2002. *Freedom in the World. The Annual Survey of Political Rights and Civil Liberties 2001-2002*. Washington D.C.: Freedom House.

Friedrich, C.J. (ed.) 1954. *Totalitarianism.* Cambridge, Mass: Harvard University Press.

—. and Brzezinski, K. Zbigniew. 1965. *Totalitarian Dictatorship and Autocracy*. Cambridge, Mass: Harvard University Press.

Fukuyama, F. 1992. *The End of History and the Last Man*. New York: Free Press.

Fuller, Lon. 1969. *The Morality of Law*. New Haven: Yale University Press.

Fusilier, R. 1960. *Les Monarchies Parlementaires: étude sur les Systèmes de Gouvernement: Suède, Norvège, Danemark, Belgique, Pays-Bas, Luxembourg*. Paris: Editions Ouvrières.

Gallagher, M. E. 2002. 'Reform and openness. Why China's economic reforms have delayed democracy', *World Politics,* vol. 54, no. 3:338-372

—. 2005. *Contagious capitalism: globalization and the politics of labour in China*. Princeton, N.J.: Princeton University Press.

Gamson, William. 1990. *The strategy of social protest*. Belmont, Calif.: Wadsworth.

Gandhi, Jennifer. 2008. *Political Institutions under Dictatorship*. New York: Columbia University Press.

—. and Adam Przeworski. 2006. 'Cooperation, Cooptation, and Rebellion under Dictatorships', *Economics and Politics,* 18:1-26.

—. and Adam Przeworski. 2007a. 'Authoritarian Institutions and the Survival of Autocrats', *Comparative Political Studies* 40:1279-1301.

—. and Adam Przeworski. 2007b. 'Dictatorial Institutions and the Survival of Autocrats', *Comparative Political Studies,* vol. 40:1279-1301.

Gang, F. et al. 1998. *Labour market aspects of state enterprise reform in China*. Paris: OECD Development Centre.

Garrett, Geoffrey and Mitchell, Deborah. 2001.'Globalization, government spending and taxation in the OECD', *European Journal of Political Research*, vol. 39, no. 2: 145-177.

Ge, S. and Tao Yang. 2011. 'Labour Market Development in China: A Neoclassical View', *China Economic Review*, vol. 22, no. 4: 611-25.

Geddes, Barbara. 1999. 'What Do We Know about Democratization After Twenty Years?', *Annual review of Political Science,* vol. 2:115-144.

Geertz, Clifford. 1973. *Interpretation of Cultures*. New York: Basic Books.

George, Alexander L. 1979. 'Case Studies and Theory Development: The Method of Structured, Focused Comparison', in Paul Gordon Lauren (ed.), *Diplomacy: New Approaches in History, Theory, and Policy*, pp. 43-68. New York: Free Press.

—. and Bennett, A. 1998. *Case studies and theory development in the social sciences*. Cambridge, Mass: MIT Press.

Gerschewski, Johannes. 2010a. 'Zur Persistenz von Autokratien. Ein Literaturüberblick', *Berliner Debatte Initial* 3:42-53.

—. 2010b. 'Three pillars of Stability: Towards an Explanation of the Durability of Autocratic Regimes in East Asia', *Paper 106 annual meeting of the American Political Science Association.* See http://papers.ssrn.com/sol3/papers,cfm?abstract_id=16575000 (2014-02-15).

—. Wolfgang Merkel, Alexander Schmotz, Christoph H. Stefes, and Tanneberg, D. 2013. 'Warum überleben Diktaturen?', in S. Kailitz and P. Köllner (eds.), *Autokratien im Vergleich*, pp. 106-132. Baden-Baden: Nomos.

Ghai, Mridula 2007. 'The Coverage Gap: Informal Labor Markets in the Developing World with Special Reference to India', paper presented at the *5th International Research Conference on Social Security* in Warsaw (March 5th-7th, 2007).

Gill, B. and Y Huang .2006. 'Sources and limits of Chinese soft power', *Survival*, vol. 48, no. 2:17-36.

Ginnikan, Wouter van. 1998. *Social Security For All Indians*. New Delhi: Oxford University Press.

Ginsburg, Tom, and Moustafa, Tamir. (eds.) 2008. *Rule by Law: The Politics of Courts in Authoritarian Regimes*. Cambridge: Cambridge University Press.

Goodman, R. and Peng, I. 1996. 'The East Asian welfare states: peripatetic learning, adaptive strategy, and nation-building', in G. Esping-Andersen (ed.), *Welfare States in Transition: National Adaptations in Global Economies*. London: Sage.

Goldthorpe, J.H. (ed.) 1984. *Order and Conflict in Contemporary Capitalism*. Oxford: Oxford University Press.

—. 1991. 'The Uses of History in Sociology', *British Journal of Sociology*, vol. 42, no. 2: 220-52.

Gosh, B. and G. Kumar. 2003. *State Politics and Panchayats in India*. New Delhi: Manohar.

Government of Andhra Pradesh. 1997. *Statistical Abstract of Andhra Pradesh: 1994*. Hyderabad: GoI.

Government of India (GoI). 1961. *Maternity Benefit Act, 1961*. New Delhi: GoI.

—. 1966. *Report of the Education (Kothari) Commission, 1964-66*. New Delhi: GoI.

—. 1972. *Payment of Gratuity Act, 1972*. New Delhi: GoI.

—. 1981. *A Technical Note on the Sixth Plan of India (1980-1985)*. New Delhi: Planning Commission.

—. 2001. *The Trade Unions (Amendment) Act, 2001*. New Delhi. GoI.

—. 2002. *Report of the National Commission on Labour*. New Delhi: GoI.

—. 2005. *National Rural Employment Guarantee Bill, 2005*. New Delhi: Government of India.

—. 2006. *National Rural Employment Guarantee Act*. New Delhi: Administration Reform Commission.

—. 2007. *The Maternity Benefits (Amendment) Bill, 2007*. New Delhi: GoI.

Government of Madhya Pradesh. 1998. *The Madhya Pradesh Human Development Report 1998*. Bhopal: GoI.

Göbel Christian. 2010. *Rural Reform in China: State Policy and Village Predicament in the Early 2000s*. Abingdon: Routledge.

Granville Austin. 1966. *The Indian Constitution: Cornerstone of a Nation*. Oxford: Clarendon Press.

Graziano, L. 1973. 'Patron-client relationships in Southern Italy', *European Journal of Political Research,* vol. 1, no. 1: 3-34.

Gould, C.C. 1993. *Rethinking Democracy: Freedom and Social Cooperation in Politics, Economy, and Society*. Cambridge: Cambridge University Press.

Gourevitch, P. 1977.'The Reform of Local Government: A Political Analysis', *Comparative Politics,* vol. 10, no. 1: 69-88.

—. 1978. 'The Second Image Reversed: The International Sources of Domestic Politics', *International Organization*, vol. 32, no. 4, 881-912

Granville Austin. 1966. *The Indian Constitution: Cornerstone of a Nation*. Oxford: Clarendon Press.

Greif, Avner. 1995. 'Political Organizations, Social Structure, and Institutional Success: Reflections From Genoa and Venice during Commercial Revolution', *Journal of Institutional and Theoretical Economics,* vol. 15: 734-40.

—. and David Laitin. 2004. 'A Theory of Endogenous Institutional Change', *American Political Science Review,* vol. 98:633-652.

Griffin, L.J., O'Connell, P.J. and McCammon, H.J. 1989. 'National Variation in the Context of Struggle: Postwar Class Conflict and Market Distribution in the Capitalist Democracies', *Canadian Review of Sociology and Anthropology,* vol. 26, no. 1: 1–37.

Grzymala-Busse, Anna. 2010. 'The Best Laid Plans: The Impact of Informal Rules on Formal Institutions in Transitional Regimes', *Studies in Comparative International Development*, vol. 45:311-333.

Guhan S. 1993. 'Social Security for the Poor in the Unorganised Sector: A Feasible Blueprint for India', in Kirit S. Prikh and R. Sudarshand (eds.), *Human Development and Structural Adjustment*, pp. 203-237.Chennai: MacMillan

—. 1994. 'Social Security Options for Developing Countries', *International Labour Review*, vol. 133, no. 1: 35-53.

Guo, Sanjuan. 2000. *Post-Mao China*. London: Praeger.

—. (ed.) 2013a. *Political science and Chinese political Studies* . Heidelberg: Springer.

—. 2013b. *Chinese Politics and Government. Power, ideology, and organization*. London: Routledge.

Gupta, Ramesh. 2003. *Pension Reforms in India: Myth, Reality and Policy Choices*. Ahmedabad: Indian Institute of Management.

Gurr, T.R. 1970. *Why Men Rebel*. Princeton, N.J.: Princeton University Press.

Habermas, Jürgen. 1973. 'Politische Beteiligung — ein Wert 'an sich'?', in Ulrich Matz (ed.), *Grundprobleme der Demokratie*, pp. 316–322. Darmstadt: Wissenschaftliche Buchgesellschaft.

Hacker, J. S. 2004. 'Privatizing Risk without Privatizing the Welfare State: the hidden politics of social policy retrenchment in the United States', *American Political Science Review*, vol. 98, no. 2:243– 60.

Hadenius, Axel and Jan Teorell. 2007. 'Pathways from Authoritarianism', *Journal of Democracy,* vol. 18, no. 1: 143-156.

Hall, P. A. 1986. *Governing the Economy*. Oxford: Polity Press.

—. 2003. 'Aligning Ontology and Methodology in Comparative Research', in J. Mahoney and D. Rueschemeyer (eds.), *Comparative Historical Analysis in the Social Sciences*, pp. 373-404. Cambridge: Cambridge University Press.

—. and Rosemary C.R. Taylor. 1996. 'Political Science and the Three New Institutionalisms', *Political Studies*, vol. 44 (December): 952-73.

—. and Soskice, David. 2001. 'An Introduction to Varieties of Capitalism', in: Peter A. Hall and David Soskice (eds.), *Varieties of Capitalism: The Institutional Foundations of Comparative Advantage,* pp. 1-70. Oxford: Oxford University Press.

Halperin, Morton, Joe Siegele and Michael M. Weinstein. (eds.) 2010. *The Democracy Advantage. How Democracy Promotes Prosperity and Peace*. London: Routledge.

Haney, Patrick J. 1997. *Organizing for Foreign Policy Crisis*. Ann Arbor, Mich.: University of Michigan Press.

Harmin, C.L. and S.S. Zhao.1995. *Decision-making in Deng's China: Perspectives from insiders*. Armonk, NY: M.E. Sharpe.

Harris, Barbara. 1984. *State and Market*. New Delhi: Concept Publishing Company

Harrison, Selig. 1960. *India: The Most Dangerous Decades*. Princeton, N.J.: Princeton University Press.

Hart, K. 1973. 'Informal income opportunities and urban employment in Ghana', *Journal of Modern African Studies,* vol. 11: 61-89.

Hausmann, Ricardo, Lant Pritchett and Rodrik, Dani. 2005. 'Growth Accelerations', *Journal of Economic Growth*, vol. 10, no. 4:303-29.

Hayek, F. 1994. *The Road to Serfdom*. Chicago: University of Chicago Press.

He, B. 2013. 'Dilemmas of China's Political Science in the Context of the Rise of China', in Sujian Guo (ed.), *Political science and Chinese political studies*, pp. 193-215.Berlin: Springer.

He, Gaochao. 2004. 'What Do Workers Want in China's Industrial Workplace?', *China: An International Journal,* vol. 2, no. 2: 323– 9.

Heilmann, Sebastian. 2002. *Das politische System der Volksrepublik China*. Wiesbaden: Verlag für Sozialwissenschaften.

Heller, P.S. 2006. 'Is Asia prepared for an Aging Population?', *IMF Working Paper* WP/06/272, December. Washington DC: International Monetary Fund.

Helliwell, John F. 1994. 'Empirical Linkages between Democracy and Economic Growth', *British Journal of Political Science*, vol. 24:225-248.

Helmke, Gretchen. 2005. *Courts under Constraints: Judges, Generals, and Presidents in Argentina*. Cambridge: Cambridge University Press.

—. and Stephen Levitsky. 2004. 'Informal Institutions and Comparative Politics: A Research Agenda', *Perspectives on Politics*, vol. 2:725-740.

—. and Levitsky, Steven. 2006. 'Introduction', in ibid (eds.): *Informal Institutions and Democracy: Lessons from Latin America*, pp.1-30. Baltimore: The Johns Hopkins University.

Hériteir, A. 1998. 'Institutions, interests and political choice', in R.M. Czada, A. Héritier and H. Keman (eds.), *Institutions and Political Choice: on the Limits of Rationality*, pp. 27-53. Amsterdam: VU-University Press.

Herring, R. 1983. *Land to the Tiller: The Political Economy of Agrarian Reform in South Asia.* New Haven, Yale University Press.

Hewitt, C. 1977. 'The effect of political democracy and social democracy on equality in industrial societies: a cross-national comparison', *American Sociological Review,* vol. 3: 508–22.

Hibbs, D.A. Jr. 1977. 'Political Parties and Macroeconomic Policy', *American Political Science Review,* vol.71: 1467–87.

—. 1994. 'The partisan model of macroeconomic cycles: more theory and evidence for the United States', *Economic and Politics,* vol. 6, no.1: 1–23.

Hicken, Allen. 2011. 'Clientelism', *Annual Review of Political Science* vol. 14:289-310.

Hicks, Alexander and Swank, D.H. 1984. 'On the political economy of welfare expansion: a comparative analysis of 18 advanced capitalist democracies, 1960–1971', *Comparative Political Studies,* vol. 17: 81–119.

—.and Misra, J. 1993. 'Political resources and the growth of welfare in affluent capitalist democracies, 1960–1982', *American Journal of Sociology,* vol. 99: 668–710.

—. and Kenworthy, Lane. 1998.'Cooperation and political economic performance in affluent democratic capitalism', *American Journal of Sociology,* vol. 103, no. 6:1631–72.

Hina Renmin University. 1998. *Research Report on Chinese Social Development 1996-1997.* Beijing: China People University Press.

Hirschmann, A. O. 1978. 'Exit, Voice and the State', *World Politics*, vol. 31, no. 1: 90-107.

Hirter, H. 1988. 'Koordinierte Verkehrspolitik. Die Entstehung und Verwirklichung einer Gesamtkonzeption', in P. Hablützel, H. Hirter and B. Junker (eds.), *Schweizerische Politik in Wissenschaft und Praxis. Festschrift für Prof. Dr. Peter Gilg.* Bern: Forschungszentrum für schweizerische Politik.

Hobsbawm, Eric. (ed.) 1982. *The invented tradition.* Cambridge: Cambridge University Press.

Hofferbert, R.I. 1966. 'The relation between public policy and some structural and environmental variables in the American states', *American Political Science Review,* vol. 60, no. 1:73–82.

—. and Cingranelli, D.L. 1996. 'Public policy and administration: comparative policy analysis', in R.E. Goodin and H.-D. Klingemann (eds.), *A New Handbook of Political Science.* Oxford: Oxford University Press.

Holbig, Heike. 2011. ‚Die Finanzkrise in China: Auswirkungen auf die Legitimität der Parteiherrschaft', in H. Albrecht et al. (eds.), *Autoritäre Regime. Herrschaftsmechanismen, Legitimationsstrategien. Persistenz und Wandel*, pp. 114-133. Schwalbach: Wochenschau.

Hollingsworth, J. P. Schmitter and Streeck, W. (eds.) 1994. *Governing Capitalist Economies. Performance and Control of Economic Sectors*. Oxford: Oxford University Press.

—. and Boyer, Robert (eds.) 1997. *Contemporary Capitalism: The Embeddedness of Institutions*. Cambridge: Cambridge University Press.

Hong, D. et al. 2004. 'Obstacles and solutions: the study of the rural Five Guarantees in post collective period', *Journal of the People University of China*, vol. 1: 3-30.

—. and Wang, H. 2002. '城市居民最低生活保障制度改革的进展 [The progress of reform in the minimum living standards scheme in urban China]', in R. Xin et al. (eds.), *2002 年: 中国社会形势分析与预测* [*The Blue Book of the Chinese Society; Analysis and Forecast of China's Social Conditions in 2002*], pp. 105-122. Beijing: Social Science Literature Press.

Horsley, J. P. 2004 .'*Guangzhou's Pioneering Foray into Open Government*', available at http://www.freedominfo.org/news/guangzhou/ (2014-01-15).

—. 2006. '*The Rule of Law in China: Incremental Progress*', available at http://www.csis.org/media/csis/pubs/090212_05rule_of_law.pdf (2014-01-15).

Hsueh, C-T. and K. T. Woo. 2005. 'The Impact of Outsourcing to China on Hong Kong's Labour Market', *American Economic Review*, vol. 95, no. 5: 1673-87.

Hu, J. 2005. 'Envisaging China's grand strategy: The ambitious goal of a prosperous people and a powerful nation', *Social Sciences in China*, Winter: 87–99.

Huawei, Lin, Michael Downey and Stephen Sonnenberg. 2004. China's Wage and Hour Laws: New Rules Governing Minimum Wages', *Stay Current*, May 2004:1-4.

Huber, Evelyne and Stephens, J.D. 1993. 'Political parties and public pensions. A quantitative analysis', *Acta Sociologica,* vol. 36: 309–25.

—. and Stephens, John D. 2001. *Development and Crisis of the Welfare State*. Chicago: University of Chicago Press.

Hung, Jing. 2001. *Factionalism in Chinese Communist Politics*. Cambridge: Cambridge University Press.

Huntington, Samuel P. 1968. *Political Order in Changing Societies*. New Haven, Conn.: Yale University Press.

—. 1984. 'Will more countries become democratic?', *Political Science Quarterly*, vol. 99, no.2: 193–218.

—. 1991. *The Third Wave. Democratization in the Late Twentieth Century*. Norman: University of Oklahoma Press.

—. 1996. *The Clash of Civilizations*. New York: Simon and Schuster.

Hurst, William. 2004. 'Understanding Contentious Collective Action by Chinese Laid-off Workers: The Importance of Regional Political Economy', *Studies in Comparative International Development* vol. 39, no. 2:94– 120.

—. 2009. *The Chinese Worker after Socialism. Cambridge*. Cambridge: University Press.

—. and Kevin J. O'Brien 2002. 'China's Contentious Pensioners', *China Quarterly*, vol. 170: 345– 60.

Hussain, A. 2003. *Urban Poverty in China: Measurement, Patterns and Policies.* Geneva: International Labour Office.

Hyden, Goran. 2010. 'Civil Society in Africa: Constraints and Opportunities for Democratic Change', in. Cheema G. Shabbir and Vesselin Popowski (eds.), *Engaging Civil Society. Emerging Trends in Democratic Governance*,pp. 249-264. Tokyo: United Nations University Press.

ILO. 1958. *Social Security: A Workers' Education Manual*. Geneva: ILO Publications.

—. 1984. *Introduction to Social Security*. Geneva: ILO Publications.

—. 1991, *Role of Trade Unions in Social Security in Asia and Pacific*. Geneva: ILO Publications.

—. 1995. *Introduction to Social Security*. [Speech by the General Director quoted in Rao (2007:47)].

—. 2000. *India: Social Protection for the Unorganised Sector*. Geneva: ILO Publications.

—. 2001. *Social Security: A New Consensus*, Geneva. ILO Publications.

—. 2002. *Indian Social Protection in the Unorganised Sector*. Geneva: ILO Publications.

—. 2004a. *An Employment Agenda for China*. Beijing: ILO Publications.

—. 2004b. *China Employment Forum, Summary Proceedings*. Beijing: ILO Publications.

—. 2005. *Social protection as a productive factor*. Geneva: ILO Publications.

—. 2006. *Decent Work in Asia: Reporting on results 2001-05*. Geneva: ILO Publications.

—. 2007. *Linkages between statutory social security schemes and community-based social protection mechanisms: A new approach*. Geneva: ILO Publications.

—. 2008. *World of Work Report: Income Inequalities in the Age of Financial Globalisation*. Geneva.

—. 2009a. *Key Indicators of the Labour Market (KILM)*. Geneva: ILO Publications.

—. 2010a. *World Social Security Report 2010/11Providing coverage in times of crisis and beyond*. Geneva: ILO Publications.

—. 2010b. *Extending Old-age Insurance Coverage in the People's Republic of China*. Available at http://www.ilo.org/public/english/region/asro/beijing/download/training/old_insur.pdf (2010-07-15).

—. 2013. *Ministries of labour: comparative overview : history, mandate, challenges world-wide database and organizational charts*. Geneva: International Labour Office.

Ichiyō, Mutō. 1998. 'Class struggle in Postwar Japan', in G. McCormack and Y. Sugimoto (eds.), *Democracy in Contemporary Japan*, pp. 114-138. Melbourne: Haöe and Iremonger.

Immergut, E.M. 1992. *Health Politics. Interests and Institutions in Western Europe*. Cambridge: Cambridge University Press.

Inglehart, R. 1997. *Modernization and Postmodernization. Cultural, Economic and Political Change in 43 Societies*. Princeton, N.J.: Princeton University Press.

Information Office of the SC. 2002. *Labour and social security in China*. Beijing: Information Office of the SC. Available at www.china.org.cn/english/2002/Apr/31774.htm (2014-01-15).

—. 2004a. *China's social security and its policy*. Beijing: Information Office of the SC. Available at www.china.org.cn/e-white/20040907/index.htm (2014-01-05).

—. 2004b. *China's social security white paper.* Beijing: Information Office of the SC. Available at http://www2.chinadaily.com.cn/english/doc/2004-09/07/content_372369.htm (2014-01-05).

Iversen, Torben. 2001. , The Dynamics of Welfare State Expansion: Trade Openness, De-industrilazation, and Partisan Politics', in Paul Pierson (ed.), *The New Politics of the Welfare State*, pp.45-80. Oxford: Oxford University Press.

—. Jonas Pontusson and Soskice, David (eds.) 1999. *Unions, Employers and Central Banks*. Cambridge: Cambridge University Press.

Jamal, Amaney A. 2007. *Barriers to Democracy: The Other Side of Social Capital in Palestine and the Arab World.* Princeton, N.J.: Princeton University Press.

Jenkins, Rob. 1999. *Democratic politics and economic reform in India.* Cambridge: Cambridge University Press.

Jing, Y. and Wang, G. 2013. 'Western Political Research Approaches and the Development of Political Science Methodology in China', in S. Guo (ed.), *Political Science and Chinese Political Studies*, pp. 84-103. Heidelberg: Springer.

Johnson, Chalmers. 1970. 'Comparing Communist Nations', in ibid (ed.), *Change in Communist Systems*, pp. 1-32 .Stanford, Ca: Stanford University Press.

Jones, E. 1981. *The European miracle, environments, economics, and geography in the history of Europe and Asia.* Cambridge University Press: Cambridge.

Josephs, H.K 1990. *Labour Law in China: Choice and Responsibility.* Salem, NH: Butterworth Legal Publishers.

Jürgenmeyer, C. 1995. ''Koexistenz und Konflikt zwischen indischen Relgionsgemeinschaften. Das Beispiel Ayodhya', in W. Kerber (ed.), *Religion: Grundlage oder Hindernis des Friedens?*, pp. 79-165. München: Kindt.

Kailitz, Steffen. 2009a. 'Stand und Perspektiven der Autokratieforschung', *Zeitschrift für Politikwissenschaft,* vol. 3:437-488.

—. 2009b. 'Varianten der Autokratie im 20. und 21. Jahrhundert', *Totalitarismus und Demokratie,* vol. 2:209-252.

—. 2010. 'Eliteneinbindung in Ideokratien', in U. Backes and S. Kailitz (eds.), *Ideokratien im Vergleich: Legitimation – Kooptation – Repression*, pp. 313-339.Göttingen: Vandenhoeck und Ruprecht.

—. and Köllner, K. (eds.) 2013b. *Autokratien im Vergleich*. Baden-Baden: Nomos.

—. and Köllner, K. 2013a. 'Einleitung', in ibid (eds.), *Autokratien im Vergleich*, pp. 3-9. Baden-Baden: Nomos.

Kalleberg, L. 1966. 'The logic of comparison: a methodological note on the comparative study of political systems', *World Politics*, vol. 12, no. 1: 69–82.

Kanamori, T. and Zhao, Z. 2004. *Private Sector development in the People's Republic of China*. Tokyo: ADB.

Katzenstein, Peter J. 1985. *Small States in World Markets: Industrial Policy in Europe*. London: Cornell University Press.

Kaufmann, Daniel et al. 2006. '*The Worldwide Governance Indicators Project: Answering the Critics*', available at http://siteresources.worldbank.org/DEC/Resources/answeringthecritics.pdf (2014-12-12).

—. et al. 2008. 'Governance Matters VII: Aggregate and Individual Governance Indicators for 1996-2007', *World Bank Policy Research Working Paper No. 4654*. Washington, D.C.: World Bank.

—. et al. 2010. 'The Worldwide Governance Indicators: Methodology and Analytical Issues', *World Bank Policy Research Working Paper No. 5430*. Washington, D.C.: World Bank.

Kaufmann, F.-X. .2009. *Sozialpolitik und Sozialstaat: Soziologische Analyse*. Wiesbaden: VS Verlag.

Keith, R. C. and Lin, Zhiqiu.2003. 'Falun Gong Problem: Politics and the Struggle for the Rule of Law in China', *China Quarterly*, vol. 175:623-642.

Keman, Hans. 1984. 'Politics, policies and consequences: a cross national analysis of public policy formation (1967–1981)', *European Journal of Political Research*, vol. 12, no. 2: 147–70.

—. 1988. *The Development Towards Surplus Welfare: Social Democratic Politics and Policies in Advanced Capitalist Democracies (1965–1984)*. Amsterdam: CT Press.

—. 1990. 'Social democracy and the politics of welfare statism', *West European Politics*, vol. 17, no. 4: 17–34.

—. (ed.) 1997a. *The Politics of Problem-Solving in Postwar Democracies*. Basingstoke: Macmillan.

—. 1997b. 'The Politics of Problem-Solving in Postwar Democracies: Institutionalising Conflict and Consensus in Western Europe', in ibid (ed.), *The Politics of Problem-Solving in Postwar Democracies*. Basingstoke: Macmillan.

—. 2002a. 'The Comparative Approach to Democracy', in ibid (ed.), *Comparative Democratic Politics. A Guide to Contemporary Theory and Research*, pp. 3-16. London: Sage.

—. (ed.) 2002b. *Comparative Democratic Politics. A Guide to Contemporary Theory and Research*. London: Sage.

Kennedy, J.J. 2007. 'From the fee for-tax reform to the abolition of agricultural taxes: the impact on township governments in Northwest China', *China Q*, vol. 189:43-59.

Kennedy, D. van. 1966. Unions, employers and government. Bombay: Manaktalas.

Kerr, C. 1960. *Industrialism and Industrial Man*. Cambridge, Mass: Harvard University Press.

—. Dunlop, F., Harbison, H. and Myers, C.A. 1973. *Industrialism and Industrial Man*. London: Penguin.

Kersbergen, K. van. 1995. *Social Capitalism. A Study of Christian Democracy and the Welfare State*. London: Routledge.

—. 1999. 'Contemporary Christian Democracy and the demise of the politics of mediation', in H. Kitschelt, G. Marks, P. Lange and J.D. Stephens (eds.), *Continuity and Change in Contemporary Capitalism*. Cambridge: Cambridge University Press.

—. 2000. 'The declining resistance of national welfare states to change?', in S. Kuhnle (ed.), *The Survival of the European Welfare State*, pp. 19-36. London and New York: Routledge.

—. and Becker, Uwe. 2002. 'Comparative Politics and the Welfare State', in Hans Keman (ed.), *Comparative Democratic Politics. A Guide to Contemporary Theory and Research*, pp. 185- 215. London: Sage.

King, Robert, O. Keohane, and Verba, Sidney. 1994. *Designing Social Inquiry*. Princeton, N.J.: Princeton University Press.

Kingdon, J. W. 1985. *Agendas, Alternatives and Public Policies*. London: Longman.

Kirchgässner, G. and Pommerehne, W.W. 1996. 'Tax Harmonization and Tax Competition in the European Union: Lessons from Switzerland', *Journal of Public Economics*, vol. 60: 351– 371.

Kirchheimer, O. 1964. 'The waning of opposition', in R. Macridis and B.E. Brown (eds.), Comparative Politics. Homewood, Ill.: Dorsey Press.

—. 1966a. 'The transformation of Western European party systems', in J. LaPalombara and M. Weiner (eds.) (1966) *Political Parties and Political Development*. Princeton, N.J.: Princeton University Press.

Kitschelt, Herbert. 2001. 'Partisan competition and retrenchment', in Paul Pierson (ed.), *The New Politics of the Welfare State*, pp. 265–302. Oxford: Oxford University Press.

—. and Obinger, Herbert. 2003: Political Parties, Institutions, and the Dynamics of Social Expenditure in Times of Austerity', *Journal of European Public Policy*, vol. 10, no. 1: 20-45.

Knight, Jack. 1992. *Institutions and Social Conflict*. New York: Cambridge University Press.

Köllner, Patrick. 2008a. Autoritäre Regime – keine weltweit aussterbende Gattung, sondern eine wachsende Herausforderung. *GIGA Focus Global 6*. Hamburg: GIGA.

—. 2008b. Autoritäre Regime: Jüngere Entwicklungen und die Perspektiven vergleichender Forschung. *Zeitschrift für Vergleichende Politikwissenschaft*, vol. 2:351-366.

—. 2013. 'Informelle Institutionen in Autokratien: Konzeptionell-analytische Grundlagen und der Fall der Kommunistischen Partei Chinas', in S. Kailitz and P. Köllner (eds.), *Autokratien im Vergleich*, pp. 272-292. Baden-Baden: Nomos.

—. G. Marks, P. Lange and Stephens, J. D. (eds.) 1999. *Continuity and Change in Contemporary Capitalism*. Cambridge: Cambridge University Press.

—. and Matthias Basedau. 2006. 'Faktionalismus in politischen Parteien: Eine Einführung', in ibid and Gero Erdmann (eds.), *Innerparteiliche Machtgruppen: Faktionalismus im internationalen Vergleich*, pp. 7-37. Frankfurt a. M.: Campus.

Koenger, W. et al. 2007. 'Labour Market Institutions and Wage Inequality', *Industrial and Labour Relations Review*, vol. 60, no. 3: 340-356.

Kohli, A. 1987. *The state and poverty in India. The politics of reform*. Cambridge: Cambridge University Press.

—. 1989. 'Politics of Economic Liberalization in India', *World Development*, vol. 17, no. 3: 305-328.

—. 2004. *State-Directed Development: Political Power and Industrialization in the Global Periphery*. New York: Cambridge University Press.

—. 2006a. 'Politics of Economic Growth in India, 1980-2005, Part I: The 1980s', *Economic and Political Weekly*, vol. 41, no. 13: 1251-60.

—. 2006b. 'Politics of Economic Growth in India, 1980-2005, Part II: The 1990s and Beyond', *Economic and Political Weekly*, vol. 41, no. 14: 1361-70.

—. 2012. 'State and Redistributive Development in India', in R. Nagaraj (ed.), *Growth, Inequality and Social Development in India. Is Inclusive Growth Possible?*, pp.194-227. Basingstoke: Palgrave Macmillan.

Kolberg, J. E. and G. Esping-Andersen. 1992. 'Welfare State and Employment Regimes', in J. E. Kolberg (ed.), *Between Work and Social Citizenship*, pp. 3-36. Armonk, N.Y.: Sharpe.

Korpi, W. 1978. *The Working Class in Welfare Capitalism*. London: Routledge and Kegan Paul.

—. 1983. *The Democratic Class Struggle*. London: Routledge and Kegan Paul.

—. 1989. 'Power, politics, and state autonomy in the development of social citizenship: social rights during sickness in eighteen OECD countries since 1930', *American Sociological Review*, vol. 54: 309–28.

Korpi, W. and Palme, J. 2003. 'New Politics and Class Politics in the Context of Austerity and Globalization: Welfare State Regress in 18 Countries, 1975–95', *American Political Science Review*, vol. 3: 425-446.

Kothari, Rajni. 1970. *Politics in India*. Boston: Little & Brown.

Korzec, M. 1992. *Labour and failure of reform in China*. New York: Macmillan Press.

Kucera, D. and Roncolato, I. 2011. 'Trade Liberalization, Employment and Inequality in India and South Africa', *International Labour Review*, vol. 150, no. 1-2.

Kumar, D. 1965. *Land and Caste in South India. Agricultural Labour in the Madras Presidency During the Nineteenth Century*. Cambridge: Cambridge University Press.

Kumar, G. 2006. *Local Democracy in India*. New Delhi: Sage Publishing.

Kumar, U. and Mishre, P. 2008. 'Trade Liberalization and Wage Inequality: Evidence from India', *Review of Development Economics*, vol.12, no.2: 291-311.

Kuruvilla, Sarosh et al. (eds.) 2011. *From Iron Rice Bowl to Informalization: Markets, Workers, and the State in a Changing China*. Ithaca, NY: Cornell University Press.

Kurzer, P. (1993) *Business and Banking. Political Change and Economic Integration in Western Europe*. Ithaca and London: Cornell University Press.

Lam, Willy. 2011. 'The Rise of the Energy Faction in Chinese Politics', *China Brief*, vol. 6, no. 7:2-4.

Landry, Pierre. 2008. *Decentralized Authoritarianism in China*. Cambridge: Cambridge University Press.

Lange, Peter. 1984. 'Unions, Workers, and Wage Regulation: The Rational Bases of Consent,' in John H. Goldthorpe (ed.), *Order and Conflict in Contemporary*, pp. 98-113. Oxford: Oxford University Press.

Lane, Jan-Erik and Svante Errson. 1994. *Comparative Politics: An Introduction and New Approach*. Oxford: Polity Press.

—. and Ersson, S.O. 1998. *Politics and Society in Western Europe*. London: Sage.

—. and Errson, S. O. 2002. 'Democratic Performance: Are There Institutional Effects?', in Hans Keman (eds.), *Comparative Democratic Politics. A Guide to Contemporary Theory and Research*, pp. 233-257. London: Sage.

Large, D. 2006. 'China's Sudan engagement: changing Northern and Southern political trajectories in peace and war', *China Q,* vol. 199:610-626.

Lauth, Hans-Joachim. 2000. Informal Institutions and Democracy. *Democratization*, vol. 7:21-50.

—. 2002. 'Die empirische Messung demokratischer Grauzonen: Das Problem der Problem der Schwellenbestimmung', in Petra Bendel , Croissant Aurel and Friedbert Rüb (eds.), *Zwischen Diktatur und Demokratie,* pp. 119-138. Wiesbaden: Westdeutscher Verlag.

—. 2010. 'Gegenstand, grundlegende Kategorien und Forschungsfragen der 'Vergleichenden Regierungslehre', in Hans-Joachim Lauth (ed.), *Vergleichende Regierungslehre. Eine Einführung*, pp. 15-37. Wiesbaden: VS Verlag für Sozialwissenschaften.

—. 2011. 'Qualitative Ansätze der Demokratiemessung', *Zeitschrift für Staats- und Europawissenschaften,* vol. 9:49-77.

Law, K-Y. (ed.) 2002. *Beyond purge and a holocaust: the cultural revolution reconsidered.* London: MacMillian.

Lee, Ching Kwan. 2007. *Against the Law: Labour Protests in China's Rustbelt and Sunbelt.* Berkeley: University of California Press.

Lee, G. 2001.'Labour Policy Reform', in L. Wong and N. Fynn (eds.), *The market in Chinese social policy,* pp. 12-37. Basingstoke: Palgrave.

Lehmbruch, G. 1974. 'A non-competitive pattern of conflict management in liberal democracies: the case of Switzerland, Austria and Lebanon', in K. D. McRae (ed.), *Consociational Democracy: Political Accommodation in Segmented Societies.* Toronto: McClelland and Steward.

—. 1979. 'Liberal corporatism and party government', in P. Schmitter and G. Lehmbruch (eds.), *Trends towards Corporatist Intermediation*, pp. 147–83 London: Sage.

—. 1984. 'Concertation and the structure of corporatist networks', in J. H. Goldthorpe (ed.), *Order and Conflict in Contemporary Capitalism*, pp. 60-81. Oxford: Oxford University Press.

—. 1993. 'Consociational democracy and corporatism in Switzerland', *Publius: The Journal of Federalism*, vol. 23, no. 2: 43–60.

—. 1999. 'Negotiated democracy, consociationalism and corporatism in German politics: The legacy of the Westphalian Peace', in T. Ertman (ed.), *The Fate of Consociationalism.* Cambridge: Cambridge University Press.

—. and Schmitter, P.C. (eds.) 1982. *Patterns of Corporatist Policy Making.* London: Sage.

Lerner, D. 1958. *The Passing of Traditional Society: Modernizing the Middle East.*

Glencoe, Ill.: Free Press. Lepsius, Rainer M. 1988. *Interessen, Ideen, Institutionen.* Wiesbaden: Westdeutscher Verlag.

Lessenich, S. 1994. 'Three Worlds of the Welfare Capitalism – oder vier? Strukturwandel arbeits- und sozialpolitischer Regulierungsmuster in Spanien', *Politische Vierteljahresschrift Zeitschrift,* vol. 35, no. 2: 224–44.

Levitsky, S and L. A. Way. 2006. 'Linkage versus Leverage – Rethinking the International Dimension of Regime Change', *Comparative Politics,* vol. 38:379-400.

—. and M V. Murillo. 2009. 'Variations in Institutional Strength', *Annual Review of Politics,* vol. 12:115-133.

—. and L. A. Way, 2010. *Competitive Authoritarianism. Hybrid Regimes after the Cold War.* Cambridge: Cambridge University Press.

Leung, J. 2006. 'The emergence of social assistance in China', *International Journal of Social Welfare*, vol. 15: 188-198.

—. and Nann, R. 1995. *Authority and Benevolence: Social Welfare in China.* Hong Kong: Chinese University Press.

Lewis, W. A. 1954. 'Economic Development with Unlimited Supply of Labour', *The Manchester School*, vol. 22:139-91.

Li, Cheng 2012. 'The Battle for China's Top Nine Leadership Posts', *Ashington Quarterly,* vol. 35:131-145.

Li, Lianjiang and Kevin O'Brien. 1999. '*Selective Policy Implementation in Rural China' Comparative Politics*', vol.31, no.2:167-186.

Li, Luqu. 2010. 'Four models of the relationship between Confucianism and democracy', *J Chin Philos*, vol. 37, no. 19:18-33.

—. et al. 2012. 'Petition Beijing: The High Tide of 2003-2006', *China Quarterly*, vol. 210: 313-334.

Li, H. and Rozelle, S. 2003. 'Privatizing Rural China: insider privatization, innovative contracts and the performance of township enterprises', *China Q,* vol. 176:981-1005.

Lieberthal, Kenneth G. 1992. 'Introduction: The 'Fragmented Authoritarianism': Model and Its Limitations', in Lieberthal, Kenneth G and David M. Lampton (eds.), *Bureaucracy, politics and decision making in post-Mao China*, pp. 1-22. Berkley: University of California Press.

—. 1995. *Governing China.* NY: Norton.

—. 2011. *Managing the China Challenge: How to achieve corporate success in the People's Republic.* Washington, D.C.: Brookings Institution Press.

—. and Michel Oksenberg .1988. *Policymaking in China: Leaders, Structures, and Processes.* Princeton, N.J.: Princeton University Press.

—. and David M. Lampton.1992. *Bureaucracy, Politics, and Decision Making in Post-Mao China.* Berkley: University of California Press.

Lijphart, A. 1968. 'Typologies of democratic systems', *Comparative Political Studies*, vol. 1: 3–44.

—. 1996. 'The Puzzle of Indian Democracy: A Consociational Interpretation', *American Political Science Review*, vol. 90, no. 2: 258–68.

—. 1999. *Patterns of Democracy: Government Form and Performance in Thirty-Six Countries.* New Haven: Yale University Press.

Linz, Juan. 1975. 'Totalitarian and Authoritarian Regimes', in Greenstein, F. I, and B. W. Polsby, *Handbook on Political Science*, pp. 175-411. Reading: Addison Wesley.

—. 2000. *Totalitäre und autoritäre Regime*. Berlin: Berliner Debatte Wissenschaftsverlag.

—. and Crépaz, M.M.L. 1991. 'Corporatism and consensus democracy in eighteen countries: conceptual and empirical linkages', *British Journal of Political Science*, vol. 21: 235–46.

—. and Alfred Stephan. 1996a. *Problems of Democratic Transition and Consolidation. Southern Europe, South America, and Post communist Europe*. Baltimore: John Hopkins University Press.

—. and Alfred Stephan. 1996b. 'Toward Consolidated Democracies', *Journal of Democracy,* vol. 7:14-33.

Liu, D.2011. *Reformen des Sozialleistungsrechts in der Volksrepublik China*. München: Nomos.

Liu, M. L. 2011.''Where There Are Workers, There Should Be Trade Unions' Union Organizing in the Era of Growing Informal Employment', in S. Kuruvilla et al. (ed.), *From Iron Rice Bowl to Informalization: Markets, Workers, and the State in a Changing China*, pp. 157-173. Ithaca, NY: Cornell University Press

Liu, X. and Yu Y. 2004. *The Health Sector in China: Policy institutional review*. Washington, D.C: World Bank.

Lipset, S.M. 1959/1981. *Political Man*. Garden City, N.Y.: Doubleday.

—. and Rokkan, S. 1967a. 'Cleavage structures, party systems and voteralignments: an introduction', in S.M. Lipset and S. Rokkan (eds.), *Party Systems and Voter Alignments: Crossnational Perspectives*, pp. 1-64. New York: Free Press.

Long, Zhaohui and Deng, Jianxin. 2005. '政府间财政转移支付: 问题及政策建议 [Chinese Intergovernmental Fiscal Transfer System: Problems and Policy Suggestions]', 改革 (*Reform*), vol. 7: 38-44.

Lohmann, H. 2009.'Welfare Sates, Labour Market Institutions and the working Poor: A Comparative Analysis of 20 European Countries', *European Sociological Review*, vol. 25, no. 4: 479-504.

Loo, B.P.Y. and Chow, S.Y. 2006. 'China's tax-sharing reforms: one system differential impact', *Asian Survey*, vol. XLVI, no. 2: 215-237.

Lowi, Theodore J. 1964. 'American Business, Public Policy, Case-Studies and Political Theory', *World Politics,* vol. 16, no. 1:671-715.

Lowenthal, Richard. 1970. 'Development vs. Utopia in Communist Policy', in Chalmers Johnson's (ed.), *Change in Communistic Systems*, pp. 33-116. Stanford: Stanford University Press.

Luo, G. 1998. 'Explanatory note of the program for reconstructing the Stat Council', Report delivered at the First Session of the Ninth national People's Congress on 6 March, in Comprehensive Bureau of the General Office of the Central Organs Establishment Commission (eds.), *The central government organs 1998*. Beijing: Reform Press. [quoted by Chan et al. 2008]

Lynn, Villa Corta. 1994. *Social protection in Asia and the Pacific*. New Delhi: Friedrich Ebert Stiftung.

Ma, J and Hou, Y.L. 2005. 'The policy process and budgeting process at the provincial level financial system in China', Comparative Economic and Social System, no 5: 34-39.

Machin, S. 1997. 'The Decline of Labour Market Institutions and the Rise in Wage Inequality in Britain', *European Economic Review*, vol. 41: 647-57.

MacIntyre, Andrew. 2003. *The Power of Institutions. Political Architecture and Governance*. Ithaca, NY: Cornell University Press.

MacKinlay, A Craig. 1997. 'Event Studies in Economics and Finance', *Journal of Economic Literature*, vol. 35, no. 1:13-39.

Macridis, Roy C. and Brown, Bernard E. 1955. *Comparative Politics: Notes and Readings*. Homewood, Ill.: Dorsey Press.

Mahoney, James 2010: *Colonialism and Postcolonial Development: Spanish America in Comparative Perspective*. NY: Cambridge University Press.

Mahoney, James 2004.'Comparative-Historical Methodology', *Annual Review of Sociology*, vol. 30, edited by Karen S. Cook and John Hagan: 81-101.

Mair, Peter. 1997. *Party System Change: Approaches and Interpretations*. Oxford: Clarendon Press.

—. 2001. 'The freezing hypothesis: an evaluation', in L. Karvonen and S. Kuhnle (eds.), *Party Systems and Voter Alignments: Looking Back, Looking Forward*. London: Routledge.

—. 2002. 'In the Aggregate: Mass Electoral Behaviour in Western Europe, 1950-2000', in Hans Keman (ed.), *Comparative Democratic Politics. A Guide to Contemporary Theory and Research*, pp. 122-142. London: Sage.

Manion, Melanie. 1993. *Retirement of Revolutionaries in China: Public Policies, Social Norms, Private Interests*. Princeton, N.J.: Princeton University Press.

Manor, J. 1988. Parties and Party System', in A. Kohli (ed.), *India's Democracy*, pp. 62-98. Princeton, N.J.: Princeton University Press.

March, J.G. and Olsen, J.P. 1989. *Rediscovering Institutions: The Organizational Basis of Politics*. New York: Free Press.

Markoff, John and White, Amy. 2009. 'The Global wave of Democratization', in C. W. Haerpfer et al (eds.), *Democratization*, pp. 55-73. Oxford: Oxford University Press.

Masilamani, S. 1995. *Economic Reforms and Trade Unions*. New Delhi: Friedrich Ebert Stiftung.

Mathur, D.C.1987. *Labour Welfare, Social Security and Industrial Relations in contract Labour in India*. New Delhi: Mittal Publications.

—. and Srkar, S. 2007. 'Growth of Employment and Earnings in Tertiary Sector, 1983-2000', *Economic and Political weekly*, vol. 42, no. 11:973-81.

Mazzuca, S. 2010. 'Access to Power versus Exercise of Power: Reconceptualizing the Quality of Democracy in Latin America', *Studies in Comparative International Development*, vol. 45:334-357.

McCarthy, John D. and Zald, Mayer N. 1977. 'Resource Mobilization and Social Movements: A Partial Theory', *American Journal of Sociology*, vol. 82: 1212-1241.

McDonald, T. J. 1996a. 'Introduction', in ibid. (ed.), *The Historical Turn in the Human Science*. Ann Arbor: University of Michigan Press.

McGuire, Martin C. and Mancur Olson, JR. 1996. 'The Economics of Autocracy and Majority Rule: The Invisible Hand and the Use of Force', *Journal of Economic Literature,* XXXIV:72-96.

McFaul, M. 2002. 'The Fourth wave of Democracy and Dictatorship: Noncooperative Transitions in Postcommunist world', *World Politics,* vol. 54:212-244.

McLean, I. and McMillan, Alistar. 2003. *The Concise Oxford Dictionary of Politics.* Oxford: Oxford University Press.

McCracken, Paul et al. 1977.*Towards Full Employment and Price Stability*. Paris: OECD.

Mefford, Dwaine. 1987. 'Analogical Reasoning and the Definition of the Situation', in Charles F. Hermann, Charles W. Kegley, Jr., and James N. Rosenau (eds.), *New Directions in the Study of Foreign Policy*, pp. 221-244. Boston, Mass.: Allen & Unwin.

Mehta, K.C.1990. *Social Security for the Unorganized.* Ahmedabad: Gandhi labour Institute.

Mehta, Prayag. 1994. *Collective Action for Social Security Entitlements*. New Delhi: Friedrich Ebert Stiftung.

Meisner, M. J. 1995. The *Deng Xiaoping Era: an Inquiry into the Fate of Chinese Socialism. 1978-1994*. New York: Hill and Wang.

Memoria, C.B. and Memoria, Santosh. 1984. *Social Security Legislation in Industrial Labour - Social Security and Industrial Peace in India.* New Delhi: Kitab Mahal.

Metcalf, D. and Li, J. 2005. 'Chinese Unions: Nugatory or Transforming?', *CEP Discussion Paper No 708*. London: Centre for Economic Performance.

Mesa-Lago, C. 1997. 'Social Welfare Reform in the Context of Economic-Political Liberalization: Latin American Cases', *World Development*, vol. 25:497-517.

Merkel, Wolfgang. 1999. *Systemtransformation. Eine Einführung in Theorie und Empirie der Transformationsforschung.* Opladen: Leske & Budrich.

—. and Aurel Croissant. 2000. 'Formale und informale Institutionen in defekten Demokratien', *Politische Vierteljahresschrift*, vol. 41:3-30.

—. 2004. 'Embedded and Defective Democracies', *Democratization,* vol. 11:33-58.

—. 2010. *Systemtransformation. Eine Einführung in die Theorie und Empirie der Transformationsforschung*. Wiesbaden: VS Verlag für Sozialwissenschaften.

—. and Aurel Croissant. 2000. 'Formale und informale Institutionen in defekten Demokratien', *Politische Vierteljahresschrift*, vol. 41:3-30.

—. Hans-Jürgen Puhle, Aurel Croissant, Claudia Eicher and Thiery, Peter. 2003. *Defekte Demokratie. Band 1: Theorie*. Opladen: Leske & Budrich.

Mertha, A. 2009. ''Fragmented Authoritarianism 2.0': Political Pluralisation in the Chinese Policy Process', *China Quarterly,* vol. 200: 995-1012.

Michels, R.[1911]1962. *Political Parties: A Sociological Study of the Oligarchical Tendencies of Modern Democracy*. New York: Collier Books.

Ministry of Civil Affairs (MCA). 1997. *Ordinance on the management of rural old aged homes (tentative).* Beijing: MCA.

—. 2005. *MOCA Minimum living Standard Scheme, Briefing Note to ILO mission.* Beijing.

Ministry of Civil Affairs (MCA). 2009. *Quarterly Statistics of the Civil Affairs in China.* Beijing: MCA. See http://www.mca.gov.cn/article/zwgk/mzyw/200902/20090200026278.shtml.

Ministry of Finance. 1993. *Economic Survey 1992-1993*. New Delhi: GoI.

—. 1999-2007. *Finance Yearbook of China*. Beijing: China Public Finance Economics Press.

—. 1999-2009. *Local Fiscal Statistical Materials*. Beijing: China Public Finance Economics Press.

—. 2000. *Economic Survey 1999-2000*. New Delhi: GoI.

—. 2009. *Budget and Finances*. New Delhi: GoI.

—. 2013. *Comprehensive Social Security for the Indian Unorganized Sector*. New Delhi: GoI.

Ministry of Health (MoH). 2004a. *The key findings of the third national health survey*. Beijing: MoH.

—. 2004b. *China Health Statistics Extract, 2004*. Beijing: Ministry of Health.

—. 2007. *Medical secure system in 2003*.Beijing: MoH.

Ministry of Labour and Employment (MoLE). 2000. *Report of the Task Force on Social Security 1999.* New Delhi: GoI.

—. 1994. *Pocket Book of Labour Statistics 1996-97*. Chandigarh: GoI.

—. 1998. *Annual Report 1997-98, 50th Anniversary of India's Independence*. New Delhi: GoI.

Ministry of Social Justice and Empowerment. 1999. *First Report of Expert Committee for Devising a Pension System For India OASIS*. New Delhi: GoI.

Ministry of Labour and Social Security (MoLSS). 2005. *2003-2005 劳动和社会保障事业发展统计公报* [*Statistical bulletin for Labour and Social Security, 2003-2005*]. Beijing: MoLSS.

MoLSS. See http://w1.mohrss.gov.cn/gb/zwxx/node_5436.htm (2010-07-15).

—. 2007. 2007 *劳动和社会保障事业发展统计公报* [*Statistical bulletin for Labour and Social Security, 2007*]. Beijing: MoLSS. See http://www.molss.gov.cn/index/index.htm (2010-07-15).

Mishra, R. K. and Raveendran, Jayasree. (eds.) 2011. *Millennium Development Goals: The Indian Journey*. New Delhi: Allied Publishers.

Mitchell, D. 1990. *Income transfer systems: a comparative study using microdata.* Unpublished PhD dissertation. Australian National University.

Mitra, K. Subrata. 1991. 'Room to Manoeuvre in the Middle: Local Elites, Political Action and the State in India', *World Politics,* vol. 43, no. 3: 390-413.

—. 1994a. *Culture and Rationality*. Delhi: Sage Publication.

—. 1994b. 'Party Organisation and Policy-making in a Changing Environment: The Indian National Congress', in K. Lawson (ed.), *How Parties Work: Perspectives from Within*, pp. 153-177. London: Praeger.

—. 1999a. 'Effects of Institutional Arrangements on Political Stability', *Annual Review of Political Science*, vol. 2: 405–428.

—. 1999b. Culture and Rationality: The Politics of Social Change in Post-colonial India. Delhi: Sage.

—. 2000. 'Politics in India', in G. Almond et al. (eds.), *Comparative Politics Today*, pp. 629-680. New York: Pearson, Longman.

—. 2002. 'Making Local Government work: Rural Elites, Panchayati Raj and Legitimacy in India', in A. Kohli, (ed.), *The Success of India's Democracy*, pp. 103-126. Cambridge: Cambridge University Press.

—. 2005. *The Puzzle of India's Government: Culture, Context, Comparative Theory*. London: Routledge.

—. 2011. *Politics in India: Structure, Process and Policy*. London: Routledge.

—. 2013. 'How Exceptional is India's Democracy? Path Dependence, Political Capital, and Context in South Asia', *Indian Review,* vol. 12, no. 4: 227-244.

—. 2014. '*Public service delivery and multi-level governance in India: Politics and the room for innovation'*, paper presented at the international conference on Public service deliverty, in November 2014, BARD, Bangladesh.

—. and Singh, V.B. 1999. *Democracy and Social Change in India: A Cross-national analysis of the Indian Electorate*. Delhi: Sage.

—. and Singh, V. B. 2009. *When Rebels become Stakeholders*. London: Sage.

Møller, Jorgen and Skaaning, Svend-Erik. 2010. 'Beyond the Radial Delusion: Conceptualizing and Measuring Democracy and Non-Democracy', *International Political Science Review*, vol. 31:261-283.

Møller, J. and W. Muni and S.-E. Skanning. 2013. 'Internationaler Strukturwandel und Autokratie' in S. Kailitz and K. Köllner (eds.), *Autokratien im Vergleich*, pp. 86-105. Baden-Baden: Nomos.

D'Monte, D. 2002. *The Decline of Mumbai and its Mills*. Delhi: Oxford University Press.

Montesquieu, C. 1989. *The spirit of the laws*. Cambridge University Press, Cambridge.

Montinola, Gabriella, Yingyi Qian and Weingast, Barry. 1995. 'Federalism, Chinese Style: The Political Basis for Economic Success', *World Politics*, vol. 48, no. 1:50-81.

Moon, J. 1993. *Innovative Leadership in Democracy. Policy Change Under Thatcher*. Aldershot: Dartmouth.

—. 1995. 'Innovative leadership and policy change: lessons from Thatcher', *Governance,* vol. 8: 1–25.

Morris-Jones, W.H. 1971. *The Government and Politics of India*. London: Hutchinson University Library.

Morris, David Morris. 1965. *The Emergence of an Industrial Labor Force in India. A Study of the Bombay Cotton Mills, 1854-1947.* Berkeley: University of California Press.

—. and Michelle McAlpine. 1982. *Measuring the Conditions of India's Poor: The Physical Quality of Life Index.* New Delhi: Promilla and Co.

Mu, Huaizhong and Liu, Qingrui. 2006. *中国养老保险制度改革关键问题研究* [*The Research on the Key Issues about China's Pension System Reforms*]. Beijing: China Labor and Social Security Publishing House.

Mulligan, Casey B., Ricard Gil, and Sala-I-Martin, Xavier. 2004. 'Do Democracies Have Different Public Policies than Nondemocracies?', *Journal of Economic Perspectives*, vol. 18:51-74.

Murphy, J. 2004. *The United States and the Rule of Law in International Affairs.* Cambridge: Cambridge University Press.

Murphy, Walter F. 2007 *Constitutional Democracy: Creating and Maintaining a Just Political Order.* Baltimore: The Hopkins University Press.

Müller, W. C. 2010. 'Party patronage and party colonization of the state', in R. S. Katz and W. Crotty (eds.), *Handbook of Party Politics*, pp. 175-189. London: Sage.

Myles, J. (1989) *Old Age in the Welfare State: The Political Economy of Public Pensions.* Lawrence: University Press of Kansas.

Nagaraj, R. 2000.' Indian economy since 1980s: Virtuous Growth or Polarisation', *Economic and Political Weekly*, vol. 35, no. 32: 2831-39.

—. 2012a. 'Development Strategies and Poverty Reduction', in ibid, *Growth, Inequality and Social Development in India. Is Inclusive Growth Possible?*, pp. 25-63. Basingstoke: Palgrave Macmillan.

—. 2012b. *Growth, Inequality and Social Development in India. Is Inclusive Growth Possible?* Basingstoke: Palgrave Macmillan.

Nayar, B. R. 1989. *India's mixed economy: The Role of Ideology and Interest in Its Development.* New Delhi: Popular Prakashan.

Naisbitt, J and Naisbitt, D. 2010. *China's Megatrends: The Eight Pillars of a New Society.* New York: Harper Business.

Nathan, A. 1973. 'A factionalism model for the CCP politics', *China Q*, vol. 53:34-66.

National Commission On Labour. 2002. *Report of the Second National Commission on Labour.* New Delhi: GoI.

—. 1969. *Report of the First National Commission on Labour.* New Delhi: GoI.

National Family Health Survey (NFHS). 2000. *Health and Family Welfare, India: 1998: 1999.* Mumbai: International Institute of Population Studies.

National Academy for Training & Research in Social Security (NATRSS). 1999. *Concepts of Social Security.* New Delhi: NATRSS.

—. 1999. *Concepts of Social Security.* New Delhi: NATRSS.

NCEUS (National Commission on Enterprises in the Unorganised Sector). 2006. *Report on the Unorganised Sector.* New Delhi: NCEUS.

—. 2007. *Report of the National Commission on the Enterprises in Unorganized Sector.* New Delhi: NCEUS.

National Statistical Commission. 2012. *Report of the Committee on Unorganised Sector Statistics*. New Delhi: GoI.

Ngok, K.L and Zhu, G.B: 2003. 'Reinventing the communist government in a transitional economy – a review of China's 1998 central government reconstruction', *Asian Profile*, vol 31, no.1: 1-14.

Nicolaidis, K. and R. Kleinfeld. 2012. 'Rethinking Europe's « Rule of Law » and Enlargement Agenda: The Fundamental Dilemma', *SIGMA Papers*, No. 49, OECD Publishing.

Nohlen, Dieter. 1994. 'Lateinamerika zwischen Diktatur und Demokratie', in Detlef Junker, Dieter Nohlen and Hartmut Sangmeister (eds.), *Lateinamerika am Ende des 20. Jahrhunderts.*, pp. 12-26. München: C.H. Beck.

—. 1999. 'Demokratie und soziale Gerechtigkeit', in Wolfgang Merkel and Andreas Busch (eds.), *Demokratie in Ost und West*, pp. 249–272. Frankfurt a. M.: Suhrkamp.

—. 2007. *Wahlrecht und Parteiensystem : Zur Theorie und Empirie der Wahlsysteme*. Opladen: Budrich.

Noorani, A.G. 1994. 'The Prime Minister and the Judiciary', in J. Manor (ed.), *Nehru to the Nineties. The Changing Office of Prime Minister in India*, pp. 94-114. London. Hurst.

Noll, H. H. 2002. *Social indicators and quality of life research. Background, achievements and current trends*. Köln: German Social Science Infrastructure Service.

Norris, Pippa. 2000. 'Global Governance and Cosmopolitan Citizens' in: Joseph S. Nye and John D. Donahue (eds.), *Governance in a Globalizing World*, pp. 155-177. Washington, D.C.: Brookings Institution Press.

—. 2005. 'Stable Democracy and Good Governance in Divided Societies: Do Power-sharing Institutions Work?', *Harvard University: Faculty Research Paper Series RWP 05-14.*

North, Douglas. 1990 and 2008. *Institutions, Institutional Change and Economic Performance.* Cambridge: Cambridge University Press.

—. 1995. 'Five Propositions about Institutional Change', in Jack Knight and Itai Sened (eds.), *Explaining Social Institutions,* pp. 15-26. Ann Arbor: University of Michigan Press.

O'Brien, K. J. 1990. *Reform without liberalization: China's National People's Congress and the politics of institutional change*. New York: Cambridge University Press.

O'Connor, Peter. 1990. 'Privatisation and Welfare Services', *Australian Journal of Social Issues*, vol. 25, no. 1: 27-39.

OECD (1999) *OECD Historical Statistics 1960–1997*. Paris: OECD Publishing (OECDP).

—. 2005. *Economic Survey of China*. Paris: OECDP.

—. 2007. *OECD Economic Surveys, India*, vol. 14. Paris: OECDP.

—.2009. *Is Informal Normal?Towards More and Better Jobs in Developing Countries*. Paris: OECDP.

—. 2010a. *Science, Technology and Industrial Outlook*. Paris: OECDP.

—. 2010b. *Economic Survey of China*. Paris: OECDP.

—. 2010c. *Tackling Inequalities in Brazil, China, India and South Africa. The Role of Labour*

Market and Social Policies. Paris: OECDP.

Offe, Claus. 1981. 'The attribution of public status to interest groups: observation on the West German case', in S. Berger et al. (eds.), *Organizing interests in Western Europe*, pp. 123-158. Cambridge: Cambridge University Press.

Olsen, J. 1998. 'Political science and organization theory: parallel agendas but mutual disregard', in Czada et al. (eds.), *Institutions and Political Choice: On the Limits of Rationality*. Amsterdam: VU-University Press.

Olson, Mancur Jr. 1965. *The Logic of Collective Action*. Cambridge: Harvard University Press.

—. 1993. 'Dictatorship, Democracy and Development', *American Political Science Review,* vol. 87, no. 3: 567–576.

Ortner, Sherry B. 1996. 'Resistance and the Problem of Ethnographic Refusal', in T. McDonald (ed.), *The Historical Turn in the Human Science*, pp. 281-304. Ann Arbor: University of Michigan Press.

Ostrom, E. 1990. *Governing the Commons: The Evolution of Institutions for Collective Action*. New York: Cambridge University Press.

Palme, J. 1990. *Pension Rights in Welfare Capitalism. The Development of Old-Age Pensions in 18 OECD Countries, 1930 to 1985.* Stockholm: Swedish Institute for Social Research.

Patnaik, P. and Patnaik, U. 2001. 'The State, Poverty and Development in India', in N.G. Jayal and S. Pai (eds.), *Democratic Governance in India*, pp. 32-66. New Delhi: Sage.

Padmadas, Sabu, Guangzhou Wang, James Brown and Bohua Li. 2005. 'Birth planning and population prospects in China and India', *Paper presented at the IUSSP XXV International Population Conference*, Tours, France, July 18th-23rd.

Pallares-Miralles, M., C. Romero, and E. Whitehouse. 2012.'International Patterns of Pension Provision II. A Worldwide Overview of Facts and Figures', *World Bank Discussion Paper,* no. 121.

Parekh, B. .2010 *Poverty in Indian Political Theory',* in Aakash Singh and Silika Mohapatra (eds.), *Indian Political Thought: A Reader*, pp. 535-560. London: Routledge.

Pearson, M. M. 2005. 'The business of governing business in China: institutions and norms of the emerging regulatory state', *World Politics,* vol. 57, no. 2:296-322.

Peerenboom, R. 2002. *China's Long March toward Rule of Law*. Cambridge: Cambridge University Press.

—. 2006. 'China and the Rule of Law: Part II', *Perspectives*, vol. 1, no.6.

Peña-Casas R. and M. Latta. 2004. 'Working Poor in the European Union', *Report of the European Foundation for the Improvement of Living and Working Conditions.*

Pennings, P., Keman, H. and Kleinnijenhuis, J. 1999. *Doing Research in Political Science. An Introduction to Comparative Methods and Statistics*. London: Sage.

Peters, B. Guy, Doughtie, J.C. and McCulloch, M.K. 1977. 'Types of democratic systems and types of public policy', *Comparative Politics*, vol. 10, no. 2: 237–55.

Perry, E. J. 2001. 'Challenging the mandate of heaven: popular protest in modern China', *Crit Asian Stud,* vol. 33, no. 2:163-180.

—. 2002. *Challenging the mandate of heaven: popular protest in modern China*. Armonk: Sharpe.

—. and Xun, L. 1996. *Proletarian power: shanghai in the Cultural Revolution*. New York: Westview.

Pampel, Fred C., John B. Williamson, and Stryker, Robin. 1990. 'Class Context and Pension Response to Demographic Structure in Advanced Industrial Democracies', *Social Problems,* vol. 37:301-16.

Pereira, Anthony. 2008. 'Of judges and Generals: Security Courts under Authoritarian Regimes in Argentina, Brazil, and Chile', in Tom Ginsburg and Tamir Moustafa (eds.), *Rule by Law: The Politics of Courts in Authoritarian Regimes*, pp. 23-57. New York: Cambridge University Press.

Phillips, D. 2006. *Quality of Life: Concept, policy and practice*. London: Routledge.

Planning Commission. 1997. *Estimate of Poverty*. New Delhi: GoI Press Information Bureau.

—. 2000. *Ninth Five-Year Plan: 1997-2002*. New Delhi: Planning Commission.

—. 2006. *Report of the Working Group on Social Security*. New Delhi: Planning Commission.

—. 2008. *Eleventh Five Year Plan(2007–2012). Volume II*. Oxford: Oxford University Press.

Pierson, P. 1994. *Dismantling the Welfare State? Reagan, Thatcher, and the Politics of Retrenchment*. Cambridge: Cambridge University Press.

—.1996. '*The New Politics of the Welfare State*', *World Politics*, 48: 143–79.

—. 2000. 'Path dependency, increasing returns, and the study of politics', *The American Political Science Review*, vol. 94, no.2: 251-267.

—. (ed.) 2001. *The New Politics of the Welfare State*. Oxford: Oxford University Press.

—. 2003. *Politics in Time: History, Institutions, and Social Analysis*. Princeton, N.J.: Princeton University Press.

Pizzorno, A. 1978. 'Political exchange and collective identities', in C. Crouch and A. Pizzorno (eds.), *The Resurgence of Class Conflict in Western Europe since 1968*, pp. 277-298. London: Macmillan.

Platteau, J.P. 1995. 'An Indian model of aristocratic patronage', *Oxford Economic Papers,* vol. 47, no. 4: 636-662.

—. and Abraham, A. 2002. 'Participatory development in the presence of endogenous community imperfections' *Journal of Development Studies,* vol 39, no. 2: 104-136.

Preworksi, Adam and H. Teune. 1970. *The logic of comparative social inquiry*. NY: Wiley.

Polanyi, K. 1957. *The Great transformation: The Political and Economic Origins of Our Time*. Boston: Beacon Press.

Potter, D. 1996. *India's Political Administration: from ICS to IAS*. New Deli: Oxford University Press.

Prabhu, K. S. and Sandhya, R. 1999. 'Financing Social Security in India', *Indian Journal of Labour Economics,* vol. 42, no. 3: 519-533.

Preworksi, Adam. 1986. 'Some Problems in the Study of the Transition to Democracy', in Guilerrmo O'Donnel et al. (eds.), *Transitions from Authoritarian Rule: Comparative Perspective*, pp.47-63.Baltimore: The Johns Jopkins Univerity Press.

Przeworski, A. and Teune, H. (1970) *The Logic of Comparative Social Enquiry*.New York: Wiley.

—. 1987. 'Methods of cross-national research, 1970–1983', in M. Dierkes, H. Weiler and A.B. Antal (eds.), *Comparative Policy Research. Learning from Experience*. Aldershot: Gower.

—. 1991. *Democracy and the Market: Political and Economic Reforms in Eastern Europe and Latin America*. Cambridge: Cambridge University Press.

Pryor, F.L. 1968. *Public Expenditure in Communist and Capitalist Countries*. London: Allen&Unwin.

Pun, N. 2005. *Made in China: Women Factory Workers in a Global Workplace*. Durham: Duke University Press.

Qi, Dongtao. 2013. 'Chinese Working Class and Trade Unions: Transformation and Predicamment in the Reform Era', in Gungwu Wang and Yongnian Zheng (eds.), *China: Development and Governance*, pp. 283-293. Singapore: World Scientific Publishing.

Qi, H. 2000. 'The evolution of Chinese township and village enterprises', in F. Richter (ed.), *The dragon millennium: Chinese business in the coming world economy*, pp. 13-34. Westport, CT: Quorum Books.

Radbruch, Gustav. 1946. 'Gesetzliches Unrecht und übergesetzliches Recht', *Süddeutsche Juristenzeitung*, vol. 105: 105-8.

Radhakrishna, R. and Subbarao, K. 1997. 'India's Public Distribution System: A National and International Perspective', *World Bank Discussion Paper 360*, Washington, D.C.: World Bank.

Radnitz, Scott. 2011. 'Informal Politics and the State', *Comparative Politics*, vol. 43:351-371.

Ragin, C.C. 1987. *The Comparative Method: Moving Beyond Qualitative and Quantitative Strategies*. Berkeley: University of California Press.

Rajni, Bakhi. 1986. *The Long Haul.* Michigan: University of Michigan.

Ramaiah, A. 1988. 'Plight of Dalits: a challenge to the social work profession', *Indian Journal of Social Work*, vol. 59, no.1: 124-146.

Ramswamy, E. A. 2000. *Managing Human Resources*. Oxford: Oxford University Press.

Rao, Madhava P. [2005] 2007. 'Social security administration in India- study of provident funds and pension scheme', *MPRA Paper No. 1919*.

Rao, Madhava P. 2011. *Social Security Administration in India. A Study of Provident Funds and Pension Scheme*. Hyderabad: ICFAI University Press.

—. Ric Shand Govinda, and K.P. Kalirajan. 1999. 'Convergence of Income cross Indian States: A Divergent View', *Economic and Political Weekly*, vol. 34, no. 13:769-78.

Rao, V. 1990. 'Laws Applicable to Voluntary Social Welfare Organisations', *Indian Journal of Social Work*, vol. 51, no. 3: 523-528

—. 2003. 'Social Welfare in Tamil Nadu Politics', *Indian Journal of Social Work,* vol. 64, no. 3: 350-372.

Rao,V and Mander,H. .1996. *Agenda For Caring : Interventions for Marginalised Groups*. New Delhi: Voluntary Health Association of India.

—. D. Rajasekhar and J.Y. Suchitra. 2006. 'The Unorganised Workers: Deprivation, Social Security and Policy Implementation', *Economic and Political Weekly*, vol. 41, no. 19: 1913-1919.

—. and Waghmore S. 2007. 'Special Issue Dalits and Development: A Reappraisal', *Indian Journal of Social Work*, vol. 68, no. 1: 21-33.

Rajasekhar, D. et al. 2011. *'Implementing Health Insurance: The Rollout of Rashtriya Swasthya Bima Yojana in Karnataka'*, Economic Weekly, vol. XLVI, no.20:56-63.

Rastogi, R.K. 1994. *Administration of Social Security*. New Delhi: Friedrich Ebert Stiftung.

Rathod, Harshada. 2007. 'Poverty Alleviation: A Case Study of Tamil Nadu', in V. Patel and M. Karne (eds.), *The Macro Economic Policies and The Millennium Development Goals*, pp. 71-82. New Delhi: Gyan Publishing House.

Rawls, Joseph. 1972. *A Theory of Justice.* Oxford: Clarendon Press.

—. 1978. 'Principles of Equality', *Mind*, New Series, vol. 87, no. 347: pp. 321-342.

—. 1979. *The Authority of Law: Essays on Law and Morality*. Oxford University Press, Oxford

Regini, M. 1984. 'The Conditions for Political Exchange: How Concentration Emerged and Collapsed in Italy and Great Britain', in J.H. Goldthorpe (ed.), *Order and Conflict in Contemporary Capitalism*, pp. 124-143. Oxford: Oxford University Press.

Remmer, Karen. 1997. 'Theoretical Development and Theoretical Decay: the Resurgence of Institutional Analysis', *World Politics*, vol. 50, no. 1: 34–61.

Reutter, Werner. 2001a. 'Einleitung. Korporatismus, Pluralismus und Demokratie', in ibid (ed.), *Verbände und Verbandssysteme in Westeuropa*, pp. 8-29. Opladen: Leske & Budrich.

Richter, T. 2007. 'The Political Economy of Regime Maintenance in Egypt: Linking External Resources and Domestic Legitimation', in O. Schlumberger (ed.), *Debating Arab Authoritarianism: Dynamics and Durability in Nondemocratic Regimes*, pp. 177-193. Stanford: Stanford University Press.

Riker, W. H. [1965]1975. *The theory of political coalitions*. Westport, Conn: Greenwood Press.

Rhodes, M. 1997. 'The welfare state: internal challenges, external constraints', in M. Rhodes, P. Heywood and V. Wright (eds.), *Developments in West European Politics*, pp. 57-74. Basingstoke: MacMillan.

—. 2001. 'The political economy of social pacts: 'Competitive corporatism' and European welfare reform', in Paul Pierson (ed.), *The New Politics of the Welfare State*, pp. 165-194. Oxford: Oxford University Press.

Rodrik, D. and A. Subramanian. 2004. 'From 'Hindu Growth' to Productivity Surge: The Mystery of the Indian Growth Transition', *IMF Working Paper WP 04/77.*

Rohenstein, B: and J. Teorell. 2008. 'What is Quality of Government? A Theory of Impartial Government Institutions', *Governance-an International Journal of Policy Administration and Institutions* 21:165-190.

Roller, Edeltraud. 2005. *The Performance of Democracies. Political Institutions and Public Policies*. Oxford: Oxford University Press.

Rose, R. and Davies, P.L. 1984.*Inheritance in Public Policy: Change Without Choice in Britain*. New Haven and London: Yale University Press.

Roßteutscher, Sigrid. (ed.) 2005. *Democracy and the Role of Associations. Political, Organizational and Social Contexts*, London: Routledge.

Rothermund, Dietmar 1993. *Staat und Gesellschaft in Indien*. Wien: BI.

—.1995a. *Indien. Kultur, Geschichte, Politik, Wirtschaft, Umwelt. Ein Handbuch.* München: Beck.

—. 1995b. 'Parlamentarische Demokratie und Föderalismus', in ibid (ed.), *Indien. Kultur, Geschichte, Politik, Wirtschaft, Umwelt. Ein Handbuch,* pp. 389-408. München: Beck.

—. 1995c. 'Genossenschaften und Gewerkschaften' in ibid (ed.), *Indien. Kultur, Geschichte, Politik, Wirtschaft, Umwelt. Ein Handbuch,* pp. 537-548. München: Beck.

Rothstein, B. and Teorell, J. 2008. 'What Is Quality of Government? A Theory of Impartial Government Institutions', *Governance-an International Journal of Policy Administration and Institutions,* vol. 21:165-190.

Ross, Fiona. 2000. '*Beyond Left and Right: The New Partisan Politics of Welfare'*, *Governance*, vol. 13: 155-183.

Rostow, W.W. 1960. *The Stages of Economic Growth: A Non-Communist Manifesto*. Cambridge: Cambridge University Press.

Rösel, J. 1994. 'Ideologie, Organisation und politische Praxis des Hindunationalismus: Lehre, Rituale und Wirkung der RSS und der BJP', in *Internationales Asienforum*, vol. 25, no. 3-4: 285-313.

Rudolph, L. I. and Rudolph, S. H. 1968. *In Pursuit of Lakshmi*: *The Political Economy of India.* Chicago: University of Chicago Press.

Ruchismita, R., and Churchill, C. 2012. 'State and market synergies: Insights from India's microinsurance success', in C. Churchill and M. Matul (eds.), *Protecting the Poor: A Microinsurance Compendium*, vol. 2, pp. 427-460. Geneva, ILO.

Rueschemeyer, D., Huber, E., Stephens, E. and Stephens, J.D. 1992. *Capitalist Development and Democracy*. Oxford: Polity Press.

Rui, Mu. 1983. 'New Development in China's Economic Legislation', *Columbia Journal of Transnational Law*, vol. 1:61-67.

Saich, T. 2001. *Governance and politics of China*. New York: Palgrave.

Sakthivel, S. and Pinaki Joddar. 2006. 'Unorganized Sector Workforce in India: Trends, Patterns, and Social Security Coverage', *Economic and Political Weekly*, vol 41, no.21: 2107-2114.

Sandbrook R. et al. 2007. *Social Democracy in the Global Periphery: Origins, Challenges, prospects*. New York: Cambridge University Press.

Sankaran, T.S., R.K.A.Subrahmanya and S.K. Wadhawan. 1994. *Development of Social Security Programmes in Developing Countries*. New Delhi: Har Anand Publications.

Sartori, Giovanni. 1970.'Concepts Misformation in Comparative Politics', *American Political Science Review*, vol. 64, no. 4:1033-1053.

—. 1976. *Parties and Party Systems: A Framework for Analysis*. New York: Cambridge University Press.

—. 1984. *Social Science Concepts: A Systematic Analysis*. Beverly Hills: Sage.

—. 1987. *The Theory of Democracy Revisited*. Chatham: Chatham House.

Sathe, S. P. 2002. *Judicial Activism in India - Transgressing Borders and Enforcing Limits*. New Delhi: Oxford University Press.

Shankar, S. and Asher, M. 2011. 'Micro-pensions in India: Issues and challenges', *International Social Security Review*, vol. 64, no.2: 1-21.

Scharpf, Fritz W. 1970. *Demokratietheorie zwischen Utopie und Anpassung. Konstanzer Universitätsreden 25*. Konstanz: Universitätsverlag.

—. 1984. 'Economic and institutional constraints of full employment strategies: Sweden, Austria and Germany, 1973–1982', in J.H. Goldthorpe (ed.) (1984) *Order and Conflict in Contemporary Capitalism*. Oxford: Oxford University Press.

—. 1987. 'A game-theoretical interpretation of inflation and unemployment in Western Europe', *Journal of Public Policy,* vol. 7: 227–57 [Special Issue edited by H. Keman].

—. 1998. 'Political institutions, decision styles and policy choices', in Czada et al. (eds.), *Institutions and Political Choice*. Amsterdam: VU-University Press.

—. 1999a. *Governing in Europe. Effective and Democratic?* Oxford: Oxford University Press.

—. 1999b. 'Demokratieprobleme in der europäischen Mehrebenenpolitik', in Wolfgang Merkel and Andreas Busch (eds.), *Demokratie in Ost und West. Für Klaus von Beyme*, pp. 672-694. Frankfurt a. M.: Suhrkamp.

—. 2004. 'Legitimationskonzepte jenseits des Nationalstaats', *Working Paper 04/6*. Köln: Max-Planck-Institut für Gesellschaftsforschung.

—. 2009. ‚Legitimität im europäischen Mehrebenensystem', in: A. Fischer-Lescano, F. Rödl, C.U. Schmid (eds.), *Europäische Gesellschaftsverfassung. Zur Konstitutionalisierung sozialer Demokratie in Europa*, pp. 297-329. Baden-Baden: Nomos.

Shepsle, K.A. 1997. 'Studying institutions: some lessons from the rational choice approach', in J. Farr, J.S. Dryzek and S.J. Leonard (eds.) (1997) *Political Sciencein History. Research Programs and Political Traditions*. Cambridge: Cambridge University Press.

—. and Weingast; B. R. 1981. 'Structure-induced equilibrium and legislative choice ',*Public Choice*, vol. 37:503-519,

Schedler, Andreas. 2009. 'The New Institutionalism in the Study of Authoritarian Regimes', *Totalitarismus und Demokratie* 6:323-340.

Schmidt, M.G. 1980. *CDU und SPD an der Regierung. Ein Vergleich ihrer Politik in den Ländern*. Frankfurt a. M.: Campus.

—. 1983. 'The welfare state and the economy in periods of economic crisis: a comparative study in twenty-three OECD nations', *European Journal of Political Research,* vol. 11: 1–26.

—. 1986. 'Comment on 'Social Expenditure and the Political Right' (by F.G. Castles)', *European Journal* of *Political Research,* vol. 14: 677–80.

—. 1989. 'Social policy in rich and poor countries: socio-economic trend and political-institutional determinants', *European Journal of Political Research,* vol. 17: 641–59.

—. 1993. 'Theorien der international vergleichenden Staatstätigkeitsforschung', in A. Héritier (ed.), *Policy-Analyse* (Politische Vierteljahresschrift Sonderheft 24), pp. 371-394. Opladen: Westdeutscher Verlag.

—. 1996a. 'When parties matter: A review of the possibilities and limits of partisan influence on public policy', *European Journal of Political Research*, vol. 30: 155–83.

—. 1996b. 'The grand coalition state', in J.M. Colomer (ed.), *Political Institutions in Europe*, pp. 62-98. London: Routledge.

—. 1997. *Demokratietheorien*. Opladen: Leske & Budrich.

—. 1998. *Sozialpolitik in Deutschland. Historische Entwicklung und internationaler Vergleich*. Opladen: Leske & Budrich.

—. 1999a. 'On the political productivity of democracies', Mauno Koivisto Lecture, *Scandinavian Political Studies,* vol. 22 no. 4: 281–94.

—. 1999b. 'Sozialpolitik im demokratischen und autoritären Staat', in Wolfgang Merkel and Andreas Busch (eds.), *Demokratie in Ost und West*. Frankfurt a. M.: Suhrkamp.

—. 2000a. *Demokratietheorien. Opladen*: Leske & Budrich.

—. 2000b. *Wörterbuch zur Politik*. Stuttgart: Kröner.

—. 2002. 'The Impact of Political Parties, Constitutional Structures and Veto Players on Public Policy', in Hans Keman (ed.), *Comparative Democratic Politics. A Guide to Contemporary Theory and Research*, pp. 166-183. London: Sage.

—. 2003. 'Zur Leistungsfähigkeit von Demokratien', in Ines Katenhusen and Wolfram Lamping (eds.), *Demokratien in Europa*, pp. 269-284. Opladen: Leske & Budrich.

—. 2005. 'Politische Reformen und Demokratie. Befunde der vergleichenden Demokratie- und Staatstätigkeitsforschung', in Hans Vorländer (ed.), *Politische Reformen in der Demokratie*, pp. 45-62. Baden-Baden: Nomos Verlag.

—. 2012. *Der deutsche Sozialstaat. Geschichte und Gegenwart*. München: C.H. Beck.

—. and Frieder Wolf. 2006. *Bildungsausgaben im inter- und intranationalen Vergleich*. Heidelberg: Inst. für Politische Wissenschaft.

—. Ostheim, T., Siegel, N.A., Zohlnhöfer, R. (eds.) 2007. *Der Wohlfahrtstaat. Eine Einführung in den historischen und internationalen Vergleich*. München: Springer.

Schmidt, Steffen W., Laura Guasti, Carl H. Landé, and Scott., F. James. (eds.) 1977. *Friends, Followers, and Factions. A Reader in Political Clientelism*. Berkeley: University of California Press.

Schmitter, P.C. and Grote, J.R. 1997. 'Der korporatistische Sisyphus: Vergangenheit, Gegenwart und Zukunft', *Politische Vierteljahresschrift*, vol. 38, no. 3: 530–54.

—. 1974. 'Still the Century of Corporatism', *Review of Politics,* vol. 36: 85–131.

—. 1981. 'Interest Intermediation and Regime Governability in Contemporary Western Europe and North America', in S. Berger (ed.), *Organizing Interests in Western Europe*, pp. 285-327. New York: Cambridge University.

—. and Lehmbruch, G. (eds.) 1979: *Trends Towards Corporatist Intermediation*. Beverly Hills: Sage.

Schumpeter, J.A. (1974) *Capitalism, Socialism and Democracy*. New York: Harper & Row.

Schwartz, Herman. 2001. 'Round Up the Usual Suspects! Globalisation, Domestic Politics, and Welfare State Change', in Paul Pierson (ed.), *The New Politics of the Welfare State*, pp. 17-45. Oxford: Oxford University Press.

Scott, W. Richard. 2008. *Institutions and Organisations: Ideas and Interests*. Thousand Oaks: Sage.

Senger, Harro von 1994. *Einführung in das chinesische Recht*, München: CH. Beck.

Sen, Amartya. 1992. *Inequality reexamined*. New York Oxford New York: Russell Sage Foundation Clarendon Press Oxford University Press.

—. 2000. *Development as Freedom*. New Delhi: Oxford University Press.

—. 2002. *Rationality and freedom*. Cambridge, Mass: Belknap Press.

—. 2003. 'The Conceptual Challenge of Evaluating Inequality and Poverty', *Economics* (quarterly), vol. 1: 257-258.

—. and Jean Dreze. 1990. 'Social Security in Developing Countries', in E. Ahman et al. (eds.), *Social Security in Developing Countries*.Oxford: Clarendon Press.

Sen, Gita. 1997. 'Empowerment as an Approach to Poverty', *Human Development Papers 1997 – Poverty and Human Development*. New York: UNDP.

—. et al. 2002. 'Structural Reforms and Health Equity: A Comparison of NSS Survey of 1986—87 and 1995-96', *Economic and Political Weekly*, vol. 37, no. 14:1342:52.

—. and D. Rajasekhar. 2012.'Social Protection Policies, Experiences and Challenges', in R. Nagaraj (ed.), *Growth, Inequality and Social Development in India. Is Inclusive Growth Possible?,*pp. 91-135 . Basingstoke: Palgrave Macmillan.

Schram, S. F. 2005. 'A Return to Politics: Perestroika, Promises and Postparadigmatic Political Science' in K. R. Monroe (ed.), *Perestroika! The Raucous Rebellion in Political Science*, pp.103-113.New Haven: Yale University Press.

Schumpeter, J. A. 1974. *Capitalism, Socialism and Democracy*. London: Unwing University Books.

Segal, A. 2003. *Digital dragon: high-technology enterprise in China*. Ithaca, NY: Cornell University Press.

Shah, Ajay. 2003. 'Investment Risk in Indian pension Sector and Role for Pension Guarantee', *Economic and political Weekly*, vol. XXXVIII, no. 8: 719–728.

Sharma, Usha. (ed.) 2006. *Labour Movement in India. Pre-Independence Period. Volume 1*. New Delhi: Vista International Publishing House.

Shanghai Ministry of Civil Affairs. 1996. *Shanghai social assistance measures*. Shanghai: MoCA. See www.shmzj.gov.cn/node8/node30/userobjectlai141.html (2014-02-01).

Sharping, T. 2003. *Birth Control in China 1949-2000: Population policy and demographic development*. Curzon, London: Routledge.

Shepsle, Kenneth A. 1979. 'Institutional Arrangements and Equilibrium in Multidimensional Voting Models.', *American Journal of Political Science* 23: 27-59.

—. 1997. 'Studying institutions: some lessons from the rational choice approach', in J. Farr, J.S. Dryzek and S.J. Leonard (eds.), *Political Science in History. Research Programs and Political Traditions*. Cambridge: Cambridge: University Press.

Shevtsova, Lilia. 2007. *Russia. Lost in Transition. The Yeltsin and Putin Legacies*. Washington: Carnegie.

Shi, S.H. 2006. 'Left to market and family – again? Ideas and the development of the rural pension policy in China', *Social Policy and Administration*, vol. 40, no. 7: 791-801.

Shi, T. 1997. *Political Participation in Beijing*. Cambridge: Harvard University Press.

Shih, Victor, Christopher Adolph and Mingxing Liu. 2012. 'Getting Ahead in the Communist Party: Explaining the Advancement of Central Committee Members in China', *American Political Science Review,* vol. 106, no.1:166-187.

Shirk, Susan. 1993. *The Political Logic of Economic Reform in China*. Berkeley: University of California Press.

Shirk, S. 2007. *China, a Fragile Superpower*. Oxford: Oxford University Press.

Shu, Gou. 2008. 'An Analysis of China's Justice System', in Li Lin et al. (eds.), *The China Legal Yearbook*, vol. 1, pp.147-154. Beijing: Brill.

Shonfield, A. 1965. *Modern Capitalism. The Changing Balance of Public and Private Power*. London: Oxford University Press.

Siaroff, A. 1999. 'Corporatism in 24 industrial democracies: meaning and measurement', *European Journal of Political Research*, vol. 36, no. 2: 175–205.

Sidel, Mark. 2010. Maintaining Firm Control: Recent Developments in Nonprofit Law and Regulation in Vietnam. *The International Journal of Not-for-Profit Law,* vol. 12, no. 3. Available at http://www.icnl.org/research/journal/vol12iss3/art_1.htm (2012-04-04).

Singh, Mahendra P. and Surya Deva. 2005. 'The Constitution of India: Symbol of Unity in Diversity', in Peter Häberle (ed.), *Jahrbuch des Öffentlichen Rechts der Gegenwart*, vol. 3, pp. 649-686. Bayreuth: Mohr Siebeck.

Singh, P. 2008. *Federalism, Nationalism and Development: India and the Punjab Economy*. New York: Routledge.

Siegel, Nico A. 2002. *Baustelle Sozialpolitik. Konsolidierung und Ruckbau im internationalen Vergleich*. Frankfurt a. M.: Campus.

Singh, Mahendra P. 2000. 'Securing the Independence of the Judiciary - The Indian Experience' *Indiana International & Comparative Law Review 245*.

Sinha, P.R.N. et al. 2006. *Industrial Relations, Trade Unions, and Labour Legislation*. New Delhi: Pearson Education.

Social Security Administration (SSA). 2002. *Social Security Programs Throughout the World, 2002*. Washington, D.C.: ISSA.

—. 2004. *Social Security Programs Throughout the World, 2004*. Washington, D.C.: ISSA.

—. 2006. *Social Security Programs Throughout the World, 2006*. Washington, D.C.: ISSA.

—. 2008. *Social Security Programs Throughout the World, 2008*. Washington, D.C.: ISSA.

—. 2010. *Social Security Programs Throughout the World, 2010*. Washington, D.C.: ISSA.

—. 2012. *Social Security Programs Throughout the World, 2012*. Washington, D.C.: ISSA.

Solinger, D.J. 1999. *Contesting Citizenship in Urban China: Peasant Migrants, the State and the Logic of the Market.* Berkley: University of California Press

—.'Why we cannot account the 'unemployed'', *The China Quarterly*, no. 167:671-688.

Som, B.N. 1994. *Challenges to Social Security- Our Response*. New Delhi: Friedrich Ebert Stiftung.

Sondrol, P. C. 1990. *Castro's Cuba and Stroessner's Paraguay: A comparison of the totalitarian/authoritarian taxonomy*. Tucson: University of Arizona.

Soskice, David. 1994. 'Reconciling Markets and Institutions: The German Apprenticeship System', in Lisa M. Lynch (ed.), *Training and the Private Sector: International Comparisons*, pp. 25-60. Chicago:The University of Chicago Press.

—. 1990. 'Wage Determination: The Changing Role of Institutions in Advanced Industrialized Countries', *Oxford Review of Economic Policy,* vol. 6, no. 4: 36–61.

State Council (SC). 1986. *Provisional regulations on the implementation of the labour contract system in state-owned enterprises*. Beijing: People's Press.

—. 1993. *Regulations on unemployment insurance*. Beijing: People's Press.

—. 1994. *Regulation concerning the work implementing 'Five Guarantees' in rural areas*. Document no. 141. Beijing: SC.

—. 1997. State *Council's announcement on establishing a national minimum living system for urban residents*. www.mca.gov.cn/article/content/WDB_ZCWJ/2003/22484945.htm (2014-01-05).

—. 1999. *Ordinance on the Minimum Standard of Living Scheme*. Document no. 271. Beijing: SC.

—. 2000. 国务院关于完善城镇社会保障体系的试点方案, 国发 (*Notification on the Pilot Project for improvement of the social security in cities*)', 42 号, released 2000-25-12.

—. 2001. *Enhancing the work of Minimum Standard of Living* Scheme. Document no. 2001/87. Beijing: SC.

—. 2006. *Ordinance on the implementation of Five Guarantees in rural areas*. Beijing: SC.

—. 2006. *Ordinance on the implementation of Five Guarantees in rural areas*. Beijing: SC.

Stefes, Christoph, Alexander Schmotz, and Merkel, Wolfgang. 2011. 'Diktatorendämmerung.

Nordafrika und Nahost: Schwache Regime und starke Oppositionsbewegungen', *WZB-Mitteilungen,* 133:25-28.

Steinfeld, E.S. 2002. *Forging reform in China: the fate of state-owned industry*. New York: Cambridge University Press.

Stenner, Karen. 2005. *The Authoritarian Dynamic*. Cambridge: Cambridge University Press.

Stephens, J.D. 1979. *The Transition from Capitalism to Socialism*. London and Basingstoke: MacMillan.

—. Huber, E. and Stephens, J.D. 1982. 'The labor movement, political power and workers participation in western Europe', *Political Power and Social Theory,* vol. 3: 215–50.

Stimson, J., MacKuen, M.B. and Erikson, R. (1995) 'Dynamic representation', *American Political Science Review*, vol. 89: 543–65.

Stone, L. 1979. 'The Rivival of Narrative', *Past and Present,* vol. 85, no. 1:3-24.

Streeck, W. 1992. *Social Institutions and Economic Performance.* London: Sage.

—. (ed.)1995. *Staat und Verbände*. Opladen:Westdeutscher Verlag.

—. 2001. 'Introduction: Explorations into the Origins of Nonliberal Capitalism in Germany and Japan', in ibid et al. (eds.), *The Origins of Nonliberal Capitalism: Germany and Japan*, pp. 1-38. Ithaca, NY: Cornell University Press.

—. 2006. 'The study of organized interests: before 'The Century' and after', in Colin Crouch and Wolfgang Streeck (eds.), *The Diversity of Democracy. Corporatism, Social Order and Political Conflict*, pp. 3-45. Cheltenham: Edward Elgar.

—. and Yamamura, K 2002. *Germany and Japan in the 21st Century: Strengths into weaknesses?* Ithaca, NY: Cornell University Press.

—. and Hassel, A. 2004. 'The Crumbling Pillars of German Social Partnership', in Herbert Kitschelt andWolfgang Streeck (eds.), *Germany: Beyond the Stable State*, pp. 101-123. London: Frank Cass.

—. and Thelen, K. 2005. 'Introduction', in ibid (eds.), *Beyond* Continuity, pp. 1-40. Oxford: Oxford University Press.

Strøm, K. 1990. 'A behavioural theory of competitive political parties', *American Journal of Political Science*, vol. 34, no. 2: 565–98.

Stykow, Petra. 2013. 'Wahlen in autoritären Regimen: Die postsowjetischen Länder im Vergleich', in S. Kailitz and P. Köllner (eds.), *Autokratien im Vergleich*, pp. 237-271. Baden-Baden: Nomos.

Sülzer, Rolf. 2008. 'Social Security in India - A System in the Making', in D. Beneck (ed.), *The social and ecological market economy: a model for Asian development?*, pp. 211-229. Eschborn: GTZ.

Subramanian, N. 1999. *Ethnicity and populist mobilization. Political parties, citizens and democracy in South India*. Delhi: Oxford University Press.

Suryanarayana, M. H. 1983. 'Treatment of Poverty in the Sixth Plan', *Arha Vijnana*, vol. 25, no. 4:419-25.

—. 1995. 'PDS: Beyond Implicit Subsidy and Urban Bias – the Indian Experiment', *Food Policy*, vol. 20, no. 4: 259-78.

—. 2001. 'Nutrition Security in India: Issues and Policies', in K. S. Prabhu and R. Sudharshan (eds.), *Reforming India's Social Sectors: Strategies and Prospects*, pp. 171-200. New Delhi: Social Science Press.

—. 2012.'Economic Development and Inequalities', in R. Nagaraj (ed.), *Growth, Inequality and Social Development in India. Is Inclusive Growth Possible?,* pp.63-91. Basingstoke: Palgrave Macmillan.

—. and Silva, D. 2007. 'Is Targeting the Poor a Penalty on the Food Insecure? Poverty and Food Insecurity in India', *Journal of Human Development*, vol. 8, no. 1:89-106.

Swaminathan, M. 2000. *Weakening Welfare: The Public Distribution of Food in India*. New Delhi: Leftword Press.

Swank, Duane H. and Hicks, A. 1985. 'The determinants and redistributive impacts of state welfare spending in the advanced capitalist democracies, 1960–1980', in N.J. Vig and S.E. Schier (eds.), *Political Economy in Western Democracies*. New York: Holmes and Meier.

—. 2001. 'Political institutions and welfare state restructuring', in Paul Pierson (ed.), *The New Politics of the Welfare State*, pp. 197–237.Oxford: Oxford University Press.

—. 2002. *Global Capital, Political Institutions, and Policy Change in Developed Welfare States*. Cambridge: Cambridge University Press.

Swidler, Ann, 1986. 'Culture in Action: Symbols and Strategies', *American Sociological Review,* vol. 51, no. 2: 273-286.

Swamy, S. 2010. *Economic development and reforms in India and China*. New Delhi: Har-Anand.

Stykow, P. 2013. 'Wahlen in autoritären Regimen: Die postsowjetischen Länder im Vergleich', in S. Kailitz and P. Köllner (eds.), *Autokratien im Vergleich*, pp. 237-272. Baden-Baden: Nomos.

Tamanaha, Brian Z. 2004. *On the Rule of Law*. Cambridge: University Press.

Tan, Q: 2013. 'Township Government Reform: Improving Local Governance', in G. Wang and Y. Zheng (eds.), China: Development and Governance, pp. 29-37. Singapore: World Scientific Publishing.

Tang, J. 2005. *城乡低保制度历史现状与前瞻* [*The Minimum Standard of Living Scheme in cities and countryside: Historical, present and future development*]. Beijing: The Institute of Sociology of the Chinese Academy of Social Policies.

Tao, R. and P. Qin. 2007. 'How Has Rural Tax Reform Affected Farmers and Local Governance in China?', *China & World Economy,* vol. 15, no. 3: 1-18.

Tarschys, D. 1985. 'The Scissors Crisis in public finance', *Policy Sciences*, vol. 15, no. 3: 205–24.

Teorell, Jan, and Hadenius, Axel. 2007. 'Determinants of Democratization: Taking Stock of the Large-N Evidence', in Dirk Berg-Schlosser (ed.), *Democratization: The State of the Art*, pp.69-96. Opladen: Barbara Budrich Publishers.

—. 2010. *Determinants of Democratization. Explaining Regime Change in the World 1972-2006*. Cambridge: Cambridge University Press.

Thakur, R. 1995. *The Government and Politics in India*. London: Macmillan.

Tharakan, P.K.M. 2004. 'Historical hurdles in the course of the People's Planning Campaign in Kerala, India', in, J. Harriss, K. Stokke, and O. Törnquist (eds.), *Politicising democracy. The new local politics of democratisation*. Basingstoke: Palgrave Macmillan.

Therborn, T. 1977. 'Capital and suffrage', *New Left Review*, vol. 103: 3-42.

Therborn, G. 1986. *Why Some Peoples Are More Unemployed than Others. The Strange Paradox of Growth and Unemployment.* London: Verso.

—. 1987a. 'Welfare states and capitalist markets', *Acta Sociologica,* vol. 30: 237–54.

—. 1987b. 'Does corporatism really matter? The economic crisis and issues of political theory', *Journal of Public Policy*, vol. 7, no. 3: 259–84.

Thelen, Kathleen. 1999. 'Historical Institutionalism in Comparative Politics', *Annual Review Political Science*, vol. 2:369-404.

—. 2004. *How Institutions Evolve*. Cambridge: Cambridge University Press.

—. and Steinmo, Sven, 1992. Historical Institutionalism in Comparative Politics,' in Sven Steinmo et al. (eds.), *Structuring Politics: Historical Institutionalism in Comparative Analysis.* Cambridge: Cambridge University Press.

Thucydides. 1951. *History of the Peloponnesian War*. New York: Modern Library.

Thun, E. 2006. *Changing lanes in China*. New York: Cambridge University Press.

Tilly, Ch. (ed.) 1975. *The Formation of National States in Western Europe*. Princeton, N.J.: Princeton University Press.

Titmuss, R.D. 1974. *Social Policy. An Introduction*. London: Allen and Unwin.

Tocqueville, A. de. [1840] 1990. *Democracy in America: I–II*. New York: Vintage Books.

Toharia, Jose J. 1975. 'Judicial Independence in an Authoritarian Regime: The Case of Contem- porary Spain', *Law & Society*, vol. 9: 475-496.

Tsebelis, G. 1990. *Nested Games: Rational Choice in Comparative Politics*. Berkeley, Calif.: California University Press.

—. 1995.'Decision making in political systems: veto players in presidentialism, parliamentarianism, multicameralism and multipartism', *British Journal of Political Science*, vol. 25, no. 3: 289–325.

—. 1999.'Veto players and law production in parliamentary democracies: an empirical analysis', *American Political Science Review,* vol. 93: 591–608.

Tsou, Tang. 1969. 'Western concepts and China's historical experience', *World Politics,* vol. 21:655-691.

—. 1983. 'Back from the Brink of Revolutionary – 'Feudal' Totalitarianism', in V. Nee and D. Mozingo (eds.), *State and Society in Contemporary China.* Ithaca, NY: Cornell University Press.

—. 1995. 'Chinese Politics at the Top: Factionalism or Informal Politics? Balance of-Power Politics or a Game to Win All?', *China Journal,* vol. 34:95-156.

Teiwes, Frederick C. 1984. *Leadership, Legitimacy, and Conflict in China.* London: Macmillan.

—. 1995. 'The Paradoxical Post-Mao Transition: From Obeying the Leaders to 'Normal Politics'', *China Journal* ,vol. 34:55-94.

UN (United Nations). 2005. *World Population Prospects: The 2004 Revision.* New York: United Nations.

UN General Assembly. 2012. 'Declaration of the High-Level Meeting of the General Assembly on the Rule of Law at National and International Level', *Resolution No. 67/1*, UN Doc. A/Res/67/1.

UNDP (United Nations Development Programme). 1999. *China Human Development Report 1999.* Beijing: China Financial and Economic Publishing.

—. 2005. *China Human Development Report 2005.* New York: UNDP.

Vaidyanathan, K.E. 2006. 'Social Protection for Children, Women and Families: The Indian Experience', Presented to the Graduate Program in International Affairs, New School. New York, 30-31 October. See http://www.unescapsdd.org/files/documents/PUB_APPJ-Vol-4-No-2.pdf (2014).

Vallléspin, Fernando. 1999 'Gerechtigkeit und Demokratie', in: Wolfgang Merkel and A. Busch (eds.), *Demokratie in Ost und West*, pp. 103–121. Frankfurt a. M.: Suhrkamp.

Valli,Vittorio and Saccone, Donatella. 2009. 'Structural Change and Economic Development in China and India', *European Journal of Comparative Economics,* vol. 6, no. 1: 101-129

Vanhanen, T. 1997. *Prospects of Democracy: A Study of 172 Countries*. London: Routledge.

Varma, A: 2004. ,'Samajwadi Party in Uttar Pradesh', *Economic and Political Weekly*, vol. 3-10: 1509-1514.

Veenhoven, R. 2002. 'Why social policy needs subjective indicators', *Social Indicators Research*, vol. 58, pp. 33-45.

Verba, Sidney. 1967 'Some Dilemmas in Comparative Research', *World Politics,* vol. 20, no.1 (October): 116-118.

—. 1986. 'Comparative politics: where have we been, where are we going?', in H.J. Wiarda (ed.), *New Directions in Comparative Politics*. Boulder, Colo.: Westview Press.

Verma, Pramod and Mookherjee, Surya .1999. *Trade Unions in India. Concepts, Cases and Case-Law*. New Delhi: Oxford & IBH Publishing.

Verma, S K and Kusum, S.K. 2000. *Fifty Years of the Supreme Court of India - Its Grasp and Reach*. New Delhi: Oxford University Press.

Venkatesh, Ashutosh. 2005. *Ethnic Conflict and Civic Life. Hindus and Muslims in India*. Oxford: Oxford University Press.

Vijay Shankar, P.S. and Shah, M. 2012.'Rethinking Reforms: A New Vision for the Social Sector in India', in R. Nagaraj (ed.), *Growth, Inequality and Social Development in India. Is Inclusive Growth Possible?*, pp.135-168. Basingstoke: Palgrave Macmillan.

Visser, J. and Hemerijck, A. 1997. *A Dutch Miracle. Job Growth, Welfare Reform, and Corporatism in the Netherlands*. Amsterdam: Amsterdam University Press.

Wadhawan, S. K. 1987. Social *Security for Workers in Informal Sector in India*. Geneva: International Labour Office,

Wagner, Adolph. 1911. 'Staat (in internationaler Hinsicht)', in *Handwörterbuch der Staatswissenschaften*, vol. 7: 727–739.

Wagner, Christian. 2006. *Das politische System Indiens. Eine Einführung*. Baden-Baden. VS Verlag.

Wagschal, U. 1996. *Bestimmungsfaktoren der Staatsverschuldung in westlichen Industrieländern*. Opladen: Leske & Budrich.

Wahman, Michael; Jan Teorell and Hadenius, Axel. 2013. 'Authoritarian Regime Types Revisited: Updated Data in Comparative Perspective', *Contemporary Politics*, vol. 19, no. 1: 19-34.

Walder. Andrew W. 1986. *Communist Neo-Traditionalism: Work and Authority in Chinese Industry*. Berkeley: University of California Press.

Waldner, David. 2001. 'Policy History: Regimes', in N. J. Smelser and P. B. Baltes (eds.), *International Encyclopedia of the Social & Behavioral Sciences*, pp. 11547-11553. Oxford: Elsevier.

Wallerstein, Immanuel. 1974. *The Modern World System*. New York: Academic Press.

—. 1997. 'Eurocentrism and its avatars: the dilemmas of social science', *New Left Rev.*, 226:93-108.

Wang, C. 2002. 'Thoughts on the Changing Era and the Modernization of the Political Party', *J Contemp World Socialism*, vol.1: 4-9.

Wang, H. 1994. *The gradual revolution: China's economic reform movement*. New Brunswick, NJ: Transaction publishers.

—. Y. Ge and Gong, S. 2007. *Regulating Medical Services in China*. New York:

Department of Social Development, Development Research Center, The State Council of P.R. China and the Milbank Memorial Fund.

Wang, K. 2008. 'A Changing Arena of Industrial relations in China: What Is Happening after 1978', *Employee Relations*, vol. 30, no.2:190-216.

Wang, Quanxing and Guan, Bin. 2003. '经济法与社会法关系初探 [A study on the relationship between economic law and social law]', in: 现代法学 [*Modern Law Science*], vol. 4: 113-118.

Wang, Y. Z. 2004. *Labour and Social Security Issues in China*. Beijing: Economic Management Press.

Wang, Yuhua. 2013.'Connected Autocracy 2013', *Annual Meeting Paper American Political Science Association 2013*.

Wang, Z. 2005. 'Political Trust', in White L (ed.), *Legitimacy: ambiguities of political success or failure in east and southeast Asia*, pp.113-140. Singapore: World Scientific Press.

Walton, G. 2001. *China's Golden Shield: Corporations and the Development of Surveillance Technology in the People's Republic of China*. Montreal: Rights and Democracy.

Ward, R.E. and Rustow, D.A. (eds.) 1964 *Political Modernization in Japan and Turkey*. Princeton, N.J.: Princeton University Press.

Watts, Ronald L .2008. *Comparing Federal Systems*. Montreal: Institute of Intergovernmental Relations.

Weaver, Kent R. 1986. 'The Politics of Blame Avoidance', in *Journal of Public Policy*, vol. 6, no. 4: 371-398.

Weber, Max. 1976. *Wirtschaft und Gesellschaft*. Tübingen: Mohr.

Wedeman, Andrew. 2004 'The intensification of corruption in China', *The China Quarterly*, vol. 80: 825-922.

—. 2012. *Double Paradox: Rapid Growth and Rising Corruption in China*. Ithaca, NY: Cornell University Press.

Weingrod, A. 1968. 'Patrons, patronage and political parties', *Comparative Studies in Society and History*, vol. 10, no. 4: 377-400.

Western, B. 1989. 'Decommodification and the transformation of capitalism: welfare state development in seventeen OECD countries', *Australian and New Zealand Journal of Sociology*, vol. 25: 200–21.

Wildavsky, A. 1980. *How to Limit Government Spending or, How a Constitutional Amendment Tying Public Spending to Economic Growth will Decrease Taxes and Lessen Inflation*. Berkeley, Calif.: University of California Press.

—. 1986. *Budgeting*. New Brunswick, N.J.: Transaction.

Widlund, I. 2000. *Paths to power and patterns of influence. The Dravidian parties in South Indian politics. Uppsala*: Uppsala University Library.

Wilensky, H.L. 1975. *The Welfare State and Equality*. Berkeley: University of California Press.

—. 1981. 'Leftism, Catholicism, and democratic corporatism: the role of political parties in recent welfare state', in P. Flora and A.J. Heidenheimer (eds.) (1981) *The Development of Welfare States in Europe and America*. New Burnswick and London: Transaction Books.

—. and Turner, L. 1987. *Democratic corporatism and policy linkages. The interdependence of industrial, labor-market, incomes, and social policies in eight countries*. Berkley: Wilensky & Turner.

Williamson, O.E. 1985. *The Economic Institutions of Capitalism*. New York: Free Press.

Wintrobe, Ronald. 1998. *The Political Economy of Dictatorship*. Washington, D.C.: World Bank.

—. 2009. 'Dictatorship: Analytical Approaches', in Carles Boix and Susan C. Stokes (eds.), *The Oxford Handbook of Comparative Politics*, pp. 263-394. Oxford: Oxford University Press.

Wischermann, Jörg. 2013. 'Zivilgesellschaften als Stütze autoritärer Regime. Das Fallbeispiel Vietnam', in S. Kailitz and P. Köllner (eds.), *Autokratien im Vergleich*, pp. 324-354. Baden-Baden: Nomos.

—. and Quang Vinh Nguyen. 2003. 'The Relationship between Civic Organizations and Governmental Organizations in Vietnam: Selected Findings of an Empirical Survey', in Ben T. Kerkvliet, Russell Heng and David Koh (eds.), *Getting Organized in Vietnam – Moving in and around the Socialist State*, pp. 185-233. Singapore: Institute of Southeast Asian Studies.

White, Gordon. 1993. *Riding the Tiger: The Politics of Economic Reform in Post Mao China* . Basingstoke: Macmillan.

White, L. 1998/1999. *Unstately power*. Armok: Sharpe.

—. 2009. *Politics booms: local money and power in Taiwan, East China, Thailand, and the Philippines*. Singapore: World Scientific.

White, Y. 2006. *The promise of a better tomorrow: China's pension system*. Hong Kong: China Law and Practice.

White, III and Lynn T. 2013. 'Chinese Political Studies: Overview of the State of Field', in S. Guo (ed.), *Political Science and Chinese Political Studies. State of the Field*, pp. 11-37. Berlin: Springer.

Wong, C. et al. 1995. Fiscal *Management and Economic Reform in the People's Republic of China*. Hong Kong: Oxford University Press.

Wong, L. and Ngok, K.L. 1997. 'Unemployment and policy responses in mainland China.', *Issue & Studies*, vol. 33, no. 1:335-355.

—. 1998. *Marginalization and social welfare in China*. London: Routledge.

Wood, A. 1999. 'Openness and Wage Inequality in Developing Countries: The Latin American Challenge to East Asian Conventional Wisdom', in R. E. Baldwin et al (eds.), *Market Integration, Regionalism and Global the Economy*. Cambridge. Cambridge University Press.

World Bank. 1986. *Poverty and Hunger: Issues and Options for Food Security in Developing Countries*. Washington, D.C.: World Bank.

—. 1990. *China: Revenue Mobilization and Tax Policy*. Washington D.C.: World Bank.

—. 1990. *China: Strategies for Reducing Poverty in the 1990s*. Washington D.C.: World Bank.

—. 1994 *Averting the Old Age Crisis: Policies to Protect the Old and Promote Growth*. World Bank.

—. 1995. *India: Policy and Finance Strategies for Strengthening*. Washington D.C.: World Bank.

—. 1996. *Primary Health Care Services. Report No. 13042-IN*. Washington D.C.: World Bank.

—. 1996. *China Pension System Reform, Report No. 15121-CHA*. Washington D.C.: World Bank.

—. 1997. *China 2020: Old Age Security: Pension Reform in China*. Washington D.C.: World Bank.

—. 2000a. *China: Overcoming Rural Poverty, Report No. 21105-CHA*. Washington D.C.

—. 2000b. *World Development Report 2000*. London: Oxford University Press.

—. 2002. *China National Development and Sub-National Finance*. Beijing: World Bank.

—. 2003. *China Country Assistance Strategy (2003-2005)*. Beijing: World Bank.

—. 2005. *China, An Evaluation of World Bank Assistance*. Beijing: World Bank.

—. 2006. *China Evaluation of the Liaoning Social Security Reform Pilot, Report No. 38183-CN*. Beijing: World Bank.

—. 2007. *World Development Indicators 2007*. New York: Oxford University Press.

—. 2008. *World Development Indicators 2008*. New York: Oxford University Press.

—. 2009a. *World Development Indicators 2009*. Washington D.C.: World Bank.

—. 2009b. *China: From Poor Areas to Poor People, China's Evolving Poverty Reduction Agenda, Report No. 47349-CN*. Washington D.C.: World Bank.

—. 2009c. *Reforming China's Rural Health System*. Washington, D.C.: World Bank.

—. 2010. *Country Partnership Strategy for the People's Republic of China -for the Period 2006-2010*. Beijing: World Bank.

—. 2011. *Social Protection for a Changing India: Main Report*. New York: World Bank.

World Health Organization. 2000. *The World Health Report 2000: Health System: Improving Performance*. Geneva: WHO.

Wurster, Stefan. 2011. 'Sustainability and Regime Type. Do Democracies Perform Better in Promoting Sustainable Development than Autocracies?', *Zeitschrift für Staats- und Europawissenschaften (ZSE)*, vol. 9, no. 4: 538-559.

Xia, M. 2000. *The Dual Developmental State: Development Strategy and Institutional Arrangements for China's transition*. Aldershot: Ashgate.

—. 2013. 'Innovations in China's Local Governance: An Assessment', in G. Wang and Y. Zheng (eds.), *China: Development and Governance*, pp. 37-47. Singapore: World Scientific Publishing.

Xu, Xianglin. 2004. ''From the Theory of Political Development to the Approach of Policy Process: Constructing the Middle-Range Theory Concerning the Chinese Political Reform'', *Journal of Chinese Social Science*, vol. 3:108-120.

Xu, Yong. 2006. '当前中国农村研究方法论问题的反思 [Reflections on the present methodologies in the Chinese rural study]', *河北学刊* [*J Hebei Acad*], vol. 26, no. 2:55-60.

—. 2007.''The Political Party Goes to the Countryside'', *Academic Monthly,* 2007/08. Available at http://en.cnki.com.cn/Article_en/CJFDTotal-XSYK200708005.htm (2014-01-15).

Yadav, R. 2008. *Social Planning & Development in India*. New Delhi: Alfa.

Yang, Dali L. 2004. *Remaking the Chinese Leviathan: Market Transition and the Politics of Governance in China.* Stanford: Stanford University Press.

—. 2007. 'China's Long March to Freedom', *Journal of Democracy*, vol. 18, no. 3:58-64.

Yang, G. 2006a. 'An institutional analysis of China's state power structure and its operation', *J Contemp China,* vol. 15, no. 46:43-68.

—. 2006b. *Institutional Change and state governance: studies of political development in China*. Beijing: The People's Press

—. and Li, M. 2013. 'Western Political Science Theories and the Development of Political Theories in China', in S. Guo (ed.), *Political Science and Chinese Political Studies*, pp. 61-84. Heidelberg: Springer.

Yin, Robert and Karen A. Heald. 1975. 'Using the Case Survey Method to Analyze Policy Studies', *Administrative Science Quarterly,* vol. 20, no. 3: 371-381.

Yip, W. and Ajay Mahal. 2008. 'The Health Care Systems of China and India: Performance and Future Challenges', *Health Affairs*, vol. 27, no.4: 921-32.

Yipeng, T. and Qi, S. 2005. *单位社会的终结: 东北老工业基地典型单位制背景下的社区建设* [*The End of 'Work unit Society': Community Development against the Background of a 'Typical Work Unit System' in Northeastern Old Industrial Bases*]. Beijing: Shehui Kexue Wenxian Chubanshe.

Yu, Ke-ping. 2008. '中国治理变迁 30 年(1978-2008) [Thirty years of governance transformation: Chinese Politics from 1978 to 2008]', *吉林大学社会科学学报* [*Soc Sci Proc Jilin Univ*], vol. 3:5-17.

—. (ed.) 2010. *The Reform of Governance*. Leiden: Brill.

Zacher, Hans F. 2001. *Rich Democracies. Political Economy, Public Policy and Performance*. Berkley: University of California Press.

Zedong, Mao. 1991.毛泽东选集第四卷 [*Selected works of Mao Zengdong*, Vol. 4). Beijing: People's Publishing House.

Zhang, Chewei. 2003. '失业率定义的国际比较及中国城镇失业率 [An International Comparison of the Definition for Unemployment and the Rate of Unemployment in Urban China]', 世界经济 [*World Economic*], vol. 5:47-54.

Zhang Li. 2001. *Strangers in the city; reconfigurations of space, power, and social networks in China's floating population*. Stanford: University Press. Stanford.

Zhang, S.F. and Tang, J. 2005. *城市低保标准仅够维持低保对象的温饱* [*The level of Minimum Standard of Living Scheme only enough for food and clothes*]. Beijing: The Institute of Sociology of the Chinese Academy of Social Science.

Zhang, Wie. 2005. *Sozialwesen in China*. Hamburg: Kovač.

Zhang, X. J. and S. Wang. 2011. 'China Has Reached the Lewis Turning Point', *China Economic Review*, vol. 22, no. 4: 542-54.

Zheng, Y. 2004. 'Humanistic socialism, political transformation and the governing ability of the party', *Paper for conference in Proceedings of the 50th International Conference on the Chinese Reform* [quoted by Yang and Li (2013)].

—. 2007. 'China's de facto federalism', in B. He et al. (eds.), *Federalism in Asia*, pp. 213-241. Cheltenham: Edward Elgar.

Zheng, Gongcheng. 2004. '自然灾害与社会安全 [Natural disaster and social security]', in: *Zheng, Hangsheng* (ed.), *中国社会发展研究报告 2004 [Research Reports on China Social Development 2004]*, pp. 29 sp. Beijing: China Renmin University Press Co. Ltd.

Zedong, Mao. 1967. *Selected Works of Mao Tse-Tung*, 4 vols. Beijing: Foreign Languages Press.

Zhiyuan, C. et al. 2000. *China human development report 1999: Transition and the state*. New York: Oxford University Press.

Zohlnhöfer, R. 2009. 'How Politics Matter When Policies Change: Understanding Policy Change as a Political Problem', *Journal of Comparative Policy Analysis*, vol. 11, no. 1: 97-115.

Zöllner, Detlev. 1963. *Öffentliche Sozialleistungen und wirtschaftliche Entwicklung. Ein zeitlicher und internationaler Vergleich*. Berlin: Duncker & Humblot.

Online data sources

Election Commission of India. 2014. '*Elections in India*', available at http://eci.nic.in (2014-09-01).

Freedom House. 2014. '*Indicators*', available at https://freedomhouse.org (2014-09-01).

ILO. 2009b. '*Economically Active Population Estimates and Projections: 1980–2020 (EAPEP), table E5*', available at http://laborsta.ilo.org/applv 8/data/EAPEP/eapep_E.html (2014-08-04).

Luxembourg Income Data Study. 2014 '*Income Inequality Measures. Luxembourg: LIDS website*', available at http://www.lisproject.org /keyfigures/ineqtable.htm (2014-04-05).

Ministry of Health. 2009. '*2009 nian Zhonggup weisheng tongji tuyao [China Health Statistical Digest 2009]*', available at www.moh.gov.cn (2009-09-05).

World Bank. 2011b. '*The Worldwide Governance Indicators (WGI) Project*', available at http://info.Worldbank.org/governance/WGI/pdf/Wgidataset.xls (2014-08-12).

Newspaper and online articles

China Daily Online. 2006. 'Central government pledges assistance to needy people', *China Daily Online*, available at www.chinadily.com.cn/english/doc/2006-01/26/content_515782.htm (2014-01-05).

—. 2007. 'China to audit social security funds', *China Daily Online*, 2007-06-07, available at www.chinadily.com.cn/china/2006-12/13/content_758099.htm (2014-01-05).

—.'China's 'unemployment rate climbs', *China Daily Online*, available at www.chinadily.com.cn/china/2006-12/13/content_758099.htm (2014-01-05).

The Hindu (Madras). 2004.'UPA Government to adhere to six basic principles of governance', *The Hindu*, 2004-05-12.

—. 2007. 'Call for general strike on Oct. 30', *The Hindu*, 2007-10-16.

—. 2008. 'General strike by trade unions passes off peacefully', *The Hindu*, 2008-08-21.

—. 2010. 'Drift, dissonance, disappointment', *The Hindu*, 2010-03-25.

—. 2011.' Rashtriya Swasthya Bima Yojana: UPA's flagship, opposition's pride', *The Hindu*, 2011-03-14.

—. 2013. 'Strike throws normal life out of gear', *The Hindu*, 2013-02-20.

—. 2014a.'Welfare benefits and vote choice', *The Hindu*, 2014-06-25.

Indian Express Newspapers (Mumbai) Ltd. 2008. ''Remember Bombay', *Indian Express Newspapers*, 2008-10-30.

Indian Today. 1998. 'Family Calling', *Indian Today*, 1998-01-12.

New York Times. 2005a. 'Deep Flaws, Little Justice in China's Court System', *New York Times*, edited by J. Kahn, 2005-09-21.

—. 2005b. 'When the Chinese Sue the State, Cases Are Often Smothered', *New York Times*, edited by J. Kahn, 2005-12-28.

Neue Zürischer Zeitung (NZZ). 2004. 'China auf der Such nach neuen Werten. Erlebt Konfuzius eine Renaissance?', *NZZ*, 2004-03-18.

—. 2013. 'Wenig Erfolg im Kampf gegen die Korruption', *NZZ*, 2013-12-04.

—. 2014a. 'Verlust der Vernunft', *NZZ*: 2014-07-02.

—. 2014b. 'Stammzellenforschung im <<Mahabharata>>?', *NZZ*, 2014-09-22.

—. 2014c. 'Wieso kapitalgedeckte Rentensysteme nicht immer die besten sind', *NZZ*, 2014-10-16.

—. 2014d. 'Rechststaatlichkeit auf Chinesisch', *NZZ*, 2014-10-22.

—. 2014e. 'Die fetten Bric-Jahre sind vorbei', *NZZ*, 2014-12-02.

People Daily's Online. 2006a. 'US$ 9000m misused from social security fund', *People Daily's Online*, 2006-11-24.

—. 2006b.'Twelve percent Chinese rural labourers participate in old-age pension', *People Daily's Online*, 2006-11-27.

Xinhuanet. 2005. 'Family planning becomes controversial topic', *Xinhuanet*, 2005-12-30.

Xiahua News Agency. 2006a. '191,849 pieces of opinions were solicited on the labor contract law', *Xiahua News Agency*, 2006-04-21.

—. 2006b. 'Investigating the Minimum Standard of Living Scheme: How many MSLS recipients are fraud cases?', *Xiahua News Agency*, 2006-04-01.

—. 2006c. 'Tackling welfare fraud, Guiyang City launched its first public hearing on the applications for the Minimum standard of Living Scheme', *Xiahua News Agency*, 2006-04-14.

—. 2007. 'New law allows job seekers to litigate against discrimination', *Xiahua News Agency*, 2007-08-30.